THE PAPERS OF WILL ROGERS

The Early Years

Volume One

November 1879–April 1904

Will Rogers (1879–1935) as an infant *(OkClaW)*.

The Papers of Will Rogers

The Early Years

Volume One

November 1879–April 1904

EDITED BY

Arthur Frank Wertheim

AND

Barbara Bair

UNIVERSITY OF OKLAHOMA PRESS : NORMAN AND LONDON

OTHER BOOKS BY ARTHUR FRANK WERTHEIM

The New York Little Renaissance: Iconoclasm, Modernism, and Nationalism in American Culture (New York, 1976)
Radio Comedy (New York, 1979)
(ed.) *American Popular Culture: A Historical Bibliography* (Santa Barbara, Calif., 1984)
(ed.) *Will Rogers at the Ziegfeld Follies* (Norman, 1992)

OTHER BOOKS BY BARBARA BAIR

(ed. with Robert A. Hill) *The Marcus Garvey and Universal Negro Improvement Association Papers,* vols. 6 and 7 (Berkeley, Los Angeles, and London, 1989, 1990)
(ed. with Robert A. Hill) *Marcus Garvey: Life and Lessons* (Berkeley, Los Angeles, and London, 1987)
(ed. with Susan E. Cayleff) *Wings of Gauze: Women of Color and the Experience of Health and Illness* (Detroit, 1993)

Library of Congress Cataloging-in-Publication Data

Rogers, Will, 1879-1935.
  The papers of Will Rogers / edited by Arthur Frank Wertheim and Barbara Bair.
  p.   cm.
  Contents: v.   1. The Early Years, November 1879–April 1904.
  ISBN 0-8061-2745-7
  1. Rogers, Will, 1879–1935—Archives.   2. Rogers, Will, 1879–1935—Correspondence.   3. Performing arts—United States—History—20th century—Sources.
I. Wertheim, Arthur Frank, 1935– . II. Blair, Barbara, 1951– . III. Title.
PN2287.R74A25 1995
792.7′028′092—dc20   94-24165
                                                                        CIP

Book and series design by Bill Cason.

The paper in this book meets the guidelines for permanence and durability of the Committee on Production Guidelines for Book Longevity of the Council on Library Resources, Inc. ∞

2   3   4   5   6   7   8   9   10

THE WILL ROGERS PAPERS PROJECT IS A DOCUMENTARY HISTORY PROJECT OF THE WILL ROGERS MEMORIAL COMMISSION, CLAREMORE, OKLAHOMA. JOSEPH H. CARTER IS PROJECT DIRECTOR AND DIRECTOR OF THE MEMORIAL. FUNDING FOR THE PROJECT HAS COME FROM THE SARKEYS FOUNDATION, THE WILL ROGERS HERITAGE TRUST, INC., AND THE STATE OF OKLAHOMA.

Contents

Documents

1. CHEROKEE HERITAGE

2. SCHOOL DAYS

4. ARGENTINA

5. SOUTH AFRICA

6. AUSTRALIA AND NEW ZEALAND

Illustrations

MAPS

PHOTOGRAPHS

Acknowledgments

THE WILL ROGERS PAPERS PROJECT IS ESPECIALLY INDEBTED TO THE BOARD of Trustees and officers of the Sarkeys Foundation for funding that established crucial underwriting for the volumes. The grant provided funds for staffing, equipment, travel, and other necessary expenses to carry out research and publication. We are very grateful to the trustees of the foundation for supporting the legacy of Will Rogers: Richard D. Bell, Jane A. Jayroe, Joseph W. Morris, Robert T. Rennie, Robert S. Rizley, Paul F. Sharp, and Lee Anne Wilson. We also very much appreciate the confidence of Cheri D. Cartwright, the director of grants for the Sarkeys Foundation, in the Will Rogers Papers Project.

State Senator Stratton Taylor and Representative Dwayne Steidley, with the backing of the Oklahoma legislature, saw that all private funds for the project were matched during a time of economic hardship. We thank the citizens of Oklahoma for their support of our effort on behalf of their native son.

This project would never have been possible without the endorsement of other key individuals. We are especially thankful for the encouragement of Will Rogers, Jr., and Jim Rogers, both of whom strongly believed in the project's mission. Dean Robert H. Henry of the School of Law, Oklahoma City University, also deserves our gratitude for his support, which helped launch the project in its early phase.

We are also very grateful to the members of the Will Rogers Memorial Commission for their endorsement of the project: commissioners Patricia Crume, John Denbo, James L. Hartz, J. Kevin Hayes, Hunt Lowry, James B. Rogers, and Charles Ward.

We very much appreciate the time and effort the staff at the Will Rogers Memorial has devoted to the project. Joseph H. Carter, director of the Memorial and the Will Rogers Papers Project, first conceived of the project, and he has been an inspiration and dedicated colleague in this effort. We would also like to thank other staff at the Memorial: Gregory Malak, curator; Marjorie Williams, fiscal coordinator; Melanie Landers, administrative assistant; Dorothy Bruffett, who photocopied and filed thousands of documents for our archives; and Donald B. O'Rourke, who proofed scanned material.

Michelle Lefebvre Carter has also given considerable time and effort to the project.

Patricia Lowe, Memorial librarian/archivist and the project's editorial assistant, provided an enormous amount of time and energy to the research and transcription process and also served as a guide to the entire Will Rogers collection at the Memorial. She also supervised the reproduction of selected images from the Memorial's photographic archive and cheerfully lent her expertise on questions large and small. Jean Anderson, editorial assistant, has managed the files and database system at the Will Rogers Papers Project office at Will Rogers Historic State Park in Pacific Palisades, California, with considerable dedication and efficiency. Their contributions have been essential to the success of the project.

Several individuals contributed to the housing of the Will Rogers Papers Project archives at the Will Rogers Historic State Park when the project was first established. Gene Asanovich, head docent, helped provide much needed space for the project in the docent office. We thank all the Will Rogers Cooperative Association and the park rangers for their support. Nancy Mendez, curator, has been very supportive in helping us to gain access to Rogers's documents at the park. Randy Young photographed Rogers's earliest scrapbook at the park for use in illustrating volume one and we are very grateful for his excellent work. Kent Rasmussen developed the database for the Will Rogers Papers Project and also provided valuable computer support as well as other advice for the project.

Robert Rosen, chair of the Department of Film and Television at the University of California, Los Angeles, supported a visiting appointment that proved very helpful in carrying out editorial responsibilities. The Interlibrary Office of the UCLA Libraries, headed by Ian Dacosta, ordered many critical documents for the project from other repositories that were vital for research. Librarians at the McHenry Library, University of California, Santa Cruz, and the Santa Cruz Public Library also contributed to the project's research.

The project is grateful for the assistance of the following archivists, librarians, curators, and scholars who provided considerable information and material for volume one: William D. Welge, director, Archives and Manuscript Division, Oklahoma Historical Society, Oklahoma City; Bradford S. Koplowitz, assistant curator, Western History Collections, University of Oklahoma Libraries, Norman; Barbara Peschel, librarian, Health Sciences Center, University of Oklahoma; Betty Bustes, Panhandle-Plains Historical Museum, Canyon, Texas; Victoria Sheffler, university archivist, Northeastern State University, Tahlequah, Oklahoma; Annabell Southern, librarian, Vinita Public Library, Vinita, Oklahoma; Derrick Austin and Lance Vanzant, archival assistants, Southwest Collection, Texas Tech University, Lubbock; Richard Fusick, archivist, Civil Reference Branch, National Archives, Washington, D.C.; Joy Dodson, public services assistant, Central Methodist College, Fayette, Missouri; Robin Courtney, librarian, City County Library, Neosho, Missouri; Devon Mahesuah, professor, Department of History, Northern Arizona University, Flagstaff; Glenn Colliver, assistant archivist, Department of History, Presbyterian Church (USA), Philadelphia; Joan McCullough, librarian, Oklahoma United Methodist Archives, Dulaney-Browne Library, Oklahoma City University, Oklahoma City; Jim Gatewood, director of public affairs, Kemper Military School, Boonville, Missouri; Marie Demeroukas, registrar, Rogers History Museum, Rogers, Arkansas; Twila D. McClure, librarian, Chelsea Public Library, Chelsea, Oklahoma; Joan Singleton, public services librarian, Bartlesville Public Library and History Museum, Bartlesville, Oklahoma; Peter Stark, map librarian, University of Oregon, Eugene; Diane Boucher Ayotte, manuscript specialist, Western Historical Manuscript Collection, Ellis Library, University of Missouri, Columbia; and Heather Lloyd, head, Special Collections, Oklahoma State University, Stillwater. Librarians and archivists at the following institutions also provided help to the project in document collection and research: the Library of Congress; the National Archives; the California State Library, Sacramento; the Oral History Project and the Rare Book and Manuscript Library, Columbia University; and the Hoover Institute, Stanford University. John R. Lovett was instrumental in providing photographs from the Western History Collections at the University of Oklahoma.

Other individuals who answered inquiries, commented on the manuscript, or provided material were E. Paul Alworth, Jack D. Baker, Genny Mae Bard, Martha Fisch, Carol Hamilton, Robert Henderson, Kathry Jenkins, Harold Keith, Howard Meredith, Peter Rollins, Emil Sandmeier, and John and Faith Wylie. Ben Yagoda was especially helpful in providing us with some of the research material he had gathered for his biography of Will Rogers. Gigi Bayliss created the maps that show the places Rogers visited during his trip abroad in 1902–4. We would like to express sincere appreciation to Wilma Mankiller, principal chief of the Cherokee Nation, for her generous reading of the manuscript.

Several people have volunteered their time to search for Will Rogers material both in the United States and abroad. Patricia Webber uncovered material at the Theatre Museum in London. A very special note of thanks is due Carol Wertheim and Jason Wertheim, both for their archival research and their support and encouragement. Thanks also to Judy Donley, Margaret and Doug Erickson, Patrice Maginnis, and Earl James Weaver for their generosity and interest during the research and editing of this volume. Historian William G. McLoughlin, who passed away during the preparation of this book, offered kind support in the early stages of the project and shared his own insights about Will Rogers's career. His publications on the history of the Cherokee Nation were an inspiration to the writing and research on the volume.

Several repositories and individuals in Australia provided information regarding the Wirth Brothers' Circus and Texas Jack: Valerie Helson, acting manuscript librarian, Australian Collections and Services, National Library of Australia, Canberra; Jo Peoples, curator, Performing Arts Collection of South Australia, Theatre Museum, Adelaide; and Mark Valentine St Leon, writer/researcher, Gleble, New South Wales.

Archivists in South Africa were also invaluable in supplying information and documents regarding Rogers's employers, James Piccione and Texas Jack. The project was aided by archivists of the Cape Archives Depot, Cape Town; the Free State Archives Depot, Bloemfontein; the Natal Archives Depot, Pietermaritzburg; and the Transvaal Archives Depot, Pretoria. Rooksana Omar of the Local History Museum, Durban, also responded to project queries. Special thanks are due to Chantelle Wyley, history subject librarian, University of Natal Library, Durban, who provided much helpful research information and guidance in the project's pursuit of South African material.

We also very much appreciate the editorial guidance of the staff of the University of Oklahoma Press, especially George W. Bauer, director, John N. Drayton, editor-in-chief, Sarah Iselin, associate editor, Patsy Willcox, production manager, and Bill Cason, designer. David W. Levy and William W. Savage, Jr., professors in the Department of History, University of Oklahoma, provided excellent advice on the project from its beginning.

THE PAPERS OF WILL ROGERS

The Early Years

Volume One

November 1879–April 1904

Introduction

The Papers of Will Rogers FEATURES THE SELECTED WRITINGS OF A BELOVED national figure, considered to be among the most popular Americans of the early twentieth century. In this series the documents are presented chronologically to enable the reader to understand the evolution of Rogers's career and his relationship to historical events.

Rogers's writings are closely integrated with the vast social changes occurring during his lifetime (1879–1935). His weekly and daily newspaper columns, magazine articles, and other pieces, estimated to total over two million words, chronicle world events and national politics from the early 1900s to the Great Depression. As an ambassador of goodwill, he traveled around the world writing cogent observations about international events. Rogers was also a very popular speaker, and his talks are classics of American oratory. Since he was a headliner in rodeo, Wild West shows, and vaudeville, on Broadway, in the cinema, and on the radio, his career as a performer mirrors the development of popular entertainment in the late nineteenth century and the first decades of the twentieth. Rogers is a leading figure in the history of American humor. His wry wit, political satire, and cowboy philosophy entertained millions of people. *The Papers of Will Rogers* is an endeavor to illuminate his importance in American popular culture as well as in social and political history.

The goal of this project is to publish the most significant documents pertaining to Rogers's career, material carefully selected from the corpus of his papers. The projected volumes encompass his personal and public correspondence, newspaper and magazine articles, speeches, and other selected writings, including important documents about him and performance reviews. The majority of the material selected is housed in the archives of the Will Rogers Memorial in Claremore, Oklahoma, the museum dedicated to preserving the Rogers heritage. Additional material stems from an extensive search for documents in many repositories in the United States and foreign archives. The edition is designed to serve both general readers and scholars. The editors hope that the publication of the volumes will contribute to an accurate record of Rogers's life and help generate a new canon of knowledge about Will Rogers and his times.

This first volume presents material dealing with Will Rogers's formative years from the time of his birth in Indian Territory in 1879 through his first trip around the world in 1902–1904. The period covered is critical to understanding the evolution of his character and career. Most of the materials pertaining to his Cherokee heritage, boyhood friendships, schooling, and his early rodeo, Wild West show, and circus performances are not readily available to readers. For these reasons the editors have elected to publish a large percentage of surviving documents from this period.

The documents in volume one illustrate the importance of familial relationships, Cherokee culture, and the history of the West to Rogers's development. Because he was raised in Indian Territory and was one-quarter Cherokee, Rogers's early life is linked to major transformations of the American frontier between 1880 and 1910 including the dissolution of the Cherokee Nation, the impact of the railroad, the restructuring of the cattle industry, and the romanticization of the cowboy. Volume one describes the beginnings of Rogers's show-business career in steer-roping contests and Wild West shows as a lariat artist—a skill he developed on his father's ranch. Included also are Rogers's earliest correspondence with family and friends and his first published writings, containing acute observations about life in Argentina, South Africa, Australia, and New Zealand during his travels abroad.

The historical significance of this body of documents exists on several levels. Letters from the Rogers family and friends sketch out what it was like to live in Indian Territory at the end of the 1800s and the turn of the century, and the difference such factors as gender, class, racial orientation, and political opportunity made. The accounts and opinions given by Rogers's sisters and female friends, and their activities, work, and associations add to our understanding of women's history; the experiences of his father and male friends add to our concepts of the economic and public history of the period, from the labor structure of the cattle industry and farming to urbanization and the growth of business enterprises, banking, commerce, and civic activism in small Indian Territory towns. The activities of Rogers's parents and siblings in the Methodist Episcopal Church South, the Home Missionary Society, the Pocahontas Club, the women's club movement, and Masonic orders also help establish the links between family and organizational history. Documentation of Rogers's participation in the Cherokee Nation school system and in denominational boarding schools originated by the missionary movement, the number of his female acquaintances who became schoolteachers, and his family members' involvement in supporting regional schools all add to the history of education in the Nation. Evidence of Rogers's own achievements in school, particularly in the areas of history and elocution, help dispel the singular focus on his behavior problems as a young boy and his dislike of education. The social history and popular culture of the Cherokee Nation are also conveyed herein with documents that present a background of dances and social gatherings, street and agricultural fairs, visiting circuses and vaudeville acts, cakewalk parties and minstrelsy, popular music and parlor games. The rodeo and roping contests that drew Rogers and many of his friends represent the confluence of the concrete economic skills of the cowboy with popular entertainment. In joining Texas Jack's Wild West Show in South Africa in 1902, Rogers made the transition from the life in which he had combined managing his father's ranch with competing in roping contests and working as a cowboy to a new career in show business and performance.

The documents in this volume also offer insights into the political history of the West. As a Cherokee and the son of an important Cherokee politician, Rogers came of age against a backdrop of federal policy and local adaptations in which tribal sovereignty was eroded, communal lands privately allotted, and mixed-blood Indians like those of his family were largely assimilated to Anglo-American values and ways. His own family history was one where the allegiances and orientations of the 1879–1904 period reached back through generations to the removal of the Cherokee Nation from the East, the reestablishment of the Nation in the West, and the Civil War. His identification with his Cherokee and Southern heritage determined in part Rogers's responses to racial divisions and labor conditions in Argentina and South Africa.

The documents presented in this volume thus are significant from many historical perspectives. Not the least of these is the fuller understanding of Rogers's origins and the thoughts and experiences that formed his character and stage personality. Volume one of *The Papers of Will Rogers* ends on the brink of Rogers's beginning his professional life as an entertainer in the United States. That professional life would come to have meaning to people of all kinds of backgrounds and walks of life who embraced Rogers for his wit and looked to him as a wry and trustworthy interpreter of American culture and politics. The particularism of his early life would give way to universalism as he translated the cultural attributes of his upbringing into a public persona that came to represent for many the essence of American character.

Chronology, 1879–1904

1879

August Will Rogers's father, Clement Vann (Clem V.) Rogers, elected to Cherokee Nation Senate, the first of five terms he served in that office.

4 November Birth of William Penn Adair Rogers, Clem V. and Mary America Schrimsher Rogers's youngest child, in the Cooweescoowee District, Cherokee Nation, Indian Territory (I.T.) at his parents' ranch near present-day Oologah, Okla.

1883

13 April Rogers's brother, Robert, dies of fever at the age of sixteen.

1885

16 December Rogers's eldest sister, Sallie, marries rancher John Thomas (Tom) McSpadden.

1887

Winter Rogers in attendance at his first school, the Drumgoole School near Chelsea, I.T.

3 March Dawes Severalty Act is passed. It mandated the individual allotment of commonly held tribal lands.

28 August–16 December "W. P. Rogers" listed as a student at the Cherokee National Male Seminary, Tahlequah, I.T.

1888

September Rogers joins his sister May as a student at the Harrell International Institute, Muskogee, I.T. Briefly returns home because of homesickness.

1890

April Mary America Schrimsher Rogers visits her son at the Harrell Institute.

28 May	Rogers's mother dies suddenly at the Rogers ranch after nursing her daughters through typhoid fever.

1891

Fall	Rogers attends Willie Halsell College in Vinita, I.T. Remains at the school until 1895.
14 October	Rogers's sister Maud marries pharmacist Captain Lane (Cap or C. L.) Lane of Chelsea, I.T.

1892

9 October	Rogers's youngest sister, May, marries businessman J. Matthew (Matt) Yocum at the Rogers ranch.
December	Rogers is listed as an honor-roll student at Willie Halsell College. He receives a "hearty round of applause" for his declamations.

1893

7 January	Rogers writes his good friend Charles White McClellan—his earliest writing in existence.
15 January	Clem V. Rogers marries his former housekeeper, Mary Bibles, at the Rogers ranch.
January	Rogers again is named an honor-roll student.
April	According to the Cherokee Nation census of 1893, Rogers is allocated a per capita distribution of funds from the sale of the Cherokee Strip.

1894

June	Rogers receives a medal for elocution at Willie Halsell.
15 October	Letter of Clem V. Rogers to Colonel C. J. Harris containing letterhead illustrating Will Rogers's Dog Iron brand.

1895

23 March	Rogers named president of the organization of Christian Endeavor, a youth organization of the Presbyterian Church.

Fall	Enrolls at the Scarritt Collegiate Institute, Neosho, Mo. Remains at the school until December 1896.

1896

August	Clem V. Rogers is appointed as a member of the Cherokee Nation commission to negotiate with the federal Dawes Commission, which was authorized to survey Nation lands and establish tribal rolls so that collective holdings could be divided into individual allotments.
December	Brother-in-law Matt Yocum is murdered at his home outside Oolagah.

1897

13 January	Rogers matriculates at the Kemper School, Boonville, Mo.
June	Rogers is injured with a slight bullet wound to the scalp while handling his rifle.
11 June	William Cheatham, who has been courting May Rogers Yocum, is found dead by the railroad tracks outside of Oolagah.
July	Clem V. Rogers and his son are falsely implicated in the murder of William Cheatham.

1898

15 March	Rogers leaves Kemper to work on ranches in the Texas Panhandle. Signs the registry book at the Johnson Hotel, Higgins, Tex. Soon he is working at W. P. Ewing's Little Robe Ranch.
April	Spanish-American War begins.
Spring–Summer	Rogers is employed by Lythe Knight for a trail drive; works at various ranches in the Texas Panhandle and travels around the Southwest.
28 June	The Curtis Act is passed, further institutionalizing the privatization of Indian Territory lands.

August	May Rogers Yocum marries Frank Stine in Texas; returns to Indian Territory.
Fall	Rogers returns home to Oologah. His father, who moves to Claremore, lets him operate the family ranch.

1899

July 4	Rogers wins first prize in a steer-roping contest at Claremore.
August	Rogers is named a honorary member of the new Pocahontas Club, founded by young women of Indian heritage in the Claremore area.
11 October	South African (Anglo-Boer) War begins.
October	At the annual St. Louis fair, Rogers participates in steer-roping and riding contests with Zack Mulhall's troupe. Competes against the Mexican champion Vincente Oropeza.
Fall	Meets his future wife, Betty Blake, who is visiting relatives in Oologah. She stays until December.

1900

17 January	Stepmother Mary Bibles Rogers dies after a lengthy illness; she is thirty-four. Clem V. Rogers moves to rooms in the First National Bank Building, where he lives for the remainder of his life, frequently visiting the homes of his daughters Sallie and Maud in Chelsea.
Winter	Rogers is fined for attempting to ride into Oologah during a smallpox quarantine.
July 4	At a reunion of Theodore Roosevelt's Rough Riders in Oklahoma City, participates in a steer-roping contest; meets Roosevelt.
1 August	Joins with many of his friends in a steer-roping contest in Vinita, I.T.
22 October	Clem V. Rogers applies for enrollment in the Cherokee Nation for himself and his son in accordance with the Dawes Commission regulations.
October	One of Will Rogers's horses drowns in the Verdigris River.

1901

January	Local newspapers report that Rogers became sick in San Francisco when either he or a friend extinguished a gas lamp in a rooming house. Goes to Hot Springs, Ark., to recover.
27–31 May	Helps organize a steer-roping and riding show at the Union Confederate Veterans reunion at Memphis, Tenn.
5 September	Wins second prize in a steer-roping contest at the Elks Convention in Springfield, Mo. Betty Blake is in the audience.
Fall	Visits the Pan-American Exposition at Buffalo, N.Y.
10 October	Appears with the Zack Mulhall's performing troupe of cowboys in a steer-roping contest at the Des Moines Seni-Om-Sed Carnival. The Humane Society prohibits the throwing and tying of steers because of danger to the animals.
22–29 October	Participates in steer-roping contests at the annual San Antonio International Fair and Exhibition, which featured the nation's best ropers and prize money.

1902

11 January	Attends his father's sixty-third birthday celebration with family at Claremore's Frisco restaurant.
ca. 20 February	Decides to travel to Argentina with friend Dick Parris, sells his share in the family cattle, leaves Oologah, and travels to Hot Springs, Ark.
16 March	Arrives with Parris in New Orleans.
19 March	Departs for New York City via the steamship *Comus*.
24 March	Arrives in New York City.
26 March	Sails for Southampton, England, aboard the S.S. *Philadelphia*.
2 April	Arrives in Southampton.

ca. 11 April	Leaves for Buenos Aires via the royal mail steamer *Danube*.
19 April	Ship stops at St. Vincent, Cape Verde Islands.
24 April	Ship stops at Pernambuco, Brazil.
28 April	Ship arrives in Rio de Janeiro, Brazil.
2 May	Ship stops at Montevideo, Uruguay.
5 May	Arrives in Buenos Aires.
7 May	Writes to the *Claremore Progress* of his experiences.
8 May	Rogers and Parris travel to the interior of Argentina.
24 May	Parris leaves Buenos Aires to return home.
31 May	South African War ends.
July	Rogers sings for sailors aboard U.S. battleship *Atlanta* and at a local concert hall in Buenos Aires.
5 August	Sails for Durban, Natal, South Africa, on the *Kelvinside*, accompanying a cargo of livestock owned by James Piccione.
11 September	Writes his father from Mooi River Station, Natal, that he is working on Piccione's horse farm.
17 November	Writes his sisters from Durban that he has been in Ladysmith.
26 November	Writes his father from Durban that he has a job driving some mules to Ladysmith.
ca. 5 December	Obtains a job as a roper, rider, and actor in dramatic skits with Texas Jack's Wild West Show and Dramatic Company.
19 December	Close childhood friend Charles White McClellan dies in Lebanon, Tenn.
25 December	Rogers sees a baseball game at a Canadian soldiers' camp.
29 December	Texas Jack's Wild West Show opens at Standerton, Transvaal, with Rogers billed as "The Cherokee Kid."

1903

28 January	The Texas Jack show plays in Harrismith, Orange Free State.
ca. 1–16 March	With Texas Jack in Durban.
17 March	Writes that the Texas Jack show will be in East London for ten days.
25 April	Texas Jack writes a letter recommending Rogers to circus proprietors.
19 May	In Port Elizabeth, Cape of Good Hope, Rogers signs a power of attorney granting his father the right to receive an allotment in his name.
20–27 June	Writes his sister from Bloemfontein that the show will be traveling to Portuguese East Africa.
21 July–5 August	Performs with the Texas Jack company in Pretoria and receives reviews in the *Pretoria News*.
9 August	Leaves South Africa by boat across the Indian Ocean for Australia via New Zealand.
17 August	Before Dawes Commission officials, Clem V. Rogers testifies on his son's behalf and Will Rogers receives an allotment certificate of 78.84 acres from his father's ranch.
August	Clem V. Rogers elected to his final term as a Downing Party candidate to Cherokee Nation Senate.
3 September	Lands in Wellington, New Zealand.
5 September	Leaves for Auckland, New Zealand.
28 September	Writes his family from Sydney, Australia.
November	Residing in Banella and Murchison, Victoria.
25 December	Spends Christmas in Melbourne.
ca. 26 December	Performs with the Wirth Brothers' Circus in Melbourne.

1904

January	Plays with the Wirth Brothers' Circus at various towns in Australia, including Wagga Wagga and Bathurst.

20 January	Performs a roping and riding act with the Wirth Brothers' Circus in Auckland, New Zealand.
5 February	Performs with the Wirth Brothers' Circus in Whangarei, New Zealand.
18 March	Leaves Auckland for San Francisco on S.S. *Ventura*.
11 April	Returns home to Oologah. Plans to perform with the Zack Mulhall show at the Louisiana Purchase Exposition (1904 St. Louis World's Fair).

Editorial Principles and Practices

DOCUMENT SELECTION FOR VOLUME ONE

VOLUME ONE OF *The Papers of Will Rogers* PRESENTS THE READER WITH printed transcriptions of documents of various types. These include handwritten personal correspondence, correspondence printed in newspapers, newspaper reports and performance reviews, school records, legal documents, and Bureau of Indian Affairs and Cherokee Nation records, including census reports, records of per capita distributions to Cherokee citizens, citizenship enrollments, and records of testimony and land allotment in accordance with federal Indian policies. Emphasis is placed on personal correspondence, especially on letters authored by Will Rogers. One hundred percent of the extant correspondence written by Rogers in the 1879–1904 period has been reproduced in volume one, along with a high proportion of letters from family members and friends written to Rogers. Some of the latter are presented in abridged form. The personal correspondence, records, newspaper reports, reviews, and other documents have not been previously published in comprehensive form in a scholarly edition.

During the 1902–4 time period two or more versions of Will Rogers's correspondence may exist. Rogers traveled abroad during this time, and recipients' copies of autograph letters home were lent by his father and sisters to their local newspapers, the *Claremore Progress* and the *Chelsea Reporter.* The publishers of those papers began to print edited versions of the letters for public enjoyment. The letters were not intended for publication, and when Will Rogers discovered that they had been printed, it caused him some consternation. He adjusted to the idea, and soon contributed his own account of his travels directly to Albert L. Kates, the owner-editor of the *Claremore Progress.* This letter, dated 7 May 1902 and printed in volume one, represents Rogers's first formal appearance in print and thus in effect documents the beginning of Rogers's career in journalism as a social commentator, foreshadowing his later syndicated columns. In cases where both autograph and published versions of a letter exist, the autograph letter signed by Rogers appears as the authority document. Letters published in newspapers have been included when no autograph version has survived. In one case both the newspaper and the autograph version have been printed to illustrate for the reader the ways in which newspaper editors revised for style Rogers's original texts to prepare them for publication. These editorial intrusions forecast his later syndicated columns, in which original drafts written by Rogers were revised, sometimes by more than one person, before appearing in published form.

In addition to transcriptions of original autograph, typewritten, or printed documents a few selected documents are presented in facsimile form. Photographs of Rogers, his family and friends, and the environment where he grew up have also been included, as have maps that elucidate the geography of the Cherokee Nation and the transformations that took place in Indian Territory in the late nineteenth and early twentieth centuries.

PLACEMENT OF DOCUMENTS

Documents are presented in chronological order, determined by date of authorship or creation. In cases where the date of creation is not known and a document appeared in published form, the date of publication is used to determine placement. Incompletely dated documents are placed at the end of a given time frame (for example, a document dated August 1899 with no specific day given would appear following all other documents in August 1899; similarly, a document dated with only a year would be placed at the end of that year, etc.). Dates construed by the editors are given in square brackets. These may have been construed either from the content of the document (e.g., mention within the document of a particular event or date or allusion to a stage in a Rogers itinerary, etc.) or from other material (e.g., a postmark on an envelope in which an original undated letter was received). The date designation of documents created on more than one day (e.g., a letter written in stages over the course of several days, or a report covering a particular time period) indicates a time span (e.g., 28 August–16 December 1887) and the document is placed according to the first date in that span. Two or more documents of the same date are arranged according to historical sequence or in the best contextual relation to documents that directly precede or follow.

Volume one has been broken into six thematic sections, each with its own introduction. Sections are based on discrete stages in Rogers's personal life or career. Section one presents material regarding Rogers's birth and family background and his family's role in the context of Cherokee Nation history. Sections two and three focus on his education as a boy and his experience as a young man doing ranch work and participating in regional roping contests. The last three sections deal with his travels in his early-to-mid-twenties to

South America (where he sought ranch work), Africa (where he turned from ranching to performing as a way of life, joining a Wild West show), and Australia and New Zealand (where he continued to add to his show-business experience by appearing with a circus). Section introductions set the context and identify some of the major themes that appear in the documents that follow. Periodically, headnotes introduce particular documents, further setting their context and supplying brief, pertinent information.

PRESENTATION OF DOCUMENTS AND EDITORIAL ELEMENTS

All documents are presented with a caption or document heading, a place and date line, an endnote or descriptive source note, and if appropriate, annotations.

Captions of correspondence assume that Will Rogers is either the author or the recipient of the letter and indicate only the other party in the correspondence (e.g., "To Charles White McClellan" or "From Sallie McSpadden"). Noncorrespondence primary documents and published third-party documents are given descriptive titles (e.g., "Cherokee Nation Census Record" or "Article from the *Indian Chieftain*"). Document headings also include the date of the document and the place it originated. The British dating style (day-month-year) is used in the captions, and "ca." (circa) is used to prefix editorially construed dates. Documents that are printed as enclosures to other documents are labeled as an enclosure, and a full descriptive heading follows in the same style as that of other documents.

Place and date lines are printed flush right at the beginning of the documentary text, regardless of where this information may have been presented in the original document. The line breaks of the place and date information are structured in accordance with the original unless their length demands alteration. When no place or date appears on the original document, the place and date line is left blank.

In letters where a recipient's address is given in the original document, the address is set flush left above the salutation, regardless of where the information may have been in the original. Salutations are similarly set flush left no matter how they appear in original correspondence. Headlines of printed documents taken from newspapers are centered and if abridged are so described in the descriptive source note.

Documents are presented with as little editorial intervention as possible. Texts are reproduced as written, with irregularities in grammar, punctuation, and spelling left intact. Paragraphs are indented. Rogers often wrote without punctuation and with irregular use of capitalization. In transcriptions of his handwritten letters two spaces have been added at the end of a sentence where no period or other punctuation was supplied in the original, in order to make his correspondence easier to read. Minor typographical errors in published documents have been silently corrected. Misspellings or abbreviations that occur in original documents are sometimes clarified in notes or with the use of square brackets. Illegible words or missing or mutilated text are indicated by an editorial message in italics and square brackets (e.g., *[word illegible], [word obscured],* or *[page torn]*). Interlineations are indicated by the use of a ▲ or ▼ symbol at the beginning and end of either superscript or subscript text. Marginal notes are quoted in annotations. Some documents that were not written by Rogers have been abridged. Abridged sections are indicated by the use of unbracketed ellipses. If ellipses occurred in the original documents, this is indicated either in the descriptive source note or by an annotation. Italics are used to render single underlined words in autograph texts and italicized text in printed documents. Double underlined words in autograph texts are rendered in italics with two underlines. Underlined blanks with roman text indicate a printed or handwritten document in which autograph or typed entries were made into the blanks.

Closings of letters are set flush right or are run into the last paragraph of the letter as they are in the original document. Signatures are set flush right, no matter how they were rendered in the original. Postscripts follow signatures, and endorsements or docketing are set flush left above the document endnote.

Descriptive source notes contain the following information: the type of document, given in abbreviated form (e.g., ALS for autograph letter signed; see Symbols and Abbreviations, following); a brief indication of the nature of the document (e.g., rc for recipient's copy); the source of the document (repository, manuscript collection, or printed source; see Symbols and Abbreviations); and any further information pertaining to the physical nature of the document or its content and presentation, including letterhead data. Facts printed, stamped, or written on an envelope are given if pertinent.

Annotations are used to clarify the text, to provide cross-references, or to identify people, places, and events. Cross-references to other documents in the volume are given by description and date of the document, with a designation of whether the document is printed above or below (preceding or following) the cross-reference, rather than by page numbers. Cross-references to the Biographical Appendix are by the name of the person profiled rather than by page numbers. Places, events, organizations, institutions, and so on are identified when they are significant to Rogers's life and career or are not widely known. Annotations fully identify individuals who are referred to in the text only by a first or last name (unless an individual appears frequently and thus is assumed to be known to the reader either in the larger context of the documents or because of previous identification). Biographical annotations of individuals are presented at first appearance. Effort has been made to identify individuals important to Will Rogers's life. In some cases biographical searches revealed no data or were limited by the obscurity of the individual and lack of public information.

Rogers family members, close friends, and people of particular significance to Rogers are profiled in the volume's Biographical Appendix. The annotation at the first appearance of such an individual's name in the text is a cross-reference to the appropriate Biographical Appendix entry. A comprehensive name index also appears at the beginning of the appendix as a guide to the reader. All other individuals named in text whom we could identify are described in annotations. Bibliographic source citations are given in annotations and in all Biographical Appendix entries in either abbreviated or shortened-title form. Complete listings of all sources appear either in Symbols and Abbreviations or in the Bibliography in the back of the volume.

Symbols and Abbreviations

TEXTUAL DEVICES

[roman]	Editorial clarification or addition to text.
[roman?]	Conjectural reading for missing, mutilated, or illegible text.
[italic]	Editorial message regarding the nature of the original text (e.g., *[line missing]*, *[page mutilated]*, or *[word illegible]*).
. . .	Text editorially abridged.
~~canceled~~	Word deleted in original.
▲▲	Text that appears between markers is written above the line in original document.
▼▼	Text that appears between markers is written below the line in original document.

DESCRIPTIVE SYMBOLS

AD	Autograph Document
ADS	Autograph Document Signed
AL	Autograph Letter
ALS	Autograph Letter Signed
AMS	Autograph Manuscript
AN	Autograph Note
ANS	Autograph Note Signed
APC	Autograph Postcard
APCS	Autograph Postcard Signed
PD	Printed Document
TD	Typed Document
TDS	Typed Document Signed
TG	Telegram
TL	Typed Letter
TLS	Typed Letter Signed
TMS	Typed Manuscript
cc	Carbon Copy
cy	Copy Other than Carbon (Correspondence)

dc   Draft Copy (of Printed Article or Correspondence)
rc   Recipient's Copy (Correspondence)

MANUSCRIPT COLLECTION AND REPOSITORY SYMBOLS

BBC-RHM   Betty Blake Rogers Collection, Rogers Historical Museum, Rogers, Ark.
BPL   Bartlesville Public Library, Bartlesville, Okla.
CAD   Cape Archives Depot, Cape Town, South Africa.
CPL   Chelsea Public Library, Chelsea, Okla.
CPpR   Will Rogers State Historic Park, Pacific Palisades, Calif.
DNA   United States National Archives and Records Administration, National Archives Library, Washington, D.C.
               RG 21 Records of the District Courts of the United States
               RG 75 Records of the Bureau of Indian Affairs
FARC   Federal Archives and Records Center, Fort Worth, Tex.
FSAD   Free State Archives Depot, Bloemfontein, South Africa
HCP-MoU   Homer Croy Papers, Western Historical Manuscript Collection, University of Missouri, Columbia, Mo.
HFP-TxLT   Halsell Family Papers, Southwest Collection, Texas Tech University, Lubbock, Tex.
IPH-OkHi   Indian–Pioneer History Collection, Oklahoma Historical Society, Oklahoma City, Okla.
JMO-OkU   John M. Oskison Collection, Western History Collections, University of Oklahoma, Norman, Okla.
JLC-OkClaW   Joseph Levy, Jr., Collection, Will Rogers Memorial, Claremore, Okla.
MFC   Mulhall Family Collection, Martha Fisch Private Papers, Guthrie, Okla.
MMC-OkClaW   Mary McClellan Comer Collection, Will Rogers Memorial, Claremore, Okla.
NAD   Natal Archives Depot, Pietermaritzburg, South Africa.
NCHF   National Cowboy Hall of Fame and Western Heritage Center, Oklahoma City, Okla.
OkClaW   Will Rogers Memorial, Claremore, Okla.
OkHi   Oklahoma Historical Society, Oklahoma City, Okla.
OkS   Will Rogers Research Project Papers, Edmon Low Library, Oklahoma State University, Stillwater, Okla.

OkTahN	John Vaughan Library, Northeastern State University, Tahlequah, Okla.
OkU	Western History Collections, University of Oklahoma, Norman, Okla.
PC	Department of History, Presbyterian Church (USA), Philadelphia, Pa.
PHM	Panhandle-Plains Historical Museum, Canyon, Tex.
SRM-OkClaW	Sallie Rogers McSpadden Collection, Will Rogers Memorial, Claremore, Okla.
TAD	Transvaal Archives Depot, Pretoria, South Africa.
URL-CLU	Department of Special Collections, University Research Library, University of California, Los Angeles
WRPP	Will Rogers Papers Project, Will Rogers State Historic Park, Pacific Palisades, Calif.

GUIDE TO ABBREVIATED CITATIONS FOR PUBLISHED SOURCES

NEWSPAPERS

BAH	*Buenos Aires Herald* (Daily), Buenos Aires, Argentina
CA	*Cherokee Advocate*, Tahlequah, I.T.
CC	*Claremore Courier*, Claremore, I.T.
CDM	*Claremore Daily Messenger*, Claremore, I.T.
ChC	*Chelsea Commercial*, Chelsea, I.T.
CP	*Claremore Progress*, Claremore, I.T.
CR	*Chelsea Reporter*, Chelsea, I.T.
CV	*Cherokee Vindicator*, Claremore, I.T.
CWM	*Claremore Weekly Messenger*, Claremore, I.T.
CWP	*Claremore Weekly Progress*, Claremore, Okla.
DC	*Daily Chieftain*, Vinita, I.T.
DE	*Daily Express*, San Antonio, Tex.
IC	*Indian Chieftain*, Vinita, I.T.
IC–S	*Indian Chieftain–Supplement*, Vinita, I.T.
ISR	*Iowa State Register*, Des Moines, Iowa
KCJ	*Kansas City Journal*, Kansas City, Kans.
LAT	*Los Angeles Times*, Los Angeles, Calif.
MCA	*Memphis Commercial Appeal*, Memphis, Tenn.
NYHT	*New York Herald Tribune*, New York, N.Y.
NYT	*New York Times*, New York, N.Y.
OBR	*Our Brother in Red*, Muskogee, I.T.

OC	*Oolagah Chief,* Oolagah, I.T.
OS	*Oolagah Star,* Oolagah, I.T.
PN	*Pretoria News,* Pretoria, Transvaal, South Africa
RCL	*Rogers County Leader,* Foyil, Okla.
TDW	*Tulsa Daily World,* Tulsa, Okla.
TJ	*Times-Journal,* Oklahoma City, Okla.
VJ	*Vinita Journal,* Vinita, I.T.
VL	*Vinita Leader,* Vinita, I.T.

REFERENCE WORKS

ADB	*Australian Dictionary of Biography.* Edited by John Ritchie. Melbourne: Melbourne University Press, 1990.
AE	*The Australian Encyclopedia.* 3d ed. Sydney: Grolier Society of Australia, 1977.
AEP	*Australians: Events and Places.* Edited by Graeme Aplin, S. G. Foster, and Michael McKernan. Sydney: Fairfax, Syme, and Weldon Associates, 1987.
AZSP	*Australia, New Zealand, and the South Pacific: A Handbook.* Edited by Charles Osborne. London: Anthony Blond, 1970.
CAE	*Collins Australian Encyclopedia.* Edited by John Shaw. Sydney: Collins, 1984.
CLG	*Columbia Lippincott Gazetteer of the World.* Edited by Leon E. Seltzer. New York: Columbia University Press, 1962.
EA	*Encyclopedia Americana.* New York: American Corp., 1970.
EFB	*Encyclopedia of Frontier Biography.* Edited by Dan L. Thrapp. 3 vols. Spokane, Wash.: Arthur Clark, 1990.
ENZ	*An Encyclopedia of New Zealand.* Edited by A. H. McLintock. Wellington: R. E. Owen, 1966.
ESA	*Encyclopedia of Southern Africa.* Compiled and edited by Eric Rosenthal. London and New York: Frederick Warne and Co., 1961.
EV	*The Encyclopedia of Vaudeville.* Edited by Anthony Slide. Westport, Conn., and London: Greenwood Press, 1994.
HDA	*Historical Dictionary of Argentina,* by Ione S. Wright and Lisa M. Nekhom. Metuchen, N.J.: Scarecrow Press, 1978.
PEP	*The Penguin Encyclopedia of Places.* Edited by W. G. Moore. 2d ed. Harmondsworth, Middlesex, England: Penguin, 1978.
SESA	*Standard Encyclopedia of Southern Africa.* Cape Town: NASOU, 1970.

WEN	*Worldmark Encyclopedia of the Nations: Africa.* 7th ed. New York: John Wiley, 1988.
WNBD	*Webster's New Biographical Dictionary.* Springfield, Mass.: Merriam-Webster, 1988.
WNGD	*Webster's New Geographical Dictionary.* Springfield, Mass.: Merriam-Webster, 1988.

FREQUENTLY CITED SOURCES

HRC	*History of Rogers County, Oklahoma.* Claremore, Okla.: Claremore College Foundation, 1979.
OCF	*Old Cherokee Families, Notes of Dr. Emmet Starr.* Vol. 1, *Letter Books A–F;* Vol. 2, *Letter Books G–L, Index to Letter Books.* Edited by Jack D. Baker and David Keith Hampton. Oklahoma City: Baker Publishing Co., 1988.
WRFT	*Roping Will Rogers Family Tree.* Edited by Reba Collins. Claremore, Okla.: Will Rogers Heritage Press, 1982.

1. CHEROKEE HERITAGE
November 1879–1883

Clement Vann Rogers (1839–1911), Will Rogers's father, as a young man, ca. 1850s (*OkClaW*).

The only known surviving photograph of Mary America Schrimsher Rogers (1839–90), Will Rogers's mother (*OkClaW*).

THE STORY OF WILL ROGERS'S FAMILY AND HIS CHEROKEE HERITAGE SERVES as a microcosm of some major themes and events in Cherokee Nation history following removal from homelands in the East in the 1830s and the reestablishment and development of the Nation in Indian Territory over the following decades.[1] A one-quarter Cherokee, Rogers's upbringing in the Cherokee Nation and his identification as an American Indian were important elements shaping his character and his perspective on American life, with both opportunities and aspects of disenfranchisement. When questioned about his heritage in a scene in one of his films, he informed a passport officer, who had inquired whether he was an American citizen, that his mother and father were both part Cherokee and he "was born and raised in Indian Territory. Course I'm not one of these Americans whose ancestors come over on the *Mayflower*, but we met 'em at the boat when they landed. And its always been to the everlasting discredit of the Indian race that we ever let 'em land."[2]

Rogers's parents, Clement Vann Rogers and Mary America Schrimsher Rogers, were both born in 1839 in the Cherokee Nation West, Indian Territory. The year of their birth was highly significant, marking a turning point in Cherokee history, as deep political and cultural struggles culminated in the forced migration of the majority of Cherokee people from the Cherokee Nation East to Indian Territory over the Trail of Tears in 1838–39. The year 1839 was also marked by three political assassinations that began the period of violent factionalization between 1839 and 1846 as new governmental institutions were developed in the reconstituted Nation. Three Treaty Party leaders—Major Ridge, John Ridge, and Elias Boudinot—were killed in the Nation on 22 June 1839 for their part in the signing of the Treaty of New Echota, or Removal Treaty, of 1835.[3] The murders represented deep social rifts that had developed in the Cherokee Nation over issues of acculturation, nationalism, and removal. They triggered a pattern of internal political violence and retribution that defined the character of the Nation in Will Rogers's parents' early childhood. As children of Treaty Party supporters, Clement Vann Rogers and Mary America Schrimsher Rogers would find their lives greatly shaped by the divisions demonstrated in the events of the year of their birth. The consequences—political, social, economic, and cultural—continued to shape the experiences of their own children, including their youngest son as he came of age in Indian Territory in the final two decades of the century.

Clem V. Rogers's life choices and his career stand, in particular, as examples of the major transitions in the history of the western Cherokee Nation. His life spanned crucial years, from the postremoval reconstruction of the Nation in his own youth to the demise of Indian Territory and the long struggle for Cherokee sovereignty during his son Will's young manhood. Clem V. Rogers, the son of slaveholders, came of age in Indian Territory in the years between the Trail of Tears and the Civil War, pioneered in the Verdigris country, served in the Confederate army, built a prosperous ranch and cattle business, participated as a politician in the Cherokee government, and became a prominent Claremore banker and business leader. His experiences highlight several pivotal phases and themes of Cherokee history in the West, including the acculturation and political influence of mixed-blood Cherokees; the erosion of communal concepts of property and traditional Indian ways; ethnic and class conflicts among Cherokees, including debates over the institution of slavery; the development of large cattle enterprises and fenced farming in the prairie districts of the Nation; responses to non-Cherokee intruders who settled and made improvements on Cherokee land, and to federal Indian policies instituting individual land allotments; the rise of small towns and increasing acceptance of norms of material accumulation and capitalistic investment; and the ultimate demise of Cherokee Nation political autonomy with the transition of Indian Territory into the state of Oklahoma.

Will Rogers's mother, Mary America Schrimsher, was born into a wealthy, slaveholding, mixed-blood Cherokee family at her family's plantation at Eureka near the Cherokee capitol of Tahlequah, Indian Territory. Through the matrilineal kinship system of the Cherokees, she was a member of the Paint Clan through her mother, Elizabeth Hunt Gunter Schrimsher (1804–77), who was half Cherokee. Her maternal grandmother, Catherine Gunter, was the daughter of a Cherokee chief; her maternal grandfather, John Gunter, was a Welsh trader and gunpowder maker in Alabama. Her father, Martin Matthew Schrimsher (1806–65), was of Welsh descent, from Tennessee. Her parents were married in Creek Path (Guntersville), Alabama, in 1831 and had established residence in the Cherokee Nation West by 1835.[4]

Will Rogers's father, Clem V. Rogers, came from a similar background. Like many other slaveholding, mixed-blood families, his parents, Robert Rogers (1815–42) and Sallie Vann Rogers (1818–82), migrated west voluntarily before the forced migration experienced by those who resisted federal confiscation of Cherokee lands. They moved from the Cherokee Nation East

(Georgia) to Arkansas in 1832 and on to Indian Territory in 1835. Clem V. Rogers's father, Robert Rogers, Jr., was a member of the Blind Savannah Clan through his mother, Lucy Cordery Rogers, who was half Cherokee. Robert Rogers, Sr., was Scotch-Irish-English. Clem's mother, Sallie Vann Rogers, a member of the Wolf Clan, was the daughter of Margaret McSwain Vann, and Avery Vann, whose father, Clement Vann, had married a full-blood Cherokee woman, Wa-wli. Clem V. Rogers was born at his parents' log home near the Baptist Mission School on the outskirts of what became the town of Westville, near the Arkansas border.[5]

The Schrimsher and Rogers families were part of the Cherokee elite. In a time when three-quarters of Cherokees were full-bloods who did not speak English, the Schrimshers and Rogerses were English-speaking mixed-bloods.[6] In a time when the great majority of Cherokees were small subsistence farmers, the Rogers and Schrimsher families had accepted ideals of "civilization" including farming on a southern slave-labor model and participation in a mercantile economy.[7] In a time when a majority of Cherokees held no slaves, the Rogers and Schrimsher families were slaveholders.[8] When a large majority of Cherokees chose to remain in their eastern homeland and resist removal, the Rogers and Schrimsher families were among those who voluntarily moved west before forced removal in 1838–39.[9]

Both the Schrimshers and the Rogerses were supporters of the Treaty (or Ridge) Party, which had originated with the signing of the Treaty of New Echota in 1835. Coming in the midst of Cherokee resistance to federal removal policies, the treaty ceded all Cherokee territory east of the Mississippi River (homelands in Alabama, Georgia, North Carolina, and Tennessee) in exchange for the promise of lands in conjunction with those occupied by Cherokees already in the West (known as the Old Settlers) who had migrated voluntarily in the years between 1794 and 1835.[10] Signed by a minority of elite Cherokees, many of whom operated large farms or were involved in mercantile trade, the treaty was opposed by Principal Chief John Ross and the vast majority of the Cherokee people.[11] The treaty, which marked the beginning of a long-standing split in political loyalties that brought generations of violence and factionalization to the Cherokee Nation West, framed Cherokee politics in a significant way from the time of removal through the Civil War and beyond. Political divisions were also partly ethnic and class divisions. The "progressives" of the Treaty Party (including Will Rogers's ancestors) tended to be wealthier, slaveholding individuals oriented toward Anglo-American norms—including the use of the English language, intermarriage with whites, acceptance of European ideas of private property and patrilineal inheritance, and affinity

Elizabeth Hunt Gunter Schrimsher (1804–71), Will Rogers's maternal grandmother, who was born in the Cherokee Nation East and settled in Indian Territory near Tahlequah (*OkClaW*).

John Gunter Schrimsher (1835–1905), Will Rogers's maternal uncle, served as a senator and judge from the Cooweescoowee District in the Cherokee Nation (*OkClaW*).

with the agricultural model demonstrated in white southern plantations operated with black slave labor—while the "conservatives" of the Ross Party tended to be small landholders and full-bloods who spoke and wrote in Cherokee and were more oriented toward traditional Native American ways.[12] His family's alliance with the Treaty Party and their culture shaped Clem V. Rogers's early upbringing and his own choices as a teenager and young man in his twenties.

When Clem V. Rogers was three years old, his father was killed in a politically motivated personal altercation when a Ross Party supporter took issue with Robert Rogers's adamant backing of the Treaty Party.[13] In 1844 Clem's mother, Sallie Vann Rogers, remarried. She wed William Musgrove (ca. 1815–80), a slaveholding wagon and cabinet maker and mercantile operator who became stepfather to young Clem and his sister Margaret.[14] A little over a decade later, Sallie Vann Rogers Musgrove financed the seventeen-year-old Clem V. Rogers's start in the cattle business in the Verdigris country.[15] William Musgrove helped him erect a log building that he managed as a small trading post, and Sallie Vann Rogers Musgrove gave him several head of cattle and some horses. She also deeded him two African American men whom his father, Robert Rogers, had held as slaves. These men, brothers Charles (Rabb) and Houston Rogers, who had been given the Rogers family name, supplied the labor that created the agricultural base of Clem V. Rogers's new ranch. While Clem V. Rogers oversaw the herd of longhorn cattle and hauled merchandise for the trading post, Rabb and Houston Rogers established the ranch's crops, including the corn used for the wintering of the livestock.[16] Clem V. Rogers's friend John Schrimsher had a ranch nearby, and Rogers rode over to court John's sister Mary whenever she came to visit. The two were married in Fort Gibson in 1858. They returned to the Verdigris country, and their first child, Elizabeth, was born there three years later, during the first months of the Civil War.

When the Confederacy was formed in 1861, Clem V. Rogers, who through his family had been acculturated to southern mores and to the economic advantages of the slave system, allied himself with its cause, as did his brother-in-law John Gunter Schrimsher. When Treaty Party leader Stand Watie was commissioned as a colonel in the Confederate army in July 1861, Rogers joined his Regiment of Cherokee Mounted Rifles.[17] He remained with the unit throughout the war, beginning as a first lieutenant, under Captain James Butler, and continuing as a captain under Watie. He was also a member of the 1862 Confederate Council that elected Watie as principal chief of the Cherokee Nation (after John Ross was taken into custody by invading Union forces and exiled to Washington, D.C., until the end of the war.)[18] As an educated, well-

Stand Watie, Cherokee Treaty Party leader and principal chief of the Cherokee Nation
during the Civil War. Clement Vann Rogers joined the Confederate army as an officer in
Watie's Regiment of Cherokee Mounted Rifles in 1861 *(Phillips Collection, OkU)*.

to-do mixed-blood and supporter of the Treaty Party, Rogers was representative of the officers of Watie's regiment. Their counterparts in the other
Regiment of Cherokee Mounted Rifles, headed by John Drew, were from a
similar class of men (although they were loyal appointees of John Ross rather

than Treaty Party backers), but unlike Watie's regiment, Drew's rank and file were primarily full-bloods of moderate means; many were members of the activist Keetoowah Society and supporters of the Ross Party.[19] The differences between the two regiments were soon made clear in skirmishes against Chief Opothleyahola and families of Creek Indians loyal to the Union who attempted to pass through the Cherokee Nation on their way north to federal territory in Kansas. Some of the fighting took place in the Cooweescoowee District, including a conflict near the Schrimsher and Rogers ranches.[20]

While Clem V. Rogers fought in these local skirmishes, Mary America Schrimsher Rogers fled from the Verdigris country on horseback with three-month-old Elizabeth. Accompanied by Rabb Rogers, she rode to her mother-in-law's home near Westville, where the baby became ill and died. Mary Rogers then continued to her own mother's place in Fort Gibson, and from there to the plantation near Tahlequah where she had grown up. The family hoped to live off the land, but as violent and destructive raids increased between pro-Union and pro-Confederate Cherokee factions, and Union army forces invaded the Cherokee Nation (in the summers of 1862 and 1863), the Schrimshers fled, like other slaveholding families, to Texas. They took up residence at a small farm near a Confederate refugee camp at Bonham, Texas, where they remained for the duration of the war.[21] Clem V. Rogers and Mary America Schrimsher Rogers's second child, Sarah Clementine (Sallie), was born in Texas in December 1863.

At war's end, Mary and Clem Rogers were twenty-six years old. The Schrimsher plantation outside Tahlequah was destroyed, as was the Rogers ranch and trading post on Rabb's Creek. Clem V. Rogers's livestock had long since been confiscated or driven away. The Rogerses' plight was representative of that faced by many Cherokee families. The devastation throughout the Cherokee Nation was severe, and Cherokees on both sides of the fighting were left destitute. A census of Union Cherokees taken during the war had found that almost one-third of the adult women were widows, and one-quarter of the children were orphans. The total Cherokee population of the Nation in 1867 had dropped to 13,566—a loss of about one-third of the Cherokee people through disease, battle, or flight since the beginning of the war.[22]

Clem V. Rogers went to Texas to join his wife and daughter, and together they returned to Indian Territory. Mary's father, Martin Schrimsher, died on the trip home. Like many Southern Cherokees, the Rogerses did not immediately return to the Cherokee Nation. Clem and Mary joined Clem's mother, Sallie Vann Rogers Musgrove, at her home in the Choctaw Nation, and put in a crop. Their third child and first boy, Robert Rogers, was born there in April

1866. The following fall the Rogerses moved back to the Cherokee Nation, near Fort Gibson, where they rented a farm from Mary's sister Elizabeth Alabama Schrimsher Adair.[23] They worked the farm for a year, then moved to Mary's mother's home in Fort Gibson, where their fourth child, Maud Ethel, was born in November 1869. Meanwhile, Clem V. Rogers worked as a teamster for the wealthy entrepreneur Oliver Wack Lipe and entered into a partnership in the cattle business with Lipe's son DeWitt Clinton Lipe. By the fall of 1870 both Rogers and the younger Lipe had moved their families back to the Verdigris country. Rogers began a second ranch there on Cherokee communal lands, up the Verdigris River from his initial ranch site on Rabb's Creek. May, the fifth Rogers child, was born in the remodeled log home at the new ranch in May 1873.

Despite severe drought in 1873 and 1874 and political upheavals in the middle of the decade, the 1870s were boom years for the Rogerses and others who had resettled in the Verdigris valley. The cattle business prospered on the sixty-thousand-acre spread, and the Rogers home became a social center under the influence of the gregarious and gracious Mary Rogers. Clem V. Rogers entered Cherokee politics as a judge for the Cooweescoowee District in 1877.[24] He was elected to his first of five terms as a senator in the Cherokee Senate in 1879, the same year as the birth of his last child, a boy named for his friend and colleague, Confederate veteran and Cherokee diplomat William Penn Adair.[25] After May's birth, Mary Rogers had lost two infants, Zoe (born and died 1876) and Homer (born and died 1878). William Penn Adair Rogers was born in the family's large two-story ranch house on 4 November 1879. He thrived, winning the attention of his older sisters and the ranch hands. When Will Rogers was four years old, his brother, Robert, seeming heir to his father's legacy as a cattle broker and rancher, fell ill and died just before his seventeenth birthday.[26]

Despite the deaths that struck the Rogers family in the 1870s and early 1880s, their experience establishing the Rogers ranch on the Verdigris River is emblematic of the reconstruction of the Cherokee Nation after the war and the shift among its mixed-blood elites from identification with the South to participation in the ways of the new West. The ranch provided Will Rogers with a youth spent among cowboys, riding the range and learning the cattle business. For Clem V. Rogers it provided large profits and a financial base for future investments. It also provided an economic foundation as he became more thoroughly involved in Cherokee Nation politics in the 1880s, working on behalf of cattle interests, resisting the encroachments of non-Cherokee intruders on Nation lands, and in 1883, defending the citizenship rights of freedmen, Shawnees, and Delawares (a position that put him at odds with the majority opinion on the Cherokee National Council).[27] The Rogers family experienced personally the major transitions that affected the Cherokee Nation as a whole in the period between the Trail of Tears of 1838–39 and the years of rebuilding after the Civil War — years that included the establishment of the ranch life that framed Will Rogers's early childhood.

1. The Cherokees were an Iroquoian people who by the time of regular contact with the English in the 1690s had occupied land in the southern part of the Appalachians for centuries. Their homeland included areas that became parts of Alabama, Georgia, Kentucky, North Carolina, South Carolina, Tennessee, and West Virginia. At the beginning of the eighteenth century the Cherokee territory included all the land between the Ohio and Tennessee Rivers and from the Blue Ridge Mountains to mid-Tennessee. Parts of that land were hunting grounds shared with other Indian peoples. Forced to succumb to the demands of white settlers and the federal government, by the end of the century the Cherokees had ceded over 97,000 square miles of land to European Americans. The Five Tribes — the Cherokees, Chickasaws, Choctaws, Creeks, and Seminoles — were all subjected to federal removal from the Southeast in the 1830s. By the time of the controversial signing of the Treaty of New Echota in 1835 and forced removal in 1838–39, the Cherokee Nation East was located primarily in a region comprising northwestern Georgia, northeastern Alabama, southeastern Tennessee, and southwestern North Carolina. Indian Territory was a region west of Arkansas set aside by the federal government for new homelands for Indians removed from east of the Mississippi River under the provisions of the Indian Removal Act of 1830. The Cherokee Nation West was located in the northeastern section of Indian Territory, near the Kansas, Missouri, and Arkansas borders, in what is today the state of Oklahoma. The Creek and Seminole Nations occupied the middle portion of Indian Territory, whereas the Chickasaw and Choctaw Nations bordered on Texas. A diminished Indian Territory was later merged with Oklahoma Territory to become the state of Oklahoma in 1907 (McLoughlin, *Cherokee Renascence*, 7, 26–30; Mooney, *Historical Sketch of the Cherokee;* Royce, *Cherokee Nation of Indians;* Wright, *Guide to the Indian Tribes of Oklahoma*, 3–27).

2. This passport office scene is from the 1930 Fox film, *So This Is London*. Rogers continued his soliloquy by reaffirming his statement in the face of scandalized expressions from a pair of onlookers: "It *was*," he said, referring to the discredit due the Indians for letting the pilgrims land. "That's the only thing that I'd ever blame the Indians for."

3. Major Ridge had been an Upper Town chief and a member of the governing National Council of the Cherokee Nation East. His son John Ridge was a leader of the proremoval Ridge, or Treaty, Party, and Elias Boudinot was the former editor of the *Cherokee Phoenix*. Like his close friend John Ridge, Boudinot was well educated and an assimilationist. Both Ridge and Boudinot were graduates of the Cornwall Seminary in Connecticut; both married white New Englanders they met while they were students there. The three men were all signers of the Treaty of New Echota, which had ceded Cherokee lands in the East and mandated removal. They were killed as an act of revenge in accordance with Cherokee law that made death the penalty for the selling of tribal land without the approval of the people in full council. Their deaths began a virtual civil war within the Cherokee Nation from 1839 to 1846, in which Cherokees of the Treaty Party (also known as the Ridge Party or Removal Party) were pitted against Cherokees of the Ross Party (also known as the National Party or Patriotic Party) over the legality of

Indian Territory, 1866–89 (Morris, McReynolds, and Goins, *Historical Atlas of Oklahoma*, 3d ed., map 33).

© 1976 by the University of Oklahoma Press

Cherokee Nation political divisions (Morris, McReynolds, and Goins, *Historical Atlas of Oklahoma*, 3d ed., map 35).

removal, the tragedies suffered by the Nation in the process of removal, the loss of the eastern homelands, and desire for political control in the West. A majority of Cherokees continued to believe the Treaty of New Echota was fraudulent. Treaty Party backers saw it as a pragmatic negotiation that accepted the loss of the homelands as inevitable and recognized that voluntary migration was preferable to forced removal. They claimed the signers were motivated by the desire to preserve the Nation's wealth and to prevent the very kind of suffering that occurred on the Trail of Tears (Conser, "John Ross and the Cherokee Resistance Campaign"; Foreman, G., *Indian Removal;* Franks, *Stand Watie and the Agony of the Cherokee Nation*, 29–34, 55–62; McLoughlin, *After the Trail of Tears*, 15–58; McLoughlin, *Cherokee Renascence*, 266ff., 367–68, 450, 451; Starr, *History of the Cherokee Indians*, 85–101, 112–19; Wilkins, *Cherokee Tragedy*, 254–78).

4. For a more detailed profile of the life of Will Rogers's mother, see the Biographical Appendix entry for ROGERS, Mary America Schrimsher.

5. For a detailed overview of Will Rogers's father's life and a profile of Mary America Schrimsher Rogers's brother, see Biographical Appendix entries for ROGERS, Clement Vann, and SCHRIMSHER, John Gunter.

6. Of those listed in the census of 1835, 77 percent were full-bloods, with small minorities of half-bloods and one-quarter Cherokees. There were 201 intermarried whites. In the 1830s members of slaveholding Cherokee families were more proficient in reading and speaking English than Cherokee. (This trend was maintained in the Rogers family. Clem V. Rogers could not speak or write in Cherokee, though he could understand some of the spoken language; Mary America Schrimsher Rogers was apparently somewhat bilingual through the influence of her half-Cherokee mother, although in her memoirs of her husband, Betty Blake Rogers says that Mary Rogers's grandmother "Catherine could not even talk to her children—she spoke no English and they spoke no Cherokee" [Rogers, *Will Rogers*, 40]. The Rogers children were raised as English speakers.) Linguistic choice was as important as ancestry in the political distinctions made between mixed-bloods and full-bloods: those of mixed ancestry who chose to converse and write only in Cherokee were considered full-bloods. In the year that the mixed-blood Rogers family settled in Indian Territory (1835), only 17 percent of Cherokees had any white ancestors, but "78 percent of the members of families owning slaves had some proportion of white blood" (Perdue, *Slavery and the Evolution of Cherokee Society,* 60; see also McLoughlin, *Champions of the Cherokees,* 256f.; McLoughlin, *Cherokee Renascence,* 329; McLoughlin and Conser, "Cherokees in Transition," 693; Thornton, *Cherokees,* 52, 53).

7. The Rogers and Schrimsher families were part of what has been described as a "small group of well-to-do, influential merchant-traders, large planters, slave-owning farmers and entrepreneurs" and artisans who had moved away from the traditional Cherokee emphasis on communal norms and matrilineal kinship to embrace "individualistic values of the acquisitive society" (McLoughlin, *Cherokee Renascence,* 327). These middle- and upper-class educated Cherokees, most of whom were English speaking mixed-bloods, emerged as leaders of the Cherokee Nation East and participated in the centralization of Cherokee political power and negotiations with federal policy makers. Many of the "Old Settlers" and early emigrationists were among the relatively more wealthy progressives who were half- or full-bloods who had married whites. Many of them were slave owners and took their slaves with them, establishing the institution in the new territory. Slaveholders, meanwhile, controlled the government of the Cherokee Nation, partly because of the wealth they had accrued (McLoughlin, *Cherokee Renascence,* 327; McLoughlin and Conser, "Cherokees in Transition"; and Perdue, *Slavery and the Evolution of Cherokee Society,* 58–60).

8. In the period between 1819 and 1827, just over two hundred Cherokee families (out of some thirty-five hundred families) owned one or more slaves. Thirty to forty families owned more than ten, and another thirty owned between three and nine. At the time of the signing of the Removal Treaty in 1835, "slavery did not permeate the Cherokee tribe but was concentrated in the hands of a very few: only 7.4 percent of tribal members held slaves," primarily wealthier mixed-blood families engaged in plantation agriculture (Thornton, *Cherokees,* 53). Slaveholders remained a minority in the Cherokee Nation West as they had been in the East. In 1848, when both Clem V. Rogers's mother, Sallie Vann Rogers, and her husband, William Musgrove, were slaveholders, and when Mary America Schrimsher's parents operated a plantation with slave labor near Tahlequah, just 10 percent of Cherokee families owned slaves. This statistic held true on the eve of the Civil War as well. In 1860, when Mary America Schrimsher Rogers and Clem V. Rogers were newlyweds and Rabb and Houston Rogers were working their land in the Cooweescoowee District, there were between thirty-five hundred and four thousand slaves in the Cherokee Nation, owned by 10 percent of Cherokee families. Several of the families to whom the Schrimshers and Rogers were related by marriage—

i.e., the Musgroves, the Bushyheads, the Albertys—were also slaveholders. Ninety percent of slaves held by Cherokees were owned by mixed-blood families (McLoughlin, *After the Trail of Tears,* 125; McLoughlin, *Cherokee Renascence,* 328, and McLoughlin, *Champions of the Cherokees,* 277, 283, 284, 380; see also Halliburton, *Red over Black,* 117; McLoughlin and Conser, "Cherokees in Transition"; Perdue, *Slavery and the Evolution of Cherokee Society;* Roethler, "Negro Slavery among the Cherokee Indians," see also Biographical Appendix entry for, ROGERS, Charles and Houston).

9. Population estimates differ, but by the year of the Treaty of New Echota, approximately 5,000 Cherokees were living west of the Mississippi River; 2,802 Cherokees had registered for removal between 1828 and 1834, but only 1,171 of these had actually emigrated. The census of 1835 enumerated 16,542 Cherokees in the East, half in the Georgia area. Approximately 2,000 Cherokees and their slaves left the Cherokee Nation East between January 1836 and May 1838 after the signing of the Treaty of New Echota and before forced removal. The great majority, some 15,000 to 16,000, were involved in the Trail of Tears. About the time of Clem V. Rogers and Mary America Schrimsher's marriage in 1858 there were, by different estimates, between 17,000 and 21,000 Cherokee residents in the Cherokee Nation West. In addition there were some 4,000 African American slaves and ex-slaves, and about 1,000 whites (Gaines, *Confederate Cherokees,* 1; Hewes, *Occupying the Cherokee Country of Oklahoma,* 33; McLoughlin, *Champions of the Cherokees,* 171; McLoughlin, "Red Indians, Black Slavery, and White Racism," 380; and Thornton, *Cherokees,* 50, 51, 52, 82–83).

10. The chronological definition of Old Settlers—western Cherokees who voluntarily left the Cherokee Nation East to settle in the West—varies. More inclusive dates, from 1794 to 1837, incorporate both the Old Settlers who moved west in migrations following the American Revolution and the so-called "early emigrants," or Treaty Party supporters who came in the mid-1830s. The more restrictive definition of Old Settlers dates from the years 1806–9 (the period of the first "removal crisis," caused by efforts of the federal agent to the Cherokees to encourage the voluntary exchange of lands in the East for tracts beyond the Mississippi) or the years of general migration from 1817 until changes in federal policy in 1828. Many of those who had earlier settled in northwestern Arkansas moved circa 1828 into the region of the Arkansas, Grand, and Verdigris Rivers, which became the Cherokee Nation West (Franks, *Stand Watie and the Agony of the Cherokee Nation,* 54; McLoughlin, *Cherokee Renascence;* Thornton, *Cherokees,* 58, 77).

Initial federal policy toward the Five Tribes focused on a program of "civilization" toward full citizenship. The formation of a federal removal policy began in earnest with Thomas Jefferson and the Georgia Compact of 1802, which put forth the idea that the U.S. government should dissolve title to Indian lands in the Southeast and relocate Cherokees and other Five Tribes members west of the Mississippi River, where, some policy makers reasoned, they would be able to live with greater cultural autonomy so that the transition from their traditional hunting and subsistence agriculture economy to an Anglicized agrarian socioeconomic model could take place in a more gradual way. Instead, early enrollments and migrations west (to Arkansas and later to Indian Territory) tended to be undertaken by those, like Will Rogers's ancestors, who were the more "civilized" members of the Cherokee Nation, relatively well-to-do, educated, and Christianized progressives, some of whom had intermarried with whites. Significant voluntary migrations took place circa 1802–8 and in 1817–19. The federal removal policy became solidified with the election of Andrew Jackson to the presidency in 1828 and the passage of the Indian Removal Act in 1830. The Removal Act signaled a shift in policy away from the notion of a sovereign Cherokee Nation subject only to federal jurisdiction, to a state's-rights argument, further opening the Nation to violations by whites.

Between 1828 and 1831 the Georgia legislature abolished recognition of the Cherokee government and its laws and claimed state authority over Cherokee lands; in 1830–32 Indian lands were surveyed for distribution to whites. By 1837 most Cherokee lands in Georgia had been confiscated by the winners in the lottery distribution system, and violence against Cherokee citizens was widespread. Forced removal began with the imprisonment of Cherokees in detention camps in May 1838 and took place in stages in the summer and fall of 1838 and the winter of 1839 (on revisions in federal policy, changing definitions of Indian sovereignty, and the ironies associated with ideas of separatism, assimilation, and acculturation, see Mardock, *Reformers and the American Indian;* McLoughlin, *After the Trail of Tears,* 3–7; McLoughlin, *Champions of the Cherokees,* 9–36; McLoughlin, *Cherokee Renascence,* xviii, 366–87, 439, 444; White, R., "The Federal Government and the Indians," chap. 4 in *"It's Your Misfortune and None of My Own,"* 85–118; and White, R., *Middle Ground;* on the politics and process of removal, see Anderson, W., ed., *Cherokee Removal Before and After;* Dale and Litton, eds., *Cherokee Cavaliers;* Filler and Guttmann, eds., *Removal of the Cherokee Nation;* Franks, *Stand Watie and the Agony of the Cherokee Nation,* 14–54; McLoughlin, *Cherokee Renascence,* 205, 207, 209, 211, 228, 411–427; Moulton, *John Ross: Cherokee Chief,* 72–86; Moulton, ed., *Papers of Chief John Ross,* vol. 1 [1809–1839]; Perdue, *Slavery and the Evolution of Cherokee Society,* 61–70, 104; Starr, *History of the Cherokee Indians,* 100–101, 103–7; Woodward, *Cherokees,* 182–218; on records of Rogers's ancestors in the Cherokee Nation East, see DNA, RG 75, Applications for Reservations, Register of Cherokees, 1817–1819, Register of Persons Who Wish Reservations Under the Treaty of July 5th 1817, record no. 218, registration of Cordery family; DNA, RG 75, 1828, List of Cherokees Wishing to Emigrate, entry for Rogers family; and DNA, RG 75, Property Valuations, 1835–39, records of Gunter and Schrimsher families).

11. The treaty was signed by seventy-five out of some fifteen to eighteen thousand people; fewer than two thousand Cherokees chose to migrate voluntarily in 1836–37 in accordance with the treaty after it was ratified. One thousand additional Cherokee full-bloods succeeded in fleeing to the mountains and escaping federal deportation. The remaining population refused to accept the legitimacy of the treaty and resisted removal. On 24 May 1838 the Cherokee people came under the rule of the U.S. Army, and General Winfield Scott's troops rounded up some sixteen thousand Cherokees and their slaves, imprisoning them in stockades and embarkation points along the Tennessee River. One of the stockades was at Gunter's Landing, near Guntersville, Ala., where Mary America Schrimsher Rogers's mother had been raised and her parents married. The first detachments of those removed by force left beginning in June 1838 and traveled by river on boats or overland. The severe heat and drought of the summer and resulting lack of safe drinking water, and the overcrowding and lack of sanitation on the boats, caused misery and disease among the travelers. As a result the remaining thirteen thousand Cherokees petitioned to remain until the approaching autumn, but the stockades were themselves overcrowded and devoid of adequate sanitation and water facilities. Epidemics broke out and some fifteen hundred to twenty-five hundred people died in the camps before departing. When contingents from the camps did leave on the roughly five-month journey, it was not until September or October 1838, and they were caught without supplies and adequate clothing in the harsh winter of 1838–39. Disease and untreated injuries continued to claim many lives, while others starved or froze to death. Mortality rates were highest among the old and very young. Over one thousand more people died in the brutal passage, and another thousand passed away within a year of arrival in Indian Territory as smallpox and other epidemic diseases struck the Nation. Approximately one-quarter of the population of the Cherokee Nation perished in the

process of removal (Conser, "John Ross and the Cherokee Resistance Campaign"; Foreman, G., *Indian Removal;* McLoughlin, "Removal and Expulsion, 1838–41," chap. 7 in *Champions of the Cherokees*, 171–202; Thornton, "Cherokee Removal: The Trail of Tears," in *Cherokees*, 54–76).

12. These divisions of ethnicity and class and their association with slaveholding and political party were not ironclad. Elites in both parties tended to be mixed-blood slaveholders. Principal Chief John Ross, for example, though he represented the interests of full-bloods, Ross Party conservatives, and those who resisted federal removal policy, was himself of largely (seven-eighths) white ancestry, a wealthy slave-owner with a large number of slaves, and a man of highly Anglicized upbringing. Stand Watie, who became the standard-bearer for the Treaty Party in 1839 after the deaths of other leaders, was three-quarters Cherokee (his mother was half Cherokee, his father a full-blood; Watie's surname was an Anglicized version of his father's Cherokee name, Oowatie). The Waties were less wealthy than the Rosses. Of the twelve framers of the Cherokee Nation Constitution in 1827 (formulated before the Ridge-Ross split), eleven were slaveholders. Together these eleven men owned some 22 percent of all slaves held in the Cherokee Nation. Their elite status is highlighted because slaveholders "comprised less than 8 percent of the heads of households" listed in the 1835 Cherokee census (Perdue, *Slavery and the Evolution of Cherokee Society,* 57; see also Franks, *Stand Watie and the Agony of the Cherokee Nation*, 2–3; Halliburton, *Red over Black*, 20–31, 69–70; Littlefield, *Cherokee Freedmen*, 13 n. 12; Perdue, "Cherokee Planters, Black Slaves, and African Colonization" and "Cherokee Planters: The Development of Plantation Slavery before Removal"; McLoughlin, "Red Indians, Black Slavery, and White Racism"; McLoughlin, *Cherokee Renascence*, 32; Moulton, *John Ross: Cherokee Chief,* 1–14; Woodward, *Cherokees*, 157).

13. Keith, "Clem Rogers and His Influence on Oklahoma History," 2.

14. Musgrove was among the sixty-eight Cherokees who owned ten or more slaves in 1860 (Littlefield, *Cherokee Freedmen*, 13n.12). Sallie Vann Rogers Musgrove joined Mrs. Jesse Bushyhead and two others in filing affidavits against the pro-abolition Northern Baptist missionary Evan Jones in 1855 for allegedly forcing them out of mission churches because they were slaveholders. Clem V. Rogers's mother shifted to the pro-slavery Southern Methodists as a result of her ostracism from the Northern Baptist mission near her home and her opposition to Jones's and other missionaries' antislavery stance (McLoughlin, *After the Trail of Tears*, 140; see also 137). In a corresponding incident, Clem V. Rogers's close friend William Penn Adair also clashed directly with Evan Jones when Jones sought to interfere with Adair taking back into slavery a black woman who had been living freely. Adair petitioned that Jones had interfered with his property rights (McLoughlin, *After the Trail of Tears*, 150). Women could hold property under Cherokee law and thus were among those who owned slaves. Sallie Vann Rogers Musgrove deeded two slaves to her son Clem the year after filing her affidavit against Jones.

15. Clem V. Rogers's start in ranching in the prairie wilderness of the Cooweescoo-wee District came during a period of material progress and development that has been called the second Cherokee renascence (the first, preceding removal, was marked by the establishment of Cherokee farms, political institutions, and educational achievements in the East in the years between 1794 and 1833). Beginning circa 1846 with the subsiding of the factional violence that tore at the Nation in the years immediately following removal, this period of relative plenty and growth ended with the onset of the Civil War in 1860–61. By the end of the war much of the material progress that had been achieved in Indian Territory since removal had been obliterated (see McLoughlin, *Cherokee Renas-*

cence). On farming and homesteading and cultural differences and social hierarchies in the Cherokee Nation in the 1850s, see McLoughlin, *After the Trail of Tears,* 69–78.

16. Theda Perdue has pointed out the perhaps obvious economic advantage held by slaveholding families in the postremoval period. Many slaveholding families began life in Indian Territory with greater material wealth than their nonslaveholding counterparts, and they augmented that wealth by utilizing slave labor to make improvements on communally held Cherokee land. Slave labor was used to "clear and fence fields, cut logs, build houses and barns, construct docks, and plant crops," enabling slaveholders to make more extensive improvements and to cultivate more acres than nonslaveholders, thus perpetuating the class divisions based on slavery and acculturation that had begun before removal (Perdue, *Slavery and the Evolution of Cherokee Society,* 71; see also McLoughlin, *After the Trail of Tears,* 125). Elite Cherokees with political power in the Cherokee government tended not only to operate large farms but to control mercantile trade and such industries as mills and fisheries, a pattern that was continued in the Rogers and Musgrove families, in Clem V. Rogers's own experience, and in that of his close colleagues such as the Lipe family (see Biographical Appendix entries, LIPE, DeWitt Clinton, and ROGERS, Clement Vann).

Historians have debated the issue of the relative benevolence of Cherokee versus white slave ownership. Theda Perdue and Michael Roethler, for example, have generally argued that traditional Cherokee values and the influence of northern missionaries tempered the institution of slavery among the Cherokees, especially among full-bloods who owned small numbers of slaves, whereas Rudi Halliburton, Jr., Daniel Littlefield, Jr., and others have maintained that conditions faced by African Americans in bondage were as harsh among Cherokee masters as among whites. William McLoughlin has taken a middle argument, citing examples of benevolence and of cruelty, and surmising that there was as much variance among Cherokees in their treatment of slaves as among whites. Both Perdue and McLoughlin have pointed out that despite a reputation for relative leniency and variations in enforcement of strict slave codes, blacks were still slaves among the Cherokees, and not equals. Cherokee elites used the power of legislation to institute slave codes restricting the rights of slaves and free blacks, and the proportion of slaves increased rather than decreased with removal from the South to Indian Territory. In 1835 there were some 16,000 Cherokees and 1,592 black slaves; by the Civil War there were some 17,000 Cherokees and 4,000 slaves (Halliburton, *Red over Black,* 39, 117; Littlefield, *Cherokee Freedmen;* McLoughlin, "Red Indians, Black Slavery, and White Racism"; McLoughlin, *After the Trail of Tears,* 121–52; and *Cherokee Renascence,* 295, 338; McLoughlin and Conser, "Cherokees in Transition"; Perdue, *Slavery and the Evolution of Cherokee Society;* Roethler, "Negro Slavery among the Cherokee Indians").

Rogers family historians and biographers have tended to stress a paternalistic relationship among the Clem V. Rogers and Rabb and Houston Rogers families. There may have been a difference in opinion on the subject between the two Rogers brothers themselves; one brother reportedly supported the Union cause in the Civil War, whereas the other remained loyal to Clem V. Rogers and the Confederate Cherokees. Clem V. Rogers hired both the brothers to work at his newly established ranch in the years of rebuilding after the war, and their children were playmates of Will Rogers as well as being variously employed by the Clem V. Rogers family (see, for example, Collings, *Old Home Ranch,* 9, 11; Croy, *Our Will Rogers,* 15; Croy interview with Clement Vann Rogers [son of Rabb Rogers], quoted in Croy, *Our Will Rogers,* 4–6; Walker interview; IPH-OkHi; see also Biographical Appendix entry, ROGERS, Charles and Houston).

Like Rabb and Houston Rogers, many former slaves returned to land they had cultivated before emancipation, becoming self-supporting wage laborers or sharecroppers, often with good relations with the families of former masters who acknowledged their revised political status. Other ex-slaves who were former Cherokee Nation residents were forcibly prevented from returning to the Nation (many had become refugees during the war; either because they were brought to Texas or other Confederate areas by slaveowners, or because they fled to Union territory in Kansas or Missouri). Others were stopped as they attempted to put in crops or make improvements in old lands, or they were turned off land they had formerly occupied by Cherokees who refused to acknowledge the citizenship rights that were granted to former slaves under the provisions of the Treaty of 1866 (see Littlefield, *Cherokee Freedmen*, 22, 23; on Clem V. Rogers and controversies surrounding the status of freed slaves in the Cherokee Nation, see Application for Enrollment in the Cherokee Nation by Clement Vann Rogers, 22–23 October 1900, below).

17. Born in Georgia in 1806, Stand Watie came to Indian Territory in 1837. He was a wealthy farmer, entrepreneur, and Cherokee politician. His brother, Elias Boudinot (Buck Watie), was among the Treaty Party leaders who were murdered in the period of political turmoil in the Cherokee Nation West after removal. Before the war Watie was an organizer for a proslavery secret society called the Knights of the Golden Circle (which later evolved into the Southern Rights Party). The society, like the Treaty Party, was composed mainly of mixed-bloods and supporters of slavery whose "principal objective" was "assisting in capturing and punishing abolitionists interfering with slavery in the Cherokee Nation" (Franks, *Stand Watie and the Agony of the Cherokee Nation*, 114–15; see also Halliburton, *Red over Black*, 119–120, McLoughlin, *Champions of the Cherokees*, 364–65, 368, 380, 390, 396). Watie was the highest-ranking Cherokee in the Confederate army and one of the last Confederate generals to surrender at the end of the war (he surrendered on 23 June 1865). When Principal Chief John Ross was removed from Indian Territory by federal forces in the summer of 1862, Stand Watie was elected principal chief of the Cherokee Nation in his place. Watie was backed in this office by the Confederate, or Southern, Cherokees, whereas Union, or Northern, Cherokees continued to honor Ross's authority in absentia. Clem V. Rogers was a strong Watie supporter (see Cunningham, *General Stand Watie's Confederate Indians;* Fischer and Gill, "Confederate Indian Forces Outside of Indian Territory"; Franks, *Stand Watie and the Agony of the Cherokee Nation;* Gaines, *Confederate Cherokees*, 5, 8–9, 59, 77, 120; Perdue, *Slavery and the Evolution of Cherokee Society*, 129; Starr, *History of the Cherokee Indians*, 143–52; Wilkins, *Cherokee Tragedy;* Woodward, *Cherokees*, 288–89. Papers of the Watie-Ridge-Boudinot families are at OkU).

Watie's regiment participated in the Opothleyahola campaigns and also in the Battle of Pea Ridge (in Arkansas). After the Pea Ridge campaign full-bloods blamed mixed-bloods in Watie's unit for atrocities that had been committed against wounded Union soldiers, including scalping. These charges were seized on by northern journalists and used in a propaganda campaign as Union newspapers denounced white Confederates for allying themselves with savages who ignored established rules of war. Upon investigation it seemed that violations were committed by members of both Watie's and Drew's regiments. Watie's forces were effective in protecting the Cherokee Nation's northern border and in making frequent raids into federal territory in Kansas and Missouri, harassing Union supply lines and troops. Watie's men also made violent guerilla raids against Ross Party supporters and pro-Union residents and suspected abolitionists, burning down homes and destroying crops and orchards. (Ross Party and Northern Cherokees made similar raids against Southern Rights families and slaveholders.) They burned the Cherokee Council House in Tahlequah in October 1863, then proceeded to

John Ross's mansion at Park Hill and burned it to the ground. In December 1863 they returned to destroy the slave cabins that had been adjacent to Ross's home. Even Watie wrote to his wife with regret over killing men whom he had considered friends before the war. After four years of service with the regiment, Clem V. Rogers rarely spoke of his experiences during the war (company muster roll and receipt rolls of C. V. Rogers, Confederate Cherokees Mounted Volunteers, 1862, 1863, in Clem Vann Rogers miscellaneous file 7, OkClaW; Fischer and Gill, "Confederate Indian Forces Outside of Indian Territory"; Franks, *Stand Watie and the Agony of the Cherokee Nation*, 114–76; Gaines, *Confederate Cherokees*, 83, 93–94; McLoughlin, "Civil War in the Cherokee Nation," chap. 8 in *After the Trail of Tears*, 201–21; McLoughlin, *Champions of the Cherokees*, 407, 411, 414; Thornton, *Cherokees*, 91).

18. On the rivalry between John Ross and the Ross Party and Stand Watie and the Southern Rights Party, and the dual government in the Cherokee Nation after Ross was exiled, see Dale and Litton, eds., *Cherokee Cavaliers;* McLoughlin, *Champions of the Cherokees*, 404–6, 408–9; Moulton, *John Ross: Cherokee Chief,* 166–83, and *Papers of Chief John Ross*, vol. 2 [1840–66]; Perdue, *Slavery and the Evolution of Cherokee Society,* 136–38; Woodward, *Cherokees*, 280–81, 284.

19. The Keetoowah Society was organized as a secret organization circa 1856–59 through the influence of the abolitionist Baptist missionary Evan Jones. Made up of full-blood conservatives who defended traditional Indian ways, the Keetoowahs were also sometimes called the Pin Indians because of the crossed pins they wore on their clothing as an emblem of their support for the society. An all-male society with several lodges that functioned as a mutual-aid association, the Keetoowahs were primarily nonslaveholding Northern Baptists who practiced syncretic religion (combining Christianity with traditional tribal rituals and beliefs). They were not English speaking and were devoted to the Cherokee hospitality ethic and other communal values that they felt mixed-blood elites had abandoned. The Keetoowahs began the war as supporters of John Ross (in opposition to Watie's regiment, who did violence to Ross supporters as well as to the Union army and Union loyalists), and through the course of the war many became supporters of abolition and the Union cause (see Mankiller and Wallis, *Mankiller,* 17, 124–25, 169, 171; McLoughlin, *After the Trail of Tears*, 153–75; McLoughlin, *Champions of the Cherokees*, 345, 347; Perdue, *Slavery and the Evolution of Cherokee Society,* 123; Thornton, *Cherokees*, 93–94; Tyner, "Keetoowah Society in Cherokee History"). John Drew's and Stand Watie's "rival Confederate units with different political loyalties" are alternately designated as the "First" or the "Second" regiment of Cherokee Mounted Rifles, depending on the political orientation of those describing them (Franks, *Stand Watie and the Agony of the Cherokee Nation*, 119; Gaines, *Confederate Cherokees*, 15; Starr, *History of the Cherokee Indians*, 143–53).

20. Whereas Watie's regiment pursued the Creeks, killing and capturing women and children as well as men in a series of clashes, the Keetoowahs in Drew's regiment were reluctant to do violence against other Indians. Many full-blood Cherokee soldiers in the unit deserted rather than do so. The ultimate fate of Opothleyahola (or Opothleyoholo) and his followers was horrific; forced to abandon wagons and supplies, they reached Kansas only to suffer horribly as refugees, freezing to death without shelter in the winter and dying of illness and starvation because they received inadequate aid from federal forces. On the conflict between Opothleyahola and his pro-Union Creeks and the Confederate Cherokees in late 1861 and early 1862, see Collings, *Old Home Ranch*, 11; Gaines, *Confederate Cherokees*, 34–42, 43–54; McLoughlin, *After the Trail of Tears*, 192–95; McLoughlin, *Champions of the Cherokees*, 400–401; Moulton, *Papers of Chief John Ross* 2:487, 491, 495; Woodward, *Cherokees*, 270–73.

Many of the hundreds of men who left Drew's regiment later became Union soldiers, thus officially splitting the Ross Party into pro-Confederate and pro-Union factions. Principal Chief Ross had for a time tried to maintain neutrality. Then, receiving little support from Lincoln or Union agents while being actively lobbied by the Confederates and Southern Cherokees, he had allied the Nation with the Confederacy. Near the beginning of the war, in the summer of 1861, approximately one-third of the Cherokee population supported Watie's Southern Rights Party and the South, including most Southern Methodists and Southern Baptists; the remaining Ross Party supporters, Keetoowah full-bloods, and Northern Methodists and Baptists were split between neutrality and support for the Union. Between February and May 1861 the adjoining Choctaw, Chickasaw, Creek, and Seminole Nations all became officially allied with the Confederacy. Ross cooperated with Union forces when they took him into custody in the summer of 1862 and spent most of the war in exile in Washington, D.C. (Abel, *American Indian as Participant in the Civil War;* Franks, *Stand Watie and the Agony of the Cherokee Nation,* 120–23; Gaines, *Confederate Cherokees;* McLoughlin, *After the Trail of Tears,* 170–75, 176–200; McLoughlin, *Champions of the Cherokees,* 387–89; Nichols, *Lincoln and the Indians*).

21. On Mary America Schrimsher Rogers's flight from the Rogers ranch, and on the Schrimsher family as refugees in Texas during the war, see Collings, *Old Home Ranch,* 11–12.

22. The census of Union Cherokees was taken in 1863. On the tremendous devastation of the Cherokee Nation in the Civil War due to Union-Confederate conflict and the guerilla warfare between internal political factions, see Littlefield, *Cherokee Freedmen,* 15; McLoughlin, *Champions of the Cherokees,* 408–12, 414. According to Gaines, no territory or state suffered a higher percentage of losses than did Indian Territory. Thirty-five hundred Cherokee men served in the Union army, and over one thousand of them died in battle, of wounds, or of disease (Gaines, *Confederate Cherokees,* 124; Thornton, "Table 9: Census of the Cherokee Nation, 1863," in *Cherokees,* 92; on the population loss experienced by the Cherokee Nation as a result of the Civil War, see also Hewes, *Occupying the Cherokee Country of Oklahoma,* 33). Hewes gives the Cherokee population in 1859 as twenty-one thousand and in 1869 (after many refugees and Southern Cherokees had returned) as fourteen thousand. The U.S. Department of the Interior reported the number as fourteen thousand in 1865. Hewes quotes a special Indian commissioner who observed that "in no part of the country was the war waged with greater destruction of property or loss of life. . . . On every hand the traveler sees the charred and blackened remains of ruined homesteads" (ibid.). In 1871 the Cherokee population in the Cherokee Nation was estimated by the U.S. Bureau of the Census as approximately eighteen thousand (Thornton, *Cherokees,* 94, 103).

23. Like many other Southern, or Confederate, Cherokees, the Rogerses did not immediately return to the Cherokee Nation. They were able to return when Reconstruction politics forged new alliances in the Nation. The Rogers family supported the Downing Party in 1866 and 1867. The Downings were a coalition party that signaled a significant realignment of Cherokee political loyalties and the desire of many Cherokees, both pro- and anti-confederacy, to reconcile their differences and develop a new program of unity. New associations were formed in the name of preserving Cherokee sovereignty against federal policies that threatened Indian autonomy, and against the encroachments of railroad companies and white intruders into Indian land. Lewis Downing, a Cherokee-speaking Keetoowah Society member, became principal chief briefly from August to November 1866 (the period when the Rogerses moved back to the Nation). Downing then ran successfully against the National Party candidate, John

Ross's nephew William Porter Ross, in the August 1867 elections. Most full-bloods backed Ross and the National Party, whereas Watie's mixed-blood Southern Party supporters (like Clem V. Rogers), reacting in part out of the long animosity they had held against the Ross family, joined the Downings. When Downing died in 1874, the Cherokee National Council chose William Porter Ross as principal chief. By 1874 the Keetoowah Society had undergone a resurgence and the Downings were supporting a Populist platform, endorsing the agrarianism of small farms versus the industrial values represented by the railroads, and attacking the corruption they saw rampant in the Ross Party government. The differences between the Downings and the Ross party sparked another period of factional violence and murders in 1874–75 that was similar to the violence between the Treaty and Ross Parties during Clem V. Rogers's childhood. Clem V. Rogers remained a Downing Party supporter throughout the rest of his political life, as did most of his friends and colleagues (on the rise of the Downing Party, see Littlefield, "Reconstruction," chap. 3 in his *Cherokee Freedmen*, 34–48; McLoughlin, *After the Trail of Tears*, 245–48; McLoughlin, *Champions of the Cherokees*, 440–43, 468, 475, 476, 478).

24. The Cherokee justice system was chaotic in the years after the war. Judges were chosen for character rather than specific knowledge of the law, and the courts operated unpredictably because of the lack of prescribed rules of procedure. Corruption was high among marshals, and lawlessness was common. A new legal code was written and adopted by the Cherokee National Council in 1874 and went into effect in 1876, the year before Clem V. Rogers became a judge. As a result lower courts were able to proceed according to more precise rules, including specific penalties designated for different types and degrees of crime. The Nation's first prison was also built in Tahlequah in this period, a few years before Will Rogers's birth. In 1884 the U.S. Congress gave the federal courts jurisdiction over certain types of violent crimes (including murder, manslaughter, and rape), and in 1889 the first U.S. District Court for the region was established at Muskogee. The Cherokee Nation courts were abolished by act of Congress in 1898 (Littlefield, *Cherokee Freedmen*, 41–44; McLoughlin, *After the Trail of Tears*, 302–7; Starr, *History of the Cherokee Indians*, 263).

25. William Penn Adair, a prominent Treaty Party leader, slaveholder, and Confederate officer, became the foremost diplomat for the Cherokee Nation in Washington, D.C., in the Reconstruction era. See Biographical Appendix entry, ADAIR, William Penn.

26. See Biographical Appendix entry, ROGERS, Robert Martin, and *WRFT,* 8–9. Robert's death foreshadowed an even greater loss that came to Will Rogers at the age of eleven when his mother, Mary America Schrimsher Rogers, died after nursing his sisters Sallie and Maud through severe cases of typhoid fever. See Biographical Appendix entry, ROGERS, Mary America Schrimsher, and "School Days," section two below.

27. On Clem V. Rogers's political career, see Keith, "Clem Rogers and His Influence on Oklahoma History." Rogers would later echo the pragmatism of his ancestors in the Cherokee Nation East. Just as the Treaty Party had once accepted removal as inevitable and had come to a legal agreement it felt best protected its interests, Rogers became reconciled to the end of the Cherokee Nation and participated as a commissioner in the allotment of Cherokee lands in preparation for statehood. His political career was capped by his participation in the constitutional convention that framed the new state of Oklahoma. On the political controversies surrounding the legal status and citizenship rights of former slaves (and non-Cherokee Indians) in the Cherokee Nation in the period between the end of the Civil War and statehood, see Littlefield, *Cherokee Freedmen*, and Wardell, "Freedmen and Citizenship," chap. 11 in *Political History of the Cherokee*

Nation, 223–40. Unlike Clem V. Rogers, who spoke out of former slaves' right to citizenship, many Cherokee leaders favored removal of the former slaves from Nation lands at federal expense. At issue was, in part, the "red" nationalism of Cherokee full-bloods versus the multiracial character of the Nation's residents. In addition to full-bloods and mixed-bloods, the Nation was home to Creek citizens and noncitizens, Delawares (adopted as citizens in 1867) and Shawnees (adopted in 1869), white men and women who were married to Cherokees, whites who had been adopted as citizens or were intruders or working on permits, ex-slaves who had been accepted as citizens under the Treaty of 1866, and ex-slaves seen as intruders because they had failed to meet the strict provisions of the treaty. Divisions between these various peoples were economic and ideological as well as racial (Littlefield, *Cherokee Freedmen,* 44–45; McLoughlin, *Cherokee Renascence,* 337).

———

Record of Birth of Will Rogers
4 November 1879
Cooweescoowee District, Cherokee Nation, I.T.

This family birth register, recording the births of Will Rogers, his parents, and his siblings, is taken from the Bible of Will Rogers's eldest sister, Sallie Rogers McSpadden.[1]

BIRTHS.

Clement Vann Rogers was born on the 11th day of January 1839.[2]

Mary A. Rogers was born on the 9th day of October 1839.[3]

Elizabeth Rogers was born on the 11th day September 1861.[4]

Sarah C. Rogers was born on the 16th day of December 1863.

Robert M. Rogers was born on the 15th day of April 1866.[5]

Maud Rogers was born on the 28th day of November 1869.[6]

May Rogers was born on the 31st day May 1873.[7]

Zoe Rogers was born on the 31st of July [January] 1876, and departed this life July 24th 1876.[8]

Homer Rogers was born on the 1st of July 18768.[9]

William Adair Rogers was born on the 4th Nov. 1879.[10]

DEATHS.

Elizabeth Rogers died December 1861.

Zoe Rogers died July 24th 1876.

Homer Rogers died Sept. 25 1878

Mama died May 28–1890.

May Stine died Sun. July 25–1909.

Papa died Oct. 28–1911.

AD. SRM-OkClaW.[11]

1. For more information on the Rogers family, see Rogers Genealogy at the beginning of the Biographical Appendix.
   Born while her mother was a refugee in Bonham, Tex., during the Civil War, Will Rogers's sister Sarah Clementine Rogers was known throughout her life as Sallie. She was named in honor of her father, Clem V. Rogers, and his mother, Sallie Vann Rogers Musgrove. She was the eldest Rogers child who survived to adulthood. She married Chelsea businessman and cattle rancher John Thomas (Tom) McSpadden in 1885, raised a family, and had a long career as a teacher, church worker, and activist in civic and women's organizations. She passed away in August 1943 (see Biographical Appendix entry, McSpadden, Sallie Clementine Rogers).
   2. Will Rogers's father, Clement Vann Rogers (often known as Clem, Clem V., or C. V.) was born to Robert Rogers and Sallie Vann Rogers in Going Snake District, I.T. (now part of Adair County, Okla.) in 1839. A noted rancher, business owner, Cherokee politician, and Claremore civic leader, he established one of the leading cattle ranches in

The earliest known
photograph of the
main house at the
Rogers family
ranch, birthplace
of Will Rogers,
near Oologah, I.T.
Rogers was born in
the room on the
first floor directly
to the right of the
entrance. *(OkHi)*.

the Verdigris country in the years following the Civil War. He died 28 October 1911 in
Chelsea, Okla., at the home of his daughter Maud Lane (see Biographical Appendix
entry, ROGERS, Clement Vann).

3. Will Rogers's mother, Mary America Schrimsher Rogers, was the daughter of
wealthy Welsh-Cherokee parents, Martin Schrimsher and Elizabeth Gunter Schrimsher. She was born at her family's plantation near Tahlequah, I.T., in 1839. She and Clem
V. Rogers had eight children, five of whom survived infancy. Will Rogers was their
second son and youngest child. Mary Rogers died at the Rogers ranch in May 1890 (see
Biographical Appendix entry, ROGERS, Mary America Schrimsher).

4. Elizabeth Rogers, the first child of Clem V. Rogers and Mary Rogers, was born at
her parents' ranch and trading post at Rabb's Creek, a tributary of the Caney River in
the Verdigris valley, near what became the town of Talala, I.T. In the early part of the
Civil War Mary Rogers fled from fighting near her home, riding with her infant daughter
on horseback to her husband's mother's (Sallie Vann Rogers Musgrove) home near Westville, I.T. Elizabeth Rogers became ill shortly after their arrival and died in December
1861 (see Biographical Appendix entry, ROGERS, Mary America Schrimsher).

5. The year was originally written as 1865; a six was written over the five, changing the
year to 1866. The confusion over the year of Robert Rogers's birth has persisted in historical
accounts of the Rogers family, with some authors reporting it as 1865 and others as 1866.
1866 is the correct date. Robert Martin Rogers was born at Clem V. Rogers's mother's
property in the Choctaw Nation, where Clem V. Rogers and Mary America Schrimsher
Rogers lived for a time upon returning from Texas after the end of the Civil War. Robert was
named for Clem V. Rogers's father and grandfather, who both were called Robert Rogers.
He loved ranch life and seemed to be well suited to inherit his father's career as a rancher
and cattleman. This promise was cut short when he died in April 1883 after a bout of
typhoid fever (see Biographical Appendix entry, ROGERS, Robert Martin).

6. The year was originally written as 1871; 1869 was then written over it. Maud
Ethel Rogers was born 28 November 1869 on the farm that Clem V. Rogers and Mary
America Schrimsher Rogers rented from Mary's sister, Alabama Schrimsher Adair
(later Rogers), east of Fort Gibson. Maud Rogers married Chelsea druggist C. L. (Cap)

Lane and was deeply involved in the charity, church, and civic life of the town. She died in Chelsea on 15 May 1925, near the end of Will Rogers's time with the *Ziegfeld Follies* (Collings, *Old Home Ranch*, 16, 21; *WRFT,* 10; see also Biographical Appendix entries, LANE, C. L.; LANE, Maud Ethel Rogers; and ROGERS, Clement Vann).

7. Actually named Mary after her mother, but always called May (for the month in which she was born), May Rogers was the youngest surviving daughter of Clem V. Rogers and Mary America Schrimsher Rogers. A light-hearted girl, in adulthood she had the most difficult life of the Rogers daughters. Her first husband was murdered, as was the man who courted her after her husband's death. She remarried, but died of illness not long after her thirty-seventh birthday (see Biographical Appendix entry, STINE, May Rogers Yocum).

8. There are many discrepancies regarding Zoe Rogers's birth and death dates. Here Sallie Rogers McSpadden mistakenly records that the baby was born in July; the actual month of her birth was January. The supplement to this document states that Zoe's headstone in the Chelsea cemetery gives her death date as 4 July 1876. In her genealogy of the Rogers family Reba Collins reports that Zoe was born and died on 31 July 1876, while Bell records that she was born 31 January 1876 at the Rogers ranch and died 4 July 1876. Family historian Ellsworth Collings wrote, "Zoe, a little girl, came July 31, 1876, but died four months later" (Collings, *Old Home Ranch*, 21; see also Bell, *Genealogy of Old and New Cherokee Indian Families*, 358; *WRFT,* 10).

9. The year was originally written as 1876; the 6 was crossed out and an 8 added, changing the date to 1878, which is the correct year of Homer Rogers's birth (and death). Homer, like Elizabeth and Zoe Rogers, was short-lived, surviving only a few months. He died as recorded on 25 September 1878, about a year before Will Rogers was born. (Some sources record his date of birth as 30 June 1878; see Bell, *Genealogy of Old and New Cherokee Indian Families*, 358).

10. William Penn Adair Rogers, the last child of Mary America Schrimsher Rogers and Clem V. Rogers, was born in his parents' ranch house near Oologah, I.T. He was named for the Cherokee statesman William Penn Adair, a close friend of his father's. Adair's wife, Susannah McIntosh Drew Adair (known as Aunt Sue), was one of the women who attended Mary America Schrimsher Rogers at the birth. There is considerable debate whether Dr. Andrew Jackson Lane (ca. 1851–96) or Dr. Richard Owen Trent (ca. 1853–88) was the attending physician at Rogers's birth. Gazelle (Scrap) Lane, the daughter of Dr. Lane, has written that her father, a pioneer physician in the Claremore/Oowala area and a close friend of the Rogers family, was the doctor who brought Will Rogers into the world (Gazelle Lane to Lewis J. Moorman, M.D., n.d., written on letter of Moorman to Lane, 19 February 1954, asking for information pertaining to Rogers's birth; Lewis J. Moorman, M.D., Papers, OkU. At the time Dr. Moorman was gathering information on the history of medicine in Oklahoma and was seeking information on the doctor who was present at Will Rogers's birth. See also Lane, interview, OkClaW; Homer Croy to Moorman, 13 June [1954], Moorman Papers, OkU).

Other family members and friends, however, suggest that Dr. Trent was the doctor who was at the Rogers home on 4 November 1879. A Fort Gibson, I.T., physician, Trent married Mary Katherine (Mollie) Brown (1859–1952), whose mother, Ann E. Schrimsher, was the half-sister of Will Rogers's mother. Madelyn Pope McSpadden (1898–1977), the granddaughter of Dr. Trent and the wife of Herbert McSpadden (1893–1980), Will Rogers's nephew, has written that Dr. Trent was the attending physician. She wrote: "From my mother-in-law [Sallie Rogers McSpadden] and Mrs. M. K. Trent I got this story. The bed was by the south window and the baby was almost there when Dr. Trent turned to the window for a better light on the cord he was preparing to use and

Will Rogers was named for William Penn Adair (1830–80), family friend and prominent Cherokee Nation politician *(Keith Collection, OkU)*.

suddenly Mrs. Rogers said 'the baby is here Doctor'" (Madelyn McSpadden to Moorman, 23 March 1954, Moorman Papers, OkU; see also McSpadden to Moorman, 2 February 1954, and Moorman to McSpadden, 22 January and 5 March 1954, Moorman Papers, OkU; Trent, *My Cousin Will Rogers*, 14).

According to the version of Will Rogers's birth given by Clem Rogers, the son of Rabb and Rhoda Rogers, who was a little boy at the time, Mary America Schrimsher

Rogers was attended by a number of women as well as by the doctor. Rogers remembered Perry Ross, a local man, riding up on his horse and telling either his aunt Sidney Ross-Rogers and/or his mother, Rhoda Rogers, along with his cousin Agnes Rogers Walker, to "Come quick. Mrs. Clem want you desperate bad. There's a birth comin'." Little Clem Rogers and the women drove the six miles to the Rogers ranch in a spring wagon, and "When we get there, my mother rush into the east room of the down stairs where the trouble was. This room at a time like this was no place for a lad of my age, so I go to the kitchen. Two or three ladies was in there with Mrs. Rogers. Finally there was a terrible screech and then a lot of little cries, like a pig under a gate. About this time [the doctor] come. He had been sent for but the river was up and he was delayed. He took charge. There was calls for hot water and bandages and there I was in the kitchen with the colored people doin' everything we could and prayin' to God everything would go well." Finally the physician emerged from the bedroom and announced to the people who had gathered in the house that a boy had been born. In his typed notes for this interview with Clem Rogers, Homer Croy transcribed the doctor's name as Dr. Lane. In his published version of the same interview, he gave the name as Dr. Trent (Croy, *Our Will Rogers*, 4–5). In a letter to Lewis Moorman about this issue Croy wrote that "Each family swears on Bibles their Grandpa was the one who done it. Miss Gazelle Lane swears to God it was her father. If you get caught between the two trenches you will need medical attention" (Croy to Moorman, 13 January [1954], Moorman Papers, OkU; notes of 1952 interview with Clem Rogers [b. 1874] by Homer Croy, HCP-MoU; see also Biographical Appendix entries, ADAIR, William Penn; ADAIR, Susannah McIntosh Drew; LANE, Andrew Jackson, M.D.; ROGERS, Clement Vann; ROGERS, Mary America Schrimsher, and TRENT, Richard Owen, M.D.).

11. The following supplement was added to the "Deaths" register in a different hand in 1963. Asterisks were placed before the above listing for Zoe Rogers and after the above listing for "Papa" (Clem V. Rogers). These asterisks were then explained in the supplement as noting information taken from tombstones in the Chelsea cemetery, 18 January 1963:

> *On the tombstone [of Clem V. Rogers] the date is Oct. 29th 1911
> Homer Rogers d. Sept. 25th 1878
> *Zoe Rogers d. July 4th 1876
> Robert Rogers d. April 13th 1883
> Maud Rogers d. May 15th 1925
> Sally C. Rogers d. August 24 1943
> Will Penn Adair Rogers d. August 15, 1935

Authenticated Roll of the Cherokee Nation
1880
Cooweescoowee District, Cherokee Nation, I.T.

In 1880 the Cherokee Nation conducted its own census (or enrollment), recording names of "persons entitled to and exercising citizenship" in the nine districts of the Cherokee Nation.[1] The first column of the census schedule was for names, the second for native or adopted status, the third for race or prior nationality, the fourth for age, the fifth for sex, and the sixth for occupation.

The census also recorded literacy (columns seven and eight were labeled "Can

Read," "Can Write") and marital status ("Yes or No," column nine), as well as detailed information on improvements and farm products in 1879.[2]

The Cooweescoowee District had the largest population of the nine Cherokee districts in 1880 (790 families, or 3,458 individuals; the entire Nation numbered 19,735). The district had almost equal numbers of males and females. The census results revealed that the district had 1,797 Cherokees, 546 ex-slaves, 1 Creek, 600 Delawares, 290 Shawnees, 220 whites married to Indians, and 4 unidentified. The district also had by far the greatest number and proportion of individuals designated as noncitizen intruders of any of the Cherokee Nation districts; indeed, almost half of the intruders in the Cherokee Nation (912 of the 1,821 registered) lived in the district where Will Rogers was born and raised.[3]

Rogers Clem V.	N.	Cher.	41.	M	Politician	Yes	Yes	Yes[4]
Rogers Mary	N.	Cher.	41.	F	DEAD.[5]	Yes	Yes	Yes
Rogers Sallie	N.	Cher.	17.	F		Yes	Yes	No
Rogers Robert	N.	Cher.	13.	M	DEAD.[6]	Yes	Yes	No
Rogers Maud	N.	Cher.	10.	F		Yes	No	No
Rogers May	N.	Cher.	7.	F		No	No	No
Rogers Col. W. P.[7]	N.	Cher.	7 m.	M		No	No	No

PD, with autograph and stamped insertions. OkHi. The copy of the original document is damaged by blots that partially obscure the first letters of the Rogers children's first names.

1. On the overall results of the census, see Hewes, "Census of 1880 as a Milestone of Development," in *Occupying the Cherokee Country of Oklahoma*, 41–44.

2. The information included number of dwellings; total acreage enclosed; total acreage planted in corn, wheat, oats, potatoes, turnips, cotton, and hay; and livestock — numbers of cattle, hogs, sheep, mules, and horses. The Cherokee Nation in 1880 was overwhelmingly agrarian, with 3,549 Cherokees classified as farmers and 13 as stockmen. There were 713 farms in the Cooweescoowee District; 29,521 acres were enclosed; and 19,815 acres were under cultivation (mainly in corn, with a small percentage in wheat). There were 20,198 registered cattle (more than twice the number in any other district) and 24,137 hogs (Hewes, *Occupying the Cherokee Country of Oklahoma*, 42, 43).

3. The Cooweescoowee District was formed in 1856 by the Cherokee National Council and named in honor of Principal Chief John Ross, whose Cherokee name was Cooweescoowee (after a mythical white water bird of tremendous size). Established out of the western portion of the Saline District, it bordered the Creek Nation on the south and the Cherokee Outlet on the west. The district was also home to most of the Delawares and Shawnees as well as the largest number of freed citizens in the Nation. The large number of people described as intruders reflects the uneasy citizenship status of former slaves. Cherokee census takers applied a strict interpretation of the Treaty of 1866 and designated only those freedmen who had returned to the Nation in the first six months after the Civil War as citizens; the rest (757 individuals) were classified as intruders. Relatively few full-blood Cherokees lived in the western prairies (see Hewes, *Occupying the Cherokee Country of Oklahoma*, 39, for a table summarizing the 1880

Maud Ethel Rogers (1869–1925), Will Rogers's sister, with whom he remained very close over the years, in a photograph taken ca. 1880 *(OkClaW)*.

census of the Cherokee Nation by district. The statistics given for population totals are from Thornton, *Cherokees*, 104–6; Hewes gives the total for Cooweescoowee District as 5,323 and for the Cherokee Nation as a whole as 25,438, noting that discrepancies in totals exist because of methods of reporting orphan populations. On the policy toward ex-slaves and the issue of ex-slaves counted as intruders, see Hewes, *Occupying the Cherokee Country of Oklahoma*, 42, and Littlefield, *Cherokee Freedmen*. On the forma-

May Rogers (1873–1909), Will Rogers's youngest sister, ca. 1880 (*OkClaW*).

Sallie Clementine Rogers (1863-1943), Will Rogers's eldest sister, in her graduation photograph from the Cherokee Female Seminary, 1880 *(OkTahN)*.

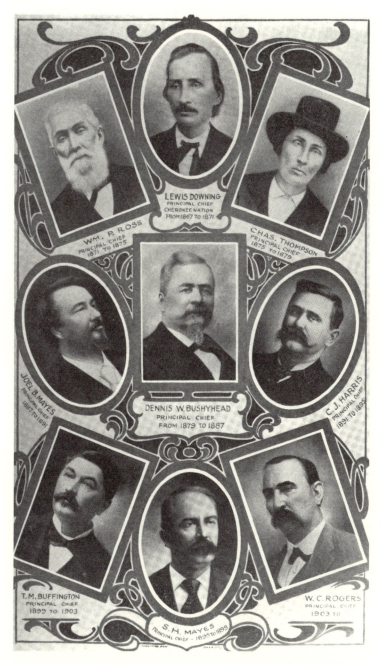

Principal chiefs of the Cherokee Nation from 1867 to 1917. William C. Rogers, the last Cherokee principal chief elected before statehood, was no relation to Will Rogers. As an influential Cherokee public official, Clem V. Rogers regularly associated with the Nation's leaders (*Oklahoma Red Book, vol. 1, General Personalities Collection, OkU*).

tion of the Cooweescoowee District, see *As I Recollect*, 54; *DC*, 28 September 1904; Shirk, *Oklahoma Place Names*, 53).

4. The schedule answers in the affirmative in the columns for "Can Read," "Can Write," and "Married, Yes or No." The census takers also recorded that Clem V. Rogers had one dwelling and four other structures on one farm with 180 total acres enclosed, 140 of them planted in corn. This crop produced 250 bushels of corn. Rogers is also listed as having 20 acres in hay, 805 cattle, 152 hogs, 2 mules, and 4 horses. His occupation is listed as "politician" rather than farmer or rancher, a reflection of his status as a Cherokee Nation senator from Cooweescoowee District (1879, 1881, 1883, 1899, 1900, 1903). Rogers was president pro tem of the Cherokee Senate in 1880 and a judge in the Cooweescoowee District in 1877, 1878, and 1879. He became a member of the Cherokee delegation that negotiated with the Dawes Commission between 1896 and 1899 (OkHi; OkClaW).

5. Mary America Schrimsher Rogers died in May 1890. The census schedule was left blank in the "occupation" column after her name and (apparently sometime after 1890) stamped "DEAD." Her entry in the 1880 Cherokee Census Index also was stamped "DEAD."

6. Robert Rogers died three years after the census was taken, at the age of sixteen. As with his mother's entries in the schedule and index, the blank occupation column after his name and his index entry are stamped "DEAD."

7. The 1880 Cherokee Census Index lists Will Rogers as No. 2337, "Rogers, W. P. Col." of Cooweescoowee District. Rella Looney of the Oklahoma Historical Society has confirmed that William Penn Adair Rogers "was enrolled as Col. W. P. Rogers" (Looney, Archivist, to J. B. Milam, Chelsea, Okla., 27 December 1940, OkHi; and Looney to Homer Croy, 9 July 1952, HCP-MoU; see also Croy, *Our Will Rogers*, 331).

Rogers Family Entries,
Per Capita Cash for Breadstuffs Receipt Roll,
Cherokee Nation Treasury
ca. 1880
Tahlequah, I.T.

Cherokee Nation land was held in common by all citizens of the Nation, who also benefitted from sales, leasing agreements, and other land use authorized by the Cherokee National Council.[1] Bonds purchased from the proceeds of land sales were held for the Nation by the federal government. Congressional appropriations were periodically distributed to all Cherokee citizens through commissions established by the principal chief and other leaders of the Cherokee Nation. Annuities were also provided for use toward support of Cherokee schools and occasional per capita payments such as those recorded in this and the following document.[2] The communal ownership of land stemmed from ancient practices in the Cherokee Nation East, where hunting grounds, pastures, and agricultural fields were held by the Cherokees as a group while improvements (homes, outbuildings, mills, crops, livestock, etc.) could be privately owned and sold.[3] Cherokee laws also regulated such things as seasonal burning, timber cutting and use, the use of salt wells and salt springs, and mineral leases, to protect resources for the common good.[4]

RECEIPT ROLL

The subscribers, do hereby acknowledge to have received of D. W. Lipe,[5] Treasurer of Cherokee Nation, the sums set opposite our names respectively, being in full of our "per capita" portion of the money appropriated by an Act of Congress for the purchase of breadstuffs, being in accordance with an Act of the National Council, dated December 3rd, 1879.

Names.	Total in family.	Amount Paid. Dolls.	Cts.	To whom Paid.	Witness.
Rogers, Clem V					
" Mary E					
" Sallie A					
" Bob					
" Maud					
" May					
" W. P.	7	115	85[6]	C V. Rogers	P L Blackstone

PD, with autograph inserts. DNA, RG 75.

1. See Starr, *History of the Cherokee Indians*, 261–62. Clem V. Rogers, for example, was active in Cherokee Nation decisions to lease Cherokee Strip land to cattlemen. As a senator he wrote and introduced a May 1883 bill authorizing such an arrangement, bringing the grazing of a large expanse of land under control of the Cherokee Strip Live Stock Association, of which he was a leading member, and formalizing the collection of tax monies for its use (see Cherokee Nation Citizen Census Record, 1883, below). Some two-thirds of the Cherokee Nation was unoccupied and sold in sections in the period between 1865 and 1891 (see Hewes, *Occupying the Cherokee Country of Oklahoma*, 11).

2. Hewes, *Occupying the Cherokee Country of Oklahoma*, 29–30. Distributions were matters of internal political debate and of Cherokee diplomacy in regard to federal action. The Downing Party platform of the mid-1870s called for per capita distribution for breadstuffs because of the shortage of food caused by the severe drought and grasshopper plague of 1873–74. The distributions provided cash to purchase food, livestock, and seed for a new crop. Funds were also distributed for use in the Cherokee school system and for Nation support of orphans. In the crisis in the mid-1870s Indian Territory missionary and federal agent John B. Jones telegrammed Clem V. Rogers's friend William Penn Adair, with the Cherokee delegation in Washington, D.C., to "Do your best for our starving people. . . . Word comes from all parts of children crying for bread" (John B. Jones to William Penn Adair et al., 23 February 1875, DNA, RG 75, microfilm M-234, roll 108, quoted in McLoughlin, *Champions of the Cherokees*, 479, see also 476–77. On the history of negotiations regarding per capita payments, see McLoughlin, *After the Trail of Tears*, 60–64).

3. Hewes has identified the "basic attitude toward the land — that it belonged to all members of the tribe" as the hallmark of Cherokee culture (Hewes, *Occupying the Cherokee Country of Oklahoma*, 1; see also Wilms, "Cherokee Land Use in Georgia before Removal"). The Cherokee Nation East had a traditional division of labor in

which men hunted and women were responsible for subsistence agricultural tasks. Villages included a communal garden cultivated by women, children, and older men. Land was held in common, and food shared. A hospitality ethic mandated the sharing of food and sustenance with any visitor in need, no matter how short the supplies. Under Anglo-European–American cultural influences, as hunting grounds were depleted (and deerskins overused as a medium of economic barter with whites), the Cherokees gradually shifted to an agrarian economy in which men increasingly took up cultivation and everyone relied on European technology and manufactured goods. Although land was still held in common, the change in the economic base of the Cherokees, in the roles of men and women and labor needs, also opened the Nation to new concepts of private property and material accumulation, including the utilization of black slave labor and the ownership of slaves. Changes in communal values and the entry into a market economy also altered ceremonies and rituals. The erosion of communal social and economic relations was encouraged by federal policies working toward detribalization and the ultimate destruction of Indian political sovereignty (see Goodwin, *Cherokees in Transition;* McLoughlin, "Changing Cherokee Ways," chap. 1 in *Cherokee Renascence,* 3–32; McLoughlin, "Red Indians, Black Slavery, and White Racism," 373, 380; McLoughlin and Conser, "Cherokees in Transition"; Purdue, *Slavery and the Evolution of Cherokee Society,* 50–56; on federal Indian policy, the demise of communalism, and the idea of individualism, assimilation, material accumulation, and self-interest as "progressive" values, see also White, "The Federal Government and the Indians," chap. 4 in *"It's Your Misfortune and None of My Own,"* 85–118). Despite increasing Anglicization and economic transitions in the eighteenth century, the communal tradition was reaffirmed in the constitution adopted by Cherokee elites (most of them slaveholders) "in July 26, 1827, which provided that all lands were common property . . . and the legislature was empowered to 'prevent the citizens from monopolizing improvements with the view to speculation'" (Hewes, *Occupying the Cherokee Country of Oklahoma,* 5). Maintenance of the political autonomy and unity of the Cherokee Nation despite economic changes remained the central issue for the Cherokees throughout the nineteenth century.

Communalism in the Cherokee Nation West was tempered by the intrusions of white settlers; by the introduction of barbed-wire fencing of individual plots, croplands, and ranches; and by the unequal distribution of wealth exemplified in livestock ownership and improvements (or lack of them) made by individual Cherokee families, and resulting monopolies of resources (see Hewes, *Occupying the Cherokee Country of Oklahoma,* 38, also 39, 41, 48. On inequity in improvements, see, for example, Hewes, *Occupying the Cherokee Country of Oklahoma,* 19–22, 24–26; Perdue, *Slavery and the Evolution of Cherokee Society,* 71–72). The Rogers family was among those who developed control over vast acreages of land and made impressive improvements, including the building of a large two-story ranch house that was beautifully furnished. Clem V. Rogers was one of the first Cooweescoowee District residents to introduce barbed-wire fencing. Through his involvement in the Cherokee Live Stock Association and in the Cherokee Nation government, Clem V. Rogers also was in a position to strengthen the claims of upper-class ranchers on common lands. Less well-to-do observers of Clem V. Rogers, for example, resented his behaving as though "he was the monarch of all he surveyed, and he pretty nearly was" (Roach, "Will Rogers' Youthful Relationship with His Father," 327). The communalism of Cherokee land use was formally ended by the Curtis Act of 1898 and the Dawes Commission's allotment of individual plots of land to verified Cherokee citizens in 1903–1910. Allotment was partially rationalized as remedying the inequities created by monopolization of resources under the communal land system, which worked against full-bloods, who generally were not involved in large-scale fencing (Hewes, *Occupying the Cherokee Country of Oklahoma*, 47, 57). On the Rogers family and allotment, see testimony of Clem V. Rogers on behalf of William P. Rogers to the Dawes Commission, 17 August 1903, below.

4. Hewes, *Occupying the Cherokee Country of Oklahoma*, 29.

5. In 1886 Clem V. Rogers's friend and former business partner DeWitt Clinton (D. W.) Lipe was appointed by Cherokee Principal Chief Dennis Wolf Bushyhead as a member of one of a series of commissions to determine citizenship claims in Indian Territory. He served along with John E. Gunter and John T. Adair. At the time Bushyhead apparently believed that the federal government's interest in establishing a citizenship roll was "to know who are really intruders in order to remove them" (*Report of the Secretary of the Interior*, 53d Congress, 2d sess., 1893, H. Doc. 1, pt. 5, serial 3210, 78, quoted in Sober, *The Intruders*, 37). Lipe was treasurer of the Cherokee Nation for two terms, 1879–83 and 1895–99 (see Biographical Appendix entry, LIPE, DeWitt Clinton).

6. As noted by the curator of a National Archives exhibition that included this receipt roll, Rogers "was less than one year old when he received a full share of an appropriation, $16.55" (DNA, RG 75, "A Matter of Identity: Chronicles of the Family in the National Archives," checklist for an exhibition in the Circular Gallery of the National Archives, July 1981, item 89).

Cherokee Nation Citizen Census Record for Per Capita Distribution 1883 Cooweescoowee District, Cherokee Nation, I.T.

In 1883, four-year-old Will Rogers and members of his immediate family were listed on a census pay roll that enabled them to receive funds from the leasing of grazing lands in the Cherokee Outlet.[1]

CITIZENS OF CHEROKEE NATION, BY RIGHT OF CHEROKEE BLOOD.

No.	Names of head and members of families separately.	Age.	Remarks.
1142	C V Rogers	45	
1143	Mary A Rogers	44	
1144	S C Rogers	19	
1145	Maudie Rogers	13	
1146	Mary Rogers[2]	10	
1147	Wm P Rogers	4	

PD, with autograph inserts. DNA, RG 75, FARC, Records of the Commissioner to the Five Civilized Tribes, microfilm publication 7RA-56.[3]

1. The manuscript census schedules were prepared under an Act of the National Council of the Cherokee Nation, 19 May 1883, and arranged according to district and

Principal Chief Dennis Wolf Bushyhead stands between John Gunter Schrimsher *(left)* and L. B. Bell *(right)*. In 1883–84, Schrimsher and Bell were delegates of the Cherokee Nation to the federal government as members of a committee formed to settle problems regarding land claims, fund distributions, and other matters. A family friend and Will Rogers's uncle by marriage, Bushyhead was married to Elizabeth Alabama Schrimsher, the sister of Mary America Rogers Schrimsher and John Gunter Schrimsher *(OkClaW)*.

thereunder alphabetically by surnames of heads of households. The census was made to distribute per capita payments ("grass" or "strip money") to Cherokee citizens from funds obtained from the leasing of tribal grasslands to the Cherokee Strip Live Stock Association for grazing cattle in the Cherokee Outlet. In the actual Cherokee Payment Roll of 1883 the six members of the Rogers family received $93; the total paid to C. V. Rogers and witnessed by William V. Carey (DNA, RG 75, FARC, microfilm publication 7RA-57, partially illegible).

The Outlet consisted of approximately 6.5 million acres of grassland in the northern part of the Indian Territory, just south of the Kansas border and between the 96th meridian on the east and the 100th meridian on the west. Recognized as a perpetual outlet to the west, this large frontier region was first granted by the federal government to the Cherokees in the Treaty of 1828 and again in Article 2 of the 1835 New Echota Treaty, in return for ceding lands the tribe owned in the southeastern United States.

The Outlet was considered prime cattle-grazing land, and the Cherokees leased the range to cattle ranchers in the Cherokee Strip Live Stock Association. As senator from the Cooweescoowee District in the Cherokee National Council, Clement Vann Rogers was instrumental in introducing a bill in 1883 leasing the Outlet to the association. The actual Cherokee Strip, a stretch of land two and one-half miles wide running 226 miles along the 37th parallel bordering southern Kansas, was ceded to the United States in the Treaty of Washington in 1866. The Cherokee Strip Live Stock Association comprised primarily ranchers and cattle industry promoters in the region and was incorporated on 7 March 1883 in the state of Kansas. The Cherokee Nation leased the land to the association for an initial period of five years and received $100,000 annually. The "strip money" was distributed each year to Cherokees by blood, excluding ex-slaves, Delawares, and Shawnees. The lease was renewed in 1888 for another five years at an annual fee of $200,000. Members of the association grazed their livestock in the region until 1890, when the federal government, pressured by railroad, business, and farming interests anxious to open up the area to white settlers, declared the leases illegal. Forced to cede the Outlet to the government, the Cherokees officially sold the area to the United States in 1893 for approximately $8.6 million, and the area was opened for settlement on 16 September 1893 (Baker, "Major Cherokee Genealogical Records"; Collings, *Old Home Ranch,* 76; Keith, "Clem Rogers and His Influence on Oklahoma History," 44–54; Ketchum, *Will Rogers,* 51; Lefebvre, *Cherokee Strip in Transition;* McReynolds, *Oklahoma,* 262–64; Morris and McReynolds, *Historical Atlas of Oklahoma,* map 20; Rainey, *Cherokee Strip,* 36–42; Savage, *Cherokee Strip Live Stock Association,* 7–10; Wardell, *Political History of the Cherokee Nation,* 237; *WNGD,* 250; Woodward, *Cherokees,* 320).

2. A reference to May Rogers.

3. Microfilm publication 7RA-56 is a 1897 copy of the 1883 census with Sequoyah District missing. In the original 1883 Cherokee Census (DNA, RG 21, FARC, microfilm publication 7RA-29), the six members of the Rogers family are similarly listed except that their last name is first, their ages are not given, and their numbers run from 1687 to 1692.

The Rogers family, except for Sallie Rogers, also appears in a similar payroll census conducted by order of the National Council in 1886. The amounts paid to those on the rolls were not designated in the records. In the 1886 payroll Will Rogers, age seven, was named as "William P.," number 1888 of those enrolled (Pay Roll by Right of Cherokee Blood, Cooweescoowee District, 1886, DNA, RG 75, FARC, microfilm publication 7RA-58 [1897 copy of 1886 payroll]).

2. SCHOOL DAYS
May 1887–March 1898

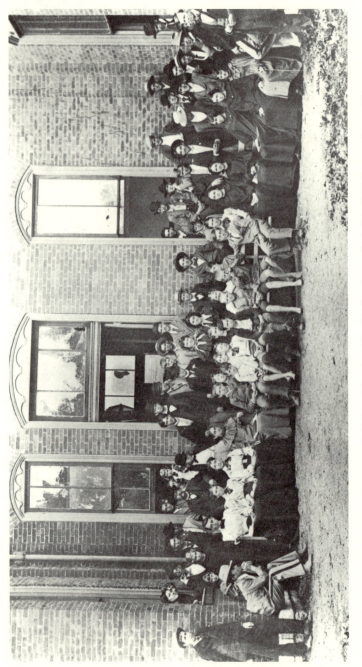

Scarritt Collegiate Institute Building, Neosho, Mo. Sitting far to the left is Will Rogers dressed in a Scarritt Guard military uniform. Also in the photograph are Maggie Nay and two other school friends, Gordon Lindsey and John Philips (*OkClaW*).

ON STAGE, RADIO, AND FILM WILL ROGERS REGULARLY PORTRAYED AN uneducated cowboy whose clever insights about society and politics stemmed more from innate wisdom than book learning. The humorist liked to strike a similar pose in his writings, which used faulty syntax and grammar for comic effect. His commonsense philosophy, which appealed to masses of Americans, allowed him to lampoon the politics of his time.

During his career Rogers joked about his lack of formal education. In 1919 he told a reporter:

> My father was pretty well fixed, and I being the only male son he tried terribly hard to make something out of me. He sent me to about every school in that part of the country [Indian Territory]. In some of them I would last for three or four months. I got just as far as the fourth reader when the teachers wouldn't seem to be running the school right, and rather than have the school stop I would generally leave. Then I would start in another school, tell them I had just finished the third reader and was ready for the fourth. Well, I knew all this fourth grade by heart so the teacher would remark: "I never see you studying, yet you seem to know your lessons." I had that education thing figured down to a fine point. Ten years in McGuffey's Fourth Reader, and I knew more about it than McGuffey did.[1]

Documents pertaining to his schooling reveal that the young Rogers attained much more than a fourth-grade education. He also attended some excellent schools that were noted at the time for their academic programs. Although he was an average C student, he did excel in certain subjects and possessed a remarkable memory that enabled him to easily pass some of his classes.

Rogers grew up in an environment where learning was respected. His parents, Clement Vann and Mary America Rogers, believed in educating their children in preparation for life. Their son was raised in a cultured household where there was an appreciation of books and music and an interest in political and economic events. As a politician and banker, Clem V. Rogers kept in touch with current affairs and the financial news by subscribing to the *New York Times*, the *Stock Reporter*, and various magazines.[2]

The family's belief in education reflected the rich cultural tradition of the Cherokees. Important to the education of Cherokees was the invention in 1821 by Sequoyah (or George Guess) of the eighty-six-character syllabary that enabled the Cherokees to read and write their own language. This easy-to-learn syllabary increased the literacy rate among the Cherokees and led to the establishment of a national press and the publication of books, religious tracts, journals, and newspapers. Among the latter were the *Cherokee Phoenix* (1828), a bilingual newspaper in English and Cherokee printed in New Echota, Georgia, and the *Cherokee Advocate* (1844), published at Tahlequah, the political capital of the Cherokee Nation. As the population increased and towns grew in the 1880s and 1890s, several English-language newspapers were founded in the Cherokee Nation, including the *Chelsea Reporter* (1896), the Vinita *Indian Chieftain* (1882), the *Vinita Leader* (1895), and the *Claremore Progress* (1893). These local papers often reported the activities of the Rogers family, and Rogers's letters abroad to his family were published in the *Chelsea Reporter* and the *Claremore Progress* in 1902 through 1904.[3]

Leaders of the Cherokee Nation recognized education as fundamental to the progress of their tribal society. Section 6, article 9, of the 1839 Cherokee constitution stated that "religion, morality and knowledge, being necessary to good government, the preservation of liberty and the happiness of mankind, schools and the means of education, shall forever be encouraged in this Nation."[4] The Cherokee National Council, the Nation's chief legislative body, authorized a common school system on 16 December 1841. The Cherokee educational system was headed by a superintendent of public instruction, a national board of education, and, at the local level, by a three-member school board in each of the Nation's districts. The districts were ordered to construct schoolhouses, and the superintendent established the standards for teacher certification and curriculum. In 1855 there were twenty-one schools, with an enrollment of 1,100 students; in 1871, fifty-nine schools; and in 1877, two years before Rogers was born, seventy-five institutions, primarily elementary schools.[5]

To support the tribal schools, the Cherokees established a special educational trust fund underwritten by revenues from the sale of land to the United States government. Will Rogers's oldest sister, Sallie Rogers McSpadden, was a teacher at a local public school and, from 1882 to 1885, at the Cherokee Orphan Asylum. "Our old Cherokee school system was an excellent one—and most thorough," she recalled. "All expenses of school supplies, books etc. were met by our Cherokee Council, the community built and furnished the buildings."[6]

As a mixed-blood Cherokee, Rogers qualified for the tribal elementary schools. The nearest school was located across the Verdigris River in Oowala, but it was often difficult to reach because of the river's high waters. Around 1887, or perhaps a year earlier, he enrolled at his first school, called the Drumgoole School, which was a public elementary school near the town of Chelsea. Drumgoole was a tribal school operated by the Cherokee Nation primarily for Indian children, but white children could attend for a fee of one dollar per month. It was a one-room, log-cabin school situated on the open prairie. McGuffey's First and Second Readers were used as textbooks.[7]

The Cherokee government also supported academies and seminaries that were equivalent to four-year high schools. The most academically prestigious were the Cherokee National Female Seminary and the Cherokee National Male Seminary. Both schools, which were opened in 1851 and located in the environs of Tahlequah, offered an advanced high-school curriculum. Classes were taught by well-educated faculty, many recruited from Ivy League universities and other eastern colleges. The seminaries also had primary and preparatory (pre–high school) departments. Graduates became the political, professional, business, and educational leaders of the Cherokee Nation.[8]

The seminaries' outstanding reputation attracted students from all over the Cherokee Nation, especially young men and women from affluent mixed-blood families.[9] Many members of the Rogers family attended one of the two seminaries. Clem V. Rogers studied at the Male Seminary for several terms, and his sister Margaret Lavinia Rogers graduated from the second class of the Female Seminary in February 1856. Will Rogers's mother, Mary America Schrimsher Rogers, may have enrolled at the Female Seminary, and her brother John Gunter Schrimsher attended the Male Seminary. Mary's sister, Elizabeth Alabama Schrimsher, graduated from the Female Seminary in February 1856 and was a classmate of Clem V. Rogers's sister Margaret. Clem V. Rogers and Mary Rogers sent their three daughters, Sallie, Maud, and May, to the Female Seminary at Park Hill, and Sallie graduated from the institution on 2 July 1880.[10]

Evidence suggests that Will Rogers also may have attended the Male Seminary for a term. The name W. P. Rogers is listed in the grade book of the preparatory department of the Male Seminary for fall 1887. This could possibly have been the famous entertainer since it was a Rogers family tradition to go there.[11]

Mission schools also played a prominent role in Cherokee education. They were established primarily to Christianize and assimilate the Cherokees into the white mainstream culture. The Moravians founded the first missionary school for Cherokees in Spring Place, Georgia, in 1801, and other schools were soon built by other religious groups, particularly the Baptists, Methodists, Congregationalists, and Presbyterians. After the removal of the Cherokees from their homeland in the Southeast, missionary societies continued to establish schools in the Cherokee Nation West. These were often the first educational institutions in the frontier Indian Territory, and several missions, such as Rev. Evan Jones's Old Baptist Mission (1839) and Samuel Austin Worcester's Park Hill Mission (1837) near Tahlequah, became significant learning and cultural centers. The mission schools offered instruction in traditional subjects and Bible studies, and their leaders were considered notable members of their communities.[12]

Clem V. Rogers grew up in a five-room log house one mile northeast of the Old Baptist Mission in the Going Snake District of the Cherokee Nation, near the present town of Westville, in Adair County, Oklahoma. His parents, Robert Rogers, Jr., and Sallie Vann Rogers, were mixed-blood Cherokees. They were considered Old Settlers since they had migrated from Georgia before the forced removal of the Cherokees in 1838. Around 1835 they moved to the area that became the center of the Old Baptist, or Ju-da-ye-tlu, Mission.[13] They sent their son to the mission school, where he was taught the fundamentals of English and mathematics. Clem V. Rogers, however, disliked school as a young boy and was often truant. He preferred roping and riding to doing homework. He never graduated from the Male Seminary and left the institution at age sixteen to work for a cattleman.[14]

As he grew older, Clem V. Rogers became increasingly aware of the importance of schooling for his children and the citizens of the Cherokee Nation. A primary reason for this change was his responsibilities as a prosperous and influential rancher, banker, and politician in the Cherokee Nation. As a senator in the National Council in 1879–80 he served on the Education Committee, where he was instrumental in appropriating funds for the support of the Male and Female Seminaries and the Cherokee primary schools. In 1882 he was appointed to the board of directors of the Worcester Academy, a Congregational mission school in Vinita; and in 1894 he was named an honorary member of the board of trustees of Willie Halsell College in Vinita. Rogers was elected president of the Claremore school board in 1899 and donated property on Fifth and Weenonah Streets in the town of Claremore for a children's playground.[15]

An equally important influence on Will Rogers's schooling was his mother. She studied at the reputable Cane Hill Female Seminary in Arkansas, and as mentioned earlier, she may have enrolled in the Cherokee National Female Seminary.[16] An accomplished pianist, Mary Rogers took music and voice lessons in school and owned one of the first grand pianos in the Cooweescoowee District. Often Mary and her son would sing together as she played the piano for invited guests in their home. Their two-story white clapboard house, bounded on the east by the Verdigris River and on the west by the Caney River, overlooked miles of unbroken rolling prairie of bluestem grass. Known as a place of warm hospitality, the Rogers home attracted friends and visitors from across the Indian Territory and neighboring states.

As the youngest son in the family, Will Rogers received considerable attention and became devoted to his mother, who was known as a sensitive, warm, and caring person. Friends remember Mary Rogers taking her son with her in a buckboard driven by a white horse whenever she travelled to visit friends. She read to him books on history and the humanities and taught him to write before he entered his first school. A member of the Methodist Episcopal Church South, Mary Rogers was considered by her friends to be a very religious person.[17] She sang in her church choir, actively participated in church work, and often entertained Methodist circuit riders when they visited her house. Will Rogers was raised in his mother's Methodist faith, and she initially wanted her youngest son to become a preacher.[18] Three of the institutions Rogers attended were affiliated with the Methodist Episcopal Church South: the Harrell International Institute, Willie Halsell College, and the Scarritt Collegiate Institute.

In the fall of 1888 Will Rogers enrolled at the Harrell International Institute. Wealthy ranchers in the Verdigris country often sent their sons and daughters away to denominational institutions. Located at Muskogee in the Creek Nation, Harrell was a boarding school primarily for young women, and was overseen by Rev. Theodore F. Brewer, a noted Methodist minister. While there Rogers took grammar-school courses as well as music and art.

Rogers, however, disliked the confinement of a boarding school, much preferring life on the open range, herding and branding cattle, hunting coyotes, roping wild turkeys, riding and breaking horses, weaning and nursing calves, and mending fences. He liked to gallop Comanche, his cream-colored pony, through the tall bluestem grass that grew wild on the range. He would hunt coyotes with his friend Bright Drake and accompany his father on short cattle drives to Chelsea. As a youngster he tended a herd of dogies, or motherless calves, and had his own Dog Iron brand.

Rogers probably remained at the Harrell International Institute until the time of his mother's death on 28 May 1890.[19] His mother, who had been nursing his sisters through severe cases of typhoid fever, became ill and died within a few days. Her sudden death hit the young Rogers very hard. Perhaps the family wanted to keep him home for a time, because there are no records of Rogers's attendance at any school during the 1890–91 academic year. Certainly there were periods when Rogers did not attend school and instead spent time at his father's ranch. Then his father would decide it was time to send his son to school again. Some biographers have mentioned that he was enrolled at the Presbyterian Mission School at Tahlequah.[20] Another account suggests he attended Vinita's Worcester Academy, where his sisters Maud and May and his brother, Robert, went.[21] But there are no extant documents proving his attendance at those two institutions.

In the fall of 1891 Rogers was sent to Willie Halsell College, an elementary

Harrell International Institute, Muskogee, I.T. (*OkHi, 19282.55*).

and secondary boarding school in nearby Vinita. An institution supported by the Methodist Episcopal Church South, it was affiliated with the Harrell School. Because Rogers was now close to home and several of his friends and relatives attended (Tom Lane, Charley McClellan, Jim Rider), he enjoyed Willie Halsell more than any other school. Schoolmates, such as Sam Cobb, Ewing Halsell, and Earl Walker, became lifelong friends. Since the school was located in the middle of a large pasture, Rogers could race his horse across campus and gallop down a path that led to town. One time he and his friends rustled a herd of cattle from a neighboring ranch, built a corral, and enjoyed riding and lassoing the untamed animals.

The environment evidently improved Rogers's grades, for the Vinita *Indian Chieftain* reported that he made the honor roll twice. Rogers also showed a flair for oral recitation, once winning a medal for elocution. Teachers and classmates recognized his remarkable retentiveness, which enabled him to easily memorize large amounts of information. First hints of his talent for entertaining audiences were in school plays and programs in which he played comic parts.[22]

While a student at Willie Halsell, the thirteen-year-old youngster began to write letters to his good friend Charles White (Charley) McClellan, who had grown up on a ranch near the Rogers's place. These letters are the earliest writings of Will Rogers that exist. Rambling from subject to subject, the correspondence reveals numerous errors in spelling and grammar and thus signals idiosyncracies that would later mark his writing style. These significant letters also suggest a restless adolescent easily bored with formal schooling and book learning and yearning for the ranch life.

After four years at Willie Halsell College, Rogers was sent by his father in the fall of 1895 to another boarding school, the Scarritt Collegiate Institute in Neosho, Missouri. The previous summer Professor J. C. Shelton, a teacher at Scarritt, had visited the Rogers's home seeking students for the school. Like the Harrell International Institute and Willie Halsell College, the Scarritt Collegiate Institute was affiliated with the Methodist Episcopal Church South. Clem V. Rogers hoped that the strict discipline at the school might be good for his son. The school's regulations were rigorously enforced by its president, Dr. Charles Carroll Wood, a former Confederate soldier.

But the freedom-loving boy defied the rules many times, sometimes missing classes and sneaking into town to attend a circus or a traveling stock-company show. Rogers would stand on the street corner and rope the country boys on their horses, as well as steers at the local stockyard. One day he roped a colt that became so frightened that it ran through a tennis net, hurdled a fence, and darted into town. His pranks, Cherokee songs, and funny stories amused his classmates, who called him the "Wild Indian." The one letter that survives from this time, to Margaret (Maggie) Nay, a local girl who had turned him down for a date, reveals Will's growing interest in the opposite sex and his adolescent self-consciousness. Rogers left school in December 1896 to attend the funeral of his brother-in-law Matthew Yocum, the husband of his sister May, who had been mysteriously murdered that month.[23]

His father next sent him to the Kemper School, a prominent military school located in Boonville, Missouri. Rogers arrived on 13 January 1897 wearing a "ten-gallon hat, with a braided horse-hair cord, flannel shirt with a red bandanna handkerchief, highly colored vest, and high heeled red top boots with spurs and with his trouser legs in his boot tops."[24] During the period he attended the school, from January 1897 to March 1898, Rogers enrolled in sophomore- and junior-level courses. As the documents from Kemper illustrate, Rogers was an erratic C student. His grades fluctuated monthly and varied according to subject. He received low marks in bookkeeping and physics, but excelled in subjects such as history, political economy, and elocution.[25]

His classmates, who called him "Swarthy" and "Rabbit" (because of his foot speed and large ears), remembered Rogers for his talent for public speaking and his ability to make people laugh. Known as the class clown, he joked his way through his orations and still received a high grade. During his last four months at the Kemper School he was at the top of his class in history. He easily memorized the dates and names in *Lyman's Historical Chart,* which catalogued the development of civilizations and countries in differently colored timelines. John Payne, a classmate, was impressed by his extraordinary memory, a faculty that would serve Rogers well on the stage and screen: "I've never met a person with a memory like Will's. We were in a Bible class under Colonel Johnston and had to learn the names of the books of the Bible by heart. Will spent only a few minutes, it seemed to me, and he had them so he could rattle them off like an alarm clock."[26]

With its strict discipline and dress code the military school conflicted with Rogers's temperament, and he rebelled against Kemper's rule and routines. He disliked wearing a military uniform every day and received demerits for his sloppy dress. Energetic and restless, he sought an outlet in roughhousing, pranks and practical jokes, and by lassoing everything in sight. Rogers would ride steers that passed the school, set off false fire alarms and cut classes. He donned an old slouch hat, an overcoat and boots, glued on a false mustache, and walked disguised into town, where he swapped stories with local merchants and farmers. Rogers received hundreds of demerits for his pranks, which he worked off by marching a solitary beat on the drill field and performing guard duty.

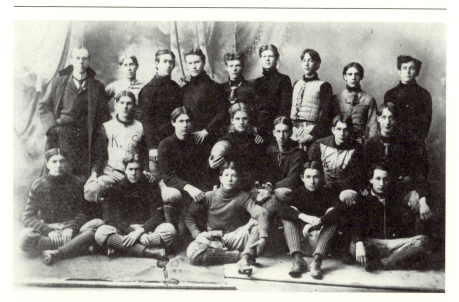

Kemper School football squad, 1897. *Bottom row (left to right):* Wallace Estill, Charlie Philips, Ben F. Johnson, Will Rogers, and John Payne. *Middle row:* Herschel Johnston, Earl Smith, Burton Mudge, Terrell Mills, Malcolm McNair, and H. P. Fairbach. *Top row:* Harry H. Smiley, Holland Scott, F. S. Spafford, F. C. H. Livingston, Mont Campbell, J. A. Kisselhorst, J. W. Wooldridge, Roy D. Williams, and Tom Hutton (*OkClaW*).

In the fall of 1897 Rogers returned to Kemper for a second academic year. The gangly country boy from Oologah was now nearly eighteen and yearned to escape the confines of the military school. He told his friend and cousin Spi Trent about his feelings: "Spi, I Really Try to be a good sport about this school business but I am gaggin at the bit. I cant keep myself inside a school room. I try, All Right, an I reckon my Body stays put but I personally am out in Green Pastures, an if you ask me, I believe thats where all the learning in the world has been written, if folks wanter bother studyin it."[27] In March of 1898 Rogers learned from William (Bill) A. Johnson, a Kemper classmate from Canadian, Texas, about an opportunity to work with a cattle outfit in the Texas Panhandle. Borrowing money from his sisters, Rogers decided to run away to Texas and "quit the entire school business for life."[28]

Although Rogers never graduated from high school, he attended school for approximately ten years and completed course work equivalent to the sophomore year in high school. He was much better educated than he liked to pretend, having frequented good schools known for their academic programs.

His record shows that Rogers had an inquiring mind and a remarkable memory, and he often performed well in subjects that interested him. With their stringent rules and strict discipline, the denominational schools and the Kemper military academy conflicted with Rogers's independent nature and inclination for the cowboy life. As he grew older, Rogers realized that he had not taken full advantage of these schools. In her memoir of her husband, Betty Rogers wrote, "Will always regretted that he hadn't taken advantage of his opportunities to get a good education; there wasn't a day of his life, he said, that he didn't regret it."[29]

1. Martin, "The Wit of Will Rogers," 107–8. American educator and college president William Holmes McGuffey (1800–1873) published a series of six *Eclectic Readers*, beginning in 1836, which were widely used in elementary schools in the Middle West and the South (*WNBD*, 635).

2. Collings, *Old Home Ranch*, 24–25; Croy, *Our Will Rogers*, 16–17; McSpadden, "Clement Vann Rogers," 398.

3. Forman, G., *Five Civilized Tribes*, 352, 412; McLoughlin, *Champions of the Cherokees*, 39; Perdue, *Cherokees*, 43–44; Wright, *Guide to the Indian Tribes of Oklahoma*, 62–63. On newspapers in the Indian Territory, see Carter, E., *Story of Oklahoma Newspapers*, 3–32; Foreman, C., *Oklahoma Imprints, 1835–1907;* Holland, "Cherokee Indian Newspapers, 1828–1906"; Littlefield and Parins, *American Indian and Alaska Native Newspapers and Periodicals, 1826–1924;* Witcher, "Territorial Magazines."

4. Starr, *History of the Cherokee Indians*, 225.

5. Davison, "Oklahoma's Educational Heritage," 354–72; McLoughlin, *Champions of the Cherokees*, 219; Starr, *History of the Cherokee Indians*, 229; Wardell, *Political History of the Cherokee Nation*, 216. On the development of the Cherokee education system in the context of Indian sovereignty, see McLoughlin, "Public Education and the Struggle for Independence, 1846–60," chap. 4 in *After the Trail of Tears*, 86–120. The National Council consisted of two bodies: a National Committee, or upper house, with two senators elected from each district; and a Council, or lower house, with three elected members from each district (Wright, *Guide to the Indian Tribes of Oklahoma*, 74).

6. Sallie Rogers McSpadden interview in IPH 76: 158–59, OkHi. An institution dedicated to educating and caring for orphans, the Cherokee Orphan Asylum was established by an act of the National Council in 1871, and it opened a year later in a building at the Male Seminary in Tahlequah. In 1875 the Orphan Asylum moved to the old Lewis Ross mansion at present-day Salina and was placed under the jurisdiction of the board of education (*DC*, 21 July 1903; Gideon, *Indian Territory*, 72–74; Johnson, "Cherokee Orphan Asylum," 275–80; Starr, *History of the Cherokee Indians*, 246; *WRFT*, 20). The requirement that Cherokee schools be taught in English "placed a serious obstacle before the vast majority of children, who spoke only Cherokee"; as a result, children, like Rogers, "of mixed ancestry obtained the greatest benefit from the schools" (McLoughlin, *After the Trail of Tears*, 87).

7. Rogers, *Will Rogers*, 44–45; Keith, *Boy's Life of Will Rogers*, 31–36. The Oowala School began as a subscription school in 1881 in a one-room log cabin owned by "Major" DeWitt Clinton Lipe, who resided in the area and was prominent in public affairs, including serving as treasurer of the Cherokee Nation for eight years (1879–83, 1895–99) (see Biographical Appendix entry, LIPE, DeWitt Clinton). A new building was con-

structed in 1884 a half mile south of the original location, and it eventually became a Cherokee national school (*As I Recollect*, 9–10; *HRC*, 280–81).

8. The Cherokee Treaty of New Echota (29 December 1835) had called for the establishment of an institution of higher learning in the West. In 1847 the National Council provided funds for the creation of the two schools. The Male Seminary opened on 6 May 1851, and the Female Seminary on 7 May 1851. John Ross, principal chief of the Cherokees, sent two officials, David Vann and William Potter, to Mount Holyoke to study the institution and recruit teachers. Ellen Rebecca Whitmore, the Female Seminary's first principal teacher, had studied at Mount Holyoke, as had teachers Ella Noyes, Sarah Worcester, and Harriet Johnson. Because the seminaries did not concentrate on teaching Cherokee traditional culture, they were primarily a force for acculturation into white society (Abbott, "History of the Cherokee Female Seminary: 1851–1910"; Agnew, "Legacy of Education," 130–31; McLoughlin, *After the Trail of Tears*, 92–93; Mihesuah, *Cultivating the Rosebuds;* Starr, *History of the Cherokee Indians*, 231–43; Sunday et al., *Gah Dah Gwa Stee*, 41–42; Tinnin, "Influences of the Cherokee National Seminaries," 59–67).

9. The seminaries enrolled both prosperous and poor students. In 1851 boarders who could afford the bill were charged forty-five dollars per academic year, but fifty needy students were permitted to attend for nothing (Starr, *History of the Cherokee Indians*, 231). William E. Sunday, who studied one year at the Male Seminary, wrote: "The richest of the Cherokee families attended school there. The boys who paid their way had to wait on the children of the poor families" (Sunday et al., *Gah Dah Gwa Stee*, 42; see also Biographical Appendix entry, SUNDAY, William Esther).

10. Sallie McSpadden's daughter, May McSpadden, also graduated from the Female Seminary on 29 May 1907, and her son Herbert (Herb) Thomas McSpadden graduated from the Male Seminary in 1910. There are no enrollment records for the seminaries before 1875 at the Oklahoma Historical Society or Northeastern Oklahoma State University, Tahlequah. Maud and May were attending the Female Seminary when it burned down on Easter Sunday, 10 April 1887. Consequently Maud was sent to the Howard Payne College at Fayette, Missouri, and May went to the Harrell International Institute at Muskogee. The Female Seminary was rebuilt on a forty-acre site north of Tahlequah and rededicated on 5 May 1889. The institution was sold to the state in 1909 and became a state normal school. It is now the site of Northeastern Oklahoma State University (Agnew, "Legacy of Education," 138–39; Collings, *Old Home Ranch*, 6–10; Love, "Rogers Family at Worcester Academy"; Mihesuah, *Cultivating the Rosebuds*, 125, 126, 130; Sallie Rogers McSpadden, newsclipping, *Oklahoma City Times*, ca. 1910, SRM-OkClaW; Starr, *History of the Cherokee Indians*, 232–42).

11. See Excerpt from Student Enrollment List, Preparatory School, Cherokee National Male Seminary, 28 August–16 December 1887, below.

12. Evan Jones, who had earlier led the Valley Towns mission in North Carolina, established a press at the Baptist Mission in the Going Snake District, where he printed religious tracts and hymn books as well as the *Cherokee Messenger* (1844), the first periodical in the Indian Territory. A Congregationalist, Worcester founded Park Hill in 1837, a complex of buildings that featured a school, church, dwellings, shops, a gristmill, and stables. It also included a two-story publishing house with bindery where Worcester published the *Cherokee Almanac*, textbooks, and religious publications in Cherokee and English. A classical scholar, Worcester translated the Bible into Cherokee. On the Jones and the Old Baptist Mission, see McLoughlin, *Champions of the Cherokees;* Mahnken, "Old Baptist Mission and Evan Jones," 174–92; and on Worcester, see Gibson, *Oklahoma*, 149–51. On the impact of missionary organizations on Cherokee education, see Foreman, G. *Five Civilized Tribes*, 412; Gibson, *Oklahoma*, 143–55;

Morris and McReynolds, *Historical Atlas of Oklahoma*, map 17; Perdue, *Cherokees*, 41–42; Starr, *History of the Cherokee Indians*, 225; Woodward, *Cherokees*, 140–43. On education in general in the Indian Territory, see Davison, "Oklahoma's Educational Heritage," 354–72.

13. During its history the area had several names including Breadtown, Cherokee, Baptist, and Baptist Mission (McLoughlin, *Champion of the Cherokees*, 185).

14. On Clem V. Rogers's education, see Collings, *Old Home Ranch*, 2–3, 6, 29; Keith, "Clem Rogers and His Influence on Oklahoma History," 1–4; McSpadden, "Clement Vann Rogers," 389–90; and Meredith, "Will Rogers' Roots," 262–63; see also Biographical Appendix entry, ROGERS, Clement Vann.

15. Keith, "Clem Rogers and His Influence on Oklahoma History," 41; Love, "Rogers Family at Worcester Academy"; McSpadden, "Clement Vann Rogers," 389.

16. Like the Cherokee National Male and Female Seminaries, the Cane Hill Female Seminary was modeled on Mount Holyoke. There was considerable interchange between the schools at Cane Hill and Tahlequah. There was also an all-male Cane Hill College, which merged with the Female Seminary in 1875 (see Ballenger, "Cultural Relations between Two Pioneer Communities"). Biographers differ on Mary Rogers's attendance at the Cherokee National Female Seminary at Tahlequah. Donald Day (*Will Rogers*, 5), Homer Croy (*Our Will Rogers*, 13), and Harold Keith (*Boy's Life of Will Rogers*, 5–6) write that she attended the seminary, whereas Collings (*Old Home Ranch*, 10) says she graduated. Clem V. Rogers may have met his future wife at the seminary through his friend John Schrimsher or through Mary's sister, Elizabeth Alabama Schrimsher, who graduated from the Female Seminary in February 1856 and was a classmate of Clem's sister Margaret Lavinia Rogers (see Mihesuah, *Cultivating the Rosebuds*, 124, 125; Starr, *History of the Cherokee Indians*, 233; see also Biographical Appendix entry, ROGERS, Mary America Schrimsher).

17. In 1844 the Methodist Episcopal Church was divided into two churches over the issue of slavery: the Methodist Episcopal Church opposed slavery, and the Methodist Episcopal Church South supported slavery. The separation remained until 1939. The Methodist Episcopal Church South was very active in converting the Cherokees through the Methodist Indian Mission Conference, which was organized in 1844 at Riley's Mill near Tahlequah. To spread the gospel, the Southern Methodists relied on circuit-rider preachers who visited homes and conducted services at Cherokee meeting houses and revival-camp meetings. Southern and northern Methodist missionary boards also established missions and schools in the Indian Territory. In 1844 there were about 3,000 Indian Methodists in the territory, and in 1886 about 5,500 Indian Methodists. Sallie Rogers McSpadden married John Thomas (Tom) McSpadden, the son of Reverend Thomas Kingsbury McSpadden, an influential Methodist circuit rider for the Southern Methodist Church in the Indian Territory and the founder of the Methodist Church in Chelsea (see Gibson, *Oklahoma*, 145, 148; *HRC*, 299–303; Stewart, "Indian Mission Conference of Oklahoma," 330–36; Sweet, *Methodism in American History*, 229–75; Vernon, "Methodist Beginnings among Southwest Oklahoma Indians," 392).

18. Collings, *Old Home Ranch*, 10; Ketchum, *Will Rogers*, 43.

19. According to biographer Richard Ketchum, Reverend Brewer wrote his father: "I regret to inform you that your son is not doing well in school and would suggest you remove him" (*Will Rogers*, 39). This letter has not been located, and documents from the Methodist newspaper *Our Brother in Red* suggest that he was not removed but remained at the Harrell Institute until the time of his mother's death in May 1890. Other sources indicate that Rogers had been home recovering from the measles in May 1890 and was moved from the ranch house during the illnesses of his sisters and the fatal illness of his mother (see Biographical Appendix entry, ROGERS, Mary America Schrimsher).

20. The story that Will Rogers went to the Presbyterian Mission School comes primarily from Keith (*Boy's Life of Will Rogers*, 48–49, 268), who interviewed people who said he had attended the school. See also Alworth, *Will Rogers*, 14, and Carter, J., *Never Met a Man I Didn't Like*, 18. The Board of Home Missions of the Presbyterian Church opened the mission school in either 1883 or 1884 for the purpose of educating both Indian and white children. In 1887 dormitory additions for boarding students were added, called Brooks Cottage, named after a Dr. Brooks. The school building burned in 1893; it was rebuilt, but closed in 1907 when statehood brought public schools (Glenn Colliver, Assistant Archivist, PC, to the WRPP, 3 December 1992; Holland, "Cherokee Indian Newspapers, 1828–1906," 565; McAfee, *Missions among the North American Indians*, PC; "Tahlequah, Oklahoma," PC).

21. O. B. Campbell, in his book *Vinita, I.T.*, writes that Will Rogers attended the Worcester Academy and even includes a school picture identifying Rogers (see pp. 69–77). The Worcester Academy was founded in 1882 as a Congregational school under the auspices of the American Home Missionary Society; it was named in honor of the Reverend Samuel A. Worcester, the influential missionary to the Cherokees. Clem V. Rogers was a member of its first board of directors. In the 1882–83 catalogue May Rogers was listed in the kindergarten group while Maud and Robert Rogers were included on the list of enrolled students. While attending the school, Robert Rogers, Will Rogers's elder brother, died of typhoid fever on 13 April 1883, two days before his seventeenth birthday. The Worcester Academy Collection at the University of Oklahoma does not include a catalogue from the year 1890–91, and Will Rogers's name does not appear in other annual catalogues in the collection. Thus it is still possible that he may have attended during those years. On the Worcester Academy, see also Garrett, "Worcester, Pride of the West"; Love, "Rogers Family at Worcester Academy"; *Worcester Academy Catalogue, 1882–1883*, Worcester Academy Collection, OkU.

22. Croy, *Our Will Rogers*, 26–30; Keith, *Boy's Life of Will Rogers*, 73–87.

23. Croy, *Our Will Rogers*, 31–35; Keith, *Boy's Life of Will Rogers*, 88–97; Rogers, *Will Rogers*, 47–48.

24. Hitch, *Will Rogers, Cadet*, 4.

25. On Kemper, see Croy, *Our Will Rogers*, 36–44; box 9, OkClaW; Hitch, *Will Rogers, Cadet;* Keith, *Boy's Life of Will Rogers*, 107–16; Ketchum *Will Rogers*, 43–44.

26. Quoted from Release 39—Morning Newspapers, 12 December [1935], OkClaW. Azel S. Lyman wrote *Lyman's Historical Chart, Containing the Prominent Events of the Civil, Religious, and Literary History of the World from the Earliest Times to the Present Day* (Cincinnati: National Publishing Co., 1873). Colonel Thomas Alexander Johnston, a veteran of the Confederate Army, served as president and superintendent of the Kemper School. Years later, Mac Koontz, a classmate, sent Rogers the copy that is now at the Will Rogers Memorial. See Croy, *Our Will Rogers*, 337; Hitch, *Will Rogers, Cadet.* Sam Cobb once explained how Rogers got the nickname Rabbit at school: "If you could see him run, you would understand. And his ears helped a lot in gaining that name" (*VJ*, 26 August 1939, clipping, box 9, OkClaW).

27. Trent, *My Cousin Will Rogers*, 39.

28. *TDW*, 7 March 1926; see also Ketchum, *Will Rogers*, 44.

29. Rogers, *Will Rogers*, 292.

Letter to the Editor
From the *Indian Chieftain-Supplement*
19 May 1887
Vinita, I.T.

By the year 1887 Rogers was attending his first school, the Drumgoole School, operated by the Cherokee Nation and located several miles southwest of Chelsea.[1] He lived with his sister Sallie and her family, who resided on a ranch a few miles from the school.[2] Rogers would ride his pony to the school on a handmade saddle that was a gift from his father. Surrounded by thousands of acres of land, the school was a one-room log cabin, and the students sat on split-log backless benches. In the spring of 1887 the Rogers family and friends attended a picnic at the school.[3]

DRUM GOOL PIC-NIC.

A PLEASANT DAY AGREEABLY SPENT BY OUR FRIENDS NEAR CHELSEA.

Mr. Editor—

On Friday, May 13th, we had a pleasant May pic-nic at Miss Ida McCoy's[4] School on Drum Gool creek. Miss Bertha McSpadden[5] was crowned queen. The ceremony was beautiful and the speeches sublime. The day was cool and pleasant and everything went off agreeably. At noon a sumptuous dinner was spread upon the grass and everybody partook of it freely. Among the many visitors were Hon. C. V. Rogers and wife, Maud Rogers, Kitty and Bessie Schrimsher[6] of Claremore;[7] John McClellan,[8] William McClellan,[9] A. J. Lane,[10] Ed. D. Hicks and family, Sallie Musgrove[11] of Oowala,[12] W. L. Green, Tom McSpadden[13] and family, of McSpadden's Ranch; Mrs. J. H. Akin, of Vinita;[14] Will Strange,[15] Joe McSpadden[16] and family of Chelsea. After dinner amusements were resumed: croquet, vocal music by the young ladies and guitar music by Green and Hicks. Total number of scholars enrolled in the school, forty nine. Mrs. Tom McSpadden exhibited the prettiest baby boy on the ground, named Clem Joel McSpadden.[17] The Indian Chieftain[18] (with supplement) was handed around to everyone. Ed Sanders[19] being the only Bunch[20] man on the ground there was little said about politics.

G.

PD. Printed in *IC-S*, 19 May 1887.

1. Located about twenty miles north of Claremore in what is now northeastern Rogers County, Chelsea was a small frontier town located on the St. Louis and San Francisco (Frisco) Railway line. The post office was established on 21 November 1882, and the town was platted by officials of the Cherokee Nation in 1885. It was incorporated under Cherokee law in 1889. The town was named by Charles Peach, a railroad surveyor, for his home, Chelsea (a London district), in England. In 1881 Henry Armstrong, a

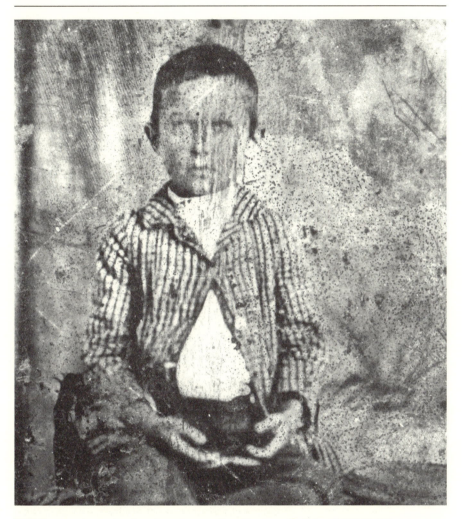

Will Rogers about the time he was attending Drumgoole School *(OkClaW).*

Delaware Indian, built the first store building near the west side of the railroad track. In 1889 oil was first discovered by Edward Byrd in the Indian Territory just west of Chelsea and near Spencer Creek. The Cherokee Oil and Gas Co. was established, and John Thomas McSpadden's family were shareholders. The town also had a flourishing flour mill, whose product was sent to neighboring states. The Frisco railway had a stockyard in Chelsea that served as shipping center for cattle and hogs from the surrounding area, and in the early 1880s abundant crops of wheat, oats, and corn were shipped via railway to Kansas City and St. Louis markets. On 16 April 1898 the town was granted a charter under the provisions of the Curtis Act. There were reported to be twenty-three business firms in Chelsea in 1901. By 1903 the population of Chelsea was approximately one thousand (Benedict, *Muskogee and Northeastern Oklahoma*, 606–7; Chelsea history material, CPL; "Chelsea: A Condensed History of Our Thriving Town," *ChC*, 30 January 1903; Gideon, *Indian Territory*, 168–69; leases of the McSpadden family giving prospecting and drilling rights to Cherokee Oil and Gas Co. on their allotments, 7 June 1902, DNA, RG 75, Cherokee Nation Box 322-1907-98221, Bureau of Indian Affairs Classified Files, 1907–39; Shirk, *Oklahoma Place Names*, 43; Workers of the Writers' Program, *Oklahoma*, 222).

2. Sallie Rogers had married John Thomas (Tom) McSpadden (1852–1936) on 15 December 1885. After their wedding they settled on Tom McSpadden's farm about six miles southwest of Chelsea. In 1892 they moved to the town of Chelsea (Kaho, *Will Rogers Country*, 25; *VJ*, 16 December 1885; see also Biographical Appendix entries for MCSPADDEN, John Thomas, and MCSPADDEN, Sallie Clementine Rogers).

3. Rogers supposedly gave his first stage appearance at a school event, when he recited the verse "I am a little star" (Kaho, *Will Rogers Country*, 26; Keith, *Boy's Life of Will Rogers*, 31–36). The few newspaper reports about teacher appointments at the school refer to it as the Drumgoole School (*IC*, 23 September 1886, 1 September 1887, and 26 July 1888), although Betty Rogers calls it the Drumgoul School (*Will Rogers*, 44–45; see also Day, ed., *Autobiography*, 6).

4. On 23 September 1886 the *Indian Chieftain* announced that Miss Ida McCoy had been appointed a teacher at the school. McCoy was educated at the Cherokee Female Seminary. On McCoy, see Cherokee Jones Allton interview, Pocahontas Club, audiotape 2, OkClaW; Keith, *Boy's Life of Will Rogers*, 33–34.

5. Bertha McSpadden (1877–1964) was the daughter of Samuel A. McSpadden (1854–1924) and Roxie Ann Green. Bertha McSpadden served as assistant postmaster of Chelsea and postmaster of Fort Gibson in the early 1900s. Samuel A. McSpadden was the brother of John Thomas McSpadden (*HRC*, 303).

6. Probably the writer was referring to Sarah Catherine (Kitty) Schrimsher (1866–92) and Elizabeth Belle (Bess) Schrimsher (1873–1957), cousins of Will Rogers. They were the daughters of Juliette Melvina Candy (1841–1930) and John Gunter Schrimsher (1835–1905), who was the brother of Mary America Schrimsher Rogers. Elizabeth Schrimsher became an active Pocahontas Club member in Claremore. She married Stephen Riley Lewis (b. 1873), an attorney, on 12 June 1907 (on the Schrimsher family, see *As I Recollect*, 41–44; Bell, *Genealogy of Old and New Cherokee Indian Families*, 371–72; DuPriest et al., *Cherokee Recollections*, 75–76; *HRC*, 515; *WRFT*, 122–23; see also Biographical Appendix entries, ROBINSON, Juliette Schrimsher; SCHRIMSHER, Ernest Vivian; SCHRIMSHER, John Gunter).

7. The Rogers ranch was located about fifteen miles north of Claremore. The town's history dates back to 1802 when the Osages established a settlement called Clermont's Town or, in the Osage language, Pasuga (Those Who Came to the Bend of the River). The ranch was located on the banks of the Verdigris River near Claremore's Mound, northwest of the present city. Considered to be a principal village of the Osages, Clermont's Town had a population of about three thousand Indians in 1821. The original town was named after Clermont II, an influential Osage chief and warrior who headed one of the three major Osage bands. He founded Clermont's Town and other tribal villages and for these accomplishments was called "The Builder of Towns." Clermont, who died in May 1828, was also called by the French Clermo, Clamore, Clairmont, and by the Americans, Claremore, from which the present city got its name. The Western Cherokees, migrants from their homeland in the Southeast, began encroaching on Osage land. The Osages felt the Cherokees were intruders, and the two Indian peoples

fought each other in many raids. In 1817 the Cherokees, with the help of other tribes, including the Delawares, Choctaws, Chickasaws, and Comanches, defeated the Osages at the Battle of Claremore Mound, or Strawberry Moon (named because it was fought during the season of wild strawberries). Most Osage warriors were on a hunting trip, which permitted the Cherokees to kill many Osage women and children and burn the town. The easy victory over the Osages precipitated more warfare, which lasted for nearly twenty years. By 1838 the Cherokees had usurped the land occupied by the Osages. In 1874 a second settlement was started by John Bullette, a Delaware Indian, who built a store two and one-half miles from Claremore's current location; and a post office was established on 25 June 1874. Growth began in 1882 when the St. Louis and San Francisco Railway reached the area, and a larger town developed around the depot. Hoping to discover oil, G. W. Eaton and others drilled a well in 1903, and they instead found artesian water at a depth of 1,100 feet. The town subsequently became well known for its radium-water bathhouses and spas, which advertised help in healing rheumatism, indigestion, eczema, lumbago, and other diseases. Located twenty-five miles northeast of Tulsa, Claremore is at present the seat of Rogers County, named in honor of Clem V. Rogers. Will Rogers bought land in the city that became the site of the Will Rogers Memorial (Benedict, *Muskogee and Northeastern Oklahoma* 1:597–601; Burns, *History of the Osage People*, 94–95, 118–24, 267–69, 282; Collings, *Old Home Ranch*, 13; Eaton, "Legend of the Battle of Claremore Mound," 369–77; Foreman, G., *Advancing the Frontier*, 134; Foreman, G., *Indians and Pioneers*, 19, 45–53, 91, 136; Kaho, *Will Rogers Country;* Shirk, *Oklahoma Place Names*, 47; Sunday, E., *Line Rider in the Cherokee Nation*, 43–44; *WNGD*, 269; Workers of the Writers' Program, *Oklahoma*, 222–23).

8. John (Sos) Foreman McClellan (1872–1949) was the son of Charles McClure and Jennie Lind McClellan and the older brother of Charles White McClellan, Will Rogers's childhood friend. He served as president of the Pocahontas Club from 1901 to 1902 and during his life was a prosperous Claremore cattleman and officer of the Farmers Bank and Trust Co. (*As I Recollect*, 68–77; DuPriest et al., *Cherokee Recollections*, 57–61; *HRC*, 289–90).

9. William Peter McClellan (1855–1926) was a Claremore rancher and livery-stable owner and the brother of Charles McClure McClellan (*HRC*, 290–91).

10. Dr. Andrew Jackson Lane (d. 1896) was a pioneer doctor in the Oologah/Claremore area and the Rogers family physician who may have attended Rogers's birth (*HRC*, 274; see Biographical Appendix entry, LANE, Andrew Jackson, and Record of Birth of Will Rogers, 4 November 1879, n. 10, above).

11. Sallie Musgrove (b. 1871) was the daughter of Francis Marion (Frank) Musgrove (1846–1895) and Clara Elizabeth Alberty Musgrove (b. 1845). Francis Marion Musgrove was the half-brother of Clem V. Rogers. Clem V. Rogers's mother, Sallie Vann Rogers, had married William Alexander Musgrove in 1844 after his father, Robert Rogers, Jr., died in 1842 (*HRC*, 333–34; *OCF* 1:164, 257; *WRFT*, 85).

12. Located just east of Oologah and north of Claremore, the Oowala community consisted of several large ranches. DeWitt Clinton Lipe (1840–1916), a noted Cherokee public official, was one of the town's earliest settlers. He operated a general merchandise store and helped establish an early school there in 1881. Oowala was Lipe's Cherokee name (*As I Recollect*, 10–11, *HRC*, 280–81; Shirk, *Oklahoma Place Names*, 157; see also Biographical Appendix entry, LIPE, DeWitt Clinton).

13. See Biographical Appendix entry, McSPADDEN, John Thomas.

14. Vinita was then a cattle-shipping and commercial town, located at the junction of two railroads, the Missouri, Kansas, and Texas (MKT, or Katy) Railroad and the Atlantic and Pacific (when the latter went bankrupt, its eastern division taken over in

1876 by the St. Louis and San Francisco Railway Co., or Frisco). The two railroads met in 1871; the town was platted in 1872. It was first called Downingville in honor of Lewis Downing, principal chief of the Cherokees in 1866 and from 1867 to 1872. It was later renamed by Elias C. Boudinot (son of the famed Cherokee Elias Boudinot who was editor of the *Cherokee Phoenix*), a mixed-blood railroad attorney, newspaper editor, tobacco manufacturer, diplomat, and "boomer" who supported white settlement and the allotment system. He named the town after his lady friend, Lavinia (Vinnie) Ream, a well-known Washington, D.C., sculptor. In a dispute with Cherokee officials over the townsite Boudinot failed in an attempt to have his own land survey of the junction accepted by the government. At first a tent town incorporated in 1873 under Cherokee laws, Vinita developed as a result of the two railroads. An 1888 report described the town's main street as six blocks long, comprising three restaurants, two meat markets, five groceries, three hotels, two drugstores, two confectionery shops, an ice cream parlor, an agricultural implements shop, and other businesses. The town became an important railroad cattle-shipping area since cattlemen could ship their cattle to St. Louis on the St. Louis and San Francisco line and to Kansas City on the Missouri, Kansas, and Texas line (Aldrich, "General Stores, Retail Merchants, and Assimilation: Retail Trade in the Cherokee Nation, 1838–1890," 125; Campbell, *Vinita, I.T.,* 1–3; Gibson, *Oklahoma,* 261–62; Gideon, *Indian Territory,* 163–66; Holden, *Ranching Saga,* 155–56; Masterson, *Katy Railroad and the Last Frontier,* 104, 126–40; Miner, "East-West Railway in Indian Territory," 562, 567; Miner, *St. Louis–San Francisco Transcontinental Railroad,* 91–101; *Our 75th Year of Community Service (1892–1967);* Shirk, *Oklahoma Place Names,* 134; Wardell, *Political History of the Cherokee Nation,* 259).

15. Will Strange was either William Strange (1836–1901) or his son William John Strange (1860–1944). The latter was a storeowner and postmaster in Chelsea (*HRC,* 409–10).

16. Joel (Joe) Cowan McSpadden (1850–98), a rancher, was the son of Elizabeth Jane Green (1821–99) and Rev. Thomas Kingsbury McSpadden (1825–77), a Methodist circuit rider and minister. Joe McSpadden was the brother of John Thomas (Tom) McSpadden, Will Rogers's brother-in-law (*HRC,* 299–300; *OCF* 1:185).

17. Clement Mayes McSpadden, Will Rogers's nephew, was born on 20 December 1886 (*WRFT,* 14; see Biographical Appendix entry, McSPADDEN, Clement Mayes).

18. The *Indian Chieftain* was an influential four-page weekly newspaper established at Vinita in 1882 by a local white merchant, George W. Green. M. E. Milford bought the paper in 1884; John Lynch Adair, a mixed-blood Cherokee and former editor of the *Cherokee Advocate,* served as its editor from 1885 to 1889. Published on Thursday, it cost $1.50 a year for a subscription, and its circulation numbered 890. A voice for the rights of the Five Tribes, its masthead announced that it was "devoted to the Interests of the Cherokees, Choctaws, Chickasaws, Seminoles, Creeks, and All Other Indians of the Indian Territory." It was financed by the Chieftain Publishing Co., which also produced the *Daily Indian Chieftain* in Vinita (started by M. E. Milford in 1899). The *Indian Chieftain* covered international, national, and local news and also published fiction, verse, legal notices, agricultural prices, and letters from subscribers. In the 1890s the *Indian Chieftain* devoted considerable space to Indian affairs, especially the allotment issue. It is still considered one of the best newspapers published by Native Americans. The paper changed its name to *Vinita Weekly Chieftain* (1902–5) and *Weekly Chieftain* (1905–12) and then ceased publication in 1912, when it was taken over by the *Vinita Leader* (Carter, E., *Story of Oklahoma Newspapers,* 31–32; Foreman, C., *Oklahoma Imprints,* 94–97; Littlefield and Parins, *American Indian and Alaska Native Newspapers and Periodicals, 1826–1924,* 390–95).

19. William Edward Sanders (1859–1939), a farmer and stockman, served as sheriff of Cooweescoowee District in 1885, 1887, and 1891 and was elected to the Cherokee senate in 1893. He later served as Rogers County commissioner for six years (*As I Recollect*, 90; *HRC*, 384; Starr, *History of the Cherokee Indians*, 511).

20. In 1887 Rabbit Bunch was a candidate of the National Party for the office of principal chief of the Cherokees, but lost in a disputed election on 1 August 1887 to Joel B. Mayes, the candidate of the Downing Party. The National Party majority in the Cherokee senate refused to canvass the returns, and armed factions belonging to both parties arrived at Tahlequah. In January 1888 armed supporters of Mayes invaded the executive office and installed Mayes as principal chief (Meserve, "Mayes," 59–60; Sunday, *Line Rider in the Cherokee Nation*, 68–69).

Excerpt from Student Enrollment List
Preparatory School, Cherokee National Male Seminary
28 August–16 December 1887
Tahlequah, I.T.

The name W. P. Rogers appears on the Cherokee National Male Seminary[1] Enrollment Book as a student in the Preparatory School[2] from 28 August to 16 December 1887. Supporting documentation suggests this student could have been Will Rogers.[3]

(For document, see page 90.)

PD, with autograph insertions. OkTahN.[5]

1. The origins of the Male and Female Seminaries date back to the Treaty of New Echota (29 December 1835), which included a provision that funds be set aside for the creation of a national academy in the Cherokee Nation West. An act of the Cherokee National Council on 26 November 1846 provided funds for the building of two high schools in the environs of Tahlequah, the Nation's capital. Construction at two different sites began that year with the building of similar stately two-story brick structures decorated with Doric columns. The buildings were completed in 1850, at which time they were considered the largest structures in the Indian Territory. The Male Seminary, located one and one-half miles southwest of Tahlequah, was officially opened on 6 May

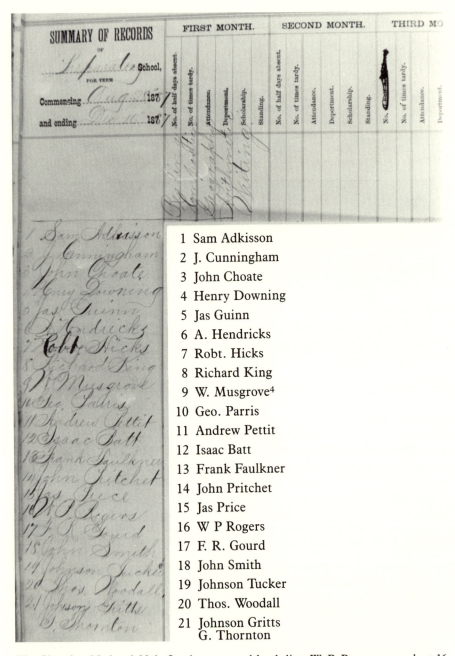

SUMMARY OF RECORDS OF _____ School, FOR TERM Commencing _____ 187_ and ending _____ 187_	FIRST MONTH.					SECOND MONTH.					THIRD MO
	No. of half days absent	No. of times tardy.	Attendance.	Deportment.	Scholarship.	Standing.	No. of half days absent.	No. of times tardy.	Attendance.	Deportment.	Scholarship.	Standing.	No.	No. of times tardy.	Attendance.	Deportment.

1 Sam Adkisson
2 J. Cunningham
3 John Choate
4 Henry Downing
5 Jas Guinn
6 A. Hendricks
7 Robt. Hicks
8 Richard King
9 W. Musgrove[4]
10 Geo. Parris
11 Andrew Pettit
12 Isaac Batt
13 Frank Faulkner
14 John Pritchet
15 Jas Price
16 W P Rogers
17 F. R. Gourd
18 John Smith
19 Johnson Tucker
20 Thos. Woodall
21 Johnson Gritts
   G. Thornton

The Cherokee National Male Seminary record book lists W. P. Rogers as student 16 in the Preparatory School during the fall term 1887 (*OkTahN*).

Cherokee National Male Seminary, Tahlequah, I.T. *(OkTahN)*.

1851 and graduated its first class in 1854. The Female Seminary, located at Park Hill three miles southeast of Tahlequah, opened on 7 May 1851.

The upper schools of the Male and Female Seminaries consisted of a four-year Academic Department including grades nine through twelve. The Male Seminary was noted for a rigorous curriculum in science, mathematics, composition, ancient and modern languages, and other subjects. The seminaries also were known for strict discipline and enforced rules, and an exhausting schedule that required students to rise at 5:30 in the morning and retire at 9:15 at night. The seminaries were modeled on eastern preparatory and finishing schools, and the Female Seminary in particular was influenced by the educational philosophy of Mount Holyoke College. During the Civil War, instruction was discontinued, and the buildings were used for a hospital, storing provisions, and other military purposes; consequently, the structures suffered considerable damage. They were eventually rebuilt; the Female Seminary reopened in 1872 and the Male Seminary in 1875. The Female Seminary burned down on 10 April 1887 and was rebuilt at a new site north of Tahlequah in 1889. The dissolution of the Cherokee tribal government, and Oklahoma statehood in 1907, eventually brought an end to the seminaries. The Female Seminary was purchased by the state of Oklahoma in 1909, when it became the first building of Northeastern State Normal School, a teacher-training institution. The last commencement exercises for the Female Seminary occurred on 27 May 1909. Because there was still a demand for a Cherokee high school, the Male Seminary became a coeducational school for the 1909–10 academic year. Many of the female students attended the merged school until the building burned down on 20 March 1910. The last graduating class received its degrees at ceremonies on 31 May 1910 at the new Normal School, which was the nucleus for the present-day Northeastern Oklahoma State University at Tahlequah. The Female Seminary building still exists and is now called Seminary Hall on the campus; the Markhoma Academy, a private school, was constructed on the location of the Male Seminary.

Since the seminaries' educational philosophy and curriculum were based on leading white schools in the East, and traditional Cherokee culture was given minimal attention, the seminaries have been interpreted as institutions promoting white acculturation among the Cherokees. There were no classes offered on Cherokee history and culture, and English was the official language. Although the schools admitted poor full-bloods, especially in the primary grades, the sons and daughters of the leading mixed-blood families of the Cherokee Nation primarily attended the seminaries. It was not unusual to find that two or three generations of a family had enrolled at the seminaries as, for example, the Rogers family did. Men and women graduates became influential politicians, lawyers, doctors, educators, and social workers in the Cherokee Nation and later in the state of Oklahoma (Abbott, "History of the Cherokee Female Seminary: 1851–1910"; Agnew, "Legacy of Education"; Mihesuah, *Cultivating the Rosebuds;* Starr, *History of the Cherokee Indians,* 231–43; Tinnin, "Influences of the Cherokee National Seminaries").

2. In 1873 the National Council voted to expand the seminaries to include a primary department—grades one through five—and a preparatory department—grades six through eight. The preparatory department was a three-year program that prepared students for the upper school, and children could enroll at any age. In the 1883–84 Cherokee National Male Seminary catalogue the preparatory department is described as follows: "The course of study in this department is arranged to prepare students for the Seminary proper. The school is thoroughly graded. Object lessons, compositions, oral, written and other exercises calculated to develop the power of written and oral expression are given. Ideas of number, form, size and actual measurement precede the more complex arithmetical operations. Map drawing, the use of excellent maps in the Seminary and topical exercises render Geography practical. The Reading exercises are supplemented by *The Treasure Trove*, a monthly for young students. The principal of this department spends an hour each Saturday with the students assisting them in selecting books from the library. During the hour students give an outline of the past week's reading" (*Cherokee National Male Seminary Catalogue, 1883–1884*, 17, copy, OkU; see also Abbott, "History of the Cherokee Female Seminary: 1851–1901," 77; Starr, *History of the Cherokee Indians,* 232).

3. Attending either the Cherokee Male or the Cherokee Female Seminary was a family tradition. May and Maud Rogers, Will Rogers's sisters, attended the Cherokee Female Seminary during the 1886–87 academic year, but left when the building burned on Easter Sunday, 1887. "W. P. Rogers" was often the name that his parents used during his childhood, especially on formal occasions (see Authenticated Roll of the Cherokee Nation, 1880, above; "W. P. Rogers, Cattle Dealer" letterhead, Clement Vann Rogers to Chief C. J. Harris, 15 October 1894, below; and Clem McSpadden to John Thomas McSpadden, August 1894, OkClaW). There is only one other William P. Rogers listed in *The Final Rolls of Citizens and Freedmen of the Five Civilized Tribes in Indian Territory* (1907 Dawes Roll, no. 2827, p. 256), and he is listed as eleven years old, which suggests that he was born after 1887. Besides Will Rogers, there is no other William P. Rogers in the 1909 Guion Miller Roll identifying members or descendants of the Eastern Cher-

okees, a roll established for the purpose of distributing U.S. government funds. Biographer Donald Day writes that Rogers attended the Male Seminary after his mother died (1890) and that he went to the school for only a short time, beginning in the fall and ending sometime before Christmas *(Will Rogers,* 19). Homer Croy writes that Rogers attended the Female Seminary but actually no males, except for sons of teachers, were admitted to the school *(Our Will Rogers,* 25; Professor Devon A. Mihesuah, Northern Arizona University, Flagstaff, to WRPP, 10 December 1992). In an interview in the Indian-Pioneer Papers, Charles T. Watts, who grew up in Claremore, said, "I can remember many times when Clem Rogers, Will's father, took him to the Male Seminary at Tahlequah" (IPH–OkHi, 45:423–24). The dates August 1887 to December 1887 also correspond to a gap in Will Rogers's education between the Drumgoole School and the Harrell International Institute.

4. William (Will, Willie, or Bill) Musgrove (b. 1873) was a cousin of Will Rogers. William Musgrove's parents, Francis Marion (Frank) Musgrove (Clem V. Rogers's half brother) and Clara Elizabeth Alberty Musgrove, operated a prosperous horse and cattle ranch several miles from Claremore. After attending the Male Seminary, William Musgrove graduated from a high school in Fort Worth, Tex., in 1895. He later operated the family farm and ranch, raising cattle and other products, and participated in steer-roping contests with Rogers. He left home in the early 1900s and resided in California until his death (Gideon, *Indian Territory,* 897–98; *HRC,* 332–34; *WRFT,* 85).

5. Seventy-six preparatory students were listed in the roll books for the Male Seminary for the term commencing 29 August 1887 and ending 16 December 1887. Those listed are from page eighty-four of the original roll book. The summary of records listed reading, composition, geography, arithmetic, and writing among the subjects studied by the preparatory students. The only grade W. P. Rogers received was a 92 in reading (Ballenger, "Early History of Northeastern State College," and Victoria Sheffler, University Archivist, OkTahN, to WRPP, 4 November 1992).

Notice from *Our Brother in Red*
15 September 1888
Muskogee, I. T.

On 15 September 1888 the Methodist paper Our Brother in Red[1] *announced that Will Rogers[2] was one of the new pupils at the Harrell International Institute[2] in Muskogee.[3] He joined his sister May, who had first enrolled at the school in January 1888.[4] Harrell, mainly a boarding school for girls, was operated by the Women's Board of Missions of the Methodist Episcopal Church South.[5] Clem V. Rogers made arrangements with its president, Rev. Theodore F. Brewer,[6] a Methodist minister, to send his son there.[7] Rogers roomed with Brewer's son, Robert,[8] but he did not enjoy the school. Later he said that he felt as if he was on an "island completely surrounded by petticoats."[9]*

H. I. I. LOCALS

Misses May Rogers and Willie, Sallie Musgrove, Vick and Nannie Lipe[10] and Ella Foreman, of Oowala are among the boarding pupils at Harrell.

PD. Printed in *OBR,* 15 September 1888.

1. *Our Brother in Red* was established in Muskogee by Rev. Theodore F. Brewer in September 1882 as an official organ of the Indian Mission Conference of the Methodist Episcopal Church South. It began as a sixteen-page monthly, but became a five-column, eight-page weekly in September 1887. It was published on Saturdays, and a subscription cost one dollar annually. Its motto was "Christian Education, the Hope of the Indians." By 1889 the paper had a circulation of more than one thousand. It carried considerable news about missionaries and meetings of the Indian Mission Conference as well as reports from various circuits in the Indian Territory. News and advertisements about the Harrell Institute were regular features of the periodical, which included a column about the local students. In 1892 Brewer was replaced as editor by Rev. William M. Baldwin. The paper moved to Oklahoma City in 1899; in 1900 it merged with the *Arkansas Methodist* at Little Rock and was renamed the *Indian Oklahoma Methodist* (Foreman, C., *Oklahoma Imprints*, 210–11; Witcher, "Territorial Magazines," 486–88).

2. The idea for a Methodist school in Muskogee was first discussed in 1878 at a meeting held in the home of Mrs. Mary E. Locke, the sister of Rev. Theodore F. Brewer. On 14 June 1879 a committee applied to Creek Chief Ward Coachman for a school to instruct Indian and white children in the "elements of sciences and agriculture and mechanical arts, with no expense to the Creek Nation" (Foreman, G., *Muskogee*, 54). The institute was officially established on 2 November 1881 and named for Rev. John Harrell (1805–1876), a Methodist missionary influential in the educational activities of the Indian Mission Conference of the Methodist Episcopal Church South, who served as a missionary in Tennessee and Arkansas before coming to the Indian Territory. After the Creek Council granted the institute a charter, the school began its inaugural session in 1881 with ninety-one students and held its first classes in the First Methodist Church (called the Rock Church) and the home of Mary E. Locke, principal of the Primary Department. With funds from the town of Muskogee and gift of $10,000 from the Women's Board of Missions, a three-story brick building was constructed on East Okmulgee Avenue in 1884. It was large enough to house boarding students, although a frame dormitory building was later added. Rev. Theodore Frelinghuysen Brewer served as the institute's first president until 1896, after which he became president of Willie Halsell College in Vinita from 1899 to 1901. An advertisement for the school, appearing in the 6 September 1887 issue of *Our Brother in Red,* reported that the school calendar was divided into two terms of five months each. The school consisted of four departments: Primary, Academic or Intermediate, Collegiate, and Music. Board cost $10.00 per month, while tuition ranged from $1.50 to $4.00. There were 135 pupils enrolled in October 1899, and seven teachers on the faculty, including a superintendent (*OBR*, August 1883, 19 October 1899; Witcher, "Territorial Magazines," 487). Harrell flourished for many years, but on 25 September 1899 the school was destroyed by fire (Robinson, "Burning of Spaulding Institute," 336–37). It was rebuilt with a gift from H. B. Spaulding, a wealthy cattleman, merchant, and former mayor of Muskogee who supported the Methodist church. The school was renamed the Spaulding Institute in his honor; later it was called the Spaulding Female College; and in 1908 its property became part of Oklahoma Women's College (*IC*, 28 September 1899). Faced with financial problems and property-tax assessments, the school closed in 1908; its buildings later were used for part of the Muskogee General Hospital (Babcock and Bryce, *History of Methodism in Oklahoma*, 189–92, 206–8, 265–66, 311–12; Benedict, *Muskogee and Northeastern Oklahoma* 1:260, 347, 452; Brewer, "Necrology: Rev. Theodore Frelinghuysen Brewer," 349–50; Foreman, C., "Dr. and Mrs. Richard Moore Crain," 73; Foreman, G., *Muskogee*, 52–55; Jackson, "Church School Education in the Creek Nation, 1898 to 1907"; West, *Muskogee*, 21, 114, 177).

3. Founded in 1872, Muskogee is located forty-seven miles south of Tulsa and is the seat of Muskogee County. It was the largest town in the Creek Nation in 1890 with a population of twelve hundred. The Creek Indians, who spoke the Muskhogean language, were often called the Muskogees. The Muskhogeans were an important Indian linguistic group, which included the peoples of the Creek Confederacy in Georgia and Alabama and others (Debo, *History of the Indians of the United States*, 9–10; Morris and McReynolds, *Historical Atlas of Oklahoma*, map 37; Shirk, *Oklahoma Place Names*, 146; *WNGD*, 803).

4. *Our Brother in Red* reported on 7 January 1888 that May Rogers was "among the new boarding students enrolled since Christmas." The *Indian Chieftain* reported on 19 January 1888 that "Miss May Rogers has gone to Muskogee to attend Harrell Institute assignment of teachers for the coming term." News about May missing school because of illness and traveling to Fort Gibson was also reported in *Our Brother in Red* (18 February, 17 March, 7 April, 14 April, and 12 May 1888).

5. Harrell began as a coeducational school, but beginning in September 1883, it became a female institution for boarding and day students. However, it did enroll male day students from the local area who were up to twelve years of age (Foreman, C., "Mrs. Laura E. Harsha," 183; Keith, *Boy's Life of Will Rogers*, 42; *OBR*, July 1883).

6. A prominent minister affiliated with the Methodist Episcopal Church South as well as an educator and editor, Rev. Theodore Frelinghuysen Brewer was born in Gibson County, Tenn., on 20 January 1845. After serving in the Confederate army under Nathan Bedford Forrest during the Civil War, Brewer was admitted into the Memphis Conference of the Methodist Episcopal Church South at Jackson, Tenn., on 10 November 1866, where he served as a circuit preacher in the Dyersburg circuit. After other appointments in Tennessee, northern Mississippi, and Arkansas, he was transferred to the Indian Mission Conference in August 1878. There he became head of the Asbury Manual Labor School for Creek Indians at Eufaula, I.T. In 1880 he was appointed to the "railroad circuit" that included Eufaula, Vinita, and Muskogee, where he was pastor of the town's first Methodist church, a stone building known as the Rock Church located at Cherokee Street and East Okmulgee Avenue. Besides founding the school and serving for over twenty years as head of the Harrell International Institute and its successors, Spaulding College and Spaulding Female College, Reverend Brewer was also president of Willie Halsell College at Vinita from 1899 to 1901. Later he served on the first textbook commission for the new state of Oklahoma, was a member of the state board of education, and a high-school inspector for the University of Oklahoma. He died on 6 April 1928 (Babcock and Bryce, *History of Methodism in Oklahoma* 1:265–71; Brewer, "Necrology: Rev. Theodore Frelinghuysen Brewer," 349–50; Clegg and Oden, *Oklahoma Methodism in the Twentieth Century*, 93–94; "Theodore F. Brewer," 232–33).

7. In August 1888, shortly before Will Rogers enrolled at Harrell, Reverend Brewer visited the Rogers ranch. He wrote in *Our Brother in Red:* "On Wednesday afternoon, after driving ten miles, and fording Verdigris river, we alighted at Mr. Clem Rogers' gate. A cordial welcome and a warm supper awaited us. Miss Maud Rogers, of Howard College, and Miss Mary Rogers, of Harrell Institute, were at home enjoying their vacations. Sister R. [Mary America Rogers] certainly knows how to make one feel at home. Our stay with this kind family was delightfully pleasant" (1 September 1888). Reverend Brewer also visited the Drumgoole and Chelsea areas, where he spent several days at the home of John Thomas McSpadden and Sallie Rogers McSpadden.

8. The son of Rev. Theodore Frelinghuysen Brewer and Mary Webster Brewer, Robert Paine Brewer was born at Fayetteville, Ark., on 3 December 1876. After attending Harrell International Institute and its successor, Spaulding Female College,

until the age of fourteen, Robert Brewer was educated at the Webb School of Tennessee and graduated from Southwestern University at Georgetown, Tex. He entered the banking business in Oklahoma, helping to organize the First National Bank of Checotah and the First National Bank of Quinton, and then was appointed president of the First National Bank of McAlester in 1916. In 1924 he became the director and president of the First National Bank of Tulsa, and later he was a bank executive in New York City (Thoburn and Wright, *Oklahoma* 3:434–35).

9. Trent, *My Cousin Will Rogers*, 32.

10. Victoria Lipe (1874–1923) and Nannie Lipe (1872–1956) were the daughters of DeWitt Clinton Lipe and Mary E. Archer Lipe (*HRC*, 280–81; see also Biographical Appendix entry, LIPE, DeWitt Clinton).

Notice from *Our Brother in Red*
22 September 1888
Muskogee, I.T.

H.I.I. LOCALS

Little Willie Rogers went home Monday, after spending a week away from his mother.

PD. Printed in *OBR*, 22 September 1888.

Notice from *Our Brother in Red*
5 April 1890
Muskogee, I.T.

Shortly before her death on 28 May 1890, Mary America Schrimsher Rogers visited Will Rogers at the Harrell International Institute.[1] Mary Rogers's death devastated her youngest child, who was closely attached to his mother.

HARRELL INSTITUTE LOCALS

Mrs. C. V. Rogers visited her little son Willie, at Harrell, Tuesday and Wednesday.

PD. Printed in *OBR*, 5 April 1890.

1. Will Rogers did not return to Harrell in the fall of 1890. According to both Homer Croy and Richard Ketchum, Rev. Theodore Frelinghuysen Brewer wrote his father: "I regret to inform you that your son is not doing well in school and would suggest you remove him" (Croy, *Our Will Rogers*, 25; Ketchum, *Will Rogers*, 39). This letter is not extant, and there is no evidence that he was removed for poor performance. He was, however, home at the Rogers ranch recovering from a bout of the measles when his sisters Sallie and Maud and Sallie's baby Mary Belle became ill with typhoid fever in May 1890 and were brought to the ranch to be nursed by Mary Rogers. His cousin Clem McSpadden also was suffering from the measles. Young Will was moved to the home of

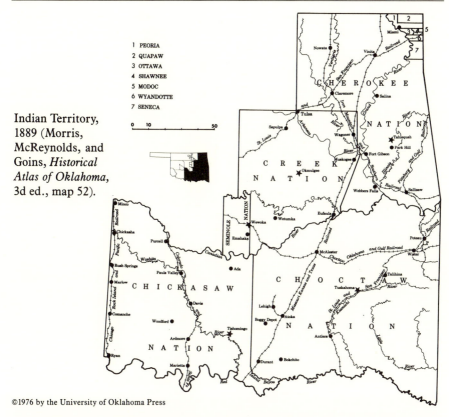

1 PEORIA
2 QUAPAW
3 OTTAWA
4 SHAWNEE
5 MODOC
6 WYANDOTTE
7 SENECA

Indian Territory,
1889 (Morris,
McReynolds, and
Goins, *Historical
Atlas of Oklahoma*,
3d ed., map 52).

Gracey Greenleaf, who worked as a cook at the ranch. He was apparently being cared for by the Greenleafs when his mother passed away. Mary Belle McSpadden died on 22 May 1890, and Mary Rogers died one week later; Maud Rogers Lane and Sallie Rogers McSpadden were still bedridden at the time. Mary Rogers's death precipitated changes at the ranch, which gradually began to decline from its heyday during the 1870s and 1880s (Keith interview with Agnes Walker, 27 June 1936, in Keith, "Clem Rogers and His Influence on Oklahoma History," 64; Walker, interview, IPH-OkHi; see also Biographical Appendix entry, ROGERS, Mary America Schrimsher).

Census of the Cherokee Nation
1890
Cooweescoowee District, I.T.

In 1890 the peoples of Indian Territory, like all Native Americans, were included in the United States census for the first time. According to the census results, there were 22,015 Native Americans living in the Cherokee Nation in 1890 (of whom 20,654 were Cherokees) and some 34,000 people of other races and ethnicities (including 5,127 African Americans, 29,166 whites, and one Chinese person), producing a

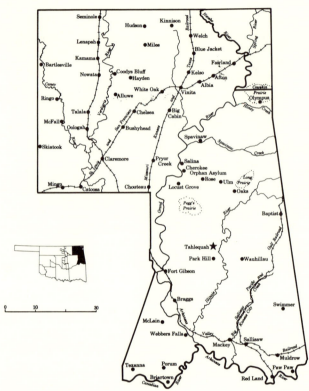

Cherokee Nation,
ca. 1889 (Morris,
McReynolds, and
Goins, *Historical Atlas
of Oklahoma*, 3d ed.,
map 36).

*total population of 56,309. Of these, 5,621 resided in the Cooweescoowee District.
Census takers reported difficulty in some cases in designating ethnicity by comparing
physical characteristics and features with responses to the question "Are you an
Indian?" People seemingly white in appearance would answer in the affirmative,
and U.S. officials encountered African Americans who spoke Indian languages and
were accepted as Indians according to Indian law and custom. Some peoples of non-
Cherokee descent were adopted Cherokees. Approximately one-half of the native
Cherokees counted were full-bloods; others, like the Rogers family, were of mixed
descent but were Cherokee by Indian law and self-identification.[1]*

*As historian Nancy Hope Sober has pointed out, "by 1890 the Indians were a
minority in their own land."[2] The five nations of Indian Territory in 1890 had a
total full-blood and mixed-blood Indian population of 51,279, an African American population of 18,636, and 110,254 white residents.[3] Over the next five years the
noncitizen population more than doubled as federal legislation dismantled tribal
sovereignty and settlement rights.*

*The first six columns of the census schedule asked for the name, native ("N") or
adopted ("A") status, race or nationality ("C" for Cherokee), age, sex, and
occupation of respondents.[3] The next three columns designated yes or no for "Can
Read," "Can Write," and "Married."*

1	2	3	4	5	6	7	8	9
Rogers Clem V	N	C	51	M	Farmer	yes	yes	yes[4]
Rogers May	"	15	F			yes	yes	no[5]
Rogers William P	"	"	10	M		"	"	"

PD, with autograph insertions.[6] OkHi.

1. Will Rogers's parents, Clement Vann Rogers and Mary America Schrimsher Rogers, were both one-quarter Cherokee (*WRFT*, vi; see also Thornton, *Cherokees*, 106–9).

2. Sober, *Intruders*, 126.

3. United States Bureau of the Census, *Population of Oklahoma and Indian Territories, 1907* (Washington: GPO, 1907), cited in Baird and Goble, *Story of Oklahoma*, 284.

4. The census reported that Clem V. Rogers was the owner of three dwellings and seven other structures on three farms, with a total of three hundred acres enclosed, all under cultivation. Rogers's improvements were valued at $15,000. His yield was recorded as three thousand bushels of corn, one thousand of wheat, one thousand of oats, two hundred of apples, and twenty of Irish potatoes. He had some three hundred fruit trees and his livestock included thirty hogs, eight hundred cattle, sixty horses, thirty-six goats, fifty domestic fowl, and five mules. He owned five plows, two of them machine plows, and a wheat drill. The Oklahoma Historical Society has reported that he also owned a reaper, a mower, a self-binder, a hack, and two farm wagons; also a piano and a clock (Rella Looney, OkHi, to Homer Croy, 12 June 1952, HCP-MoU).

5. Will Rogers's sister May was born in 1873 and would have been seventeen, not fifteen, at the time of the 1890 census. Her age was listed correctly in the 1880 census. Will Rogers's mother, Mary, died on 28 May 1890, and his brother, Robert, had passed away on 13 April 1883. His sisters Maud and Sallie were listed separately. Maud married in 1891, and Sallie in 1885 (*WRFT*, 10).

6. On 28 July 1897 the National Council authorized a manuscript list of names appearing on the 1890 U.S. Census Record. The list was arranged by district and alphabetized by surname. The list contains an individual's name, 1890 roll number, age, and sex. The names of Clem V. Rogers (no. 4331), May Rogers (no. 4332), and William P. Rogers (no. 4333) appear on p. 195, Cooweescoowee District. All three are listed as N.C. (native Cherokee), and their age and sex are the same as in the 1890 U.S. Census Record (FARC, Fort Worth, RG 75, microfilm 7R60-1).

Notice from the *Indian Chieftain*
15 October 1891
Vinita, I. T.

In the fall of 1891 Rogers enrolled as a boarding student at Willie Halsell College in Vinita, approximately thirty-six miles from the Rogers ranch. Willie Halsell College was situated on 160 acres of pastureland on the northern edge of town. A coeducational school with an enrollment ranging from 150 to more than 200 students, it offered courses from the first grade through high school and was known as the

Will Rogers at about age twelve, when he was a student at Willie Halsell College *(OkClaW)*.

Willie Halsell College, Vinita, I.T. Tom Lane is standing farthest right in the back row. In front of his left shoulder is a student with a light-colored hat who resembles Will Rogers (*OkClaW*).

largest private school in the eastern part of the Indian Territory. Rogers attended Willie Halsell College for four years from 1891 to 1895.[1]

WILLIE HALSELL INSTITUTE NOTES.

Tom Lane,[2] the musician of the Institute, went home yesterday to attend the wedding of his uncle. He was accompanied by Willie Rogers, brother of the bride.[3]

PD. Printed in *IC*, 15 October 1891.

1. Willie Halsell College was founded in 1887 as Galloway College by the Indian Mission Conference of the Methodist Episcopal Church South to provide education and religious instruction. It was named in honor of Bishop Charles B. Galloway, who headed the Indian Mission Conference in 1886 and 1887 and helped initiate the idea for a school at Vinita. Classes were first held in the local Methodist church. Its founding was

William Electious Halsell, a prosperous rancher in Indian Territory and Texas, was the benefactor of Willie Halsell College, which was named for his daughter. Will Rogers frequently visited Halsell's Mashed-O Ranch in Texas (*HFP-TxLT*).

Ewing Halsell, who became a successful rancher like his father, William Electious Halsell, attended Willie Halsell College with Will Rogers. The two became lifelong friends (*HFP-TxLT*).

stimulated by the need for another Methodist school in the Indian Territory and a desire to offer the citizens an educational option beyond the tribal schools. A historical note in the 1894 annual catalogue pointed out the success of the Harrell Institute in Muskogee. "It was found that Harrell could not fully meet the demand [for students]," the catalogue reported. The church thus decided to establish another school at Vinita, and one of its chief founders was Rev. L. W. Waters, Methodist pastor at Vinita. As provided in the 1866 treaty between the Cherokee Nation and the United States, the Cherokee Council granted 160 acres of land just north of the city's limits to the college for "educational and religious purposes" (*1894 Annual Catalogue of Willie Halsell College*, 16). In 1894 Vinita had a population of two thousand and was the second-largest town in the Cherokee Nation with one national bank, four hotels, four churches, and two newspapers. The town also had a successful school, the Worcester Academy, a popular Congregational mission school, which opened in November 1882 and was supported by the American Home Missionary Society (Campbell, *Vinita, I.T.,* 69–72; Garrett, "Worcester, Pride of the West," 386–96).

Willie Halsell classes were first held in the Methodist church in September 1890, and sixty students were enrolled at the end of the first year. The school commenced construction of a school building, and classes were held in the unfinished building in September 1891. Funds for its completion were contributed by William Electious Halsell, a wealthy cattleman and banker who donated land as well as money to complete the four-story brick-and-stone main building (Halsell donated $3,000; the town of Vinita, $7,000; and the Board of Foreign Missions of the Methodist Episcopal Church South, $7,000). In honor of Halsell's gift the board of trustees renamed the school for Halsell's deceased daughter, Willie, who had died from meningitis on 11 July 1884 at the age of ten (Holden, *Ranching Saga,* 137–38; *IC,* 2 July 1891; *OBR,* 11 June 1891). The newly named Willie Halsell College graduated its first class in June 1894. A few blocks from the school, on Smith Street, was a two-story dormitory for the boys called the Annex, built in 1893 and run by "Aunt Laura" Cooper. Rogers resided in the Annex and also boarded with a local family (Mr. and Mrs. W. W. Miller). Room and board was $10.00 a month, and tuition in 1894 varied from a low of $6.80 for students in the primary department to $14.80 for juniors and seniors. Clem V. Rogers was on the school's honorary board of trustees. Although Willie Halsell College enrolled several hundred students at its peak, it was plagued by financial problems by 1905. Statehood in 1907 and the availability of tax-supported public schools also contributed to its demise. In 1908 W. E. Halsell bought the property to pay off the school's debt. The Hall-Halsell Elementary School was eventually built on the site *(1894 Annual Catalogue of Willie Halsell College;* miscellaneous material, box 9, OkClaW; Babcock and Bryce, *History of Methodism in Oklahoma,* 267–99, 310–11; Branda, *Handbook of Texas: A Supplement* 3:370; Campbell, *Vinita, I.T.,* 73–77; Holden, *Ranching Saga,* 156–58; see also Biographical Appendix entries, HALSELL, William Electious, and HALSELL, Ewing).

2. Thomas Lipe Lane, the son of Dr. and Mrs. Andrew Jackson Lane, was a neighborhood friend with whom Rogers was especially close during his school years (see Biographical Appendix entries, LANE, Andrew Jackson, M.D., and LANE, Thomas Lipe).

3. Rogers and Lane attended the wedding of Maud Rogers to Captain Lane (C. L. or Cap) Lane on 14 October 1891, held at the Rogers ranch. C. L. Lane was the nephew of Dr. Andrew Jackson Lane, Tom Lane's father (Paula Love to Homer Croy, n.d., HCP-MoU). The *Indian Chieftain* reported on the Lane-Rogers wedding: "Only the immediate relatives of the contracting parties were present. The bride was neatly attired in a cream colored mohair, trimmed with wool lace and ribbons, while the groom wore a black cut-away and presented in every respect an ideal groom. After the ceremony the guests proceeded to the dining room and partook of as choice a breakfast as one could wish for. The happy couple will make Chelsea their future home" (22 October 1891). Among the presents were a team of horses from Clem V. Rogers, a lamp from Dr. and Mrs. A. J. Lane, and a cow and calf from May Rogers (see Biographical Appendix entries, LANE, Captain Lane, and LANE, Maud, Ethel Rogers).

Article from the *Indian Chieftain*
13 October 1892
Vinita, I. T.

NOTES FROM THE COLLEGE.

—The Willie Halsell College commenced its school year on Sept. 5th, under most favorable conditions. Although the college is a comparatively young candidate for favor, its aims are broad, and hopes soon to rank high among educational institutions of its kind. Prof. Rowsey[1] has progressive ideas; and he is blessed with a spirit which prefers being abreast of the age to being shackled by the rules of outgrown methods.

—September 30th closed a very prosperous month. Have now a large enrollment and more constantly coming in. Mr. Wills[2] from West Virginia and Mr. Doyer from St. Louis, have recently been enrolled. Miss Hortense Glover, from Tennessee, a very efficient literary teacher, will soon be added to our corps of teachers.

—One of the most interesting and beneficial features of the college are the literary societies which have been recently organized—the Apollonian, Calliopean, and Philomathean—for the young men, young ladies and children of primary department.[3] These societies are for the purpose of assisting in the work of sustaining and enlarging the scope and usefulness of the school.

—The calisthenic exercises for the cultivation of physical strength and muscular elasticity which are given to the pupils of the school at the close of each day's work, by Miss Croom,[4] and the vocal training given at the opening of school by Miss Selleck, also deserve special mention.

—Two elegant upright pianos and an organ have recently been purchased and which add greatly to the muscial department.

—Several car loads of gravel are in readiness to construct a walk direct from college to Main st. as soon as it rains; when we will have a building which delightfully supplements the natural advantages of the location, being situated in the midst of the smiling prairie where every advantage of our outdoor amusement and exercise can be obtained under the most delightful conditions, affording, in fact, all the benefits of country life with the resources of instruction in the city available.

—The work of this school is based upon such just and righteous principles—its scope is so broad, its aims so far reaching and inclusive in their cognizance of the pupil and the community that we hope that its host of friends may be able to rejoice at the new era of usefulness and prosperity upon which it is just entering.

PD. Printed in *IC*, 13 October 1892.

1. William Eugene Rowsey, a graduate of Vanderbilt University, served as Willie Halsell College's second president from 1892 to 1896. He married Eva Patton, the valedictorian of the first graduating class. After his tenure at Willie Halsell College he became a prominent lawyer and banker in Muskogee. He served as president of the Bank of Commerce and director and treasurer of the Muskogee Electric and Gas Co. He also served as deputy U.S. clerk, Northern District, for five years. Rowsey was the principal speaker at the second annual reunion of students held in Vinita on 6 October 1934. Rogers also attended the reunion, as did some of his schoolmates: Ewing Halsell, Earl Walker, Sam Cobb, and Henry Knight. (Rogers had been invited to the first reunion in August 1933, but could not attend because of a movie commitment). Rogers rode in a parade and after he was introduced by Rowsey, gave a speech at the reunion event (Rowsey, who had just returned from a trip abroad, said: "I found people in every country who asked me about Will Rogers. The man we all knew as 'Rabbit' Rogers, of school days, has become more popular than any king, emperor, or potentate") ("Will Rogers Treks to His Old 'College,'" *NYT,* 23 December 1934; see also Babcock and Bryce, *History of Methodism in Oklahoma,* 268; Dewitz, *Notable Men of Indian Territory,* 188; *TDW* 27 August 1933 and 30 September 1934; "Will Rogers Chronology," 6 October 1934, OkClaW; Will Rogers to Earl Walker, ca. 27 August 1933, telegram, box 9, OkClaW; "Will Rogers Meets Old Friends Who Knew Him as Rabbit in Their Cowboy Days," *Kansas City Star,* 25 November 1934).

2. Charles W. Wills.

3. The 1894 annual catalogue described the school's literary societies as follows: "The college has four literary societies which meet every Friday afternoon in their respective rooms. Each society is under the immediate supervision of one or more of the faculty who render all the encouragement and assistance necessary. The Apollonian Society is composed of the young men. The Calliopean Society consists of the young ladies. The Philomatheans is the name of the society made up from the sixth and seventh grades. The Busy Workers are the primary pupils. These societies afford opportunity for practice and improvement in Forensic Discussion, Elocution and Composition, and we URGENTLY REQUEST every parent to interest himself in this special feature of this work, and thus encourage the pupils" (*1894 Annual Catalogue of Willie Halsell College,* 18).

4. Cordelia Croom.

Notice from the *Indian Chieftain*
29 December 1892
Vinita, I.T.

At Willie Halsell College, Rogers took courses in the preparatory department (fifth and sixth grades) and was also listed as a pupil in elocution and art. With some foreshadowing of his future talents, Rogers excelled in elocution.[1] One of his first public appearances was at a school function in which he received "a hearty round of applause" for his declamations.

The College Entertainments.

The entertainments given at the close of the fall term of Willie Halsell college by the Apollonian and Calliopean societies last Thursday and Friday evenings were quite a success. While the programme of each evening was excellent and the parts well sustained, the second evening was more enjoyable. Several of the parts deserve especial mention. The oration by John Barrett, "Shadows on the Mirror," was good, also the recitation by Miss Cooper, "Van Bibber's Rock." The vocal solo by little Birdie Ironside was very sweet and too much praise cannot be given her. Willie Rogers was inimitable in each of his declamations and never failed to receive a hearty round of applause. Considered as a whole both evenings' entertainments reflect great credit upon the institution, showing the unmistakable marks of careful and patient labor on the part of the faculty. Prof. Rowsey is an able educator, and is nobly assisted by the other members of the faculty. The institution over which they preside holds in no slight degree the destinies of this country within its hands; it should be the pleasure of all to do their utmost to extend its powers for doing well the work which is at hand.

Friend.

PD. Printed in *IC*, 29 December 1892.

1. The 1894 annual Willie Halsell College catalogue described the programs in elocution as follows: "ELOCUTION. The course of study in this department will cover two years. Its object will be not merely to drill pupils to 'recite pieces', but to make them good readers. Careful and thorough training will be given in articulation, vocalization, and production of tone, by lessons based on scientific principles. Exercises in reading and reciting passages from best authors will also be a daily practice. Special attention is given the Delsarte System, it having been found that no system yields so much to the grace, physical control and expression of pupils, enabling them to appear to great advantage. Such an art is no mean addition to a lady's charm" (*1894 Annual Catalogue of Willie Halsell College*, 23–24). Rogers once wrote about his years at the school: "I took elocution I stopped it just in time or I would have been a senator" (Will Rogers to Earl Walker, ca. 27 August 1933, telegram, box 9, OkClaW).

Roll of Honor, Willie Halsell College
December 1892
Vinita, I.T.

Roll of Honor.[1]

The fall session of the college closed last Friday, Dec. 23rd. Written examinations were in progress during the week and the marks ran very high.

Below is a partial list of the pupils in the academic and collegiate departments who averaged above 90 in daily grade for the month of December:

John McCracken	99 1-2
Walter McKeehan	98 1-2
John L. Denbo	98 1-3
Walter C. Jones	98 1-7
Jno. C. Barrett	97 9-10
C. Hunt	97 4-5
Willie Akin	97 4-5
Jesse Jones	97 2-7
Chas. Mehlin	96 3-5
J. L. Kell	96 3-5
C. W. Wills	96 1-6
Oneida Cooper	95 5-6
J. M. Oskison[2]	95 9-10
Eva Patton	100
Chas. Walker[3]	95 1-2
Mable Cook	93 4-5
Ludie Hall	93 2-5
P. T. Dwyer	94 4-5
H. P. Evans	93 4-5
Janie Hunt	92
Flora Foreman[4]	91
Ibbie Thomas	91
Willie Rogers	90 2-3

Several others would have followed in the above list had not absence lowered their grades.

The average of the entire school on examination was about 93.

W. E. Rowsey, President.

PD. Printed in *IC*, 29 December 1892.

1. The 1894 annual catalogue described the Roll of Honor as follows: "A Roll of Honor is published at the end of each month in the Indian Chieftain and Vinita Globe. This is composed of the fifteen pupils making highest marks during the month. Great interest is manifested in this honor, and the grades run very high. A deduction of 5 is made for each absence from any class." There were 165 pupils enrolled in the school in 1892–93 (*1894 Annual Catalogue of Willie Halsell College*, 16, 20).

2. Born near Tahlequah, I.T., John Milton Oskison (1874–1947) was the son of John Oskison and Sarah E. Shanks, a Vinita family engaged in the cattle business. Oskison graduated from the Willie Halsell College in 1894 and then attended Stanford Univer-

In 1934 Will Rogers attended a reunion of his Willie Halsell College classmates in Vinita. *Left to right:* Jim Highland, Jim Rider, Harry Williams, Billy Friend, Henry Knight, Sam Cobb, Will Rogers, George Franklin, and Earl Walker *(OkClaW).*

sity, graduating with a B.A. degree in 1898. He next went to Harvard University, where he did graduate work in English. Of Cherokee descent, Oskison was a successful novelist and short-story writer whose work often dealt with the Indian Territory. His short stories appeared in such magazines as *Scribner's, North American Review,* and *Century Magazine.* He also served as an editorial writer on the *New York Evening Post* and as an associate editor on *Collier's Weekly.* His first novel was *Wild Harvest* (1925), which was followed by other works of fiction including the best-seller *Brothers Three.* When Rogers could not attend the school's first reunion in 1934 he sent a telegram to his schoolmate Earl Walker: "Now that I find that they are celebrating the passing out of Willie Halsell Institute well there were guys went there that would have put even Harvard or Yale out of business   I believe John Oskison was the only one we really got educated but they taught a lot of em to go out and lead fine useful lives to their communities" (Will Rogers to Earl Walker, ca. 27 August 1933, telegram, box 9, OkClaW). Oskison claimed that he, Will Rogers, and two other friends attended the 1893 Chicago World's Fair together. Oskison's second wife, Hildegarde Hawthorne, was the granddaughter of Nathaniel Hawthorne. Oskison died of a heart ailment on 25 February 1947 (John M. Oskison, "A Tale of the Old I.T.," JMO-OkU; Dale and Wardell, *History of Oklahoma,* 513; Gibson, *Guide to the Regional Manuscript Collections,* 134–35; *Story of Craig County,* 531–32; Workers of the Writers' Program, *Oklahoma,* 91).

3. Charles Paul Walker (1877–1957) and his brother Earl Walker (1876–1957) were schoolmates and good friends of Will Rogers. They were the sons of the Vinita ranch foreman and law officer Joseph Newton Walker (1854–1919). Charles Walker became a relief agent for Wells Fargo Express Co. in Bisbee, Ariz. Earl Walker became a bookkeeper and cashier in the First National Bank of Vinita and retired from banking in the early 1950s (*Story of Craig County,* 652–53).

4. A resident of Vinita, Florence Foreman (1880–1954) was the daughter of Albert Foreman (b. 1847) and Mary Ann Davis (b. 1850) (*Story of Craig County,* 351–52).

To Charles White McClellan
7 January 1893
Vinita, I.T.

*Charles White McClellan, a neighborhood friend, lived on his father's large ranch in
the Oowala community several miles from the Rogers place. He and Will Rogers
were very close friends and spent much time together, riding, roping, and going to
parties. While attending Willie Halsell College, Rogers wrote several times to
McClellan, who was enrolled in the Cherokee National Male Seminary at Tahlequah.[1] The following letter is the earliest piece of Will Rogers's writing in existence.*

Willie Halsell College
Vinita, Ind Terr
Jan 7th 1893

Mr Charley Mcclellan

My little friend I thought that I would write you a few lines to see how you
are a getting along   what are you doing out at home now   are you going to
school now   you all got in a lot of cattle from the strip[2] dident you   I heard
that you had got in a 1,000 head of cattle   how many did you get in from the
strip   did you go out to the strip with them after the cattle   did you get in any
horses with the cattle. do you ever go to see your girl at the ▲ Oologah ▲ section
house   her big sister mamie[3] is my girl and the little one is yours   I have got
the pretiest girl in the country   she is John Gores[4] sister   she lives at
Bluejacket[5] about twelve miles from here   dont you tell any of them fellows
from out there,   have you got that little cutter[6] that I let you have   have you
got any more cotterages [cartridges?] for it   you can just keep it till I get to see
you and I will get it then   have you ever shot any thing with it   I heard that
you shot horses are any thing that dident suit you   I did not get to see you
while I was out there Xmas   did you have a good time Christmas   I had a
pretty good time while I was out there   wait till next summer we will have the
time then. when I get back. I wish that I could come home in time to go on all of
the spring works but I guess that I can not get home from here till the middle of
June and they will be over by then[7]   I will close   answer soon   from

Willie. P. Rogers

ALS, rc. MMC-OkClaW.

1. A Chas. McClellan was listed among the students attending the Preparatory
School at the Male Seminary during the term commencing February 1893 and ending 30
June 1893 (Ballenger, "Early History of Northeastern State College"; see Biographical
Appendix entry, McCLELLAN, Charles White).

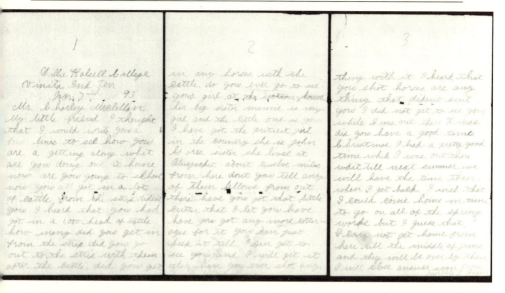

The earliest known existing letter of Will Rogers was sent to his friend Charley McClellan (*OkClaW*).

2. Charles McClure McClellan (b. 1847), the father of Charles White McClellan, was a prosperous cattleman and horse breeder in the Oowala area of the Cooweescoowee District. McClellan also grazed his cattle on thousands of acres in the Cherokee Outlet or "Strip," as it was commonly called (DuPriest et al., *Cherokee Recollections*, 57–59; Sunday et al., *Gah Dah Gwa Stee*, 100–101). His leasehold was located in part of the Otie Reservation near the present site of Perry, Okla. The chief ranch house was on Black Bear Creek, west of Pawnee. Maps of the Outlet identify these ranches as the McClellans Private Ranch and the McClellan Cattle Co. (Dale, *Range Cattle Industry*, 141; Morris and McReynolds, *Historical Atlas of Oklahoma*, map 41). Cherokees who had made improvements on land in the Outlet were permitted allotments of eighty acres at a cost of $1.40 per acre. The McClellan family, including Charles White McClellan and his parents, Charles M. and Jennie L., as well as his brothers and sisters (John F., Mary E., Jessie, Susan, Stephen, and Lela), were granted allotments (*As I Recollect*, 68–77; Chapman, "Cherokee Allotments in the Outlet," 416; DuPriest et al., *Cherokee Recollections*, 58–59, 190).

3. Mary (Mamie) Gore (b. 1867) was born in Bluejacket, I.T. Her sister Daisy and brother John were boyhood friends of Rogers (*Story of Craig County*, 369–70).

4. Daisy Gore (1879–1965) from Bluejacket, I.T., was listed as a schoolmate of Will Rogers in the *1894 Annual Catalogue of Willie Halsell College* (p. 8). She was the daughter of Sallie Bluejacket (1843–1924) and Jonathan Gore (1833–1906), a pioneer settler in Bluejacket, a lawyer, and county attorney. Daisy Gore married Sam Crockett, a skilled Vinita musician. Her brother Jonathan, Jr. (John, 1875–1936) was a good friend of Will Rogers at the school (*Story of Craig County*, 369–70).

5. Located about twelve miles north of Vinita on the Missouri, Kansas, and Texas

(Katy or MKT) railroad line in Craig County, Bluejacket was named for Rev. Charles Bluejacket (ca. 1817–97), a Shawnee chief, an early settler of the town, and its first postmaster. The town was founded in 1871 when a depot and a tent town were constructed as a result of the MKT railroad. Many Shawnee Indians, who had migrated from Kansas, inhabited the town. In the 1890s it was an important depot for shipping cattle, hay, and grain on the MKT from the surrounding region (Collings, *Old Home Ranch*, 1; Croy, *Our Will Rogers*, 340; Shirk, *Oklahoma Place Names*, 25; *Story of Craig County*, 57–61, 255).

6. A slang expression for a revolver.

7. Rogers was probably referring to the spring roundup when his father's ranch hands and other ranchers in the area would round up the young calves and brand them. In the spring roundup cowboys would also separate the herds for returning cattle to their home ranges. In the summer the young Rogers worked on his father's ranch helping to round up cattle for shipment to market in the fall. In the fall roundup cattlemen and their hands would separate their stock from the collective herd and drive them to a railroad depot for shipment to market. In the years of the open range before barbed wire, all the cattle in a region grazed together. The roundups in Clem V. Rogers's region were well organized. Clem V. Rogers and cattlemen from the area extending from Vinita to Tulsa would meet in August at Claremore or Wagoner during the first week of April to plan the spring roundup; the fall roundup meeting occurred in the first week of August. Both roundups were divided into four large sections each with a separate outfit having its own boss. One section had to be completed before another was started (Collings, *Old Home Ranch*, 42–43; Gibson, "Cowboy in Indian Territory," 147; Holden, *Ranching Saga*, 127–28).

To Charles White McClellan
28 January 1893
Vinita, I.T.

Willie Halsell College
Vinita Ind. Ter.
Jan 28th '93.

Mr. Chas. McClellan, Kind Friend,

I wrote to you a long time ago and you did not answer it. I would have liked to heard from you   how are all of your cattle   are any of them dying out in that part of the country.[1] I would like to be out there with you   do you go to school now   your papa got in some cattle from the strip dident he   I heard that he had got in a lot of cattle   how many did he get in   were they big steers or earlings [yearlings?] have you got that pop that I let you have when you was up here   is it ever broke with you yet   keep it till I come out there and I will get it from you   well I will close   answer soon

from your friend
Willie Rogers.

ALS, rc. MMC-OkClaW.

1. Winters in the Indian Territory were usually severe and compounded by blue northers, harsh blizzards that brought temperatures below zero as well as sleet and snow. As a consequence many cattle would freeze to death (Gibson, "Cowboy in Indian Territory," 147–48).

Roll of Honor, Willie Halsell College
January 1893
Vinita, I.T.

ROLL OF HONOR.

The following are the pupils in the academic and collegiate department of Willie Halsell College, constituting the roll of honor for month ending January 27th, 1893:

John Denbo	99 1-6
James Kell	98 7-10
J. W. McCracken	98 1-7
Walter McKeehan	98
James Moore	98
Charles Hunt	97 9-10

Will Rogers
and his good friend
Charley McClellan
(*OkClaW*).

Clinton Adams	96 5-6
Charles Mehlin	96 7-10
H. P. Evans	96 3-5
C. W. Wills	96 1-2
J. M. Oskison	95 2-3
J. C. Barrett	94 1-2
Frank Donelson	92 5-6
Alice Cooper	92
Charles Walker	91 3-5
Lucile Fortner[1]	91
Flora Foreman	92 3-7
Ewing Halsell[2]	90 1-5
Mabel Cook	90 2-3
Willie Rogers	90 5-6
Dora Franklin	90 6-7

The grades throughout the school were satisfactory. In the primary department the averages were very good.

The above grades were based on recitation and attendances.

W. E. Rowsey,
President Willie Halsell College.

PD. Printed in *IC*, 2 February 1893.

1. Lucile Fortner (d. 1963), part Cherokee, was the daughter of Dr. Benjamin F. Fortner and Lucy Jennie Gunter (1854–1928). After graduating from Willie Halsell College, she attended the Conservatory of Music in Cincinnati and then became principal of the Department of Music at the Cherokee National Female Seminary. She married Ewing Halsell on 28 June 1899 (Clinton, "Indian Territory Medical Association," 41; Holden, *Ranching Saga*, 207–10, 531–33; see also Biographical Appendix entry, HALSELL, Ewing).

2. The son of William Electious Halsell, the rancher Ewing Halsell (1879–1965) was a boyhood friend of Rogers at Willie Halsell College, and the two remained close friends thereafter (see Biographical Appendix entry, HALSELL, Ewing).

To Charles White McClellan
24 February 1893
Vinita, I.T.

Willie Halsell College
Vinita Ind Terr
Feb 24th 1893

Mr Charley McClellan[1]

dear friend   I am sitting it school this morning and did not have nothing to do so I thought that I would write to you   you must not let every body in the whole country see that letter   I dont want everybody to see it   I made a mistake and put yours in her envelope and hers in yours   I dont know how I come to do it though   Have you and tom[2] got shot guns or rifles or what kind   about what time in June will you go home or or you going home before school is out   I guess that I will stay up here till school is out   it is out about the 15 of June   we get to go home then   we will miss all of the roundups wont we   do you ever write to your girl at Talala[3]   she is a dandy little gal   who is toms girl   he would not tell me who she was   I am a going out home on a visit in about a month or to   do you have day scholars down there[4]   I would like to be down there and go to school   I am a getting tired of this place   I want to go some place else   does bill Musgrove[5] go to school down there   well I must close   I will hafto write to tom and it is about time for my fifth reader class so I will close   answer soon   from your friend

W. Rogers.

ALS, rc. MMC-OkClaW. Envelope hand-addressed to Charley McClellan, Tahlequah, Male Seminary.[6]

1. McClellan was attending the Cherokee National Male Seminary at Tahlequah (surviving envelopes of this letter as well as letters of 13 March 1893 and 28 March 1893

are addressed to the Male Seminary). McClellan was also listed as a Preparatory School student (Ballenger, "Early History of Northeastern State College," 99).

2. Thomas Lipe Lane had attended Willie Halsell in 1891 and evidently left to enroll at the Cherokee National Male Seminary. His name is listed with Charles McClellan on the list of students attending the Male Seminary's Preparatory School between February 1893 and 30 June 1893 (Ballenger, "Early History of Northeastern State College," 98–99). Lane eventually reenrolled for the 1893–94 term at Willie Halsell College, where he roomed with Rogers (see Will Rogers to Charles White McClellan, 28 March 1893, below; *1894 Annual Catalogue of Willie Halsell College*, 9; DuPriest et al., *Cherokee Recollections*, 63; *HRC*, 274; Keith, *Boy's Life of Will Rogers*, 57–59; and Biographical Appendix entry, LANE, Thomas Lipe).

3. Talala, a town about six miles north of Oolagah, was founded in 1890 and named for Captain Talala, a Cherokee military officer who fought in the Civil War. The name means "woodpecker." A major railroad shipping headquarters for cattle, the town was located on Clem V. Rogers's ranch property (*As I Recollect*, 178; Collings, *Old Home Ranch*, 1, 33, 35; Shirk, *Oklahoma Place Names*, 202).

4. The Cherokee National Male Seminary was primarily a boarding school, but did admit some day students (Agnew, "Legacy of Education"; Starr, *History of the Cherokees*, 231).

5. Rogers was referring to his cousin William Musgrove (see Excerpt from Student Enrollment List, Cherokee National Male Seminary, 28 August–16 December 1887, n. 4, above). A William A. Musgrove was listed among the students in the junior class at the Male Seminary (Ballenger, "Early History of Northeastern State College," 99).

6. The envelope for this letter, postmarked [25?] February 1893, is not extant in the OkClaW correspondence files; however, it does appear as a facsimile reproduction in Collings, *Old Home Ranch*, 27.

To Charles White McClellan
13 March 1893
Vinita, I.T.

Willie Halsell College
Vinita I.T.
Mar 13th 1893

Mr. Charley McClellan

My dear friend   I have just been putting off to write to you for over a week and have not wrote yet but I will now   you ought to come up here to school[1]   this is a dandy place up here   I am getting in a hurry to get home   it is getting spring and I dont like to go to school but we wont get home for a long time yet for school isent out till June   is tom[2] down there yet   tell him to write to me   I want to hear from him   Raleigh Flournough[3] from Chelsea is up here   he come yesterday evening   has any more of the boys got expelled since those other two did   wasent chick pain[4] one of them. I am going home the first of April and stay a week and help brand calvs and colts   is any of the boys sick

Standing before the Claremore, I.T., home of Dr. Andrew Jackson Lane, one of the Rogers family physicians, are three of his sons, all friends of Will Rogers. *Left to right:* Gordon Lane, Tom Lane, an unidentified child, and Denny Lane. Tom Lane was an especially close friend of Rogers during his youth *(gift of Noel Kaho, OkClaW)*.

down there   I herd that they was all sick and most of them were going home   well I am in school so I cant write you a long letter for I havent got time   I will close   answer soon   from

Willie R.

ALS, rc. MMC-OkClaW. Envelope hand-addressed to Master Charley McClellan, Tahlaquah, Male. Sem., C[herokee]. N[ation]. Return address printed VINITA, Cherokee Nation, Ind. T.

1. McClellan eventually enrolled at Willie Halsell College, and the presence of his friend in the boarding school made Rogers's attendance there more tolerable (Keith, *Boy's Life of Will Rogers*, 76).
2. Thomas Lipe Lane.
3. In his 28 March 1893 letter to McClellan (see following), Rogers refers to Raleigh

De Flournoy (b. 1876) as his roommate. He was the son of De Hardiman Flournoy (1848–1908) and Anna Wilson Flournoy (b. 1855) (*HRC*, 140; *OCF* 1:214; Starr, *History of the Cherokee Indians*, 137, 559).

4. Chick Payne was related to Doc Payne, a cowboy on the Rogers ranch (Collings, *Old Home Ranch*, 39, 61).

To Charles White McClellan
28 March 1893
Vinita, I.T.

Willie Halsell College
Vinita. I.T.
Mar 28th 1893

Mr. Charley McClellan

my dear friend   I thought that I would write you to see how you are doing down there   I got your letter this evening and was very glad to hear from you   tell tom lane if he dont answer my letter I will whip him when I get him out home   does any of the boys down there ever get fired   the[re] was 2 turned out for 2 weeks and then they can come back. they was fired yesterday   prff [prof?] caught them in the girls room eating cake and having a fine old time   have you got you a girl down there   you must not drop your little Talala girl   she is a dandy   who is your girl down there   tell me   I wont let anyone know who it it [is]   you ought to be up here   we have boys and girls all board here and we take them to church every sunday night and have dances and do anything that you want to   I sure have lots of fun up here   Raleigh Flournoy is up here going to school   I room with him and booth McSpadden[1] and henry Beard and Jim *[word deleted]* Kell   but Jim is gone home[2] and so just three of us is in here now. Jim went home to go to work on the ranch   well I must close I am getting sleepy   answer soon   I dont get a letter only once a month   from your friend

Willie P. Rogers.

ALS, rc. MMC-OkClaW. Envelope hand-addressed to Master Chas. McClellan, Tahlequah, Male Sem, I.T. Return address W. P. Rogers, VINITA, Cherokee Nation, Ind. T.

1. Thomas Booth McSpadden (b. 1880) was the son of Florence Ellen Hoyt (1858–1939) and Joel (Joe) Cowan McSpadden (1850–98), the brother of John Thomas McSpadden (*HRC*, 299–300).

2. James L. Kell came from Chelsea (*1894 Annual Catalogue of Willie Halsell College*, 9).

Cherokee Nation Citizen Census Record
for Per Capita Distribution
1893
Cooweescoowee District, Cherokee Nation, I. T.

Will Rogers was listed with his father and stepmother, Mary Bibles Rogers,[1] in the Cherokee Census of 1893, which was used as a basis for per capita payments of funds received from the sale of the Cherokee Outlet to the federal government in 1893.

Census of <u>Cherokee by Blood</u> Citizens residing in <u>Cooweescoowee District,</u> Cherokee Nation, authorized by an Act of the National Council, approved April 15, 1893.

No.	Name	Age	Male	Female
3233	Clem V. Rogers	54	Male	
3234	Mary Rogers	27		Female
3235	Willie P. Rogers	13	Male	

PD, with autograph insertions.[2] DNA, RG 75, FARC, Fort Worth, Records of the Commissioner to the Five Civilized Tribes, microfilm publication 7RA-54.

    1. Clem V. Rogers married his neighbor and housekeeper Mary Bibles (sometimes referred to as Mary Bible) at the Rogers ranch on 15 January 1893 (see Biographical Appendix entry, ROGERS, Mary Bibles).
    2. The census was conducted by district, with separate sections within each district for Cherokee citizens, adopted whites, freedmen, and Shawnee, Delaware, and Creek peoples who were residents of the Cherokee Nation (Baker, "Major Cherokee Genealogical Records," OkClaW).

Excerpt from Annual Catalogue of Willie Halsell College
June 1894
Vinita, I. T.

The Willie Halsell College included a primary department (first through fourth grades), a preparatory department (two years), and a collegiate department (freshman through senior classes). Military uniforms were advised for boys; girls wore woolen uniforms. In the 1893–94 academic year the coeducational school had a faculty of nine. The register of students listed 209 students, including Will Rogers's cousins Will Musgrove and Ernest Schrimsher from Claremore; Ella, Booth, and Clarence McSpadden from Chelsea; Ewing Halsell from Vinita; and "Willie Rogers" from Oolagah. The majority of the students were from Indian Territory; Rogers was the only student from Oolagah. Besides elocution, he also studied art and was a pupil in the pencil, charcoal, and crayon class. At the commencement exercises in 1894 Rogers was awarded a medal for elocution.[1] He remained at the school through the 1894–95 academic year.

MEDALS

At Commencement the following gold medals were awarded:

Scholarship—Offered by Mrs. W. C. Patton, and awarded to Miss Eva Patton, whose average during entire year including examination was 99.8.

Deportment—Offered by Dr. B. F. Fortner,[2] was drawn by Miss Eva Patton, Misses Dimmie Byrd, Narcie Walker, Marguerite Highland, Fannie Mae Browning and Messrs. Thos. Lane and Earl Walker also drew for it.

Elocution—Offered by Robt. O. Perkins, Henderson, Tenn., and awarded to Miss Josie Crutchfield.[3] The judges of the contest thought Willie P. Rogers entitled to a medal and the privilege of a duplicate was given him.

Instrumental Music—Offered by Miss L. R. McClatchy and awarded to Miss Lucile Fortner.

Vocal Music—Offered by Miss G. B. Spence and awarded to Miss Louis Skinner.

Oratory—Offered by W. S. Dugger,[4] awarded to John M. Oskison.

Debater—Offered by A. L. Society, awarded to H. P. Evans.

C. L. Society—Offered by Mr. James S. McCrary and awarded to Miss Lalla Croom, Pinson, Tenn.

Housekeepers—Offered by Mrs. L. W. Johnson and awarded to Miss Lucy Carey.

PD. From *1894 Annual Catalogue of Willie Halsell College, A School for Boys and Girls* (Vinita, I.T.: The Indian Chieftain Printers, 1894), 20. OkClaW. Signed by W. S. Dugger, teacher of Modern Languages, Sciences, and Oratory.[5]

1. The commencement awards were also announced in the *Indian Chieftain,* 14 June 1894.
2. Dr. Benjamin F. Fortner (1847–1917) was one of the leading physicians in the Indian Territory. Born in Texas and a graduate of Vanderbilt University's medical school, he first practiced medicine in Arkansas and in 1879 moved to Claremore, where he was also engaged in the livestock business. He established his medical practice in Vinita in 1884 and in 1887 began a partnership with Dr. Oliver Bagby. A respected Vinita citizen involved in many civic and educational movements, he served on the boards of Galloway College (later Willie Halsell College) and the Worcester Academy. He also served as a surgeon for railroad and insurance companies. Fortner helped organize the Indian Territory Medical Association in 1881 and served as its first president. This pioneer medical organization was merged into the Oklahoma State Medical Association in 1906. Fortner retired from medicine in 1917 just before his death from a heart attack at the age of seventy (Clinton, "The Indian Territory Medical Association," 23–41; Holden, *Ranching Saga,* 207–8; *Story of Craig County,* 79).
3. On 7 June 1895, Josie Crutchfield (1875–1946), part Cherokee, married William

Electious Halsell. She was the niece of Mary Alice Crutchfield (1854–94), Halsell's first wife. She and her husband had elegant homes in Vinita and Kansas City, where they led an active social life (Holden, *Ranching Saga*, 171–79, 257–71, 269; *OCF* 1:243; see also Biographical Appendix entry, HALSELL, William Electious).

4. William S. Dugger, a faculty member, taught modern languages, sciences and oratory. He served as president of the school from 1902 to 1905 (Babcock and Bryce, *History of Methodism in Oklahoma*, 311). On 10 January 1909 Dugger wrote a letter to Clem V. Rogers (published in the *Claremore Messenger*, 15 January 1909), stating how much he had enjoyed his son's vaudeville performance at the Orpheum in Memphis.

5. The name of W. S. Dugger is written on the front cover of the 1894 annual catalogue at the Will Rogers Memorial, suggesting that this was his own copy (OkClaW).

Clement Vann Rogers to Principal Chief Colonel Johnson Harris
15 October 1894
Oolagah, I.T.

In July 1893, C. J. Harris,[1] principal chief of the Cherokee Nation (1891–95), appointed his friend Clem V. Rogers to serve on a commission to appraise improvements made on the properties of intruders (unauthorized residents of Indian Territory) in July 1893. In October Rogers wrote Harris using stationery printed with a "W. P. Rogers, Cattle Dealer" letterhead and illustrated with Will Rogers's Dog Iron brand. Clem V. Rogers discussed issues he faced in his position on the commission.

Oologah Oct 15th 1894

Col. C. J. Harris
Tahlequah, I.T.
[Word illegible] & Friend

I just got back home from the Vinita fair[2] and found your letter   Also one from Pernot & one from the Commissioners at Indian Affairs saying for me to meet at Vinita on the 22nd of this month to finish up our work.[3]

Pernot is at Eureka Springs[4]   Will write him today.

[Order?] the Sherriff to furnish us a man to assist us in our work. Did you [discuss?] the Negroe question while in Washington[?][5] If the Negroes are left off we can get through in a short time. If left on will be longer getting through our work. I wish you would lend Judah Wiley to assist us and Nation Indian arrangements for an attorney.

The Intruders are coming into the country nearly every day   Harris you certainly ought to stop Blackwell in his Town lot sale at David near Chelsea. You cant expect our [Solicitor?] to do any thing in trying to stop this man Blackwell.[6] We had a tip top fair at Vinita last week took in over $2350.00 People are well up here   Crops are looking well that is wheat.

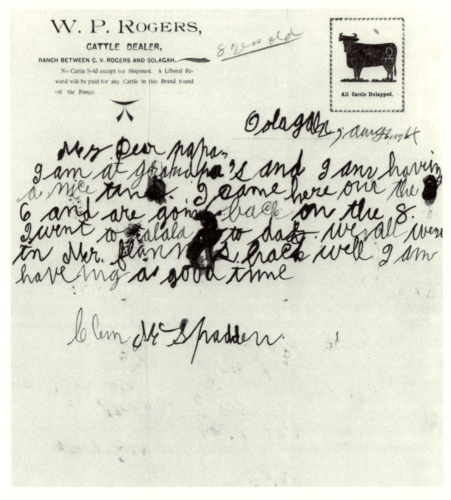

Rogers's eight-year-old nephew, Clem McSpadden, wrote his father, Tom McSpadden, using stationery featuring Will Rogers's Dog Iron brand on a longhorn steer and a letterhead with Rogers's name listed as a "cattle dealer" *(OkClaW)*.

Try and meet us at Vinita on the 22nd of this month   I am anxious to finish up the work, for the Council can take some action in the [sell?]ing of the places of these Intruders.

Hoping you and family are well is the wish of a true Friend

C. V. Rogers

ALS. OkHi, Indian Archives Division. On W. P. Rogers, Cattle Dealer, letterhead.[7]

1. Besides being principal chief, Colonel Johnson Harris (1856–1921) served as an official of the Cherokee Nation in several capacities. He was elected senator from the Canadian District (1881–85) and from the Tahlequah District (1899), secretary (1895–99), delegate to Washington, D.C. (1889, 1895), and treasurer (1891). Born in Georgia, Harris moved with his parents to the Canadian District in the Cherokee Nation in the 1870s and attended the Cherokee National Male Seminary at Tahlequah. His second marriage on 4 March 1891 was to Mamie Elizabeth Adair, the daughter of William Penn Adair and Sarah Ann Adair. A successful rancher and a member of the Downing Party, Harris was selected as principal chief by the council upon the death of Chief Joel B. Mayes in December 1891 and served in that capacity until 1895. During his tenure as principal chief Harris opposed the federal government's allotment policy initiated through the Dawes Commission (Dewitz, *Notable Men of Indian Territory*, 74; Meserve, "Chief Colonel Johnson Harris," 17–21; Starr, *History of the Cherokee Indians*, 564).

2. Clem V. Rogers was a past president of the Vinita Fair Board (1890) and served on its board of directors for many years. The annual Vinita fair began in 1882 and was the town's largest exposition. The fair included agricultural exhibits, livestock judging, horse racing, a ladies' riding contest, a pigeon-shooting contest, and a ladies' department exhibiting needlework, among others. The fairgrounds contained a racetrack, exhibit buildings, and an amphitheater. By the late 1890s the fair had lost popularity. The property was sold to S. S. Cobb for $1,000 in 1899 ("Early Fairs," *Story of Craig County*, 90; McSpadden, "Clement Vann Rogers," 396).

3. Joshua Hutchins of Georgia and P. H. Pernot of Indiana, appointees of Pres. Grover Cleveland, also served as commission members. William P. Thompson served as the attorney for the Cherokee Nation and accompanied Rogers on his tours of properties. The work of the commission took over two years to complete and included interviews with over three thousand families regarding the valuation of buildings and fences erected on Indian land, crops planted, trees felled, etc. The commission's final report was accepted by the Department of the Interior in August 1895 (*IC*, 27 July 1893; Keith, "Clem Rogers and His Influence on Oklahoma Territory," 68–70; McSpadden "Clement Vann Rogers," 394–95; Sober, *Intruders*, 109–10; Wardell, *Political History of the Cherokee Nation*, 285–89).

Rogers had long objected to the lawlessness that accompanied the "great wrongs by white men not citizens" who made improvements and planted crops contrary to Cherokee Nation regulations and whose numbers and success in getting Indian officials to ignore their actions threatened the ongoing authority and unity of the Nation (Rogers to Chief Dennis Bushyhead, 11 August 1885, quoted in McSpadden, "Clement Vann Rogers," 394, and Keith, "Clem Rogers and His Influence on Oklahoma History," 55).

Rogers's participation on the intruder commission is also discussed in his other letters to Principal Chief C. J. Harris, 25 October 1894 and 18 November 1894, Clement Vann Rogers file, OkClaW.

4. A health resort noted for its many medicinal springs, Eureka Springs is located in northwest Arkansas, thirty-five miles northeast of Fayetteville (*WNGD*, 382).

5. Clem V. Rogers was no stranger to the issue of the status of freed slaves and their legal designation as either citizens or intruders. He had served on a three-person Cherokee Nation committee in 1883 that issued a report regarding the rights of African American ex-slaves and Shawnee and Delaware minorities in the Cherokee Nation to share in federal per capita payments made to legal residents of the Nation. The freed slaves and non-Cherokee Indian peoples, officially incorporated into the Cherokee Nation after the Civil War, had been excluded from the payments. They petitioned for a fair share of the federal distribution. Rogers and his fellow committee members, E. E.

Starr and H.T. Landrum, ruled that it violated the Cherokee constitution to deny the petitioners their share of the payments. The Cherokee Senate nevertheless refused to accept the recommendation of the committee; the payments were mandated by an act of the federal Congress in October 1888. The Cherokee Senate was acting on a long tradition of excluding African American residents of Indian Territory from citizenship and property rights. The tribal constitution of 1839 specifically denied African Americans the right to own improvements of "horses, cattle, hogs or firearms," to learn to read or write, or to intermarry with Indians (Sober, *Intruders,* 83). The question of the rights of African Americans to land and improvements and their status as citizens or intruders stemmed from the contradictions generated by the Cherokee National Council's very narrow application of the stipulations and time limits regarding the ability of former slaves to make claims on property during Reconstruction. Appraisals of improvements were complicated by Cherokee unwillingness to honor many African American claims to citizenship rights. Black residents of such areas as that east of the Verdigris River in Cooweescoowee District, who claimed Cherokee citizenship by blood, were labeled as late arrivals or intruders. The legal disputes over the status of the freedmen extended well into the 1890s and the period of enrollment in the early 1900s. The final report filed by Rogers's commission included data from 315 claimants by blood and 70 freed slaves, with over 2,000 people, black and white, designated as intruders. The improvements subject to appraisal included only those made before August 1886 (Keith, "Clement Vann Rogers," 56; Sober, *Intruders,* 83–89, 109–12; Wardell, *Political History of the Cherokee Nation,* 233–37).

6. David Blackwell was a notorious intruder who had established the town of David northwest of Chelsea. The Cherokees called him King David. Although he claimed Cherokee heritage, the Cherokees believed he was an intruder and tried unsuccessfully to expel him from his property. The town survived until 1897 when it was destroyed by a tornado that killed one woman. Blackwell became a booster of Chelsea and died in 1903 (*HRC,* 52).

7. During 1894 both Clem V. Rogers and Clem McSpadden wrote letters using "W. P. Rogers, Cattle Dealer" letterhead. Will Rogers, popularly known as W. P., was nearly fifteen years old at the time. The full letterhead read: "W. P. Rogers, Cattle Dealer, Ranch Between C. V. Rogers and Oolagah. No Cattle Sold except for Shipment. A Liberal Reward will be paid for any Cattle in this Brand found off the Range." A graphic of a three-pronged brand was featured below the text of the letterhead, and on the right was another graphic of a longhorn steer with Will Rogers's Dog Iron brand, captioned "All Cattle Dulapped." Rogers's Dog Iron brand was modeled on the shape of andirons at his father's ranch. He used the brand on the calves his father gave him; his father used CV for his cattle and J4 for his horses (Clem McSpadden to J. T. McSpadden, Oolagah, August 1894, OkClaW. Clem McSpadden's letter to "My Dear papa" was written on a W. P. Rogers letterhead when he was eight years old and visiting his grandfather C. V. Rogers's ranch).

Cherokee Nation Payment Roll for Per Capita Distribution 1894
Cooweescoowee District, Cherokee Nation, I.T.

In 1894 Will Rogers, his father, and stepmother again received funds from the sale of the Cherokee Outlet.

We, the undersigned citizens of the Cherokee Nation, by right of Cherokee blood, do hereby acknowledge to have received of E. E. Starr, National Treasurer of the Cherokee Nation, the sums set opposite our names respectively, in full of our shares in the per capita distribution authorized by an Act of the National Council, dated May 3rd 1894.[1]

Names of Head and Members of Families.	Amount.	To whom Paid.	Witness to Payment.
3644 Rogers Clem V.			
3645 " Mary.			
3646 " Willie P.	797.10	C V Rogers[2]	L B Bell[3]

PD, with autograph insertions.[4] DNA, RG 75, FARC, Fort Worth, Records of the Commissioner to the Five Civilized Tribes, microfilm publication 7RA-38.

1. This payment roll was popularly known as the Starr Roll, named for the National Treasurer Ezekial Eugene Starr (1849–1905), who was elected treasurer of the Cherokee Nation on 23 December 1891. In this position he distributed over seven million dollars to citizens of the Cherokee Nation. A merchant and farmer, he was also elected senator from the Flint District on 6 August 1883 (Baker, "Major Cherokee Genealogical Records," OkClaW; Bell, *Genealogy of Old and New Cherokee Indian Families,* 402; *OCF* 2:85; Starr, *History of the Cherokee Nation,* 655).
2. Clem V. Rogers also accepted payment of $797.10 on behalf of the three-person Perry Ross family, with the payment witnessed by L. B. Bell (registrants 3632 through 3634). Individuals received $265.70, couples $531.40, families of three $797.10, families of five $1,328.50, etc.
3. A Cherokee official, L. B. Bell served in several positions for the Cherokee Nation, including as a delegate for the signing of an agreement with the Dawes Commission on 9 April 1900 and as senior counsel for the Nation in 1900 regarding the enrollment of freed slaves (Wardell, *Political History of the Cherokee Nation,* 234, 323, 329).
4. The Starr Roll was organized by district and thereunder alphabetically by payees' names (organized by family), amount received, signature of person receiving payment, signature of witness, and any remarks.

Notice from the *Claremore Progress* 23 March 1895 Claremore, I. T.

Wednesday evening the organization of the Christian Endeavor was completed at the Presbyterian church by the election of the following officers: President, Willie Rogers; Vice president, Miss Elen Spencer; Secretary, Miss Maggie Russel; Treasurer, Mr. Wallace. Meetings will be held every Wednesday evening at the church.[1]

PD. Printed in *CP,*[2] 23 March 1895. "Church Notes" column.

1. The First Presbyterian Church of Claremore was built in 1889. A wooden frame structure, it was replaced in 1902 by a building constructed of native stone (*HRC*, 474). The Organization of Christian Endeavor was a protoecumenical youth group that originated in Wisconsin in the late nineteenth century. It included youngsters of high-school and college age (Dr. Robert Henderson, Professor Emeritus of Religion, University of Tulsa, telephone interview by Arthur Wertheim, 22 November 1992). On 18 December 1890 an article in the *Indian Chieftain,* describing a meeting held at the Claremore Presbyterian Chruch on 13 December 1890, announced, "The Young People's Society of Christian Endeavor, recently organized in connection with this church, gives promise of much good."

2. The *Claremore Progress* was begun in 1893 by the Claremore Printing Co. and its owner Joe A. Kline. Kline was wounded at San Juan, Cuba, while serving as a sergeant in Theodore Roosevelt's Rough Riders (L troop) and later was a performer in Buffalo Bill's Wild West show (Jones, *Roosevelt's Rough Riders,* 254, 310; Roosevelt, *Rough Riders,* 265). The paper went through two other owners in 1893; Kline sold it to J. G. Cash, and Albert L. (A. L. or Pop) Kates bought it from Cash. An easterner from New Jersey, A. L. Kates built the paper into an effective community journal using an extensive pony-express network to obtain news. Originally a four-page weekly appearing Saturday, the *Progress* featured local events and personages, especially articles about the town's most influential citizens, including Clem V. and Will Rogers. It also covered surrounding communities in columns entitled "Oolagah Oozings," "Inola Inklings," "Catoosa Items," and "Collinsville Coolings." Clem V. Rogers gave Kates his son's letters during the period between 1902 and 1904 when he was in Argentina, South Africa, Australia, and New Zealand. The *Claremore Progress* and the *Chelsea Reporter,* another nearby local newspaper, were thus the first publications to print Will Rogers's writings. The *Claremore Progress,* a daily newspaper, is still in existence today (Carter, E., *Story of Oklahoma Newspapers,* 31; Foreman, C., *Oklahoma Imprints, 1835–1907,* 63–64; *HRC,* 9; see also Biographical Appendix entry, KATES, Albert L.).

Cherokee Nation Citizen Census Record
Post-August 1896
Cooweescoowee District, Cherokee Nation, I.T.

Census of <u>Cherokees by Blood</u> Citizens of <u>Cooweescoowee</u> District, Cherokee Nation. Authorized by an Act of the National Council, Approved August 21, 1896.

No.	Name	Age	Male	Female	How far from Precinct	Proportion of the Blood
123	Clem V. Rogers	58	Male		4 ms.	1/8
	William P. Rogers	17	"		" "	1/4
	Mary Rogers (Nee Bibles)	30		"	" "	1/8

PD, with autograph insertions. DNA, RG 75, FARC, Fort Worth, Records of the Commissioner to the Five Civilized Tribes, microfilm publication 7RA-19.

To Margaret Nay
27 November 1896
Neosho, Mo.

In Fall 1895 Rogers enrolled at the Scarritt Collegiate Institute[1] at Neosho,[2] Missouri. The school was named after Dr. Nathan Scarritt, a Methodist minister and wealthy real-estate owner from Kansas City who gave a large endowment to the institute. Called the "Wild Indian" by his classmates, Rogers was known for cutting classes, roping students and steers, telling funny stories, and teaching his friends Cherokee songs.[3] When Rogers invited Maggie Nay,[4] a local girl, to a party, he was rebuffed and wrote the following letter to her.[5]

Neosho Mo
Nov 27. 96.

My Dearest Friend if you can not be my Sweetheart

I received the note a little bit ago and was more than glad to hear from you but was *sorry* to hear my fate. I did not think of getting such a note but it is all right of course   I am as sorry as can be but then if your mother does not want you to go with me why it is all right. I would hate to do anything Contrary to her will. I know I drink and am a wild and bad boy and all that but Then you know that Marvin[6] is a model boy   he never did anything in his life   he is as good as an *angel*   I am an outcast I suppose   so of course dont do anything that will get you with a ["]*drunkard as I am*"

And as far as me not coming back after Xmas I will be here[7]   but then that is all all right   I know how it is when you dont want to go with a boy   a girl has to make up a good excuse to tell him   so you see that is the case with you   you want to make things as smoothe as possible   so that is all right   but I would rather you would have just told me the straight truth that you did not care to quit Marvin and go with me   I would not have got mad at you for it and that would have been all that there was to it.

I was a fool for trying to go with you any way   I might have known you would have not gone with me.

but then you said for me to write to you when I went home. but what do you ask me that for for you would be Marvins Sweetheart and he would not like for you to be writing to me and going with him. and then you would not want to be writing to a *drunkard* like I am. I am to far below you to write to "*you*"

and then you do not want my picture you want the one you are going with not I.

Margaret (Maggie) Nay, a friend in Rogers's youth (*courtesy of Carol Hamilton, Prairie Village, Kans.*).

Well I suppose you have heard enough of this <u>*Drunkard*</u> that they call Will Rogers. so I will close   hoping you all a merry evening   as I expect I had better not go as your Mother might object to me. and as Jess[8] says that no decent person would speak to me. and I know all of you are decent   but I am *very* sorry that I can not come.

but don't think that I am mad at you in in the least and I like you more than I ever did before for the truth never hurts me.

I will send this by Harry Basye as he is going up

I will close.

from a drunkard who likes you but whom you never cared for.

Now please dont let any one see this Maggie and I will not let any one[9] see your note

your would like to be S——

AL, rc. OkClaW.

1. Scarritt Collegiate Institute was founded by the Neosho Circuit of the Methodist Episcopal Church South on 3 February 1878. It was first called the Neosho Seminary, and in 1880 it became the Neosho Collegiate Institute. Financial problems plagued the school, and it was forced to close in June 1887. It reopened in 1888 when Nathan Scarritt paid $5,000 of its debt, and consequently it was renamed in his honor. Scarritt hired Dr. Charles Carroll Woods as president. A graduate of Central College at Fayette, Mo., and a recipient of a D.D. from Trinity College of North Carolina, Woods served as president for eight years, during which time the school flourished. He increased the enrollment to about 400 students, which included pupils from the Indian Territory. Woods introduced a popular student military unit called the Scarritt Guards, which performed at county fairs and reunions. Located in the north half of block 8 of McCord's Addition, the school consisted of four buildings in 1891. The girls lived in a dormitory, while the boys boarded in rooms in the town. Will Rogers was a member of the 1896 Scarritt football team. The school began to decline in the late 1890s, and in 1908 it closed. The property of Scarritt Collegiate Institute was sold in 1913 to the local school district, which built a public school on the land. The assets of Scarritt were transferred in 1908 to Morrisville College, a Methodist school at Morrisville, Mo., which became the Scarritt-Morrisville College. When this college closed in 1925, it combined with Central College in Lexington, Mo., which eventually merged with Howard Payne College in Fayette, Mo. This college was absorbed by Central Methodist College, still in existence today in Fayette (Louise D. Prettyman to Homer Croy, 8 March 1952, HCP–MoU; Croy, *Our Will Rogers*, 335; *Joplin Globe*, 23 August 1953; *Neosho, City of Springs*, 110–11).

2. Neosho was founded in 1839 when a log storehouse was erected. Soon other businesses were established around its central square, and after the Civil War the town became a thriving business community. The seat of Newton County in southwest Missouri, Neosho was considered a regional "center of education, culture and art" in the 1890s (*Joplin Globe*, 23 August 1953; see also *Neosho, City of Springs*, 113–14; *WNGD*, 821).

3. Croy, *Our Will Rogers*, 30–35; Keith, *Boy's Life of Will Rogers*, 88–97.

4. See Biographical Appendix entry, VEERKAMP, Margaret Nay Price.

5. The following letter was sent in 1952 to Homer Croy by Margaret Nay Price who

was living in Neosho. Croy was then working on a biography of Rogers and quoted from the letter in his book *Our Will Rogers,* 32–33. Price sent the document with the following letter written to Croy on 16 July 1952:

2 days *after* Bastille Day.
Dear Mr. Croy:
    I am sorry for my discourtesy in not answering your first note sent from Claremore, but I have been all this time trying to find the one note of Will Rogers which I possess. I put it away for safe keeping & did too good a job of hiding it.
    Now that I have found it, I do not believe you will care to use it, but I know you will like to see it, so I am sending it in this letter. I do not have any of the letters he wrote me from Kemper. You see, we did not know he was going to be famous one day. How this note ever survived the years is a mystery. I was amazed to find it in my mothers things after her death.
    I really didn't know Will Rogers *too* well. You see we were such *kids* then. You, no doubt, remember how small town kids do. We were of the *gang* stage & would meet & all go in a crowd. We might *pair off* after we got to our destination &, in that way, I'd be with Bill but that was about the extent of our friendship.
    When he came back to Neosho the fall this note was written, I was barely 14 & was going around with another college boy, so Will did not try to see me. Then there was a party of some sort, & he asked me to go. It was his first real definite approach & I was *thrilled to death*—out of this world!—and then my mother would not let me go. It was lifes darkest moment & I evidently was tactless enough to tell him *why* I couldn't go. That is why I thought you could not use the note. Some people might really think he *was* a drunkard, & of course he was *not,* and you would not want to give such an impression.
    A German family, who lived a few miles out, made & sold wine & it was quite 'wicked' for the boys to go out to this place. Probably all of them together didn't drink a bottle—but my mother heard a tale of some of the boys getting too much and falling off their bicycles. Things were quite different in 1896. Mothers were very careful about their little girls and my mother wasn't *sure* about these *wild Indian boys from the Territory,* hence her refusal to let me go, and my broken heart.
    Soon after the episode of this note, Will was called home because the husband [Matthew Yocum] of one of his sisters was killed—and he did not come back after Christmas. Went to Kemper instead.
    I am also sending you a little picture he sent me from Kemper. It looks as if he might have started wearing the double breasted blue serge even then. I had some other little things he sent me from Kemper, but a young man who wrote a youth's book of Will Rogers took these things & did not return them.
    There was another picture I had of Will & 2 other boys which was reproduced in the K.C. Star, but the original has been lost. I can tell you very little about Will. It really has been about a thousand years since then. I don't think he went with the girls very much. He was just a little *shy* in that way & then he couldn't have been over 15 or 16. He did go a little with Jess Price (now Mrs. Gurney Lowe of 2654 Grand Ave, Huntington Park, Calif[)]. I understand she is too ill to write a letter, but her husband is quite a good writer & just *might* give you a few hints. Also you might write

to *Gordon Lindsay* of *Chouteau, Okla.* He went to school here with Will and was in the picture in the K C Star. He was still in Chouteau some 10 yrs ago.

I never saw Will but twice after he left here. Saw him in the Follies in N.Y., but did not try to see him personally, & later saw him when he appeared in Joplin.

They called me *Maggie* when I was small. I was usually referred to as 'Little Maggie Nay.' When we saw him in Joplin he said something to my husband about being so much heavier and then he looked up with that grin of his, pointed to me and said "*She aint* any bigger."

Well, really, I seem to be telling you more of my self than of Will Rogers. I'm sorry I can't help you more. I just do not *know* any more. I've no objection to you using the note, but would not like to create the impression that Will drank too much. Also I hope you will not use my name any more than is necessary. I've no desire to get in the lime light, thru my slight connection with him. Will you *please* try not to lose the note & picture. I think I shall send it to you by registered mail. Very Sincerely,

Margaret Nay Price (Mrs Garland Price).

(Margaret Nay Price to Homer Croy, 16 July 1952, HCP-MoU)

6. Marvin McDonald from Pleasant Hill, Mo. He was going to a college in Neosho and was Price's boyfriend (Margaret Nay Price to Homer Croy, n.d., HCP-MoU).

7. Rogers never returned to the Scarritt Collegiate Institute after Christmas vacation and enrolled instead at the Kemper School in January 1887.

8. Jess or Jessie Price was also one of Rogers's friends. She later married Gurney Lowe and lived in California (Croy, *Our Will Rogers*, 336).

9. "Any one" is written over "your n . . ." and then the sentence continues "see your note." Rogers seems to have changed "I will not let your n . . ." [be seen by anyone] to "I will not let any one see your note."

Kemper School Matriculation Book Entries
5 January–11 February 1897
Boonville, Mo.

Will Rogers's signature on page 52 of the matriculation book indicates that he enrolled at the Kemper School[1] in Boonville,[2] Mo., on 13 January 1897. He remained at Kemper until March 1898. A boys' military school noted for its academic program and training in discipline, it attracted sons of wealthy families from the Indian Territory as well as other areas in the Southwest.[3] Rogers was one of five boys who entered the school in the winter session of 1897.

11. 3, 1880	Edwin Ruthman McKee.	(Ent Jany 5, 1897.
11. 4, 1880[4]	William Penn Rogers.	(Ent Jany 13, 1897.
8. 24, 1880	Myron L. Boyer.	(Ent Jany 16, 1897.
7. 5, 1880	Paul Trotter Brown	(Ent Feby 11, 1897.
9. 5, 1882	Benjamin Madison Pike.	(Ent Feby 10, 1897.

The 1896 Scarritt Collegiate Institute football team. *Seated (left to right):* Craig, Geyer, Rogers, Catron, Armstrong, Keys, and Boyd. *Middle row:* Davidson and Woodward. *Standing:* Maupin, Pierce, Hamilton, Hughes, Funk, and McDonald *(OkClaW).*

AD. From Lt. Col. A. M. Hitch, *Will Rogers, Cadet: A Record of His Two Years as a Cadet at the Kemper Military School, Boonville, Missouri* (Boonville, Mo., 1935), 6.

1. Kemper Military School was founded in 1844 as the Boonville Male Boarding School, and a year after its founding it was renamed the Male Collegiate Institute. In 1854 it became the Kemper Family School, and during the Civil War it was called Kemper and Taylor's Institute. In 1896 it became the Kemper School, and in 1899 its name was changed to Kemper Military School, which still exists today as the Kemper Military School and College (A. M. Hitch, president of the Kemper Military School, to Homer Croy, 12 July 1952, HCP-MoU). The school had fifty-two students during the 1896–97 term and seventy-two students during the 1897–98 term (Hitch, *Will Rogers, Cadet,* 8).

2. Located in central Missouri, Boonville is situated on the Missouri River twenty-five miles west of Columbia. In 1861 it was the site of the first Civil War land battle in the state *(WNGD,* 162).

3. Two of Kemper's graduates were Cap Lane '85, Rogers's brother-in-law, and Clem McSpadden '02, Rogers's nephew (Hitch, *Will Rogers, Cadet,* 23; see Biographical Appendix entries, LANE, Captain Lane and McSPADDEN, Clement Mayes).

4. Will Rogers's year of birth (1879) was erroneously reported as 1880 in the matriculation book.

Kemper School Report Card
26 March 1897
Boonville, Mo.

An explanatory note that accompanied this report card explained that students were ranked on a scale of "100 for perfection and 0 for total failure." An average of 67 was the lowest grade allowed to maintain satisfactory status in any given subject area. The grades in the subjects printed in italics were figured at a value of one-fourth in determining the student's overall average of lesson grades. "Deficiencies in deportment" were expressed by demerits, and "more than 25 demerits in a month indicate unsatisfactory conduct, that should receive the attention and censure of parents." Although Rogers's grades were satisfactory in all subjects except Algebra, his deportment was considered unsatisfactory.[1]

KEMPER SCHOOL

MONTHLY REPORT

BOONVILLE, MO. March 26 1897

Grades of ___Will Rogers___ for _6th_ school month ending with date.

Mental Arithmetic ___		Astronomy ___	
Practical Arithmetic _82_		Geology ___	
Algebra _62_		Zoology ___	
Geometry ___		Psychology ___	
Trigonometry ___		Reading ___	
English Grammar _82_		*Letter-Writing* _82_	
Rhetoric ___		*Composition* _76_	
English Literature ___		*Book-keeping* _68_	
Latin ___		*Bible* _70_	
German ___		*History, U.S.* _100_	
Greek ___		*History, General* _81_ [2]	
French ___		*Elocution* _85_ [3]	
Geography ___		*Drawing* ___	
Physical Geography _80_		*American Literature* ___	
Physiology ___		*Political Economy* ___	
Physics ___		*Civil Government* ___	
Chemistry ___		Av. of Lesson Grades _79_	

DEMERITS for month _50_ [4]

PD, with autograph insertions. OkClaW.

1. Rogers's classes in 1897 were considered a second-year (sophomore) high-school course load. History, elocution, letter writing, composition, and Bible met once a week,

KEMPER SCHOOL·

MONTHLY REPORT·

BOONVILLE, MO., *March 26* 1897

Grades of *Will Rogers*

for *6th* school month ending with date.

Mental Arithmetic		Astronomy	
Practical Arithmetic	82	Geology	
Algebra	62	Zoölogy	
Geometry		Psychology	
Trigonometry		Reading	
English Grammar	82	Letter-Writing	82
Rhetoric		Composition	76
English Literature		Book-keeping	68
Latin		Bible	70
Greek		History, U. S.	100
German		History, General	81
French		Elocution	85
Geography		Drawing	
Physical Geography	80	American Literature	
Physiology		Political Economy	
Physics		Civil Government	
Chemistry		Av. of Lesson Grades	79

DEMERITS for month 50

Rogers's grades in history and elocution at the Kemper School revealed his talent for memorization and public speaking—skills that served him well in his later career (*OkClaW*).

while the other classes met four times a week. In his second year at Kemper (1897–98) Rogers took third-year high-school level classes that included arithmetic, algebra, grammar, physics, political economy, letter writing, composition, Bible, history, elocution, and reading (Hitch, *Will Rogers, Cadet,* 7).

2. The textbook Rogers used in history was Azel. S. Lyman's *Historical Chart,* which consisted of timelines linked to countries and civilizations. According to John Payne, Rogers's roommate, Rogers could quickly memorize his history assignment: "That Lyman's Historical Chart, how well I remember that, and the names, how I have labored over them, and old Will could just read the thing over once or twice, go into the recitation room and get a 100" (Hitch, *Will Rogers, Cadet,* 8).

3. Every Saturday one-fourth of the Kemper pupils were required to give a declamation. The course was taught by W. A. Annin, a Princeton graduate, who stressed correct pronunciation and decorum. Dan Cosgrove, a classmate, recalls that Rogers would "clown" during his recitation, "bring down the house and get the highest grade" (Hitch, *Will Rogers, Cadet,* 8).

4. Rogers received many demerits for his pranks and practical jokes, which included roughhousing, lassoing students, tardiness, inattention to dress, and a messy room. Students had to walk a beat for an hour for each demerit, and his classmates remember him often marching guard as a penalty for his demerits (Hitch, *Will Rogers, Cadet,* 16–17). Rogers once wisecracked, "I spent two years at Kemper, one in the guardhouse and one in the fourth grade" (Rogers, *Will Rogers,* 52).

Article from the *Claremore Progress*
5 June 1897
Claremore, I.T.

Willie Rogers, son of Hon. C. V. Rogers, met with an accident Thursday evening which came near costing him his life. He was handling a winchester rifle and in setting it down it was accidently discharged, the ball passing through his hat and inflicting a slight scalp wound.[1]

PD. Printed in *CP,* 5 June 1897. Reprinted from *OC.*

1. Rogers was showing neighborhood friends the manual of arms he had learned at the Kemper School when the rifle hit the ground hard and discharged. The bullet grazed his forehead and left a scar on his left temple (Croy, *Our Will Rogers,* 42–43; Trent, *My Cousin Will Rogers,* 38–39).

Article from the *Kansas City Journal*
18 July 1897
Kansas City, Kansas

On 7 December 1896, John Matthew Yocum, husband of May Rogers, Will Rogers's sister, was murdered.[1] The assassin or assassins shot Yocum, a farmer and hotel manager, through the couple's bedroom window as he was preparing to go to bed.[2] Five local African Americans were arrested for the crime, but they were

North entrance, Kemper School, Boonville, Mo. *(OkClaW)*.

eventually released, and the murder was never solved.[3] Another murder occurred on 11 June 1897 when the body of William Cheatham was found near the railroad tracks one-half mile outside Oolagah. At the time Cheatham, who worked in a livery stable, was courting May Rogers Yocum.[4] On 14 July 1897, Walter Deskey, alias W. E. Milstead, was arrested for the murder.[5] Four days later the Kansas City Journal *reported that Milstead confessed that Clem V. Rogers had "prevailed on him to do the deed, and that Rogers' son, Bill [Will] Rogers, was with him when the shooting occurred."*

THE YOCUM MYSTERY.
PROSPECT IS GOOD NOW FOR ITS UNRAVELING.
LOOKS BAD FOR MRS. YOCUM.
A CONFESSION WHICH IMPLICATES MRS. YOCUM'S FATHER.
UNKNOWN YOUNG MAN ADMITS THAT HE FIRED THE SHOT THAT KILLED CHETINE,[6] MRS. YOCUM'S LOVER–SENSATIONAL DEVELOPMENTS EXPECTED.

Claremore, I.T., July 17.—(Special.)

The mystery surrounding the murders of Matt Yocum in December last, and one Chetine, last month at Oologah, as reported in The Journal at the time of their occurrence, is being unraveled and brings to light a fiendish and deep-laid plot in which one of the leading families of the Nation appears to be implicated. It will be remembered that Yocum was shot in his own house about 8 o'clock at night, just as he was in the act of retiring, the miscreant firing a load of buckshot through the window. Chetine, who had been playing some attention to Mrs. Yocum since her husband's death, was waylaid as he was returning from her house about 10 o'clock at night and shot with a load of buckshot. Death was instantaneous in both cases. In the Yocum case a party of negroes was suspected of having committed the crime and they were finally arrested in Kansas and turned over to the Cherokee authorities. They were released the other day—the court discharging the cases against them for lack of evidence. The second murder occurred, however, while they were still in custody, and the similarity of the two cases, with Mrs. Yocum figuring in both, aroused a sense of indignation where the sentiment is rarely experienced, and every effort is being put forth to unravel the matter.

The result of this investigation, so far, is the arrest of a young man[7]—name not known—who has confessed to the killing of Chetine, implicating as the instigator of the crime, Clem V. Rogers, the well known stockman, Cherokee politician and father of Mrs. Yocum.

He admits that he fired the shot that killed Chetine, but asserts that Rogers prevailed on him to do the deed, and that Rogers' son, Bill Rogers, was with him when the shooting occurred. This revelation, if, indeed, it can be designated by that term, has occasioned no surprise in local circles, as public sentiment has for some time connected Rogers with both crimes. It is asserted by the authorities that a close investigation will implicate Mrs. Yocum as an accessory in the murder of her husband, as the night on which he was killed she had, contrary to custom, pinned up a corner of the window curtain. It was through this window that the shot was fired and this is held to have a bad appearance against her. It was through her own statements that attention was diverted to her father as a possible instigator of the crime. At the time of Chetine's death she stated with much bitterness and apparent grief that her "father's money had killed her husband and now had killed the only man she loved." Public sentiment, almost to a unit, is against Rogers and it is confidently believed that the next few days will develop some very sensational facts.

The officers are extremely reticent and it is hard to learn the full extent of the evidence so far against him. The motive, further than that Yocum had betrayed his daughter and was only prevailed on to marry her by her father paying him a large amount of money, is not known. No motive can be learned from the last murder.

PD. Printed in *KCJ*, 18 July 1897.

1. May Rogers married Matt Yocum on 9 October 1892. She and her husband had managed the DeVann Hotel in Claremore, which was destroyed by fire in January 1896, and they also owned a farm near Oologah (*HRC*, 376; *IC*, 13 October 1892; *WRFT*, 28). At the time of his murder Yocum was being tried for embezzlement (*CP*, 15 February 1896 and 13 February 1897; see also Biographical Appendix entries, STINE, May Rogers Yocum, and YOCUM, J. Matthew).

2. Yocum was shot in the side and died almost instantly. Another shot hit the headboard of the bed where his wife and child were sleeping. The *Indian Chieftain* reported that "the victim was just getting into bed when the first shot struck him and cried out to his wife. 'Oh, May, help me! May, help me!' Mrs. Yocum thought a lamp had exploded and drew down under the bed clothes holding her child. Tracks at the window indicated that the assassin had stood there some time waiting for his opportunity" (*IC*, 17 December 1896; see also *VL*, 10 December 1896).

3. The five African Americans who were arrested and released for lack of evidence were Albert Tucker, Ben Greenleaf, Houston Rogers, Jasper Rogers, and Clem Rogers. The latter three were sons of Charles (Rabb) Rogers. Clem Rogers and his brothers were favorite playmates of the young Will Rogers (Walker, interview, IPH-OkHi; *CP*, 9 January, 23 January, 30 January, 4 March, 6 March, 9 June, 12 June, and 26 June 1897; *IC*, 17 December 1896, 7 January, 21 January, and 24 June 1897; Collings, *Old Home Ranch*, 7, 22–23; Keith, *Boy's Life of Will Rogers*, 16–23; see also Biographical Appendix entries for ROGERS, Charles (Rabb) and Houston; ROGERS, Clement Vann; and WALKER, Agnes Rogers).

4. *KCJ*, 13 June 1897. In this news story Cheatham is identified as a man named Chelom.

Matthew Yocum, Will Rogers's brother-in-law, who was mysteriously murdered in 1896 (*OkClaW*).

5. On 17 July 1897 the *Claremore Progress* reported that "Deskey [Milstead] first came to Oolagah about the first of April and it is believed that money was his motive for the crime, as no other reason for the hellish deed can be assigned."

6. The murdered person is described as William Cheatham in subsequent news reports.

7. Walter Deskey, alias W. E. Milstead.

Article from the *Indian Chieftain*
22 July 1897
Vinita, I.T.

On 22 July 1897 the Indian Chieftain *printed a follow-up story suggesting that Milstead's confession was a fabrication. The newspaper further reported that Clem V. Rogers was anxious to discover the instigator of the* Kansas City Journal *story of 18 July 1897.*

W. E. Milstead, charged with the killing of Wm. Cheatam near Oolagah a few weeks ago, was brought here for a preliminary examination before Commissioner McClure yesterday. Deputy Charley Lamb arrested Milstead near Sedan,[1] Kansas, on Wednesday of last week.

The story of the murder of Will Cheatam at Oolagah last spring is one of the most mysterious and altogether remarkable occurrences that ever happened in this country. The evidence against Milstead seems to be wholly circumstantial, but it has been hinted that some remarkable developments may come during the preliminary investigation now going on before Commissioner McClure.

The night of the murder of Bill Cheatam in April there had been some kind of a show in Oolagah in the evening, after which Cheatam accompanied Mrs. Yocum to her home about a mile and a quarter from town. The couple walked out to the place, and as Cheatam was returning alone, about a quarter of a mile from the town he was shot, evidently from ambush, with a number twelve shot gun, as the wads picked up on the spot afterwards proved, the charge taking effect in his head, neck and breast.

Next morning the body was found and the alarm given, and all sorts of stories circulated about the killing. The dead man held in his right hand a revolver, and it is said that he left the door of Mrs. Yocum with the revolver in his hand after having been admonished by her not to return the way they had come.

The statement wired from Claremore to the Kansas City Journal Monday implicating Clem V. Rogers, the father of Mrs. Yocum, in the murder of

Cheatam, and stating that W. E. Milstead, the prisoner, had made a confession that he had been hired to commit the deed by Rogers, is evidently a fabrication, and utterly and entirely false. Milstead stated here yesterday that he had made no confession, and that he hardly knew Clem Rogers when he saw him. Rogers went to Kansas City yesterday to investigate the charges made in the Journal and to trace up the author.

PD. Printed in *IC*, 22 July 1897.

    1. Sedan is located in Chautauqua County in southeast Kansas (*WNGD*, 1094).

Article from the *Indian Chieftain*
12 August 1897
Vinita, I.T.

Suspected of instigating the Kansas City Journal *story was Thomas A. Latta,[1] a Claremore resident. In early August 1897 he was arrested for criminal libel.*

Tom A. Latta, of Claremore, was arrested some days since for criminal libel, and his case set for trial before Judge McClure, in this city, Monday. Latta is the person who sent the dispatch to the Kansas City Journal stating that Milstead had confessed the killing of Cheatham and that Clem Rogers had paid him to do so. Milstead's discharge by the commissioner discounted this story completely and places Latta in a very uncomfortable situation, as under the statute he can be sent to the penitentiary. It is also stated that the Journal and the Wichita Eagle will both have to defend good sized libel suits for publishing the defamatory matter.

PD. Printed in *IC*, 12 August 1897.

    1. A journalist, Thomas A. Latta of Claremore started a newspaper called the *Tribune* in Collinsville, I.T. Latta was also editor of the *Claremore Messenger* in 1902 and 1903. In 1904 he founded the *Bartlesville Enterprise* as a weekly and began a daily edition in 1905. He was also owner of the *Sapulpa Light* around the turn of the century, and was employed as an editor by the *Tulsa World* in 1907. Born in Indian Territory in 1872, he was the son of John and Anna Latta, Indian missionaries (*CP,* 1 November and 21 November 1902; Foreman, C., *Oklahoma Imprints, 1835–1907*, 58, 59, 63, 215, 219).

Article from the *Indian Chieftain*
19 August 1897
Vinita, I.T.

The charges against W. E. Milstead were dismissed in July 1897.[1] The case against Thomas Latta continued for nearly two years from August 1897 until October 1899, at which time the criminal libel charges were dropped.[2]

Commissioner McClure held Thomas A. Latta to the grand jury Tuesday in the sum of $700, on a charge of criminal libel, and Clem V. Rogers and his son Willie were parties who suggested the prosecution and furnished the evidence upon which Latta was held. The Kansas City Journal of Sunday, July 18, 1897, contained a very sensational article written by Latta in which it was stated that W. E. Milstead, the man charged with the murder of Will Cheatham at Oolagah, some two months ago, had confessed to the crime, and had implicated Clem Rogers and his son. The statements contained in the article were wholly without foundation, and were calculated to injure Rogers immeasurably. Mr. Flemming, managing editor of the Journal, came down and made a statement before the commissioner as to who the author of the article in question [had been].

PD. Printed in *IC*, 19 August 1897.

1. On 29 July 1897 the *Vinita Leader* reported that "the case against Milstead in the Cheatham case was dismissed and the prisoner discharged on account of there being no evidence worth having. It was unfortunate that the arrest was made, but a wise thing was done in dismissing the case at once."
2. *VL*, 19 October 1899.

Kemper School Transcripts
January–May 1897
September 1897–March 1898
Boonville, Mo.

As the transcript from his last months at the Kemper School suggests, Rogers continued to receive average grades and at times excelled in some subjects. He received 109 demerits during his second month, but no demerits for his fourth month. Rogers, who was now eighteen, left the school on 9 March 1898 not due to poor grades or demerits but because of his growing dislike of school, especially the regimentation of the military academy.

53rd yr	4th mo. 12/6/96–1/25/97		5th mo. 1/28–2/25	6th mo	7th	8th[1]
Arith	85		87	82	82	67
Gram	65		72	82	67	68
Bk	75		71	68	66	57
Hist	70		80	81–	68–	79–
				100	85	98
Eloc	95		88	85	77	92
av	76	Alg	80	69	75	68
m	20/45	Lwr	70	82	81	73
d	0	Comp	70	76	75	84
		Bible	80	70	73	38
		av	79	PGeog 80	76	79
				av 79	av 75	av 71
		m 17/38		m 22/39	m 23/39	m 25/39
				d 50	d 59	d 73

54th yr 1897–98

	1st Mo	2nd	3rd	4th	5th to 3/9/98
Arith	81	92	78	75	81
Alg	85	71	62	81	94
Gram	81	77	74	79	71
Physics	55	57	65	71	65
Lwr	85	83	83	85	88
Comp	79	82	85	85	64
Bible	91	92	70	82	60
Hist	80	95	92	99	92
Eloc	80	80	0		
Polit Ec	90	89	81	84	83
av	73	av 77	av 74	Read 73	80
				av 74	av 75
d	65	d 109	d 75	d 0	d 45

AD, transcripts. Kemper School records.[2]

1. Rogers began his schooling at Kemper on 13 January 1897, thus the dating of this document from January 1897. This transcript and the one that follows have been placed chronologically in the volume according to the last date in the time periods covered (rather than the first) because of the nature of the documents.

Cadet Will Rogers dressed in a Kemper School military uniform *(OkClaW)*.

2. The abbreviations used for the subjects Rogers took are as follows: Arithmetic (Arith), Grammar (Gram), Bookkeeping (Bk), History (Hist), Elocution (Eloc), Algebra (Alg), Letterwriting (Lwr), Composition (Comp), Physical Geography (PGeog), Political Economy (Polit Ec), and Reading (Read). Other abbreviations used in the transcripts were average (av), merits (m), and demerits (d).

3. ROPING AND RANCHING
March 1898–January 1902

With his hand and hat on the rail in the front row, Zack Mulhall poses next to his fourteen-year-old daughter, Lucille, at the 1899 St. Louis Annual Fair. Directly above Mulhall and standing near the top of the stairs is Will Rogers. He has his hands on the shoulders of two cowboys; the one on Rogers's right is Vincente Oropeza, who also competed at the fair (*OkClaW*).

SEEKING ADVENTURE, WILL ROGERS LEFT THE KEMPER SCHOOL IN MARCH 1898 and roamed the Southwest for approximately six months, holding several jobs as a ranch hand. He traveled to Higgins, a small railroad town in the Texas Panhandle, where he found work at a nearby ranch owned by W. P. (Perry) Ewing. Rogers wrangled horses, helped in the roundup and calf branding, and joined a six-week cattle trail drive, accompanying four hundred head of cattle 165 miles to Medicine Lodge, Kansas. The trail drive gave Rogers an opportunity to experience the rugged life of a cowpuncher. He guarded the herd at night and got drenched in a prairie thunderstorm, and his horse was caught in quicksand at a treacherous river crossing.[1]

After nearly three months on the Ewing ranch, Rogers rode horseback to Amarillo, where he found work as a cowhand with Lythe (Light) A. Knight, a Plainview, Texas, cattleman.[2] He tended a large herd of cattle to Liberal, Kansas, and performed other chores on the ranch. When Rogers returned to the Panhandle country in 1934, he wrote about these experiences in his weekly newspaper column:

> That plains was the prettiest country I ever saw in my life, as flat as a beauty contest winner's stomach, and prairie lakes scattered all over it. And mirages! You could see anything in the world—just ahead of you—I eat out of a chuck wagon, and slept on the ground all that spring and summer of 98.[3]

Anxious to see more of the West, he rode railroad baggage cars to various places in New Mexico and Colorado.

In the fall of 1898 Rogers returned home and discovered that his father had left the ranch in the care of an Illinois tenant farmer. That August Clem V. Rogers had decided to sell his cattle and move with his second wife, Mary Bibles Rogers, to Claremore, where he was a director and vice president of the town's First National Bank. The elder Rogers was also very involved with Cherokee political affairs. In 1899, he was elected for a fourth time to the Cherokee Nation Senate as a representative from the Cooweescoowee District. Clem V. Rogers realized that he had a large ranch to manage, and he asked his son to oversee the property. He hoped that his nineteen-year-old son would settle down and become a successful cattle rancher.[4]

In the years since Will Rogers's birth the Verdigris country had undergone great transformation. The discovery of coal and the construction of railroads caused vast economic changes as the area became increasingly attractive to investors, farmers, mine operators, railroad companies, and retail merchants.

The building of railway lines across the Cherokee Nation stimulated a boom in the growth of towns. In 1871 and 1872 the Missouri, Kansas, and Texas Railroad (the MKT or Katy) was constructed across Indian Territory from southern Kansas to northern Texas. In 1871 the Atlantic and Pacific (later called the St. Louis and San Francisco or Frisco) was built from Seneca, Missouri, to meet the MKT line. The junction of the two railroads became known as Vinita, platted by the Atlantic and Pacific in September 1871 and soon destined to play a role in Will Rogers's history. Present-day Claremore was founded on 19 September 1882 when the Frisco railway line was extended from Vinita to Tulsa. By 1886 the Frisco had penetrated as far south as Sapulpa. That year Congress permitted the Kansas and Arkansas Valley Railway (also known as the St. Louis, Iron Mountain, and Southern Railway, and later as the Missouri Pacific Railroad) to establish a line from Fort Smith, Arkansas, to Coffeyville, Kansas.[5] This rail line bisected Clem V. Rogers's ranch in 1889, cutting it into two parts. On 12 September 1889 the first train traveled through his property. The operation of the railway line caused the establishment of Oologah, originally a switch stop six miles southwest of the Rogers ranch. By 1899 an Indian agent reported eighty-nine small settlements in the Cherokee Nation; most, like Vinita, Oologah, and Claremore, were a product of railroad stations. Formerly unbroken prairie lands of bluestem grass were now dotted with small towns, some of which would become associated with Will Rogers.[6]

The railroads fundamentally changed the demographics of the Cherokee Nation, bringing hoards of white laborers and other non-Indian intruders into the area. Many white railroad construction workers, tenant farmers, and coal miners lacked temporary permits and lived in the area illegally. The question of intrusion and U.S. government jurisdiction over the Indian Territory caused considerable debate in the Cherokee Nation. Whereas full-blood Cherokees generally opposed intrusion and the abolition of tribal governments, arguing for Indian self-sufficiency, mixed-bloods supported statehood and U.S. citizenship, even though many disliked the intruders. In the late 1870s William Penn Adair, for whom Will Rogers was named, helped lead the resistance to the early boomers who promoted opening the territory to homesteaders.

Clem V. Rogers opposed the intrusion of white traders, town boomers, and tenant farmers, and he regretted the lack of law enforcement to keep them out. Rogers and other large cattle ranchers recognized that the conversion of the open range to small farm operations would mean the demise of valuable grazing pastures for their livestock. "We are *fast fast* drifting into the hands of white men," he warned Dennis Wolf Bushyhead, principal chief of the Cherokee Nation, in August 1885.[7] In the Cherokee Senate he introduced a bill prohibiting intruders from entering the Indian Territory, but it failed to pass. Intruders continued to encroach on Cherokee property, build houses, and farm the land. When Congress approved payment to the intruders for their improvements on Cherokee land before 11 August 1886, Rogers was appointed to a three-person commission in 1893 to appraise their property.[8]

The demographics of the Indian Territory changed dramatically in the 1880s and 1890s. By 1885 there were 25,000 white people in the Indian Territory; five years later there were 140,000 whites in a total population of approximately 210,000. In 1900, when Rogers was twenty-one and managing his father's ranch, the Five Tribes were definitely a minority in their own lands, as noncitizens outnumbered Indians seven to one. White settlement made the population of the Indian Territory burgeon from 197,000 in 1890 to 390,000 in 1900, to 691,736 in 1907, when a census was taken in relation to statehood.[9] The federal government was determined to reduce large tribal holdings into individually owned plots of land through an allotment system. The Cherokee communal system held that title to all land was held in common and vested in the tribe rather than individual property owners. Each citizen was allowed to lease as much land as he or she wished for cultivation or grazing and could own the improvements.[10] The system accelerated the growth of large landholdings, especially by entrepreneurial mixed-blood Cherokees such as Clem V. Rogers. From the 1870s onward, corporations eager for Indian resources, land-hungry railroad companies, and potential white settlers brought tremendous pressure on the government to dissolve the land system and the sovereignty of the Cherokee Nation.[11]

A series of acts essentially eliminated Indian tribal holdings through a forced allotment of lands in severalty. The Dawes General Allotment (Severalty) Act in 1887 mandated U.S. citizenship and individual allotment of land to Indians, counteracting tribal allegiances and communal patterns of land use. In 1893 the Dawes Commission was empowered to negotiate with the Five Tribes for the allotment of tribal lands. The passage of the Curtis Act on 28 June 1898 abolished tribal government and subjected the Five Tribes to federal jurisdiction. In 1896 Congress authorized the Dawes Commission to survey tribal lands and to establish tribal rolls so that holdings could be divided by allotment. As a member of two Cherokee delegations in 1896 and 1898, Clem V. Rogers was directly involved in negotiations with the Dawes Commission on the allotment question.[12]

By 1898 Clem V. Rogers realized that the Cherokee Nation was doomed and that his large holdings would be broken up. The political turmoil was certainly one reason he moved to Claremore that year and decided to let his son manage the ranch. After considerable discussion and delay, the Cherokees finally reached an

In 1898 Principal Chief Samuel Mayes appointed Clement Vann Rogers as a member of a Cherokee Nation committee to negotiate with the Dawes Commission dealing with land claims, allotments, intruders, and other disagreements with the federal government. Committee members, *front row (left to right):* H. C. Lowrey, George Sanders, Robert Bruce Ross (chair), and Percy Wyly. *Back row:* Clement Vann Rogers, William Wirt Hastings, George W. Benge, William P. Thompson, and David Faulkner *(OkTahN)*.

agreement with the Dawes Commission in August 1902, which allowed each enrolled citizen an allotment of 110 acres of average value. On 22 October 1900, Clem V. Rogers applied for allotments for himself and for his son with an agent of the Dawes Commission. Allotment of Cherokee land was conducted between 1903 and 1907. On 17 August 1903, Clem V. Rogers received a certificate of allotment for 69.93 acres, and Will Rogers for 78.84 acres. By 1907 Clem V. Rogers's 60,000-acre ranch was divided into hundreds of allotments legally possessed by other Cherokees. Although he shrewdly bought back some of his neighbors' property, his days as a Cherokee cattle baron had ended.[13]

At the same time that federal policy was undermining tribal sovereignty, economic forces were transforming the agronomy of the Cherokee Nation. During the last two decades of the nineteenth century diversified farming, dominated by fenced pastures and plowed fields producing marketable crops, gradually displaced large cattle ranches dependent on open-land grazing. Farmers migrating from Kansas settled on the prairie north of Clem V. Rogers's ranch, making grazing land beyond the boundaries of his property more difficult to find.[14] A clever businessman, Rogers adapted to these changing conditions by switching from grazing longhorns on the open range to feeding high-grade breeds of shorthorns in fenced acreage. To improve his stock and to profit from the expanding domestic and export market for beef, he purchased purebred Durham shorthorns and Hereford bulls. In order to keep his prized cattle from straying into his neighbors' acres, he erected a barbed-wire drift fence approximately five miles long on the northern side of his property in 1891. Before the coming of the railroad to the Cherokee Nation, Clem V. Rogers drove his fattened cattle to a depot at Coffeyville, Kansas, for shipment to Kansas City and other markets. After 1889 he could transport his cattle from nearby Chelsea on the Frisco line and from Talala on the Kansas and Arkansas Valley Railway line, located three and one-half miles north of his cow camp.[15]

Clem V. Rogers also expanded his operations and engaged in extensive commercial farming. He bred some of the finest horses in the area, entered into the hog-raising business, and produced large numbers of turkeys, geese, chickens, pigeons, and other fowl. Huge amounts of acreage were now used to grow rich harvests of wheat, corn, and oats as well as horticultural products such as garden vegetables and fruits. When he produced a record crop of thirteen thousand bushels of wheat in 1895, the *Claremore Progress* called Clem V. Rogers the "Oologah wheat king."[16]

The first twenty years of Will Rogers's life corresponded to the vast transformations and political turmoil in the Cherokee Nation. Fundamentally he disliked the barbed wire, the railroads, and the intruders—preferring instead the freewheeling cowboy life of the open range with its roundups, branding, and line riding. Later he reflected nostalgically on this bygone era:

> I have always regretted that I didn't live about thirty or forty years earlier, and in the same old country—the Indian Territory. I would have liked to have gotten there ahead of the 'nesters,' the barbed wire fence and so-called civilization. I wish I could have lived my whole life then and drank out of a gourd instead of a paper envelope.[17]

Basically the day-to-day operations of the ranch bored Rogers, and he let the tenant couple who lived in the main house care for the farm.[18] For a time Rogers bunked with his distant cousin Spi Trent in a makeshift log cabin built on the property. He enjoyed spending long hours with his friends, especially riding his horse across the plains with Charles McClellan. He participated in

Will Rogers *(left)* on Comanche, his favorite roping horse, with an unidentified cowboy at the 1899 St. Louis Annual Fair *(OkClaW)*.

steer-roping contests and attended horse shows, local parties, and dances. His neglect of responsibilities on the ranch irritated his father, but there was little Clem V. Rogers could do to change the nature of his son. Yearning to discover new places, Rogers spent considerable time away from the ranch. He escorted shipments of cattle to St. Louis, Kansas City, and California. In 1901 he traveled to the Pan-American Exposition in Buffalo and returned to Texas for a brief time.[19]

Rogers relished the cattle roundups, the branding of calves, and the cowboy comradery around the campfire. He was an avid horse breeder and trader and collected the territory's finest saddles, ropes, spurs, and boots. He was always eager to buy quality roping horses for his stable and purchased ponies from Zack T. Miller, co-owner of the well-known 101 Ranch and the 101 Real Wild West Show in Oklahoma Territory.[20]

His favorite horse at this time was Comanche, a cream-colored pony with a white mane and tail that was raised by the young Anderson Rogers, son of Houston Rogers, Clem V. Rogers's former slave, who worked at the Rogers ranch and lived nearby. Because of his speed and agility Comanche gained a reputation as a great roping horse, and Rogers used him in many steer-roping contests during this time. Rogers's friend Jim Hopkins, a champion steer roper, called Comanche "the best horse that was ever wrapped up in so much hide."[21]

The steer-roping contests were the precursors of modern-day professional rodeo. Those events evolved from the roping and riding skills that working cowboys used on the cattle range and during the roundup. Equestrian contests gave cowboys an opportunity to display and test important occupational skills needed for their rigorous work, as well as exhibit their horsemanship. Steer roping, for example, required skills used to rope and restrain a sick steer on the open range, to "cut out" a steer from a large herd, and to collar cattle for branding. The cowboy contests started when hands from the same outfit began competing against one another in bronco riding and steer roping as a form of recreation and as part of cow-camp entertainments. Roping and riding contests were also held among outfits during social times on the semiannual roundups. Competitions soon began to be held in the town square of the railhead at the conclusion of a long cattle drive.[22]

During the 1880s and 1890s cowboy competitions commenced in western towns, primarily on Sundays and holidays. These popular entertainments, featuring the best local working cowhands in steer-roping and bronco-riding contests, were often held on the outskirts of town. People would travel miles on horseback and in wagons to watch the proceedings. The competitors would combine their entrance fees to create purses awarded to the winners. When merchants began to organize events to promote their town, these contests became more formalized with prize money donated by citizens and firms, and champions were attracted from all over the country. The largest events occurred at county fairs, commercial expositions, conventions, stampedes, Fourth of July celebrations, and "Frontier Days" celebrations.[23]

Rogers's participation in these cowboy competitions played a formative role in the development of his show-business career, and these were his first introductions to performing before a large audience. During the period from 1899 to 1901, Rogers appeared in steer-roping contests at fairs in St. Louis (1899), Des Moines (1901), and San Antonio (1901) and at the Rough Riders reunion in Oklahoma City (1900) and the Union Confederate Veterans reunion in Memphis (1901), among others. A pioneer showman who organized many of these events was Zack Mulhall, an Oklahoma Territory ranchman, railroad livestock agent, and Wild West show producer.[24] He recruited Rogers and other skilled cowboys from the Indian Territory for roping and riding contests at county fairs, cattlemen conventions, commercial expositions, and local parks—indeed, just about anywhere he could get a crowd. Although he rarely finished among the top three contestants, Rogers developed a reputation as a skilled steer roper during his time.

Rogers's talent for roping had evolved when he was a young boy on his father's ranch. His sister Sallie remembered her brother spending considerable time as a child roping a large post-oak stump in the backyard. When he was ten years old, his father gave him eight dogies, or motherless calves, and he regularly practiced roping the young animals. The young Rogers learned by watching and imitating Dan Walker, an African American cowboy and top roper, who was considered the head cowhand on the Rogers ranch. In 1893 Rogers attended the World's Columbian Exposition at Chicago, where he saw Mexican vaqueros perform roping stunts with Buffalo Bill's Wild West show.[25] Here Rogers was enthralled by the lasso tricks of Vincente Oropeza, who was billed as "the greatest roper in the world."[26]

Local cowboy friends also helped perfect his skills, including Jim Hopkins, Charles McClellan, Frank Musgrove, Johnnie Lipe, and Jim Rider, an expert thrower of the Johnny Blocker, a turned-over loop that was particularly effective for roping hornless cattle. Rogers also learned at steer-roping contests by watching champion ropers such as the Texan Clay McGonigle, Tom Vest, Abe Wilson, and others. These experiences provided the foundation for his trick-rope artistry on the vaudeville stage.[27]

Steer roping required considerable dexterity and challenged the best of the cowboys. At the turn of the century the contests were held on large grounds where there was enough space for the competitor to chase the steer. The animal was given a head start of 50 to 100 feet until it reached a chalk line, at which point the horse and rider would begin to charge after the steer so that the rider could attempt to rope the animal by the horns or around the neck while pitching a rope over the opposite side of the animal, an action called the trip. As the rider dismounted to go after the catch, a well-trained horse kept the rope taut so that the rider could bind three feet of the steer with a short rope. After the roper had finished, the contestant would raise his hands signaling for time. The roper with the fastest time won first prize.[28]

Besides engaging in steer-roping contests, Rogers led an active social life with neighborhood friends and relatives his age. His companions included the brothers Thomas, Gordon, and Denny Lane; Herman and Clint Lipe; Jim and Austin Rider; his cousins Clem and William Musgrove; Spi, Dick, and Tom Trent; and the McClellan brothers, Charles, Sos, and Steve. Rogers and his friends participated in many social and recreational activities held in the region, including picnics, hayrides, oyster suppers, swimming and cakewalk parties, and outdoor stomp dances. The outdoor Saturday-night stomp dances held at the nearby community of Oowala, as well as the swimming parties by the Verdigris River, attracted large crowds. On the hayrides Rogers would lead a large group of boys and girls in singing. He also hosted lively parties at the ranch, where a wooden platform for dancing was constructed in the yard. Other activities occurred at the Pocahontas Club, a social organization for the area's young Indian women, who admitted Rogers and several of his male friends as honorary members.[29]

Friends remembered the young Rogers as the star of these parties. At the dances in Claremore he called out the figures of the quadrille, a popular square dance. Gazelle Lane, a neighborhood friend, recalled that Rogers led the outdoor stomp dances: "What energy! He could dance all night, and when the dance was over, would be going as strong as when the dance had started."[30] Rogers developed an avid interest in the popular music of the late 1890s. He purchased the latest ragtime and minstrel sheet music at stores in Kansas City, where he also heard the blackface comic and singing team of Bert Williams and George Walker perform on the vaudeville stage. Rogers entertained his friends at parties by imitating minstrels and such singing popular tunes as "Coon, Coon, Coon" and "I Ain't Got a Dollar I Can Call My Own." Susan McClellan Wear, the sister of Charles McClellan, remembers him visiting her family's house regularly on Sunday afternoons to sing the newest songs. These activities, including singing tenor in a local quartet, signaled Rogers's interest in the world of show business.[31]

At this time Rogers was known as a dapper young man who bought the latest fashions at Kansas City and at other cattle-market towns. He enjoyed courting several local girls, including Belle Price and Kate Ellis. He was especially fond of Ellis, and there were rumors of an impending marriage.[32]

In the fall of 1899 an important turning point in Rogers's life occurred when he met his future wife, Betty (Bettie) Blake.[33] She came from a prominent family of nine children from Rogers, Arkansas, a small town in the northwestern part of the state near the Indian Territory border. The twenty-year-old Blake, who was recovering from typhoid fever, traveled to Oologah to visit her sister Cora and her husband, Will Marshall, who was a depot station agent in the town. After a chance encounter at the Oologah station the two frequently spent time together at social gatherings, sharing their mutual interest in popular music and singing. While she played the piano, Rogers sang popular tunes. After Blake returned home, Rogers corresponded with his new friend.

Betty Blake at age eighteen in 1897 *(OkClaW)*.

Two surviving letters (5 January 1900 and 14 March 1900) reveal his growing fondness, but also his uneasiness about being an "Injun Cowboy" in her eyes. Their meeting in 1899 was the beginning of a long and stormy romance—a courtship that eventually led to their marriage in 1908.[34]

1. *Amarillo Daily News Globe*, 20 February 1926; Croy, *Our Will Rogers*, 45–47; Day, *Will Rogers*, 25–26; Keith, *Boy's Life of Will Rogers*, 126–37; see also Biographical Appendix entry, Ewing, Frank.

2. Croy, *Our Will Rogers*, 47; Keith, *Boy's Life of Will Rogers*, 138–40; on Knight,

see also *Amarillo Sunday News Globe*, 14 August 1938, and Biographical Appendix entry, KNIGHT, Lythe A. (Light). Rogers probably left the Ewing ranch around 8 June, for he spent the night at the Johnson Hotel in Higgins, Tex., on that date. In one of his weekly articles, written in 1932, Rogers recounted an experience he had at Higgins when a cowboy from the Box T Ranch plowed up the main street *(Daily Oklahoman*, 3 November 1932, reprinted in Gragert, *Will Rogers' Weekly Articles* 5:202–3; see also Day, *Will Rogers*, 26).

3. *TDW,* 29 July 1934, reprinted in Gragert, *Will Rogers' Weekly Articles* 6:139.

4. Collings, *Old Home Ranch*, 76–79.

5. In the treaty of 1866 the Cherokee Nation permitted the construction of two railroads in their land, one north and south, and the other east and west. The Atlantic and Pacific and the Missouri, Kansas, and Texas railways were the first two railroads to enter Indian Territory in the early 1870s. Further construction of railroads was held up due to the problem of land grants in the Cherokee Nation. Pressed by railroad lobbyists, Congress declared in 1886 that the Indian Territory was under federal jurisdiction and that Congress could grant rights-of-way, thus clearing the way for more railroad construction.

The Kansas and Arkansas Valley Railway was incorporated in November 1885 and obtained a charter in 1886 to build a line from Fort Smith, Ark., to Coffeyville, Kans. Work began in 1887, and by late October 1889 the railway had reached the Kansas border. The track ran through the town of Claremore and northward across Clem V. Rogers's ranch property, then on to Coffeyville. The railway stimulated the growth of Indian Territory towns such as Oologah and Talala and made it easier for Clem V. Rogers and other Verdigris-country cattle ranchers to ship their stock. By 1900 two more lines had been built, so that by 1907 there were nine lines and branches. The St. Louis, Iron Mountain, and Southern Railway Co. was incorporated in April 1874 as a consolidation of the St. Louis and Iron Mountain Railroad Co. (one of the oldest railroad companies, chartered in 1851), the Cairo and Fulton Railroad Co. (chartered in 1853), and the Cairo, Arkansas, and Texas Railroad Co. The Kansas and Arkansas Valley Railway was sold to this corporation in 1909. The St. Louis, Iron Mountain, and Southern Railway and the Kansas and Arkansas Valley Railway became part of the Missouri Pacific Railroad in 1917 (a conglomerate of 148 different railroad corporations) (Lefebvre, *Cherokee Strip in Transition*, 42–43; Robertson D., *Encyclopedia of Western Railroad History* 2:141, 143, 144; Self, "Building the Railroads," 198–99; Wardell, *Political History of the Cherokee Nation*, 257–60).

6. Gibson, *Oklahoma*, 263; Hewes, *Occupying the Cherokee Country of Oklahoma*, 53; *HRC*, 13; McReynolds, *Oklahoma*, 270–77; Morris and McReynolds, *Historical Atlas of Oklahoma*, map 52; Wardell, *Political History of the Cherokee Nation*, 255–89. On Oologah's founding see *History of Oologah*, 9; Sunday, *Line Rider in the Cherokee Nation*, 38–44.

7. Quoted from Collings, *Old Home Ranch*, 57.

8. Clement Vann Rogers to Principal Chief Colonel Johnson Harris, 15 October 1894, above, and Clement Vann Rogers to Harris, 25 October and 18 November 1894, OkClaW; Keith, "Clem Rogers and His Influence on Oklahoma History," 68–70; McSpadden, "Clement Vann Rogers," 395; Wardell, *Political History of the Cherokee Nation*, 284–86.

9. Dale and Wardell, *History of Oklahoma*, 285–88; Hewes, *Occupying the Cherokee Country of Oklahoma*, 48; McReynolds, *Oklahoma*, 278–307; Wardell, *Political History of the Cherokee Nation*, 255–89. Population figures are from McReynolds, *Oklahoma*, 277, 307; see also Baird and Goble, *Story of Oklahoma*, 284.

10. See Graebner, "Public Land Policy of the Five Civilized Tribes."

11. White, *"It's Your Misfortune and None of My Own,"* 115–16.

12. Keith, "Clem Rogers and His Influence on Oklahoma History," 76–80.

13. Collings, *Old Home Ranch*, 97–104; Thornton, *Cherokees*, 116–17.

14. Collings, *Old Home Ranch*, 58–59, 105–7; Dale, *Range Cattle Industry;* Graebner, "History of Cattle Ranching in Eastern Oklahoma," 311; Hewes, *Occupying the Cherokee Country of Oklahoma*, 48–50.

15. Collings, *Old Home Ranch*, 47–48; Morris, McReynolds, and Goins, *Historical Atlas of Oklahoma*, 3d ed., map 52; see also Dale, *Range Cattle Industry*, 147–70. Rogers's barbed-wire fence is reported in *IC*, 26 February 1891.

16. Collings, *Old Home Ranch*, 73; see also 55–65.

17. Rogers, *Will Rogers*, 56.

18. Betty Blake Rogers remembers visiting the ranch in late 1899 and noting the deteriorating conditions: "We were met by the farmer's wife. The house was cold, ill-kept and bare of furniture. As I remember, the whole place was run down and neglected, and I knew it had little resemblance to the hospitable home where the Rogers family had been born and raised" *(Will Rogers*, 18).

19. Rogers returned for a time to the Ewing ranch near Higgins, Tex. (Keith, *Boy's Life of Will Rogers*, 142–43; Trent, *My Cousin Will Rogers*, 144–45). Rogers may also have worked around 1901 at the XIT Ranch. Rogers has been identified in a photograph, dated 1901, that was taken with other cowboys at chuck-wagon time at the XIT's Yellow House division (Will Rogers was identified by Lula Allen, who lived on a ranch in the area and whose brother is in the picture; see Carl Williams to Byron Price, 5 May and 9 May 1980, Carl Williams Collection, PHM). The photograph without identification has been reproduced in Haley, *XIT Ranch of Texas*, 210f., and in Duke and Frantz, *6,000 Miles of Fence*, 102f.; see also 75–76).

20. Collings, *Old Home Ranch*, 86; see also Collings and England, *101 Ranch*, 77–78.

21. O'Donnell, "My Friend Will," 19. See also Collings, *Old Home Ranch*, 61–62, 85–89; Keith, *Boy's Life of Will Rogers*, 45–48; Ketchum, *Will Rogers*, 60–61; and Biographical Appendix entry, ROGERS, Charles (Rabb) and Houston. According to writer Arnold Marquis, Rogers acquired Comanche around 1890 after his mother died, when the horse was five years old. Comanche stood about fourteen hands and weighed 950 pounds (Marquis, "Will Rogers and His Horses," 28–29). Another favorite horse during this time was Robin.

22. Collings, *Old Home Ranch*, 91; Fredriksson, *American Rodeo*, 3–5; Gipson, *Fabulous Empire*, 224; Keith, *Boy's Life of Will Rogers*, 148–49; Lawrence, *Rodeo*, 36, 78–82; Robertson, M., *Rodeo*, 86–87; on the cowboy life in general, see Frantz and Choate, *American Cowboy*, 33–82.

23. Although cowboy roping and horse-racing contests reportedly took place in Santa Fe, N. Mex., as early as 10 June 1847, full-scale competitions did not start until later. Prescott, Ariz., claims to be the first community to have an organized contest as early as the Fourth of July, 1864. This town was seemingly among the first to charge admission and award a prize on the Fourth of July, 1888, when a medal was awarded to Juan Leivas for tying a steer in one minute and seventeen seconds. A bronc-riding contest between cowboys representing different ranches occurred at Deer Trail, Colorado Territory, on 4 July 1869. Pecos, Tex., held an early rodeo on 4 July 1883 when local cowboys roped and rode longhorn steers on the main street. Winning steer ropers received expensive saddles as prizes at the Texas State Fair in Austin in 1882 and at an 1886 fair in Albuquerque, New Mexico Territory. Cheyenne, Wyo., began its famous

Frontier Days in 1897, whereas the popular Calgary Stampede started in 1912. Although the Rodeo Association of America was formed in 1929, professional rodeo cowboys formed the Cowboys' Turtle Association in 1936. The Girls Rodeo Association was established in 1949, and the Cowgirl Hall of Fame in Hereford, Tex., today honors the best women riders (Fredriksson, *American Rodeo*, 4–5, 171–76; Lamar, "Rodeo," in Lamar, ed., *Reader's Encyclopedia of the American West*, 1028; Lawrence, *Rodeo*, 80–81; Roach, *Cowgirls*, 119, 124; Slatta, *Cowboys of the Americas*, 128–31, 146–47, 210; Westermeier, *Man, Beast, Dust*, 30–35).

24. For more information see Biographical Appendix entry, MULHALL, Colonel Zack.

25. According to Harold Keith, Will Rogers went to the Chicago World's Fair with his father (*Boy's Life of Will Rogers*, 62–72). John M. Oskison, a Willie Halsell schoolmate, writes that he, Will, and two other friends (Frank and Jim Walker) went by themselves the day after school finished. They traveled by train, stopping overnight in St. Louis and going on to Chicago, where they slept in a cheap hotel and ate twenty-five-cent meals. Oskison writes: "We spent a wholly satisfying week scuttling from exhibit to exhibit, riding the Ferris wheel and the intramural railway, trying the shows on The Streets of Cairo that proved less exciting than the promises of their barkers, and testing other attractions of the Midway Plaisance. To us the discovery, in a western supply house exhibit, of a wonderful silver-decorated saddle and bridle priced at two hundred and fifty dollars was far more important than the Rembrants and Corots in the Palace of Fine Arts. However, we did like Rosa Bonheur's 'Horse Fair.' Will endorsed it heartily. 'Them overgrown broncs wouldn't be any good to ride, but they'd sure make a he-man plow team!'" (Oskison, "A Tale of the Old I.T.," chap. 2, p. 9).

26. A copy of the 1893 program printed in Russell, D., *Lives and Legends of Buffalo Bill*, 376–77, lists as act number nine "*Group of Mexicans* from Old Mexico, will illustrate the use of the Lasso, and perform various Feats of Horsemanship." See also Collings, *Old Home Ranch*, 25–26, 80; Keith, *Boy's Life of Will Rogers*, 62–72; Ketchum, *Will Rogers*, 43. Rogers competed against Oropeza in steer roping at the St. Louis annual fair. See Biographical Appendix entry, OROPEZA, Vincente.

27. Collings, *Old Home Ranch*, 91; O'Donnell, "My Friend Will," 20–21; on Rider, see Keith, *Boy's Life of Will Rogers*, 148–156, and Biographical Appendix entries, RIDER, James Hall, and McGONIGLE, Henry Clay.

28. Croy, *Our Will Rogers*, 75–76; Keith, *Boy's Life of Will Rogers*, 149; Charles H. Tompkins to Homer Croy, 1 August and 11 August 1952, HCP-MoU. Steer roping is also called "steer jerking" and "steer tripping." Because this event has caused considerable injuries to steers, it is outlawed in most states. In contests today the roper must rope the steer's horns (Lawrence, *Rodeo*, 36–37, 176–77).

29. For recreational activities see *As I Recollect*, 163; Croy, *Our Will Rogers*, 58–59; HRC, 34.

30. Croy, *Our Will Rogers*, 59. See also Biographical Appendix entry, LUCKETT, Lasca Gazelle Lane.

31. Wear, interview, OkClaW; see also *As I Recollect*, 162–63; Croy, *Our Will Rogers*, 55–56; O'Donnell, "My Friend Will," 1. On Williams and Walker see Gilbert, *American Vaudeville*, 283–87.

32. *As I Recollect*, 162; Croy, *Our Will Rogers*, 55–56. See also Biographical Appendix entry, ELLIS, Kate.

33. For more information on Rogers's wife, see Biographical Apendix entry, ROGERS, Betty Blake.

34. Rogers, *Will Rogers*, 12–20.

Johnson House Registry Book
15 March 1898
Higgins, Tex.

*A Kemper classmate, William (Bill) A. Johnson,[1] from Canadian, Tex., told Will
Rogers about the excitement of working for large cattle outfits in the Panhandle.
Borrowing money from his sisters Sallie and Maud, Rogers traveled to Higgins,
Tex.[2] As his signature on the hotel registry suggests, Rogers arrived on 15 March
1898 and stayed at the Johnson House hotel.[3] He soon got a job nearby on W. P.
(Perry) Ewing's ranch, where he worked for several months as a ranch hand helping
with branding, round ups, and driving a herd of cattle to Kansas.[4]*

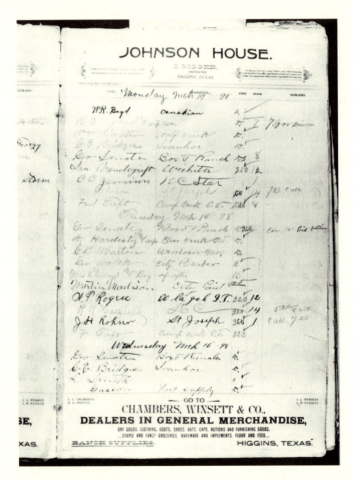

AD. OkClaW. Photo-facsimile reduction of the original.

1. Johnson, who lived in nearby Canadian, was a friend of Frank Ewing, whose father, W. P. Ewing, owned the Little Robe Ranch. It was probably Johnson who told Rogers about the Ewing ranch. See Biographical Appendix entry, JOHNSON, William A.

2. Higgins, a town in the Panhandle two miles from the Oklahoma border, is located in southeastern Texas in Lipscomb County, the center of a wheat and cattle region. The town was founded in 1887 when the Atchison, Topeka, and Santa Fe Railroad reached the Texas border from Indian Territory. The railroad's townsite agent, L. E. Finch, platted the settlement, which he named for G. H. Higgins, a Massachusetts stockholder in the Santa Fe line. Higgins became a railroad town and market center for ranches in the area. The town of Higgins has erected a historical marker in the city park which reads: "WILL ROGERS . . . one of America's best loved humorists whose stage act gently mocking man's foibles was highlighted by rope tricks learned here (Higgins) in his youth. Born in Oklahoma, in 1898 (threatened with discipline for pranks) he left school and came to Texas. He became a cowboy on the Little Robe Ranch, near Higgins, and made a lifelong friend of young Frank Ewing, son of his employer. In 1902 he joined a wild west show and was famous by 1918" (Robertson and Robertson, *Panhandle Pilgrimage*, 274, see also 272; *CLG*, 783; Webb, *Handbook of Texas* 1:807).

3. The Johnson House, a frame structure located near the railroad depot, was built in 1888 by its first owner, J. F. Johnson (1858–1927), the father of William A. Johnson. Born at Rover, Tenn., Johnson lived in Kiowa, Kans., before moving to Higgins, where he also built the town's first general store. Around 1897 he and his wife, Elizabeth Winsett, moved to Canadian, where they opened up another store and a bank. A successful pioneer rancher and banker, he was president of the Southwest National Bank of Canadian. The hotel was renamed Hotel Higgins after Johnson sold the establishment. Rogers also signed the Johnson Hotel registry on the nights of 16 March and 8 June 1898 (Johnson House Hotel Registry, OkClaW; *History of Lipscomb County*, 1; Stanley, *Higgins Texas Story*, 5, 8).

4. W. P. (Perry) Ewing's Little Robe Ranch was actually located on Little Robe Creek about twelve miles southwest of Higgins across the state line in what is now Ellis County, Okla. The township of Little Robe had previously been a hunting ground of the Cheyenne Indians, and the ranch was named after a well-known chief. According to Frank Ewing, it took several days before the Ewing family knew Rogers was in Higgins because the ranch was so isolated. Rogers became a lifelong friend of Frank Ewing, son of W. P. Ewing (Frank Ewing interview, 79:498–99, IPH-OkHi; see also *History of Lipscomb County*, 411; Croy, *Our Will Rogers*, 45–46; "Notes and Documents [Little Robe Township, Ellis County]," 344; Shirk, *Oklahoma Place Names*, 126; and Biographical Appendix entry, EWING, Frank).

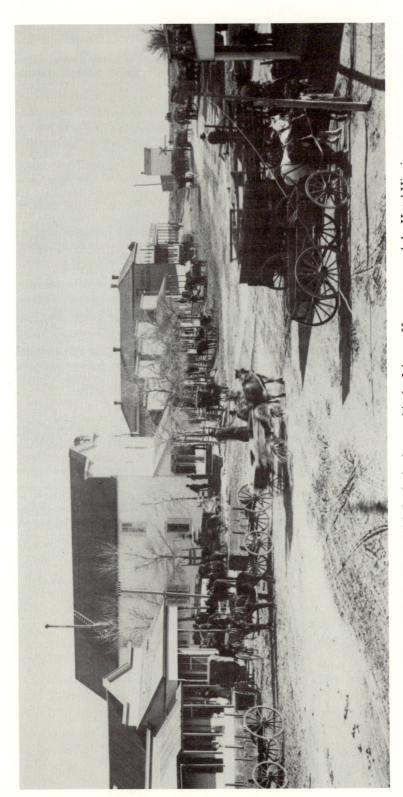

View of Higgins, Tex., 1905. In the background is the Johnson House, renamed the Hotel Higgins (PHM, *A History of Lipscomb County*).

Application to the Mutual Life Insurance Company of New York
9 September 1898
Talala, I.T.

THIS APPLICATION

Made to the Mutual Life Insurance Company of New York as the basis and a part of a proposed Contract for Insurance [sub]ject[1] to the Charter of the Company and the laws of the State of New York. I hereby agree that all the following statements and answers, and all those that I make to the Company Medical Examiner, in continuation of this application, are by me warranted to be true, and are offered to the Company as a consideration of the contract, which I hereby agree to acc[ept], and which shall not take effect until the first premium shall have been paid, during my continuance in good he[alth] and the policy shall have been signed by the Secretary of the Company, and issued. I further agree that in any distribution of surplus, the principles and methods which may then be in use by the Company for such distribution, and its determination [in] the amount apportioned to such policy shall be and are hereby ratified and accepted by and for every person [w]ho shall have or claim any interest in the contract.

1. My full name is ___William Penn Rogers___
2. I reside at ___near Talala.___
   In the City of ___near Talala___
   County of ___Cherokee Nation___
3. My former residences were ___—near Talala, I.T.___
4. My place of business is ___Talala I.T. (nearby)___
5. My P.O. address is ___Talala I.T.___
6. My present occupation is ___Cattle raising___, in the following branch of business or trade _____
7. My other occupations are ___several___
8. My former occupations have been ___Going to School ▼ same as above ▼___
9. The full name of the person to whom the insur[ance will be] payable is ___—Estate___

10. Residing in _____
11. The relationship of said Beneficiary to me is _____

(The Children or Executors, if any, are named, and the Children or Executors of _____)

12. The insurable interest of the said Beneficiary in the *[word obscured]* proposed for insurance, other than that of family relationship, is ____

_____

13. I hereby apply for insuran[ce] on my life on the ___Income Life___ plan ___20___ Payments ___20___ Year Distribution.

14. Amount, $ ___5000—___ Contingent Additions or Mortuary Allotment, $_____ Deferred Annuity, $_____

15. The Premiums are to be p[aid] _____ annually for ___20 years___

16. I was born on the ___[4th]___ day of ___November___ 1879. in ___—near___ Talala Cherokee Nation___

17. I am a citizen or subject of ___United States___

18. I have been accepted for insurance under the following policies in this Company: ___None___

19. I am insured in other Comp[ani]es and Associations, as follows: ___None___ and in no others.

20. No application has ever been made to any Company or Association for insurance upon my life on which a polic[y] has not been issued on the plan and premium rate originally applied for, except to the following Companies or Associations: ___no___ and no such application is no[w] pending or awaiting decision in any corporation. ___no___

I hereby warrant and agree that during the next [t]wo years following the date of issue of the Contract of Insurance to which application is hereby made, I will not travel or reside in any part of the Torrid Zone, or North of the para[llel] of 60° North Latitude, and will not engage in any of the following hazardous occupations or employments: retailing intoxicating liquors, handling electric wires and dynamos, *[word partially obscured]*ting, mining, submarine labor, aeronautic ascensions, the manufacture of highly explosive substances, service upon any railroad train or track or in switching or in coupling cars, or [o]n any steam or other vessel, unless written permission is expressly granted by the Company.

I further warrant and agree that I will not eng[age] in any military or naval service in time of war, during the ordinance of the said contract, without first obtaining written permission from the Company.

I also warrant and agree that I will not die by my own act, whether sane or insane, during the period of one year following said date of issue.

I have paid $_____ to the subscribing Soliciting Agent, who has furnished me with a binding receipt therefor, signed by the Secretary of the Company, making the insurance in force from this date, provided the application shall be approved, and the policy duly signed by the Secretary of the Head Office of the Company and issued.

Dated at Talala [Sept.] 2nd 1898.

{Signature of person whose Life}   William Penn Rogers

[Sentences obscured]. [I have] known this applicant for *[words obscured]* and saw him sign this application.   *[signature illegible]*
Soliciting Agent[2]

PDS, with autograph insertions. Mutual Life Insurance Co. of New York, "Gift to the Nation," OkClaW.

1. The original application was folded in sixths and apparently taped later at the creases, sometimes obscuring portions of the text in the folded areas.

2. The application, no. 914486, was stamped on 9 September 1898 and processed by hand on 10 September 1898 for life insurance in the amount of five thousand dollars due in twenty payments over twenty years at an annual premium of $141.40.

Enclosure:
Medical Examiner's Report
2 September 1898
Talala, I. T.

MEDICAL EXAMINER'S REPORT

1. What is your full name?   William Penn Rogers   Age   19   Are you Married or Single?   Single

2. Have you ever had any of the following diseases? [For] each illness state date, number of attacks, duration, severity, complications and result.

Yes or No.

A. Dizziness, unconsciousness, epilepsy or convulsions of any sort? Paralysis? Apoplexy? or any diseases of the nervous system?   No

B. Headaches, — severe, protracted or frequent?   No

C. Sunstroke?   No

D. Discharges from ear or any other chronic discharges?   No

E. Chronic or persistent cough or hoarseness, or spitting or coughing of blood, asthma or shortness of breath, or any chest or lung disease?   No

F. Disease or any functional disturbance of the heart?   No

G. Dyspepsia or Indigestion? — No

H. Chronic or habitual Diarrhea — No

I. Severe, protracted or repeated intestinal colic? — No

J. Colic, due to renal or hepatitis or other derangement of the liver? — No

M. Hemorrhoids, fistula or any other disease of the rectum? — No

N. Gravel, bladder or kidney disease? — No

O. Syphilis or other venereal disease? — No

P. Stricture? — No

S. Any chronic disease of the [word obscured]? — No

T. Cancer or tumors or ulcers of any kind? — No

4. What are the full particulars of any other illness, constitutional diseases or injury you have had, giving date, duration and remaining effects, if any? None [1]

5. Has your weight recently increased or diminished, and from what cause? No

6. Are you on the U.S. invalid pension roll—if so, for what disability? No

7. Give name and address of physician last consulted None When and for what complaint? XXX

8. a. What were your past and what are your present habits in the use of alcoholic or other stimulants? Do not use them

b. In the use of chloral, morphine and other narcotics? Do not use them

9. Have you ever been under treatment at any asylum, home or sanitarium? No If so, when, how long and for what? XXXX

10. Are you now in good health so far as you know or believe? Yes

11. Family Record of the Applicant[2]

	Living.		Dead.			
	Age?	Health?	Age?	Specific cause of death?	How long sick?	Health, previous to last illness?
Father,	60	Good				
Father's Father				Dont know		
Father's Mother			65	Malarial fever	few days	Good
Mother,			48	Typhoid fever		Good
Mother's Father			70	Killed by Cyclone		Good
Mother's Mother			81	Old age		Good
[section of page obscured]						
Brothers						
Number living,						
Number dead,						
			18	Typhoid fever	2 weeks	Good
Sisters						
Number living,						
	29	Good				
	27	Good				
Number dead,						
2				[Died in] infancy		

Name and P.O. Address
Of each living member of family

Parents   C. V. Rogers, Claremore, I.T.

Brothers _____

Sisters (If any married give husbands name and address).

    J. T. McSpadden &
    C. L. Lane [Chelsea, I.T.]
    Mrs. May Yocum
    Fort Worth, Texas

11 + To Be Answered When the Person Examined is a Woman

A. Have you had any menstrual disorder, or symptoms of uterine or ovarian disease, or any disease or tumor of the breast? _____

B. Have you borne children, and if so, how many and how recently?

_____

C. Have you suffered abortions or serious troubles in labor? _____

D. Date of Marriage? _____ E. Are you now pregnant? _____

F. Have you passed the climacteric? _____ G. Are you engaged to be married within the next two years? _____

I certify that my answers to the foregoing questions are correctly recorded by the Medical Examiner.

Dated at ___Talala I.T.___ State of ___Cherokee Nation___
the ___2nd___ day of ___Sept.___ 1898
Witness: ___E. Y. Bass___ M.D.[3]   ___William Penn Rogers___
                                                          Signature of the Person Examined

12. Figure and general appearance? ___Erect___ 13. Apparent age? _18_ years.

14. Weight? _145_ lbs. 15. Height? _5_ feet _7_ inches. 16. Race? ___White___

17. Measurement of abdomen at level of umbilicus? ___32 *[fraction obscured]*___ inches.

18. Of the chest under vest, at level of 4th rib, at full inspiration? _34 1/2_ inches.

19. Of the chest under vest, at level of 4th rib, at de[compressed?] expiration? _31 1/2_ inches.

20. Number of respirations per minute? _20_

21. Is there anything abnormal in the character of the respirations? _No_

22. Is there any indication of disease, either acute or chronic, of the respiratory apparatus? _No_

23. State the rate and other qualities of the pulse ___76 full & strong___

24. Is it intermittent or irregular? _No_

25. Is there any indication of disease of the heart? _No_

26. Is there any thickening or degeneration of the r[en]al or temporal arteries? _No_

27. Is the hepatic area sensitive on percussion or enlarged or diminished in size? _No_

28. Test urine voided at time of this examination, and state whether clear or turbid ___Clear___

a. Specific gravity? 1022   b. action? Acid

c. Presence of Albumen? None   d. Of sugar? None

e. Result of examination [with] the Microscope? XXX

f. Do you know that the applicant passed the urine you have examined? Yes

29. How long have you known the applicant? Seven years

30. Give some mark of identification None—

31. Is there any bodily malformation? Or impairment of sight or hearing? Or loss of any part of any member? If so, give full particulars. No

32. Has the applicant been successfully vaccinated? Yes

33. Has the applicant h[ernias]? If so, state kind and proper truss to be worn No

34. In your opinion is the [applicant] affected by residence or occupation? No

35. Are you satisfied that everything has been fully stated as to the physical condition, habits, and personal and family history of the applicant? Yes

36. Do you without reservation recommend the applicant for insurance? Yes

37. What person or persons other than the applicant and examiner were present at this examination? None

I certify that I have made this examination at Talala, I.T. on this 2nd day of September 1898} E. Y. Bass, M.D.

Medical Examiner

Remarks.

There was never any consumption in family on neither side.

PDS, with autograph insertions. The Mutual Life Insurance Co. of New York, "Gift to the Nation," OkClaW.

1. Rogers is not including childhood diseases and accidental injuries here; we know, for example, that he was just recovering from a bout of the measles when his sisters contracted typhoid fever and his mother died after caring for them in May 1890. He also injured himself when the gun he was using accidentally discharged while he was showing off drills he had learned while at military school to local friends in June 1897 (*CP,* 5 June 1897).

2. Rogers's memory regarding the specifics of his family differs in some respects from documented evidence. His mother, who was born in October 1839, was fifty years and seven months old (not forty-eight) when she died. His brother, Robert, died two days before his seventeenth birthday (not at age eighteen). Sallie McSpadden was thirty-five years old in 1898, Maud Lane was twenty-nine, and May Yocum was twenty-five. May was living in Fort Worth, Tex., temporarily in September 1898, but her last name

was Stine, not Yocum. She had married Fort Worth resident Frank Stine in August 1898. Rogers lists his deceased brother Robert with two of his living sisters; below that he states that two Rogers siblings died in infancy. That number was actually three (Elizabeth, Zoe, and Homer). His mother's father, Martin Matthew Schrimsher, died on the return migration home from Texas after the end of the Civil War—the explanation that a cyclone was involved in the death seems to be an original one. Schrimsher was fifty-nine at the time of his death, not seventy. Rogers's mother's mother, Elizabeth Hunt Gunter Schrimsher, was seventy-four at the time of her death in 1877. Rogers's father, Clem V. Rogers, would not be sixty until his next birthday in January 1899.

3. Dr. E. Y. Bass of Talala was a member of the Indian Territory Medical Association and a specialist in pediatrics. He was practicing medicine in Talala in the early 1890s. By 1905 he was one of two doctors in the growing town, sharing a private practice with Dr. Freer (and later, with Dr. Ramsey). His office was one of several service and business establishments in Talala, including a general merchandise store and W. C. Rogers's large clothing store (Clinton, "The Indian Territory Medical Association," 43; *HRC*, 247, 294, 337).

Notices from the *Cherokee Vindicator*
28 October 1898
Claremore, I.T.

Rogers returned to his home in the fall of 1898 after working as a ranch hand in Texas and other western states. In August of that year his father moved to a home in Claremore.¹ Clem V. Rogers was named vice president and a director of the First National Bank in Claremore and became increasingly involved in the politics of the Cherokee Nation.² When his son returned to Indian Territory, Clem V. Rogers decided to let him manage the family ranch and gave him a herd of cattle with which to stock it.³

W. P. Rogers, son of C. V. Rogers of this city, was down from Talala Monday visiting his parents. Mr. Rogers reports his cattle in good shape for the winter.

C. V. Rogers, at his home, corner of Sixth Street and Muskogee Avenue, has a system of lights that are as fine as any electric lights ever produced. The light is made by a machine purchased from the Bay Light Gas Machine Co. of Fort Smith, Ark. and are very cheap, considering the quality of light furnished. The plant was put in about two months since and Mr. Rogers would not do without them for double their cost.

The lights are bright and steady and one small jet lights a large room. Mr. Rogers says the cost for seven lights every night in the year will not exceed $15 and there are no lamps to clean and the machine that runs the lights are no

When Rogers visited Amarillo in 1926 he met his old friends from the Higgins area. *Left to right:* T. H. Black, William A. (Bill) Johnson, Will Rogers, and Frank Ewing *(PHM)*.

trouble whatever. If you have not seen these lights it would pay you to investigate them. Every business house in the city should have them.[4]

PD. Printed in *CV,* 28 October 1898.[5]

1. Will Rogers's mother, Mary America Schrimsher Rogers, had died on 28 May 1890. Clem V. Rogers married his former housekeeper, Mary Bibles, on 8 June 1893. Around 13 November 1897 Clem V. Rogers purchased a two-story house at Sixth and Muskogee Streets in Claremore, previously owned by G. H. Harlow, and he and his wife made it their home. Mary Bibles Rogers died on 17 January 1900 from complications from surgery necessitated by meningitis. On 27 January 1900, Clem V. Rogers moved to rooms in the First National Bank building in Claremore, and he lived there until his death in 1911 *(CP,* 20 January and 27 January 1900, 3 November 1911; Collings, *Old Home Ranch,* 78; see Biographical Appendix entries, ROGERS, Clement Vann, and ROGERS, Mary Bibles).

2. Clem V. Rogers's friend, William E. Halsell, founded the First National Bank of Vinita in 1891; its charter was granted on 8 March 1892. In 1894 Halsell established the First National Bank in Claremore and became its president. At first it was located in a makeshift tent on the corner of what is now J. M. Davis Boulevard and Will Rogers Boulevard; eventually a small building was constructed. As vice president, Clem Rogers served on the board of directors with Halsell, W. A. Graham, J. O. Hall, F. A. Neilson, J. G. Rocker, J. M. Taylor, F. B. Fite, and R. L. Comer. C. F. Godbey was the treasurer

(DuPriest et al., *Cherokee Recollections,* 155; Holden, *Ranching Saga,* 159–60; see also Biographical Appendix entry, HALSELL, William Electious).

Clem V. Rogers was appointed to several commissions by the Cherokee government in the 1890s. In 1893 he served on a commission to appraise the improvements intruders (primarily white settlers) had made on the land they occupied in the Cherokee Nation. In 1896 he was appointed to a delegation to reach an agreement with the Dawes Commission regarding the dispensation of Cherokee landholdings and other matters. In 1898 he was appointed to another delegation to deliberate with the Dawes Commission over citizenship and allotment issues. The Congressional Act of 3 March 1893 empowered the Dawes Commission to negotiate with the Five Tribes to dissolve their tribal governments and to arbitrate allotment agreements (Keith, "Clem Rogers and His Influence on Oklahoma History," 68, 78–79; Wardell, *Political History of the Cherokee Nation,* 318–22; Woodward, *Cherokees,* 320).

3. Collings, *Old Home Ranch,* 78–79.

4. Apparently Clem V. Rogers was one of the first people in the town to have electricity. On 7 January 1901 the Claremore city council issued a charter to J. V. Wofford and Co. for electric lights, pending an affirmative committee report *(HRC,* 21).

5. The *Cherokee Vindicator* newspaper was published in Claremore and printed in 1898 and 1899 by Callaway and Callaway. It carried international, national, and local news; its masthead motto was "Take What Is in Sight and Rustle for More" *(CV,* 21 October 1898–12 May 1899, OkClaW).

Notice from the *Cherokee Vindicator*
28 April 1899
Claremore, I. T.

Sightseeing tours were a popular recreational activity in the Claremore area. Farmers and ranchers would form a caravan of wagons, buggies, and hackneys and would travel to a neighboring state.[1] Tourism continued with the coming of the railroad. Will Rogers joined one of these excursions to San Antonio in April 1899.[2] The trip gave Rogers an opportunity to see many historic sites associated with the city's Spanish-Mexican heritage and the Texas revolution and to discover the Hispanic roots of cowboy culture.[3] He would return in October 1901 as a participant in steer-roping contests held at the San Antonio International Fair.

Will[4] Rogers, son of C. V. Rogers of this city, and Austin Rider[5] of Talala arrived home this week from a trip to San Antonio, and other points in Texas. The boys report a pleasant time.

PD. Printed in *CV,* 28 April 1899.

1. *HRC,* 34.
2. On 12 April 1899 the Vinita *Daily Chieftain* reported: "A delightful Place May Be Easily Visited. There will be quite a number of persons go[ing] to San Antonio next Wednesday on the Katy excursion, but it is possible some of our people are overlooking 'a good thing.' There is probably no place within the confines of the United States, of equal distance, so unlike the United States and so much Spanish and Mexican as San

Antonio. Probably half the population are able to converse in Spanish and a great many in no other language. Then it is by far the pleasantest spot in Texas to visit, at this time of year, to say nothing of the special attractions provided and the historical incident connected with the city. The M. K. and T. will sell a round trip ticket for this excursion at $10; train leaves at 4:12 a.m., April 19. Passengers may return on any train leaving San Antonio up to 24th." The *Daily Chieftain* reported that Will Rogers was in San Antonio on excursion in its 12 April and 26 April 1899 editions.

3. San Antonio was founded as a Franciscan mission (San Antonio de Valero, later the Alamo); and the presidio of San Antonio de Bexar in 1718. It became the civil municipality of San Fernando in 1731. The three consolidated in the 1790s and became a city in 1809. Predominantly Spanish in culture, San Antonio figured importantly in the Mexican and Texan revolutions. In the 1860s and 1870s it became known as a colorful Wild West town and an important livestock center in the heart of the Texas cattle country. Rogers's familiarity with San Antonio and its Spanish culture helped form the basis of his curiosity and interest in Argentina *(Historic San Antonio, 1700–1900;* O'Neill et al., *San Antonio Historic Survey;* Smith, H., *Charm of Old San Antonio; WNGD,* 1062–63).

4. This newspaper story probably represents the first time that Rogers was referred to as Will rather than Willie or W. P. in print.

5. Austin Rider (b. 1871) was the brother of James (Jim) Hall Rider, a cowpuncher friend and an excellent roper, who worked on a nearby ranch (Austin Rider, enrollment no. 4101, Census of 1890, Cooweescoowee District, p. 185, OkHi; Eastern Cherokee Application of James H. Rider [Miller Roll], 1906, OkTahN; Keith, *Boy's Life of Will Rogers,* 148–56; *OCF* 1:1; see also Biographical Appendix entry, RIDER, James Hall).

Article from the *Claremore Progress*
8 July 1899
Claremore, I.T.

Many communities in the Indian Territory and in western states held colorful Fourth of July celebrations that included steer roping and other equestrian events featuring local cowboys. The Independence Day rodeos would later become a tradition in many towns across America.[1] Claremore held a Fourth of July celebration in 1899 that attracted a large crowd from the surrounding area. Rogers entered the steer-roping contest, winning first prize. It was his first performance before a crowd and, as Rogers later wrote, had a great influence on his career.[2]

CLAREMORE'S BIG CELEBRATIONS.

The Third and Fourth of July were gala days in Claremore. The big two days' celebration came off on schedule time and was a success in every feature. Early on the morning of the Third the people began to arrive and the town was full of pleasure seekers until the programme was concluded on the evening of the Fourth. The attendance from the country, and neighboring towns was estimated at 2,500 persons, but when Claremore turned out en masse on the Fourth there were perhaps 4,000 persons on the grounds. . . .

The morning of the Fourth dawned dismally. Rain fell in torrents, and the prospects for getting out the American bird to idolize and honor on its birthday seemed forlorn. But all the drooping spirits were revived when the rain ceased, the sun came forth, the band began to play and the fun started. . . .

The last on the program, and the most exciting of the days' sports, was the roping contest. Ten entered the contest, but only a few of them were in any way successful. Will Rogers won first money, roping and tieing his cow in 52 seconds.[3] Sam Dickson won second in 1 minute and 7 1/2 seconds, and W. S. Miles secured third prize in 1 minute and 19 seconds. The other contestants had bad luck of one kind or another and failed to get in the race.

The free beef and bread were liberally partaken of and out of ten beeves slaughtered only the bones were left to tell the tale. All in all, Claremore's celebration was the biggest event in the Territory this year. Everybody will come next year.

PD. Printed in *CP,* 8 July 1899.

1. Robertson, M., *Rodeo*, 94.
2. On 4 July 1932, Rogers attended a rodeo at Nowata, Okla. The event caused him to reminisce about the 1899 Claremore event in his weekly article: "I was just thinking when I was looking at that show the Fourth, it was at a little Fourth of July celebration at Claremore just 35 miles from this one, on July Fourth, 1899, (Boy that's 33 years ago) they had a steer roping, and I went into it. It was the first one I ever was in; the very first thing I ever did in the way of appearing before an audience in my life. Just such a show as I was looking at now, (only ours was not so skilled, all these things have advanced). Well, as I look back on it now I know that that had quite an influence in my little career, for I kinder got to running around to 'em, and the first thing I know I was just plum 'Honery' and fit for nothing but show business. Once you are a showman you are plum ruined for manual labor again" (*TDW,* 17 July 1932).
3. Rogers won $18.50 (*CC,* 7 July 1899).

Article from the *Claremore Progress*
19 August 1899
Claremore, I.T.

This article reports Will Rogers's participation in a cakewalk party. The cakewalk was both a type of ragtime music and a high-kicking, strutting dance style that was popular from 1897 to the beginning of World War I. Derived from slave culture and based on syncopated piano music, the cakewalk became a dance craze in the 1890s. Young people across the country participated in cakewalk parties and annual cakewalk jubilees, or championships, that featured winning dancers from small-town contests. As the lyrics of one 1899 song put it: "Never saw the like in all my days / Everybody's got the ragtime craze . . . / Cakewalk music, it fills the air, / You can't escape it 'cause it's everywhere."[1]

Brilliant "Tacky" Party.

Quite a happy affair in the social world was the "tacky party" given by Misses Clara and Mattie Hagood at their home east of Oolagah, on Wednesday evening, August 10. An important feature of the evening was the "cake walk." The prize, a generous sized ginger cake, was awarded to Vic Foreman[2] and Willie Rogers. Every body did well, however, and deserved some of that "ginger bread," which they got, with the recipe for making same to "take home to ma."

At a late hour the guests took their departure with many declarations of a most delightful time. . . .[3]

PD. Printed in *CP,* 19 August 1899.

1. The cakewalk developed in slave culture before the Civil War, as slaves entertained one another by mocking the self-satisfied behaviors of elite whites. A cake was awarded as a prize to "the couple performing the most elaborate or original routine" (Ewen, *All the Years of American Popular Music,* 119). It was adopted into minstrel acts and later into vaudeville. The dance craze of the 1890s emerged in part out of white imitation of blacks in minstrel shows, and cakewalk music of the period was characterized by derogatory and satiric images of African Americans created and perpetuated by black and white composers and performers, music publishers, and largely white consumers. As one historian of the period has pointed out, "cover illustrations adorning sheet music of the 1890s became more colorful and insulting to blacks than at any time in the history of American popular song" (Dennison, *Scandalize My Name,* 354). The editors of the *Musical Courier* (1899) took a critical view of the new phase of popular culture. "A wave of vulgar, filthy and suggestive music has inundated the land," they stated. "The pabulum of theatre and summer hotel orchestras is coon music. Nothing but ragtime prevails and the cakewalk with its obscene posturings, its lewd gestures. It is artistically and morally depressing and should be suppressed by press and pulpit" (Whitcomb, *After the Ball,* 16; see also Will Rogers to Folks, 28 January–6 March 1903, n. 3, below).
2. Victoria (Vic) Lipe Foreman (1883–1968) was the daughter of Ada Carter McClellan Foreman (1853–1936) and Stephen Taylor Foreman (1848–91) (son of the Presbyterian missionary Rev. Stephen Foreman [1807–81]). Victoria Foreman studied at the Cherokee National Female Academy and Central College in Lexington, Mo. With her sisters, Ada Foreman (1881–1919) and Jennie Foreman (1878–1959), she was one of the founders of the Pocahontas Club in 1899 and served in various capacities, including president. She married James Stevenson Kennedy on 18 May 1906, and they were the parents of four children (*As I Recollect,* 33–40; DuPriest et al., *Cherokee Recollections,* 6–7, 10, 14, 106, 282; *HRC,* 194–95, 289; Starr, *History of the Cherokee Indians,* 637; see also Article from the *Claremore Progress,* 19 August 1899, n. 2, below).
3. The article went on to list the guests, who included some of Rogers's closest boyhood friends: Casper and Clint Lipe, Charles McClellan, Tom and Gordon Lane, as well as Rogers's sister May Stine and her new husband, Frank Stine, with May's son Johnny Yocum.

Article from the *Claremore Progress*
19 August 1899
Claremore, I. T.

POCAHONTAS CLUB[1] ENTERTAINED.

The Pocahontas Club was entertained at the residence of Mrs. Ada Foreman[2] Thursday of last week.

Each member and quite a number of visitors enjoyed themselves immensely. The art exhibition was very attractive and created a great deal of amusement. Miss Hattie Johnston, one of the guests, won the prize by naming the greatest number of the exhibits, the prize being a beautiful bouquet of tea roses. Charley McClellan received the booby prize, a lovely bunch of bachelor buttons. . . .

Will Rogers, Herman[,] Casper and Clint Lipe were received into the club as honorary members.[3]

Refreshments were served at seven o'clock, consisting of melon, ice cream and cake.

The club will meet at Mr. & Mrs. C. M. McClellan's[4] next Thursday.

PD. Printed in *CP,* 19 August 1899.

1. The Pocahontas Club was founded on 29 June 1899 by some young girls who were neighbors in the Oowala community, which was located across the Verdigris River and about seven miles from the Rogers ranch. The founders were the daughters of the area's pioneer families, the Lipes, Lanes, McClellans, Starrs, Foremans, Bards, and Dannenburgs. On 29 June 1899 the first meeting was held at the home of Dr. and Mrs. A. J. Lane and included Nannie and Lola Lipe; Mary Bell and Lettie Starr; Mary, Pearl, Susan, and Lela McClellan; Jennie, Ada, and Vic Foreman; Elizabeth, Sally, Mae, and Love Bard; Trixie Dannenburg; Ida Mae Collins; and Gazelle (Scrap) Lane. On 14 July 1899 a meeting to complete the club's organization was held at the Lane home and hosted by the Lane daughters, Gazelle and Ida Mae Collins. Membership in the club was limited initially to women of Indian descent, but a month later they decided to admit several of their brothers and local boys, including Will Rogers, as honorary members. Rogers supposedly played a major role in convincing the female members to let him and his friends join the club. Other honorary members included Tom Bard; George Collins; Thomas, Gordon, and Denny Lane; Herman, Casper, and Clint Lipe; Sos, Steve, and Charley McClellan; Will and Clem Musgrove; and Emmett Starr (Starr, who grew up in Oowala, later became a physician and was the author of the pioneer *History of the Cherokee Indians;* see *As I Recollect,* 165–67; *HRC,* 402).

Rogers was very friendly with the Oowala boys and girls, often visited their homes, and regularly attended club meetings. The club was social and functioned as a meeting place during the summer for the local boys and girls, many of whom went away to boarding schools. They met in homes of various members, where they staged parties with contests and guessing games, discussed literature, and ended the evenings with refreshments. They also organized picnics, hayrides, square dances, swimming parties, jack-

Members of the Pocahontas Club photographed about 1901. *Top row (left to right):* Ada Foreman, Lettie Starr, Flora Foreman. *Middle row:* Trixie Dannenberg, Bess Schrimsher, Nancy Eva (Nannie) Lipe, Cora Hicks, Lola Vann Lipe, Bessie Barrett, Gazelle (Scrap) Lane, Mary Starr. *Front row:* Mary McClellan, Ida Collins, Juliette Melvina (Bunt) Schrimsher, Zoe Bullette, and Mattie Easton. Rogers was an honorary member of the club *(Claremore Progress Publishing Co.).*

rabbit chases, and mound-climbing trips, and staged local traditional Indian stomp dances. The club, which is still in existence today, aims to foster the history, traditions, and culture of Indian tribes. Membership is granted to individuals with Indian (primarily Cherokee) roll numbers or to direct descendants of enrolled Cherokee Indians. Each year the Pocahontas Club presents a ceremony honoring Rogers at the Will Rogers Memorial on 4 November, the anniversary of his birth *(As I Recollect,* 1–2, 162–64; *CP,* 23 August 1902; DuPriest et al., *Cherokee Recollections;* Love, "The Pocahontas Club"; Sunday et al., *Gah Dah Gwa Stee,* 14).

    2. Born at Cane Hill, Ark., Ada Carter McClellan Foreman (1853–1936) was the daughter of Sarah Truesdale McClellan (b. 1823) and Evan White McClellan (1811–82). She married Stephen Taylor Foreman on 28 April 1874. In 1874 they moved from Cane Hill to the Cooweescoowee District and became pioneer ranchers in the Oowala area. Her brother, Charles McClure McClellan, was married to her husband's sister, Jennie Lind Foreman McClellan. When her husband died in 1891, she was forced to raise her five daughters (Sarah, Jessie, Jennie, Ada, and Victoria) and two young sons (Taylor and

Perry) in their ranch home near Oowala. She was involved in many educational and religious actives in the Claremore area. In 1935 she returned to Cane Hill, where she died in 1936 (*As I Recollect*, 25–28, 33–40; DuPriest et al., *Cherokee Recollections*, 6–7, 10, 14, 106, 282; *HRC*, 194–95, 289; Starr, *History of the Cherokee Indians*, 637).

    3. Herman, Casper, and Clint Lipe were the sons of Margaret Emma Thompson Lipe (b. 1849) and Clark Charlesworth Lipe (1847–1901), a merchant, cattleman, and Cherokee public official. The Lipe family lived near the Verdigris River east of Oologah. The three sons and another brother, Clarence (1891–1971), were neighborhood friends of Rogers in his youth. John Casper Lipe (b. 1878) was a graduate of the Cherokee National Male Seminary in 1899 and Spauldings Commercial College in Kansas City. He later resided with his wife, Anna Belle Price (b. 1887), in Rogers County. In 1901 Clint Lipe was killed in a fall from a horse while helping Will Rogers and others during a roundup. Rogers rode a horse to the nearest doctor, but Lipe was dead before the doctor arrived to give him aid (Croy, *Our Will Rogers*, 91–92, 218; DuPriest et al., *Cherokee Recollections*, 6, 9; *HRC*, 279–80; O'Beirne, *Indian Territory*, 310–11; *OCF* 1:57, 2:119; Starr, *History of the Cherokee Indians*, 568).

    4. This refers to Charles McClure McClellan (1845–1927) and Jennie Lind Foreman McClellan (1850–1911), parents of Charles White McClellan, Will Rogers's young friend. The McClellans had a ranch on the Verdigris River near Oowala (*HRC*, 289; see also Biographical Appendix entry, McClellan, Charles White).

Notice from the *Indian Chieftain*
5 October 1899
Vinita, I. T.

Will Rogers once wrote in his weekly syndicated article that his show-business career dated from his appearance at a roping and riding contest at the annual St. Louis fair in 1899.[1] Colonel Zack Mulhall,[2] a pioneer showman and railroad livetock purchasing agent who owned a large ranch in Oklahoma Territory, organized this contest and many others. During the next several years Rogers and other cowboys from the Indian Territory appeared in many roping and riding events at fairs, carnivals, conventions, and exhibitions.[3]

ROPING AND RIDING.

Territory Entries at St. Louis Fair Contest.[4]

Among the list of those entered in the St. Louis fair riding and roping contests appear the following, residents of this territory:

Ed Ramsey, Inola.[5]
W. P. Rogers, Oolagah.[6]
B. B. Posey, Wagoner.[7]
C. W. Burns, Claremore.
C. C. Jackson, Chouteau.[8]

Ribbon from the 1899 St. Louis Annual Fair roping contest, which Rogers called an important turning point in his show-business career *(OkClaW)*.

Hick Miller, Ft. Gibson.[9]
J. W. Bell, Chouteau.
George Moore, Chouteau.

PD. Printed in *IC*, 5 October 1899.

1. Rogers wrote: "My business career kinder dates from the time I first run into the Col. It was in 1899 at the St. Louis fair, (not the World's fair) just the big St. Louis fair they held every year. They had decided as an attraction they would put on a Roping and Riding Contest. They were not called Rodeo's, or Stampedes, in those days they were just what they are, a 'Roping and Riding Contest.' Well I was pretty much of a Kid, but had just happened to have won the first and about my only Contest at home in Claremore, Okla., and then we read about them wanting entries for this big Contest at St. Louis. Well some one sent in my name, and the first thing I knew I was getting transportation for myself and pony to the affair. . . . I dident get very far in this St. Louis Contest. I made the serious mistake of catching my steer and he immediately jerked me and my Pony down for our trouble. But that gave me a touch of 'Show business' in a way, so that meant I was ruined for life as far as actual employment was concerned" *(CWP,* 15 October 1931).

2. Mulhall, whose real name was probably Zachariah P. Vandeveer, spelled his nickname either Zach or Zack. Newspaper articles and playbills referring to Mulhall and his Wild West show use both forms. In correspondence he spelled his name Zack, and this spelling will be consistently used here in references to Mulhall (Olds, "Story of Lucille," 10; Stansbury, *Lucille Mulhall,* v; see also Biographical Appendix entry, MULHALL, Colonel Zack).

3. Mulhall's troupe of riders and ropers also included a cowboy band. At St. Louis he hired the St. Louis First Regiment Band and dressed them in cowboy outfits. Later the band went under different names including the Rough Riders' Band, Mulhall's Cowboy Band, and the Frisco Line Territorial Band (a publicity ploy since Mulhall then worked as a livestock agent for the St. Louis and San Francisco railway line). At these contests Mulhall would challenge the audience to compete against the band members in steer roping and bronco riding. Mulhall cleverly put some of his best riders in the band, including Rogers, who pretended to play the trombone. Rogers was often called on to compete in the audience contests (Cheney, "Lucile Mulhall, Fabulous Cowgirl," 14–15; Day, ed., *Autobiography,* 13; Day, *Will Rogers,* 30–31; Ketchum, *Will Rogers,* 62; O'Donnell, "My Friend Will," 21–22; Stansbury, *Lucille Mulhall,* 11–19).

4. After the Civil War the growth of St. Louis was stimulated by the railroad. Consequently, it became a leading midwestern agricultural, trade, and manufacturing

center and had a population of 575,238 in 1900. The 1899 event in which Rogers participated was the city's annual fair. In 1904 St. Louis held the Louisiana Purchase Exposition (the centennial celebration of the Louisiana Purchase, an event popularly known as the St. Louis World's Fair), where Rogers performed in Zack Mulhall's Wild West show and other productions (*EA* 24:145–51; *WNGD*, 1051).

5. Located in southern Rogers County, Okla., Inola's post office was established in 1890. Inola means "black fox" in Cherokee (Shirk, *Oklahoma Place Names*, 109).

6. Oologah was founded in 1889 as a railway switch stop on the Kansas and Arkansas Valley Railway, which ran from Coffeyville, Kans., to Van Buren, Ark. The town was named for either Houston Benge, whose Cherokee name was Oologguhah, or for the Cherokee chief Dark Cloud. The town grew in the 1890s along with its cattle, coal, and wheat production. The Rogers ranch was located a short distance northwest of Oologah (*As I Recollect*, 178; *History of Oologah*, 9; Shirk, *Oklahoma Place Names*, 156).

7. The county seat of Wagoner County, Okla., Wagoner's post office was established in 1888. The town, which is located about thirty miles south of Claremore, was named for "Big Foot" Wagoner of Parsons, Kans., a train dispatcher (Shirk, *Oklahoma Place Names*, 215; *WNGD*, 1312).

8. Located in southwestern Mayes County, Okla., Chouteau's post office was established in 1871. The town is named for Jean Pierre Chouteau (Shirk, *Oklahoma Place Names*, 46).

9. An important military post located on the Grand River and established in 1824, Fort Gibson was used by the federal government until 1890. The town surrounding the fort was incorporated on 27 November 1873. It was named for Col. George Gibson, chief of the Army Commissary Department. Will Rogers's maternal grandmother and grandfather—Elizabeth Gunter Schrimsher and Martin Matthew Schrimsher—had a town house at Fort Gibson. Clem V. Rogers and Mary America Schrimsher were married there in 1858 (Collings, *Old Home Ranch*, 10; Gideon, *Indian Territory*, 160–63; Hewes, *Occupying the Cherokee Country of Oklahoma*, 22–23; Shirk, *Oklahoma Place Names*, 81–82; *WRFT*, 110–11).

Notice from the *Claremore Progress*
7 October 1899
Claremore, I.T.

Willie Rogers left early Wednesday morning for St. Louis where he will take part in the roping contest at the fair there. A car was furnished him by the Frisco for his horse and feed.[1]

PD. Printed in *CP,* 7 October 1899.

1. The St. Louis and San Francisco railroad (formerly the Atlantic and Pacific), known locally as the Frisco, ran through Claremore. Rogers and the other cowboys shipped their roping horses by freight car and often rode in the caboose to care for them (Croy, *Our Will Rogers*, 75).

Article from the *St. Louis Post-Dispatch*
8 October 1899
St. Louis, Mo.

Rogers appeared in several events at the St. Louis Annual Fair in both roping and riding contests. On October 7 Rogers appeared with some of the best ropers in the world in a contest that was described as the "International Championship of the World at Roping Steers." The great Mexican roper Vincente Oropeza, whom Rogers had seen perform earlier at the 1893 Chicago World Columbian Exposition, participated in this event.[1]

Cow-Punchers in the Arena
An Exciting Exhibition of a Great Western Sport
Astonishing Feats of Horsemanship and Thrilling Rough-Riding
After Cattle—How the Steers Were Thrown and Tied

Three inches of rope, or the lack of it, rather, prevented Bob Miller from making $700 in a little more than a minute at the Fair Grounds yesterday afternoon. Skill and pluck won the coveted prize for Gus Pickett of Decatur, Tex., the champion cow puncher of the world.

Thousands of persons were witnesses to Miller's bad luck and Pickett's good fortune—thousands of men and women who yelled themselves hoarse in appreciation of a typical American sport—cow roping. The exhibition was conceded by experts who saw it to be the best of its kind ever seen here. There was never an instant when the contest was not intensely exciting. Not one of the men entered failed to show the stuff that was in him—the nerve and cool determination that is a staple article in the Western cattle country.

The contestants were the best in their line, men born with the spirit of adventure and reared in the saddle. They came from all parts of the country west of the Mississippi and two of them from a point east of it. The inducement to competition was alluring. The prizes consisted of $700 for the best roper, $200 for the second and $100 for the third.

Contestants were required to lasso and throw a steer and tie at least three of its feet together in such a way that it could not rise. The prizes went to those who did this in the shortest time.

The roping was done in the field of the mile race track. In the center of the field a pen had been erected in which to confine the steers. The man who was to do the roping took his position to the right of the gate of this pen, as viewed from the grand stand. Fifty yards from the gate a horseman was stationed with a red flag which he dropped as the steer passed him. This was the signal for the

Vincente Oropeza, the famed Mexican rope artist, inspired Will Rogers when he saw Oropeza perform with Buffalo Bill's Wild West show at the Chicago World's Fair in 1893. Rogers later competed against Oropeza in steer roping at the St. Louis Annual Fair in 1899 *(Keith Collection, OkU)*.

contestant to ride in pursuit of the steer. When the steer heard the hoof beats behind him he would scamper away across the field with the rider almost at his flank swinging his lariat and preparing to throw.

Of a sudden the loop of rope would go sailing through the air. If it settled over the horns of the steer the battle was on in earnest. It is one thing to get a rope over a steer's horns and another to throw him up, like a Thanksgiving turkey. As soon as he feels the rope he becomes a four-footed, double-horned demon. The rope must be thrown over his back and about his legs. Then comes a quick swerve of the horse and a sudden jerk. If the rider is skillful and the horse well trained Mr. Steer's feet are pulled from under him and he goes about three feet in the air and comes down so hard the breath is knocked out of him. Then nothing remains but to tie him.

But you've got to get him down first.

Each man in yesterday's contest was allowed only two casts of the lariat. . . .

Then the crowd got its first taste of the true quality of this Western sport, when B. B. Posey of Wagoner, I.T., started in pursuit of an active young steer. He overtook it within 100 yards of the pen, but missed his first throw. The steer swerved and made for the west end of the field, with Posey following closely, gathering his rope for the second throw as he went.

Over near the water jumps he threw his lasso. The loop settled over the animal's horns. Quick as a shot the cowboy rode around the bull and a second later the first fall was scored. Posey, notwithstanding his miss on the first throw, had the bull securely tied one minute and thirty-four seconds after it was liberated from the pen. It was a great performance which won him applause, not only from the crowd in the grand stand but from his competitors as well. His score remained the best until after the programme was half finished.

W. P. Rogers of Oologah, I.T., had a long chase before he could get close enough to lasso his steer and the best time he could make was 2:39. . . .

Vincente Oropeza, the champion roper of Mexico, was the next out. A bad horse probably lost him the money. He dropped his steer on the second throw and completed the tie-up in 3:39. . . . Then came Gus Pickett of Decatur, Tex., the champion of the world, with a record of 32 seconds. Pickett threw and tied his steer so quickly it took the crowd's breath away. He overtook it a few yards from the signal flag, lassoed it and got around it, threw it and tied it almost before anybody realized what was happening. . . .

Pickett, who won first prize, went into the contest with his left leg in plaster of paris. It was broken a few weeks ago.

PD. Printed in the *St. Louis Post-Dispatch*, 8 October 1899. Headlines abridged.

1. Vincente Oropeza appeared in several other events during the fair. An article describing Oropeza's participation in a 5 October riding event appeared in the *St. Louis Post-Dispatch* of 6 October 1899 along with a drawing of Oropeza, called the "Champion Roper of Old Mexico." Oropeza was simultaneously performing with Buffalo Bill's Wild West show at the fair. The cowboys also provided entertainment on the last day of the fair when the famous African American cowboy Bill Pickett displayed his famous bulldogging technique and "showed the crowd how a steer could be subdued without the use of a rope" (*St. Louis Post-Dispatch* 9 October 1899). On the same program the young Lucille Mulhall beat champion rider Bruce Norton in a horse race. She had also displayed her riding talents at the 5 October event. See Biographical Appendix entry, OROPEZA, Vincente.

To Betty Blake
5 January 1900
Oolagah, I.T.

Will Rogers first met his future wife, Betty (Bettie) Blake,[1] during her visit to Oologah in late fall 1899. She had come from her home in Rogers,[2] Ark., and was recovering from typhoid fever. During her stay of several months in Oologah she lived with her sister, Cora Blake Marshall, and brother-in-law, Will Marshall, who was a railroad station agent in the town. By chance Rogers encountered Blake in the depot, where he was picking up a package containing a banjo. They spent much time together at social gatherings and enjoyed their mutual fondness for the popular music of the times.[3] Betty Blake would play the piano while Will Rogers sang. Shortly after she returned home before Christmas,[4] Rogers sent her the following letter.

Oolagah. I.T. Jan. 5th ~~Agency~~ ▲ 1900 ▲

Miss Bettie Blake
Rogers Ark

My Dear Friend
No doubt you will be madly surprised on receipt of this *Epistle* But never the less I could not resist the temptation and I hope if you cannot do me the *great* favor of *droping* me a few lines you will at least excuse me for this I *cant help* it.

Well I know you are having a great time after being out among the "Wild Tribe" so long. Well I have had a great time this Xmas myself have not been at home three night in a month taken in every Ball in the Territory and everything else I hear of.

I was in Fort Gibson again last week to a Masque Ball I had a time but the Ball came near being a failure it was managed by Sidney Hagood which accounts for it.

The Oologah, I.T., train depot, where Will Rogers first encountered Betty Blake in 1899 (*OkClaW*).

I see Sandy[5] and the other folks real often. Kate[6] is still as pretty as ever and going with Doctor Place.[7] Lil[8] is just the *cutest* girl I know and I am as silly about her as ever.

Say you people never did come out home as you said you would and see us "Wooly Cowboys" rope a wild Steers   I have some pictures of it I think and if you want them I will send them to you if you will send me some of those Kodak Pictures you had up here of yourself and all those girls. Now isent that a "mamoth inducement for you" To have your pictures in lovely "Indian Wigwam"

I never have had that Swell Ball that we talked of when you were here   But if you had staid we would of had it but you would not stay long enough for us to show you a hot time we were just getting acquainted good when you left   If you will only come back up here we will endevor to do all that we can to make you have a time   all kinds of late songs but I know they are old to you there. dances. Skating. Sleigh Riding. Horse Back Riding of which you are an expert, and in fact every kind of amusement on the face of Gods footpiece

The first page and closing lines of Will Rogers's first letter to his future wife, written shortly after Betty Blake met him for the first time in Oologah (*OkClaW*).

Well I guess you have had ample suffiency of my nonsense so I will stop. Hoping you will take pity on this poor heart broken Cowpealer and haveing him rejoiceing over these ball prairies on receipt of a few words from you   I remain your True friend and Injun Cowboy

W P Rogers.

Oolagah
I.T.

ALS, rc. OkClaW. On United States Indian Service[9] letterhead.

1. The daughter of James Wyeth Blake (1845–82) and Amelia Crowder Blake (1845–1922), Bettie (Betty) Blake was born on 9 September 1879 in Silver Springs, Ark., and died in Pacific Palisades, Calif., on 21 June 1944. Silver Springs was renamed Monte Ne in 1900 by William Hope (Coin) Harvey (1851–1936), who built a luxurious pleasure and health resort in the town consisting of hotels, casino, auditorium, amphitheater, dance pavilion, and other structures. The building of a gigantic pyramid in Monte Ne celebrating civilization's achievements was never finished because of his death. Harvey gained fame in the 1890s as a colorful Populist and free-silver advocate, and as the author of *Coin's Financial School* (1894), a book advocating free silver to solve economic problems. One of Betty Blake's early beaus was Tom Harvey, a son of Coin Harvey (Croy, *Our Will Rogers*, 60–69; Ketchum, *Will Rogers*, 67–68). Newspaper articles about Betty Blake at this time in the *Rogers Democrat* refer to her as Bettie, and Will Rogers mostly called her Bettie during their courtship (BBC-RHM). After her marriage to Will Rogers she spelled her first name Betty. See Biographical Appendix entry, ROGERS, Betty Blake.

2. Located in Benton County in northwest Arkansas, Rogers was founded in 1881 as a railroad town on the St. Louis and San Francisco (Frisco) railway line. On 10 May 1881 the first Frisco passenger train arrived at Rogers and the depot was officially opened. Rogers grew quickly, boasting a population of thirteen hundred in 1882. The town was named in honor of Capt. Charles W. Rogers, popular vice president and general manager of the Frisco railroad. When Betty Blake's father died in 1882, the family moved five miles northwest to Rogers, Ark., where her mother became a dressmaker (BBC-RHM; Workers of the Writers' Program, *Arkansas*, 308–10; Miner, *St. Louis–San Francisco Transcontinental Railroad*, 96–98, 155–56; Snelling, "One of the Blake Girls"; *WNGD*, 1025).

3. Betty Blake studied piano and once gave a piano recital in Rogers, Ark. On 3 September 1899 the *Rogers Democrat* reported that she played the guitar before a group called the "Mas Luz" Circle. Several members of the Blake family were employed by the Frisco railroad, including her brother-in-law Will Marshall, her brother James K. (Sandy) Blake, and her sister Anna with her husband, Lee Adamson. In 1904 Betty Blake worked as a billing clerk for the Frisco railroad at Jenny Lind, Ark., where her brother Sandy was a depot agent (BBC-RHM; recital program, n.d., OkClaW; on Betty Blake's early life, see also Croy, *Our Will Rogers*, 60–69; Keith, *Boy's Life of Will Rogers*, 146–47; Ketchum, *Will Rogers*, 67–69; Rogers, *Will Rogers*, 12–21).

4. On 21 December 1899 the *Rogers Democrat* reported in its column called "Local Items" that "Miss Bettie Blake, who has been [in] Oolagah, I.T., for several months with her sister, Mrs. W. L. Marshall, returned home Monday night."

5. James K. (Sandy) Blake, Betty's brother, who later was a railway station agent at Nowata, I.T. (Snelling, "One of the Blake Girls," 43).

6. Kate Ellis's father Jake Ellis, and her mother operated the hotel in Oologah, and it was there at a supper that Will and Betty became better acquainted. It was rumored that Kate Ellis and Will Rogers had a close romantic attachment and intended to marry, but her father opposed it because he felt Rogers was too wild. Ellis and Rogers corresponded with each other while he was abroad in 1903. She became a schoolteacher and later married Robert W. Lewis and settled in Independence, Kans. (see Kate Ellis to Will Rogers, 15 February 1903, below; Croy, *Our Will Rogers,* 55, 71, 218–19, 342–43; Rogers, *Will Rogers,* 15–16; see also Biographical Appendix entry, ELLIS, Kate).

7. A Doctor Place was known as "Oologah's bachelor physician" (Rogers, *Will Rogers,* 15). Rogers could also have been refering to the Oologah physician Dr. Edgar Pleas (d. 1933) (whose name was pronounced like "place"), a graduate of the University of Arkansas Medical Department (see *History of Oologah,* 9; Clinton, "Indian Territory Medical Association," 32, 42, 43; Collins, R., *Will Rogers: Courtship and Correspondence,* 24).

8. Lil Ellis, sister of Kate Ellis.

9. The United States Indian Service was the federal government agency responsible for providing a wide range of services to tribal organizations. Under the secretary of the interior and as part of the United States Bureau of Indian Affairs (created in 1824), the Indian Service consisted of a large number of Indian commissioners, agents, field workers, inspectors, commissioners, and other employees involved in implementing the federal government's Indian policy (Stuart, *Indian Office*).

Article from the *Claremore Progress*
3 February 1900
Claremore, I.T.

When a smallpox scare in Oologah and other surrounding communities occurred, the town council passed a quarantine law that prohibited people coming into the town. When Rogers rode his horse into Oologah to get his mail and attempted to disregard the quarantine, he was arrested by the city marshal and fined by the mayor, William E. Sunday.[1]

Oolagah is enforcing its quarantine with a vengeance. Will Rogers, who lives near there, went into town one day this week and he was taken before the mayor and fined $5 for passing the quarantine line.[2] While their method of "fumigating" is a novelty in that line, it will probably prove effective against the present variety of "smallpox."

Deaths from smallpox in Claremore to date, none; cases recovered to date, 101; diagnosis of cases by Dr. Fortner that failed to pan out according to his diagnosis, three; sore arms from vaccination to date, 999; confined as result of vaccination, five; falling off in cases as a result of cold weather, 89 percent; those afraid of the disease, one—he from Vinita.[3]

PD. Printed in *CP,* 3 February 1900.

1. On 2 January 1900 the Claremore city council ordered the town marshal to prohibit from entering the city any visitors by train who were suspected of having smallpox. The Kansas and Arkansas Valley railway refused to pick up passengers and the Frisco railroad stopped mail delivery. When people supposedly afflicted quickly recovered, the scare proved false (Keith, *Boy's Life of Will Rogers,* 143–45; *HRC,* 18–19; Sunday et al., *Gah Dah Gwa Stee,* 78–79; see also Biographical Appendix entry, SUNDAY, William Esther).

2. Sunday, the mayor at the time, wrote that Rogers was fined $19.85 and that his friend Gordon Lane, who accompanied him, was fined the same amount. "Will wrote me out a check for both fines using the saddle for a table," recalled Sunday (Sunday et al., *Gah Dah Gwa Stee,* 78–79; see also *History of Oologah,* 11).

3. On 27 January 1900 seventeen cases of smallpox were reported in Claremore by Dr. Benjamin Fortner from Vinita, yet the fear of a large outbreak proved to be unfounded *(HRC,* 18–19).

Notice from the *Daily Chieftain*
10 March 1900
Vinita, I.T.

C. V. Rogers returned to Claremore yesterday from a tour through New Mexico looking for a location for a stock ranch, which he expects to put in charge of his son William when stocked.[1]

PD. Printed in *DC,*[2] 10 March 1900.

1. The Vinita *Daily Chieftain* also had reported on 17 February 1900 that Clem V. Rogers was planning to travel to New Mexico to locate a cattle ranch, and the newspaper then went on to say that he would put his son in charge of the ranch. On 12 April 1900 the Vinita *Indian Chieftain* reported that Clem V. Rogers had returned from New Mexico and was "favorably impressed with the country as a stock country." The ranch was never purchased.

2. The *Daily Chieftain* began in Vinita in the fall of 1891, edited by John Lynch Adair, former editor of the *Weekly Chieftain.* It had an irregular and short run until 1892, but reappeared on 3 October 1898 as the *Daily Chieftain* when it was published by M. E. Milford, publisher of the weekly *Indian Chieftain* and edited by D. M. Marrs. The four-page paper was published daily except Sunday and cost $4.80 annually (Foreman, C., *Oklahoma Imprints, 1835–1907,* 97; Littlefield and Parins, *American Indian and Alaska Native Newspapers and Periodicals,* 124–25).

To Betty Blake
14 March 1900
Oolagah, I.T.

This letter from Will Rogers to Betty Blake suggests a strain in their relationship.[1] Rogers had learned that Blake's friends were teasing her about her "Indian

Cowboy," and he felt intimidated about her social circle.[2] They saw each other twice in 1900, in the spring at Springfield, Mo., where Rogers participated in a steer-roping contest, and in the autumn at a street fair held at Fort Smith, Ark. They did not see each other again until they met at the 1904 St. Louis Louisiana Purchase Exposition.[3]

Oolagah Indian Territory
March, fourteenth, Nineteen Hundred.
"Headquarters Dog Iron Ranch"[4]
"Hillside Navy"

My Dear Bettie.

Now for me to attempt to express my delight for your sweet letter received would be utterly impossibe so will just put it mild and say I was *very very* much pleased.

I was also surprised for I thought you had forgotten your Cowbow (for I am yours as far as I am concerned)

Well I am still in the Land of the *Broncho* and the *Texas Steer* have not gone to New Mexico yet   dont know that I will go now for my Father is back and he dont much want me to go   I hope that I wont now for I can live in hopes of seeing you some day   I do wish you could come out this Spring   I will do everything in my power to make you have a good time even if the company was not so enjoyable.

I know you had a fine time when your Sweetheart[5] was down to see you. Oh! how I envy him for I would give all I possessed if I only knew that you cared something for me   for Bettie you may not believe it or care any thing about it but you do not know that you have made life miserable for one poor boy out in the B.I.T.[6]   but never the less you did for I think of you all the time and just wish that you might always have a remembrance of me for I know that I cant expect to be your sweetheart for I am not *"smoothe"* like boys you have for sweethearts   But I know you have not one that will think any more of you than I do although I know they may profess to   Now Bettie I know you will think me a Big fool (which I am) but please consider that you are the one that has done it   but I know you did not mean to and I ought not to have got so broken up over you but I could not help it   so if you do not see fit to answer this please do not say a word about it to any one for the sake of a broken hearted Cherokee cowboy.

Now Bettie if you should stoop so low as to answer this please tell me the plain truth for that is what you should do and not flirt with me for I would not be smoothe enough to detect it.

I have some New Songs to send you   also those pictures I promised   I was very glad to get your pictures and *thank* you very much for them   I have had lots of compliments on them especially yours.

I am going to Fort Smith[7] some time soon and if you will permit I can probaly come up but I know it would be a slam on your Society career to have it known that you even knew an ignorant Indian Cowboy.

I still have lots of pretty ponies here   if you will come out I will let you pick the herd

Well Bettie please burn this up for *my* sake   Hopeing you will consider what I have told you in my undignified way and if not to please never say anything about it and burn this up

I am yours with love

Will Rogers.

ALS, rc. OkClaW.

1. Except for a few postcards from later dates, there is no correspondence extant from Betty Blake Rogers to Will Rogers. Comments in Will Rogers's letters suggest that she often did reply to his letters. Evidently these letters must have contained very personal and sensitive material that Mrs. Rogers did not wish to make public.

2. The Blake family, which consisted of seven girls and two boys, was considered to be one of the most socially prominent families in Rogers, Ark. Betty's mother owned a large house at 307 East Walnut Street. All the daughters were active in the town's social affairs. Betty Blake worked as a typesetter at the *Rogers Democrat,* the local newspaper, and as a billing clerk at the Frisco station at Jenny Lind, Ark. ("Blake Home with its Seven Attractive Daughters Was Center of Much Social Activity," clipping, BBC-RHM; Snelling, "One of the Blake Girls," 9; see also Biographical Appendix entry, ROGERS, Betty Blake).

3. Day, *Will Rogers,* 38–39; Ketchum, *Will Rogers,* 69–70; Rogers, *Will Rogers,* 82.

4. Rogers named his father's ranch the Dog Iron Ranch after his own "Dog Iron" brand. Modeled after an andiron from the ranch's fireplace, the brand was first used on the dogies, or motherless calves, his father gave him around 1890 (Collings, *Old Home Ranch,* 80; see also Clement Vann Rogers to Principal Chief Colonel Johnson Harris, 15 October 1894, above).

5. One of Betty Blake's sweethearts was Tom Harvey, the son of Coin Harvey. He was editor of the local paper at Monte Ne (Ketchum, *Will Rogers,* 68, 116, 140).

6. Residents often referred to the "B.I.T.," or Beautiful Indian Territory. After statehood Lillie Cloud, a Foyil, Okla., resident, penned "Farewell to the B.I.T.: In Memoriam of the Indian Territory Which Became a State Nov. 16, 1907," promising "Beautiful Indian Territory, we can never forget you" (Foyil, Okla., *Statesman,* 30 November 1907).

7. Fort Smith is located in west Arkansas on the Oklahoma border at the confluence of the Arkansas and Poteau Rivers. To keep the peace between the Cherokees and the Osages in the area and to protect white settlers, trappers, and explorers, the United States established a log stockade at the site in 1817. It was named for Gen. Thomas A. Smith, the commander who ordered the fort's construction. Fort Smith served as a gateway for the movement of the Five Tribes into Indian Territory in the 1820s and 1830s. Cherokee removal parties traveled via the Trail of Tears that went through Fort

Smith. Construction of a new fort was started in 1838; the town was incorporated in 1842; and the U.S. Army post remained until 1871. The Federal District Court at Fort Smith was authorized to enforce the law in Indian Territory since tribal courts had no jurisdiction over white settlers. Railroads and coal mining stimulated the growth of the city at the end of the nineteenth century. Now the center of a manufacturing and agricultural area, Fort Smith is the second largest city in Arkansas (Workers of the Writers' Program, *Arkansas*, 142–52; Lamar, *Reader's Encyclopedia of the American West*, 44; *WNGD*, 409).

Notices from the *Claremore Progress*
9 June 1900
Claremore, I.T.

During the time Will managed his father's ranch, the Rogers home was known for its lively parties. Will enjoyed inviting all his friends and neighbors over for a good time and had a wooden platform constructed in the yard for open-air dances.[1]

Will Rogers gave a party and dance at his father's place near Oolagah Tuesday night. Quite a number of Claremore young people were invited. The following were in attendance from here: Misses Boone[2] and Julian,[3] Drs. Duckworth[4] and Hayes[5] and John Matheson. They all report a pleasant time.

Mrs. Maude Lane and son, of Chelsea, were the guests of Mrs. Lane's father, C. V. Rogers, Wednesday. They were returning from a visit to the old home place near Oologah.

PD. Printed in *CP,* 9 June 1900.

1. Croy, *Our Will Rogers*, 58; Day, *Will Rogers*, 29.
2. Maude Hightman Boone (1879–1958) was the wife of Alonzo Havington Boone (1869–1957), a descendant of Daniel Boone. Their ranch was southwest of Tiawah, a town near Claremore (*HRC*, 114).
3. Born in Missouri, Geraldine Julian Hays (d. 1862) was the daughter of Wilson Gilmore Julian, owner of a mercantile store in Claremore and founder of a subscription school. A talented musician, she taught piano in Claremore and Catoosa. In addition to being a member of the First Christian Church, she was very active as an officer in several Claremore civic and social clubs and was a founder of the town's public library. Noted for her charm, she married Dr. William Franklin Hays in 1903 (*HRC*, 227–28).
4. Dr. Franklin Muron Duckworth (b. 1873) graduated from St. Louis Medical College in 1897 and was a member of the Indian Territory Medical Association (Clinton, "Indian Territory Medical Association," 29, 37, 43, 48; *OCF* 1:181).
5. After graduating from Kentucky University Medical School and finishing postgraduate work at Rush Medical College in Chicago, Dr. William Franklin Hays (1886–1937) began his practice in Claremore in 1897. He formed a partnership with Dr. Jesse Bushyhead. A prominent Claremore citizen, Hays was president of the Rogers

County Medical Society, vice president of the Bank of Claremore, and co-owner of the town's pharmaceutical drug store. Hays and his wife, Geraldine Julian Hays, lived at Seventh and Seminole Streets, where they raised three daughters (*CP,* 26 February 1937; *HRC,* 227–28).

Notice from the *Vinita Leader*
14 June 1900
Vinita, I. T.

Will Rogers was supposedly the first person in the Indian Territory to own a horse-drawn buggy with rubber tires. He would go to many social events in the buggy pulled by Robin, one of his favorite horses. To keep the tires in good shape, he suspended the buggy by ropes from the beams in a shed.[1]

OOLAGAH ITEMS.

W. P. Rogers has received a new buggy, which is provided with rubber tires. It is the first of its kind ever brought to this vicinity and is quite an attraction.

PD. Printed in *VL,*[2] 14 June 1900.

1. Day, *Will Rogers,* 29.
2. Founded on 20 March 1895 as the *Cherokee Champion,* this newspaper became the *Vinita Leader* on 13 August 1895. Because of early financial problems, it went through a series of owners including L. B. Bell, Davis Hill, W. L. Trott, J. O. Hall, and L. W. Buffington. French Staunton Evans Amos, a founder and first president of the Oklahoma Historical Society, served in various capacities as editor, manager, and publisher from 1897 to 1919. A Democratic paper, the *Vinita Leader* gave extensive coverage to Cherokee political and legal affairs and to local news. An article describing the paper's history declared that it "was the first paper in Vinita to adopt the all at home print form, and the first to make the subscription price $1 a year. It was, in all probability, the first paper in the Cherokee Nation to swear to the number of subscribers, the first to use power presses, the first to use a telephone and electric lights. It hopes to be the first to use Vinita ice and to use water from Vinita waterworks. It tries to be true to the best interests of the Cherokee Nation and of Vinita" (*VL,* 7 February 1901). The paper merged with the *Craig County Democrat* in 1959 (Foreman, C., *Oklahoma Imprints, 1835–1907,* 98–99; Littlefield and Parins, *American Indian and Alaska Native Newspapers and Periodicals, 1826–1924,* 375–77).

Article from the *Claremore Courier*
15 June 1900
Claremore, I. T.

A national reunion of Theodore Roosevelt's Rough Riders[1] was held in Oklahoma City[2] from 1 to 4 July 1900. As part of Zack Mulhall's Wild West show, Rogers participated in steer-roping contests that featured champion ropers from across the country. He met Theodore Roosevelt, then governor of New York, who was campaigning for the vice presidency on the Republican ticket with presidential candidate William McKinley.[3]

THE ROPING CONTEST.
LARGE NUMBER OF ENTRIES FOR
THE COWBOY EVENT AT
OKLAHOMA CITY.

The roping contest that will be given at the Rough Riders' reunion here in July promises to be one of the greatest contests of that kind ever held in the country and those who are here from a distance will have the pleasure of witnessing one of the finest exhibitions of this western sport ever given in this country.

Manager Dowden has already received entries from more of the first class cowboy ropers than ever entered into a like contest in the country. Among those he has secured are E. M. (Bud) Daggett and Leonard Trainor[4] of Chelsea, E. V. Schrimsher,[5] Steve McClellan,[6] Ben Heiney and Billy Rogers of Claremore . . . all of Indian Territory.[7] Miss Mulhall[8] will also rope a steer. There are others from Texas and other cattle points who have signified their intention of taking part in the tournament, but their entries have not yet been received. The contests will be given at the Driving park and from the number of entries there is certainty the entertainment will be one of the principal features of the reunion.[9]

PD. Printed in *CC*,[10] 15 June 1900. Reprinted from the Oklahoma City *Times-Journal*.

1. As a lieutenant colonel in the Spanish-American War (1898), Theodore Roosevelt led the Rough Riders, officially known as the First United States Volunteer Cavalry. The regiment became famous for its charge up San Juan Hill during the United States's invasion of Cuba. The Rough Riders included many cowboys from the West, and among its twelve troops were two from Indian Territory (Troop L and Troop M). Noting the large number of soldiers from its area, the *Vinita Leader* reported that sixty-one Rough Riders from Vinita were either wounded or killed in the war (24 January 1901). Biographer Donald Day writes that Rogers attempted to volunteer for the Rough Riders in Amarillo in 1898, but was rejected by a recruiting sergeant as too young (*Will Rogers*, 27). The first Rough Riders reunion was held in Las Vegas, New Mexico Territory, in June 1899. The second reunion in Oklahoma City, which ran from 1 to 4 July, was especially meaningful to Roosevelt, who was a friend of many of the Oklahoma Rough Riders. His appearance attracted an immense crowd to the city, and his train, which arrived on 2 July, was greeted by thirty thousand people. The next day Roosevelt, riding a black charger, led a grand military and civic parade that featured nearly one hundred Rough Riders as well as Civil War veterans, many cowboys and Indians, and bands.

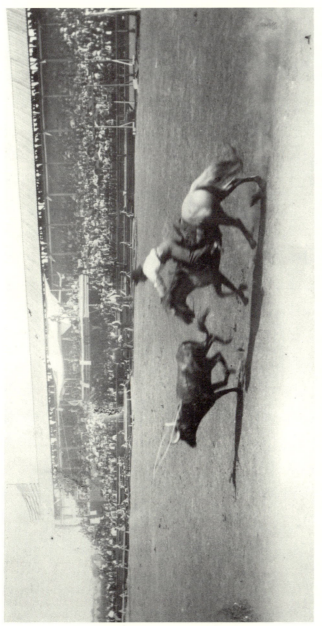

Competitor in the steer-roping contest, Rough Riders Reunion, Oklahoma City, 1900 (*Scrapbook A1, OkClaW*).

A leather ribbon from the Rough Riders Re-union, from one of Will Rogers's scrapbooks *(Scrapbook 1902–4, CPpR).*

After the parade thousands of people crowded into Kramer's Park to hear his speech, in which he supported statehood for Oklahoma Territory and expansionism. In the afternoon he attended the steer-roping contest and saw Rogers and the other cowboys perform. As a devotee of the Wild West and the rugged individual as well as a Dakota cattle rancher, Roosevelt certainly must have been attracted by the feats of the cowboy ropers. The success of the Oklahoma City event also led to the appearance of Zack Mulhall's cowboy band in the 1901 presidential inaugural parade as an escort to newly elected Vice President Roosevelt. In the fall of 1901 President Roosevelt (who had assumed the presidency after McKinley's assassination) was thinking of appointing Mulhall as governor of Oklahoma Territory. According to Fred Olds, the idea backfired due to Mulhall's "reputation as a gunman, his life style and Democratic affiliation" (Olds, "Story of Lucille," 12; see also *Daily Oklahoman*, 28 June 1900; Faulkner, *Politics, Reform, and Expansion*, 242–47; Jones, *Roosevelt's Rough Riders; Mulhall Enterprise*, 1 March and 8 November 1901, Mulhall file, OkClaW; Roosevelt, *Rough Riders;* Smith, B., "Theodore Roosevelt Visits Oklahoma," 264–67; Stansbury, *Lucille Mulhall*, 18–19; White, G., *Eastern Establishment and the Western Experience*, 79–83, 149–70).

2. Oklahoma City, the present capital of Oklahoma, was founded on 22 April 1889, which was the first day of the Land Run of 1889. On that date thousands of people, as a result of the 1889 Springer Amendment, occupied the Unassigned Lands, or Oklahoma District, claiming land on a first-come basis *(Directory of Oklahoma State Almanac, 1989–90*, 534–35; Gibson, *Oklahoma*, 293–95; *WNGD*, 886).

3. The *Daily Oklahoman* of 4 July 1900 reported: "Colonel Roosevelt and staff attended the roping contest at the park in the afternoon, the governor riding the black charger that had carried him in the parade. He spent most of the time with the cowboys, but wherever he went the crowd cheered him wildly. Men and women crowded around his horse anxious to shake their hero by the hand and none of them were disappointed." There were two roping contests, on 2 July and 3 July. A reported twenty-five thousand people attended the second event, advertised as "roping and tieing thirty wild steers" *(Daily Oklahoman*, 28 June and 4 July 1900). Several competitors, including Rogers, broke their ropes in the contest (Collings, *Old Home Ranch*, 92; Keith, *Boy's Life of Will Rogers*, 15; O'Donnell, "My Friend Will," 21; Stansbury, *Lucille Mulhall*, 15).

4. Leonard Edward Trainor (1879–1940) became a lifelong friend of Rogers and acted as his stand-in in Rogers's films. See Biographical Appendix entry, TRAINOR, Leonard Edward.

5. Ernest Vivian Schrimsher (1875–1942) was a cousin of Will Rogers. Ernest Schrimsher's father, John Gunter Schrimsher (1835–1905), was the brother of Mary America Schrimsher, Will Rogers's mother *(HRC*, 385; Starr, *History of the Cherokee Indians*, 509, 527, 651; *WRFT*, 120; see also Biographical Appendix entry, SCHRIMSHER, Ernest Vivian).

6. Stephen Frank McClellan (1884–1912) was the youngest son of Charles McClure and Jennie Lind McClellan and the brother of Charles White McClellan, Will Rogers's boyhood friend. Educated at Cherokee schools and the University of Arkansas, he married Joella Bradshaw in 1915 and they had two children. Around 1900 he had a serious fall off his horse, suffered a concussion, and was unconscious for many days. Will Rogers supposedly took care of him at night (O'Donnell, "My Friend Will," 4–5). A cattleman, Steve ran the McClellan ranch in Oolawa after his parents' death and used the livestock brand "STV" *(As I Recollect*, 77; *HRC*, 289–90; Sunday et al., *Gah Dah Gwa Stee*, 101).

7. Other competitors in the Oklahoma City contests from Oolagah were Spi Trent, Clint Lipe, and Richard Parris (clipping, "The Cowboy Tournament," 3 July 1900, Jim O'Donnell [Hopkins] file, OkClaW; *CP,* 16 June 1900).

8. Lucille Mulhall (1885–1940), the daughter of Zack Mulhall, was only a teenager at this time. A good friend of Rogers, she would become one of the country's best-known cowgirls. At the event she displayed her riding and roping skills. Theodore Roosevelt was especially impressed by her riding feats in the steer-roping contest in Oklahoma City and cheered her performance. Lucille and her sister Agnes were guests of honor at a dinner for the Rough Riders given after the performance, and a few days later Roosevelt visited the Mulhall ranch. Roosevelt urged Zack Mulhall to make Lucille a star of his troupe (Cheney, "Lucile Mulhall, Fabulous Cowgirl," 15, 58; Fisch, oral history, WRPP; MFC; Stansbury, *Lucille Mulhall,* 17, 19; see also Biographical Appendix entry, MULHALL, Lucille).

9. In addition, the Rough Riders reunion featured riding contests, band concerts, a military ball, trotting races, fireworks, and a theatrical production reenacting the Battle of San Juan Hill.

10. The *Claremore Courier* was an eight-page weekly published in Claremore in 1899 and 1900 at a subscription cost of $1.00 yearly. It was the successor to the *Cherokee Vindicator* and was published by W. H. Edmundson (editor) and A. A. Bessey (manager) (Foreman, C., *Oklahoma Imprints, 1835–1907,* 63).

Notice from the *Claremore Courier*
15 June 1900
Claremore, I.T.

Will Rogers, Spi Dick and Tom Trent came in from Oolagah Wednesday night to attend a dance that didn't materialize.[1]

PD. Printed in *CC,* 15 June 1900.

1. Among Will Rogers's friends at this time were the brothers Richard Owen (Dick) Trent (b. 1880), Thomas Brown (Tom) Trent (b. 1887), and Spi (Martin) Trent (1884–1959). They were distant cousins of Will Rogers through his mother's (Schrimsher) line and sons of Mollie Minx Brown (b. 1859) and Dr. Richard Owen Trent (1859–88) of Muskogee. Spi Trent was especially associated with Rogers at this time. Clem V. Rogers had rented the main house at the Rogers ranch to a tenant farmer and his family, and because Will Rogers did not like living with them, he and Spi Trent built a log cabin on the property and for a time lived there together (Collings, *Old Home Ranch,* 79–89; Day, *Will Rogers,* 29; Commission, *Final Rolls of Citizens and Freedmen of the Five Civilized Tribes,* 256; Ketchum, *Will Rogers,* 58–59; *OCF* 2:156; Trent, *My Cousin Will Rogers,* 45–56; *WRFT,* 121; see also Biographical Appendix entries, TRENT, Richard Owen, M.D., and TRENT, Spi).

Lucille Mulhall, champion roper and rider and good friend of Will Rogers, at about sixteen years of age *(Baldwin Collection, OkU)*.

Notice from the *Claremore Progress*
23 June 1900
Claremore, I.T.

A number of our young people participated in a social hop at the opera house[1] Thursday night. A large crowd was present and despite the warm weather a good time was had. Several young people from a distance were in attendance, among them being Miss Bell West, of Wagoner; Messrs. Will Rogers, Tom and Spie Trent, Casper and Clint Lipe, of Oolagah, and Richard Parris, of Tahlequah.[2]

PD. Printed in *CP*, 23 June 1900.

1. The opera house was Claremore's main place of entertainment where dances, plays, and musical performances were staged. For example, on 26 March 1898 the *Claremore Progress* reported the upcoming appearance of the Oakes Comedy company and the Swiss Bell Ringers. A new opera house was constructed in 1902 (*HRC*, 14).

2. Born and raised in Tahlequah, Richard Parris (1877–1922) was working as a hand on the Rogers ranch. Parris would go to Argentina with Rogers in 1902 (see Biographical Appendix entry, PARRIS, Richard).

Notices from the *Vinita Leader*
2 August 1900
Vinita, I.T.

OOLAGAH ITEMS.

W. P. Rogers and Spy Trent left for Pryor Creek[1] to attend the roping contest.

❧

C. V. Rogers, of Claremore, Mrs. Tom McSpadden, of Chelsea, Mrs. Gulager and daughter, Mary,[2] from Tahlequah and Dick Trent from Fort Gibson were in Oolagah Wednesday and drove out to spend the day with W. P. Rogers.

PD. Printed in *VL*, 2 August 1900.

1. Pryor Creek took its name from a creek located near the town. On 26 January 1909 its name was changed to Pryor. It is located in Mayes County in northeastern Oklahoma, forty-one miles northeast of Tulsa (Shirk, *Oklahoma Place Names*, 172; *WNGD*, 985).

2. Martha Lucretia Schrimsher Gulager (b. 1845) was the sister of Will Roger's mother, Mary America Schrimsher Rogers. Martha Schrimsher married Frederick William Gulager (b. 1844) on 27 January 1869, and they were the parents of four children. Their only daughter, Mary Elizabeth Gulager, was born in 1880 and graduated from the Cherokee National Female Seminary in 1900 (*OCF* 1:56; Starr, *History of the Cherokee Indians*, 638, 657; *WRFT*, 120, 125).

Article from the *Indian Chieftain*
2 August 1900
Vinita, I.T.

The roping contest on the Willie Halsell College campus was typical of informal events staged on the open prairie at this time. Several of Rogers's schoolmates participated in the contest, and practically everyone in town attended.

Will Rogers *(second from the left)* with his cousin Spi Trent and friends Mary McClellan and Pearl McClellan on an outing *(OkClaW)*.

ROPING CONTEST.

BERT OSKINSON[1] CAPTURES FIRST PRIZE IN 50 SECONDS.

As an offset to the failure and disappointment of the Woodley picnic, Vinita gave a free roping contest at the college campus yesterday afternoon that was exciting enough to satisfy the most fastidious cattle man on the range, and afforded an entertainment that was very near perfect in its line. The grounds where the contest took place were splendidly suited to the occasion. About 50 acres of smooth open prairie that had been mown two or three weeks and the grass was up just high enough to make a beautiful green sward with a gentle slope to the east and without a tree or shrub, or break of any kind to mar the scene. About 15 high headed, longhorned Texas steers were driven into the arena about 5 o'clock and corralled on the outskirts. Fifteen cowboys rode leisurely into the campus and lined up fronting the long line of buggies, carriages, traps, phaetons, with a numerous sprinkling of equestrians and pedestrians, and the snapping of cameras all along the line indicated that something more enduring of the occasion than mere memory would be preserved.

The following cowboys entered the contest, and drew numbers for their turns at the roping. Bert Oskison, Jim Rider,[2] Jim Hopkins,[3] Will Rogers, Heber Skinner,[4] Spy Trent,[5] John Weir, Joe Knight and Alex Franklin.[6] John Franklin[7] and Robt. L. McClure were selected as timekeepers and W. E. Halsell[8] as judge. Sam Cobb[9] and Jim Walker[10] cut the steers out from the bunch and turned them singly into the open. The cowboys dashed in according to number and the work began. Bert Oskison won the first premium, $25, roping and tying his steer in 50 seconds. Second money, $15, was won in 58 seconds by Jim Hopkins, and Alex Franklin won third in 61 seconds. Pretty nearly everybody in Vinita and large numbers from the country turned out to see the contest and the streets of the town were well nigh deserted while it was in progress. Heber Skinner came in three seconds of being a winner and was considered one of the most skillful ropemen in the bunch.[11]

PD. Printed in *IC*, 2 August 1900.

1. Albert (Bert) James Oskison (1879–1930) was the half brother of the novelist John Oskison. He was raised on the Oskison farm four miles west of Vinita and attended Willie Halsell College with Will Rogers. A skilled roper, he joined Rogers in several roping and riding events at this time. Bert Oskison first became a farmer and rancher in Colorado Springs, Colo., but he soon returned to Craig County, where he owned a farm fifteen miles north of Vinita in the Wolfe District. In 1918 he and his wife, Lizabeth Elvira Gleason (1885–1971) moved to a home in Estella, where they raised three children. Bert Oskison died in a saw accident (*Story of Craig County*, 531–33).

2. On Jim Rider, see Biographical Appendix entry, RIDER, James Hall.

3. On Jim Hopkins, see Biographical Appendix entry, HOPKINS (O'Donnell), James Dennis; see also *DC*, 3 June, 5 September, 6 September, 18 September, 28 September, and 5 October 1901; *IC*, 19 September, 26 September, and 17 October 1901, 15 October and 22 October 1903).

4. A top roper, Heber Skinner (b. 1874) participated in many early cowboy competitions with Will Rogers and the Zack Mulhall troupe. A member of a pioneer Craig County family, he became a prosperous cattleman in the Vinita area. In 1902 he married Martha Riley (b. 1880), a graduate of the Cherokee National Female Seminary and Payne College in Fayette, Mo., and they became the parents of two children (*Craig County Democrat*, 31 August 1933; *DC*, 1 June, 17 July, 22 July, 29 July, 7 September, 15 October 1901; *OCF* 1:253; Starr, *History of the Cherokee Indians*, 653; *Story of Craig County*, 11).

5. On Spi Trent, see Biographical Appendix entry, TRENT, Spi.

6. Alex Franklin was the son of George Washington Franklin (1860–1906), a Vinita rancher (*Story of Craig County*, 354–55).

7. John Franklin (1862–1943), the brother of Alex Franklin, was a successful Vinita farmer specializing in Hereford cattle, Duroc-Jersey hogs, and drought-resistant corn. In 1899 he married Stella Brodie (d. 1969), for whom the nearby town of Estella (eight miles northwest of Vinita) was named in 1900 when Johnson served as its postmaster. He

also served as a senator in the Cherokee National Council and as Craig County commissioner, and helped organize the Vinita Production Credit Association (Shirk, *Oklahoma Place Names,* 74; *Story of Craig County,* 356).

8. On W. E. Halsell, see Biographical Appendix entry, HALSELL, William Electious.

9. Sam Cobb from Vinita is listed as a schoolmate of Will Rogers in the 1894 Willie Halsell College catalogue (p. 7). Cobb joined with Rogers in many of the Mulhall troupe events. He apparently was related to the family of Sam Sylvester Cobb (1840–1923), a successful merchant, rancher, and banker in Vinita *(Story of Craig County,* 296–97; see also James H. Rider to Will Rogers, 2 September 1902, nn. 3, 9, below).

10. James A. Walker from Prairie City, I.T., is listed as a schoolmate of Will Rogers in the 1894 Willie Halsell College catalogue (p. 11).

11. Rogers would always have great affection for the group of ropers from Willie Halsell College whom he knew from his school years. On the eve of the Willie Halsell reunion in 1933 Rogers sent a telegram to classmate Earl Walker: "I still believe Earl Walker, Heber Skinner, Sam Cobb, Sunny Knight, John McCracken, Charley Mehlin, and dozens of fine Indian Territory girls who went to old Willie Halsell are as great a contribution to American life as 'Pretty Boy Floyd' " (Will Rogers to Earl Walker, ca. 27 August 1933, telegram, box 9, OkClaW).

Article from the *Indian Chieftain*
13 September 1900
Vinita, I.T.

ROPING CONTEST.
DAY'S FESTIVITIES AT SPRINGFIELD, MO.
. . . SECOND DAY.

Amid deafening rounds of applause at the fair grounds Thursday afternoon, Heber Skinner, of Vinita, lassoed, threw down and tied a steer in 34 seconds. This time is 13¾ seconds better than the best time the day before, 10 seconds better than any made at the Oklahoma Rough Rider's reunion, and is within 1½ seconds of the world's record.

The contest Thursday was, as [a] whole, more interesting than the one the day before. Better time was made, the bronco riding was more exciting and the crowd was larger. Not only was the amphitheater filled, but thousands of spectators were ranged all around the half-mile speed ring, within which the exhibition was carried out.

The bronco riding was scattered through the program instead of being given all at once, so that there was a freedom from monotony. Music was furnished by Hobart's Military band.

Jim Hopkins of Pryor Creek and Joe Knight of Vinita, tied for the second prize in 58 seconds. Hopkins' throw was right in front of the grand stand and he made a good showing, throwing his steer twice. The money was divided between them. . . .

Alex Franklin of Vinita made two pretty throws and tied his steer in 1:18, and Billy Rogers of Claremore made his tie after three throws in 1:29. . . .[1]

PD. Printed in *IC*, 13 September 1900.

1. Rogers's friends Charley McClellan, Dick Parris, Jim Rider, and Leonard Trainor participated as contestants in the steer-roping competition, as did his cousins Ernest Schrimsher and Spi Trent. Lucille Mulhall was the hit of the first day of festivities. She thrilled the crowd with equestrian feats (*IC*, 13 September 1900).

Notice from the *Vinita Leader*
4 October 1900
Vinita, I. T.

W. P. Rogers had a fine horse drowned in the Verdigris river this week while trying to swim across.[1]

PD. Printed in *VL*, 4 October 1900.

1. Edward Sunday, who worked as a line rider for Clem V. Rogers in the early 1870s and was a founder of Oologah, wrote about the incident. He said that Will Rogers "always was showing off with his roping. He used to come to town on a little black pony. One day he came through on his way to a rodeo in Claremore; there wasn't a bridge across the river, just planks across the railroad bridge that footmen could cross on, and Will tried to walk the narrow board with his rope on his horse, leading him through the water. The horse started to swim and stopped halfway across. When Will tightened up on the rope, the horse got strangled and drowned (*Line Rider in the Cherokee Nation*, 62–63; see also Biographical Appendix entry, SUNDAY, William Esther).

Application for Enrollment in the Cherokee Nation by
Clement Vann Rogers
22–23 October 1900
Claremore, I. T.

Following the 1887 passage of the Dawes General Allotment (Severalty) Act and the 1893 passage of the Indian Appropriation Bill, the Commission to the Five Civilized Tribes, or Dawes Commission, was delegated to negotiate with tribal leaders in Indian Territory in regard to individual allotment of previously commonly held Indian lands. Allotment agreements were signed by the Choctaw and Chickasaw Nations in 1897; the Cherokee Nation ratified the agreement on 7 August 1902. In the spring of 1900 the Dawes Commission began compiling tribal roles of Indian citizens in preparation for making land assignments. Here Clem V. Rogers applies for enrollment for himself and his son, in accordance with Dawes Commission regulations.[1]

DEPARTMENT OF THE INTERIOR
COMMISSION TO THE FIVE CIVILIZED TRIBES,
CLAREMORE, I.T., OCTOBER 22, 1900.

In the matter of the application of Clement V. Rogers for the enrollment of himself and child as Cherokees by blood; being sworn and examined by Commissioner Breckinridge,[2] he testified as follows:

Q Give me your full name?   A. Clement V. Rogers.
Q How old are you?   A 61 years old last January
Q What is your post office?   A Claremore.
Q You live in Cooweescoowee district do you?   A Yes, sir.
Q Who is it you want to have enrolled?   A Myself and son.
Q Are you a Cherokee by blood?   A Yes, sir.
Q How long have you lived in the Cherokee Nation?   A I was born here.
Q Lived here all your life?   A Yes, sir.
Q What is the name of your son?   A William P. Rogers.
Q How old is he?   A He xxxxxx will be 21 on the 4th of next month.
(Clement V. Rogers on 1880 roll, page 161, No. 2331, Clem V. Rogers, 2337, Col. W. P. Rogers, Cooweescoowee district. Clement V. Rogers on 1896 roll, page 244, [N]o. 4093, Clem V. Rogers, Cooweescoowee dist. William P. Rogers on 1896 roll, page 244, No. 4094, Wm. P. Rogers, Cooweescoowee district.)
Q Your son is living at this time is he?   A Yes, sir.
The applicant applies for the enrollment of himself and one child. He is identified on the rolls of 1880 and 1896 as a native Cherokee. He has lived in the Cherokee Nation all his life, and he will be listed for enrollment as a Cherokee by blood. His son, still a minor, is identified on the rolls of 1880 and 1896, he is living now, and will be listed for enrollment as a Cherokee by blood.

Bruce C. Jones, being duly sworn, says that as stenographer to the Commission to the Five Civilized Tribes he correctly recorded the proceedings and testimony in the above case, and the foregoing is a true and complete transcript of his stenographic notes thereof.

Bruce C. Jones

Sworn to and subscribed before me this the 23rd of October, 1900.

[signature illegible — C. Breckinridge?]

Commissioner.

TDS. OkHi.

1. Enrollment sessions for Cherokees were scheduled at Bartlesville, Catoosa, Chelsea, Claremore, Muldrow, Nowata, Oolagah, Pryor Creek, Tahlequah, Vinita, and Welch. Freed-slaves enrollment took place in 1901 (Littlefield, *Cherokee Freedmen*, 226, 227, 231). On allotment, detribalization, and assimilation/individualization as federal Indian policy in the years following the Civil War, see Fritz, *Movement for Indian Assimilation, 1860–1890*. See also Brown, L., "The Dawes Commission"; Debo, *And Still the Waters Run;* Littlefield, "Dawes Commission," chap. 9 in *Cherokee Freedmen*, 214–48; and Wardell, *Political History of the Cherokee Nation*, 325–27.

2. Clifton Rhodes Breckinridge (1846–1932) served as one of the three commissioners on the Dawes Commission. He was first appointed in 1901 and served until the commission expired by law on 1 July 1905. The two other members were Tams Bixby and Thomas B. Needles. Born at Lexington, Ky., he was the son of John C. Breckinridge, vice president of the United States under James Buchanan and a Confederate general. After serving in the Confederate army and navy, Clifton Breckinridge attended Washington and Lee University in Virginia and became a cotton planter at Pine Bluff, Ark., from 1870 to 1883. He then served as a congressman from Arkansas and minister to Russia (1894–97). After his duties as a Dawes commissioner, Breckinridge was president of the Arkansas Valley Trust Co. between 1906 and 1914. He died at Wendover, Ky., on 3 December 1932 (Foreman, G., "Clifton R. Breckinridge," 118–19).

Enclosure:
Cherokee Nation Roll
22 October 1900
Cooweescoowee District, Cherokee Nation, I.T.

(For document, see page 207.)

1. The enrollment and political rights of groups that achieved citizenship status in the Cherokee Nation after the Civil War—including Delawares, Shawnees, and freed slaves and their descendants—were the subject of a series of disputes within the Cherokee Nation and between the Nation and the federal government through the Reconstruction period until the end of the century. The treaty of 1866 contained several articles granting citizenship rights to ex-slaves, including Article 9, which declared that freed slaves and their descendants who were residents in the Nation, or who had returned to residency within six months, were to have all the same rights as native Cherokees. Since many former slaves had become refugees in the war, the time limitation set by this provision created complications in ex-slaves' claims to citizenship,

CHEROKEE NATION.
CHEROKEE ROLL.

(*Not including Delawares, Shawnees, or Freedmen.*)[1]

RESIDENCE: Cooweescoowee *DISTRICT*,
POST OFFICE: Claremore, IT

CARD NO. _____
FIELD NO. 4747

Dawes' Roll No.	NAME.	Relationship to Person first Named.	AGE.	SEX.	BLOOD.	TRIBAL ENROLLMENT.		
						Year.	District.	No.
No. 1 11383	Rogers, Clement V.	X	61	M	¼	1880	Coo.	2331
No. 2 11384	" William P.	Son	20	M	¼	1880	"	2337[2]

No. 1 on 1880 Roll   as   Clem V. Rogers

No. 2 " 1880 "   "   Col. W. P. Rogers

No. 1 " 1896 "   page 244 No. 4093   as Clem V. Rogers Coo. Dist.

No. 2 " 1896 "   244 No. 4094   " Wm. P. Rogers   "   "

[STAMPED:] Date of Application for Enrollment. OCT 22 1900
CITIZENSHIP CERTIFICATE ISSUED FOR NO. [11383] AUG 17 1903
CITIZENSHIP CERTIFICATE ISSUED FOR NO. [11384] AUG 17 1903

PD, with autograph insertions. OkHi.

many African American former residents were rejected as intruders upon application. Many organized in response to this rejection and petitioned in protest to federal agencies. Their citizenship status remained a matter of political dispute, augmented over the issue of the distribution of federal payments to Cherokee citizens for the sale of Cherokee Nation lands.

Freed slaves whose status was ambivalent, and Shawnees and Delawares who had been incorporated into the Nation after the war, memorialized the Cherokee Nation to be included in the distribution of funds in 1883. Clem V. Rogers was on the three-member committee chosen to make a formal statement on the claims for inclusion. Rogers and the committee reported that the lands of the Nation "were and are the common property of citizens" and no citizen "can be legally deprived of his or her right and interest" in them (Wardell, *Political History of the Cherokee Nation*, 233–34). The Cherokee National Council, however, refused to follow the committee's recommendation to recognize these three groups' citizenship rights, and the status of the Shawnees, Delawares, and freedmen remained in controversy.

Federal legislation, passed in 1888, declared that the non-Cherokee citizens should share in appropriations. Citizenship censuses, or tribal rolls, were used as the basis for determining individual appropriations. The 1880 census indicated the enrollment of 15,307 Cherokees, 1,976 African Americans, 672 Delawares, and 503 Shawnees. An 1889 census prepared by federal agents (the Wallace Roll) indicated 3,524 African American claimants. Meanwhile, monies earned by the Cherokee Nation from the lease of Cherokee Outlet lands were distributed only to Cherokees by blood; former slaves, Delawares, and Shawnees were excluded and sued for their share of this revenue. The Delawares and Shawnees were paid, but the freedmen were embroiled in controversies over the accuracy of the Kern-Clifton Roll conducted in 1896–97. That census contained 2,530 authenticated names and a total of 4,552 ex-slaves claiming citizenship in the Nation ("Roll of Cherokee Freedmen, 1896–1897," "Applications for Enrollment of Freedmen, 1897," DNA, RG 75; Littlefield, *Cherokee Freedmen*, 148–248; Teall, *Black History in Oklahoma*; Wardell, *Political History of the Cherokee Nation*, 223–40; see also Franklin, *Blacks in Oklahoma*).

2. The Cherokee Roll also indicated information about the tribal enrollment of parents. Under columns for "Name of Father," "Year," and "District," and "Name of Mother," "Year," and "District," was written "Robt. Rogers dead G[oing] Snake Sallie Rogers dead Coo." for Clement Vann Rogers, and "No. 1" and "Mary Rogers [dead] Illinois" for William P. Rogers.

Article from the *Chelsea Commercial*
18 January 1901
Chelsea, I.T.

During a trip to California in the fall of 1900 Will Rogers stayed at a San Francisco rooming house lighted by gas. He was accustomed to kerosene lamps in the Indian Territory and inadvertently either he or a friend blew out the gas lamp upon retiring.[1] Luckily, someone smelled the gas, found Rogers, and rushed him to a hospital. After he returned home, his father sent him to recover at Hot Springs, Ark., a health resort noted for its thermal and mineral springs.[2]

Almost Fatal Accident.

W. P. Rogers, brother of Mrs. J. T. McSpadden and Mrs. C. L. Lane of this city, recently shipped some cattle to California, and while in a San Francisco hotel went to bed, leaving the gas burning. A young man who made the trip with him as helper blew out the gas and retired. When both parties came to rights they were in a hospital recovering from what came near being a fatal asphyxiation. Mr. Rogers congratulates himself upon his fortunate escape.[3]

PD. Printed in *ChC*,[4] 18 January 1901.

1. There is some debate regarding who precipitated the incident. Biographer Homer Croy has written that Will Rogers was alone in the room and that he blew out the gas (Dal Walker to Homer Croy, 30 July 1952, HCP-MoU; *Our Will Rogers*, 72–73). But Betty Rogers, quoting her husband, suggests a leak might have caused the incident (*Will Rogers*, 58–59). She writes that Rogers had accompanied a trainload of cattle to the William Randolph Hearst ranch at San Simeon, Calif.

In an unpublished autobiographical manuscript Rogers wrote:

I worked on ranches and finally I and another boy went to California with a shipment of cattle and up to Frisco and that night something happened. He says he didn't blow the gas out. Maybe there was a leak. I was asleep when he come in. Anyhow they dug us out of there the next morning and hauled us to a hospital and believe me bub I didn't know a fighting thing till late that night. That was just bull luck. The main doctors gave me up but a lot of young medical students [did not] and just by practicing on me they happened to light on some nut remedy (that no regular doctor would ever think of) and I came alive. Well I landed back home pretty badly buggered up. This stuff had located in my system. I went to Hot Springs to boil it out and when I would get in a hot room they would all think the gas was escaping some place. (Rogers, "How I Got into Show Business")

Another story, probably incorrect, states that three men died and that the incident occurred in Bakersfield ("Rogers Lived, 3 Died as Pal Blew Out Gas, *New York Daily News*, 30 August 1935, clipping, Will Rogers box, Museum of the City of New York).

2. Hot Springs is a city in west-central Arkansas, some forty-seven miles from Little Rock and not far from what was the eastern border of the Cherokee Nation, I.T. Settled in the early nineteenth century, the area became a U.S. government reservation in 1832. Later Hot Springs National Park was created there (1921) (*WNGD*, 515). Clem V. Rogers had earlier taken his ailing wife, Mary Bibles Rogers, to the baths at Hot Springs in hopes that they would help her recover her health in 1899–1900.

3. In an article entitled "Overcome By Gas" published on 24 January 1901 by the *Vinita Leader*, the following story was reported: "Some months ago Will Rogers, son of Clem V. Rogers, left home for New Mexico. Later he went to San Francisco. There he and a stockman went to bed in a hotel. Before they did so they turned out the gas, but must have not done it well, for it escaped and in the morning they were found as if dead. It took four hours to bring Rogers' friend around and nine hours to revive Rogers himself. It left Rogers in a debilitated condition and he is now in Hot Springs seeking better health."

Will Rogers bicycling in front of the Rogers family ranch, which his father let him oversee for several years before Will left for Argentina in 1902. Betty Blake Rogers later reminisced that Rogers courted her by doing tricks on his bike when she visited Oologah (*gift of the National Broadcasting Co., OkClaW*).

On 16 March 1901 the *Claremore Progress* reported that "Will Rogers returned to his home to Oologah from Hot Springs, Wednesday morning. He had about recovered his health, which was caused by a bed fellow not turning the gas off in a hotel in California."

4. Established in 1895, the *Chelsea Commercial* was a weekly newspaper published by J. W. Quinn (Foreman, C., *Oklahoma Imprints, 1835–1907*, 60–61).

Article from the *Claremore Progress*
30 March 1901
Claremore, I.T.

Minstrel shows were an extremely popular form of American entertainment from the 1840s to the 1890s. They had evolved from Jim Crow dance and song routines of the 1830s. White entertainers, performing in blackface, imitated African American dances, songs, dialect routines, and comic skits. In the shows the members of the minstrel companies accentuated negative plantation stereotypes and caricatures of African Americans. Traveling companies performed across the nation in leading theaters, and minstrelsy was especially popular in the northern cities, where it gave white audiences an opportunity to work out ambivalent feelings on slavery and race. Although a declining form of theater entertainment by 1900, the shows were still popular in communities that had their own amateur minstrel troupes. In March 1901 Will Rogers participated in an amateur minstrel night in Claremore where he performed a comic solo and dialect yarn and entered the cakewalk contest.[1]

A GREAT SUCCESS.

The entertainment given last Friday night by the home talent minstrels was all that was anticipated and far exceeded the expectation of the large audience that greeted them. It was a success in every way—financially, socially and as a dispeller of the blues.

From the time the curtain went up until the close, the audience was kept in a merry mood, and the troupe were showered with compliments at its close.

P. E. Saddler, the interlocutor,[2] had the "show" in full control during the evening, and the manner in which he conducted his difficult part, reflected credit upon him.

Joe M. LaHay,[3] as bones, and R. Lee Comer,[4] as tambo, were warm numbers and held up their end of the entertainment like old timers.

Excellent solos were rendered by Miss Ida May Collins,[5] Mrs. C. F. Godbey,[6] Miss Mayme Headen, and Miss Mary Bullette.[7] Messrs. Joe M. LaHay, Thos. Lane, Scipio Young, Will Rogers and J. O. Yahn. . . .

Messrs. Scipio Young and Byron Haymes, caught the crowd with old plantation and breakdown dancing. They were warm numbers and had to respond to encores.

Messrs. Rogers and Yahn, besides solos, contributed to the evenings entertainment by some excellent dialect yarns.

George Bullette helped out the ragtime[8] music with a masterful manipulation of the bones.

The entertainment closed with a cake walk,[9] the contest being for a large iced pyramid cake. The couples contesting were introduced by Mrs. A. A. Bessey in a graceful manner by conducting them once around the stage, when they were left to put forth their best and fanciest steps. The contesting couples were Mr. J. O. Yahn and Mrs. J. M. LaHay, Mr. Byron Haymes and Miss Madge King, Mr. Will Rogers and Miss Mary Bullitte, Mr. Thos. Lane and Miss Mayme Headen, Mr. Bones and Miss Tambo. This was one of the best features of the entertainment, and they all acquitted themselves with credit.

Mr. Bones and Miss Tambo, taking the burlesque end of [the performance] to a perfection.

Mr. Will Rogers and Miss Mary Bullette were awarded the cake by the judges.

PD. Printed in *CP,* 30 March 1901.

1. There is a large literature on minstrelsy. See, for example, Lott, "Love and Theft: The Racial Unconscious of Blackface Minstrelsy"; Roediger, "Black Skins, White Masks"; Toll, *Blacking Up;* ibid, *On with the Show,* 81–109; Wilmeth, *Variety Entertainment and Outdoor Amusements,* 119–29.

2. The minstrel show's framework consisted of the actors sitting in a semicircle on the stage. In the center sat the "interlocutor," who served as the master of ceremonies and the director. In the show's first segment the interlocutor carried on a comic repartee with the endmen, called Bruder Tambo and Bruder Bones, who respectively played a tambourine and a pair of bones. The comic exchange between the interlocutor and the endmen was highlighted by rapid-fire puns, jokes, riddles, and malaprops. The second segment was the "olio," or variety section, when each actor performed a solo. The show usually ended with all the actors staging a skit (Nye, *Unembarrassed Muse,* 164; Toll, *On with the Show,* 89).

3. Joseph Martin (Joe) LaHay (1864–1911) was a close friend and colleague of Clem V. Rogers and a leading Cherokee Nation politician and Claremore booster. He was an attorney and served as the mayor of Claremore for seven terms, including one in 1899 and another in 1902–3.

LaHay was born during the Civil War at a Confederate refugee camp at Boggy Depot, in the Choctaw Nation, I.T., the son of John D. LaHay and Helen Martin LaHay. His father, who served with Clem V. Rogers in Stand Watie's Cherokee Mounted Regiment, was killed during the war. Joe LaHay attended Cherokee Nation public schools and graduated from the Osage Mission school in Kansas. His mother remarried after the death of his father, and his stepfather was killed in a coal mine at Krebs in the Choctaw Nation in 1879, whereupon Joe LaHay helped support the family by working first around the mines and then as a bookkeeper and cashier for the Osage Coal Mining Co. He married Annie Russell (1864–1951), a Scottish immigrant, in Missouri in 1886. In 1888 they moved to Claremore, where they established their family, which eventually included four children. They were charter members of the Presbyterian Church, and Joe LaHay was elected the town's first mayor. Annie Russell LaHay helped organize Claremore's first public library. Joe LaHay was district clerk for Cooweescoowee (1893–95), a member of the Cherokee Senate for two terms (1897–99, 1903–5), a delegate to Washington (1897–99), and treasurer of the Cherokee Nation (1899–1903). He was also a delegate to the Democratic National Convention in Chicago in 1896. He apprenticed to Indian Territory lawyers before passing the bar in 1898 and established his law practice in Claremore. Like Clem V. Rogers, the LaHays owned a farm outside of town but made their home in Claremore.

LaHay had many forms of collaboration with Clem V. Rogers. Both were members of the Knights of Pythias (LaHay was the grand chancellor of Indian Territory). They were involved in organizing the First National Bank of Claremore together, and LaHay and Clem V. Rogers's son-in-law Matthew Yocum (first husband of May Rogers Yocum Stine) were business partners. They rented the second floor of the Halsell Hall building, where LaHay used part of the floor for office space and Yocum used other rooms for overflow when the De Vann hotel rooms were full; they sublet the remaining rooms. LaHay and Clem V. Rogers, fellow Downing Party stalwarts, were both members of the Claremore City Council and were elected as senators from the Cooweescoowee District in the last official elections for the Cherokee National Council in 1903 (see July-August 1903 documents, below). LaHay was the last president of the Cherokee Senate before statehood. An opponent of merging Indian Territory with Oklahoma Territory to form a state, he played a strong role as a member of various committees in the Sequoyah Convention (1905), which convened to draft a constitution to create a separate Indian state named Sequoyah (the constitution was accepted by a large majority of Indian Territory citizens in an election, but was rejected by Congress).

The LaHays and the Rogerses were longtime personal friends and attended many social gatherings together. Joe LaHay was a popular man and had an excellent singing voice. The local *Claremore Progress* featured his long-running professional ad ("Will practice in all of the courts of Indian Territory") and also gave accounts of LaHay's antics at "home talent" minstrel shows, cakewalks, and costume parties and as toastmaster at civic events. LaHay and Clem V. Rogers both died in 1911. The LaHays were then residents of Muskogee; he had moved his law practice to Muskogee from Claremore soon after statehood (*CC*, 11 August 1899; *CDM*, 18 September 1901; *CP*, 22 December and 29 December 1894; 1 July and 8 July 1899; 20 January 1900; 30 March, 13 July, and 5 October 1901; 1 February, 12 April, 3 May, 24 May, 6 September, and 18 October 1902; 3 January and 4 April 1903; 16 September 1905; *CR*, 10 July 1903; *CWM*, 6 November 1903, 22 September 1905; *DC*, 5 November 1903, 10 June 1904; Gibson, *Oklahoma*, 327–29; Gideon, *Indian Territory*, 313–14; *HRC*, 10, 24, 60, 271–72; *Inola Register*, 25 January 1907; Maxwell, "Sequoyah Convention"; Starr, *History of the Cherokee Indians*, 270–71; Thoburn and Wright, *Oklahoma* 3:530–31).

4. R. Lee Comer was a businessman in Claremore. His brother John Leonard Comer married Mary Ermina McClellan, the sister of Charles White McClellan (*HRC*, 153).

5. Ida Mae Collins (1867–1938) was the eldest daughter of George O. Collins (d. 1871) and Lucinda Elliott Journeycake. Her mother married Dr. A. J. Lane in 1877. She grew up in the Oowala community and attended Vinita's Worcester Academy and the Cherokee National Female Seminary until it burned on 10 April 1877. Ida was a founding member of the Pocahontas Club in 1899 and served as its first president in 1899–1900. She was also a talented pianist, a singer, and a schoolteacher. Ida Collins married C. L. Goodale on 1 August 1906 and lived in Collinsville and Tulsa, where she was active in church, civic, and club activities (*As I Recollect*, 19–24; DuPriest et al., *Cherokee Recollections*, 1–2; see also Biographical Appendix entry, LANE, Andrew Jackson, M.D.).

6. Mrs. C. F. Godbey was the wife of the cashier of Claremore's First National Bank.

7. Mary A. Bullette (b. 1886) was the daughter of Helen Conkle and John L. Bullette (b. 1852), a prosperous Claremore merchant and rancher of Delaware Indian descent. A pioneer in the area, John Bullette established a mercantile business in old Claremore in 1880 and then moved it five miles north to the present-day location of the town. He also served as clerk of the Cooweescoowee District (1881–83) and as executive secretary to Principal Chief Joel B. Mayes and C. J. Harris. A farmer and owner of coal-mining interests, Bullette owned a large two-story structure in Claremore. Mary and her sister Mabel Zoe were often at the Pocahontas Club affairs (Croy, *Our Will Rogers*, 55; Gideon, *Indian Territory*, 390–91; O'Beirne, *Indian Territory*, 443–45).

8. Pure or classical ragtime began as the instrumental music of black composers and

performers, notably Scott Joplin. In the 1870s and 1880s ragtime flourished in cities with large African American populations, such as St. Louis, Memphis, and New Orleans. Known for its buoyant beat and syncopated rhythms, ragtime became very popular in the 1890s and the early 1900s as white composers and music publishers exploited the form by blending African American rhythms with white American melodies. Ragtime tunes with lyrics ridiculing blacks and perpetuating stereotypes, called "coon songs," were integrated into the minstrel shows in the 1890s (Nye, *Unembarrassed Muse*, 318–19; Toll, *On with the Show*, 118).

9. On the cakewalk see article from the *Claremore Progress*, 19 August 1899, above.

Article from the *Claremore Progress*
18 May 1901
Claremore, I. T.

A highlight of Will Rogers's early career as a steer roper was the United Confederate Veterans reunion[1] held at Memphis, Tenn., in May 1901. Rogers helped organize a group of cowboys to stage a riding and roping show at the reunion, which attracted over 100,000 veterans. He enlisted many of his friends to compete in the show, including Charley McClellan, Jim Hopkins, and Dick Parris, who would accompany him to Argentina the following year. Besides competing, Rogers acted as the master of ceremonies, or "barker," who introduced the roping contests from the grandstand.[2]

WILL GO TO MEMPHIS.

A number of cow boys of the Cherokee Nation have formed a stock company to give exhibitions of bronco busting and cattle roping during the Confederate re-union at Memphis the later part of this month.

J. C. Law and Will Rogers went to Memphis this week to make arrangements. The gentlemen's driving park near the city has been tendered the boys free and they will have full charge of the show and pocket all the receipts, the city doing all the advertising for them free. While the expenses will be heavy as all the horses and cattle will have to be shipped in, it is believed that the affair will be a financial success and the tenderfoots from the east will have a chance to see life as it is lived among the boys on the plains.[3]

Miss Mulhall, the noted equesterian, will be with the combination.[4]

A large number of the boys from Claremore will go down, among them being: Will and Clem Musgrove,[5] Charlie McClellan, Dick Parris, Frank Rucker,[6] Ernest Schrimcher, Tom Lane, Jim Sharp and Henry Walkley.[7]

PD. Printed in *CP,* 18 May 1901.

1. Formed in 1889, the United Confederate Veterans (UCV) organized all veterans who had served in the Confederate army during the Civil War into one major umbrella

organization. The UCV flourished in membership in the 1890s and early 1900s. The annual reunion of the UCV, held at different cities, was a very popular event in the South with many convention speakers, meetings, entertainment, and a colorful parade (White, W., *Confederate Veteran*, 33–48).

2. The contingent arrived on 25 May and began performing on 27 May for four days. On the afternoon of 26 May the cowboys gave a free exhibition of steer roping and bronco riding at Montgomery Park (*MCA*, 26 May 1901; see also Croy, *Our Will Rogers*, 56–58; Keith, *Boy's Life of Will Rogers*, 157–63).

3. The horses and steers were shipped from Texas (*MCA*, 26 May 1901).

4. An advertisement for the show in the *Memphis Commercial Appeal*, 29 May 1901, proclaimed "Montgomery Park, Cowboys and Indians, Grand Roping Contests and Indian Parades and War Dances, Miss Lucille Mulhall, The Daring Bronco Rider Will Appear Daily and Rope the Wildest Texas Steers, 2 Carloads Long-Horned Texas Steers, 2 Carloads Texas Broncos, 40 Indians and Texas Cowboys, Contests Daily at 3 p.m."

5. Clement Rogers Musgrove (1882–1911), the brother of Will (or Bill) Musgrove and a cousin of Will Rogers, was named after Clem V. Rogers. Educated at the Oowala School and the Male Seminary, he once worked on Clem V. Rogers's ranch. He married Veta Harris in 1905, and they were the parents of two children. A Claremore resident, he served as county clerk of Rogers County in 1920 (*As I Recollect*, 95–96; Collings, *Old Home Ranch*, 39; *HRC*, 333–34; *OCF* 1:194; Starr, *History of the Cherokee Indians*, 576; *WRFT*, 85).

6. Born in Randolph County, Mo., Frank Marshall Rucker (1866–1953) came to Indian Territory in the 1880s and established a ranch on his wife's (May Dora Taylor) allotment between Claremore and Pryor, near Blackie's station. His property was soon one of the largest cattle ranches in the area, consisting of approximately twenty thousand acres and over nineteen thousand head. He served as a U.S. deputy marshal during the late 1880s and early 1890s. His ranch also produced quality horses, hogs, and mules. With his brother Dr. John Garther Rucker, a Claremore physician, he owned a general store and the Mason Hotel in Claremore, and helped found two banks, the First National Bank of Claremore and the Farmer's Bank and Trust Co. In 1905 he built an early telephone system that ran from Vinita to Wagoner (*HRC*, 381–82; *OCF* 1:39).

7. Henry Kirkham Walkley (b. 1875) was elected councilor from the Coow-eescoowee District in 1905 (*OCF* 2:128).

Article from the *Commercial Appeal*
31 May 1901
Memphis, Tenn.

THE COWBOYS' SHOW
Their Exhibition an Unusually
Clever One, and Was Enjoyed by the Crowd

The "Cow Punchers" held high carnival at East End Park yesterday afternoon and the riding, busting broncos, roping, racing and Indian war dance kept the large crowd amused and entertained until late in the evening.

The outfit consists of forty cow boys, with a sprinkling of half breeds, all fresh from the spring round ups in the vicinity of Claremore, Indian Territory.

The boys are from different ranches and came as sightseers and to have a good time during the reunion.

Frank Rooker[1] is boss of the outfit and a jollier set of good fellows never were brought together.

The first half of the entertainment was taken up in roping and some good sport was furnished as two car loads of Texas "dogies" or range cattle had been received during the day. Each rider rode for his steer at the drop of the flag as it came from the cattle chute and some pretty individual work was witnessed.

Heber Skinner from Vinita, Indian Territory, won first money, $50, for roping, throwing and tieing down a steer in 31¼ seconds, beating his record of Wednesday and coming within four seconds of the world's record. Rucker won second money in 37 seconds and Wakley third in 43¼ seconds.

Charley McLellon, a quarter blood Cherokee and his seventeen-year-old brother, Steve, are among the most daring and skillful riders, but Charley was badly hurt Wednesday by his horse falling under him in throwing a steer and did not ride yesterday. Charley McLellon is a typical looking Indian, with long black hair, black eyes and high cheek bones. He is a college man, having attended Cumberland University at Lebanon, Tenn., and was in the junior class last year.[2]

Shorty Provine rode a bucking broncho without bridle and guided his horse with a hackamore. His riding was loudly applauded but was eclipsed when a wild steer of the long-horn variety was roped and saddled and ridden by one of the bronco busters. Messrs. Sharpe, Franklin, Rogers and Hopkins entertained the crowd with fancy roping on horse back while several cowboy races from the eight pole were exciting and interesting. The cowboys are camped at the park. They will give daily exhibitions Friday and Saturday afternoon, beginning at 3 o'clock and return to their homes Sunday. The public have never before had an opportunity of seeing cowboy life as it really exists in the West today and it will prove interesting. The sport is exciting but not brutal and is very enjoyable. The performance concludes each day by a buck and war dance by the half breeds and cowboys.

PD. Printed in *MCA*, 31 May 1901.

1. Probably a reference to Claremore cattle baron Frank Marshall Rucker (see article from the *Claremore Progress*, 18 May 1901, n. 6, above).

2. Founded in 1842, the Cumberland College of Tennessee is today an independent private junior college offering associate of arts and associate of science degrees. Lebanon is located in Wilson County in north-central Tennessee, about thirty-one miles east of Nashville. Susan McClellan Wear, Charles White McClellan's sister, was also a student at Cumberland College and recalls attending the roping contest and later having dinner

Portrait of Charles (Charley) McClellan taken when he was a student at Cumberland College, Lebanon, Tenn. McClellan died from typhoid fever in 1902 while attending the college (*Keith Collection, OkU*).

with her brother and Rogers. Charley McClellan died on 19 December 1902 from typhoid fever while still a student at the college (Cass and Birnbaum, *Comparative Guide to Junior and Two-year Community Colleges*, 122; *CP,* 27 December 1902; Susan Mc-Clellan Wear interview, Pocahontas Club, audiotape 16, OkClaW; *WNGD,* 657; see also Biographical Appendix entry, MCCLELLAN, Charles White).

Article from the *Daily Chieftain*
6 September 1901
Vinita, I.T.

Rogers entered the steer-roping contest at an Elks Convention in Springfield, Mo., where the cowboy entertainment was organized by Zack Mulhall. Rogers got second prize behind his good friend Jim Hopkins. One of the spectators was Betty Blake, and he tried to impress her with his roping.[1] At the street parade Rogers and the other cowboys wore purple shirts and had fun roping the spectators. At the parade's head was Charles McClellan, who wore a full headdress of eagle feathers.[2]

TERRITORY BOYS

GROUND STEERS IN STIRRING STYLE AT SPRINGFIELD THURSDAY.

JIM HOPKINS WINS FIRST PRIZE IN FAST TIME,

WHILE OTHER TERRITORY REPRESENTATIVES DO AGILE STUNTS

FOR THE ENTERTAINMENT OF THE VAST THRONG.

The roping contest at Springfield Thursday was largely a territory affair.

Jim Hopkins, who annexed the first prize in the fast time of 45 seconds, though registered from San Antonio, is a product of the territory range.

Sam Cobb executed the most spectacular stunt of the day. The elastic larynx of the agile steer he had circled with the noose snapped the rope before the bovine had disturbed the dust. Tying his rope together, with his horse on the run, he grounded the animal in 2 minutes and 3 seconds.

Dick Parris, of Tahlequah, missed second prize by his failure to jolt the last kick out of his steer. The animal, after being tied in 46 seconds, unloosened a wind-mill uppercut that snapped the throngs, and Parris' chances.

W. P. Rogers, of Oologah, won out on his good time of 50 seconds.

The following is the list of men who took part and the time made by each. . . .

PD. Printed in *DC,* 6 September 1901.

1. Betty Rogers remembered her husband riding Comanche, his favorite horse, and wearing a Stetson. She recalled, "Comanche was very fast, and Will's cowboy yell could be heard over all the others as he raced his pony around the arena at a dead run" (Rogers, *Will Rogers,* 21). Evidently, their relationship remained unchanged, and he would not see her again for nearly three years. It was here that a New Yorker supposedly offered

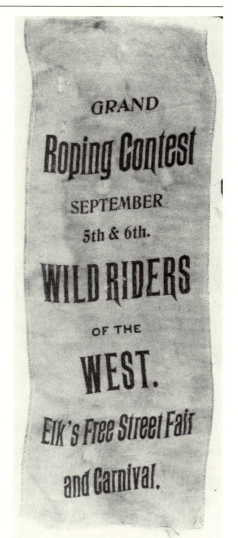

Advertisement for the roping contest at the Elks Convention. "I saw Will . . . in Springfield, Missouri, which was near my own Arkansas town, at a rodeo during the convention of the Elks Lodge," recalled Betty Blake Rogers in her memoir of her husband (*Will Rogers,* p. 20) (*OkClaW*).

Rogers five hundred dollars for Comanche after seeing the horse perform. Rogers refused, saying, "there is not money enough in that grandstand to buy old Comanche" (O'Donnell, "My Friend Will," 19).

2. Croy, *Our Will Rogers,* 74; Keith, *Boy's Life of Will Rogers,* 163–64; Ketchum, *Will Rogers,* 70.

Article from the *Claremore Progress*
21 September 1901
Claremore, I.T.

Rogers was considered the life of the party at Saturday night outdoor stomp dances. He would sometimes dress up as an Indian and during the dances bellow a war whoop. The Pocahontas Club held "An Evening with Hiawatha," which was well attended by friends from the surrounding area. Dressed in an Indian costume, Rogers stole the show with his attire and singing.[1]

AN EVENING WITH HIAWATHA.

Col. and Mrs. F. A. Neilson[2] entertained the Pocahontas Club and its friends in a pleasant and unique manner Friday evening last.

The rooms of their elegant home were decorated in an attractive manner with Indian curios.

At 9:00 o'clock roll was called by President J. F. McClellan,[3] and each guest was presented with a paper arrow bearing his or her name, after which ensued a warm contest. A cloth with a large heart marked on it with red chalk being drawn across the folding doors. Each guest being blindfolded was conducted into a darkened room and directed to fire their arrow as near as they could guess to [the] center of [the] heart. The first prize, a buckskin money purse of Indian make with heart shaped bead work, was won by Miss Nettie Frakes.[4] The second prize, a miniature bow and arrow, by Miss Zoe Bullette.[5] The booby, a peace pipe fell to Miss Vic Foreman. Prof. J. M. Yorke then sang "Hearts" by Horris; after which were passed divided hearts with heart quotations from Hiawatha, each half heart bearing half the quotation and a bead of real wampum. Partners for refreshments finding each other by numbers and quotations. The guests seated themselves on fancy Indian blankets spread upon the floor in true Indian style, and were served with refreshments consisting of ice cream, sherbert, cake and fruit.

Mr. Will Rogers appeared in full Indian costume, of war paint, tomahawk and other paraphernalia, and favored the company with several excellent songs, which were highly appreciated.

Owing to [the] storm coming up, it was 2:00 a.m. when the wagonette was ordered to take the guests home, when they departed highly pleased with their evening's entertainment and delighted with their host and hostess. . . .

PD. Printed in *CP,* 21 September 1901.

1. Croy, *Our Will Rogers,* 59.
2. F. A. Neilson owned a mercantile store in Claremore (*HRC,* 259).

3. John Foreman (Sos) McClellan (1872–1949), Charles McClellan's older brother, was president of the Pocahontas Club in 1901 and 1902. By its second year of operation the boys in the club were holding offices. A successful rancher, McClellan owned a ranch in the northeast Claremore area and used the SOS brand that derived from his nickname. He was also an officer of the Farmers Bank and Trust Co. (DuPriest et al., *Cherokee Recollections,* 57–59; *HRC,* 289–90; John Foreman McClellan, Jr., interview, Pocahontas Club, audiotape 12, OkClaW).

4. Nettie Frakes was the daughter of Dora and Hiram Frakes, the first proprietors of Claremore's Sequoyah Hotel. Nettie Frakes served as Chelsea postmaster and married twice, to James E. Milam and to C. W. McHenry (DuPriest et al., *Cherokee Recollections,* 61).

5. Mabel Zoe Bullette (b. 1881) was the daughter of Helen N. Conkle and John Bullette and the sister of Mary Bullette. She married Dr. Frank Muron Duckworth (b. 1873) (Gideon, *Indian Territory,* 390–91; O'Beirne, *Indian Territory,* 443–45; *OCF* 1:181).

Article from the *Daily Chieftain*
27 September 1901
Vinita, I.T.

Cow Boy Party.
At the Beautiful Residence of
Mr. and Mrs. W. L. Trott.[1]

Did you ever go to one?

If you haven't you have missed a treat, for this was one of the most successful parties ever given in Vinita.

The cow boys, in response to the unique little invitations, were all there dressed in their roping costumes, and Miss Dot Fay received the guests in a most admirable and graceful manner. Everybody was made to feel at home.

A large placard was hung across the brilliantly lighted hall on which was written "Welcome," Go on and have a "time."

The house was beautifully arranged and everything had been prepared with the greatest of care for the pleasure of the guests by Mr. and Mrs. Trott. Delightful music and dancing were indulged in, which added a great deal of merriment to the occasion. At ten o'clock the boys were provided with a little book which contained the names of eight different kinds of cattle, with the letters transposed and each one drew a card on which was a young lady's name to help him "do the guessin'." After a long careful study it was decided that Tom Isbell[2] had won the prize—a fine leather whip, and the second prize was awarded Miss Maud Miller, who was assisting him.

The guests were then invited to the softly lighted veranda, where a delightful lunch was served and thoroughly enjoyed by all.

Will Rogers *(top left)* poses with some young friends from the Claremore/Oologah area *(Scrapbook 1902–4, CPpR).*

It was among the "wee small hours" when the guests, profuse in their thanks to their hostess, left for their homes to dream about the pleasant hours spent. The occasion was long to be remembered by all present.

Those present were . . . Sam Cobb, John Skinner,[3] Geo. Franklin, Will Rogers, of Claremore, Will Orme of Tulsa. . . .[4]

PD. Printed in *DC,* 27 September 1901.

1. Born in Woodberry, Tenn., in 1844, William Lafayette Trott settled in Vinita in 1868 after serving in the Confederate army. A Vinita pioneer, he opened a livery business and in 1884 established a lumber yard. He ran unsuccessfully for the Cherokee Nation Senate in 1891 and was later elected mayor of Vinita. In 1869 he married Louisa J. Moore, and they were the parents of two children (O'Beirne, *Indian Territory,* 277–79; Starr, *History of the Cherokee Indians,* 605).

2. Born in Fort Gibson, I.T., Thomas J. Isbell was the son of L. P. Isbell, an early Vinita police chief and U.S. deputy marshal. Tom Isbell joined Theodore Roosevelt's Rough Riders in the Spanish-American War, serving as a private in Troop L, according to the official "Muster-out Roll." He was once described as the first soldier in his

"regiment to kill a Spaniard" (*ISR*, 11 October 1901). First Lt. John R. Thomas of Troop L recalled Isbell leading an advanced patrol when he "spied the first Spanish picket some distance in advance of him. Quick as lightening his Krag-Jorgenson plugged the Spaniard, and he never moved after he fell in the trail" (quoted in Benedict, *Muskogee and Northeastern Oklahoma* 1:279). According to the Muster-out Roll, Isbell was wounded in Cuba on 25 June 1898 at the battle of Las Guásimas, shot in the neck, hip, and thumb. In his account of the Rough Riders, Theodore Roosevelt wrote: "Thomas Isbell, a half-breed Cherokee in the squad under Hamilton Fish, was among the first to shoot and be shot at. He was wounded no less than seven times. . . . He did not receive all of the wounds at the same time, over half an hour elapsing between the first and the last. Up to receiving the last wound he had declined to leave the firing-line, but by that time he had lost so much blood that he had to be sent to the rear. The man's wiry toughness was as notable as his courage" (Roosevelt, *Rough Riders*, 106; see also Jones, *Roosevelt's Rough Riders*, 127, 306). Lieutenant Thomas remembered the wounded Isbell having to walk four miles to a hospital. "He had a thumb shattered, two bullets through his scalp at the base of his brain, two in his body, and a bullet through his arm" (quoted in Benedict, *Muskogee and Northeastern Oklahoma* 1:280). Roosevelt's Rough Riders, officially the First United States Volunteer Calvary, contained two troops from the Indian Territory, which included twenty-five cavalrymen from Vinita. A total of 103 soldiers from the Indian Territory served as Rough Riders. Another Vinita citizen, Tilden Dawson, was supposedly the first American killed in the conflict. After the Spanish-American War, Isbell joined Buffalo Bill's Wild West and Congress of Rough Riders of the World, performing with sixteen other Rough Riders in a mock battle recreating the victory of San Juan Hill during the show's tour in 1899. A talented rider and roper, Isbell next appeared with Zack Mulhall's cowboy performers, appearing with Rogers in the 1901 Des Moines Seni-Om-Sed Carnival. He later rejoined the Buffalo Bill show, performing a bronco-riding act in England and other countries in 1903. Isbell moved to California in 1914 (see Jim Rider to Will Rogers, 2 September 1902, below; Campbell, *Vinita, I.T.*, 129–30; *IC*, 13 October and 19 October 1899, 19 September 1901; Jones, *Roosevelt's Rough Riders*, 341; Roosevelt, *Rough Riders*, 266; Russell, D., *Lives and Legends of Buffalo Bill*, 419; *Story of Craig County*, 47; White, G., *Eastern Establishment and the Western Experience*, 153).

    3. John Kell Skinner (b. 1881) was the son of Vinita ranchman and merchant Nathaniel Skinner (b. 1851) and Nannie Kell Skinner (1861–89). John Skinner attended Vinita's Worcester Academy and Willie Halsell College. He worked as a professional cowboy at many ranches during his lifetime. Known for a strong temperament and an inability to get along with people, he roamed from one job to another. He was employed by Ewing Halsell to work at his ranches in Oklahoma and Texas between 1942 and 1946. After that he obtained a job near Roswell, N. Mex., and was last heard from in 1954 (Holden, *Ranching Saga*, 413–20; O'Beirne, *Indian Territory*, 271–73; *OCF* 1:228).

    4. A total of thirty-seven people attended the party.

Notice from the *Claremore Progress*
5 October 1901
Claremore, I.T.

Will and Clem Musgrove, Ernest Schrimsher and Will Rogers left over the Frisco yesterday afternoon for Kansas City at which place today the cowboys of the southwest will have a parade, headed by the famous Teddy Roosevelt cow boy band.[1] From there they will go to Des Moines, Iowa, where they will take part in the roping contests at the cattlemens' convention to be held there.[2] There will be twelve Territory cow boys in the outfit.

PD. Printed in *CP,* 5 October 1901.

1. Probably a reference to Zack Mulhall's band, which had marched in the inaugural parade of President William McKinley and Vice President Theodore Roosevelt in March 1901. Roosevelt had seen the band perform at the Rough Riders reunion in Oklahoma City and invited them to the event. The band appeared under several names, including Mulhall's Cowboy Band and Colonel Mulhall's Frisco Line Territorial Band, which advertised the St. Louis and San Francisco Railroad, for which Mulhall worked. The previous issue of the *Claremore Progress* had carried a full-page profile of Theodore Roosevelt (*CP,* 28 September 1901; see also 12 October 1901; Cheney, "Lucile Mulhall, Fabulous Cowgirl," 58; Stansbury, *Lucille Mulhall,* 16–21).
   2. See article from the *Iowa State Register,* 11 October 1901, following.

Article from the *Iowa State Register*
11 October 1901
Des Moines, Iowa

Zack Mulhall's show appeared at the state fairgrounds every afternoon as part of the Des Moines Seni-Om-Sed Carnival.[1] The show featured Mulhall's cowboy band and two dozen of the best steer ropers in the country. Among them were Will Rogers, Lucille Mulhall, and other expert ropers from the Indian Territory. One event in particular signaled the danger to cattle in steer-roping contests.

STEER ROPING MODIFIED

HUMANE SOCIETY PREVENTS THROWING
AND TIEING OF CATTLE AT THE
FAIR GROUNDS.

ENTERTAINMENT GOOD, HOWEVER—HORSE SHOW
AND MIDWAY HINDERED BY RAIN—
PROGRAMMES.

Attorney Dunshee, representing the Humane Society, turned the cold damper on the steer roping contest feature of the Seni Om Sed carnival on Thursday afternoon [10 October], and because of the demand that the steers must not be thrown and roped, that part of the programme was not quite as exciting as it was during the first days of the contest.[2] There were plenty of other features to amuse, however, and the big crowd of 3,000 that went out to the grounds, despite the fact that it was raining, had a good time.

Because of the restrictions of the Humane Society, the steers were simply roped and not thrown. The cowboys were disgusted with the bonds of restraint that were placed upon them and did not enter into the game with their usual spirit, but just the same they put up a very clever exhibition. Rogers, the cowboy from the Cherokee Nation, roped his steer in 12 seconds, a record that it would be hard to beat, but two or three of the other competitors were close up on the score.

Sam Cobb, of the Indian territory, rode a quarter mile dash against Miss Lucille Mulhall, of Mulhall, Okla., and lost, Miss Mulhall winning in 26¼ seconds.

The exhibition will be repeated this afternoon, and despite the efforts to those who are trying to interfere, the management say that there will be a show that will be a hummer.

There are several men in the aggregation of cowboys who were with Roosevelt in his regiment of Rough Riders, and they are an interesting group. Isabel, for instance, a cowboy from the Indian country, was the first man of the Rough Rider regiment to kill a Spaniard in the Spanish-American war. . . .[3]

PD. Printed in *ISR*, 11 October 1901.

1. Rogers and the other local cowboys performed from 7 to 12 October at the fair grounds. The fair's name derived from Des Moines, spelled backwards. Advertisements for the show featured "Exciting Wild West Steer Roping Contests, With Daily Street Parades of Wild Cow Boys and Indians, Accompanied by the Famous Cowboy Band." The carnival week at Des Moines also included a horse show, street performances, night parades, theatrical presentations, DeKreko's Congress of Nations, and a free outdoor vaudeville show in which the Mulhall troupe displayed their roping abilities (*ISR*, 4 October and 8 October 1901; see also Stansbury, *Lucille Mulhall*, 19, 23, 25).
2. The restrictions were caused by several incidents during an earlier steer-roping contest. Several steers needed to be roped three or four times before being thrown; one steer had a horn broken, and another suffered a broken leg. Humane societies began to criticize the treatment of cattle and horses in cowboy contests as early as the 1890s. The societies especially singled out steer roping for its cruelty to animals. Because many steers were injured and killed in these events over the years, steer roping has been prohibited as a spectator sport in most states except Arizona, Oklahoma, Oregon, Utah, and Wyoming (Fredriksson, *American Rodeo*, 145–52; *ISR*, 9 October 1901; Lawrence, *Rodeo*, 36–37, 176–77).
3. The article went on to report on the saddle horses at the fair and the horse-show

program. The Seni-Om-Sed program for Friday and Saturday was also printed, with the Mulhall show scheduled first at the fairgrounds on Friday afternoon.

Notice from the *Claremore Progress*
12 October 1901
Claremore, I.T.

Accompanied by Spi Trent, Rogers traveled to Buffalo, where he attended the Pan-American Exposition. Considered one of the most elaborate world's fairs of its time, the exposition stressed the themes of peace and progress.[1]

C. V. Rogers this week received word from his son Will, who is taking in the Pan-American Exposition, that he is having a great time.[2]

PD. Printed in *CP,* 12 October 1901.

1. The Buffalo Pan-American Exposition, which ran from 1 May to 2 November 1901, attracted over eight million people. The exposition was called the "Rainbow City" because of the bright color schemes of the buildings, which were designed primarily in a Spanish Renaissance style. A guidebook declared that the primary objective of the exposition was to "illustrate progress during the century just closed and lay a strong and enduring foundation for international, commercial and social unity in the world" (Rydell, *All the World's a Fair,* 127). It was originally conceived as a fair demonstrating closer relationships between North, Central, and South America. A major feature was the 389-foot Electric Tower, designed by the architect J. G. Howard, demonstrating technological progress. The exposition's midway, named the Pan, comprised a variety of amusements (a large seesaw, a rotating "aero-cycle," and a "Trip to the Moon"), restaurants, ethnographic villages, and a prominent exhibit entitled the "Evolution of Man." The exhibits symbolized predominant American attitudes at the turn of the century. The villages displaying the cultures of African Americans, Native Americans, Africans, Asians, and Hispanics, although endorsed by leading anthropologists, served to justify racial stereotypes and eugenic theories. The Filipino village and an exhibit on the Philippines (which was ceded by Spain to the United States in the 1898 Treaty of Paris ending the Spanish-American War) reinforced support of the nation's growing empire abroad. On 6 September 1901, the day after delivering a speech at the exposition celebrating American progress, Pres. William McKinley was assassinated by the anarchist Leon Czolgosz in the Temple of Music. Although 8,120,048 people attended the fair, McKinley's assassination affected attendance, and the exposition lost $578,000. A popular attraction on the midway was Col. Frederick T. Cummins's Indian Congress, which featured sham battles, Indian heroes, military scouts, and "long haired painted savages in all their barbaric splendor" (Rydell, *All the World's a Fair,* 149). According to Spi Trent, Rogers saw many of the exhibits on the midway, including probably the Cummins show and its star attraction, Geronimo, the famous Apache chief and warrior, who also appeared with the Cummins show at world expositions at Omaha (1898–99) and St. Louis (1904). The midway attractions must have given the young Rogers an introduction to the possibilities of a career in show business. Rogers would join the Cummins Indian Congress and Wild West Show at the St. Louis Louisiana Purchase Exposition in 1904 (Allwood, *Great Exhibitions,* 106–7, 182; Rogers, *Will Rogers,* 82–86;

Russell, *Lives and Legends of Buffalo Bill*, 383–84; Rydell, *All the World's a Fair*, 126–51; Trent, *My Cousin Will Rogers*, 146–48).

2. Rogers probably traveled to the exposition before he went to Des Moines and San Antonio for the steer-roping events, and the letter or postcard had taken time to get to his father.

Article from the *Daily Express*
23 October 1901
San Antonio, Tex.

From Des Moines, Rogers traveled to San Antonio, where he participated in steer-roping contests at the annual San Antonio International Fair and Exhibition. The steer-roping exhibitions were considered among the largest contests of the time and featured the nation's best ropers and top prize money.[1]

FAIR CROWD GROWS BIGGER AND BIGGER

THE ROPING CONTEST WAS THE BIG FEATURE OF THE DAY
AND WAS THE MOST EXCITING AFFAIR OF THE KIND EVER SEEN IN TEXAS—
THE STEERS WERE WICKED AND FOUGHT HARD—
THE NECK OF ONE WAS BROKEN.

. . . A multitude of people greater by four thousand than on Monday witnessed the second day's roping contest at the Fair grounds Tuesday morning.[2] It was the greatest outpouring of people ever seen at a roping contest in Southwest Texas. They crowded the grand stand to suffocation, hung and sat on the fences, stood on the race track. They were all well repaid, for some good records were made and many feats of skill performed. It was plainly demonstrated that the people want roping contests and in consequence another contest will be held on next Monday morning which, it is expected, will prove fully as interesting as those pulled off Monday and Tuesday.

Ross Kennedy of Sabinal, one of Tuesday's ropers, gets first money, $700, his record being 46 seconds. John Hewitt of San Angelo takes second money, $350 with a record of 52 seconds. . . .

Ross Kennedy, who wins first money, did a spectacular feat in turning his steer a back somersault. It was later found that the steer's neck was broken.

CONTEST IN DETAIL.

Riley Smith of Beeville, the first cowpuncher to throw the lasso, made a record of 54 seconds. His steer was a big red one and was apparently startled when released from the pen, for he almost stood still before attempting to run.

Eugene Irvin, second man up, tied his steer in 1.22. Irvin would have established a brilliant record had his horse not fallen with the steer. Irvin got up and jumping on his horse circled around the steer dragging the latter down. The grand stand cheered him. . . .

W. P. Rogers, Vinita, I.T., threw his steer several times. Rogers had a black Bremer ox which the judges declared to be a "snap." That the animal was tricky is not doubted. Rogers' time 1.36.

L. E. Blackaller, Frio, Tex. He caught on the first throw and got his steer down near the backside fence. He found it necessary to throw this steer for the second time. Time 1.07.

John Merril, Round Rock. Merril had a big ox and a poor horse. He established a record of 1½ minutes to tie his steer.

Dan McCrohan, San Angelo, had a fighting animal to handle. In trying to throw his animal, man, horse and all went down. Then the steer went after the man. McCrohan had to dodge the enraged brute. The latter was thrown on the third attempt. Time was 2.05. . . .

TUESDAY'S OFFICIAL TIME.

Ross Kennedy	46
Riley Smith	54
Sam Anderson	56
John McLean	1.03
L. E. Blackaller	1.07
Bob Lansford	1.15
Clay McGonigle[3]	1.20
Eugene Irvin	1.22
John Merril	1.30
Jim Reagan	1.35½
W. P. Rogers	1.36
Jack Heard	1.38½
W. R. Capps	1.38½
C. R. Miller	1.51
J. Kelley	2.02½
Dan McCrohan	2.05
Will Hill	2.06
Len English	2.17
Green Holland	3.32

The prizes awarded to the ropers will be distributed at the Fair grounds this morning.[4]

PD. Printed in *DE*, 23 October 1901. Headlines abridged.

1. The San Antonio International Fair ran from 19 to 30 October. It featured exhibitions of livestock, machinery, and farm products as well as a variety of entertainment including harness races, Professor Conterno's Celebrated Band, football games, motorcycle contests, and an event entitled "Battles of Our Nation." Each day the fair had a theme such as "Confederate Day," "San Antonio Day," and "Military Day." Cattle-roping contests were advertised for 21 October and 22 October. Ropers came from Indian Territory, Texas, Colorado, and other states (*DE*, 14 October 1901).

2. Because of the large number of ropers (forty-nine) the competition was held over two days. Rogers did not compete on the first day, Monday, 21 October. Charles H. Tompkins, the rodeo producer, who first met Will Rogers at this fair, wrote about the type of steers in the San Antonio contest: "The steers for this contest were furnished by Coleman and Kearns, two fine South Texas cowmen of those days of over 50 years ago. George W. Saunders was the man who promoted these ropings, and that famous old-time cowman and roper, John Blocker, was the field marshal. The steers were Brahmas and wild as deer; the cowboys dubbed them 'Billies.' They were steers weighing around 900 pounds each, and many of them could out run a fast horse. They were brought in a few days before the contest and were kept off feed and water for 24 hours so that they would not be sluggish and could run fast." (Tompkins, "My Association with Will Rogers," 7).

3. Henry Clay McGonigle (1879–1921) was considered one of the best ropers during the early years of cowboy contests between 1900 and 1920. Rogers first met him at the San Antonio event, and they became acquaintances (Porter, W., *Who's Who in Rodeo*, 84–85; *TDW*, 7 March 1926; see also Biographical Appendix entry MCGONIGLE, Henry Clay).

4. The prize money was $500 for first place, $400 for second, and $250 for third.

Article from the *Daily Express*
29 October 1901
San Antonio, Tex.

In the team competition Rogers's "thoroughly wild" steer jumped the fence and ran into the nearby race track. It took over seven minutes to rope the animal. There is a story that Rogers broke down and cried, feeling he had disappointed his teammates from the Indian Territory.[1]

ANOTHER BIG OUTPOURING OF PEOPLE

TREMENDOUS CROWDS STILL CONTINUE TO FLOCK TO THE SAN ANTONIO INTERNATIONAL FAIR.[2]

THE ROPING CONTEST.

THE BIGGEST CROWD ON RECORD TO WITNESS A CONTEST TOOK THE GRAND STAND.

The largest crowd ever assembled in San Antonio to witness a roping contest came to the Fair grounds Monday morning to see nine selected "cowpunchers" throw lassos on twenty-seven of the wildest and wooliest steers seen in this city. The contest was arranged immediately after the close of the one held last Tuesday. The cowboys making the best records in last week's contests were secured. A great deal of interest was manifested in the affair and cash purses aggregating $800 were hung up for the cowboys to go after. The latter also raised a purse of $225 for the man making the best individual record. The nine men entered were divided into teams of three each. Coleman & Keeran entered a team composed of Jim Proctor, L. E. Blackaller and Jack Hill. Preston Austin and John W. Kokernot entered Clay McGonigle, Jim Hopkins and Joe Gardiner[3] as their team. W. P. Rogers, Jack Heard and Green Holland, the Territory team, were entered by Gus Witting. The winning team was to receive $400, the second $250 and the third $150. There was a heavy play in the books on all the cowmen before the contest was commenced but after the first nine steers were turned loose bets could not be secured on some of the entries, no matter what odds were offered by the books.

The crowd itself was one of the most interesting features of the contest. Probably three-fourths of the people who went to the grounds in the forenoon came for no other purpose than to see the roping. Long before the first steer was liberated there was no available room in the grand stand. Then the visitors began searching for points of vantage along the fences. These were soon a black mass of humanity. The fences were lined from a point 100 yards north of the grand stand past San Juan hill, and little knots of people were to be seen in all portions around the race track. San Juan hill had never been crowded so densely before, and the room not taken up by visitors was filled with carriages. The stock barns were improvised grand stands. It was a great crowd and a good humored one, for they stuck almost until the last steer was spread out, and that was 2 o'clock. The sport lasted for three hours and was the best of its kind ever pulled off in the Alamo City.

The Contest in Detail.

Green Holland of the Territory team was the first roper. A big long-horned steer and full of ginger fell to his lot. Holland gave chase and caught the steer after a long sprint. The latter was securely tied in 1.05½.

Jack Hill was the second man up and coming from Twohig, had a black Bremer steer assigned to him. His animal was a bad ox and thoroughly versed in sprinting. Hill threw up his hat in 1.16½.

Clay McGonigle of Midland, Tex., was called to the post. On the books he was played as favorite. McGonigle holds the best record for tying steers and thoroughly understands the art. He repeated his star performance by breaking all records made in this city. His brilliant work was due partly to the fact that his horse could not be beaten for just such work. A red and white spotted steer came bellowing out of the pens and as he passed the stakes McGonigle shot out after him. He chased his game but a short distance and roped splendidly. His ox was "busted wide open," and the roper lost no time in getting his legs tied. The record was 44¼ seconds.

W. P. Rogers of the Indian Territory was next up. He ran his steer to the back side fence and missed on the first throw catching the steer's hind foot. The animal kept his pace until on the race track, where he was thrown and tied. Time 2.15. . . .

Rogers, the second time up, had a bob-tailed steer to contend with. He was a thoroughly wild animal and was out to show the cowboys a good time. He did. Rogers missed the first throw and when he finally got his lasso on the animal's horns his saddle turned, then the rope had to be cut. Rogers went after another rope, and after more chasing, got the steer tied in 7.16. . . .

Jack Hill's third steer made a complete circle of the pen and after a long chase he was thrown near the back side fence. Time 2.17.

Clay McGonigle caught a fast ox. The animal got up after the first throw and the roper had to go after him again. Time 1.11.

Rogers tied his [third] steer in 2.37½.

The steer got loose later and the record was thrown out.

Blackaller did more good work for the third time. He had a hard steer to handle and after three attempts, tied him. Time 1.12.

Joe Gardiner had to run his steer into tall timber before getting him down. He threw his rope three times. Time 2.04¼.

Jack Heard made no time with his third steer and gave up the chase. . .

THE WINNERS.

According to the decision of the judges the team entered by Coleman & Keeran gets first money. . . . Austin and Kokernot's team winners of second money. . . . Witting's team no record by reason of Heard giving up in attempting to rope third steer.

The prize of $225, gotten up by cowboys in the contest goes to L. E. Blackaller for individual roping, his record being 3.35½ for three steers.

PD. Printed in *DE*, 29 October 1901. Headlines abridged.

1. Croy, *Our Will Rogers*, 74–76; Keith, *Boy's Life of Will Rogers*, 166. Charles H. Tompkins wrote that Rogers's "steer was just jumping from the center field to the race track when Will caught him. He got a side run on Will, and Will's saddle turned under

his horse's belly and that ended their time as far as time was concerned (Tompkins, "My Association with Will Rogers," 8). Tompkins would later hire Rogers for his Wild West show at the 1904 Louisiana Purchase Exposition at St. Louis.

  2. The program for Tuesday, 29 October 1901, printed at the top of the *Daily Express* report on the fair, included Woodmen of the World Day, Conterno's Band concert, a vaudeville show, races, and a premium stock parade.

  3. Joseph (Little Joe) Gardner from San Angelo, Tex., was considered among the best steer ropers in the early 1900s. He was a partner of Clay McGonigle. Around 1922 Rogers visited Gardner's ranch in Sierra Blanca, Tex., to help brand calves (*TDW,* 7 March 1926; Westermeier, *Man, Beast, Dust,* 45).

Article from the *Claremore Progress*
18 January 1902
Claremore, I. T.

As the patriarch of the Rogers clan, Clem V. Rogers's birthday was always the occasion for a large family celebration to which close friends were also invited.

IN HONOR OF HIS SIXTY-THIRD BIRTHDAY.

C. V. Rogers celebrated his sixty-third birthday Saturday by entertaining at dinner his children, grandchildren and a few friends at an elegant dinner at the Frisco restaurant. Mrs. Gibbs[1] had prepared one of those excellent dinners for which she is noted and the guests did ample justice to it.

A pleasant afternoon was spent at Mr. Roger's rooms in the bank building.

The following guests were present: Mr. and Mrs. C. L. Lane and three children, of Chelsea; Mr. and Mrs. J. T. McSpadden and five children, of Chelsea; Mrs. May Stine and two children of Talala; Mr. Will Rogers, of Oologah. . . .

PD. Printed in *CP,* 18 January 1902.

  1. Mrs. Joseph L. Gibbs, Sr., took in boarders and served meals in a building formerly occupied by Boling's Pharmacy in Claremore. Her husband ran Gibbs's Livery Stable in town. In 1902 the Gibbses opened "an elegant restaurant" opposite the Frisco depot that they called the Globe Restaurant. Joe Gibbs, Jr., opened a bowling alley in the same period (*CP,* 21 September and 28 September 1901, 25 October and 21 November 1902).

Clement Vann Rogers in a formal portrait that reflects his stature as a prominent rancher, banker, and public official in the Cherokee Nation (*OkClaW*)

4. ARGENTINA
February 1902–July 1902

A dapper Will Rogers as a young man *(Scrapbook A1, OkClaW)*.

WANDERLUST STRUCK WILL ROGERS IN EARLY 1902. ALREADY RESTLESS AND
on the move, appearing in regional rodeos and roping contests with his friends,
Rogers was frustrated with the style of ranching mandated by the modernization of the Verdigris country. Now that open grasslands had been fenced and
divided, long cattle drives were replaced by the shipping of livestock by
railroad. Faced with an increased emphasis on crop farming, Rogers began to
dream of opportunities in a more open country and to think of alternatives
beyond inheriting his father's place—on a diminished scale—as a cattleman in
Cooweescoowee District. He considered the rangelands of Texas, which were
nearby and familiar territory to friends and family members and places where
the old rules of frontier life and of managing large herds of cattle seemed to
remain more intact. He decided instead on the larger adventure of Argentina, a
country whose economy was based on the livestock industry. There the huge
cattle belt on the pampas seemed to promise a chance for a young cowboy with
experience on his own family's ranch to learn Argentine ways of ranching and
to work his way up to becoming a cattleman in his own right.[1]

Rogers announced his decision to a rather stunned Clem V. Rogers, who
despite his surprise supported his son and helped him in the sale of the
Rogers-ranch cattle at market. The proceeds of the sale went to Will for his
trip. Will recruited his close friend Dick Parris,[2] whom he had known from
Tahlequah and who had worked as a ranch hand on the Rogers ranch, to come
with him to Argentina. Parris and Rogers had shared experiences on the
regional rodeo and roping circuits, and Parris was popular in Oolagah and
other Cherokee Nation towns, where he was known, like Rogers himself, for
his charm and folksy humor. The two young men set out in March 1902 for
New Orleans, where they hoped to book passage to South America. They soon
learned that their travel would be more complicated than they had imagined.
They took in the sights and the theater in New Orleans, seeing a prime example
of success and fame in show business when they viewed Julia Marlowe in her
extremely popular historical melodrama, *When Knighthood Was in Flower*.[3]
Rogers was impressed with the performance and the play, which satirized
England from an American's point of view. He soon had a chance to do

something of the same, for he and Parris journeyed briefly to New York and then on to England.

This period was one of major transitions in Rogers's life, and also in the world around him. He was headed for Argentina, where a virtual revolution was occurring in land use, agriculture, demography, the migration of labor, and the growth of cities and towns—changes not unlike those occurring in Indian Territory, where modernization had transformed the Verdigris country drastically since the time when Clem V. Rogers had first established his ranch there. Rogers arrived in England just as the Victorian era had drawn to a close with the death of Queen Victoria in 1901, and Britain was preparing for the coronation of its new king, Edward VII. British society was also dealing with its role in the South African War, which was to end within weeks. Both the reconstitution of the monarchy and the changes in British colonialism signaled by the war delineated the period when Rogers visited England as a new political era. Little did Rogers know when he visited London—with news about the end of the war in the air—that he would soon be moving to South Africa himself and witnessing the aftermath of the war firsthand.[4]

Parris and Rogers did some sightseeing in London, where Rogers formed some opinions of the British and of British culture and poked Yankee-style fun at the monarchy. He also went to a performance by Dan Leno, the leading singer-comedian in British popular theater.[5] The two tourists finally set sail for their intended destination, stopping in ports in Europe, the Atlantic islands, and Brazil before arriving in Buenos Aires in early May 1902. Rogers wrote home to his family about the trip, entertaining them with descriptions of the people and places he had seen. He arrived in Buenos Aires full of optimism, declaring the city one of the most beautiful he had ever beheld. Buoyed up by a talk with the American consul, who was himself a cattleman who had amassed quite a fortune during his years in Argentina, Rogers and Parris prepared to venture into the country's interior to look for work.

After time in the city and one trip into the cattle belt to seek employment, Dick Parris had had enough. He told Rogers he wanted to go home and try his hand in Texas, and Rogers paid for his passage back to the United States. Parris bore gifts for the Rogers family and left Will alone in Argentina at the end of May 1902.

Rogers rather quickly learned that Argentina was not what he had hoped. There was little opportunity there for a young American with minimal capital to begin even a small ranching enterprise. Like the flood of immigrants from Italy and Spain who had come to Argentina hoping to earn enough through day labor and agricultural work to eventually buy land, Rogers learned that

Richard (Dick) Parris, who accompanied Will Rogers to Argentina. Later in life he became a Bartlesville, Okla., rancher and deputy sheriff (*Bartlesville, Okla., Public Library*).

ownership and control of ranchland in the prime areas of the interior were monopolized by a small circle of Argentine elites who also dominated the nation's politics.[6] Although the country had experienced an economic boom in the 1880s and would have another resurgence of well-being between 1904 and 1912, Rogers arrived during a recession when wages were on a downward spiral and inflation was high. Rents and food prices exceeded the average monthly earnings of working families in Buenos Aires, and unemployment, even in agriculture, was common.[7]

Modernization of the pampas had in many ways paralleled the very phenomena that Rogers was seeking to escape in Indian Territory. British-financed railroad systems created new market possibilities along the frontier and brought with them new entrepreneurs and towns. The rising importance of sheep raising and agriculture, along with innovations in cattle breeding to meet the needs of foreign markets, meant fencing, the devaluation of old skills in handling cattle, and a new diversification of ranch labor. The free-agent gaucho way of life—romanticized in 1902 much as the cowboy and Wild West images were idealized and translated into popular culture in the United States—was irrevocably altered by these changes in the cattle industry. The gaucho for well over a century had been a nomadic wild-cattle hunter and handler, living closely dependent on his horse and maintaining his own separate subculture on the pampas. By the end of the nineteenth century he had become more of a *peón de campo,* a seasonal and migratory cowhand and ranch worker, often facing irregular or nonexistent employment and suscept- ible to the laws and labor needs of the ranching elite. Never a landowner, the Argentine equivalent of the cowboy had little security and faced eviction from small homesteads established on the huge spreads of land whose titles were often held by an absentee owner.[8]

There are ironies to be seen in the contrast between Rogers's place in Indian Territory and in Argentina. Both regions were transformed by huge popula- tion increases that changed the ethnic composition of rural and urban society. Both experienced massive development through the establishment of rail- roads, urbanization, migration, and a diversification of the economy. In both Indian Territory and Argentina frontier life and the norms associated with it were passing away. While the Cherokee Nation resisted the encroachments of intruders, of non-Indian migrants who sought work and hoped to establish small farms in Indian Territory, Rogers went abroad, a foreigner to Argentine culture and society, looking for similar opportunities for himself, and not finding them in a country where land was monopolized by the owners of huge estates. The quite-privileged son of a leading cattleman, property owner, businessman, and statesman of reputation in his own country, Rogers without capital or land in Argentina was relegated to the bottom ranks of the social hierarchy. The very processes that had limited his chances of finding work as a ranch hand in Argentina were mirrored in Indian Territory: the breakup of tribal lands into private property, the fencing of formerly open range; and the movement of people like his father from ranch to town or city, where the focus was on commercial and civic affairs, and the rental of ranches to tenants or their management by others from afar. In Argentina, estancia owners typically lived in Buenos Aires, where they were involved in enterprise, investment, and politics. Their large ranches meanwhile were rented in portions to tenant farmers, or managed by others who employed the gaucho-turned-peón-de- campo. Like Rogers, many of these gaucho ranch workers were part Indian in heritage.

Rogers had sympathy for the gaucho class, but could not find a place for himself between their downtrodden state and that of the Englishmen who served as overseers or managers of the ranches, whose status and means were

Portrait of Juan Moreira, famous Argentinean gaucho and literary figure, from one of Will Rogers's scrapbooks (*Scrapbook 1902–4, CPpR*).

beyond his own and whose detachment from the actual work of the ranches left him feeling little respect. He also was critical of Argentine ways of running and handling cattle and horses, finding them at odds with the time-honored methods he had been taught in Indian Territory. Not only did he find it difficult to fit in or find work in the interior, Rogers also felt alienated from the many other men who had come to Argentina, as he had, from foreign ports in search of work and social mobility. English-speaking immigrants were a small minority, and Rogers had difficulty learning Spanish or its Anglo-Argentine or Italo-Argentine varieties. He was disgusted by the political corruption practiced in small and large ways around him. Rogers turned for society to the English-speaking popular theater and to leisure activities centered around the docks where American sailors came into port. He entertained on board the ships and made friends with people performing in the theater, singing a little himself. In Argentina, as in the other countries to which he would travel, show business kept appearing as a viable and happier alternative to a ranching way of life.

Although his original hopes proved unrealistic, the lessons he learned in his travels were invaluable. One lesson, he confessed with appreciation to his father, was the value of money; but he also learned to enjoy life on his own. His experiences in England, aboard ship, and in Buenos Aires and the Argentine hinterlands helped give him an international perspective at the same time that he became more aware of his own identity as an American. His letters home to his father, friends, and sisters, as well as his first published reports in his hometown newspaper, offer us our first glimpse of Rogers as a commentator who offered wry humor and pointed opinions on the common affairs of life. Thus his time in Argentina not only represented a gradual transition away from his family legacy in Indian Territory, which included a career in ranching, but also foreshadowed his future career both as an entertainer and as a columnist commenting on the news of the day.

At the end of July 1902, after barely three months in Argentina, Rogers wrote his family to inform them that he felt he had learned what the country had to offer and was moving on. Instead of returning home, he secured work on a big shipment of livestock headed for Natal, South Africa. He left Buenos Aires in the first week of August 1902.

1. As Rogers summed it up, "I had heard that the Argentine Republic was a great ranch country so I sold a bunch of my cattle and took a boy named Dick Parris with me and we hit the trail for South America" (transcription of autobiographical notes, OkClaW). For biographical accounts of this period of Will Rogers's life and his trip to Argentina, see, for example, Croy, *Our Will Rogers*, 76–79; Day, ed., *Autobiography*, 16–26; Keith, *Boy's Life of Will Rogers*, 166–72; Ketchum, *Will Rogers*, 75–78; Rogers, *Will Rogers*, 63–69.

2. Like Rogers, Parris was a mixed-blood Cherokee who was known for his sense of humor. He grew up in Tahlequah, attended school there, and made a living working on Cherokee Nation ranches and participating in regional rodeos. Parris was twenty-five years old, and Rogers twenty-three, when the two friends set out together for Argentina. See Biographical Appendix entry, PARRIS, Richard.

3. For information on Julia Marlowe's career and *When Knighthood Was in Flower,* see Derrick, "Julia Marlowe"; Marlowe, *Julia Marlowe's Story,* and Will Rogers to Sisters and Folks, 18 March 1902, n.4, below.

4. On the Victorian era and the monarchy of Edward VII, see Betjeman, *Victorian and Edwardian London;* Fulford, *Queen Victoria;* Hardie, *Political Influence of Queen Victoria;* Lee, *King Edward VII.* On the British involvement in and reaction to the South African War, see Blanch, "British Society and the War"; Nasson, "Tommy Atkins in South Africa"; and Porter, B., "Pro-Boers in Britain."

5. Dan Leno (1860–1904), who was known as the "greatest of all British music hall comics," appeared in the United States only once in his career (*EV,* 308). He starred at the Olympia Music Hall in New York in March 1897, returned to London, and made no other appearances outside Britain. Rogers saw him perform on 7 April 1902, perhaps receiving further encouragement for a career in theater and entertainment (see Will Rogers to Sisters and All, 4 April 1902, n.6, below).

6. On the political economy and social history of Argentina in the late-nineteenth and early-twentieth centuries, including issues of land ownership and immigrant labor, urbanization, the market economy, and the cattle and agricultural industries, see *HDA;* Munck, Falcon, and Galitelli, *Argentina;* Scobie, *Argentina;* idem, *Buenos Aires;* idem, *Revolution on the Pampas;* Slatta, *Gauchos on the Vanishing Frontier;* Smith, P., *Politics and Beef in Argentina;* Spalding, *La clases trabajadora Argentina;* Taylor, *Rural Life in Argentina;* Weil et al., eds., *Handbook for Argentina.*

7. On changes in labor, wage issues, and unemployment at the beginning of the 1900s in Argentina, see *BAH,* 20 August 1902; Munck, Falcon, and Galitelli, *Argentina,* 43–45; Scobie, *Buenos Aires;* Slatta, *Gauchos on the Vanishing Frontier,* 30–56.

8. On the social history of the gaucho and on the gaucho as a romantic and nationalistic symbol in Argentine culture and literature, see Becco and Calcena, *Gaucho; HDA,* 346–48, 348–49; Molas, *Historia social del gaucho;* Nichols, M., *Gaucho;* Paullada, *Rawhide and Song;* Slatta, *Gauchos on the Vanishing Frontier;* idem, "Cowboys and Gauchos."

Aerial view of the Rogers family ranch near Oologah. Although photographed in the 1940s or 1950s, Rogers's birthplace still looked much as it may have looked in the late 1890s, with miles of prairie around it *(OkClaW)*.

Notice from the *Claremore Progress*
22 February 1902
Claremore, I. T.

Despite Clem V. Rogers's efforts to make his son the heir to his ranching business, giving Will responsibility for managing the ranch and financial control over its cattle, young Will, now in his early twenties, continued to look for greater variety and wider horizons. As biographer Homer Croy has put it, the "red soil of Oklahoma made his feet itch." In early 1902 Rogers amazed his father by announcing that he wanted to sell all of his cattle and travel to Argentina with his long-time friend Dick Parris. He felt limited on the family farm and was attracted by the allure of the open range life that remained in Texas and in Argentina. Rogers hoped that the profits earned from the sale of his cattle would pay his travel expenses and help establish a place for him in the cattle industry in Argentina.[1]

Will Rogers has disposed of his herd of cattle and all his feed and announces his intention of going to South America to look into the matter of going into the cattle business there.

PD. Printed in *CP,* 22 February 1902.

1. Croy, *Our Will Rogers,* 76. Sources differ on the details of the transaction; some say that Clem V. Rogers bought back the cattle (which he had initially given to Will Rogers), and others say that they were sold (or perhaps subsequently resold) at auction in Kansas City. The amount of money gleaned from the sale is also variously reported between two thousand and three thousand dollars. For example, Betty Rogers reports that Will "went to Claremore to have a talk with his father about South America. Uncle Clem was not pleased. He wanted Willie to stay at home, but after a heated argument it seemed to him that the only solution was to let Willie go his own way. With characteristic generosity, he agreed to buy back the cattle that he had given Willie in the first place, and paid him some three thousand dollars for the herd" (Rogers, *Will Rogers,* 61–62). Historians Ellsworth Collings and Richard Ketchum draw on Betty Rogers's version of the events, and Rogers's cousin Spi Trent (who was living at the Rogers ranch at the time) also says that Clem V. Rogers purchased the cattle (Collings, *Old Home Ranch,* 94; Ketchum, *Will Rogers,* 70; Trent, *My Cousin Will Rogers,* 148). Biographer Homer Croy, however, says that "Will took the cattle to Kansas City and sold them with a profit of two thousand dollars, a handsome sum" (Croy, *Our Will Rogers,* 76).

From Clement Vann Rogers
13 March 1902
Claremore, I.T.

Will Rogers and Dick Parris traveled (apparently via Hot Springs, Ark.)[1] to the southern port of New Orleans, where they mistakenly believed they could get direct passage to Argentina. Here Clem V. Rogers lets his son know that he has forwarded some money to Will in New Orleans. The Rogers family would soon hear from Will about his time in that Louisiana city.

Claremore, I.T., <u>March 13</u> *1902*

Dear Willie

Hot Spring. My Health continues good. We had a good rain here Monday night & Tuesday All day. & it is nice & warm today. Willie we sent you your money to day to the Commercial Bank at New Orleans[1] $1300.00. I also sent you a Telegram about sending the money to the Commercial Bank at New Orleans, La. Keep the Telegram & this letter & you wont have any trouble about being identified at the Bank their. Sallie Maude & May & all the children are well. Write when you can

Your Pa

C. V. Rogers

ALS, rc. OkClaW. On C. V. Rogers Bank Building letterhead. Envelope hand-addressed to W. P. Rogers, Hot Springs, Ark., care of Sam Bowman.

1. The local *Vinita Leader* reported, "W. P. Rogers left Thursday for Texas where he will stop a short time and then go on to Argentine Republic, South America, where he will engage in the cattle business" *(VL,* 27 February 1902). Rogers actually spent some time in Hot Springs, Ark., in early March 1902 before he and Dick Parris proceeded on their trip.

Enclosure:
Bank Draft
Claremore, I. T.
24 March 1902

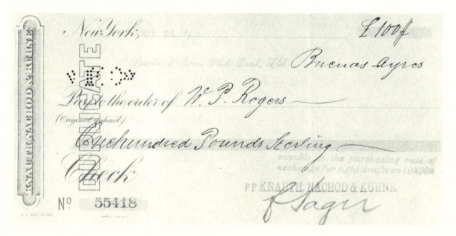

PD, with autograph insertions. OkClaW. Duplicate bank draft.

Rogers also received a Western Union telegram from C. F. Godbey, a cashier in Claremore, notifying him, "We sent draft to Commercial Natl Bank New Orleans." Like Clem V. Rogers's letter, the telegram was addressed to Rogers in Hot Springs, Ark. (Godbey to Rogers, 13 [March] 1902, OkClaW).

To Sisters and Folks
18 March 1902
New Orleans, La.

This is the first of many letters that the Rogers family received from Will Rogers
documenting his experiences in his convoluted travels to Argentina and beyond.
Here he describes his and Dick Parris's activities in New Orleans.

New Orleans. La.
March 18. 1902

My Dear Sisters and Folks[1]

Well We are here   arrived Sunday Night and find that we can not get a boat direct from here   but you can get a ticket from here via New York for Bueanos Ayers[2] for about 150 apiece that is first class   there is no second class   just first and the steerage.

We leave here in the Morning (Wednesday) at 9 oclock on the steamship Comus. and it is due to arrive in New York on Next Monday Morning   and then will have to wait probaly several days before we can get a boat out of there

We have seen most all of New Orleans   been down to the wharf most all day seeing them unload and load the big ships.[3]

Went to see Julia Marlowe[4] in When Knighthood was in Flower. last Night   it was simply fine.

We sent our baggage aboard this eve consisting of a big trunk of mine which has both our saddles and all our outfits in it and some of our clothes and we each have a grip with the rest of our togs in them.

It is regular spring down here   grass is away up and trees are all green and everything is as pretty as can be.

I will write you a long letter on the boat and mail to you when we get to N.Y. I guess if I am not to sick.

This seems an afful long way but it is the way they all go from here to that far down in S.A. It will take about 25 days from N.Y. to B.A.

We are in good Spirits and feeling fine.

I dont have time and there is no use to write to each of you   I will write to both in one so this is for all. give all the children Uncle E.[5] love and tell them I will have lots to tell them when I see them.

I cant tell you where to write to for I dont know where I will be so I will write as often as possible.

AL, rc. OkClaW. Envelope hand-addressed to Mrs. C. L. Lane, Chelsea, Ind. Ter.

1. This letter to Sallie McSpadden, Maud Lane, May Stine, and their families was addressed to Maud Lane. During his travels Rogers sent letters to either Sallie or Maud (in addition to those sent to his father). He intended that they share them with all the family and interested neighbors and friends. His sisters referred to reading the letters aloud to their children and passing them around to friends of the family. Sallie McSpadden, Maud Lane, and Clem V. Rogers corresponded regularly with Rogers. Their letters sometimes reached him months after they were mailed from Indian Territory, as he continued to move from place to place during his travels. His sister May Stine and some friends also were occasional correspondents between 1902 and 1904.

2. Buenos Aires, the capital of Argentina, is located on the eastern rim of the pampas. The country's main port, it is located on the estuary of the Río de la Plata in east-central Argentina, about 130 miles from the sea. First colonized by Spain in 1536, Buenos Aires developed over the centuries into the political, cultural, commercial, and industrial center of the country. Historically there has been much tension between Buenos Aires and the rural provinces. The city had a separate constitution from the provinces in the midnineteenth century. It has long dominated national commerce and controlled the Argentinian government. Large waves of European immigration were attracted to the city in the 1880s and the early 1900s. When Rogers lived in Buenos Aires, it was very cosmopolitan, "highly European in construction, citizenry, and culture" (Scobie, *Buenos Aires,* 13). Suburbs developed in the late-nineteenth and early-twentieth centuries as new towns and neighborhoods were established along the railroad corridors leading to and from the city. By 1910, after the boom in renewed immigration that came a few years after Rogers's departure from Argentina, the city had a population of 1,300,000 (for an account of what the average traveler would have encountered arriving in Buenos Aires by ship in 1910 versus 1870, see Scobie, "Study in Contrasts," chap. 2 in *Buenos Aires,* 13–69; see also Sargent, "1900–1930: The Creation of Greater Buenos Aires," chap. 5 in *Spatial Evolution of Greater Buenos Aires,* 93–105; Scobie, *Argentina,* and idem, "Buenos Aires as a Commercial-Bureaucratic City, 1880–1910").

3. New Orleans was an important deepwater port located between the Mississippi River and Lake Pontchartrain and a principal market for southern industrial and agricultural products, including cotton and rice. On the important role of dockworkers in the labor history of New Orleans in this period, see Arnesen, *Waterfront Workers of New Orleans,* and Rosenberg, *New Orleans Dockworkers.* On the history of New Orleans in the late-nineteenth and early-twentieth centuries, see Blassingame, *Black New Orleans, 1860–1880;* Carter et al., eds., *Past as Prelude: New Orleans;* Jackson, *New Orleans in the Gilded Age: Politics and Urban Progress; WNGD,* 837, 839).

4. Julia Marlowe (1866–1950) (also known as Fanny Brough and Sarah Frances Frost), a prominent actress in the United States and Great Britain, was born in Cumberland, England, the daughter of shopkeepers. Her father immigrated to the United States in 1870, and the family soon followed, living first in Kansas and then in Ohio. Julia, then called Fanny Brough, was raised primarily by her mother, who ran a hotel in Cincinnati. Her mother introduced her to the works of William Shakespeare and encouraged her to work in the chorus line of the local opera, where she came to the attention of the actress Ada Dow. After theatrical training, she made her debut under the name Julia Marlowe in a tour of New England in 1887. Despite excellent reviews, Marlowe constantly struggled financially and was eventually forced by economic strain to perform in works other than Shakespeare's. The play in which Will Rogers saw her perform in New Orleans, *When Knighthood Was in Flower,* was a melodramatic historical romance about the life of Mary Tudor, the sister of Henry VIII. A huge popular success,

it had tremendous advance sales and bookings in several cities over a two-year run. This success reversed Marlowe's previous impoverishment. As her authorized biographer put it, "This was the play that freed her" (Russell, C., *Julia Marlowe*, 299–300). The play, by Paul Kester, was an adaptation of a novel by Charles Major. Marlowe went on to establish a well-regarded Shakespearean company with the actor Edward Hugh Sothern, who became her husband in 1911. Marlowe was famous for her physical beauty and the quality of her voice. Personally a proponent of women's rights, professionally she represented to audiences the "quintessence of Victorian womanhood and . . . upright behavior" (McArthur, *Actors and American Culture*, 158). In a period when the acting profession often was considered disreputable, especially for women, she insisted on creating a "high moral influence" through her parts and was part of the trend in which the centrality of personality became a dominant school in American theater (Wilson, G., *History of American Acting*, 150).

Seeing *When Knighthood Was in Flower* in New Orleans in 1902 may have had quite an influence on Rogers as he set off to make a living as a rancher abroad—only to soon become discouraged and turn to a show-business career instead. At the very time that Rogers was struggling as a young man with decisions about what to do with his life, Marlowe demonstrated both the viability and ultimate respectability of a career in public performance and the attraction of a life in popular theater. *When Knighthood Was in Flower* revolved around the central figure of Marlowe and was in effect a one-woman show (and, in some scenes, a comedic monologue)—not unlike Rogers's own acts later in his career, which were solo performances focused around the strength of personality and the cultural qualities that his personality was popularly seen to represent. Like Rogers's later acts, much of the humor of *Knighthood* involved satirical commentary on political authority (in *Knighthood*, represented by the king). Marlowe's role in *Knighthood* also foreshadowed many of the themes of Rogers's later casting as the hero of the 1931 film version of Twain's novel *A Connecticut Yankee in King Arthur's Court*. In the very ahistorical scenario of the play, an American schoolgirl was transported to the English court, whereupon she "told a crowned king where he got off and nightly the audience went wild with enthusiasm at the telling" (Russell, *Julia Marlowe*, 296; see also Chinoy, "Art versus Business: The Role of Women in American Theatre"; Derrick, "Julia Marlowe"; James et al., eds. *Notable American Women* 2:497–99; Marlowe, *Julia Marlowe's Story* [as told to E. H. Sothern]; McArthur, *Actors and American Culture*, 18, 33–34, 47, 55, 148, 155, 158; Wilson, *History of American Acting*, 145–50).

5. "Uncle E" was an affectionate pseudonym Will Rogers used with his nieces and nephews.

To Sisters and All
4 April 1902
Southampton, England

Will Rogers and Dick Parris sailed on the S.S. Philadelphia *from New York to Southampton, England, departing in March 1902. Here is the first of two letters written home about their experiences in England.*

Southampton.[1] England

April 4th. 1902.

My Dearest Sisters and all.

Well Old *Dunker Dee*[2] Landed after Eight long days of heaving forth every thing he looked at. got on the boat at 10 oclock   ate a big dinner and then the thing come off   went to my little 1 1/2 by 5 and did not arise till the *Engineer* squalled out Southampton   then I sallied out   looked like a freak. after that dinner on Wednesday could not look towards anything   not even water till Monday   then after various attempts got a lemon and an Orange that never managed to find the way back.

Now I want to chirp to you now that if they would of been any turning back there I would of took out a small stack   for when you hear people say you get over it in a day or so you put it down that they have been taking foolish powders   for I and lots of the rest of them was all out on the whole trip   then when I could eat the last two days   they dident have anything I could eat. Dick was only sick about one day   Oh how I did think about all the good beans and good things we ever did have to eat at home. But now I feel good   we got in Wednesday Night at 10 oclock. they search your baggage for *Spirits* and *Tobacco.* dident find any in mine for I dident chew and my Spirits had all left me on that boat   if I had any at all I contributed them to the *big blue* before I met them. I dont know but what we may have to pay something on our saddles in S.A. for I think they ride bareback. then we took a *"handsome"* not a Lady. but a kind of a dog cart and went to a hotel. We get a nice room almost papered with pictures of Queen Victoria[3] who certainly had a stand in with the Photographer   We pay 2 shillings for both (now search out your Almanac and see what that is)   I've tried to learn the measly stuff till i am blue in the face   the penny is the principal thing   and the half penny   the penny looks about like our $20 gold pieces   I think I have got a great lot of coin and feel in my geans and when I go to pay for any thing its only a pipe dream for it takes them all for one apple or Orange   they are the only familiar Characters Ive met.

Every time We eat or get any thing they speal out what its worth   I just hand them a pound   that is all I know   which is about a five spot over there   and trust to the lord that they will take pity on my ignorance and do me half way right   anyway they'll hand me back a double hand full of something and strut off   I have got enough money in *bulk* to start in some kind of business. but when I count it (or if some one else did) there would not be enough there to make the first payment on a soda cracker.

That Machine[4] Maud has got there that talks so fast aint one. two. three. with the slowest creature over here. why they would make it *"go to the rear and find a damp place and fade away"* Our English must be a kind of slow process. I went up to a Man for some information yesterday and he throwed open the throttle and broke out on one of those chained ligntning [speeches?] and I flagged him at the first quarter and asked him (in my speediest tone   which by the way he seemed to tire of before I got done) if that I was perfectly willing to pay him for his over time if he would kindly relate it over again as though he were speaking of some of his poor or dead relation.

Their dress is about the same as ours all but the shoes   and you couldent imagine anything half so big and clumsy   why those old buckle plow shoes over home would be "dancing pumps" over here   all of them Dukes. Dudes. Earls and hod-carrier[s].

And this *food* over here is altogeather different by name and by nature. oh I am almost starved for something cooked over in America. We are only 40 miles from London and as we cant get out from here till a week from today   we will go up there and spend a few days as it is just as cheap living   We will see some great sites there I suppose but we are prepared for the *worst*.

We may call on his Royal Nibs the king.[5]

Our boat leaves here on the 12th for Buenos Aeyers   will be 20 or 25 days on that trip   I tell Dick he has got to get me drunk to get me on another boat   we go by Rio Janerio[6] and Montivideo.[7] an then B.A. I just sent Dick out to hunt the post office and he is back saying all the letters have to be weighed and then he stamps them and you pay

This information I am putting you next to is quite a weighty matter and I look to have to draw on my inside pocket to send this.

But By By will write you from London or here after being there   before we sail

Lots of Love to all. I am fast regaining my lost flesh for the next episode
Your Loving Bro and Uncle

.E.

Nowhere in Particular.

ALS, rc. OkClaW.

1. Southampton is a city in Hampshire in the south of England, located on a peninsula between two river estuaries, opposite the Isle of Wight. England's principal port and the chief passenger port for the British Isles, it has long been the terminal for many trans-Atlantic shipping lines. Originally a Roman and Saxon settlement, it became a naval base and was severely damaged by German bombing during World War II (*PEP,* 734; *WNGD,* 1135).

2. "Dunker Dee" was a term of endearment that Will Rogers's nieces and nephews used to refer to him (see May McSpadden to Will Rogers, 31 August 1902, below).

3. Queen Victoria (1819–1901), for whom the Victorian era is known, was queen of

the United Kingdom from 1837 until her death. She was the only child of Edward, the Duke of Kent. Beloved for portions of her reign, she withdrew from public life for a long period after the death of her husband, Albert, in 1861. She assumed new stature in the final years of her life, during the South African War. Her reign represents the gradual revision of the British monarchy from primarily political to ceremonial functions. Victoria, who especially in her later years was rather short and squat, was not known for her physical beauty (thus Rogers's comment that the portrait of her in his hotel room was so flattering she must have "had a stand in with the Photographer") (Fulford, *Queen Victoria;* Hardie, *Political Influence of Queen Victoria;* Mullen and Munson, *Victoria: Portrait of a Queen*).

4. Rogers is referring to his sister's Victrola.

5. Edward VII (1841–1910), the former Prince of Wales and the eldest son of Victoria and Albert, became king on the death of his mother on 22 January 1901. Born at Buckingham Palace, Albert was a poor student and a philanderer as a youth, and as a result he was excluded from most affairs of state. He married Alexandra, the daughter of Prince Christian of Denmark, in 1863. He was king for nine years, until his death (Cowles, *Gay Monarch;* Lee, *King Edward VII*).

6. Rio de Janeiro, the major commercial seaport of Brazil, is located in rolling hills on the shores of Guanabara Bay. Founded in the sixteenth century and settled by the French, it became a passageway for mineral wealth and exports after the discovery of gold and diamonds in the eighteenth century. It was the capital of Brazil before the capital was shifted to Brasília in 1960 (Levine, *Historical Dictionary of Brazil,* 186; *WNGD,* 1019).

7. Montevideo, the capital of Uruguay, is a seaport on the Rio de La Plata estuary, about 135 miles east (and across the water) from Buenos Aires. Montevideo was a major export center for the cattle industry, including wool, meat, hides, and other animal products, and the site of stockyards and slaughterhouses. The city was settled by the Spanish in the early eighteenth century and was occupied variously by the British, the Argentinians, the Portuguese, and the Brazilians, as well as the Spanish. It became the capital of independent Uruguay in 1830 *(WNGD,* 786–87).

To Sisters and All
4 April 1902
Southampton, England

As Will Rogers continued upon his travels, his family members began publishing his letters home without his knowledge. His father usually shared letters with the Claremore Progress; *his sisters Maud and Sallie, with the* Chelsea Reporter. *This letter in the* Reporter *represents Will Rogers's first publication, a foreshadowing of his later career as a commentator with his own syndicated newspaper column.*

This document is reproduced here to commemorate Rogers's first appearance in print. It also can be compared to the matching document that precedes it to illustrate the ways in which editors modified Rogers's original letters for publication.

FROM WILLIE ROGERS.

Southampton, Eng.
April 4, 1902.

My Dear Sisters and All: —

Well I landed after eight long days of heaving forth everything I looked at. We left New York at ten o'clock; I ate a hearty dinner and then the thing came off; I went to my little 1 1/2 × 5 and did not arise till the engineer squalled Southampton. After that dinner on Wednesday I could not eat a thing until Monday, then, after various attempts, I got a lemon that never managed to find the way back. I want to say to you now that if there had been any way of turning back I would have taken out a small stock. Dick was only sick a day or two.

I feel splendid now. We arrived Wednesday night at 10 o'clock. Our baggage was searched for tobacco and spirits; they did not find any in mine for I don't chew and my spirits had all left me on that boat if I had any at all I contributed them to the briny deep before I met that officer.

After we landed we took a hanson not a lady but a kind of cart, and went to a hotel; we got a nice room almost papered with pictures of Q Victoria who must have had a stand in with the photographer.

I tried to learn their money till I'm blue in the face; their penny looks like our $50.00 gold pieces. I think I've got a great lot of money and feel in my jeans to pay for something and find its only a pike dream for it takes it all to pay for an apple or an orange, the only familiar characters I've met in bulk. I have enough money to start in some kind of business, but when I count it I find there is not enough to make the first payment on a soda cracker.

That talking machine Maud has isn't one two three with the slowest creatures here.

They would make it "go to the rear and fade away." Our English must be a slow process. I went up to a man for some information yesterday, and he throwed open the throttle and broke out on one of those chained lightning spikes when I flagged him at the first quarter and asked him (in my speediest tone) to kindly relate it again as though he was speaking of some of his poor or dead relations, and that I would pay him for his over time.

You cant imagine any thing half as big and clumsy as the shoes they wear here I have old buckle plow shoes at home would be dancing pumps over here. The food is altogether different both by name and nature. Oh I am almost starved for something cooked in America. Dick has just returned from a trip to the P.O. saying our letters must be weighed then we stamp and pay for them.

This information I am putting you next on is quite a mighty matter and I expect to have to draw on my inside pocket to send this letter. Well good bye we'll write you again after having visited London, as it only 76 miles from here. I am fast regaining my lost flesh for the next episode.

> Your loving brother and Uncle.
> Will T. Rogers.

No where in particular

PD. Printed in *CR*, 25 April 1902.

To Sisters and All
13 April 1902
Southampton, England

FROM WILLIE ROGERS.
SOME INTERESTING FACTS ABOUT
ENGLAND

> Southampton, Eng.
> April 13, 1902.

Dear Sisters and All: —

Well Dick and I have visited London and find it the biggest case of a town it has ever been my misfortune to see.

We visited the House of Parliament, where all the great doings of the state are carried on, also Buckingham Palace where the King and Queen will reside during the "big blow-out." Then we went to West Minster Abbey where all the great men of England have monuments erected to their memory and dull as I am I felt a curious sort of sensation creep over me while looking at this, although I knew very few of the men personally.[1] Here all the old armour, chains and crowns worn by all the English sovereigns are kept, but the one that opens your eyelashes most is the one that King Edward will be topped with.

The whole city is being torn up and rebuilt for the coronation.[2] I think they are going to stop up the Thames to make more room for the people. You have dreamed of the great London Bridge. Well, I was on that bridge as well as visited the London Tower.[3] On every street corner is a monument to some brave, heroic old man who met his death on the field. What a pity they haven't some of that old stock left to make a stand for them, now, in South Africa.[4]

The work here seems all to be done by girls.[5] All the ushers in in the theaters, the bar-tenders, waiters and all are girls. They are real pretty, but all look alike and talk so fast I don't know what they are saying.

There is no end of theaters in London, but they are not up to the Americans in either tragedy or comedy.[6] The only advantage I have seen over our American cities, is that here they have large parks or play-grounds all through the city for the children, and you see thousands of them playing there all the time.[7]

We passed some very beautiful places between Southampton and London. All so well improved, but not a vacant foot of land on the way. We leave here tomorrow for Buenos Ayres, and I'll have a long letter to mail you at the first point at which we touch land, which I think will be a Port above Rio Janerio, then on by Montevedio, so don't be uneasy if you don't hear from me for a month or six weeks.

Lovingly
Willie

PD. Printed in *CR*, 16 May 1902.

1. The House of Parliament, also known as the New Palace of Westminster, was built between ca. 1840 and 1850 by Charles Barry. A Victorian Gothic building with the famous "Big Ben" clock tower, the palace houses the British House of Lords and House of Commons. Buckingham Palace, located at the west end of St. James Park, was built by John Sheffield, the Duke of Buckingham, in 1703 and remodeled between ca. 1825 and 1830 for George IV. Queen Victoria first occupied the mansion as a permanent residence for the British sovereign in 1837; her son Edward VII also resided there. Westminster Abbey was a Benedictine cathedral in the 1500s before it was converted to a collegiate church. It became the state church of England because of its proximity to Westminster Palace. The site of royal coronations, it also houses Poets' Corner and is the final resting places of royal figures (Crowl, *Guide to Historic Britain*, 521, 520, 523–24; Darwin, *Lure of London*, 16, 24; Harris and Millar, *Buckingham Palace and Its Treasures;* Jeffries, *Century of Buckingham Palace;* Loftie, *Westminster Abbey*).

2. Although Edward VII became king in January 1901, his official coronation did not take place until August 1902. On 28 June 1901 the king issued a proclamation announcing that the coronation would occur in June 1902. The ensuing year was full of preparations for the ceremony, including city renovations and a massive distribution of honors (1,540 peerages, knighthoods, and other decorations were conferred in 1902). A few days before the scheduled grand event, Edward fell ill with appendicitis and underwent surgery. The postponed celebration took place on 9 August 1902, with processions through the streets representing all the regions and races of the British Empire, cannon fire in Hyde Park, a coronation journey by the king and queen from Buckingham Palace to Westminster Abbey, and the coronation ceremony itself, in which the king was crowned by the archbishop of Canterbury in the Abbey. As one historian has put it, this "series of public functions . . . were designed to associate with the Coronation main sources of Imperial strength" (Lee, *King Edward VII* 2:110; see also 102–10).

3. London Bridge was designed to span the Thames River by John Rennie and his son, Sir John, in 1831 (Old London Bridge, which had houses built upon it, was farther downstream). The bridge became the main causeway for clerks, merchants, and other white-collar commuters who lived in the suburbs of London and worked in the city. It was renovated between 1886 and 1894. It was, as one historian has described it, "the road

from commerce to domesticity and back again" (Green, *Streets of London,* 34). The Tower of London, or White Tower, was built ca. 1078 under the direction of William the Conqueror; its exterior was altered in the seventeenth century by Christopher Wren. The Tower includes many sections, including St. John's Chapel (the oldest church in London), armories that display sixteenth- and seventeenth-century weapons, a bell tower, curtain walls, a moat, and the Jewel House, where the crown jewels and regalia of the various monarchs are held. The tower is also the burial place of many ill-fated figures, including Ann Boleyn (Betjeman, *Victorian and Edwardian London,* pl. 13; Crowl, *Guide to Historic Britain,* 513; Darwin, *Lure of London,* 10; Wilson, D., *Tower*).

4. The South African War had begun in October 1899 and was drawing to a close as Rogers visited London. It officially ended 31 May 1902. Rogers would soon be witnessing the aftermath of the war firsthand (see "South Africa" section, following).

5. Though domesticity was the ideal among both middle- and working-class British women, a survey conducted in London in 1904 reported that four out of five married women worked out of financial necessity. In 1902 there may also have been a reserve-army-of-labor effect as young women occupied some jobs traditionally filled by young men who were away at the war (Oakley, *Woman's Work,* 50; see also Anderson and Zinsser, "Earning Income," in *History of Their Own,* 248–77; Hobsbawm, *Workers: World of Labor,* 131–51, 194–213).

6. In Rogers's autobiographical notes, Rogers remembered that he and Parris "happened to ooze our way into an Opera House and saw Don [Dan] Leno. I dident know he amounted to anything but he was as big a man in England as Joe Kraler in Muskogee. I happened to save the program and after years learned he was a top mounter on all the show notices" (transcription of autobiographical notes, OkClaW). The program Rogers saved from a Monday evening, 7 April 1902, performance, featured Dan Leno as act nineteen of twenty-four. Harry Ford, Phil Ray, Florence Baines, and George Robey were the other comedians in the show, which also included acts by burlesque artists, a ventriloquist, dancers, jugglers, acrobats, singers, and musicians (unidentified theatre programme, London, 7 April 1902, Will Rogers Scrapbook, 1902–4, CPpR).

7. In the early nineteenth century city planners and educators developed new theories about the utilization of public space. In part a reaction to child labor and the lack of sanitation in many areas of the city, the change reflected a new view of children and an emphasis on physical education as a means to build health, character, and values such as team spirit and a sense of fair play. As a result the number of public parks, children's playgrounds, and sporting grounds located in London increased steadily over the century. Battersea Park, for example, was planned in the 1840s and opened to the public in 1858, including large playing fields, a lake, gardens, and skating facilities. Public laws passed at midcentury transformed space in crowded residential neighborhoods to public use as old churchyards were converted to children's playgrounds. By the time Rogers visited London, there were over one hundred such children's parks in the older and more crowded sections of the city (Betjeman, "Parks," *Victorian and Edwardian London,* 104–11; Moncrieff, "Parks and Palaces," *London,* 215–39; Rasmussen, "London Parks," *London,* 307–38).

To Clement Vann Rogers
19 April 1902
St. Vincent, Cape Verde Islands

St. Vincent. Cape Verde Islands.[1]
April 19. 1902.

My Dear Father.

I will try and write you a short letter and tell you that I am allright and feeling good   we are Steaming along the west coast of Africa and will soon be into St Vincient at one of the Cape Verde Islands adjoining Africa and is situated excactly on the Equator   it is quite warm during the days but is cool at nights.

We take coal here and Passengers and Freight and will be here all day then sail for Portambuco.[2] on the coast of Brazil. this is the *9th* day out and we will be about 14 more days on board. We have seen parts of England. France. Spain. Portugal. Africa already which is considerable country   We are getting offul tired of this and are in a hurry to land and get to work if we find we will like the country.

We are on board one of the largest boats   there is about 500 men work on it all togeather and there is about 300 Passengers most of them emigrants Portugese that are 3rd Class.

I wrote you a card from Lisbon Portugal.[3] Our last stop. did you get it.[4] I hope all are well at home and you are feeling as good as when I left just two months ago today. probaly I will be able to hear from you before long. I think we will have to learn to talk Spanish for that is the principal language.

There is every class of people in the world on this boat   we are bout the only Americans on board.

I was only Seasick a day or so on this trip and feel fine now   This old boat is rocking so I can hardy write

Well I will close   I dont know how long it will take this letter to reach you. I will write you every chance I can.

Lots of Love to all the folks and most of all to you from your

Loving son,
Willie.

ALS, rc. OkClaW.

1. St. Vincent (Sao Vicente) is one of the Cape Verde Islands. The main town of this eighty-eight-square-mile island is Mindelo, a coaling station. Settled by the Portuguese in the 1460s, the island figured in the expansion of the African slave trade in the early 1500s. Its prosperity declined with the official abolition of the slave trade in the

nineteenth century. The Cape Verde Islands are a group of ten volcanic islands and five islets in the Atlantic Ocean, divided into Windward and Leeward groups. They are located almost four hundred miles off the west coast of Senegal, between 14°47' and 17°13' north latitude and 22°40' and 25°22' west longtitude. The islands produce sugar, tobacco, fruit, and fish and serve as a coaling station for trans-Atlantic vessels such as the one Rogers traveled upon. Cape Verde became a Portuguese overseas province in 1951. The Partido Africano da Independencia da Guine e Cabo Verde (African Independence Party of Guinea and Cape Verde) was formed in 1956 and led a successful nationalist war (1963–74). Guinea-Bissau gained its independence in 1974, and Cape Verde became an independent republic in 1975 (Davidson, *No Fist Is Big Enough to Hide the Sky;* Lobban, *Historical Dictionary of Guinea-Bissau and Cape Verde,* xiii–xv; Shaw, C., *Cape Verde; WNGD,* 218).

2. Pernambuco (Recife), a seaport city at the mouth of the Capibaribe River, is the capital of the state of Pernambuco in eastern Brazil. The city is located near Point Plata, the "easternmost point of South America," and is one of the major ports of Brazil, handling sugar, cotton, and other agricultural exports. It was first settled in 1535 and was occupied by the Dutch for part of the seventeenth century. A United States naval and air base was established there during World War II *(WNGD,* 943, 1006).

3. Lisbon, the seaport capital of Portugal, is the country's main port. Built on terraced hills, the city was an ancient Iberian settlement that was occupied by Phoenicians, Carthaginians, Romans, and Moors. It became a primary European commercial center during the period of Portuguese colonial expansion and voyages of discovery. It was held by Spain from 1580 to 1640 and briefly by the French in the early nineteenth century. The Atlantic seaport maintains trade in olive oil, timber, wine, fish, and other goods and is a shipbuilding and sugar refining center *(WNGD,* 675).

4. The *Claremore Progress* reported that "C. V. Rogers received a postal from his son Willie this week. It was mailed to [from] Lisbon, Portugal, and stated that he was on his way to South America" (3 May 1902).

To Sisters
19 April 1902
St. Vincent, Cape Verde Islands

St. Vincent,
Cape Verde Islands
April 19, '02

My Dear Sisters: —

Well as we are steaming into St. Vincent, on one of the Cape Verde Islands and will be here all day I'll have a chance to write and let you know how I am. This place is just north of the Equator and is very warm, but the nights are cool. Of course it is much warmer on the land. We have about 200 Portugese and Spanish emigrants on board, all third class or steerage passengers that are going to Brazil. There seems to be every kind of woolie in the world on this boat. I can't understand a soul but Dick, and he is getting so he talks just like some of these folks.

We have very good food. Our six o'clock dinner is splendid, we have five different courses. This morning they gave a practice exhibition of letting down all the life boats. It was a fine sight. They blew a whistle and there were men running from every little hole to their places. The boats were lowered in just a few seconds. You see there are about 500 men employed on the boat. You would think there were only about 100. Then there are 300 passengers. It is one of the largest boats.

It is a sight to see how all these ports are garrisoned, and the vast expense it takes to fix them up. of course New York has the finest lay out.

These Islands belong [to] the French[1] and there is a French Man-of-War here. We saw all the Portugese war fleet in the Lisbon harbor. We stopped at Vigo,[2] which is a lovely place, last Sunday evening. At all these places we anchor in the harbor and the small boats come to us, and there are so many fruit peddlers come with all kinds of fruit that is very cheap.

I hope you are all as well as when I left, for I can't get to hear from you. It has been just two months ago today since I left home and will be two more weeks before we reach Buenos Ayres   When we go home we will go up the west coast.

I will write you again from Pernambuco, our next stop. Lots of love to each of you.

Willie.

PD. Printed in *CR*, 30 May 1902. Printed along with Rogers to Sisters, 24 April 1902, Pernambuco, Brazil, under one headline: "Two Letters from Willie Rogers. Some Interesting Facts About His Trip to South America."

1. Rogers was mistaken; the Cape Verde Islands were occupied by the Portuguese.
2. Vigo, a seaport in Pontevedra province, Spain, is located on the Estuary of Vigo, an inlet of the Atlantic Ocean. It is the home of lumber, leather, and fishing industries (*WNGD*, 1299).

To Sisters
24 April 1902
Pernambuco, Brazil

Pernambuco, Brazil.
April 24, 1902

My Dearest Sisters: —

I will now state you a few more facts about the country in which we do not live. I wrote you a card from Lisbon and a letter from St. Vincent, on an island we passed Saturday. Oh, what a horrible place that was, it was so hot and all the people were negroes and didn't wear enough clothes to cover a postage stamp. It was a dry sandy desert. There were hundreds of little negro boys who swam around the boat and when the passengers would throw coins in the water they would dive to the bottom of water 100 feet deep for them. They were the finest divers and swimmers I ever saw. We now see the South American coast for in a few hours we will be at Pernambuco but we will not be allowed to go ashore nor can any one come aboard for they have the Benbonic Plague there. Our next stop will be at Rio de Janerio and then to Buenos Ayres on the 4th of May.

We crossed the equator yesterday at 4 o'clock. It was very hot, but has been raining ever since and is now quite cool.

This trip is getting just a bit old and we will be glad to land.

We learn there are very few Americans in Argentina so Dick and I will have to learn to talk Spanish. You must look over this writing for the boat is trying to "turn a cat." There are lots of sharks following us, some 50 to 75 feet long. We have discovered two Americans among the first class passengers. We enjoy our long talks with them. They are very wealthy. Most of the other first class passengers are English. Well, I will write again from Rio de Janerio, as we get there in four more days.

Give my love to all,
Willie.

PD. Printed in *CR*, 30 May 1902. Revised version printed in *CR,* 31 May 1902.

To Clement Vann Rogers
24 April 1902
Pernambuco, Brazil

WILL ROGERS TELLS OF HIS TRAVELS.

Pernambuco, Brazil,
April, 24, 1902

My Dear Papa:

As we will soon be at another port I can mail you another letter. We will be here about eight hours, then on down the coast. We will get to Buenos Ayres about the 4th of May.

We are having very good weather. We crossed the equator yesterday evening and it has been raining on us the past two days. I am feeling well and weigh more than I ever did.

I hope you are all doing O. K. and are well at home.

I don't know when you will get this letter. I wrote you from St. Vincent in the ocean last week.

I will write as often as I can and let you hear how I am doing. There is nothing of interest since I last wrote you, so I will close.

Lots of love to all.

Lovingly, Willie.

PD. Printed in *CP,* 31 May 1902.

To Clement Vann Rogers
1 May 1902
Montevideo, Uruguay

Most travelers who approached Buenos Aires by trans-Atlantic voyage stopped in Brazilian and other ports along the eastern coast. Near the turn of the century "Montevideo provided a European environment, unimpressive with its low, white-washed buildings, tiny downtown center, and village atmosphere."[1]

Montivideo. Uruguay.
May 1st. 02.

My Dear Papa:

I will write you again as we will get into Montivideo tomorrow that is only a days run from Buenos Ayres. we go within about 35 miles of B.A. and then on up there on the train we will be quarinteened on board the Ship about two days after we get there before they will let us go ashore for there is some Bubonic Plague at some of the places we stopped at.

We stopped for 36 hours in Ri De Janerio that is the capitol of Brazil and a very large place. I wrote you a card from there. Each one of these are separate countries of their own   they are just like the U.S. and old Mexico they have their own Money and it is all different from the other.

We will have to learn to speak Spanish before we will be able to do much   we are going to try and get work at some of the ranches and we will soon learn.

We will get into B.A. about the 4th or 5th of May if we are not held too long in quarintine. I will be able to write you something probaly in the next letter of the country.

We have seen all kinds of Fruit growing Pine Apples. Oranges. Bananas. and any kind you want all very cheap.

We are getting here in the Fall   it is just begin to get cold   July and August are their coldest months and January and February are the warmest   it hardly ever gets cold enough to snow so they say.

I am well and feel fine   hope you are all well   I would like to hear from you all.

Well I will close

Lots of love to all your
Loving Son Willie

ALS, rc. JLC-OkClaW.

1. Scobie, *Buenos Aires*, 14.

To Sisters
7 May 1902
Buenos Aires, Argentina

FROM WILLIE ROGERS.

Bunos Ayres,
May 7, 1902.

My Dear Sisters: —

Well we are here at last, got here on the 5th of May. We were quarantined for two days on board, before we were allowed to land.[1]

This is a beautiful country and a very fine city, the prittiest I ever saw. There are about one million inhabitants.[2] We are stopping at an English hotel, "The Phoenix,"[3] where English is spoken. We start for the interior tomorrow, by rail for about 500 miles,[4] then we will get us some horses and see if we can get a job, although wages are almost nothing,[5] but we want to learn how they handle cattle here, which is very different from what it is in the United States, then, we want to learn the language too.[6]

The cities here are built something on the order of San Autionia, Tex. All the houses are on the Spanish plan, with lots of openings through the roof, and court where they have all kinds of palms and flowers.[7]

They have an abundauce of fruit here. I dont know what half of it is.

I guess Clem will be at home by the time this reaches you. I hope he got through all right and covered himself with glory like his old uncle did.[8]

Some high official died here and was buried to-day. It was a state funeral and of course the grandest I ever saw.

Such a fine hearse with 10 fine black horses. The police and soldiers were all mounted and presented a splendid appearance. The police here are always mounted on very fine horses, though they are small.

Hoping you are all well I am

Lovingly
Willie.

PD. Printed in *CR*, 20 June 1902.

1. Although Buenos Aires had long served as a major port, until late in the nineteenth century it had poor anchorage and ocean vessels anchored miles from he city, necessitating the transfer of cargo and passengers with launches through shallow water and then by horse or oxen and cart. It was not until the decade before Rogers arrived in the city that "concrete basins, docks, and dredged channels finally created a modern port out of the mud banks of Buenos Aires" (Scobie, *Argentina*, 96). During this period of modernization and increased shipping services, the cost of passage was such that immigrant workers arriving from European ports were able within a few weeks to earn enough to cover the cost of their round-trip passage. In the early 1900s the system of migratory agricultural labor, in which European workers (called *golondrinas*, or swallows) would arrive for seasonal work and then return home, was organized to the extent that the government maintained a processing area between the docks and the principal railroad station that "rushed farm workers off the ships and onto trains in record time" (ibid., 119, 131).

2. The population of Argentina and of its main port city, Buenos Aires, burgeoned in the late nineteenth century because of large waves of European immigration and internal migration from rural areas to the city. From 1880 to 1900 the population grew by over 2,000,000, a net increase of approximately 85 percent. The overall population of the country increased from 1,800,000 in 1869 to 4,000,000 in 1895 to 8,000,000 in 1914; some 5,000,000 immigrants, mostly from Italy and Spain, migrated to the coastal cities, primarily Buenos Aires, in this period. Historian James Scobie reports that the population of the metropolis of Buenos Aires "increased nine times between 1869 and 1914" and "topped the million mark around 1905" (Scobie, *Buenos Aires*, 136, 205; see also *Anuario Geografico Argentino* [Buenos Aires, 1941], cited in Taylor, *Rural Life in Argentina*, 57; and Scobie, *Argentina*, 5, 32, 33, 61, 119, 131–35, 147).

3. The major hotels were beyond the means of most immigrants arriving in Buenos Aires, most of whom took up residence in crowded *conventillos* (tenements) in the downtown core, near potential work sites. An overwhelming number of *conventillo* dwellers in the Central City were foreign born. By the period when Rogers lived in the city *conventillo* conditions had improved over what had existed earlier in the late 1800s. Most *conventillos* had central concrete patios and sanitary facilities. Though rooms were small, many had windows. Crowding remained a problem, however, as workers lived with many people in one room, struggling to meet steadily escalating rents. Many new arrivals lived their first days in Argentina in the Immigrants' Hotel, which in the late 1800s was "a filthy, unventilated horsebarn in the center of Buenos Aires and after the turn of the century a gloomy, concrete edifice near the northern port area. Others found their way into shabby hotels, joined the households of already established friends or relatives, or lived as vagabonds along the waterfront or in the parks" (Scobie, *Argentina*, 131). Though Rogers would later become familiar with these more typical options for immigrants looking for work—locating other Americans, taking up residence in a boarding house, and finding himself at times in a city park when efforts to find work had failed—he began his stay in Argentina at one of the better hotels. The Plaza and the Palace were the grandest hotels of the period, and "other hotels of note" were the "Majestic, Paris, Grand, Phoenix, Royal, and a host of others of lesser degree" (Koebel, *Argentina Past and Present*, 147; see also Scobie, *Buenos Aires*, 151–57).

4. Buenos Aires was located on the eastern edge of the expansive grasslands of the interior. The railroad system, constructed between 1880 and 1910, radiated outward from Buenos Aires to the hinterlands, effectively subordinating the provinces to Buenos Aires by orienting the economy of the country toward an export trade in which British-

financed railroads funneled raw materials from the rural areas to the commercial centers and docks of the coastal city, and manufactured goods were transported from the coastal cities for consumption in the interior. Workers were also channeled from the city to agricultural and livestock jobs in the interior. The railroads developed in a spokelike pattern without connecting links, and frequently the only way to travel cross-country was to take a train to the nearest port city (Rosario, Bahía Blanca, or Buenos Aires) and then out again along one of these spokes. There was no other efficient way of reaching the interior until decades after Rogers's time in Argentina. A five-hundred-mile rail trip would have carried Rogers well into the interior along lines that ran westward toward Mercedes and Mendoza, northwestward toward Córdoba, or southwestward to Bahía Blanca. His first trip into the interior seems to have been northward toward Córdoba; his second was westward (Scobie, *Argentina*, 137–46; idem, *Buenos Aires*, 91–100, see also fig. 7, "Expansion of the National Railroad System, 1870–1910," 93).

5. Rogers arrived in Argentina during an economic depression between two booms of economic growth, one in the 1880s and another between 1904 and 1912. The boom of the 1880s signaled a revolution in the national economy, a period of immigration, ethnic change, and major changes in rural life. The introduction of widespread agriculture and the modernization of the cattle industry (ca. 1850–1910) effectively destroyed the gaucho subculture while creating new kinds of work for ranch hands. Like the gaucho, Rogers conceived of work with cattle as primarily equestrian. The introduction of fencing and the shift from hunting and handling of semiwild cattle to the management of semitame herds in fenced pastures deemphasized the long-honored skills of horsemen, reduced the number of workers necessary to handle herds, and created a wide social split between ranch laborers who worked primarily on foot and those on horseback. New immigrants were primarily employed as agricultural laborers and in ranch tasks such as ditch digging, bricklaying, carpentry, and fence construction. More traditional cattle hands found themselves un- or underemployed as the number of workers on ranches fluctuated with the seasons. According to the 1908 census, only "43 percent of adult male livestock workers found year-round employment in Buenos Aires province" (Slatta, *Gauchos and the Vanishing Frontier*, 32). The influx of immigrant labor on ranches also brought criticism of traditional gaucho work methods from foreigners who questioned conventional Argentine ways of breaking horses and running herds. Worker turnover was high at individual ranches. By the 1890s and well into Rogers's time in Argentina, wages for ranch hands had fallen sharply as prices for consumer goods and land had risen. The average wage for a ranch hand in 1901 was thirty-one paper pesos per month, plus food. Overall wages for common and skilled laborers in Argentina in the 1890s and first years of the 1900s were half what they had been in the boom period of the 1880s. The decline in wages was matched by an increase in rents and, in city areas, by greater evidence of hunger and homelessness. A few months before Rogers arrived in Buenos Aires, *La Prensa* published a series of articles demonstrating the plight of workers with families, whose average monthly expenses far exceeded the average monthly wage of a day laborer. Wages for urban working people did not begin to rise until 1905 (Scobie, *Buenos Aires*, 136–38, 140–41; Slatta, "Gaucho to Peon: Changing Ranch Labor," chap. 3 in *Gauchos and the Vanishing Frontier*, 30–56).

6. Walter Larden, the English author of a comparative account of work life and changes at his Anglo-Argentine brother's estancia in 1888–89 and 1908–9, wrote of the hybridization of English and Spanish on the ranches. Whereas Rogers professed a desire to learn and use the Spanish language—a process that seems to have come harder to him than to Dick Parris—Larden was alarmed at what he termed the invasion and injury done to the English language by the incorporation of Spanish words and phrases and the

revision of English terms for Spanish use. Larden's viewpoint seems to have been more typical of the Anglo-Argentine vision than Rogers's assumption that he should try to learn Spanish. The British, in urban areas at least, lived in largely separate communities. They "frequently could not speak Spanish and knew little of the country outside a British school, a British club, and a British firm" (Scobie, *Argentina,* 135; see also Larden, "Anglo-Argentine English," *Estancia Life,* 112–14).

7. The architecture of the central part of Buenos Aires underwent changes in style with adjustments in upper-class residential patterns. Up to 1870 the single-story elongated patio-style house that had originated in colonial times continued as the norm, with an occasional second story. At the end of the century rising land values caused expansion upward with the construction of two-family, two- and three-story homes with patio-style floorplans. After a huge commercial economic boom that began in 1880, wealthy families began to look more to Europe for architectural inspiration. As a result of Italianate and Parisian influences multistory *palacio* mansions and *petits hotels* were built on large square lots rather than the traditional rectangular ones. Housing remained oriented to the Plaza de Mayo. The upper class effectively "remodeled the city into the Paris of South America" (Scobie, *Buenos Aires,* 130). The changes affected interior design as well as urban planning as the style of decoration moved from the Spanish to the baroque. The older Spanish-style buildings constructed on narrow lots (which were similar to those that Rogers was familiar with in San Antonio) continued to be used for new housing in the suburbs, and working-class *conventillos* in the downtown also were built with an interior patio. After 1900 owning or renting a small traditional-style house on the outskirts of the city came more within the reach of skilled working people and artisans who were able to travel to work in the Central City by streetcar (ibid., 127–35, 156, 178–80).

8. A reference to Will Rogers's nephew Clem McSpadden, who was completing his final year at Kemper Military School in Boonville, Missouri. Rogers is making fun of his own comparatively poor performance while at the same school (see Clement Vann Rogers to Will Rogers, 17 June 1902, below; see also Biographical Appendix entry, McSpadden, Clement Mayes).

To Clement Vann Rogers
7 May 1902
Buenos Aires, Argentina

Buenos Aires. A.R.S.A.[1]
May 7th 1902.

My Dear Papa

We arrived in B.A. all O.K. we were held on board the ship two days as they had heard there was a case of yellow fever[2] on board but it was a mistake we got in here the night of the fifth.

This is the largest city in South America it has one million people and is the prettiest place I ever saw.

They talk all Spanish but we are at an English hotel we are going to start to some town in the interior tomorrow and try and get work. Wages are almost nothing down here.

Clement Mayes (Clem) McSpadden, Will Rogers's nephew, graduated from the Kemper Military School in 1902 (*OkClaW*).

We have been around twice and seen the American Consul.[3] he is a nice fellow and has been in the country for 25 years and is a cow man   he says there is lots of money to be made down here with a good lot of Capital as you buy land and it is advancing at the rate of 100% a year and he thinks will continue to do so   he has made a great deal of money here and has lots of land now.

Of course I dont know what I can do with what little I have   I dont expect I will be able to do much for awhile.[4] And we are going to try and get work if we can.

I will write you as soon as we get located for a little bit. hope you are all well   I am as ever your

Lovingly Son Willie

ALS, rc. JLC-OkClaW.

1. Argentine Republic, South America.
2. Experience with deadly cholera, typhoid, and yellow fever epidemics had made government officials stringent in taking precautionary measures. Yellow fever struck the Río de la Plata area in 1870, and ships that had been in port at Santos or Rio de Janeiro in Brazil were subject to strict quarantine. Yellow fever occurred again the following year, reaching epidemic proportions in February. Although it was not understood until 1900 that the mosquito was the carrier of the disease, officials did perceive a correlation between high incidence of the disease and stagnant water and poor sanitary systems. As the epidemic progressed, strict regulations were put into effect, including evacuation of city blocks and disinfection of latrines. By April 1871 hundreds of people per day were dying of the disease and the city was effectively shut down, with government offices closed and services suspended. The specter of the epidemic "continued to guide public concern" for decades, especially in regard to new arrivals reaching and moving into the *conventillos* of the city (Scobie, *Buenos Aires*, 122–24, 153).
3. The vice-consul who advised Rogers may possibly have been Jorge Alejandro Newbery (1875–1914), a prominent Argentinean civil engineer, scientist, athlete, and pioneer aviator who was born in Buenos Aires and educated at Cornell University and Drexel University in the United States. His grandparents were residents of New York. Rogers kept Newbery's card in his scrapbook. On the card were written the names of Thomas Duggan and Patrick Ham—"the largest ranchers in A.R." (Will Rogers Scrapbook 1902–4, CPpR).
Newbery studied with Thomas Edison in Philadelphia, and in 1895 he graduated from Drexel with a degree in electrical engineering. He returned to Buenos Aires, where he became an administrator and engineer in charge of municipal gaslighting services for the city government. He published *Consideraciones generales sobre la municipalización de los servicios de alumbrado* (Buenos Aires: Annals of the Scientific Society of Argentina, 1904), participated in international electrical engineering conferences, and directed experiments in electric lighting in Paris in 1905. He was an avid boxer, rower, runner, fencer, swimmer, yachtsman, wrestler, and soccer, rugby, and polo player. Distinguished in sportsmen's circles in Buenos Aires, he was a strong advocate of physical education. His interest in aviation began in the first years of the century, when he began participating in experimental elevation flights in hot-air balloons in Argentina and Uruguay. He was a founding member and officer of the Argentinean Aero Club, and

served as president of the club from 1906 to his death. He set a series of South American and world flight records for distance and elevation between 1908 and 1914. He became a minister with the Escuela de Aviación Militar, the first flight school in Argentina, in September 1912, and carried out numerous exploratory flights of South America. He set a world record for flight over water in October 1913 with fellow aviator Enrique Lubbe on a trip to Montevideo and in the following February overtook the world record for altitude. He also conducted meteorological research in flight in mountainous terrain. He died when a plane he was piloting lost power and crashed in March 1914. He remains a hero in the history of aerial navigation in Argentina, and a street, a railroad station, and a school in Buenos Aires are named in his honor. One of his biographers has called him "el conquistador del espacio," the conqueror of space or distance (subtitle of Larra, *Newbery;* see also Osvaldo Cutolo, *Nuevo diccionario biografico argentino* 5:46–47; and Piccirilli, Romay, and Gianello, *Diccionario historico argentino,* 5:435–36).

4. Rogers would soon learn that even his meager hopes in regard to landownership were naive and that he was overly optimistic in his tendency to see a role model in the likes of Dr. Jorge Newbery the U.S. vice-consul, who, like other members of the elite, had established himself as a "cowman" in Argentina. Newbery's advice that there was "lots of money to be made down here with a good lot of Capital" hinged rather on the latter part of the phrase than the former. Rogers later summed up his fortunes in Argentina by writing, "Well I didn't prosper and do much good down there" (transcription of autobiographical notes, OkClaW). Whereas in the American West policies had encouraged settlement of small farms and ranches through generous land laws, which focused on occupancy and development as precursors to formal ownership, in Argentina the ownership of land was monopolized by an elite, with large land grants distributed as political rewards. Originating in the colonial era with grants made by the Spanish crown, the land-tenure system became self-perpetuating, so that a few property owners (the *latifundia,* or large-ranch or estate holders) controlled vast expanses of land. In the second decade of the nineteenth century 538 individuals owned over nineteen million acres of land in the pampas. Settlers with small family farms were either tenants or squatters with no land rights associated with their occupancy; they were subject to eviction if the land they had settled on became part of a title acquisition (Slatta, *Gauchos and the Vanishing Frontier,* 92; Larden describes such an eviction in his account of his brother's estancia, in *Estancia Life,* 44).

Landowners controlled not only the land itself but the justice and legal systems that regulated its use. Vagrancy and work laws, for example, were used to conscript gauchos either into military service on behalf of the wealthy or into wage work on the estancias. The landed elite were mainly absentee landowners; living in the city, they hired others to manage their properties or rented land to farmers in limited tenancies. Like Rogers, many immigrants came to Argentina with the hope of doing temporary ranch-hand or agricultural labor and working their way up to landownership. Most European laborers came with the hope of owning a family-size farm; instead they became laborers or tenant farmers. Perhaps only 5 percent of laborers were able to achieve tenancy. The experience of most was institutionalization as hired laborers. As land became more valuable, owners were less inclined to sell "and the march of tenants up the agricultural ladder literally ceased"; even individuals with some accumulated capital were unable to purchase land (Taylor, *Rural Life in Argentina,* 205). As James Scobie has commented on the dream of social mobility and land in Argentina, "the self-made man . . . did not exist" in any real sense; some immigrants to the urban areas were able to acquire skills and savings, marry, and eventually use earnings to buy a small plot on the outskirts of Buenos Aires (Scobie, *Buenos Aires,* 212). While there were few opportunities for

Albert (A. L. or Pop) Kates *(far left)* and his family, photographed about 1900. *Left to right:* Kates's sons, Jack, Harry, and Bill, and his wife, Nellie. As the publisher of the *Claremore Progress,* Kates printed Rogers's first publications, letters from abroad, in 1902–4 *(courtesy of Jerry Kates, Gladewater, Tex.).*

immigrant laborers to acquire land in the province of Buenos Aires, immigrants were able to establish small farms in other provinces (Munck, *Argentina,* 44–45; Scobie, *Argentina,* 114; Slatta, *Gauchos and the Vanishing Frontier,* 91–105, 106–25, 126–40; Taylor, "Ownership and Distribution of Land," chap. 8 in *Rural Life in Argentina,* 174–208).

To the *Claremore Progress*
7 May 1902
Buenos Aires, Argentina

Whereas previous letters home had been published without his knowledge, this letter was written expressly for publication in the local Claremore newspaper. It represents Will Rogers's first deliberate piece of journalism.

TELLS OF HIS TRAVELS.

Buenos Ayres, Rep. S. A.,
May 7th, 1902.

Readers of the Progress:–

Hello, comrades!

We have at last landed in South America after an exceedingly hard struggle. There may be places farther away than this, but it is a "pipe" they are no harder to get to.

On arriving in New Orleans we found that there were no boats to Buenos Ayres, but that from New York we could go direct. So we went forth on our first voyage on anything bigger than the Verdigris.[1] Well old hands, it is not what its cracked up to be. Five days to New York and then we happened to another spasm of hard luck. No boat for B. A. for three weeks, but found we could go by way of England for the same price and quicker as they were faster boats. We stayed in New York for three days, and then were off for South Hampton, England, on the steamer Philadelphia. I only lasted on deck to see the big guns at Sandy Hook[2] and it was all "up" with me. I went to my bunk and didn't get out until we were tied to the dock at South Hampton. I thought die I would. Any time an old nestor tells you sea sickness is not bad, he hasn't been on anything larger than Dog Creek.[3] I couldn't eat a thing for six days with any success, (you know friends that Willie is sick when he can't eat). We were eight days and had very rough weather.

We were in England twelve days; up to London, which is a great place, but its not got a "look in" with New York for speed. No electric cars and no street cars at all in the main squeeze of town. Hitch a thrasher engine to a string of covered wagons and you have an English train, as fast, as comfortable, and as handsome. If you call that prosperity, excuse me.

We saw the Houses of Parliment, London Tower and all the places of interest, the chair where his royal highness will be crowned in. All the crowns of his "decestors," and all the royal jewelry and finery. It looked pretty good.

We saw his big Nibs at a distance. Don't think he recognized us though.

We sailed on the eleventh of April on the royal mail steamer Danube, which called in at several different ports for cargo and passengers. We would get to go to ashore for several hours. First in Rupert, France; then Vigo, Spain. Saw what was left of the Spanish navy. Lisbon, Portugal, which is a beautiful place; by the Canary Islands,[4] to the Cape Verde at St. Vincent, crossed the equator the twenty-second of April, and it was good and hot, but got cooler soon. Then to Pernambuco, on the northeast coast of Brazil; Bahia,[5] and then Rio

DeJanerio, where we stopped for thirty-six hours. It is a city of 800,000 inhabitants and has the finest harbor in the world. It is a great fruit growing country. We next stopped at Montivideo, which is the cleanest and healthiest city in South America; then to Sanata, thirty-five miles from Buenos Ayres. Large boats cannot go clear up the river. We were quarantined for two days before we could land. Republics are quarantined against each other all the time.

We then went by rail to Buenos Ayres. We landed the fifth day of May after a twenty-five days trip from England, seven thousand miles. I never got so I would not get sick when it got rough. It would be "up" to the ocean with me. Those boats do everything but rare up and fall back.

Buenos Ayres is the prettiest place I ever saw. Houses are all built on the Spanish plan, with an open court clear to the roof. The street cars, trains and almost everything is on the United States plan. Much more like it than England. It has one million population and is the largest city in South America.

As I want to tell the cow men of the country, I went to see Mr. Newbrey [Newbery], the United States Consul, who has been here for twenty-five years, and is a land and cattle owner. He has made a great deal of money here, and says there are fortunes to be made by persons who have capital to buy land which is actually advancing one hundred per cent a year, and will continue to do so for a time. It is practically a new country and lots of foreign capital is coming in.[6] The export of cattle almost doubles each year, the surplus being shipped to the various foreign countries on foot and frozen.[7] The seasons are exactly the reverse of yours, for it is now fall here. July and August are the coldest months, but not so cold as home only in the south and the mountains.

They are breeding up the herds here now and are getting more good cattle.[8]

They figure on a fifty per cent increase when they do not feed at all. Only the very best cattle are fed. There are no diseases in the south or west. Taxes are very low. In parts they raise lots of Alfalfa and it is a great wheat country.[9]

There are lands here they will give to a person if he will live on them and become an Argentine citizen. It is also a great sheep country.[10]

They are expecting a war with Chili any day,[11] but the consul says that will not have any effect on conditions. You can't buy land from the government, but have to deal with some individual. There is certainly money in it for the man able to buy it.

We start for the interior to-morrow to try and strike a lay on some of the big ranches. We go about five hundred miles by rail and then overland to our destination. Wages are very low. We are trying to learn Spanish, as that is the only language.

A NEW
SPANISH DICTIONARY,

BASED UPON THE

LATEST EDITION OF THE DICTIONARY
OF THE SPANISH ACADEMY.

CONTAINING THE

SCIENTIFIC, MILITARY, COMMERCIAL
TECHNICAL & NAUTICAL TERMS,

And brought right up to date.

PART I.—SPANISH-ENGLISH.

PART II.—ENGLISH-SPANISH.

ENGLISH BOOK EXCHANGE
333 FLORIDA 333 BUENOS AIRES

London:

HIRSCHFELD BROS.

22 & 24, BREAMS BUILDINGS, FETTER LANE, E.C.

1900

"We are trying to learn Spanish, as that is the only language." Title page from a Spanish-language dictionary that Rogers presumably purchased in Buenos Aires. The dictionary is part of Rogers's library collection at the Will Rogers State Historic Park (*CPpR*).

I will be able perhaps to tell you of the ranches and cattle and how they handle them, in another letter.

We have not heard a word from home since we left. There are very few Americans in this country,[12] but quite a number of Englishmen.

Hoping you are all having a time, I am as ever yours.

Will Rogers.

PD. Printed in *CP,* 21 June 1902.

1. A reference to the Verdigris River, which extended north to south through the Cherokee Nation; it also ran through the Rogers family ranch in the Cooweescoowee District (Collings, *Old Home Ranch,* 18–19).

2. Sandy Hook is a peninsula on the coast of New Jersey about fifteen miles south of the southernmost tip of lower Manhattan Island. Six miles long, it encloses an inlet of Raritan Bay and is the cite of a lighthouse guiding ships to and from New York harbor (*WNGD,* 1,065).

3. Another reference to familiar territory back home; Will Rogers's uncle, John Gunter Schrimsher, settled on Dog Creek at about the same time that Clem V. Rogers settled in the Cooweescoowee District in the 1850s (Collings, *Old Home Ranch,* 9).

4. The Canary Islands are a volcanic and mountainous island group in the Atlantic Ocean off the northwest coast of Africa, some eight hundred miles southwest of Spain. The islands were divided into two provinces of Spain in 1927: Santa Cruz de Tenerife (four islands) and Las Palmas (six islands, three of which are uninhabited). They were an important stop along the European trade routes between West Africa and the New World (*WNGD,* 214).

5. Bahía (Salvador, or Sao Salvador), a seaport city on All Saints Bay in eastern Brazil, is the capital of the state of Bahía. Located about 220 miles south-southwest of Pernambuco, it was founded by Thomé de Sousa in the early sixteenth century. A major port, it is important to the shipping, tobacco, leather, textile, and hardwood industries in Brazil (*WNGD,* 1059–60).

6. Much of the foreign capital Rogers refers to was British. British investment in nineteenth-century Argentina funded much of the commerce, public works, mines, railroad development and streetcar systems, stockraising and meat packing—the major areas of the country's infrastructure and economy. British-backed railroads directed trade to Buenos Aires, which in turn served as a hub that made the country's economy dependent on exports and world markets. Overseas trade was in turn dominated by British shipping. Although British people made up a minority of immigrants, they represented an upper echelon of merchants, bankers, entrepreneurs, cattle raisers, and farmers who managed much of the capital investment of the country and were part of an Anglo-Argentine oligarchy that dominated political and economic affairs. This trend escalated in the economic boom of the 1880s, which was generated by the policies of the "Generation of Eighty," those who sought modernization and development on the basis of foreign investment and immigrant labor. The dependency on outside forces, markets, and resources became one of the central issues of Argentine politics in the twentieth century (Ferns, *Britain and Argentina in the Nineteenth Century; HDA,* 371–74; Scobie, *Argentina,* 86, 100–102, 135; idem, *Buenos Aires,* 74–75, 90–91, 97, 100).

7. Cattle were central to the Argentine economy since their introduction in the 1550s. The slaughter of wild cattle for beef and hides gave way in the early 1800s to the production of cattle for hides and for sale to the *saladeros,* or salted-meat-processing

industry, for conversion into dried meat and by-products. By 1850 ranchers had diversified into sheep and wool as well as cattle, and by 1900 the *frigoríficos*, refrigerated meat-processing plants, had superseded the *saladeros*. Salted beef and shipment of live cattle dominated the export industry until the end of the nineteenth century (*HDA*, 166–68; Slatta, *Gauchos and the Vanishing Frontier*, 5; Smith, P., *Politics and Beef in Argentina;* Taylor, *Rural Life in Argentina*, 214–15).

8. Refrigeration of livestock carcasses for export was first used with sheep rather than cattle, stimulated by British investors looking at Argentina as an alternative to Australia as a source of mutton. These investors were willing to extend the financing to develop packing plants in Buenos Aires. Sheep breeders began to modify their strains for the commercial production of mutton for export, and by the mid-1880s cattle raisers were doing the same with beef cattle, turning toward more selective breeding and better pasturage to supply meat for British consumers. The exporters of on-the-hoof stock or refrigerated meat paid more per head than did the *saladeros*. As a result of the new emphasis on breeding for the export of meat, the shorthorn, "producer of the famous marbleized roast beef," became common on *cabañas* (stockbreeding ranches for raising purebred animals) in Argentina (Scobie, *Argentina*, 117). The *cabañas* were located primarily in the humid part of the pampa, in what remains the cattle-breeding belt. With the changes in breeding came changes in ranching, including extensive use of fencing to separate stock of different breeds and the cultivation of special feedlots for animals that would be shipped live to trans-Atlantic markets (Scobie, *Argentina*, 116–17; Slatta, *Gauchos on the Vanishing Frontier*, 235; Taylor, *Rural Life in Argentina*, 214–21).

9. On cattle estancias new tasks were developed for laborers adapting to new methods of raising and managing livestock, including the growing and harvesting of alfalfa for winter pasture and for feed in city stockyards. The agricultural development of the pampas was responsible for the great economic growth Argentina experienced at the end of the 1800s. In the last decades of the nineteenth century cultivated acreage increased many times over, to almost ten million acres of farmland. Exports climbed in response, with cereals making up half the value of exports in 1900. "Wheat was the first cereal crop to break the virtual monopoly of livestock in Argentine agriculture" (Taylor, *Rural Life in Argentina*, 224). Wheat farming began to be a big enterprise at the end of the century with the introduction of farm machinery, improvements in railroad transportation, and the influx of immigrant agricultural laborers. Argentina became a "major producer of wheat" in the world market, "with annual exports from several harvests in the 1890s topping one million tons" (Scobie, *Argentina*, 119). By 1905 wheat and other cereal crops exceeded livestock and meat products as the primary export (Scobie, *Argentina*, 119–20; idem, *Revolution on the Pampas;* Slatta, *Gauchos on the Vanishing Frontier*, 45–46; Taylor, *Rural Life in Argentina*, 133, 219, 223–26).

10. Sheep were introduced into Argentina at the same time as cattle (they were introduced from Peru and Paraguay in the 1500s), but the sheep-raising industry did not become firmly established in the province of Buenos Aires until the first half of the 1800s. Diversifying livestock (beyond cattle and horses) opened the way to agricultural development by intensifying land uses, raising the value of land, and attracting immigrants. Just as the early cattle industry focused on trade in hides rather than beef, the sheep industry relied on shipments of wool. Wool and sheepskins were the country's primary nonmeat exports by 1885, and after 1901 frozen mutton shipments also became a valuable export. In the early part of the twentieth century Argentine-raised merino wool supplied textile industries in England, France, Germany, and the United States. Lincoln and Romney Marsh sheep were bred toward the end of the century, both for wool and mutton, and by the turn of the century Lincoln breeds dominated the market.

Sheep were also used to produce tallow. Sheep raising was initially concentrated in the Buenos Aires and Santa Fe provinces, but after the Indian wars of the 1870s the frontier area of Patagonia became a primary sheep-raising region. Sheep-raising estancias often thrived on immigrant labor. In the province of Buenos Aires many shepherds, shearers, and *puesteros* — salaried renters who tended sheep in fenced pastures or grazing lands — were native workers. Many other sheep estancias had English-speaking managers from Britain, Australia, or New Zealand, and Irish and Basque immigrants were commonly hired as herders. Sheep ranching was less labor-intensive than cattle ranching, with one shepherd handling perhaps five times as many animals during the grazing period than the average cattle ranch hand. Toward the end of the century mechanization caused a severe economic crisis among the migratory shearers, who depended on seasonal employment, as their labor was supplanted by the use of shearing machines (Scobie, *Argentina,* 113; Slatta, *Gauchos on the Vanishing Frontier,* 141–47; Taylor, *Rural Life in Argentina,* 221–23).

11. The threat of war with Chile ran high after 1900 over boundary dispute issues. After negotiations, the Pactos de Mayo agreements were signed by the Argentine Republic and Chile on 28 May 1902. In the set of four agreements the two countries came to terms with ways to address the boundary problems and agreed to limitations in naval armaments (*HDA,* 663; Scobie, *Buenos Aires,* 241).

12. The general census of 1909 reported that Americans made up 2.9 percent of the total population of the Federal District of Buenos Aires; 54.5 percent of residents of the district were Argentines, with Italian and Spanish residents the most common non-native nationalities. In 1904, 45 percent of the population of Buenos Aires were foreign-born, as were 55 percent in the Central City (Scobie, *Buenos Aires,* 260, 263).

To Folks
23 May 1902
Buenos Aires, Argentina

Dick Parris had enough of Argentina after a few weeks in Buenos Aires and a trip to the interior. Homesick and discouraged about his chances to find meaningful work in cattle ranching in Argentina, he told Will Rogers he was ready to return home. Rogers used a portion of his much-depleted remaining funds to pay for his friend's passage back to the United States. Parris left Buenos Aires on 24 May 1902 and returned home to Indian Territory on 3 July 1902, bearing gifts from Rogers for members of his family.

Buenos Aires, A.R.S.A.
May 23. 1902.

My Dear Folks

As Dick is going to go back to America I have some things to send to you[1] and Sallie.

I went up into the Interior about 800 miles and looked around for a few days but was not able to strike anything   but am not in the least discouraged for I am going out west from here in a few days. Dick has decided to go to Texas so he leaves in the morning for N.Y.   has to go back the same way we came   I am liable to show up at any minute so look out   I send you these pieces of lace   they are considered very rare   are made by the Native Indians of the Republic of Paraguay.[2] are very expensive even here   and a large duty on them   but Dick will see that they are not found   there is one for you. Sallie.   and May send hers to her please.

The fierce looking ▲ Corn ▲ knife in there is for Papa   I did not know what would interest him so I will send the most common thing here[3] for everybody carries the biggest knives you ever saw   but are not so *bad*. tell him to put that with his *Curios*.

The *goards* and silver things ▲ Bombillars ▲ are for you and Sallie   they put the Tea in them and then suck it up with the other   they are used by the Natives of this country.[4]

I have a little collection of coins of each country I have been in and got each one in their respectave countrys   I will put in for one of you   their are ten with the old penny I have carried the rounds. You see I am making so much money I have to send it home on the installment plan.

Tell the children that I will try and bring them something   it will not be much unless business picks up   but it may be something.

You see this is no place to make money unless you have at least $10.000 or more and then you may do some good   but still if it had a lot of Americans here it would be good   but Lord there is none at all. Lots of all kinds of people but Americans   the biggest part of the capital is English but I do hate them   and you dont have any Idea how jealous they are of Americans   they wont hire an American.

I have seen them on the Ranches   I was out at the biggest one in S.A.   when I was up North they work all Natives   only the head men are English.[5] I have not seen an American Cattle Man and as for American Cow Boys I guess I am the only one there   they all go back   These Natives are bad looking but are not so bad I dont think if you treat them good   and they are very cowardly   I will send you some views of the camp pictures so you can see how they dress and what kind of Saddles they ride.[6] All wear those big pants and carry corn knives   I carry a pistol   they are afraid of a pistol.

This is a beautiful place and has a lovely level country all around it.   it is winter here but it is like Spring at home

Please write to May and Papa when you get this and tell them I am allright and will write to them at once but wont have time just now

Did you get the address Dick sent to papa   hope you did and have written   I will perhaps hear from you by the Middle of July   hope you are all well.

I am trying to learn Spanish   I think I can say 6 words   did know 7 and forgot   one there is very ~~few~~ ▲ little ▲ English spoken down here.

Well you must write all the news you ever did know   for remember I havent heard a word since I left   address the same place as before

With lots of love to all   I am as ever your loving

Brother
Willie

ALS, rc. OkClaW. Envelope hand-addressed to Mrs. C. L. Lane, Chelsea, Indian Territory, United States of America.

1. A reference to Maud Lane. Rogers wrote, "Dick came back to America from there but I stayed; I layed around a lot of those ranches" (transcription of autobiographical notes, OkClaW).

2. Paraguay, the smallest republic in South America, is bounded by Argentina, Bolivia, and Brazil. It is the only Western Hemisphere colony of Spain where Indian culture and language predominate rather than Spanish. The Guaraní language is more common than Spanish. The patterns of cultural separatism and amalgamation, struggles over land use, and the political repression of Indian peoples by European colonists and their descendents in Paraguay and Argentina have their parallels to the history of the Cherokees and other Indian peoples in the United States and Indian Territory. Argentina at the time of Spanish colonization had a relatively small population of native peoples. Estimates vary, but there were perhaps 300,000 Indians of some twenty different groups living in the region at the time of conquest; 530,000 in 1700, and 210,000 in 1810. A mestizo Indian-Spanish population developed during the period of colonization as Indians were converted and acculturated to European values, culture, and needs. Spaniards and Indians alike adapted to the use of horses, transforming most Indian economies from an agricultural to a nomadic hunting base. Indians also supplied labor for the Spanish in fields, towns, and transportation. Indian resistance to European and mestizo settlement in the eighteenth and nineteenth centuries included raids against ranches, livestock, and settlements. The Spanish and independent governments responded with a policy of Indian control and repression, culminating in the Indian wars of the 1870s, including the government's "Conquest of the Desert" campaign against Indians in Patagonia in 1878–79 (*HDA*, 412–14; Rolinski, *Historical Dictionary of Paraguay,* 178–79; Taylor, *Rural Life in Argentina,* 54–56).

3. In his letters home Rogers made various comments about gauchos carrying long knives and their reaction to his own pistol. In his study of gaucho culture, Richard Slatta has observed that:

All gauchos carried a sheathed knife, or *facón*, ranging up to seventy centimeters (twenty-seven inches) in length, thrust through the back of the tirador. The facón was vital for work (killing, skinning, and castrating animals and repairing equipment), eating, and defense. This sword-like knife, repeatedly outlawed because of the many murders committed by facón-wielding gauchos, shrank to a more modest length by the end of the century. Although firearms became common during the last quarter of the century, the facón remained the favored instrument because of its versatility. (*Gauchos on the Vanishing Frontier,* 74)

4. The drinking of *mate,* "a highly caffeinated Paraguayan tea," was an important part of the gaucho diet and social ritual (Slatta, *Gauchos on the Vanishing Frontier,* 5). The tea was made by steeping tea leaves in a small pear-shaped gourd; the gourd would be passed around a circle of tea drinkers and the mate sipped through a *bombilla,* or communal straw, made of silver or other metal. The gourd would be filled and passed around several times in a ritual that began and ended each work day. Wealthier Argentines also drank mate, or *mate cimarrón,* unsweetened tea, from individual bombillas and gourds decorated with silver, copper, or wood. For the gaucho, mate drinking was an important expression of camaraderie. It could also be brewed in ways that conveyed meaning; that is, mate brewed with milk traditionally conveyed respect; sweetened mate, friendship. Gauchos employed as ranch hands often were given a supply of caffeine-rich tea by their employers, along with tobacco and meat (Barreto, *Mate: Su historia y cultura;* Slatta, *Gauchos on the Vanishing Frontier,* 78–79, 80, 81).

5. Absentee Argentine landowners would often hire Englishmen to manage their estancias and supervise temporary gaucho labor. In the early twentieth century approximately six out of ten estancias were operated by a hired resident manager rather than an owner. In visiting his England-born brother's estancia in 1908, Walter Larden observed that "all over the country there are now estancias belonging to married Englishmen who had none of the rough pioneering work" and who employed peon labor. His brother had started his ranching by managing his estancia on shares for a British firm that had invested in the land. By 1908 he too had hired a manager—an Englishman born in Uruguay—who oversaw the work of native Argentines (Larden, *Estancia Life,* 72; see also 44, 81).

6. Rogers described the gaucho-style saddle in detail in a later letter (see Will Rogers to the *Claremore Progress,* 7 July 1902, below). Gaucho dress was distinctive and reflective of gaucho subculture. Gauchos wore their hair long and dressed in short-brimmed hats, bright-colored shirts with *tiradors* (wide belts adorned with coins or silver ornaments), and trousers "of immense capacity" (Slatta, *Gauchos on the Vanishing Frontier,* 74). They carried their facónes and wore a poncho (usually hand-woven) and light, flexible, handmade boots, or *botas de potro,* fashioned from delicate portions of young horsehide. The toe of the botas de potro would sometimes be left open "to permit one or more exposed toes to clutch the small wooden stirrup" used on the traditional gaucho saddle. The botas de potro began to give way to hard European-manufactured boots at the end of the century. Facónes grew shorter, and manufactured fabrics replaced hand-woven ones. "In dress, ranch workers became largely indistinguishable from the immigrant farmer or urban day laborer except in the most traditional regions" (ibid., 74–76, quotes 75, 76; see also Nichols, M., *Gaucho;* Paullada, *Rawhide and Song*).

To Sisters
9 June 1902
Buenos Aires, Argentina

WILLIE ROGERS,
DON'T LIKE THE COUNTRY.

Buenos Ayres,
Argentenia
South America,
June 9, 1902

My Dear Sisters:

I expected to write to you sooner, but did not so will write now. Did you receive the package I sent by Dick? He left here for home on the 24th of May. I have been in B.A. most of the time, except what time I was in the country. I was on one of the biggest ranches in South America; but find ranch life here different from what it is at home. Our cowboys cant stand to work with the Peons or natives, for you have no place to sleep and only get beef, bread and a native kind of tea as diet.[1] So many Americans come here with a small capital but they can do no good, for the government has no land for sale and it takes a large piece of land to keep a bunch of cattle or sheep on. Oh it is nothing like North America. I tell you, you don't know what a good country you have till you see others. After seeing this country all of our people who have money enough go home and those who do not, work till they have saved up money enough for their home passage. Winter is coming on and it is getting quite cold here now. We find the language a great drawback. It is almost absolutely necessary that you speak Spanish if you are to go into business or to work for wages. Then the manners and customs of the people are so very different from ours. Here you are shoulder to shoulder with every nation on the globe, for every ship brings in four or five hundred passengers that are to live by labor alone. A few with capital. It is almost impossible to get a paying position for there are hundreds waiting even with a pull, to take every vacancy. As for working with cattle, we cant begin to compete with the natives here for we can't speak Spanish, we don't know the country, we can't live on their diet, we can't endure the hardships nor work for from $5 to $8 per month in our American money.[2] In hiring you, you are expected to work the first year for nothing. The only work that we understand how to do is done by the head men who are all or nearly all English.

As I now see things I don't expect to make any money here, but I would not take a fortune for my trip. Here is a bit of advice for my old comrades. "Just stay where you are boys, that is the best country on the globe for a person who was raised there. There you are among people while here you are with every kind of old "Nestor" in the world."

Marry and stay at home boys, for this country is overrated.

My health is good and I feel fine but I do wish I could hear from you all, but I guess it will be the middle of July before I can get your letters. I may stay here some time yet and I may turn up at home at any time. But don't be alarmed about me. Write me long letters and give all the boys and my friends my love. Write at once.

Lovingly Yr. bro.

Willie.

PD. Printed in *CR*, 1 August 1902.

1. Mate and fresh beef, usually roasted quickly over an open fire, were the staples of gaucho diet. On special occasions these might be supplemented by corn mush sweetened with honey or sugar or made with spiced meat, or beef soup made with squash, rice, and onions. Vegetables and bread were not commonly eaten. Rural gaucho families rarely grew vegetables or produced dairy products. Diet was also determined by class. On one ranch in 1900 and 1901, peons "ate rice, farina, rough salt, meat, and mate," while the manager supplemented his diet with luxuries like coffee, sugar, and fruit (Slatta, *Gauchos on the Vanishing Frontier,* 47). In the early 1900s some ranchers tried to diversify the food supplied to workers on the grounds that a more nutritional diet would result in a healthier work force. Others tried to limit or restrict the communal drinking of mate, mainly because of the time the ritual took out of the work day (ibid., 47–49, 76–78).

2. Rural wages had dropped to a low of 5.6 pesos in 1895 and gradually increased in the first decade of the 1900s. Wages in 1902 and 1903 were the same as in 1899: 33 paper pesos a month, or approximately 14 gold pesos. In 1908 in Buenos Aires province "160,000 workers found year-round employment on ranches, but another 133,000 were without permanent jobs" (Slatta, *Gauchos on the Vanishing Frontier,* 48–49). The *Buenos Aires Herald* reported that "large numbers of farm hands are at present unemployed" (20 August 1902). Rogers recalled in drafting his memoirs that "those good native gauchos or peelers down there get $15 a month in rag money—that's 42¢ on the $1.00 of regular money" (transcription of autobiographical notes, OkClaW).

To Clement Vann Rogers
17 June 1902
Buenos Aires, Argentina

Buenos Aires.
June. 17. 1902.

My Dear Father.

I will write you again and tell you that I am getting along alright and well.

I have been out into the interior about 800 miles and seen the country which looks like a good cattle and farming country

The work and cattle business here is nothing like it is at home   they have big ranches but they do not use the judgement in handleing them that is used at home   the head men are men that have had no experience at all and it is all left to the *Peons* or Natives who get about 5 dollars a month in our money and have to live like dogs. There is hundreds of men to every job of work   there is no American Men much handleing cattle here   it is all English.

It is no place for a man that hasent got plenty of money to buy his land and his cattle also for the cowman it is alright but for the cowboy it is no good unless he has the job with an American before he comes.

There is hundreds of people coming in on every boat from every country in the world you hear hundreds of different languages spoken all the time.

I have been well paid for my trip for I have learned lots on the trip. you dont know how good your country is till you get away from it   just tell all of those boys that want to come here to stay right there   that is good enough.

Dick went back about a month ago   I think he was going to Texas to work   I dont think there is much use of me staying here and I may start home any time.

They are trying to get a bill through the congress to have the Argentine Government lease or sell land to any one who wants it   that will probaly pass in a month or so   then a man with money can make something if he knows where to buy.

But after all the Territory is the best I guess even to invest in land.

It is getting a little cold here as it is winter

There is lots of cattle horses and Sheep shipped from here every day on all the boats for South Africa as they dont let them ship live cattle to England now from this country.[1]

I guess you got Dicks letter telling you where to write to me at.   and that I should hear from you before long

I guess you can probaly collect enough that is owed me up there to pay my insurance which comes due the 10th of September.[2]

Earnest Schrimpsher owes me $20 besides what the other boys do. Please see that they take good care of my *ponies* and dont let anyone use them.

Well I will close   write all the news. I do hope you all are as well as when I left   I may not be here to get the letter but then I might

I guess you are in the new hotel and have your fine barn done and all by now[3]   Give all who might ask of me my best regards   I will write the paper a letter about the country in a few days and tell all the boys to stay at home for that is the best place in the land for them

I do hope this will find you well and dont worry about me for I will be alright and I am in fine health and will write more often from now on. I may see you soon though.

I will close with all my love to a Dear Father I am your loving son

Willie.

[P.S., written on the back of page four:] address me in care of Edward Meyers.[4] 621 Avenida De. Mayo. Buenos Aires. A.R.S.A.

ALS, rc. OkClaW.

1. In 1900 England closed its ports to Argentine livestock because of hoof-and-mouth disease *(aftosa)*. The disease first began appearing in herds of cattle in Buenos Aires in 1870 and posed great concern to leaders of the cattle industry, specifically the Sociedad Rural Argentina (Argentine Rural Society), a group founded in 1866 by the landowning elite to foster stockraising, breeding, and agriculture, with emphasis on raising beef for the British market. New methods for shipping beef were developed partly in response to the disease, and once the British ban was in place, "overnight, the packing plant became the major purchaser and outlet for Argentine cattle" (Scobie, *Argentina,* 120). The ban had a devastating effect on those in the business of shipping livestock. Live cattle exports (as opposed to salted or refrigerated beef, etc.) constituted 43 percent of meat exports in 1897, but only 8 percent by 1907. The local British press in Buenos Aires regularly reported on the issue, expressing hopes that the restrictions would be lifted and that England would recognize that "Argentina has adopted the required measures to prevent the introduction of foot and mouth disease." An editorial frankly stated that the time "when the British ports shall be opened to our cattle is the indefinite date set in the popular mind for the beginning of the promised 'good times'" for economic recovery ("Meat Trade," *BAH,* 8 August 1902 and editorial, *BAH,* 7 August 1902; see also "British Ports," *BAH,* 7 August 1902; *HDA,* 398–99, 902; Scobie, *Argentina,* 120).

2. Rogers is referring to the annual payment for his life insurance policy, due on 10 September of each year (see Application to the Mutual Life Insurance Co. of New York, 9 September 1898, above).

3. In 1899 Clem V. Rogers traded horses he had purchased from Texas for investment in a newly constructed brick hotel, the Sequoyah, located near the town depot. He lived in rooms in the Lindel Hotel on the second story of the First National Bank

building, and while his son was away, he built a new stone and brick livery stable. A journalist who interviewed him in 1898 and 1899 described his upstairs apartment as "full of more antique furniture and Indian relics than I had ever beheld before in my life. The walls of the building were lined with beautiful Indian blankets, bows, arrows, old guns of ancient models, and every conceivable thing made by an Indian, and all of the very highest class make" (Carselowey, "Some Interesting Facts about Will Rogers," IPH-OkHi; Collings, *Old Home Ranch*, 61–62, 63, 78, 80; see also Clement Vann Rogers to Will Rogers, 17 June 1902, following, nn. 4, 16).

4. Edward Meyers was apparently an American from Chicago. Will Rogers saved his business card with the address of Miss Edith M. Meyers (Meyers's daughter?) on 44th Avenue in Chicago handwritten below Edward Meyers's printed name (Will Rogers scrapbook 1902–4, CPpR).

From Clement Vann Rogers
17 June 1902
Claremore, I.T.

Like other towns developed along the railroads, Claremore was undergoing a period of growth in the early twentieth century. With a population of about 1,500 people, it had come to rival older town centers like Tahlequah and Fort Gibson in size. Clem V. Rogers, as one of the local leaders "who believe[d] in the future of Claremore," was an important contributor to this growth.[1] In addition to his livery stable and hardware store (which he owned in partnership with Herb Moore) he invested in several other Claremore businesses, including the DeVann and Sequoyah hotels. At the time of writing this letter to his son, he was a member of a committee meeting to plan the construction of a new court building, and he was interested in building a new opera house. As the editor of the Claremore Progress *observed, "with a brick hotel, a brick opera house, a brick Masonic Temple, a rock Presbyterian Church, two rock livery barns and three residences in the course of erection," developments were taking place that "our town may well be satisfied with."[2]*

Claremore, I.T., June 17th 1902.

Buenos Aires S.A.
Dear Willie

We have got all the card & letters you have wrote back Home to me & the Girls, including the letter on May the 1st & May 7th. My Health have been good every since you left. The Girls & their children are all well. Clem come out at Boonville all ok.[3] Tom, Sallie, Cap, Bessie Schrimsher & me all went up to see him finish. He is now at Home. Claremore have now 2 good Brick Hotels.[4] I still keep my same room. your 2 Poneys are fat & nice up at Home. No one have ever rode them   Them & old Minnie run in the front Pasture.

Good Crops on my old Home place   Wheat, corn, & oats. Wheat is all cut.[5] They are cutting oats now. Corn is sure fine up here. Hay Crop will be good.

Clement Vann Rogers's stone livery stable in Claremore did a thriving business (*OkClaW*).

Cap & Maude are now in their new House.[6] Tom & Sallie had their House fixed up[7] Stine & May are still at the Ta.la.la. Hotel yet.[8]

Spi is still at Okmulgee.[9] They like him fine. Bunt Schrimsher married a Kansas man by the name of Robinson.[10] Her People were all opposed to the match. They live here in Claremore. Judge Jennings[11] Daughter married last week to one [Downing?] & are now at Tahlequah.

John Drakes Daughter[12] is to be married on the 22nd & Ella McSpadden on the 25th to Dr. Morrisons son,[13] at Chelsea. Cap Lanes Brother gets married next back in Texas. Maude is going down to the wedding[14] Ernest S.[15] & Willie Musgrove are still around Town here but the Girls dont seam to pay any attention to them. Crops are sure good in this country   Wheat. Corn. Oats. Cotton. & Hay.

Sequoyah Hotel is sure fine. Frakes & wife Run it. The Lindel Hotel here the old Bank building is pretty good. Gibbs & wife run it. I stop here with them. My stone stable is finished but I havent got it Rented yet. It is sure a nice building.[16] Crutchfields stable is about finished.[17] It is built out of Rock also. Dr. Bushyhead have been in St. Louis going to School about one month. His

Early scene of Claremore, I.T. Located in the black building in the center of the photograph were the offices of the *Claremore Progress*. This is now the intersection of Will Rogers Boulevard and Muskogee Street. The offices of the *Claremore Progress* have been on the same block for over 100 years *(Sprangel Collection, OkU)*.

wife & children & aunt Eliza[18] is going to California next week & spend the summer. I will go up Home tomorrow to look after my Crops. Alf[19] is still got his cattle in your Pasture. He hasent paid the last $200.00 yet. but I will try & get it in time to pay your insurance policy which is due about the latter part of August. Mine comes due about that time also.

To day Claremore had a good rain. Which will very near make corn. I saw Sallie, Maude, & Clem at Pryor Creek yesterday   they will go back Home tomorrow. Joe Lahay[20] & me drove over there yesterday & come back the same day. My Stone Livery Barn cost me about $4000.00. To day I wrote to Miss Miller at Vinita[21] to send me your Ring that she has of yours. Kates got a letter from you & will Publish it in his Paper this week[22] & will send you & Dick several copies. Write when you can is the wish of your Pa

C. V. Rogers

[P.S. on the back of the envelope:] Hello. Willie—first letter ▲ *[word illegible]* ▲ from home got in on the morning of July 25.

ALS, rc. OkClaW. On C. V. Rogers, Bank Building letterhead. Envelope addressed to W. P. Rogers, Buenos Aires, South America, Care of Edward Meyers, 334 Callis Piedras.

1. *CV,* 21 October 1898.
2. *CP,* 12 October 1901.

Captain (Cap) Lane, Will Rogers's broth-
er-in-law and husband of Maud Rogers
Lane. A pharmacist and banker, Cap
Lane was a prominent Chelsea booster
(*OkClaW*).

3. A reference to Will Rogers's nephew Clem McSpadden's graduation from
Kemper Military School in Boonville, Mo. Clem McSpadden did very well at the school;
he graduated with lieutenant status and "carried off the highest honors of the class"
(*CR*, 6 June 1902). Clem McSpadden's grandfather Clem V. Rogers; his parents, Tom
and Sallie McSpadden; his uncle Cap Lane; and his mother's cousin Elizabeth (Bess or
Bessie) Schrimsher of Claremore all attended his graduation at Boonville on 29 May 1902
(guest book signatures in Hitch, *Cadet Days*, 23; see also *CWM*, 30 May 1902). Clem
McSpadden was sixteen years old at the time of his graduation from Kemper (see *CR*, 30
May, 7 September, 12 October, and 24 December 1901, 3 January 1902; see also
Biographical Appendix entry, MCSPADDEN, Clement Mayes).

4. Buildings made of brick or stone were seen as contributing to the permanency
and stature of Indian Territory towns and were symbols of the commitment of their
residents to town life. A 1903 account of Chelsea, for example, offered statistics on
businesses that were housed in "stone and brick buildings" (twenty-three out of forty,
with four more stone and brick buildings under construction) as evidence of the
thriving nature and modernity of the town (*ChC*, 30 January 1903). In Claremore, as in
Tahlequah and other centers, older wooden buildings gave way at the turn of the century
to new, taller buildings of more solid construction.

The new Sequoyah Hotel, the long-anticipated three-story "brick hotel" with a
marble lobby, opened with fanfare in Claremore in May 1902 (*IC*, 8 May 1902; see also
DC, 1 May and 2 May 1902). The construction of the hotel had been news in Claremore
since Missouri developer J. M. Bayless began plans to erect a brick hotel in August 1901.
The official opening was a major social event in the town, with a public band concert and
a sit-down dinner and dance for nearly three hundred guests. Sallie McSpadden and
Maud Lane were among those who attended. The new building included a complete
system of indoor plumbing and electric lights and was touted as "being one of the finest

[hotels] in the Southwest" (*CP,* 3 May 1902). Mayor Joe LaHay served as toastmaster at the dinner dance, and Pocahontas Club members gave a representative of the hotel owner, J. M. Bayless, a painting of Sequoyah for the hotel's lobby. Mr. and Mrs. Frakes were the hotel managers for its first year of operation; they retired in April 1903.

The Lindel Hotel, another Claremore establishment, was located in the brick First National Bank building. Clem V. Rogers roomed there after the death of his second wife, Mary Bibles Rogers, in 1900 until his own death in 1911. The Lindel Hotel was managed by Mr. and Mrs. Ed H. Gibbs (Lindel Hotel letterhead, Will Rogers to Sisters, 20 April 1904, OkClaW; *CDM,* 18 September 1901; *CP,* 3 August, 31 August, 21 September, 28 September, 9 November, and 14 December 1901; 8 February, 12 April, 19 April, 3 May, 10 May, and 24 May 1902; 4 April, 11 April, and 18 April 1903; 15 December 1911; *CWM,* 18 September 1901 and 16 January 1903; Collings, *Old Home Ranch,* 76, 78; Hewes, *Occupying the Cherokee Country of Oklahoma,* 53; *HRC,* 16, 19, 20, 23–25, 495).

5. When he lived at the Rogers ranch, Clem V. Rogers was one of the first Cooweescoowee District ranchers to diversify into wheat; he introduced it as a crop on a large scale in the fall of 1891, when he became committed to converting the cattle ranch to a successful farm. His first wheat field was north of what became the town of Oologah, near Four Mile Creek. Wheat thrived in the soil and weather conditions of the Verdigris country, and yields and profits on the Chicago market were high for the first harvest in 1892. Record yields were achieved in 1895, leading the *Claremore Progress* to describe Clem V. Rogers as the "Oologah wheat king" (*CP,* 27 July 1895). Before the 1890s the great majority of acres under cultivation in the district were planted in corn (used in livestock feed). Railroad developers were among those who promoted the planting of wheat as a staple crop (as part of the transition of the country from open-range cattle ranching to farming), and they made seed wheat available. By the 1890s the major Verdigris-country farms included fields of alfalfa, corn, oats, and wheat. Each year Rogers usually put four hundred acres of land in wheat, one hundred each in oats and in hay crops, and two hundred in corn, with additional acreage planted for pasture. The ranch also had a vineyard, orchards, and fields planted in barley, rye, and vegetables. Wheat was the primary cash crop. With allotment Clem V. Rogers's sixty-thousand-acre ranch shrank to a farm made up of land allotted to the Rogerses and bought or leased by them from neighbors who had received adjoining allotments. After moving to Claremore, Clem V. Rogers caught the railroad from town to his ranch each weekend to supervise the small-scale farming being done there by tenants. By the time of statehood the farm had seriously deteriorated, and Rogers no longer took an active part in its management (Collings, *Old Home Ranch,* 70–74, 94, 97, 104, 105–07; Hewes, *Occupying the Cherokee Country of Oklahoma,* 43).

6. Cap and Maud Lane had established their home in Chelsea in the 1890s, and Cap Lane's drugstore business prospered. In 1901 the Lanes had their house extensively remodeled and painted. Disaster struck as the work was being completed in May 1901. As Cap Lane put it in a notice in the local paper, "On the 2nd of this month I had the misfortune to lose my dwelling house and contents by fire" (*CR,* 16 May 1901). Accounts of the cause of the fire differed. Some said it began with a spark from the smokehouse, and others said that it started when a fire set in the yard by workers, cleaning up remnants from carpentry done on the house, spread to the newly painted home and destroyed it. The family was not harmed. The Lanes decided to rebuild on a new site on the southern outskirts of Chelsea. They called their new, large two-story home, with full attic, Sunset Farm and moved into it in time to celebrate their eleventh wedding anniversary there in October 1901. It became a social center for visitors and for

Home of Cap and Maud Lane, Chelsea, I.T., about 1902–3, with some of Will Rogers's nieces and nephews gathered by it. *Left to right:* Herb McSpadden, mounted on Spot; Gunter Lane, holding horses; Ethel Lane, in the saddle of the second horse, with Irene McSpadden behind her. On the porch are Estelle Lane, Pauline McSpadden, and Helen McSpadden *(OkClaW).*

neighborhood children (Collings, *Old Home Ranch,* photo, 118; *CR,* 12 October and 17 October 1901; see also Biographical Appendix entry, LANE, Maud Ethel).

7. After living on a farm outside Chelsea, Tom and Sallie McSpadden moved into town in 1892 and built a house there that they called Maplewood. The grounds included small ponds that local children used for skating, and the McSpaddens donated land adjacent to the house to the town for a permanent public park for children's enjoyment. Tom and Sallie McSpadden lived at Maplewood until their deaths in 1935 and 1943, respectively. Tom McSpadden owned many properties in Chelsea. As the *Chelsea Reporter* put it, "the rent roll of Tom McSpadden is the largest of any man in Chelsea" (*CR,* 15 February 1901). He was often involved in building, moving, or remodeling houses that he then rented out (*CR,* 17 January 1901, 15 August 1902, 2 October and 23 October 1903, 28 April and 14 July 1905; see also Biographical Appendix entries, McSPADDEN, John Thomas, and McSPADDEN, Sallie Rogers).

8. May Rogers had managed the DeVann Hotel in Claremore with her first husband, Matthew Yocum, in the 1890s. Under different management, the hotel burned to the ground in a fire that destroyed a section of the downtown at the beginning of 1896. At the end of the same year Yocum, whose financial dealings had come into question, was murdered. May Rogers Yocum purchased the Oologah Hotel from J. Epsy Bell and

managed it on her own after her husband's death. In 1898 she married for a second time. She and her new husband, Frank Stine, took over the management of the Talala Hotel in 1900 or 1901. They had the hotel renovated and upgraded the facilities. Frank Stine opened a soda fountain and butcher-shop business in Oologah in late 1902, and in 1903 the Stine family moved to the McDaniel Hotel. In October 1903, May Stine wrote to Will Rogers that they had "quit the Hotel. . . . Frank runs a butcher shop in the winter and a Ice Cream parlor in Summer" (May Rogers Yocum Stine to Will Rogers, 4 October 1903, below). During this period the Stines also helped supervise the running of the Rogers ranch (*CP,* 27 December 1902 and 4 April, 20 June, and 10 October 1903; *HRC,* 376; see Biographical Appendix entries, STINE, Frank, and STINE, May Rogers Yocum).

9. Before Rogers left for Argentina, his close friend and distant cousin Spi Trent had spent time with him working at the Rogers ranch near Oologah. Clem V. Rogers paid for Trent's education at Spaulding Business College in Kansas City, and Trent worked at his family's hardware and general mercantile business in Okmulgee. He was still living in Okmulgee in January 1903 when he went to Claremore to attend Clem V. Rogers's sixty-fourth birthday party. In the following year he passed through Claremore on his way to take up a new position in Oklahoma City (*CP,* 2 March 1901, 17 January 1903; *CWM,* 1 January 1904; Trent, *My Cousin Will Rogers,* 145–49; see also Biographical Appendix entry, TRENT, Spi).

10. Will Rogers's cousin Juliette (Bunt) Schrimsher married Abraham Van Dyke Robinson in October 1901. The couple traveled to Kansas after the wedding and returned to live in Claremore in June 1902. Robinson (who was known as Dyke) was originally from Missouri, and he worked in a hardware store in Claremore owned by Clem V. Rogers from 1901 to 1903. He apparently had a fiery personality. New in town and a non-Cherokee, he was regarded at the time of his courtship of Bunt as an outsider to Cherokee society. Bunt Schrimsher was teaching public school in Claremore when she met Dyke Robinson. Bunt and her sister Bess were favorites of Clem V. Rogers's, and he and Bunt often had joint birthday celebrations (his birthday was 11 January and hers 12 January). Bunt had also been close to Clem V. Rogers's second wife, Mary Bibles Rogers. The Schrimshers and the Rogers families were privately worried about the relationship between Bunt and Dyke Robinson, and Will Rogers's sisters wrote to him about their doubts. These misgivings seem unwarranted, however, as the marriage was a long and successful one and Bunt and Dyke Robinson went on to become leading citizens in Claremore. They raised a family of four children and were active in Claremore church and civic affairs and in local Democratic politics. Bunt Schrimsher Robinson became the president of the Pocahontas Club, and Dyke Robinson became the postmaster of Claremore (*CDM,* 11 January and 21 January 1901; *CP,* 12 January, 3 August, and 7 September 1901 and 18 January 1902; *CR,* 17 January 1901; *CV,* 20 January 1899; *CWM,* 25 October 1901; see also Biographical Appendix entry, ROBINSON, Juliette Schrimsher).

11. Judge Harry Jennings was a Republican circuit court judge whose jurisdiction as a U.S. commissioner included Bartlesville, Claremore, Catoosa, Coweta, Okmulgee, Sapulpa, and other towns in Indian Territory and Oklahoma Territory, with headquarters in Tulsa. The *Claremore Progress* reported on his appearances in courts in different cities, including terms in the civil courts at Claremore and Nowata. Jennings was born in London, educated at London's St. John's Wood College, and came to the United States in 1871. He settled in Bartlesville in 1892 and founded and served as editor of the *Bartlesville Magnet* newspaper in 1896. He remained a U.S. commissioner until statehood, but was reassigned from the Nowata circuit in the summer of 1902, much to the

chagrin of the local attorneys there, who regarded him with "respect and good will" (*CP*, 12 July 1902). In the fall of 1902 Judge Jennings continued his interest in the newspaper business, purchasing the *Claremore Messenger* from a Mr. Kirkpatrick and Tom A. Latta and managing it as a Republican organ. The name of Judge Jennings's daughter has not been identified (Campbell, H., "Reminiscences," 380; *CP*, 29 March, 12 July, 25 October, 1 November, and 15 November 1902; Foreman, C., *Oklahoma Imprints, 1835–1907*, 58).

12. John Polk Drake (1844–1916) and his family were neighbors of the Rogerses, owning a ranch across the Verdigris River near those of the McClellans and the Lipes. John Polk Drake was a veteran of the Confederate army from Tennessee. He married Emily Jane Walker (1844–1921), a mixed-blood Cherokee and daughter of a Treaty Party family, in Fort Gibson, I.T., in 1877. They came to the Verdigris country in the following year and began a farm and horse-breeding ranch. They moved to Chelsea in 1890. Their daughter John Ella (Johnny) Drake (1883–1974) married Charles Henry (Charlie) Love (1878–1922), a Delaware Indian who had come to the Cherokee Nation in 1900, in Chelsea on 22 June 1902. The Drakes had five daughters, Mary, Bessie, Johnny, Emma, and Nannie. In other letters written in 1902, Will Rogers's sisters reported that Emmie Drake was seeing a Dr. Bolt and also told Rogers about the activities of Emmie's sister Bess. May McSpadden also confirmed in a letter to her uncle that Johnny Drake was planning to marry Charley Love. Bright Drake (1876–1959), cousin to the Drake girls, was a close childhood friend of Will Rogers, and as boys the two worked cattle drives together from Clem V. Rogers's ranch to John Polk Drake's range and on to Chelsea. Johnny Drake Love and Charley Love were ranchers and farmers and had three children (May McSpadden to Will Rogers, 22 June 1902, OkClaW; Sallie McSpadden to Will Rogers, 30 October 1902, below; *HRC*, 176, 176–77, 282; *OCF* 1:20).

13. Sallie Rogers McSpadden and Tom McSpadden's niece, Ella Bailey McSpadden (1881–1958) of Vinita, married Harry Morrison (1881–1947) in 1902. Ella McSpadden was the daughter of Florence Hoyt McSpadden and Tom McSpadden's brother Joel Cowan McSpadden, and therefore was a sister of T. R. McSpadden. Harry Morrison was the son of Dr. G. W. Morrison (1840–1924) of Chelsea, a veteran of the Confederate army from Maryland who had come to Vinita in 1870–71 as a company doctor for the MKT railroad, and Olive Ruth Davis Morrison, who was a widow running the Vinita boardinghouse for railroad officials when Dr. Morrison came to town. The Morrisons moved to Chelsea in 1889, and Dr. Morrison had a private practice. Harry Morrison became a farmer rancher and the owner of a Chelsea grocery store. The Morrisons were close to the McSpaddens, and Sallie McSpadden referred to the young couple in her letters to Will Rogers as Ella and Harry (May McSpadden to Will Rogers, 22 June 1902, OkClaW; Sallie McSpadden to Will Rogers, 30 October 1902, OkClaW; *HRC*, 299, 303–04, 329).

14. Cap Lane was from Clarksville, Tex., where his father, Robert Gordon Lane, was a doctor. His father and brother R. C. Lane visited Chelsea from Texas in July 1901. Another brother, Tom Lane, lived in Claremore. Maud Lane left Indian Territory for Texas at the end of June 1902 to attend R. C. Lane's wedding to Myra Shelton in Paris, Tex. She went to Clarksville on the same visit to see Cap Lane's old home (*CP*, 9 August 1902; *CR*, 27 July 1901 and 27 June 1902).

15. A reference to Ernest Schrimsher, Bunt Schrimsher's older brother and another of Will Rogers's cousins. Ernest Schrimsher married Susan Philips of Nowata on 27 October 1902, some four months after Clem V. Rogers wrote this letter. Susie Philips was educated in the Cherokee public school system and had graduated from the Cherokee Female Seminary in 1895. She taught in the Cherokee school at Nowata. Ernest and Susie Schrimsher were married in Nowata in late October 1902 and moved to a new

house they built on a farm outside Claremore a few months after their marriage. They had six children, including a set of twins (*CP,* 12 July, 1 November, and 15 November 1902, 28 February 1903; Starr, *History of the Cherokee Indians,* 651; see also Biographical Appendix entry, SCHRIMSHER, Ernest Vivian).

16. The building of Clem V. Rogers's two-story stone-and-brick livery stable was part of Claremore's boom. Rogers began the stable in October 1901. He went up to Coffeyville to inspect a livery barn there and proposed "to have the latest conveniences in the new one he intends to erect" (*CP,* 5 October 1901). He purchased a lot on the northeast corner of Second Street and Missouri Avenue and moved the old hotel that was on the property to a new location. The construction of the new Sequoyah Hotel was going on at the same time, and the local residents felt that removal of the old building "strongly illustrates the progress made by our town" (*CP,* 12 October 1901). This same issue reported that "C. V. Rogers has about completed plans for his new livery barn and it will be a daisy," two stories high, built in an L shape, with the main building forty by one hundred feet and its extension around the corner thirty by fifty feet. The front of the building was made of pressed brick, and the side and rear walls of stone. Construction on the foundation began at the end of October 1901, and the walls went up in January 1902. By April 1902 Rogers was advertising the livery barn for rent at "reasonable terms" (*CP,* 12 April 1902). He found a tenant a month after he wrote this letter to Will Rogers. The Claremore Livery and Transfer Co. moved into "Rogers' handsome rock livery barn" at the end of July 1902, and they were considered to "have the finest quarters of any livery barn in the Territory" (*CP,* 26 July 1902). Years later the stable was remodeled and became the Yale Theater (*CP,* 5 October, 12 October, 26 October, and 9 November 1901, 4 January, 12 April, and 26 July 1902; *CWM,* 25 October 1901 and 25 July 1902).

17. The Crutchfields were longtime Cooweescoowee District residents. Tom Crutchfield was a neighbor of the Rogerses along the Verdigris River, and Joe Crutchfield was one of the teachers at the West Point School near John Gunter Schrimsher's ranch. J. K. Crutchfield purchased George W. Walkley's livery barn and lot at the corner of Third Street and Catalayah Avenue in Claremore in the summer of 1899. He remodeled and repainted the building and operated a horse and mule exchange on the premises while making plans to build a new and larger barn. The new barn was finished in 1902 (*As I Recollect,* 44; *CP,* 28 July 1899; *HRC,* 159–60).

18. Dr. Jesse Bushyhead was Will Rogers's cousin and close friend (he was the son of Mary America Schrimsher Rogers's sister, Elizabeth Alabama Schrimsher Adair Bushyhead, and Dennis Wolf Bushyhead, principal chief of the Cherokee Nation). A prominent Claremore physician, he maintained excellence in his medical practice by learning new medical theories and approaches in postgraduate courses. He apparently returned to his alma mater, Washington University/Missouri Medical College in St. Louis, Mo., in 1902 to engage in such additional training. He married Fay Reynolds (a non-Cherokee woman from Arkansas who had been the assistant head of the Claremore public school for two years) in October 1898, and the couple had one daughter and four sons who were raised in Claremore. Dr. Bushyhead maintained an office over Hill's Drug Store in Claremore and advertised his professional services regularly in the *Claremore Progress* (*CP,* 1 July 1893, 28 September and 5 October 1901, 1 February, 19 April, and 6 September 1902, 14 October 1905; see also Biographical Appendix entry, BUSHYHEAD, Jesse Crary, M.D.).

Eliza Missouri Bushyhead Alberty (1839–1919) was the sister of Jesse Bushyhead's father, Dennis Wolf Bushyhead. The Albertys, like the Bushyheads, were an old mixed-blood Cherokee family who had been slaveholders before the Civil War. The same age as Will Rogers's parents, Eliza Bushyhead was educated at the Cherokee National Female

A prominent Claremore physician, Dr. Jesse C. Bushyhead *(second from left)* was the son of Principal Chief Dennis Wolf Bushyhead and Elizabeth Alabama Schrimsher Adair Bushyhead. Dr. Bushyhead was thus Rogers's first cousin as well as a close friend of the family. Assisting Dr. Bushyhead are Drs. White, Battles, and Lynn (patient unidentified). Bushyhead's office was located on the second floor of the First National Bank of Claremore *(OkClaW)*.

Seminary. She married twice, in 1859 to David Rowe Vann (1831–70), and in 1871 to Bluford West Alberty (1828–91). She lived in Tahlequah, where she ran the National Hotel. She was a very close friend of both Maud Lane and Sallie McSpadden and was a frequent guest in their homes in Chelsea and a participant in social events they sponsored, including the Chelsea Embroidery Club and the Women's Home Missionary Society. She also spent long periods of time staying with Fay and Jesse Bushyhead, and she socialized with Clem V. Rogers when she was in Claremore.

The Bushyheads had ties to California as well as to Indian Territory, in that Dennis Wolf Bushyhead had gone there to try his hand in mining during the gold rush of 1848—

49 and stayed nearly eighteen years. Fay Bushyhead and her children left Claremore with Aunt Eliza Alberty for an extended visit to California in midsummer 1902 and returned in the spring of 1903. Fay Bushyhead gave birth to a twelve-pound son in San Diego in November 1902. Dr. Jesse Bushyhead joined his family in San Diego in the following month (Maud Lane to Will Rogers, 24 July 1902, below; *CC*, 28 June 1899; *CDM*, 21 January 1901; *ChC*, 18 January 1901; *CP*, 21 September 1895, 17 September, 24 September, 3 October, and 26 November 1898, 19 October 1901, 18 January, 10 May, 11 October, 15 November, and 27 December 1902, 12 October and 4 November 1906; *CR*, 17 January 1901; *CWM*, 20 April, 27 April, and 25 May 1906; *DC*, 8 April 1902; 19 February and 5 November 1903; Keith, "Clem Rogers and His Influence on Oklahoma History," 61; Littlefield, *Cherokee Freedmen*, 13n.12; Mihesuah, *Cultivating the Rosebuds*, 125; *OCF* 1:272; *WRFT*, 78).

19. A reference to Alf Cunningham. The Rogers family apparently knew two Alf Cunninghams. The older Cunningham was one of the top cowboys at the Rogers ranch during its heyday in Will Rogers's childhood and a very close friend of the Rogers family. He had been in the Confederate army and had accompanied the Schrimsher family (Will Rogers's mother's family) back to Indian Territory from Texas after the war. He became the foreman of the Rogers ranch and was known to greet party guests in grand style at the ranch's hitchrack when Mary America Schrimsher Rogers sponsored one of her famous get-togethers. Cunningham had apparently gone through some rough periods in his life before coming to the Rogers ranch and was a recovering alcoholic. He was considered "Clem's most trusted cowboy, dependable and honorable and was respected by all who knew him" (Collings, *Old Home Ranch*, 38). The younger Alf Cunningham (to whom Clem V. Rogers may be referring in this letter) was born in 1860 and married Laura Lombard (b. 1874) in 1898 (Collings, *Old Home Ranch*, 24, 30n.8, 38; *OCF* 2:99).

20. Joe LaHay, the popular mayor of Claremore and the treasurer of the Cherokee Nation in 1902, was a leading Downing and Democratic Party politician and a very close friend, business partner, and political colleague of Clem V. Rogers. He and Rogers served on several civic, fraternal, and political committees together and often traveled in consort to do business in Tahlequah (see article from the *Claremore Progress*, 30 March 1901, n.3, above).

21. Probably a reference to Miss Maud Miller of Vinita, a member of Will Rogers's social set in the Verdigris country. Maud Miller won a prize for a word game with Rogers's friend (and fellow roper and Wild West show performer) Tom Isbell at a party she and Rogers attended at the home of Mr. and Mrs. W. L. Trott in Vinita in 1901 (see article in the *Daily Chieftain*, 27 September 1901, n.2, above). Rogers may have been seeing Miss Miller before he left Indian Territory.

Will Rogers asked Clem V. Rogers about the status of the ring in his 31 July 1902 letter home and requested that his father not publish the information about Miss Miller and the ring when sending his letters to the local papers. Rogers may have been concerned about his father locating jewelry of his that was of some monetary value since he was suffering financial hardships in Argentina (see Will Rogers to Clement Vann Rogers, 21 July 1902, below).

22. A reference to A. L. Kates, the publisher of the *Claremore Progress* (see Biographical Appendix entry, KATES, Albert L.)

From May McSpadden
22 June 1902
Chelsea, I.T.

May McSpadden[1] was Will Rogers's niece, the daughter of Sallie Rogers McSpadden and Tom McSpadden. She was eleven years old at the time she wrote this letter.

You know where I live, Chelsea, I.T.
June, 22, 1902

Dear Uncle Willie:

How glad we are to know that we can write to you.

Well Clem covered himself with glory as his uncle did and he brought home his sheep skin too.

Clem got the scholarship medal, do you know what that is? I suppose you do tho. Today is Sunday.

Uncle Willie ain't you getting pretty lonesome down there without us? I expect you will be mosing back to the United States pretty soon.

We are all well and doing fine. Uncle Willie I think it is so funny for you to write and spell and yet don't know your A, B, C's, dont you think so? . . . .

We are all going to write to you.

I hope you and Mr. Paris are well and will stay that way till you get back to the United States because I am afraid they don't have doctors down in South America. . . .

If you want to give mama a present you can give her a white snake skin.

Goodbye
May McS.

Clem said, "Tell him to send me a Boa Constricter."

ALS, rc. OkClaW.

1. See Biographical Appendix entry, POOLE, May McSpadden.

Left to right: Irene, Herb, and May McSpadden, some of the children of John Thomas (Tom) McSpadden and Will Rogers's sister Sallie Rogers McSpadden (*OkClaW*).

From Pearl Yocum
25 June 1902
Claremore, I.T.

June 25, 1902

Friend Willie

as uncle Jim[1] is writeing I will tell you how my white face calf is getting a long   she is just as fat as she can be and has got to be nearly a cow and I am so proud of her   old Comancha[2] is just as fat as he can bee   he comes up evry night, and I think he is looking for you but dont see you   I go out to the fince and rub him and kill horse flies off of him and pet him a little   the colt is fine   his grode lots   wee mis you verry much

Wee are can[n]ing Blackberies and when you come home I will make you a cobler   Papa and Mama send their best wishes to you[3]

I will close by asking you to answer soon

I remain as ever your little friend

Pearl Yocum

ALS, rc. OkClaW.

1. James Cleveland (see James Cleveland to Will Rogers, 25 June 1902, following).

2. Comanche was Will Rogers's beloved horse. Clem V. Rogers had bought Comanche for his son when the horse was five years old. Comanche was wise and athletic, admired among Indian Territory cowboys and rodeo riders as a superb steer-roping horse. Herb McSpadden (Sallie Rogers McSpadden's son, who became the manager of the Rogers ranch) summed up Comanche as "outstanding" among Will Rogers's horses (Rogers was a good judge of horses and over time owned many): "He was cream colored with white mane and tail, square made, fourteen hands high, and weighed about one thousand pounds. Comanche was intelligent, fast, and a good roper." Rogers himself said, "I had an awful good little horse that really put me in the business" (both quoted in Collings, *Old Home Ranch*, 85). Rogers frequently told stories about Comanche's skill in the roping ring, including a time when he loaned Comanche to another cowboy at a roping contest in Springfield, Mo. The roped steer broke away and fled from the dismounted cowboy as he was trying to tie him, "but old Comanche, when the steer crossed the rope, turned and busted him all by himself" (Day, ed., *Autobiography*, 12). Comanche would "put you up so close to a steer that you didn't rope him, you just reached over and put a Hackamore on him" (Collings, *Old Home Ranch*, 85; for another account of Comanche's prowess in the ring, see p. 93; see also Will Rogers to Sisters and Folks, 27 November 1903, n. 3, below).

3. The Yocums were tenants at the Rogers ranch after Will Rogers left the ranch for Argentina, but little is known about them. Ellsworth Collings has noted that the family living at the ranch as tenants during the time that Will Rogers was managing the ranch for his father in the 1890s was from Illinois. Since young Pearl Yocum and her parents seem to have been well acquainted with Rogers and fond of him, it is possible they were residents of the ranch during his tenure there. The Yocums may very well have been of some relation to Will Rogers's sister May Rogers Yocum Stine's first husband, Matthew Yocum. May and her second husband, Frank Stine (Matthew Yocum's first cousin), lived at the Rogers ranch to look after things when Will Rogers went away to compete in roping contests, and so there was a direct connection between the ranch and the Yocum-Stine family (see Biographical Appendix entries for STINE, May Rogers Yocum, YOCUM, J. Matthew).

By October 1902 the Yocums and Jim Cleveland were no longer at the ranch, and there was apparently some financial dispute and hard feelings between them and Clem V. Rogers. Maud Lane wrote to Will Rogers that "when old uncle Jimmie left he took everything he could haul off." Clem V. Rogers tacitiurnly reported in October that "Cleveland and Yocum is not on the Home place" and that he was collecting money from them. After the Yocums and Cleveland left the ranch, John Lipe took care of Will Rogers's ponies (Clem V. Rogers to Will Rogers, 21 October 1902 and 9 February 1903; Maud Lane to Will Rogers, 31 October 1902; Kate Ellis to Will Rogers, 15 February 1903, all in OkClaW and below; Collings, *Old Home Ranch*, 78, 79).

From James Cleveland
25 June 1902
Oologah, I.T.

Oolagh I.T.
6/25/1902

Mr. W. P. Rogers

I recived youre leter of the 13 and was glad to hear that you was in good health   well Willie you can rest easy about your horses   they are all write They have not had a bridle on sins you left and i dont intend they shal have   they are both in good helth and fat   I have just got through harvesting wheat   i about 2/9 crib oats is as fine as i ever saw   corn is out of site   i have the finest ~~crop~~ ▲ *[word illegible]* ▲ of corn i ever saw   we are all write at this writing   i want to hear from you often   tell Dick that i would like to see him and swap swap[1] a five with him and hear him laf   your pa was up to the ranch a few day ag[o] and was pleased with crop   Willie i wish you and Dick was hear to gou to the 4 of July at Talala   they are going to have a roping contest   i think you could mak it warm for the boys   your your frins and cinection are all well as far as i no   ther has bin very litt[l]e sickness in the neighborhod   we hahv had a fine season for corn this year   plenty rane   grass is fine as I ever saw on rang   grass in pasters is wast high   I am busy fencing [fixing?] for Thrasher   i had good luck to get my thr*[remainder of word illegible]* to come to the [east?].[2]

Wille tak good care of your Self and dont get in no troble with them wolles down there

i will close

give Dick my best rgrads   best wishes for both of you   hoping you may do well.

write soon

James Cleaveland

ALS, rc. OkClaW. Envelope hand-addressed to W. P. Rogers, Buenos Aires South America c/o Ed Meyers, 334 Calle Piedras. Return address, Jas Cleveland, Oologah, Ind. T.

1. The word swap appears as the last word on page one of the original letter and the first word on page two.
2. Cleveland is referring to threshing (thrashing) the harvested grain crops.

From Sallie McSpadden
2 July 1902
Chelsea, I.T.

July 2, 1902
Chelsea. Ind. Ter.

My Dear, Dear Willie:

Every single day we think of and talk about, love you and want oh, so badly to see you. I have waited to write because Maud and papa each told you the news and I did not want you to get all our letters at once. Every one enjoys reading your letters very much. I have been having them printed in the Chelsea Reporter and that keeps all your friends posted. Maud is still in Texas.[1] Expects to return Saturday. The children stay with me all day and go home at night. My children take it [their?] time about going home with them. Papa was up Saturday and stayed till Monday. Herbie and Gunter[2] went back with him and I went down and spent the afternoon yesterday expecting to bring the boys home with me, but Herb wanted to go on to Uncle John's[3] so I let him go. He will return Thursday. Papa fitted them out with new clothes. He had Johnnie[4] there also. Oh, papa has the loveliest Milton velvet carpet you ever saw. It is an Indian design. He has had his room all renovated, papered and bought him a wardrobe. It looks so much better. Tom[5] has gone out to see about the thresher. You know we always have to cook for them so on the "glorious fourth" we will be threshing wheat. We have a very good crop this year. Corn is fine. Lots of fruit, I mean strawberries, cherries, black and huckleberries and peaches and not quite so many apples, still a great abundance for our family use. I am putting up some kind of fruit every day for we expect you home for Christmas, sure. . . .

Papa says Uncle Jim[6] looks after your horses splendidly. Says they are as fat as can be and are never ridden. So you see they are just waiting for you to come back. Miss Rachel[7] always asks about you and enjoys your letters so much. She is so nice. The children all swear by her. May says you must teach her to talk Spanish when you come home. With lots of love from every one and the sincere hope of seeing you soon. I am

Your affectionate
Sister Sallie

ALS, rc. OkClaW. Envelope hand-addressed to W. P. Rogers, Buenos "Ayres," South America, [c/o] Edward Myers, 334 Calle Piedras. Meyers's address was crossed out and a note written explaining "not here." Forwarded via return address to American Consul, Cape Town, South Africa. Stamped "unclaimed"; handwritten note: *"gone to* to Mooi River Station, Natal." The back of the envelope is addressed care of J. Piccione, Mooi River Station, Natal.

Wedding picture of Will Rogers's sister Sallie and John Thomas (Tom) McSpadden, taken in 1885 and reprinted at the time of their fiftieth wedding anniversary (*SRM-OklaW*).

1. Maud Lane was in Clarksville and Paris, Tex., attending the wedding of her husband Cap Lane's brother, R. C. Lane, and visiting the Lane family.
2. Will Rogers's nephews Herb McSpadden and Gunter Lane (see Biographical Appendix entries for LANE, James Gunter, and McSPADDEN, Herbert Thomas).
3. Will Rogers's uncle (his mother's brother), John Gunter Schrimsher.
4. A reference to either Johnnie Yocum, the son of May Rogers Yocum Stine, or to Johnnie Drake, the daughter of a close friend of Clem V. Rogers's and a playmate from Will Rogers's youth.
5. Tom McSpadden.

6. Jim Cleveland.

7. Rachel Hanson, a local schoolteacher and friend of Sallie McSpadden. Rachel and Georgia Hanson were members of Sallie McSpadden's Chelsea Embroidery Club and were frequent guests at the McSpadden home (*CR*, 16 May and 17 October 1902).

From Dick Parris
4–8 July 1902
Tahlequah, I.T.

Tahlequah, Ind. Ter. July 4[1] *1902*

My Dear Old Pard

Well here I am at last back home after a hell of a Voyage   say kid you must sure come back cause there aint no place like home.

I arrived on the 3rd of July and they were going to have a Dance that night   Well

Everybody is Well up at your place and Everything is allright. the people all want to see you very bad   there is no news hardly at all   nothing you would care to hear   none of them old girls married yet but some of them has got to tell Parris no or he is going to tie up with some of them and that very quick. Well I dont want to ever see that country again and hope you will be back all right in a few months   well tell Old Myers to write and Bob

Well Ill ring off for this time so Write soon and tell me all the news.

Your Pard

Dick Parris

ALS, rc. OkClaW. On Brown Drug Co. Prescription Druggists letterhead, West Side Public Square, Tahlequah.[2] Envelope hand-addressed to Mr. W. P. Rogers, "Burnos Aires," South America, care of Edward Meyers 334 Calle Piedras. Return address printed M. Thompson Drug Co., Druggists, Tahlequah, Ind. Ter. Note on the back of the envelope: "40¢ due Palmer on this letter."[3]

1. The second page of this letter was dated 8 July 1902.

2. The letterhead continued "Fine Drugs, Chemicals, Perfumery, Toilet Articles, &c. . . . Finest Brands of Foreign and Domestic Cigars."

3. Ed Meyers attached a note to this letter reading: "*Bill*, Opened this by mistake, also to put in smaller envelopes   Say that damed old Kid put on a two cent stamp   durned if these dagos here didnt tax me for 40¢ on account of it   double postage   Meyers."

To the *Claremore Progress*
7 July 1902
Buenos Aires, Argentina

Tells of Ranch Life Argentine.

Buenos Ayres, S.A., July 7, 1902.

To The Progress: —

I have been here over two months and have made two trips into the country of about eight hundred miles each, and been on some of the big ranches and seen considerable country, but a very small part of what is here, as Argentine alone is half as large as the United States.

I don't think from what I have seen and heard that the unsatisfactory conditions of the country are in the land, climate or natural resources, as the land is generally good and they raise most everything, but the fault is in the people especially the governing class.

It is supposed to be the same kind of government as the United States,[1] but the men who are in control are always the worst in the country, and it is said to be the most corrupt and unstable of any government in the world.[2]

There is no energy or get up in the natives and they of course are the ones in power. They only think of dressing and showing off to the extent of their means. The country is very deep in debt and a dollar of their money is worth only forty-three cents and they vary all the time. The laws in regard to law breakers and criminals are never enforced.

All the leading enterprises are owned and managed by foreigners, but they risk their money where a war or revolution will take it all, for they have no protection whatever. There has been a big war scare on with Chilli, but that has quieted down, but they do not know how long it will remain so. There are very few North Americans as it is said they get disgusted with conditions and go back. There are a few in the town, but none in the country. There are thousands of every other kind of people under the sun here. The most of the capital is English and there are lots of that nationality here, but an Englishman's and an American's ways are altogether different. There is more land here to the amount of people than any country I ever struck. The government will not sell land, but they will give you about fifteen hundred acres if you will become a citizen of the country, but it will be away back where you can't get a way out with what you raise and they will tax you to death. You will have to serve in the army and fight in case of war. The American consul is now trying to get a law passed to sell anyone land and let them pick it where they please and pay for it yearly. That would give a cow man a chance.

The most of the emigrants that come can't make a living and starve out. They can't pay the exhorbant taxes and they go back. There are a lot of Boers coming over here now to settle, but it is said they will not stay.

As to the stock business, it pays pretty well, but now that the English ports are closed against this cattle it is hurting the trade. This country supplies So. Africa. Only enough are killed here to supply this country. There are no packing houses here.

This is a great sheep country, but I think the hog business would beat them all, for a hog is worth more here than a cow or horse and are very scarce. Cattle and horses are worth about what they are at home.

The ways on the ranches here are no more like America than anything. A man with a pull, though he be English city bred, will come here and go to managing a big ranch. Probably he will not know how to ride, but here they don't think it takes any experience to manage a ranch, and it does not the way they manage it. They don't know what it is to use any judgement or common sense in handling a bunch of cattle. The head men consider that the hands (that is the Peons or natives) know all about it and it is not necessary for them to know anything. I was on one of the big ranches here for several days and here are a few of the things that I actually witnessed. They will give you an idea how far behind the times they are. Oh, it is disgusting for anyone from America, and that is why they will not stay. They drive the cattle in a run and I asked the boss if it did not run too much of the fat off, and he gave me the horse laugh and said: why they fill right up again. In cutting out, there are from three to five men to each animal and no one to hold the herd until they get out two or three, then they all go. They would not begin to believe that a horse knew enough to cut out a cow without guiding and one man to the head.

They have good fat horses and plenty of them, but they are never learned anything. They are not very tall, but are short and very heavy made. They do not pitch near as bad as you see them there. They don't think of rounding up a herd of cattle with less than thirty men. There is no such thing as a "chuck wagon." Your grub is tied onto your saddle, as it can be made into a regular "carry all." It is two pieces of wood the length of our saddle skirts and fastened together across the front and back that lays long ways on the back, then it is covered over with sheep skin, old sacks or any old thing that strikes their fancy, and it is just a big pack, right flat all over and about a foot and a half wide. The stirrups are little round things, something like our race stirrup, but not so big, as they can only just get the tip of the toe in. There is not a man that would think of putting his foot flat into a stirrup. The stirrups are fastened by a small piece of leather to the old frame and no fenders. Your whole leg don't hang down, only from the knee hangs over the edge of the pack. The rope is fastened into a ring that is put behind right where our back cinch ring is. My saddle and all have been a big show ever since they seen it. As for roping, riding or for any old thing, they can't each the "punchers" in America. They all use a raw hide rope and are doing good to catch one out of three and always run with him at least one hundred yards, slowing him up. They are not at all reckless. They are a cowardly lot. The all carry knives in their belt from a foot and a half to two feet and very few have guns, and if a man points a gun at a whole bunch, he can put them all to flight.

They pay the men about eight and ten dollars a month in American money. A boss about twenty-five dollars and managers on some of the ranches from forty to fifty dollars.

All the Americans I have met here are only living to get back to America. Any part of the states are better for a man without lots of money, than this place, and the beauty of it is you are among "people," not a lot of "dagoes" from all over the world and all having a different lingo. It would be alright for a man with a lot of money to bring down an American outfit and run a ranch on the American plan, he can get rich, for these dagoes would give his American cow punchers a wide berth, and they could have things their own way. Here you are not allowed to put a brand on the brute any larger than your hand and it is almost impossible to read it, but they do not pay any attention to brands as each outfit is supposed to know their own animals by the flesh marks and the brands are only looked for in case of dispute.

It is the middle of winter here now. It is not very cold but always damp and rainy. The Fourth of July passed off quietly here. Once in a while you would see an American flag, but no "roping contests."

Well, I must shove off, and my parting words are for all you people to fight shy of this part of the globe. You never know a country until you leave it, and so stay where you are.

Adieu and my best wishes to all.

Will Rogers.

Printed in *CP,* 23 August 1902.

1. The Argentine Constitution of 1853 was similar to the U.S. Constitution. It provided for a representative, republican form of government with a federal system — a national government, headquartered in Buenos Aires, and twenty-two provincial governments, with a division of power between national and regional authority. The constitution also mandated certain freedoms, including the freedom of the press and the

prohibition of slavery. The presidency, however, was construed in the Spanish tradition of the caudillo (political strongman). The president was to serve a four-year term, be Roman Catholic, and was granted power to suspend civil liberties in the national interest. The Argentine legislature consisted of a Senate, with a minimum of two senators from each province, and a Chamber of Deputies, with representation based on the population of the various provinces. Politics until the early twentieth century were "for all practical purposes . . . a fiefdom of a limited number of powerful families that, apart from regional rivalries, were in basic agreement on their government's form and objectives. Until 1916 the oligarchy determined who would be president by agreeing on a candidate and then having him elected" (Weil et al., *Area Handbook for Argentina*, 200; see also "Governmental System," chap. 8, 185–94, and "Political Dynamics," chap. 9, 195–216).

2. The agricultural transformation of the pampas and the commercial development of Buenos Aires into a railroad hub and world port strongly influenced Argentine politics. With the revolution in the country's political economy after 1880, political power became more centralized—concentrated, as commercial wealth was, in the coastal region. The president, backed by an oligarchy of well-to-do capitalists and landowners, had constitutional authority to intervene in provincial affairs, and used the new railroad and telegraph systems as well as the power of conscription to maintain nationalist control over the rural areas. In the 1890s organized opposition began to emerge with the formation of the middle-class Unión Cívica Radical (Radical Party), and in the early 1900s a working-class labor movement developed, including the Federación Obrera Argentina (Argentine Workers' Federation) in 1901, the organization of the general strike of November 1902, and the formation of the Unión General de Trabajadores (General Workers' Union) in 1903. In the 1890s two Argentine presidents turned their offices over to their vice presidents amidst conflicts between the federal government and the provinces (Pres. Miguel Juárez Celman was forced out of office in 1890, and Pres. Luiz Saenz Peña resigned in 1895). Coup attempts were made in 1890, 1893, and 1905. Political unrest was matched by the instability of the national currency and massive inflation. Julio Argentino Roca, who had been president during the boom years from 1880 to 1886, was reelected in 1898 and remained president until 1904. Politics were dominated by the Partido Autonomista Nacional (National Autonomous Party) (PAN), which represented the interests of merchants, bankers, estate owners, developers, and financiers. The PAN controlled elections through "local bosses whose henchmen flagrantly abused the electoral system," and payoffs and bribes characterized the work of government officials from customs inspectors to judges (Weil et al., *Area Handbook for Argentina*, 20). The abuses committed by Roca's elite group made workers, students, immigrants, and other gorups call for the reform of corrupt practices and an end to political domination by the PAN. The Radical Party, led by Hipólito Yrigoyen, boycotted elections after 1898 to protest the corruption and called for electoral reform)including regularized voting registration and the use of secret ballots rather than voice voting, which made it possible for landholders and political administrators to monitor votes and thus intimidate workers and tenants) and a two-party system. Anarchists and the Socialist Party also won adherents among industrial workers and urban laborers. Yrigoyen was elected president in 1916, and during his term many members of the traditional oligarchy were ousted from office. Labor rights and land and tenancy reform remained volatile issues (*HDA*, 794; Munck, *Argentina*, 47, 49; Scobie, *Argentina*, 146–47, 189, 195–203; Spalding, *Clases trabajadora Argentina;* Weil et al., "Political Confusion and Economic Growth (1890–1943)," in *Area Handbook for Argentina*, 19–22, 200–203, 275).

To Sisters
21 July 1902
Buenos Aires, Argentina

Buenos Aires
July 21. 1902.

My Dear Folks at Home

Well I will pen you a small document to keep you posted on my where are you. I am now back from a second "cruise" into the plains of the *Goucho*.[1] havent been able to do any one out of any considerable sum of colateral but am living in perfect ease. picking up a few unthought of facts but no loose change.

I never felt better or lighter hearted in all the days of my Persimonhood   a dollar dont look any bigger to me than it ever did

Well I put from this land sometime between the 1st and the 10th of August for Capetown[2] South Africa with a ship load of stock   I dont know just when we will start   the boat will be here tomorrow and it takes some time to clean up and load her full cargo   I dont know what the biggest part of the cargo is   I guess all kinds of live stock.

It takes about 18 to 20 days to the cape.   ships generally carry from 500 to 1000 head of stock and about 20 to 30 Peons or men to feed and care for them. I am a full fledged *Peon*.

You see a man cannot land in South Africa according to the law unless he has 100 Pounds or $500 in our coin   but this man[3] wants some men to work for him and he will land me and I will Probaly work for him   you get 2 pounds or $10.00 for going over and 4 pounds if you come back   you see they use them cleaning out the ship   I will stay for they say it is a pretty good place.[4] you see they speak English and there is lots of Americans there

This is a bum land for any one that hasent got this coin but there is lots to be made if a man had the *mon*. I just begin to see what a little I did know about this world   I know 10 times more about my own country than I did before I left   I will get all the information I can for that is all I will have when I again approach the B.I.T.

I wish you people had a little of this cold weather up there   it gets pretty chilly here of course no snow but it is damp and rains lots.

Not much doing here on the 4th of July. a few lonesome but good looking "old glorys" waving over this *dago* land.

I have been having a great time   one of the "U.S. battleships." the "Atlanta"[5] was here for a couple of weeks and I almost lived on board   learning them all the latest coon songs[6] I knew   for it had been 2 years since they left   they had a minstrel troup[7] among themselves and seemed to have a good time   wanted me to enlist and join them   they told me when I got "on the rocks" and wanted to go to Gods country that they would make up enough to send me back

two of the boys deserted them here   both officers   one of them a fullblood "Oneida" Indian from New York state[8] the only Fullblood in the navy   he is here   just ate supper with me.   he is going back home

There is a Texas Cow boy here that I think will go with us to South Africa

You ought to hear me singing in an English Speaking Concert hall where all the Sailors[9] and men off of the all the boats go ~~in dock~~ at night

I havent heard a line from home and I want you all to write me a long letters to Capetown in care of the American Consul there and I will get them alright   Tell any of my friends that would like to hear from me that I would be pleased to hear from them and will reply personally (not through my secretary) at once on receipt of said Epistle.

If things are not exactly satisfactory to your "Royal Nibs" in those parts I may return to the U.S. ▲ Shores ▲ by a chartered *"shift"* thence overland on foot (as I can see the landscape better) *via* Catale and Whiteoak[10]

What I think of the people of this portion of the globe wouldent look good in print and I can leave it without doing serious injury to my palpitator.

Well I must shove off. hope to hear from you soon and my parting sylables are "dont worry bout me   get along yourself"

Lots of love to all and I do hope you are all well.

                                                  from your loving Uncle E.

Care of American Consul ▲ Capetown ▲ South Africa.

ALS, rc. OkClaW. Envelope hand-addressed to Mrs. C. L. Lane, Chelsea, Indian Territory, U.S. of America. Revised version printed in *CR*, 5 September 1902.

1. A reference to the pampas, vast fertile plains of the east-central region of Argentina. The gauchos were a nomadic social group who maintained a highly masculinized culture based on cattle herding. Emerging in the mideighteenth century, gauchos hunted and killed wild cattle for meat and hides. As the cattle industry was modernized, increasing limitations were put upon traditional gaucho ways of life. By the end of the nineteenth century the traditional gaucho had become a folk hero, memorialized in romantic gaucho literature and lauded by nationalists who looked to him as a symbol, or embodiment, of values of individualism, independence, and courage that they felt were uniquely Argentine. The real gaucho had become a migratory cowhand and ranch worker, or *peón de campo*, whose customs and skills were eradicated or devalued as the pampas were converted to fenced ranches and farms. Earlier in the nineteenth century, gauchos were often negatively stereotyped as primitives or deviants given to violence and criminality.

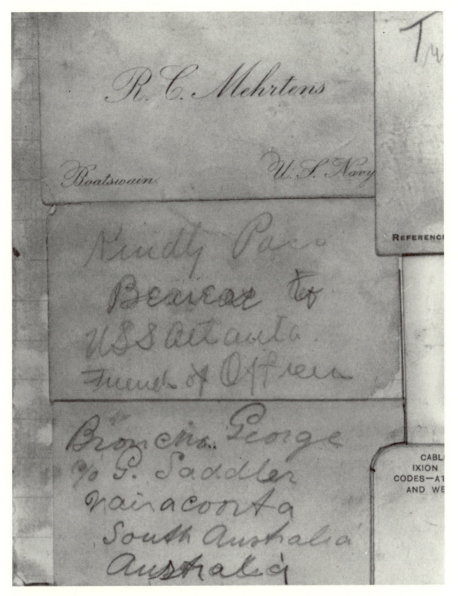

Will Rogers's pass to board the U.S.S. *Atlanta* is featured here amidst other cards he collected on his 1902–4 travels *(Scrapbook 1902–4, CPpR)*.

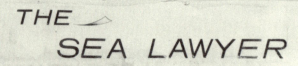

THE
SEA LAWYER

SPECIAL PUBLICATION OF U. S. S. ATLANTA

Buenos Aires, Argentina, June 26th, 1902

U. S. S. ATLANTA

BEAN SOUP.

Take thirty-six gallons of water and subject it to a warm influence until it steams. Then drop in three bars of Navy saltwater soap and allow them to dissolve. Add five dozen heavy-chested beans, and allow them to boil until they begin to swell and look uncomfortable.

Then remove the beans and lay them aside to form the nucleus for a baked bean breakfast. Next take a boat-hook or some equally convenient weapon, and agitate the liquid conglomeration until the soap begins to make its presence manifest. Serve with side arms. The above is sufficient for 250 men. If the crew consists of a larger number use more water. If there is a liberty party use less beans.

STEW (CANNED WILLY).

Take a can each of corn, peas, beans, tomatoes, a potato, an old cabbage and a flat cap full of rice. Also a few chunks of old bread, sour dough, cracked hard tack, and any other old odds and ends for which there is no use. Then add enough flour to make a mild bluff. Add salt and pepper. In the absence of pepper use gunpowder. Mix the whole into one homeogenous medley and drop into forty gallons of boiling water. Then call a few cans of Choice Roast Beef, and when they come open them quickly with cleaver and drop the contents into the boiling melody before they have time to escape. Stir with boat hook and boil for eighteen consecutive seconds. Serve with funny stories and stand by with cocked revolver.

In Buenos Aires, Will Rogers entertained sailors aboard the U.S.S. *Atlanta*. This issue of the ship's newspaper *The Sea Lawyer* was saved in his scrapbook from the period. The sailors may have named the stew recipe after Rogers (*Scrapbook 1902–4, CPpR*).

Many gauchos were mestizo, of mixed Spanish and Indian descent; others were of African-Argentine heritage. Traditional gaucho subculture shared some values and ways of life with the Indian subculture, including worldviews that emphasized stoicism, mysticism, and a pantheistic concept of nature; the use of *boleadoras,* or bolas, and lances in hunting cattle; and migratory, equestrian lifestyles that were at odds with that of the *terratenientes,* or large landowners who converted the open grasslands of the pampas to private property.

Gaucho families were landless; most lived in modest homes constructed on property owned or claimed by others, and thus were susceptible to eviction. Gaucho men were also particularly susceptible to forced and voluntary conscription into military service in the Argentine army or frontier militias (partly due to landowners' influence over the enforcement of vagrancy laws), thus adding to the popular association of gauchos with violence. The romantic image of the gaucho as a free agent beneath the open sky was much at odds with the impoverishment and discrimination faced by actual gaucho families. In the first part of the 1900s the gaucho look—distinctive dress, hair styles, and material culture—became a fad in urban areas of Argentina. Gaucho songs and romantic literature about the gaucho also gained popularity, much as Wild West shows in the United States fed a popular nostalgia for idealized images of the frontier past (Becco and Calcena, *El gaucho;* Estrada, *Apuntes sobre el gaucho Argentina; HDA,* 346–48, 348–49; Molas, *Historia social del gaucho;* Nichols, M., *Gaucho;* Paullada, *Rawhide and Song;* Slatta, "Cowboys and Gauchos"; Slatta, *Gauchos on the Vanishing Frontier).*

2. Before unification in 1910, the Atlantic seaport city of Cape Town, in southwestern South Africa, was the capital of the large province of Cape Colony. Cape Town remained the capital of the Cape after the formation of the Union of South Africa in 1910. It is now the legislative capital of the Republic of South Africa. Located on Table Bay on the Cape of Good Hope, it was settled by Dutch immigrants between 1652 and 1795. Captured by the British in 1795, it was returned to Dutch rule in 1803 and retaken by the British in 1806. The oldest European-settled city in South Africa, it remains one of two principal seaports and is the country's second-largest manufacturing center *(ESA,* 89–90; Pakenham, *Boer War,* 6; *WNGD,* 218).

3. Rogers worked for James Piccione aboard the *Kelvinside,* which sailed with a large cargo of livestock from Buenos Aires to Durban, Natal, South Africa, on 5 August 1902. A prosperous cattle and horse breeder with a large farm in Natal, Piccione was well known among British livestock breeders and landowners and the Anglo-Argentine elite who were involved in the livestock industry, horse racing and breeding, and agriculture—the social set that belonged to the Sociedad Rural Argentina and frequented the Jockey Club in Buenos Aires (see "South Africa" section, below, and Biographical Appendix entry, PICCIONE, James).

4. A few weeks after Rogers departed for South Africa, the *Buenos Aires Herald* ran an editorial on South Africa, warning its readers that it was not a promising place for unemployed laborers to go looking for work or for those with little capital to look for business ventures: "According to shipmasters and disappointed exiles who have recently returned from the Cape, the ports there are fairly congested with unemployed who have flocked thither in the expectation of securing work . . . while the conditions of the inland country, only recently escaped from the devastations of war, are such that the authorities restrict emigration from the coast, and even a landing at any port is allowed only under severe restrictions. In a word, it would seem that one might better remain here than fly to perhaps greater ills in South Africa" *(BAH,* 28 August 1902).

5. Rogers saved a satiric newsletter produced by the U.S.S. *Atlanta.* Called *The Sea Lawyer* and printed in Buenos Aires on 26 June 1902, the little pamphlet featured a

photograph of the ship and such items as a recipe for "Stew Canned Willy," which was perhaps named in Will Rogers's honor. Ingredients included cans of corn, peas, beans, and tomatoes, old sourdough bread, and salt and pepper. Cooks were advised "in the absence of pepper use gunpowder." The stew should be stirred with a "boat hook and boil[ed] for eighteen consecutive seconds. Serve with funny stories and stand by with cocked revolver" (Will Rogers Scrapbook, 1902–4, CPpR; see also illustration of *The Sea Lawyer*).

6. So-called coon songs were ragtime compositions with lyrics that dealt, usually in a highly derogatory way, with African American subjects. The words and the sheet-music cover art for these songs (with such titles as "Hush, My Little Coon," "My Pickaninny Babe," "I'll Eat Watermelon Till I Die," "I Loves You Sadie, Deed I Do!," and "Mammy's Little Dinah") presented crude images of African Americans that carried racist stereotypes to an exaggerated extreme. They played on and perpetuated racist ideas of black submissiveness, laziness, dishonesty, and stupidity; presented black people as animals; and associated black sexuality with infidelity and vice. Songs such as "Coon! Coon! Coon!" reinforced assumptions of white superiority by presenting the theme of the black person who longed to be white ("I wish my color would fade . . . / I'd like a different shade . . . / I wish I was a white man / 'Stead of a / Coon! Coon! Coon!") (Dennison, *Scandalize My Name*, 394). Others romanticized the era of slavery.

The songs were extremely popular in the nineteenth century and remained so in theater and vaudeville until 1910. The coon song was of folk origin, but was commercialized by such as vaudevillian Ben Harney, a black performer who passed as white, and then by white promoters and white entertainers who parodied blacks. The songs were highly rhythmic, used broken phrasing and elongated syllables in words, and unlike the "proper" parlor songs popular with young ladies, frequently dealt with bawdy themes and sexual double entendres. They were often intended to be humorous, with black life, black language, black foodways, black physical features, and black intelligence the subject of their lampoons. African American leader, writer, and musician James Weldon Johnson described coon songs as "crude, raucous, bawdy, often obscene" and full of racial stereotypes regarding sexuality and food (Johnson, *Along This Way* [reprint, New York: Viking, 1969], 152–53, quoted in Tawa, *Way to Tin Pan Alley*, 185). From the late 1890s on, "coon songs" and "ragtime" were often used interchangeably to refer to a kind of syncopated music that was not necessarily racially derogatory in character (Dennison, *Scandalize My Name*, 348–424; Ewen, *All the Years of American Popular Music*, 117–19; Tawa, *Way to Tin Pan Alley*, 9, 181–93, 212–15; Wenzel and Binkowski, *I Hear America Singing*, 51, 70; Whitcomb, *After the Ball*, 26–29).

7. Minstrelsy, usually an all-white-male blackface performance, began in the 1830s and remained popular after the Civil War, when it began to be supplanted by variety, which had both male and female performers (variety was in turn the precursor of vaudeville). In the 1890s the average song-and-dance man in minstrelsy made between ten and thirty dollars a week when performing, often with long lapses between bookings. Minstrel troupes often functioned on the verge of bankruptcy. Several minstrel troupes appeared in Claremore in this period, and home minstrel shows were also popular. Rogers later appeared in blackface performances when he entered show business in South Africa (see article from the *Claremore Progress*, 30 March 1901, above; see also *CP,* 25 October and 20 December 1902; Lott, "Love and Theft: The Racial Unconscious of Blackface Minstrelsy"; Suthern, "Minstrelsy and Popular Culture"; Tawa, *Way to Tin Pan Alley*, 61, 74).

8. The Oneidas were an Iroquoian-speaking Native American community that at

the time of European contact occupied some five to six million acres of land in what became central New York state. The fur trade transformed the Oneidas from partici-pants in a self-sufficient regional economy to employees of Europeans within the world economy. Cultural assimilation was furthered through the influence of missionaries, and the introduction of new diseases brought suffering and a loss of Indian population. Many of the Oneidas supported the American cause in the Revolutionary War, which brought them into conflict with pro-British Iroquois. From 1785 to 1842 New York state entered into over thirty land treaties with the Oneidas; the net result was the Oneidas' loss of their tribal homeland. Removal of Oneidas to Wisconsin took place in the 1820s and 1830s, leaving the Oneida people geographically and politically split in modern times between communities in New York, Wisconsin, and Ontario, Canada (Bloom-field, *Oneidas;* Campisi, "Ethnic Identity and Boundary Maintenance in Three Oneida Communities"; Campisi and Hauptman, eds., *Oneida Indian Experience;* Donaldson, *Six Nations in New York;* Geier, "Peculiar Status").

The Sea Lawyer newsletter contained a column about the man Rogers refers to in this letter. Chapman Shenandoah (b. 1873) was described in the column (reprinted from the *Indian Advance* of Carson City, Nev.) as the "only full blooded Indian in the U.S. Navy." He was born on an Oneida reservation in New York. Illiterate, he was a mechanical genius, able to examine engines and construct versions of them from memory in his own workshop. He spent seven years as a student at Hampton Institute, Hampton, Va., where he was an assistant in the campus machine shop. He enlisted in the U.S. Navy during the Spanish-American War and was stationed in San Francisco and New York; reenlisting after the war, he shipped out on the *Atlanta*. Will Rogers and Chapman Shenandoah had more than their Indian heritage in common. Shenandoah was described as "one of the most popular Chief Petty Officers on board the *Atlanta*. He is fairly bubblying over with good nature and his dry wit keeps his shipmates in convulsions of laughter" (Will Rogers Scrapbook, 1902–4, CPpR).

9. Sailors, along with day laborers, soldiers, and servants, occupied the bottom of the occupational ladder in Buenos Aires. Immigrants newly arrived in the city often tried to secure work as stevedores at the ports. Along with sailors, they made the dock areas the center of social as well as work life (Scobie, *Buenos Aires,* 211–12).

10. When he wrote "shift," Rogers perhaps meant "skiff." Catale and White Oak were Indian Territory towns. Catale is located in present-day Rogers County three miles northeast of Chelsea. The name of the town in Cherokee means "in the valley." White Oak is in present-day Craig County seven miles west of Vinita. It was founded about 1895 just north of its present site. The St. Louis and San Francisco Railroad built a spur and stock pens in the town, which subsequently became an active shipping point for cattle being transported to Kansas City and St. Joseph, Mo. The town also became well known for its ceremonial stomp dances performed by local Shawnee, Delaware, and Cherokee people (Shirk, *Oklahoma Place Names,* 222; *Story of Craig County,* 161–66).

To Clement Vann Rogers
21 July 1902
Buenos Aires, Argentina

Buenos Aires, S.A.
July 21. 1902

My Dear Father

I will write you again   I wrote to the paper a few days ago and that is why I did not write to you also as I knew you would know that I was alright.

Well I have been out in the country and am now back in Buenos Aires   there is no show for a person here unless he has a good big capital   but still I have got a lot of learning and experience out of this trip.

I am going from here over to South Africa between the first and 10 of ~~this~~ August and you can address my letters to me in care of the American Consul at Capetown.

I am going with a ship load of stock horses mules and cattle.

There is lots of stock goes from here   it is about 4500 miles and it takes about 18 to 20 days on a cattle boat   they send from 500 to 1000 head on one boat and about 20 to 30 men to care for them.

You have to have a lot of money ~~to~~ before they will let you land   but they man that owns this lot of stock promised me to land me and I will work for him.

It is lots better place than this for they all speak English and there is lots more Americans there.

I may come back to the U.S. from there   I think I will go to work for Halsell[1] and stay there when I get back

I am feeling fine and in the best of health

It is tolerably cold here now and lots of rain

I have not heard a line from any one yet   guess I havent had time quite

I dont hear any news only from New York as they are the only papers we get after they are 5 weeks old. but no news about our country in them.

Well there is nothing of interest to tell you so I will close. have Uncle Jim take good care of my ponies. write me soon and a long letter and tell any one that might feel an interest in me to write me at Capetown South Africa Care of the "American Consul."

lots of love to all from your loving son

Willie.

ALS, rc. OkClaW. Envelope hand-addressed to C. V. Rogers, Claremore, Indian Territory, U.S. of America. Revised version printed in *CP,* 30 August 1902.

1. A reference to W. E. (Bill) Halsell, one of the major cattle ranchers of the Verdigris country and a close acquaintance of Clem V. Rogers. Halsell was one of the main stockholders in the First National Bank of Vinita, which was chartered in 1892. He joined Clem V. Rogers in founding the First National Bank of Claremore in 1894. Both men served as directors. Halsell became president and Rogers vice president of the bank. They built a brick building to house the bank of Main Street in Claremore. Before Will Rogers returned home to Indian Territory, W. E. Halsell and Clem V. Rogers had a major falling-out over the 1903 Cherokee Nation elections (Maud Lane to Will Rogers, 17 August 1903, below; Collings, *Old Home Ranch*, 30n.7, 76–77, 94; *CV*, 13 January 1899; Holden, *Ranching Saga*, 159; see also Biographical Appendix entry, HALSELL, William Electious).

To May Stine
21 July 1902
Buenos Aires, Argentina

Buenos Ayres, S.A., July 21.

Mrs. May Stine, Talala, I.T.

My Dear Sister:

I will write you again as I want to tell you where to write to me. I will shake this land between August 1 and 10 and sail for South Africa on a big cattle boat in care of cattle, and will not come back to this point. It is no good for an American.

There is an old Texas "punch" going with me. Tell all the boys there is nothing doing down here.

I have not heard a word from anyone and you must write me all the news.

I didn't get to rope any on the Fourth of July, as these dagoes don't know what a contest is. They are the greenest and hardest lot I have ever seen. I have been out on lots of the ranches and been with them but did not go to work for them. They only pay seven or eight dollars a month and nothing to eat.

It will take about 18 or 20 days to go to Cape Town from here. If I don't like it there I may come home.

Tell old Cain and Keys[1] my address and tell any of those old boys to write.

There is nothing doing, so I will close with my best wishes.

Yours lovingly, Will Rogers.

PD. Printed in *CP,* 30 August 1902.

1. References to Will Rogers's friends Jim or E. B. Keys and another friend of Rogers who is always referred to as "Cain" — pals of Rogers on the rodeo and roping-contest circuit. James H. (Jim) Keys was born in 1876. Edward (E. B.) Keys was probably Jim Keys's brother (*OCF* 1:132; see also James H. Rider to Will Rogers, 2 September 1902, below).

From Maud Lane
24 July 1902
Chelsea, I.T.

July 24–1902
Chelsea
Cher. Nat.

My Own dear Dear Boy.

How I do want to see you   it seems more than a year since you went away from home. Dick[1] got home all right and sent me the box of things you got for us   my dear brother how can we ever thank you enough for the lovely collars you sent us   I never saw any thing like those collars   the day they came Sallie and I were going to Claremore to tell Aunt Eliza Alberty goodby   she and Fay[2] started to Cal. that day and we just took the box on down to Claremore with us and Telephoned sister May to come down and she did so we had a good time and all of us enjoyed seeing all the things. I let Sallie have first choice of the collars and she took the large squair cream one and I let May take next choise and she chose the black one so I got the very prettiest one of all and you have no Idea how nice it looks on me and I intend that my girls shall each graduate (if they are so fortunate) in it and they shall both marrie in it, as for the cute little goards I want to use mine all the time   I have tryed it and think that the tea tast[e]s so very much better out of the goard but the children are quite distressed to know what they do when it is ice tea   Gunter[3] says there is no room for ice   I told them that over where you are they do not have any ice so Gunter does not want to go there. Papa was so pleased with the knife and nearly every one in Claremore came in to see our things   all the ladies wanted the lace and all the men went wild over the knife, Papa kept the coins and the views we divided among we four. It would have made you quite home sick could you have looked in and seen us sitting flat on the floor pouring over the things you sent. We had heard that you came back with Dick and stop[p]ed in Sanfrisco Cal. and each morn and night when Cap[4] would come home I would ask for a letter from you till Dick sent the box and letter.

Well I guess by this time you have the letter I wrote you some time ago and I did not intend waiting so long before sending you another letter but I have had my hands most full. . . .

I have not seen papa for some time   he has been quite busy seeing after the crops on the home place. I cant think of anything to write and dont know when this will reach you but do hope you are either on your way home or going to start at once for we all want you to come back so badly there's not a day that we

Maud Rogers Lane, Will Rogers's sister *(OkClaW)*.

dont talk of you and wish you was at home   We all send just lots of love and kisses for our dear boy who is so far away in distance but who is ever with us in thought   we never cook white beans that Ethel[5] doesn't want to send you some   she just insisted on sending you a box of eatibles and said she knew you wanted something   Now please answer this letter in person.

Lovingly
Maud

ALS, rc. OkClaW. Envelope hand-addressed to Mr. W. P. Rogers, Buenos "Ayres," South America, care of Edward Myers, 334 Calle Piedras. Forwarded via Consulado Americano,

Capetown, Sud Africa (written in Edward Meyers's hand as the return address), and c/o J. J. Piccione, Mooi River Station, Natal.

1. Dick Parris.
2. Fay Reynolds Bushyhead.
3. Gunter Lane.
4. Cap Lane.
5. Maud Lane's ten-year-old daughter, Ethel (see Biographical Appendix entry, HEDGES, Ethel Lane).

From Sallie McSpadden
27 July 1902
Chelsea, I.T.

July 27. 1902

Dear, Dear Willie:

Your last letter written June 9 was received last evening and how I do wish you could see us read one of your letters. I take a central seat and Tom with the baby[1] sits very near so he can hear every word. Then each child gets just as near as possible and even Helen[2] is as still as a mouse, so as to hear what "Uncle E" has to say. Oh, how very much we love to hear from you and every one loves to read your letters. Mrs. Bone said she had learned more from your letters than from her geography. The lace collars you sent us were the lovliest things I ever seen. We took them to Claremore just to show them and how the ladies did envy us. Our embroidery club met soon after at Mrs. Scotts and we took our lovely collars there and I do wish you could have heard the "ohs, and ahs, and how I wish I had a brother off to send me such nice presents." I really don't know [how] to thank you. I intend for each one of my girls to graduate in this collar. Of course I've never in my life had anything half so fine and lovely and every one who has seen it has complimented your excellent taste as well as bewailed your poor pocket book. The goards were a great curiosity and were highly appreciated. Thank you, you are the very dearest old brother in the world and I want you to hurry and come home, though I am glad you have had such a delightful trip. It has been worth a fortune to you and I only wish I could have been with you. I do enjoy seeing new sights and places. . . .

Tom has been getting up his cattle to ship this last week. He has had so many stolen from him, he will not have more than three loads to market this year but he does not owe a dollar so we will have a little surplus after all. Herbie[3] came in after hunting for three days, with a face as long as a fence nail, to tell me that all three of his steers were gone. You know he has had a little

Members of the Women's Home Missionary Society, Methodist Episcopal Church South, Chelsea, I.T., photographed about 1903 at the home of W. C. Poole. Will Rogers's sisters, Sallie Rogers McSpadden and Maud Rogers Lane, were very much involved in the southern Methodist church. *Front row (left to right):* Mrs. W. C. Poole (with plume in her hat), Mrs. Fisher (who ran the Fisher Hotel in Chelsea), Bertha McSpadden, Mrs. Jim Kell (holding dog), Mrs. W. C. Strange, and Miss Henson. *Top row:* Mrs. Horace Adams (by post), Mrs. John Tibbs (wife of the Frisco railroad agent in Chelsea), Mrs. W. R. Greer, Mrs. Bone (whose husband was a physician in Chelsea), Mrs. Samuel A. McSpadden (sister-in-law of Tom McSpadden), Mrs. John D. Scott (whose husband was a director of the Bank of Chelsea), Maud Rogers Lane (to the right of the post), and Sallie Rogers McSpadden (standing far right) *(OkClaW)*.

brand (HX —) of his own, and did not put his papa's brand on so it offered a good opportunity for idle fellows to drive them off. Herb loves old Yak as well as you do Commanche, and no matter how late in the afternoon they are out he will never eat until his pony has been unsaddled, watered and fed. The other children have to pet Herb a good half a day, to get him to let them ride on Yak. May is always wishing you were home but all the children wish that, as well as we grown folks. Miss Ida Scudder enjoys your letters so much, and really you have developed into quite a letter-writer since you left us. Your descriptions are just fine. . . .

I really can not begin to give you all the messages your friends send to you or I would be writing all the time. Every body is interested in you and in hearing from you, that is why we have your letters printed. The "Chelsea Reporter" has made a reputation for itself since you have been away   Each member of the family join me in sending you lots and lots of love and we all hope soon to have our dear old boy safe at home with us again.

Your loving sister

Sallie

ALS, rc. OkClaW. Envelope hand-addressed to Mr. W. P. Rogers, Buenos "Ayres," Argentina, c/o Edward Myers, 621 Avenida De Mayo. Marked *"Not here."* Readdressed to American Consul, Cape Town, South Africa. Forwarded c/o J. J. Piccione, Mooi River, Natal.

1. Sallie's husband Tom McSpadden and their infant daughter, Pauline, born September 1901 (see Biographical Appendix entry, Love, Pauline Elizabeth McSpadden).
2. Two-and-a-half-year-old Helen McSpadden, born October 1899 (see Biographical Appendix entry, Eaton, Helen McSpadden).
3. Nine-year-old Herb McSpadden, who in adulthood would follow in his father's footsteps as a rancher and become the manager of the old Rogers home ranch (see Biographical Appendix entry, McSpadden, Herbert Thomas).

To Clement Vann Rogers
31 July 1902
Buenos Aires, Argentina

Buenos Aires.

July 31. 1902

My Dear Father.

I will write you again as I guess I will get away from this country about the third of Sept or 4 more days.[1] I have give this place a trial and I know that it is no place or for that matter any other place any better than the U.S. for a man with a small capital or none at all. I only want to see the country now as you say Alf owes me enough to pay my Insurance this fall and what other is owed me will pay for the next year and I do not owe any one a cent I dont think.

I never cared for money only for what pleasure it was to spend it and I am not afraid of work and so as I am now I feel better than I ever did in my life and am in good health   so dont you all worry about me because I am not making money for if I did I would spend it and as long as I dont I cant

I have spent a world of money in my time but I am satisfied as some one else has got the good of some of it   it has not been all on myself and if you will only give me credit for just spending my own as I think I have I will be as happy as if I had a million.

All that worries me is people there all say oh he is no account   he blows in all of his fathers money and all that kind of stuff Which is not so. I am more than willing to admit that you have done everything in the world for me and tried to make something more than I am out of me (which is not your fault) but as to our financial dealings I think I paid you all up. and everyone else

I only write these things so we may better under[stand] each other.

I cannot help it because my nature is not like other people to make money and I dont want you all to think I am no good simply because I dont keep my money   I have less money than lots of you and I dare say I enjoy life better than any of you and that is my policy. I have always delt honestly with every one and think the world and all of you and all the folks and will be among you all soon as happy as any one in the world b̶u̶t̶ ▲ as ▲ then I can work and show the people that I am only spend[ing] what I make.

Send this up to the Girls as I have not time just now to write to them as they are shaping up the stock getting ready to go in a few days   I will write you a long letter as soon as I land which I guess will be about the 25 of Sept.

I got your letter and the papers from you and the girls but no letter from them

I see they are all marrying off pretty fast up there   I will haf to hurry home or I will be left out. Tell me about that ring you said you wrote to Miss Miller for and have you that diamond stud I left in your desk.[2]

I will close hoping to hear from you all soon   dont think about me for I am the happiest one in the lot and will get along all O.K.

Address my mail to Me at Capetown in care of the American Consul. South Africa.

although we go about 600 miles around the other side of it to port natal[3] I guess I will get it all right. you address at Capetown.

With all my love I am your loving son

Willie.

ALS, rc. OkClaW. Lower right portion of pages torn.

1. Rogers wrote "Sept" but meant "August."
2. A circle is drawn around this portion of the letter regarding the ring, and Rogers has added a marginal note: "dont publish this about the Ring." Clem V. Rogers gave his son a diamond stud pin to try to encourage him to continue his education, but as Will Rogers explained to his roping-contest friend Charles Tompkins, while proudly exhibiting the pin, "My father gave it to me to stay in school. But school was too much for me and I lit out" (Croy, interview with Charles H. Tompkins, *Our Will Rogers*, 75).

3. Port Natal (Durban) is an Indian Ocean seaport located on the southeastern coast of South Africa in the province of Natal. It was settled in 1824 as Port Natal and renamed Durban in 1835 after Sir Benjamin D'Urban, who was appointed governor of eastern Cape Colony in 1833. The city was built around the largely landlocked Bay of Natal (Durban Bay) on an area that had originally been swamp. Durban became the site of the first railway in South Africa in 1860. In the same period it became the destination of indentured Indian laborers emigrating to work on sugar plantations in Natal. By the 1870s Durban had become a major rail center and a seaside resort. Its harbor underwent improvement and was opened to large ships in 1904 (*ESA*, 149–50; Pakenham, *Boer War*, 15–16; *WNGD*, 348).

5. SOUTH AFRICA
August 1902–August 1903

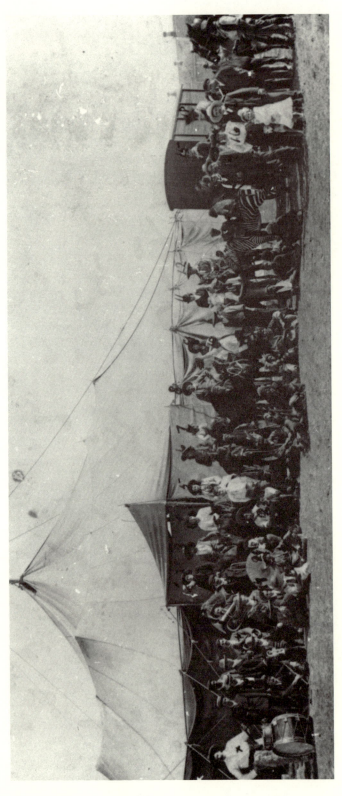

Texas Jack's Wild West Show and Dramatic Company, South Africa, 26 May 1903. Identified as follows: *X*, members of the cowboy band; *1*, Clarence Cook (bareback rider); *2*, George Andres (Australian Bushman); *3*, Ernie Ward (Australian trick rough rider); *4*, Harry Ward (trapeze artist and heavy-weight lifter); *5*, Miss Williams (a.k.a. Mrs. Cox, horse trainer and star performer); *6*, Texas Jack (rider, roper, and owner of the show); *7*, Mrs. Texas Jack (rider); *8*, Will Rogers (The Cherokee Kid, roper); *9*, Miss Alvarez (rider); *10*, Johnnie Cox (assistant manager and trainer); *11*, Mrs. Fitzsimmons (wife of the manager); *12*, W. F. Hampton (a.k.a. Buckskin Bill, star rider from Denver, Colo.); *13*, Mr. Fitzsimmons (manager); *14*, Mr. Alvarez (clown); *15*, Montana Brown (rider); *16*, Mrs. Ajax; *17*, Mr. Ajax (flexible marvel); *18*, Checieto Amego (Argentine gaucho rider); O, Zulus and Indians from India, painted as North American Indians; *19*, Comedian; *20*, Carlo (contortionist); *21*, M. Victor (a.k.a. Ming Hi, Chinese clown); *22*, Tony Rogers (clown); *23*, Scottie; *24*, Harry Fisher (jockey) *Scrapbook A1, OkClaW*).

IN THE SUMMER OF 1902 WILL ROGERS TRAVELED FROM ARGENTINA TO South Africa as a laborer aboard a British Ship. His original hopes of establishing himself as a rancher in Argentina had been dashed; his funds had been depleted by his complicated route of travel, the departure of Dick Parris from Argentina, and his disappointing encounter with underemployment. Feeling that he had learned about Argentina and what the country had to offer, Rogers sought a berth as a keeper of livestock for a huge shipment of animals from South America to Africa. He was hired by an Irish-born South African investor and farmer, James Piccione,[1] a wealthy man who trained top thoroughbred horses for the international racing circuit and who owned one of the largest horse-breeding and livestock estates in Natal. Rogers helped care for Piccione's livestock on the voyage across the Atlantic and had an agreement that Piccione would put forth the funds necessary to support Rogers's application for a work permit upon arrival in Durban, Natal. Piccione secured Rogers's entry when they reached that South African port, and Rogers helped drive the livestock north to Piccione's farm, located near the British garrison at Mooi River Station, south of Ladysmith, Natal. When he stayed on the estate for several weeks to work off his commitment to Piccione, he was amazed by the wealth displayed at the farm with its prize animals and deluxe facilities and outbuildings. He worked at a variety of tasks, including exercising and caring for horses, riding horses for inspection for prospective buyers, and helping the farm's veterinarian and blacksmith. His time in the Mooi River area was his introduction to the severely hierarchical South African society and to the landscape, which was freshly scarred by the recently ended South African War.[2]

Rogers arrived in South Africa less than three months after the close of the South African War (often called the Boer, or Anglo-Boer, War), which had begun in 1899. This turn-of-the-century war was emblematic of the complex revolution taking place in the South African political economy, and of the clash of cultures and ethnicities induced by British colonialism and Afrikaner migration into lands formerly occupied and ruled by African peoples.[3]

As in the United States, the turn of the century signaled what was regarded metaphorically as the close of the frontier in South Africa.[4] There were political parallels between what was occurring in the former frontier of Indian

Territory during Rogers's absence and what he witnessed while a resident in Natal. Rogers had already seen the end of the open-range ranching life in Indian Territory, the shift toward fenced farming and commerce, the introduction of the railroads, the changes in cattle markets, and the building of new small towns. At the turn of the century, as the tenets of the Curtis Act (1898) took effect under the Dawes Commission in Indian Territory, the citizens of the Cherokee Nation were subjected to enrollment and private land allotment in preparation for the dissolution of tribal government and the formation of the state of Oklahoma.[5] In South Africa in the same period black Africans and immigrant Indian laborers found themselves increasingly dispossessed and discriminated against as British and Afrikaner settlement expanded and colonial power became more invasive, overtly restrictive, and entrenched. A white infrastructure of towns, cities, transportation systems, mines, and markets was created—an urban and industrial response largely caused by the discovery and exploitation of great mineral wealth in diamonds and gold. At the close of the war Afrikaner nationalists saw the former Boer republics of the Transvaal and the Orange Free State fall under British jurisdiction, eventually to be realigned into the new political entity of the Union of South Africa (1910).

Rogers encountered in South Africa a population dominated numerically by black Africans and politically by British and Afrikaner minorities. The Dutch had begun colonization of the country at the Cape in the 1600s, and the British had become a presence in the late 1700s and early 1800s. British repression and settlement spurred the Afrikaner exodus, or Great Trek, from the Cape westward across the Orange River into African lands between 1835 and 1837. British and Afrikaner conflicts continued as the Boers concentrated in Natal in the late 1830s, and Natal was annexed as a British colony in 1843. The independence of the Afrikaner republics was shaken by the discovery by whites of mineral wealth, first diamonds in Kimberley, which became annexed to the Cape Colony, and later gold in the Afrikaner territories. The first president of the Transvaal Republic, Paul Kruger, led an Afrikaner rebellion against British rule in 1880–1881, (the First Boer War, or to the Afrikaners, the First War of Independence), and as a result the Transvaal obtained limited independence. Five years later gold was discovered on the Witwatersrand. The gold rush that ensued flooded Afrikaner-controlled regions with *uitlanders*, or foreigners, and with foreign capital.[6]

The political subjection of independent African chiefdoms, long pressured by white expansion, came during the same period (1870–98). By the time of Rogers's arrival in South Africa in 1902 all the African chiefdoms had been subjected to white control. The once-powerful Zulu, with whom Rogers came

Photographs of a Zulu leader and young men from one of Will Rogers's scrapbooks *(Scrapbook 1902–4, CPpR).*

in contact in Natal, had been conquered by the British in the year of Rogers's birth (1879), though their traditional enemies had been the agrarian Transvaal Afrikaners. Zululand was incorporated into the British colony of Natal in 1897, two years before the outbreak of the South African War and five years before Rogers's arrival.[7]

The South African War began in October 1899 as the Afrikaner republics declared war and began invasions of the British colonies. The broad region around Ladysmith, Natal, in which James Piccione's farm was located, was the scene of protracted warfare, the physical effects of which were still evident to Rogers as he traveled in the area at the war's end. The Afrikaner forces lay siege to Ladysmith in 1899–1900, and in the years after the siege was broken, the British mounted a "scorched earth" policy of attrition in which Afrikaner homes and farms were destroyed and livestock slaughtered. Africans were also caught by the violence as the British burned villages that they claimed might harbor Afrikaner fighters. Many African farmers, laborers on Afrikaner farms, and residents of mission stations became refugees. Many blacks were also placed in concentration camps, as were Afrikaner civilians, mainly women and children, the wives and offspring of men fighting the war. Thousands of people died in the camps because of disease — more than were killed in battle on either the British or Afrikaner sides. After the war many found the farms where they had lived or labored destroyed or in disarray, and a severe shortage of seed for new crops caused widespread hunger. The war formally ended with the signing of surrender papers at Pretoria on 31 May 1902. In its aftermath reconstruction efforts were focused on white farms. Black Africans continued to be relegated to the lowest rungs in the labor structure.[8]

Presented with this situation, Rogers, perhaps not surprisingly, identified strongly with the Boers. Like the Cherokees, the Afrikaners had been subjected to a history of relocation and migration. The Cherokee people also valued their cultural heritage and political independence, and were all too familiar with political repression by Anglo-Americans. Like Rogers's family, most Afrikaners were farmer-ranchers who had experienced some form of frontier life. In the 1830s the Boers, or Voortrekkers, had moved under British pressure from lands in the Cape Colony eastward. In the same decade the Cherokees were subjected to forced federal removal from their lands in Georgia, Alabama, Tennessee, and North Carolina westward to areas that once had been part of the Louisiana Purchase. Cherokees who had earlier in the century moved from their homelands in the East to Arkansas (the "Old Settlers") had also been forced by the encroachments of white settlement to move farther west.[9] The Cherokees and the Afrikaners thus had parallel histories of ethnic repression, agrarianism, and migration. The values and the mystique of the Afrikaner soldier—of the independent mounted rifleman in the commando units—also were similar to those of the cowboy hero in the United States. And, the Afrikaners in their relations with native Africans were not unlike Rogers's own Confederate, slaveholding family. As a result, Rogers, although part Native American, did not identify with black native Africans or their disenfranchisement. Nor did he, as an American Indian, feel ties of kinship with the Asian Indian laborers working in Natal who were heirs to a contract-labor system that had begun late in the nineteenth century.[10]

The documents in this section demonstrate not only Rogers's observations of South African society and concurrent political transformations in Indian Territory, but also aspects of the social history and popular culture of the times. Meanwhile, the letters of Rogers's sisters highlight the differences within the family that gender made. They were entrenched in cooking, cleaning, and caretaking roles in their domestic lives, as well as parochial leisure activities and family rituals—local fairs, visits, and trips to nearby cities or states for weddings and graduations or because of illnesses or shopping needs. In a 27 August 1902 letter to Will, his sister Maud wistfully expressed the wish that she too could be a man so that she could travel and see the world. Rogers's unmarried close woman friend, Kate Ellis, became a schoolteacher to make her living, and his men friends like Jim Rider and Dick Parris continued to work as ranch hands and to participate in the rodeo contest circuit. Some of them also joined Wild West shows, converting skills developed in their real work on ranches and in the cattle drives into performance art. Clem V. Rogers, while still reporting news about the ranch and its crops, had made a transition, like other Americans, from an agrarian economy to commerce in the small town. He developed his business enterprises in the town of Claremore, and also continued his important role in local Cherokee politics. Land allotment figures large here as Clem V. Rogers participates in the Cherokee enrollment on both his own and his son's behalf and, after receiving a power of attorney from Will, takes out allotments in their names.

The distribution of tribal lands into individual allotments that began while Rogers was in South Africa was a closing chapter in the politics of land policy in Indian Territory that had begun in his youth. There was intense outside pressure for white occupation of Indian lands in Will Rogers's early years. In the last decades of the nineteenth century the discovery of coal in the region and the building of railroads created a new economic infrastructure with small towns and markets, making the area increasingly attractive to non-Indian farmers, mine operators, railroad companies, people in professional and retail occupations, and investors. Native American leaders split between those (primarily of full Indian heritage) who opposed the white intrusions and the abolition of tribal governments and argued for Indian self-sufficiency, and those (primarily those of mixed heritage) who argued that assimilation of the Five Tribes of Indian Territory into eventual state citizenship was inevitable and economically advantageous. Many white beef contractors and cattle ranchers allied themselves with Cherokee ranchers in opposition to white settlement, recognizing that the conversion of the open range to cultivation and small farms meant the demise of large grazing contracts and the compromise of their own businesses and way of life.[11] As sections of the territory were being opened to outsiders, and other areas were occupied by increasing numbers of intruders, there was also federal pressure to break down tribal holdings into individually owned plots of land.[12] Supported by reformers who advocated the cultural, economic, ideological, and political assimilation of Native Americans to the dominant white ways, allotment was seen as the "most important means of destroying tribalism."[13]

The Tin Pan Alley fad that dominated popular culture in the early 1900s is also much in evidence in the correspondence between Rogers and his sisters and friends. He tells his family of songs being sung at evening gatherings at the Piccione farm, and his sisters tell him the titles of their favorite new songs and send him sheet music. Kate Ellis and Rogers both incorporate the titles of songs jokingly into their letters. Rogers's interest in the songs, particularly in what he and the sheet music industry called "coon" songs, represents his place in the transition from nineteenth-century minstrel and variety shows to burlesque theater, the cakewalk, ragtime, and the vaudeville circuit, which Rogers would join in 1905. The minstrel show was the first stage entertainment for which popular songs were written. Burlesque used heavy-handed parody and caricature in musical productions. Variety shows emerged in the 1870s, when the circus also became increasingly popular. The sentimental ballad reigned, as did work songs of the railroad and the field, and cowboy songs. In the last decade of the century the publishing of popular songs shifted from music shops to small commercial publishing houses, and by the early 1900s popular sheet music had become a big business centered along Twenty-eighth Street in New York, dubbed Tin Pan Alley. The career of Charles K. Harris exemplified the trend; his "After the Ball," a song to which Rogers refers in one of his letters, was the first popular song to sell several million copies of sheet music.

The unfortunately named and conceived coon song became a rage in musical theaters in the 1890s. Its popularity lasted for two decades. The lyrics of most of these songs portrayed satiric images of black people and often perpetuated extremely negative stereotypes that depicted African American men as lazy, unintelligent, dishonest buffoons or sexually predatory, violent bullies. In stage performance the songs were "shouted" rather than sung, usually by white women singers such as May Irwin, who developed the technique in stage musicals. The songs were written by both black and white composers, mostly vaudevillians. The cakewalk entered vaudeville in the same period. Having originated in black slaves' parodies of white plantation owners, it was incorporated into minstrel shows by whites in blackface. In the 1890s the cakewalk became a dance craze in small towns across the country (including, as we have seen in the "Ranching and Roping" section, those in Indian Territory). The 1901–2 songs that Rogers enjoyed, which he apparently performed informally in South Africa, were syncopated songs designed as piano music, written in styles adapted from black classical ragtime. The terms *ragtime* and *cakewalk* were both sometimes used alternatively to refer to an eclectic body of songs produced through Tin Pan Alley.[14]

When Will Rogers sought out the show-business entrepreneur Texas Jack at the end of 1902 and demonstrated his skill with a rope, he began participating in another major phenomenon of American popular culture of the late 1800s and early 1900s—the Wild West show. Part circus, part rodeo, part historical melodrama and parade, the Wild West show was a means by which the American West that Rogers had seen as a small child became converted into legend. Texas Jack's Wild West Show and Dramatic Company was one of many small offshoots of the bonanza created by Buffalo Bill's Wild West, which began in 1883 and played to audiences of thousands in the United States and Europe into the next century.[15] Texas Jack, an orphan, had taken his name from a benefactor, Texas Jack Omohundro, who was a close friend of William F. (Buffalo Bill) Cody. He performed in a traveling circus in the United States, England, and several British colonies before he had started his own traveling company. His show included trick riders, acrobats, a contortionist and strong man, a mock Pony Express ride, and Texas Jack as a sharpshooter. The second part of the show featured melodramas about Texas Jack's life in the West, starring white performers who had acts in the other portions of the show as scouts and pioneers, frontiersmen, and Native Americans. Rogers joined the show as a bronco rider and trick-rope artist. He also played small parts as Native American or African-American characters in the dramatic sketches. Rogers credited Texas Jack with teaching him the ropes of show business, including how to work a crowd and do an act.[16] His experiences in Argentina and Natal had taught him that he had few prospects in making a living as a cowboy, and he had no hope, with his meager or nonexistent capital, of achieving independence on a ranch abroad. He subsequently turned to popular performance as a way of making a living and, in doing so, laid the foundation for his future career.

1. See Biographical Appendix entry, PICCIONE, James. For Rogers's accounts of his life in South Africa, including his time at Piccione's farm and with Texas Jack's Wild West Show and Dramatic Co., see Day, ed., *Autobiography,* 19–23, and typed transcriptions of Rogers's autobiographical notes, OkClaW.

2. On Rogers's trip from Argentina to South Africa and his experience working at the horse-breeding ranch near Mooi River Station, Natal, see Ketchum, *Will Rogers,* 77–79, and Rogers, *Will Rogers,* 67–75.

3. On the South African War and this period in South African History, see Bailes, "Military Aspects of the War"; Cammack, *Rand at War;* Pakenham, *Boer War;* Warwick, ed., *South African War;* Wilson and Thompson, eds., *Oxford History of South Africa.* Back home in Indian Territory, the local Chelsea and Claremore papers carried news of the war with sympathy for the plight of Boer farmers (see, for example, "Capetown Wants More Troops," *ChC,* 18 January 1901; "Transvaal War," *ChC,* 11 January 1901; "Re-Stocking Boer Farms," *CP,* 19 April 1902, and "Australian Pro-Boers," *CP,* 26 April 1902).

4. For comparisons of the South African and North American frontiers, see Lamar and Thompson, eds., *Frontier in History.*

5. On the individual allotment of the tribal lands, the land rushes opening the Twin Territories (Indian Territory on the east and Oklahoma Territory on the west) to outside settlers, and the transition to the statehood of Oklahoma in 1907, see Gibson, "Centennial Legacy of the General Allotment Act"; Gibson, *History of Oklahoma,* 114–25; McReynolds, *Oklahoma,* 278–317; Odell, "Divide and Conquer"; Otis, *Dawes Act and*

the Allotment of Cherokee Land; Wardell, *Political History of the Cherokee Nation,* 312–34; and Williams, "Pictorial Essay on the Dawes Commission."

6. On the impact of the discovery of mineral wealth by whites and the career of Paul Kruger, see Fisher, *Afrikaners* and *Paul Kruger;* D. Hobart Houghton, "Mining Revolution," in Wilson and Thompson, eds., *Oxford History of South Africa 2:10–21* and also *2:307–14;* Johnstone, *Class, Race, and Gold;* and Richardson and Van-Helten, "Gold Mining Industry in the Transvaal."

7. On Zulu history and culture, see Cope, *Izibongo: Zulu Praise-Poems;* Guy, *Destruction of the Zulu Kingdom;* Kennedy, *Art and Material Culture of the Zulu-speaking Peoples;* and Vilakazi, *Zulu Transformations.*

8. On the effect of the war on civilians and on British and Afrikaner policy toward African peoples, see Guy, *Destruction of the Zulu Kingdom;* Spies, "Women and the War"; Warwick, "Black People and the War."

9. On nineteenth-century Cherokee history and the period of Cherokee removal, see Anderson, ed., *Cherokee Removal Before and After;* Davis, K., "Chaos in the Indian Country: The Cherokee Nation, 1828–35;" Ehle, *Trail of Tears;* Evants, *Cherokee Removal;* Thornton, *Cherokees,* 47–115; Wardell, *Political History of the Cherokee Nation;* and Woodward, *Cherokees,* 192–304. As in the Afrikaner experience with the discovery of gold on the Witwatersrand and the resulting land rush of outsiders, the loss of Cherokee sovereignty and collective land rights in the Cherokee Nation East was influenced in part by the discovery of gold in areas within the Nation.

10. On the experiences of Indian immigrants and residents of South Africa, see Bhana, *Settling Down Roots: Indian Migrants in South Africa, 1860–1911;* Bhana, ed., *Essays on Indentured Servants in Natal;* and Bhana and Pachai, eds., *Documentary History of Indian South Africans.*

11. Indian lands had been lost in war-compensation settlements following the Civil War. Many outsiders also came to work in mines and other fields. In 1885 the Chester Arthur administration successfully lobbied Congress to pass an act authorizing the cession of Cherokee, Creek, and Seminole lands in the western part of Indian Territory. Negotiations continued in the late 1880s, and in 1889 the Springer Amendment was approved opening the Unassigned Lands, or Oklahoma District (well over a million and a half acres), to claims by white settlers, and instigating a land rush in April 1889 — the first of a series of rushes as additional lands were opened in the following years. Will Rogers was ten years old when the 1889 land rush occurred. In May 1890 the Oklahoma Organic Act created self-government for Oklahoma Territory, the western twin to Indian Territory. By the time Rogers was twenty-one, the Five Tribes were a distinct minority in their own republics: noncitizens outnumbered Indians seven to one. On these issues see Baird and Goble, *Story of Oklahoma,* 284; Collings, *Old Home Ranch,* 104; McReynolds, *Oklahoma,* 278–307; Odell, "Divide and Conquer: Allotment among the Cherokees"; Sober, *Intruders,* 120–26. In 1890 noncitizens outnumbered citizens in the Cooweescoowee District over two to one (12,322 noncitizens, 5,621 citizens). White intruders and mixed-blood Cherokee families (Cherokees who had intermarried with whites) had dominated the population of the district since the Civil War (Hewes, *Occupying the Cherokee Country of Oklahoma,* 38, 48).

12. The effects of the passage of the Dawes Act of 1887, combined with the Curtis Act of 1898, institutionalized federal policy breaking tribal holdings into individual parcels allotted to persons of Indian heritage. Allotment represented the end of Indian sovereignty. In the 1890s the Dawes Commission was authorized by Congress to determine tribal citizenship, enroll citizens, and survey and allot Indian lands. The Dawes Commission (also known as the Commission to the Five Civilized Tribes) was

created in 1893 to apply the 1887 Dawes (or General) Allotment Act to the Five Civilized Tribes by negotiation with Indian leaders regarding allotment. In 1895 a survey plot of Indian Territory was prepared by the U.S. Geological Survey in preparation for allotment. By that year the Dawes Commission had accrued power to prepare tribal rolls and make land assignments to Native American residents without tribal permission. Cherokee full-bloods opposed the breakup of commonly held tribal lands into private allotments and resisted the dictates of the commission. They were eventually assigned lands by the commission with the aid of federal marshals. Clem V. Rogers served as a member of the Cherokee Nation delegation that dealt with the Dawes Commission. The commission functioned until July 1905, when its responsibilities were taken over by the Interior Department. The commission found some 90,000 individuals eligible for enrollment out of some 300,000 applicants, and distributed some twenty million acres of land (Brown, L., "Dawes Commission"; Gibson, "Centennial Legacy of the General Allotment Act"; Gibson, *History of Oklahoma*, 118–19; Littlefield, *Cherokee Freedmen*, 214–48; Mankiller and Wallis, *Mankiller*, 168–69; White *It's Your Misfortune and None of My Own*, 85–118; Williams; "Pictorial Essay on the Dawes Commission"; see also "Ranching and Roping" section introduction).

13. Francis Paul Prucha, "Introduction," to Otis, *Dawes Act and the Allotment of Indian Lands*, x. See also Carlson, *Indians, Bureaucrats, and Land*. See also Application for Enrollment in the Cherokee Nation by Clement Vann Rogers, 22–23 October 1900, above.

The views expressed by one member of the Board of Indian Commissioners in 1890 summed up the prevailing Anglo-American prejudices about land, Native American polities, and Native Americans themselves: "This might seem like a somewhat rapid reduction of the landed estate of the Indians, but when it is considered that for the most part the land relinquished was not being used . . . the sooner the tribal relations are broken up and the reservation system done away with the better. . . . The fact that individual ownership of property is the universal custom among the civilized people of this country would be a sufficient reason for urging the handful of Indians to adopt it" (Commissioner Morgan, writing in 1890, quoted in Otis, *Dawes Act and the Allotment of Indian Lands*, 85).

14. On American popular music crazes, racial representation in American popular music at the turn of the century, and the impact of Tin Pan Alley music promotion, see Dennison, *Scandalize My Name*, 345–424; Ewen, *All the Years of American Popular Music;* Tawa, *Way to Tin Pan Alley;* and Wenzel and Binkowski, *I Hear America Singing*.

15. On the Wild West show and Cody's career, see Biographical Appendix entry, CODY, William F. (Buffalo Bill).

16. On Texas Jack and Rogers's experience with Texas Jack's Wild West Show and Dramatic Co., see primary materials, box 25, OkClaW, and Will Rogers Scrapbook, 1902–4, CPpR; *PN*, 20 July, 22 July, 23 July, 24 July, 25 July, 27 July, 29 July, 30 July, 31 July, 1 August, 4 August, and 5 August 1903; Mayor's Office, Pretoria, to Homer Croy, 19 August 1952, and enclosures: clipping from *PN*, 18 August 1952, and *Pretoria News* Office to Homer Croy, 14 August 1952, HCP-MoU; Croy, *Our Will Rogers*, 81–86; Ketchum, *Will Rogers*, 81–84; Logan, *Buckskin and Satin: The Life of Texas Jack;* Rogers, *Will Rogers*, 76–81. See also Biographical Appendix entry, TEXAS JACK.

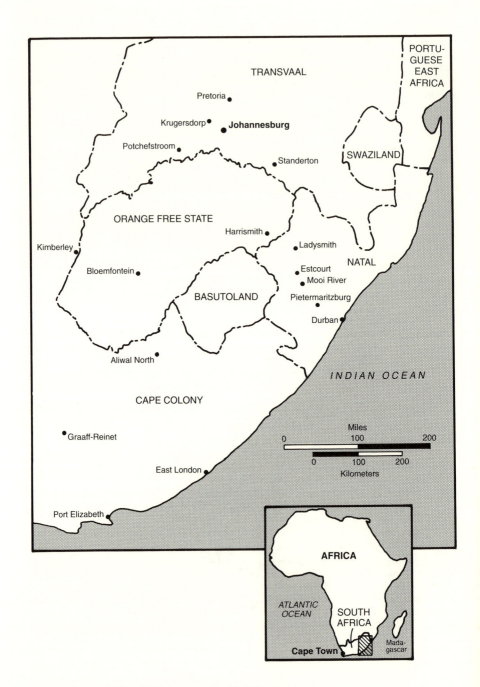

Eastern South Africa, 1902 *(map art by Gigi Bayliss).*

From E. B. Camp
19 August 1902
Buenos Aires

Having exhausted the considerable funds he had earned from the sale of the cattle from the home ranch in Indian Territory, and having grown weary of his prospects in Argentina, Rogers secured work with the wealthy farmer and horse breeder James Piccione,[1] who had purchased a large amount of livestock in Argentina and needed workers to care for the animals during transport to his estate in South Africa.[2] The Kelvinside, to which Rogers's friend E. B. Camp[3] refers, was the ship Rogers sailed on to accompany the livestock to South Africa. Rogers called it a "menagerie ship not only a cattle boat but every kind of animal."[4] The shipment included hundreds of cattle, mules, horses, and sheep. The trip took a month, and the ship hit heavy weather off the coast of South Africa, but arrived safely in Durban, Natal. Rogers was hired to help drive the stock to Piccione's horse farm near Mooi River Station, some fifty miles from Ladysmith, Natal.[5]

Buenos Aires
19 August 1902

Dear Rogers: —

Several steamers are leaving for South Africa during this week and it seems to me quite the proper thing that one of them should carry a letter from Camp to Rogers — so here goes.

The first thing I want to do is to express my appreciation of the Winchester and the trunk. I had intended thanking you before you left, but as you know, the boat got away earlier than I expected and so there was no opportunity. The Indian decided not to take the trunk, although I offered it to him for $1.50 (rag money) and the second-hand "dago" wouldn't have it, so it is still "for sale"; the Winchester will travel with me when I leave this dog-goned hole and very likely go back with me to the good old States.

Was very sorry not [to] get down to the docks for a few words before you started, but was delayed by a man that I was after for a job and then, too, I didn't think she would go until next day. I told "Tex" about sending the money to your address, but he will probably bring it himself as he expects to be away very soon for the Cape. He has "seen Scott" and that gentleman has got him a job as second man in charge of the sheep on board the "Haversham Grange" which leaves this week for Capetown. Tex had a row with the Dutchman and quit the hotel; he took a room in Calle Corrientes and is eating with me here at Harry's. . . .

Haven't seen anything of Meyers[6] since you took to the Kelvinside mules. By the way, the Kelvingrove has not got away yet, but will probably do so tomorrow — "mañana."[7]

Am going to enclose with this letter, an article about Piccione's shipment on the Kelvinside.[8] Perhaps you will be interested and if you show it old Picc., perhaps he will give you a better job. . . .

The group of acrobats that were with Frank Brown[9] (the four with a girl) are now playing at the Cosmopolitan, but I have not seen them, as I do not associate with the Music Hall crowd these days. . . .

And now my dear boy, how about this memorable trip across the South Atlantic on the good ship "Kelvinside"? Did she roll? Was Willie sick? Did the mules Kick? Was there plenty for Willie to eat? Could he eat what he got? Do you think that a well-preserved mixture of pony-piss and sheep-shit will ever become fashionable as perfume? Were your slumbers peaceful and your dreams always pleasant?

I shall expect very soon to receive a poem by William P. Rogers, entitled —————— Twenty one days on a floating dung-hill, or the experiences of Don Guillermo as chambermaid to a flea-bitten mule.

You may not believe me, but I really am getting tired of life in dear old Buenos Aires, this charming city of "vino y putas," and am seriously thinking of taking my departure. Am making arrangements for a slight augmentation of my now meagre exchequer. If I am so fortunate as to secure a position here before long, it may keep me until some time in January. If I do not find something to do, shall probably leave for Capetown in October or November.

Don't fail to write and let me know just how things are in South Africa. If you have not already started me a letter, do so when this is received, addressing to

Yours

E. B. Camp

in care of the

American consul

Consulado Notre Americano

Buenos Aires

Republica Argentina

ALS, rc. OkClaW. Envelope addressed to Mr. W. P. Rogers, c/o American Consul, Capetown, Sud Africa. Forwarded c/o J. J. Piccione, Mooi River Station, Natal.

1. See Biographical Appendix entry, PICCIONE, James.
2. Rogers later told fellow vaudevillian W. C. Fields that in taking the job aboard the *Kelvinside* he had "accepted a position as chambermaid for a parcel of mules" (news release, "Will Rogers Cried and Cut Up his Rope," Will Rogers Memorial Fund, 10 December 1935, OkClaW). W. C. Fields wrote that he first met Rogers, who became a good friend in their *Ziegfeld Follies* years, in 1903 when both were working in show business in South Africa and Australia. Fields was on the vaudeville circuit, and Rogers was traveling as a Wild West or circus performer. If this story is true, it is most likely that

Fields encountered Rogers in South Africa (Fields, *W. C. Fields by Himself,* 19–20, 153; see also Wertheim, ed., *Will Rogers at the Ziegfeld Follies,* 192–95).

3. No biographical information has been located regarding Rogers's friend E. B. Camp or the mutual acquaintances he mentions in this letter. Like Edward Meyers, Camp appears to have been a fellow American.

4. Type transcription of Rogers's autobiographical notes, OkClaW.

5. The Mooi River was a major stockbreeding region. The British garrison of Mooi River Station was situated south of Ladysmith on a railway that ran from Durban to Ladysmith and on to Johannesburg. The station was located between Estcourt and Willow Grange. The town of Mooi River developed in the same area on the farm called Mooirivier, owned by Jacobus N. Boshoff (1808–81), who was the president of the Orange Free State from 1855 to 1859. Mooi River (which means "beautiful river" in Afrikaans) became a municipality in 1959 (Bulpin, *Discovering Southern Africa,* 486–87).

Natal, a province in eastern South Africa, is bounded on the north by the Transvaal, Swaziland, and Mozambique, on the east by the Indian Ocean, and on the west by Lesotho and the Orange Free State. It comprises a long coastal plain and central midlands two to four thousand feet above sea level. Its primary towns and cities include Dundee, Durban, Ladysmith, Newcastle, and Pietermaritzburg. The area was occupied by the Nguni people, ancestors of Zulu- and Xhosa-speaking peoples. The coast of Natal was sighted by Europeans (aboard the ships of Vasco da Gama) in 1497, and European settlement began at Port Natal in 1824. The area was reached by Voortrekkers (Boers [Afrikaans for "farmers"], or Afrikaners [white South Africans who spoke the Afrikaans language], who made the Great Trek) between 1835 and 1838. It became a British colony in 1843 and a separate colony in 1856. Zululand (which occupied the coast northeast of Natal, below Portuguese East Africa, and had been ruled earlier in the nineteenth century by a strong Zulu monarchy) was annexed by the British in 1897, and other districts in the north were incorporated in 1903. Immigration of indentured Indian laborers began in 1860 (Brookes and Webb, *History of Natal; ESA,* 357; Pakenham, *Boer War; WNGD,* 814).

6. A reference to Edward Meyers, an American acquaintance of Will Rogers who lived in Buenos Aires and handled Rogers's mail for him after he left Argentina.

7. The *Kelvingrove* was a sister ship to the *Kelvinside.* It was in port at Buenos Aires preparing to depart for South Africa. The *Buenos Aires Herald* of 19 August 1902 announced that the "S.S. Kelvingrove will receive mails for South Africa all day to day" at dock 1. Camp evidently sent this letter to Rogers via the *Kelvingrove.*

8. See enclosure, following. The daily *Buenos Aires Herald* listed the S.S. *Kelvinside,* a British vessel, among the ships at dock 1 on 31 July 1902. It remained listed for the first few days of August, was docketed to sail on Tuesday, 5 August, and the following day the *Buenos Aires Herald* "Shipping News" column noted that the *Kelvinside* had been cleared and had left port for South Africa with a cargo of livestock ("Br. S.S. Kelvinside, dock 1, to Port Natal, live-stock").

9. Frank Brown (1858–1943) was an English-born clown of international prominence who became one of early twentieth-century Argentina's most popular entertainers. He was born into a family of acrobats, tightrope walkers, and tumblers in Brighton, England. His brother Henry, an acrobat and clown, was called the "Shakespeare jester" in his appearances in London, and Frank began following in his footsteps at an early age. He apprenticed with the Henry Manley Circus and appeared as an acrobat in Moscow in 1877 and in circuses in Mexico and New York in the following year. He came to Buenos Aires with the Carlo Brothers as part of an international tour in 1879

that included performances in Jamaica, England, France, Russia, and many parts of Latin America. The Carlo Brothers Circus with Frank Brown featured an eighteen-act program with music, a trampoline act, a miniature circus, pantomime, tumbling, hurdling, equestrienne, and trapeze acts, and Brown doing comedy. Other performers that appeared with Brown were the Nelson Family, Frederick Carlo, Señorita Amelia, Addie Austin, Harry Carlo, Alfredo Leopold, and J. C. Lamont.

Brown took up residence in Buenos Aires in 1888, and became a widely known and popular attraction for children's entertainment on Sunday afternoons, providing amusement for three generations of Argentineans. He suffered a muscular injury in 1893 and as a result changed his act, eliminating the gymnastic and tumbling aspects and focusing on being exclusively a clown. Frank Brown's own circus, based in Buenos Aires, did numerous benefits to raise money for the care of poor children. Brown was praised as a great all-around comic artist, who used political elements in his humor and appealed to sophisticated adults of both genders and all races as well as to the young. His publicity materials announced him as the King of the Clowns, who sustained constant hilarity for the intelligent public. Brown retired in 1924 and lived in Colegiales with his companion, Rosita de la Plata (Castagnino, *Centurias del circo criollo*, 49–66).

Enclosure:
News Item
ca. 5 August 1902
Buenos Aires

The departure and cargo of the Kelvinside *are described in this unidentified newsclipping[1] preserved in Will Rogers's scrapbook.*

MR. PICCIONE
HIS SHIPMENT TO S. AFRICA.

This popular and well-known gentleman made a happy exit from our midst on Tuesday evening[2] on board the Kelvinside bound for Durban, South Africa.

Mr. Piccione takes with him by far the most valuable consignment of livestock that has ever left the country, consisting as follows: 50 thoroughbred stallions, brood mares, colts and fillies, purchased principally from the well known studs of Messrs Saturnino Unzue, Villanueva, Samson, Duggan, Luro, etc. Amongst these are the race horse Bonnie Dundee, one of the fastest sprinters in the country, Atahnalpa, Charabon, etc., as well as a lot of very promising youngsters. Delfin, another plucky purchase of Mr. Piccione,

James J. Piccione, wealthy land owner and noted horse breeder, was Rogers's employer in South Africa *(Twentieth Century Impressions of Natal)*.

unfortunately died from pneumonia before being shipped. The remainder of the horses consist of a really well bred lot of Clydesdale colts and mares from the estancia of Mr. John Shaw, and also a number of high-class harness horses.

The horned cattle, some 300 in number, comprise 160 beautifully bred young heifers specially selected and tamed on the Entre Rios estancia of Mr. Unzue, and a lot of heifers from the Saralegue camp in Santa Fe. These are all "tick" cattle, which Mr. Piccione says is absolutely necessary for the South African camps which are infested with "tristeza," and, consequently, will be rendered immune to this dread disease. There are about 2,000 breeding sheep on board—Rambouillet, Hampshire Downs and cross-bred Romney Marsh; the two former from the best flocks of Mr. Unzue's estancia, "San Jacinto" Mercedes, and the Romneys from Mr. Harrison of Halsey. The lower holds of the "Kelvinside" are filled up with mules between 600 and 700 in number. Altogether, the consignment is very valuable and well chosen, Mr. Piccione being a well-known expert in everything appertaining to horse-flesh. His return may be expected before the end of the year, having to take over Peppermint at the end of the racing season, and also to attend to shipment of 2,000 heifers purchased from Mr. Unzue.[3]

A large number of Mr. Piccione's personal friends witnessed his departure from the docks and one and all heartily cheered this Nature's nobleman to the echo and wished him a safe passage and speedy return. Amongst others we noticed Messrs Samson, Kincaid, Getting, Hamilton, Capt. O'Neill, Lumb, Drury, Shaw, Miller, Cunningham, Whiting, etc.

PD, unidentified newsclipping. Will Rogers Scrapbook, 1902–4, CPpR.

1. The source of this article that Camp sent to Rogers has not been identified; it was possibly from the *Buenos Aires Weekly Herald,* an English-language Buenos Aires newspaper that included news about social affairs involving the British community and the arrivals and departures of vessels in port. It did not appear in the daily *Buenos Aires Herald.*
2. 5 August 1902.
3. James Piccione was renowned for his knowledge of horses. He owned a large string of successful racehorses including Peppermint and Bonnie Dundee, both mentioned in this article. Crediting Piccione with the establishment of the livestock trade between Argentina and South Africa, the *Buenos Aires Herald* (24 July 1902) reported that Piccione purchased Peppermint from Mr. Samson for fifty thousand dollars. Piccione also supplied British colonial officials and farmers with mules and was a cattle and sheep breeder, developing strains of animals resistant to regional South African illnesses by interbreeding with stock from South America.

Piccione exported large shipments of stock from Argentina to South Africa from the 1890s well through at least the second decade of the 1900s. He lobbied regularly for colonial officials to improve harbor and dockside conditions in Durban that hampered his operations. In October 1910 the Society for the Prevention of Cruelty to Animals brought proceedings against him "in respect of the cargo of mules brought over from the

Argentine for the Government last year." Piccione countered the charges with renewed demands for better facilities for the transport of livestock in Durban, including the construction of proper gangways to discharge cargoes of livestock and the acquisition of a new site for a veterinary compound (the current one necessitated herding untrained animals through traffic). These requests had been made before he left on another trip to Argentina in May 1910. His suggestions were backed by the chief veterinary surgeon, who wrote of animals being held at the wharf without food or water because of difficulties unloading them, but harbor officials deemed the establishment of a new compound impossible (Jas. Piccione to the Under Secretary of Agriculture, 14 October 1910, and minute paper re J. Piccione, Mooi River, 14 October 1910, NAD, PV5, vol. 152, ref. 4400/1910; "J. Piccione," in *Twentieth Century Impressions of Natal*, 540, 541, photograph of Peppermint, p. 540).

From Maud Lane
27 August 1902
Chelsea, I. T.

Although Will Rogers and his family members wrote frequently while he was absent from the United States, there were long periods during his many moves and travels in which he received little mail. In this August 1902 letter his sister Maud expresses some frustration with her domestic lot and wishes she could have some of the opportunities for independence and movement available to Will as "a man." Her musings point out the difference gender made in Rogers family members' lives. Will was the boy and baby brother. His father looked to his only surviving son as the heir to his ranching business and had provided the financial means and livestock for Will to make a living in charge of the family ranch—an investment that Will converted into funds that paid for the first months of his world travels.[1] Will was also a single person with responsibilities only to himself, and thus was able to widen his horizons beyond Indian Territory in a way that social conventions denied to his sisters and, indeed, to many of the young men he knew.

Aug 27—1902
Chelsea
Cher. Nat.

Our Own dear, dear Brother

I cant understand why you have never heard from any of us   we have all written and addressed the letters just as you directed but for some cause they have failed to reach you   how I do wish I could see you this eave for I am quite tired and there has not been three days at one time I have not had company in the house and now to cap it all Cap and each of the children are sick   nothing serious   just enough to be very cross and want to see someone doing something all the time   you cant know how very tired I am of company and it is so hot   I am so behind with my sewing and all my summers work. . . .

How I do wish I was with you and seeing all the wonderful things you are seeing   that is the only thing makes me wish I was a man so I could travel and see something. So you do not know that we received the things you sent us by Dick and how are we ever to thank you enough. . . .

Please write often as we are always so anxious to get your letters   All join me in just lots of love to our dear boy. Come home just as soon as you can get here.

Lovingly,
Maud.

ALS, rc. OkClaW.

1. These funds, used to book transportation and hotel lodgings for himself and his friend Dick Parris, were soon depleted. Rogers learned to make his own way in very meager circumstances, moving through a series of temporary manual-labor jobs in Argentina and South Africa before turning to show business.

From May McSpadden
31 August 1902
Chelsea, I. T.

Chelsea, I. T.
Sunday.
Aug, 31, 1902.

Dear Uncle Willie.

Uncle Willie when you go to South Africa please do not let the natives grab you.

Chelsea is going to have a fair 3rd- 4th- & 5th of September.[1]

They are going to have races, a bull fight, roping contest and autimobile race and just every thing, & I wish you could be here.

Papa has a 1st cousin visiting us, she is from Tennessee & her name is Alberta Green.[2]

Uncle Willie if you can you must be back home by Christmas because we will miss your presents.

Clem is going to Vanderbilt Unniversity this term.[3]

Herb and I started to Chelsea Academy August, 18, 1902.[4]

I am in the sixth grade this term, and Herb is in the fourth.

Dunker Dee we do want to see you of so bad, and if you knew how bad we wanted you I know you would come home in a jiffy.

There was a show passed through Chelsea and had a elephant, camel, lion, & lioness, two baby lions, wild-hog, 2 white parrots, trimmed with green, 2 hieaners, 2 monkeys, 1 green parrots, and that was all.[5]

I hope you are getting along nicely. Lisse and Maude McS start to the Seminary after the fair.[6]

Have the Boa Constrictors got after you yet?

We like so much to hear your good sweet letters.

I have learned lots about ~~History since~~ Geography since you left, for we have tracked up you[r] travels two or three times.

I must close,

Your loving little tinsy niece.

May McSpadden

ALS, rc. OkClaW.

1. May's father, John Thomas (Tom) McSpadden, was director of the Chelsea Fair from 1901 to 1915. The fair, held in early September, was a popular regional event that drew "a good per cent of the Claremore population" in addition to the residents of Chelsea (*CR*, 11 September 1903). Clem V. Rogers often entered horses into its races. The *Claremore Progress* reported that he was attending the Chelsea Fair in September 1902. In the following year one of his driving horses took second money in a competition at the fair. It later broke away from its handler and ran through the crowd, wagon in tow, but no one was harmed. Horse-show events and rodeo and roping contests were featured at the fair, as were livestock judgings and agricultural displays. Sallie McSpadden often won prizes for her sewing and floral designs. Beginning in 1901, Claremore also hosted a small September street fair made up mainly of fund-raising craft booths and games hosted by local churches and organizations. The last Chelsea Fair was held in 1915 (*CP*, 21 September 1901, 6 September 1902, and 5 September 1903; *CR*, 11 September 1903 and 30 September 1904; *HRC*, 310).

2. A Bertha McSpadden Green (b. 1894) is listed in *OCF* 2:129.

3. Clem McSpadden entered Vanderbilt University in Nashville, Tenn., after he graduated from Kemper Military School in Boonville, Mo. He went away to college with high expectations placed upon him by the Chelsea townspeople. In September the local paper reported that Tom McSpadden had accompanied Clem to Vanderbilt so that he could start the school year and that Clem had "carried off the highest honors at Boonville, Mo., and will no doubt do the same at Nashville" (*CR*, 12 September 1902). Clem visited home for the Christmas and New Year's holidays and returned to Chelsea after completing the school year in June 1903. Clem apparently had some difficulties at Vanderbilt. He did not return to school there after the first year. His aunt Maud Lane confided to Will Rogers that she "never did expect a great deal of him [Clem]" but that "I must say he is even worse than I thought. I dont think he learned one thing at Vanderbilt but I tell you it took the money for him [to go there], something like $130.00 a month that came near breaking his fathers heart and when he did not stand head of his class Sallie nearly died, so they will not send him back this year[. H]e will have to farm awhile but I fear he will not make a very good one [farmer]" (Maud Lane to Will Rogers, 12 July 1903, OkClaW). Maud continued to share her doubts about their nephew with her brother in a subsequent letter, commenting that "I think the young man led a very swift life last winter" and that "Sallie has begun to see that Clem is not perfect—and it is just about killing her" (Maud Lane to Will Rogers, 17 August 1903, OkClaW). In September 1903, Clem McSpadden enrolled at the State School of Mines in Rolla, Mo. In the following year he went to work for the Oklahoma and Cherokee Central railroad,

working the line from Nowata to Bartlesville (*ChC*, 30 September and 14 October 1904; *CR*, 7 September 1901, 26 December 1902, 2 January, 19 June, 18 September, and 25 December 1903, 8 January 1904; *IC*, 1 January and 8 January 1903; see Biographical Appendix entry, MCSPADDEN, Clement Mayes).

4. May McSpadden (sometimes called Mazie) was nine years old when she wrote this letter. She and her younger brother Herbert Thomas (Herb) McSpadden attended the Chelsea Academy in their home town. Cousin Ella McSpadden was the McSpadden children's governess before she left for school in Jackson, Tenn. Tom and Sallie McSpadden were strong supporters of education in Chelsea and had contributed to the building fund for the academy. It was a nonsectarian private school begun under the auspices of the Cumberland Presbyterian Church. The school building was a modern "two-story stone structure, quarried out of rock found near the town of Chelsea" (*ChC*, 30 January 1903). It first opened in September 1894, when May was a toddler and Herb still a baby. G. A. Beardon was the principal of the school in 1903. The school had some 120 students and four regular teachers (*CR*, 30 May and 7 September 1901; Gideon, *Indian Territory*, 169; see also Biographical Appendix entries for MCSPADDEN, Herbert Thomas, and POOLE, May McSpadden).

5. Chelsea, Claremore, Vinita, and other towns in the Cherokee Nation were frequent hosts to traveling shows and fairs. The *Claremore Progress* for 13 September 1902 advertised a large tent show of *Uncle Tom's Cabin*. The *Claremore Courier* for 24 August 1900 advertised "John Robinson's 10 Big Shows Combined with Spectacular Solomon & Queen of Sheba," a show that reportedly featured "44 camels harnessed to a $20,000 golden chariot!" John Robinson's shows were well known to Claremore residents. The acts he brought to Claremore in 1898 included a full three-ring circus, wild-animals displays, a strong man, aerialists, acrobats, and fancy bicyclists and horseback riders (*CV*, 28 October 1898). He was still bringing his acts to Claremore in 1905, when the "Four-Ringed Circus, Big Double Menagerie, Hippodrome and Wild West" show boasted a "double herd of elephants," "Captain Winston and his Talented Aquatic Thespians, the Educated Seals," clowns, one hundred shetland ponies, and a "Stupendous Realistic Production [of the] Battle of Wounded Knee" (*CP*, 21 October 1905). Pawnee Bill brought his Wild West and Far East show (featuring "Many Strange and Peculiar People") to Claremore a week before Robinson arrived with his extravaganza (ibid.). Adam Forepaugh and the Sells Brothers also brought shows to the region, including acts done at Madison Square Garden and the kinds of menageries May McSpadden mentions in this letter (*IC*, 17 August 1899). Will Rogers would have been familiar with these shows and fairs as well as with the rodeo contests in which he participated before going abroad. They foreshadow his own involvement in Texas Jack's Wild West Show, the Wirth Brothers' Circus, the 1904 St. Louis World's Fair, and the vaudeville circuit.

6. Elizabeth (Lizzie or Peach) McSpadden (b. 1883) and Maude Hoyt (Maudie) McSpadden (b. 1885) were May McSpadden's cousins. They were part of the social circle of young people who were frequent guests at Chelsea-area parties and dinners in the summers of 1901 and 1902. They were the daughters of Florence Hoyt McSpadden (b. 1858) and Joel Cowan (Joe) McSpadden (1850–98) (one of Tom McSpadden's six brothers), who had married in 1879 and lived on a farm on the western outskirts of Chelsea. Lizzie and Maude McSpadden had attended Willie Halsell College from 1894 to 1901 and then had started as students at the Cherokee Female Seminary in Tahlequah. They were students at the seminary in the 1901–2 and 1902–3 school years. They boarded at the school and returned home to visit for Christmas and summer vacations. (*CR*, 13 July, 17 August, 31 August, 7 September, and 24 December 1901, 26 December

1902; *HRC*, 299, 300; Mishesuah, *Cultivating the Rosebuds*, 129; *OCF* 1:184–85; Starr, *History of the Cherokee Indians*, 237; see also Sallie McSpadden to Will Rogers, 25 April 1903, n. 2, below).

From Clement Mayes McSpadden
31 August 1902
Chelsea, I.T.

Here Will Rogers's nephew Clem McSpadden writes about the coming of the railroad to Tahlequah. Tahlequah and Fort Gibson were the only major Cherokee towns until the railroads came to the western prairies of the Cherokee Nation, causing dozens of new towns to spring up around railroad stations and post offices.[1] Tahlequah, the capital of the Cherokee Nation, was its largest town in 1902, with a population of about 1,800. Before August 1902, when the railroad connection was made, it had been the only major town in the Nation not situated on a railroad. Many travelers had approached it overland from Fort Gibson, which had been made part of the rail system much earlier.[2] Like many of the older centers in Indian Territory, Tahlequah underwent a boom in development around the turn of the century. Old wooden buildings were torn down and replaced with new two-story brick-and-stone establishments.

Chelsea, I.T.
Aug. 31, 1902.

Dear Uncle Willie:

I will now proceed to jot you a small article as it may give you some notion of how things are going on here. I am well and hope that you also are progressing favorably with Mother Nature.

Tahlequah has a railroad now. It was completed to Tahlequah on the third of August and the big celebration day was the fifth. I was down there and took in every thing there was to take in. The railroad comes in on the left of that Maravian Church, leaves the Male Seminary to the right and goes up by the Presbyterian Mission.[3] The depot is on the hill about a hundred yards from Jim Thompson's house. It is said by every one to be the most crooked railroad in the U.S.[4]

We had a big time down there on Celebration Day. There were about 5000 people there. The trains began to run on that day, and about 900 or 1,000 people came in from Fayetteville[5] on an excursion. Every body was at the train. Whenever a train comes in every body sets out for the depot, foot and horse. They had speaking and other sports and in the evening they gave a big ball. I sure went to that. Rosanna Harnage[6] and I. Do you know the young lady? There was a stomp dance led by old Gee Dick[7] just before the ball, and we went to the opera house about 9 o'clock. Sure had a fine time there, and there were a lot of girls and boys said they wished you were there, as it did not seem right unless you were there with all of your fun

Every body down there was wanting to know about you. I tell you that you sure have got a good "stand in" there.

Clem.

ALS, rc. OkClaW.

1. Tahlequah, established where the Barren Fork and the Illinois Rivers forked, had been the largest of the three main towns (along with nearby Park Hill and Fort Gibson) in the Nation since the 1850s, when it boasted the "legislative buildings, the Supreme Court building, the office of the *Cherokee Advocate,* a post office, eight stores, five hotels, three blacksmith shops, a tailor shop, a saddlery, a tannery, a shoemaker shop, a dentist, and several law offices, as well as residences of those who worked in the town. In 1849 a brick Masonic Temple had been built, and the leading members of the nation belonged to it. The town's population was about 1,600" (McLoughlin, *After the Trail of Tears,* 81, citing information from Carolyn Foreman, "History of Tahlequah," typescript, Foreman Papers, Thomas Gilcrease Institute of American History and Art, Tulsa, Okla.).

In the census of 1880, Tahlequah, Fort Gibson, and Vinita (in Cooweescoowee District) were the only three incorporated towns. The next two decades saw great transformation. The Lanes and McSpaddens's hometown of Chelsea, for example, was surveyed in 1884 and officially incorporated in 1891. Characteristic of other prairie towns that sprang up because of the railroads, it described itself by its proximity to major railways: as promotional literature for the town put it, "Chelsea is situated in the north central part of the Cherokee Nation, on the St. Louis and San Francisco Railway, and is midway between the M. K. and T., and the Missouri Pacific Railways" (*ChC,* 30 January 1903). Vinita and Claremore were on the same St. Louis and San Francisco line as Chelsea, with Claremore on a railway crossroads. By 1899 there were eighty-nine towns in the Cherokee Nation (most of them with just a few hundred residents), a remarkable result of the railroads and increasing settlement. By 1903 all of the largest towns in the Nation, including Tahlequah, were located on railways (Hewes, *Occupying the Cherokee Country of Oklahoma,* 52, 53; Wardell, "Map of the Cherokee Nation, 1895," in *Political History of the Cherokee Nation,* 274f.).

2. Fort Gibson, west of Tahlequah, was located on the Kansas and Arkansas Valley Railway, the same railroad that ran northwest by southeast through Claremore (Wardell, "Map of Cherokee Nation, 1895," *Political History of the Cherokee Nation,* 274f.; see also Hewes, *Occupying the Cherokee Country of Oklahoma,* 55. Figure 5 in *Occupying the Cherokee Country of Oklahoma* (p. 14) is a map of the Cherokee Nation; it shows the location of major towns and railroads in 1902, but before the railroad through Tahlequah was completed).

3. The Moravian mission was the first house of worship built in Tahlequah and was initially known as the Union Church. It was later joined by Baptist and Presbyterian missions. The Presbyterian "Mission site was authorized by the National Council of the Cherokee Nation at their sessions of 1884 to be located at Park Hill in Tahlequah District," including the "Park Hill Chapel and school House, situated near the former residence of the late Stephen Foreman at Park Hill in said district" (representatives of the Cherokee Nation and the Presbyterian Board of Home Missions to Dennis Wolf Bushyhead, 17 November 1885, Cherokee National Records, microfilm CHN 100, OkHi). A school had been maintained by the Cherokee Nation in the capital since 1844;

in 1887 the Woman's Board of Home Missions of the Presbyterian Church opened the Tahlequah Girls' School and Brooks Cottage for boys on a beautiful site overlooking the town. In the 1890s two different fires destroyed school or dormitory buildings, which were replaced, and in the transitions the school merged with the former mission department at Dwight School and became both a day and boarding school for young people. The Woman's Board later withdrew as public schools were established circa 1907 (McAfee, *Missions among the North American Indians*, 52–53; timeline notes, boarding and day school operation in Tahlequah, Okla., Presbyterian Historical Society, Philadelphia).

4. J. F. Thompson was the head of Cherokee Lodge 10 of the A. F. and A. M. secret society in Tahlequah. The Muskogee, Oklahoma, and Western Railroad ran from Muskogee to Fayetteville, Ark. (west of the Arkansas border via a successor company, the Ozark and Cherokee Central Railway). The line went from Muskogee northeast to Fort Gibson (which is twenty-two miles southwest of Tahlequah) through Tahlequah and on to Westville near the western boundary of Arkansas. It had been approved by Congress in January 1897 and was completed in March 1903. The section through the Cherokee Nation was seventy-four miles long (Gideon, *Indian Territory*, 171–74; Self, "Building of the Railroads," 200).

5. Fayetteville, Ark., is located in the northwestern part of the state, fifty miles north of Fort Smith. A summer mountain resort, it is home to the University of Arkansas (founded in 1871). The Battle of Pea Ridge took place near Fayetteville on 7–8 March 1862 (Cherokee Confederate forces participated, including Watie's Cherokee Mounted Regiment, in which Will Rogers's father, Clem V. Rogers, and his uncle John Gunter Schrimsher were enlisted). Fayetteville was incorporated as a city in 1906 (*WNGD*, 392–93).

6. Rosanna Harnage, a young and well-respected local teacher, was the fifth assistant principal of the Cherokee Female Seminary in Tahlequah in 1902–3. A 1901 graduate of the seminary, she married Frederick McDaniel (*CP,* 12 July 1902; Mihesuah, *Cultivating the Rosebuds*, 122, 128).

7. Gee Dick was listed as a full-blood Cherokee, age sixty-five, in the *Final Rolls of Citizens and Freedmen of the Five Civilized Tribes in Indian Territory*, 351 (enrollment no. 18551).

From Sallie McSpadden
1 September 1902
Chelsea, I.T.

Chelsea, I.T.
Sept. 1—1902.

My Darling Brother:—

May and Clem are both writing to you, but I want to write also and tell you how sorry I am that you have never received any of our letters. . . . I think we must have received every single letter and postal that you have written. And as every body is always asking about you we have every one published.   How they are enjoyed! Not only by us but by all the host of friends you have all over the country. We are so glad you are well and to know that you are in splendid spirits. . . .

We are all very well and are preparing for the great Chelsea Fair which will come off Wednesday, Thursday, and Friday of this week. How I wish you were here. We are expecting papa, Uncle John & Bess beside the Lipe girls.[1] . . . Beside our little local attractions of needlework, fruit, etc., races, roping contests etc. we are to have an automobile race and a Mexican bull fight which two things are very drawing cards. . . .

I got four new songs. they are "I've grown so used to you" "You're only a Volunteer" "Down Where the Cotton Blossoms grow" "Any old Place I hang my hat is home sweet home to me."[2] They are all real pretty. The last one is an especially popular song and I am sure you would like it. The sentiment would suit you exactly. but I hope and trust you may decide to soon and forever more hang your hat in the Beautiful Indian Territory. But I'd a thousand times rather have you traveling all over the world than married to some of these "rattie" old girls. We will anxiously await your next letter. Wish lots and lots of love and the prayer that the best of every thing may attend you and bring you safely home. I am

Lovingly

Your sister

Sallie

ALS, rc. OkClaW. Envelope hand-addressed to Mr. W. P. Rogers, Cape Town, South Africa, c/o American Consul. Readdressed and forwarded c/o Mr. Piccione, Mooi River, Natal.

1. References to Clem V. Rogers, John and Bess Schrimsher, and Nannie, Victoria and Lola Lipe.

2. "I've Grown So Used to You" was composed by Thurland Chattaway (1872–1947) and published in 1901. Chattaway wrote for *Ev'ry Month,* a magazine edited by Theodore Dreiser in New York in 1896.

"You're Only a Volunteer" may be a reference to the Paul Dresser song "Mr. Volunteer," also published in 1901. Dresser (1857–1906), whose real name was Dreiser, was the brother of Theodore Dreiser. He was a financial backer of *Ev'ry Month.* He began his musical experience working in minstrel shows. A film was made of his life in 1942, named after one of his songs, "My Gal Sal."

"Down Where the Cotton Blossoms Grow," another 1901 song, was written by the team of Harry Von Tilzer (1872–1946) and Andrew Sterling (1874–1955). Von Tilzer was one of the most important popular composers from the late 1890s through the mid-1920s. His songs included "A Bird in a Gilded Cage," "Wait Till the Sun Shines, Nellie," and "I Want a Girl (Just Like the Girl that Married Dear Old Dad)." Sterling, whose Tin Pan Alley career spanned roughly the same time period as Von Tilzer's, wrote the lyrics for "Meet Me in St. Louis." He began his career writing parodies of popular songs for vaudeville performers.

"Any Old Place I Can Hang My Hat Is Home Sweet Home to Me" was composed by Jean Schwartz (1878–1956) with lyrics by William Jerome (1865–1932). Schwartz's first publication was a cakewalk called "Dusky Dudes," written for piano and published in 1899. Schwartz performed with Jerome in vaudeville before the two collaborated in writing music for Broadway shows (1901–13). Jerome had begun his career performing in minstrel shows, and in 1908 he worked for the *Ziegfeld Follies.* Will Rogers responded to Sallie's praise of Schwartz and Jerome's song by sending her his own revised lyrics, which parodied his own travels away from home (see Will Rogers to Folks, 17 November 1902, printed in *CR,* 2 January 1903, and *CP,* 3 January 1903, and reprinted below; see also Bloom, *American Song,* 545; *EA* 9:376; Ewen, *All the Years of American Popular Music,* 111–12, 155–58, 175–76; Kinkle, *Complete Encyclopedia of Popular Music and Jazz* 2:703, 837, 931, 3:1358, 1718, 1807, 1893–94).

From James H. Rider
2 September 1902
Talala, I.T.

Jim Rider was one of Will Rogers's close friends on the rodeo-contest circuit. He had been one of Rogers's classmates at Willie Halsell College in Vinita. This letter, which reports on the activities of several of Rider and Rogers's mutual friends, chronicles the kinds of options Rogers might have chosen had he stayed at home. Several of the young men Rogers knew on the roping-contest circuit in Indian Territory ended up making a living in Wild West shows in the United States in the same period that Rogers made a similar career choice in South Africa.

In 1902 Rider owned a fine Spanish-tooled western saddle that had been crafted in San Francisco and was widely admired among cowboys in Indian Territory. When Rogers decided he wanted to try his luck in Argentina, he bargained with Rider for the saddle. He traded his own saddle, a new saddle blanket, and fifty dollars for Rider's coveted saddle, and the prized item went with him to Argentina and South Africa.[1]

Talala, IT
USA
9-2-02

Mr. W. P. Rogers
c/o American Consul
Cape Town
South Africa

My Dear old pal:—

I dident even dream of lining one out to you away off down in South Africa. You will have to excuse me Will for not answering your letter as I kept waiting to hear from you after you got there. I would give most anything to see you. I am at Vinita[2] now and have been here for three weeks. We had a roping here the 24th and 25th of last month. Sam Cobb[3] got first in 35. . . . They roped cows and yearlings. Cain's rope bounced off both days just a little hard luck was all but I am getting used to a little things like that.

They had a contest at Talala the 4th of July. John Cochran got first in 37½ and Booth[4] got second in 40 and the next morning we all went to that hell of a

James (Jim) Rider standing at a chuck wagon at the Mashed-O outfit, 1937. A classmate of Rogers at Willie Halsell College and an expert roper, Rider taught Rogers the Johnny Blocker rope throw. Rider named his son after Rogers *(Keith Collection, OkU).*

place you call Collinsville.[5] We roped mules there and the rules was that you either had to get the neck or neck and one front foot. . . .

I missed my steer the first throw and up set my loop around his big piss quasa neck the second throw and went all the way and never looked back   I was mounted on Robbin[6] and we parted that little Sea grass just like it was a twine string. I went back and picked up my rope and went on and tied him. I think it was the best work I ever done considering every thing and I was the only man out of about 18 that caught around the neck with out any feet in my loop. I have quite kicking about missing and having hard luck but I would like to have what I won fair and square. They are going to have a roping at Chelsea the 4 and 5th next Thursday and Friday   I would give any thing if you was here to take it in with us. It dont seem like there is any thing doing if you aint along. These boys get to braggin on some button prick being an awful fast tie   I tell all of them there aint no body can catch any quicker, quit his horse or

tie half as quick as Rogers   they belly ache a little while and then own up to it.
They cant do any thing else. Skinner married. he married Mattie Riley, Jack
Rileys daughter[7] I guess you know her dont you? he lives out about Caney
Kans.[8] Sam Cobb is working for his Uncle S. S. Cobb.[9] They have got a big
string of cows at Summit[10] in the Creek Nation and Sam stays down there.
Trainor is with Pawnee Bills Show.[11] Hop is with Buck Skin Bob's wild west and
Tom Isibell[12] is with Buffalo Bill's.[13] Ned Mc is some where in Colorado   Keys[14] stays over near Rudy. he bought 200 head of steers last winter but
[I] think he has sold them and his father is talking of getting a small ranch in
the Eastern part of Colorado. I sold my steers   got 25.00 and $30.00   I havent
got a thing left but Montie and Bomp a little bay bronc I got from Jeff Tyner.[15] I
guess I will turn them over to[o]   and JO sold all of his cattle but about 400
head of 2's and they are for sale   he aint going to far any more in this country. I
am thinking of going down where Ollie is in South Western Texas. I dont know
just where I will windle up at but it is a cinch I wont stop until I strike a place
that suits me and where they get up and work them cow boy style   I want to go
where they go up and line them every day   I dont care if I dont see a man but
once a year. May and Frank[16] were well and in good spirits when I left over
there. I saw CV[17] as I came through Claremore   he was showing me that large
knife you sent him. Every one that ever saw it says it is the finest thing they ever
saw of the kind. . . .

Well old boy as this is the last sheet of paper I will have to quit unless I go
down in town and get more   it dont seem like I have written any thing that you
would like to hear. I saw Comanche and your bay colt along early in the summer
and they were looking fine. Well old pal I will have to quit but I sure hate to.
hoping this will get to you and find you well and having a good time I will close.
Always remember me as your best friend.

Jas H Rider

ALS, rc. OkClaW.

1. Croy, *Our Will Rogers*, 77; see also Biographical Appendix entry, RIDER, James
Hall.

2. Vinita had a regular fair with roping contests. Jim Rider and Will Rogers had
often competed there together in the past (Collings, *Old Home Ranch*, 91).

3. Rider refers to three different persons named Sam Cobb in this letter. This is a
reference to Will Rogers's schoolmate and fellow roper Sam Y. Cobb (1878–1949) of
Vinita (see article from the *Indian Chieftain*, 2 August 1900, n. 9, above; see also (*Story of
Craig County*, 296–97, and n. 9 below).

4. Booth McSpadden.

5. Collinsville, I.T., was a town in the southwestern portion of Cooweescoowee
District, west of Claremore on the railroad line that ran north through Bartlesville. It

was established in 1897 and named after Dr. H. H. Collins, an early resident. After statehood it was part of Tulsa County. It is seventeen miles north-northeast of Tulsa and is located among oil and gas fields (Hewes, *Occupying the Cherokee Country of Oklahoma*, 14; Shirk, *Oklahoma Place Names*, 51; *WNGD*, 277).

6. Robin (sometimes spelled Robbin) was one of Will Rogers's favorite roping ponies. He was a large sorrel that Rogers purchased at a roping contest for $125 after seeing a competing roper ride the horse and tie a steer in record time. Will's friend Jim Hopkins often rode Robin in roping contests (Jim Rider to Will Rogers, 26 February 1903, below; see also Collings, *Old Home Ranch;* Marquis, "Will Rogers and His Horses").

7. Born in 1874 in Denton County, Tex., Heber Skinner was a prominent Vinita cattle rancher. He married Martha (Mattie) Riley (b. 1880) on 11 March 1902. She had attended the Cherokee Female Seminary and graduated from Payne College in Fayette, Mo. (*OCF* 1:253; Starr, *History of the Cherokee Indians*, 653).

8. Caney, Kans., is in Montgomery County in the southeastern part of the state, twenty miles southwest of Independence. Like the Cooweescoowee District, the Caney area had corn and wheat farms and later was part of the regional development of oil fields (*WNGD*, 215).

9. Rider is referring to Samuel Sylvester (S. S.) Cobb (1840–1923) and his nephew Samuel S. Cobb (b. 1865). The elder Cobb was born in Morganstown, Tenn., and became a Vinita entrepreneur and civic leader. He served in the Union Army during the Civil War and became an officer. He and his brother John B. Cobb came West after the war's end and established a trading post in Indian Territory. S. S. Cobb came to Vinita in 1888 and went into the mercantile business with Will Rogers's friend Heber Skinner's brother-in-law, G. B. McGlasson. Cobb was also a cattleman, and he brought cattle from the Cherokee Strip to his ranch in the Vinita area. He continued to diversify his business investments in Vinita, adding a dry goods store, a barber shop, and the Cobb Hotel (a forty-room establishment designed for men coming in from out of town to do business, and built in 1890) to his shares in the mercantile and grocery business. Cobb was also active in the First National Bank. He was one of the founders of the Vinita branch and served as its first president when it was organized in 1892. He also owned significant real estate in the Vinita vicinity. S. S. Cobb married Mary Ellen Vore (1855–1941) of Webbers Falls, I.T., in 1883. The couple had five children: Mary, Sam (known as "Att"), Hutton, Artie, and Clarice.

S. S. Cobb's nephew, Samuel S. Cobb (also known as S. S. Cobb), was the son of John B. Cobb and Eva Clingan Cobb. Like his uncle, he was born in Tennessee. His family migrated to Tahlequah by train and wagon in 1870. John B. Cobb had become a Cherokee citizen by marriage, and he established a farm near Wagoner, I.T. Samuel S. Cobb studied at the Cherokee Male Seminary and at the State Agricultural College in Manhattan, Kans. He graduated from the latter in 1889 and took an office position with the Muskogee newspaper *Our Brother in Red*. His uncle put forward capital for the younger Cobb to manage a drug store in Wagoner, I.T. (the two were coowners of the building and the store's stock). Merchants in those days acted as bankers for local farmers, in effect loaning money by accepting mortgages on farms or livestock and extending credit for merchandise. Samuel S. Cobb became the Wagoner postmaster in August 1890. He was described as "six feet one inch in height . . . a young man of prepossessing appearance, affable and courteous in manner and well educated" *Story of Craig County*, 296–97; McFadden, "Intruders or Injustice?," 447; O'Beirne, *Indian Territory*, 270; Wilson interview with S. S. Cobb, WPA Writers Project, 1938, IPH-OkHi).

10. A post office was established at Summit in the Creek Nation in 1896 and was maintained there until 1915. Summit, located six miles southwest of Muskogee, was at the highest point on the Katy Railroad between the Arkansas and the North Canadian River (Shirk, *Oklahoma Place Names*, 200).

11. Leonard Edward Trainor (b. 1879) married Laura May Ruler (b. 1881) in 1898 (*OCF* 1:39; see Biographical Appendix entry, TRAINOR, Leonard Edward). For information on Pawnee Bill's Wild West and Far East show, see Biographical Appendix entry, LILLIE, Gordon William (Pawnee Bill).

12. Thomas J. Isbell went on Buffalo Bill's Wild West show tour of England in 1903. Like Leonard Trainor and Heber Skinner, Isbell had participated in steer- and calf-roping contests with Will Rogers between 1899 and 1901. Isbell and Skinner entered into a small business raising hares in 1901 (*DC*, 1 June, 17 July, 22 July, 29 July, 5 September, 7 September, 15 October 1901; *Story of Craig County*, 77; *IC*, 15 October 1903; see also article in the *Daily Chieftain*, 27 September 1901, n. 2, above).

13. Buffalo Bill's Wild West was the prototype for other such shows that toured the United States and abroad in the late 1800s and early 1900s. The shows combined the performance art of the circus, stage melodrama, and rodeo and used the skills of real cowboys, bronco riders, trick ropers, and sharpshooters. They enjoyed a heyday of popular support from their inception in the 1880s through the first decade of the 1900s. Pawnee Bill (Gordon William Lillie), a resident of Indian Territory, was one of Buffalo Bill's (William F. Cody's) chief competitors until the two men merged their well-known shows in 1910. The partnership was a financial failure and ended in 1913. Buckskin Bob, like Buckskin Bill, was a cowboy name used by a variety of Wild West show promoters and performers (see Biographical Appendix entry for CODY, William F., and LILLIE, Gordon William).

14. Jim or E. B. Keys.

15. Possibly Jefferson Carter Tyner (b. January 1872) (*OCF* 1:163).

16. Will Rogers's sister May Rogers Yocum Stine and her husband, Frank Stine.

17. Will Rogers's father, Clem V. Rogers.

To Clement Vann Rogers
11 September 1902
Mooi River, Natal, South Africa

In working in Natal, Rogers went to a region that had been critical in the recently ended South African War.[1] The war, which began in October 1899 and officially ended on 31 May 1902, just several weeks before Rogers's arrival in South Africa, had pitted the British in the self-governing Cape Colony and Natal colonies against the two Boer (or Afrikaner) republics, the Transvaal and the Orange Free State. The effects of the war were still very apparent, and British and allied troops remained stationed in the area although hostilities had formerly ceased.

Here Rogers writes a quick note to let his father know he has arrived safely and is working with stock at James Piccione's large horse farm. When he wrote out notes for his autobiography, Rogers described his work upon arrival in South Africa as "a job in the country breaking horses for the British Gov[ernment]."[2]

Mooi River Station
Natal. South Africa
Sept 11, 190[2]

My Dear Father

I have not had any time to write as I have been as busy as I could since I came   we made it over alright and I am out in the country 150 miles from where we landed   I am with the man that owned the stock on the boat working for him   it is cold here   we are up in the mountains   so far I am working with all kinds of stock   I will write you a long letter soon   tell Kates[3] I will write him a letter from here about this country soon.

I have only got a minute so I will close   love to all   write to the Girls and tell them I am here and doing fine. write to me in care of the American Consul at Capetown.

Lots of Love to all.

from your loving Son
Willie

ALS, rc. OkClaW.

1. The war was known to the Afrikaners (Boers) as the Second War of Independence. The Afrikaners invaded Natal in three columns at the beginning of the war and besieged the British at Ladysmith. The beginning of the war is usually dated from the seizure of a Natal railroad line at Harrismith on 11 October 1899 (Brookes and Webb, *History of Natal*, 202–9; Fisher, *Afrikaners*, 149–96; Pakenham, *Boer War*).

2. Rogers, "Boer War in South Africa," transcriptions of autobiographical notes, OkClaW. See also Day, ed., *Autobiography*, 20–21.

3. A reference to A. L. Kates, publisher of the *Claremore Progress*. Rogers wrote the letter for Kates on 22 September 1902, and Kates published it in the *Claremore Progress* on 1 November 1902 (it is reprinted below; see also Biographical Appendix entry, KATES, Albert L.).

From Spi Trent
11 September 1902
Okmulgee, I.T.

OKMULGEE,[1] IND. TER.

Mr. W.P. Rogers
Africa I don't know

Dear old Coz Bill.

Well you have never written me a word since you left. I never could hear from you only the little news I could get from Uncle Clem, why dont you write to me   you know Will that I would apreshate a letter from you more than any one.

I dont know how much you wil apreshate this   I am wrteing to you just as soon as I heard where to address my letters to   so Will I think you ought to answer this just as soon as you can.

Uncle Clem wrote to me yesterday a told me where to address my letter.

Will if there is any thing that I can do you dont hesirtate to write me because I will never forget what you have did for me   when do you think you will come home. every one would like to see you. there will be a big Ropeing contest I think in Springfield Mo next month so be sure and come home for that. I think you have seen enough country to do you. why did Richard[2] come back. I havent heard a word from him.

I have a good position keeping Books here. that is all I have to do. there ▲ are ▲ two of us and we sure have to work. but it is a nice place to word [work], when you write you must tell me all about yourself and that country. I would sure lite to be with you old boy. we would never seperrate would we. you must tell me just when you think you will be home.

I would write you a longer letter but I dont ▲ know ▲ wheather you will get this or not. I will sure write you a good one next time if you get this.

so good by answer Soon, at once from your Loveing Coz

S E Trent

ALS, rc. OkClaW. On Parkinson, Trent Mercantile Co. letterhead, James Parkinson, president, W. C. Trent, vice president, C. J. Shields, secretary, and J. C. Trent, treasurer and manager.[3] Envelope hand-addressed to W. P. Rogers, c/o American Consul, Cape Town, South Africa, and forwarded care of J. J. Piccione, Mooi River Station, Natal.

1. Okmulgee, I.T. (also known for part of the nineteenth century as Okmulkee), was the capital of the Creek Nation. A council house (capitol) and post office were established there ca. 1868–69. The name is from the Creek words *oki mulgi,* meaning "boiling waters." The town was named after the Creek town of Okmulgee in Russell County, Ala. For many years the closest railroad was at Muskogee, some forty miles northeast, and major mercantile stores were based a few miles northwest of the town in Shieldsville. The coming of an extension of the Frisco railway line in 1900 spurred a fantastic growth in the local population; the town had some two hundred people in the spring of 1900, and by 1901 this number had increased to nearly one thousand. Okmulgee became the county seat of Okmulgee County, Okla., after statehood (Gideon, *Indian Territory,* 149–51; Shirk, *Oklahoma Place Names,* 155).

2. Dick Parris.

3. The Trent family mercantile business was started by James Parkinson, president of the company, a Mason and a pioneer in the Okmulgee area, and W. C. Trent, a merchant who came to Indian Territory from Arkansas in the early 1870s. The two partners founded Parkinson and Co. in 1900. They reorganized the firm as the Parkinson, Trent Mercantile Co. in 1902, with Trent as vice president and his son, Josiah Charles Trent, as treasurer and manager. The 1902 letterhead advertised a capital stock of $100,000 and dealership in "dry goods, clothing, shoes, groceries, hardware, implements, furniture, lumber and building material of all kinds." The Trents later bought

out Parkinson's share of the business and conducted the mercantile establishment (the largest in Okmulgee) until 1920 (the year of Josiah Charles Trent's death). The Trents also owned a lumberyard, a threshing-machine distributorship, an automobile agency, and much Okmulgee real estate. They invested with James Parkinson in the Parkinson Hotel and were active in Okmulgee civic affairs, fraternal orders, and the Methodist Episcopal Church South. The Trent-Parkinson Building was a large two-story brick Romanesque building with the mercantile store on the first floor and offices on the second. It is now on the National Register of Historic Places as part of the historic downtown district of Okmulgee, Okla. Will Rogers's cousin Spi Trent was the son of Dr. Richard Owen Trent and Mollie Brown Trent (Dewitz, *Notable Men of Indian Territory,* 133; Bill Hoge, "Oologah Oozings" [on death of Spi Trent], *CP,* ca. 6 March 1960, OkClaW; Thoburn and Wright, "Josiah Charles Trent," *Oklahoma* 3:630; Trent, *My Cousin, Will Rogers,* 149; Weisiger, "National Register Lists Oklahoma Properties"; *WRFT,* 121; see also Biographical Appendix entry, Trent, Spi).

To the *Claremore Progress*
22 September 1902
Mooi River, Natal, South Africa

In this rare letter written directly for the Claremore Progress, *Rogers gives a more comprehensive description of his travel from Argentina and his reactions to South Africa. He identifies strongly with the Boers, who, like the Cherokees in the United States, had a strong sense of separate cultural identity and were primarily small farmers and ranchers. Just as the Cherokees had been relocated from the East to Indian Territory in the West because of federal repression, the Boers migrated eastward to the land they occupied in the Orange Free State and Transvaal in the 1830s to escape British policy in the Cape. Afrikaner culture and economy was disrupted by the arrival of* uitlanders *much as Indian life in the Cherokee Nation West was subject to the arrival and growing political influence of intruders. Just as there was little identification with African Americans among Rogers's social set in Indian Territory, so Rogers did not identify with the native Africans who made up the majority of the South African population (though he does record the racial division of labor and the discrimination they faced). With the European incursion into their lands and the growing strength of colonial powers and capital investment, native Africans were subjected to confinement on native reserves and the denigrations of separate black and white settlement and labor patterns. Rogers expressed a similar disassociation in his judgment of laborers from India, denying any parallels between their situation and abilities and those of American Indians.*

IN SOUTH AFRICA.

Mooi River, South Africa,
September 22, 1902.

To the Progress, Claremore, I.T., U.S.A.

I shoved off from Buenos Ayres on the 5th of August for South Africa on board one of the large cattle steamers bound for Port Natal, 1,000 miles above

Capetown, on the eastern coast of Africa. We were in a specially fitted steamer that had on board 750 head of mules, 300 cows, 700 sheep, 300 work horses, 50 thoroughbred race horses, 40 little Shetland ponies, besides feed and water for all the stock. The trip is very hard on horses, as they are not allowed to lie down during the entire voyage of eighteen days. Only fifty horses died from sickness during our trip. We had some rough weather off the south end of Africa. Five ships which were a day or so ahead of us, went down with all on board. We struck the latter end of the storm and barely escaped another. While we were in port unloading, one of the worst storms known for years wrecked sixteen sail ships at anchor in the bay, and filled the mouth of the harbor so full of sand and wreckage that ships cannot pass.

Importing stock has been a great business here since the beginning of the war and will be until all the farms are restocked, for there is practically nothing in the country now and all the farms are bare and property destroyed.[1]

The man I am with[2] shipped this load of animals to this point to restock his farm, that is said to be the finest in Africa. He is worth $35,000,000 lives on his farm and maintains the finest racing stables in the country. He has a private race course and his stables are veritable palaces, being heated by steam and lighted by electricity. He also has a system of waterworks. His 6,000 animals are fed on alfalfa at $50 per ton. So you see that stock is very valuable in this land.[3]

It is just beginning of spring here and we have numerous cold rains.[4] The grass is just coming up. This compares with March or April at home. This is a hilly, mountainous country with no timber.

There was a lot of fighting all around here[5] and the largest English remount camps are alongside of us, where they kept fresh horses for the Tommys at the front. They still have about 12,000 horses here.[6] Most all of the English here were in favor of the Boers, for they knew the actual conditions of affairs, and knew that the English were robbing the people of their country. It will only be a short time until this country will be no good, for all of the English colonies have been done for, the same as this will be. Times are not near so good now as before the war and wages are on the decline.

The Boers must have been great fighters and very shrewd,[7] for you will find where they planted cannon in seemingly inaccessible places, by which they trapped the English at all points. But they could not hold out against overwhelming numbers and all of the money used to wipe them out.

I advise all to fight shy of this country, especially if they are not carpenters, bricklayers or shrewd tradesmen. All common labor is done by kaffirs or negroes. You have to see them to realize what wild looking people they are. All

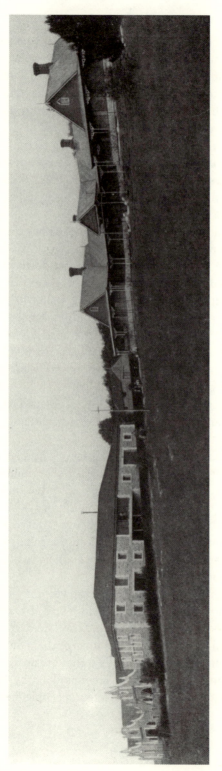

James J. Piccione's stables and residence, Mooi River, Natal (*Twentieth Century Impressions of Natal*).

have rings, chains and all kinds of old scrap iron in their ears and nose. Lots of them have horns tied on their heads and any old thing they may take a fancy to. As to the other wearing apparel there is little to speak of. They travel at a run all the time and always singing. They are as crazy as snakes. They are all branded and marked according to the tribe they belong to. We are in Zululand and they are the hardest layout of the lot. Some of them actually walked and helped us drive the mules over the mountains, a distance of 200 miles, for they don't get to ride.[8]

The conveyance in towns is a two wheel doings that a large guy with horns hitches himself in. You get in and he's off in a long trot that he keeps uphill and down. There is also a lot of other cheap labor here done by Indians from India.[9] They are almost black and about as locoed as the negroes. They are nothing like the American Indians. They don't know much.

There is not much game here since the war. However, there are a lot of ostrich here, and farther inland are the lions and big animals.

American manufacturers are rushing their machinery into this country, but it is said to be too complicated for these dagoes to work. But the American horses and mules were the best here during the war, and they had animals from all over the world.

This is a great place for driving oxen. There are never less than twelve and often as many as thirty oxen to one wagon. All mule teams are from four to eight pairs to each wagon. This is necessary on account of the rough country.

Military law rules here and before you can land you have got to have £100 ($500) or the promise of a job. Also you cannot go from one part of the country to another without a pass, and that is hard to get.

I see very few Americans here. I guess they know a good thing and stay in a good country, and I think William will take their tip and do likewise when I again land in Yankee land, (as the foreigners call it), so at some near date you may receive some accurate information as to the experience of a young "nipper before the mast" on a cheese box bark bound for the Saviour's terra firma.

Hoping to be an "eyeball" witness to you all soon, I am, as ever, yours truly,

Will Rogers.

PD. Printed in *CP,* 1 November 1902.

1. In the last two years of the war the British strategy aimed at the foundations of Afrikaner culture and society. British troops under F. S. Roberts and H. H. Kitchener's command became occupied with the destruction of Afrikaner homes, wagons, livestock, and property. Soldiers taken prisoner were shipped away to camps in Ceylon, India, and other remote regions, while Afrikaner civilians, mostly the wives and children of men involved in the fighting, were put in local concentration camps.

Thousands of Africans were also put in camps, removed from white farms or from their own lands or mission stations. Tens of thousands of Africans and Afrikaners died in these camps of disease. More individuals died in the camps than were killed in action on either the Boer or the British side in the war; over twenty thousand of them were children. Livestock, particularly horses, were confiscated and slaughtered by the thousands to prevent their use by the Boer forces. Afrikaner farmhouses, barns, and outbuildings were set afire. African huts and villages were also burnt by British troops, and Africans as well as Afrikaners joined the ranks of scattered refugees. There was looting by both British and the Afrikaner forces in Natal. Reports indicate a large number of assaults on native Africans employed by the British army, on civilian Indian and Chinese shopkeepers and traders, and on Boer women in concentration camps, were committed by the British or members of their white colonial contingents. The destruction of property and animals and reports of the spread of diseases and of assaults against women were in part tactics calculated to induce Boer men to lay down their arms (Bailes, "Military Aspects of the War"; Harrison, *White Tribe of Africa;* Nasson, "Tommy Atkins in South Africa"; Pakenham, *Boer War;* Pretorius, "Life on Commando"; Spies, "Women and the War"; and Warwick, "Black People and the War").

2. James Piccione.

3. James Piccione's Greenfields stock farm near Mooi River Station (sometimes also called Greenlands or Greenfield) was by all accounts a huge, rich estate with impressive facilities. The stables were modern in design, built of masonry with air conditioning and heating systems, and fifty large box stalls had the horses' names engraved on brass plates on the doors. The facilities, 350 by 50 feet, were described by one British observer as "lofty and commodious" and "fitted with every convenience that wealth and experience can suggest," so much so that the "animals are tended like children" and "are better housed than thousands of human beings" ("J. Piccione," *Twentieth-Century Impressions of Natal,* 540). Indeed, during the South African War, some fourteen hundred men were sheltered in the stable and the surrounding buildings. The farm also featured a large manor house with several wings, many outbuildings equipped with modern farm machinery powered by steam, and a training racecourse with a five-furlong straight stretch going into the finish line.

Piccione also owned several other farms, including ones at Ankeny, Bettle, and Ipolelo. As to his net worth, he was known to have been offered thirty-five thousand pounds for Greenfields alone and to have declined the offer. The refusal was "not to be wondered at when one sees the place in the freshness of a spring morning, with its stone walls, its broad verandahs, its tennis courts, and so on" (ibid., 542). One of his more successful racehorses, Peppermint, was rumored to be worth over six thousand pounds. Piccione, while more wealthy than Clem V. Rogers, shared many of Will Rogers's father's passions. Clem V. Rogers also loved fine horses and raced horses locally; in the time that his son worked at Piccione's horse farm with its extravagant facilities, Rogers had himself just opened the largest and most modern livery stable in Claremore (see Biographical Appendix entry, Piccione, James).

4. Normal annual rainfall ranges from twenty-eight to forty inches at Durban to about forty to eighty inches in some inland areas of Natal, with summer and winter seasons coming at opposite times of year from those that Rogers had known in Oklahoma (Wilson and Thompson, eds., *Oxford History of South Africa* 2:55).

5. The Boer invasion of Natal of October–November 1899 extended on several fronts south down from the Transvaal and east from the Orange Free State, converging in the Ladysmith area and moving from there down past Estcourt and Willow Grange (towns on the railroad line) to Mooi River Station (see map of invasion, Pakenham, *Boer*

War, 127). Significant battles in the area included those at Elandslaagte, northeast of Ladysmith, on 21 October 1899, and at Ladysmith (Modderspruit) in the last week of October 1899, in which the Boers outmaneuvered the British partly through the use of large bombardment guns (what Rogers's refers to as "cannons"). The Boer guns outranged those in use by the British and were fired from strategic positions. The town and British camp at Ladysmith went under siege (see map of siege, 1899–1900, Pakenham, *Boer War,* 264). The landscape of the area around Ladysmith, and the inadequacy of British maps, made disrupting the siege difficult. The terrain, broken by ravines, outcrops, and rocky kopjes, served as "a natural fortress for the besiegers," in contrast to the exposed veld further south. The British found, in their repeated attempts to recapture the Ladysmith area, that the conditions enabled the Boers to be "every-where—and nowhere" (Pakenham, *Boer War,* 149, 151). The initial British strategy in the Natal campaign (under General Sir Redvers Buller's command) was a "fatalistic acceptance of pitched battles at his opponents' strongest points" (Bailes, "Military Aspects of the War," 82). Casualties were severe. The battle at the closest British garrison above Mooi River, at Willow Grange, took place on 22–23 November 1899. The warfare made refugees out of many residents of Natal, while other civilians found themselves caught as prisoners in the siege (Bailes, "Military Aspects of the War"; Pakenham, *Boer War,* 136–40, 142–55, 265–69; and, on use of large bombardment guns by the Boers, see Brian Willan, "Siege of Mafeking," 142–43).

6. British soldiers would change their mounts at Mooi River Station, and many horses were maintained there for army use. Piccione supplied horses to the British, and Greenfields was only a few miles from the station. Rogers liked to go there to socialize with the British soldiers. Later in life he told stories of how the use of unbroken or partially trained horses from the Americas or Australia "killed and crippled more soldiers than the Boers did" because the British recruits were unused to riding them ("they would holler 'Company Mount,'" he said, and "in ten seconds you couldn't see anything but loose horses and Tommies coming up and digging the dirt out of their eyes") (Rogers, *Will Rogers,* 73). Reports that Rogers worked breaking and training horses for the British Army in South Africa came from his work with horses at Greenfields and his activities at the Mooi River Station during the period that he worked in the area (Pakenham, *Boer War,* 7, 127; see also transcriptions of autobiographical notes, OkClaW).

7. Rogers's praise for the shrewdness of Boer fighters was echoed by British and civilian commentators at the time. As one historian has written, "Boer styles of warfare exercised a peculiar fascination over British military commentators. Many, especially civilians not forced to grapple with it, wrote rhapsodically of their enemy's prowess" (Bailes, "Military Aspects of War," 69). As a cowboy fresh from his own ranch and territorial upbringing, Rogers could identify with the popular image of the Boer soldier as an independent, fast-thinking, wily rifleman working in consort with his fellows atop a good horse, adapting well to guerrilla warfare while regretting the farm left behind (for a discussion of this image and of the Afrikaner vision of the war as "a national cause fought by a people's army," see Pretorius, "Life on Commando," 103–22, quote from p. 103).

8. The South African War took place in a region where 80 percent of the population was black. In Natal, black Africans outnumbered whites ten to one. The Zulus, descendants of a kingdom that had been a formidable military and political power under the leadership of Shaka early in the nineteenth century, had been subjugated after warfare with British colonialists and Afrikaner settlers in the latter 1800s. The last independent king of the Zulus was Cetshwayo, who "revitalized Zulu military power,

only to see his kingdom sacrificed in the Anglo-Afrikaner struggle for South African supremacy" (Lipschutz and Rasmussen, eds., *Dictionary of African Historical Biography*, 44). The Zulus were conquered by the British in 1879, and Zululand was incorporated into the British colony of Natal in 1897 (Guy, *Destruction of the Zulu Kingdom*).

The Zulus, comprising many clans and subclans descended from different houses in their system of *umuzi* (kraals) and genealogical groupings, were relegated by Europeans to less-desirable lands. While Europeans settled "the coastal belt, the interior grasslands, and the midlands bench," which were suitable for farming and raising livestock, the most impoverished Zulus were relegated to the hinterland and "rough and inaccessible" areas "delimited at an early date as Native Reserves" (Fair, *Natal Regional Survey*, n.d., 3:27–28, quoted in Vilakazi, *Zulu Transformations*, 2 n. 3). These areas had little arable land, and many Zulu families depended on male migratory labor. Many Zulu men took temporary manual-labor jobs in rural areas and traveled to nearby cities and towns for temporary low-wage employment.

The Zulus are known for their complicated beadwork and symbolic personal adornment, dress, and hairstyles, which establish identity and communicate social differentiations such as marital status, rank, and military standing, to those, unlike Rogers, who were familiar with their meaning (Kennedy, *Art and Material Culture of the Zulu-Speaking Peoples*).

During the South African War, black African transport and mule drivers, construction workers, horse tenders, trench diggers, and other laborers were essential to the British campaign. Many Afrikaner commandos were accompanied to the battlegrounds by African personal servants. Both sides used African peoples for scouting and intelligence work. After the war African refugees suffered the most from the scorched-earth policy of the British, which left farms and villages decimated, stock animals dead, and seeds in severe shortage. As Peter Warwick has pointed out, "the rehabilitation of white agriculture was given first priority in the programme of rural reconstruction" (Warwick, "Black People and the War," 206). Impoverishment and starvation among Africans was rampant in areas that had been most heavily utilized by the British army, and after British victory black Africans continued to be relegated to work as manual laborers and in the lower ranks of work in mines, farms, and towns (Warwick, "Black People and the War," 186–209).

9. In 1860, in response to British prejudices against the Zulus as farm laborers, indentured Indian migrant workers were brought to Natal to work on sugarcane plantations. They were primarily Hindus of the lower castes and included both men and women. They worked under contracts toward obtaining citizenship and land rights. After serving their indentures they often entered diversified areas of the service economy, purchased land and supplied produce, opened small shops, or participated in the fishing industry. In the 1880s the Afrikaner republic of Transvaal restricted Indian residential, trade, and property rights, and in the early 1890s the Afrikaner Orange Free State began deporting Indians. Indian emigration was ended in 1911, by which time over 150,000 Indians had come to South Africa to work as contract laborers. Indians outnumbered Europeans in Natal in the census of 1904.

Most Indian residents in Natal backed the British during the South African War. Many British officers brought Indians with them to South Africa as servants. After the war's end Alfred Milner's administration rewarded Indian loyalty by placing further civil restrictions upon Indian South Africans and supporting the prohibitions against further Indian immigration long urged by Afrikaner nationalists. Under Jan Christian Smuts, Indians and all Asians were subjected to compulsory registration and excluded from the Transvaal. Mohandas Gandhi, then an attorney in Johannesburg, began his political career of resistance against British imperialism by urging noncooperation with the registration and pass system and passive resistance in crossing the Transvaal and Natal borders (Bhana, ed., *Essays on Indentured Servants in Natal;* Bhana and Pachai, *Documentary History of Indian South Africans;* Brookes and Webb, "The Coming of the Indians," chap. 9 in *History of Natal,* 85–92; Kuper, *Indian People in Natal;* Millan, *People of South Africa;* Pillay, *British Indians in the Transvaal;* Stultz, *South Africa,* 33–34).

According to a 1906 source, Piccione employed approximately forty-five Zulu and Indian laborers at Greenfields (*Twentieth Century Impressions of Natal,* 540). During the period that Rogers worked at the farm, Piccione had at least six Indian contract workers. He wrote to immigration officials in Durban that "three of my indentured Indians intend returning to India & the other three intend looking for work elsewhere." He went on to explain that the Indians had "been off work for a considerable number of days through sickness etc.," for which he had deducted from their wages, and "also three of them deserted & were arrested by the Police & sent to Proom for upwards of a week each, one of the them received 10 lashes." Piccione deducted from the wages of those three unfortunates "during their absence," and reported that they would "have to make up the time lost by sickness etc. & desertion before their term of indenture with me is completed, as their wages & rations cost more than" the daily sum deducted. He ended his letter with the inquiry "When may I expect the twenty Indians I have applied for?" (Jas. Piccione to the Protector of Indian Immigrants, Durban, 15 October 1902, NAD, II, vol. 1.112, ref. 1 2246/1902).

To Folks
5–9 October 1902
Mooi River, Natal South Africa

Mooi River Station
Oct 5. 1902.

My Dear Folks.

Well after so long ~~an~~ a time I have at last a few spare moments so I will detain you with a few scattering facts gathered from the various places it has been my misfortune to see.

Fact No one 1 am feeling as fine as a racer   working pretty hard but sorry to say a little shy on food. for there is no place I have been that you get the good old Grub that you will get ▲ even ▲ in the poorest parts of America   I have been at this place about 5 weeks working for the Man that owned all the stock on the boat   he is about the richest old *bloak* there is in this country   he would be worth $35 Million in America   he lives right here at the farm   In the time that I have been here I have done more different kinds of odd jobs than I thought there were on a big farm and racing stable   I will try and give you a few of the things that I have already done   the principal thing of course is to help feed and care for some of the Thoroughbreds and then to take a lot of them out for an exercise gallop every day which is a *cinch* for these horses are supposed to be the best in this country   not a one of them under $3 thousand dollars in our money   Oh you should of view me up on one of those little saddles for they wont let my saddle get in the same lot with them   for all the riding Saddles are little padded English style

Then other time I am at ~~wor~~ work with the vetinary in the hospital as they have lots of crippled and sick horses and mules dying and we have to throw down all the wild ones to perform on them. I get to use my saddle on a big old horse and I drag off all the dead ones which is about one or two a day. then I have been helping the blacksmith Shoeing horses this week at my odd times. then I have helped dock a lot of horses   that is cut their tail off up short for driving in traps and carriages and then to roaching mules. Then helping seperate horses and mules. but here is where I get put though in the center of one of the big rock barns   there is a big place like a show ring for horses   well when any buyers come here comes his Nibs and sings out *"yank"* (as that is all I am known by) bring out such a horse   well I walk him out then he will start me in a run with the scoundrel around and around him a hollering at you all the time for he is the only man that I ever saw that could holler louder and more at a person than Papa. then he will pump that man with more lies in a minute than you could think of in a year then out with another and so on till I am faged out. I have only rode one wild horse   another boy here that worked in South America was going to ride one here one day and he threw him and I by some miracle or other rode him and whipped him and I think I ruined my future chances for they said that was too rough fashion for them   so I guess I will not get to ride any more soon on those kinds of horses for the way that they do things is altogeather different from our way.

Well today has been an unusually busy day   it is Sunday and there was a couple of big buyers come to see the thoroughbreds   Well we worked like a fool getting all cleaned up and horses rubbed down   then out they come   well there is only two of us that ever take the horses out to show   well we had to present every one on the farm and a lot of them are not brought out often and you are only allowed to have a halter on them   well they will jerk and pull you from one end of the ring to the other

Well this eve after that was finished what did the Rube do to show them some excitement   He has what is called a Riding School   It is ~~ol~~ only a building about 100 feet long and 20 wide with a solid board jump in the middle about 4 ft   there is not another thing in it   ground as hard as rock   Well he puts a mare in there loose that had only been ridden a time or so   he turned her loose and all the visitors and Ladies and all were in there to see them make her jump the hurdles as this was the first one that he has had in it since we came   Well they get a lot at each end with long whips and get after her and make her jump this high thing which is as solid as rock   well they were having great sport When I hearing the Melee rushed in to see and no sooner had I turned up till he balled out at me to jump up on her back and ride her over. We had all seen the jump there and had said we would not jump a horse over it but he took me by surprise and before all hands on this farm I got up   I told him I had never ridden over hurdles but guess I could try   Now fancy being on a horse with not a thing on it bridle or nothing and a lot of *Dagoes* after it with whips and a solid 4 ft wall in front of you for the 1st time. Well I had no more than got up and planted my Lunch Hooks with a death grip into the mane and they took after her   well she cleared it alright and they kept up us at it till she give out and I got so I could do it pretty good   But what was the worst of it   he had a long Ox whip about 30 ft long and sometime he hit me and sometime the mare   Well I think now he is going to School several at it and I am to be the Steeplechase jockey.

He took about 12 of us of the boat and said he would give us work for you cannot land in this country unless you have $500 or a job   We do not know what wages we are getting   no one has asked him   but I dont think he will have work for all of us as he is selling out pretty fast. he has about 20 Negroes work here too and about 30 Indians from India   they all sign to work for a man for 5 years   We are about 3 miles from this Station   it is only a small Station but there is lots of English Soldiers camped all around

Has there been a letter published in the progress that I wrote from here[1] I wrote it a couple of weeks ago. I have only got 2 letters since I left America   one from Papa and one from Uncle Jim[2] and a batch of Chelsea and one of Claremore Papers   I have not got any mail since I arrived here   you see it gets so far behind and has so far to come and through so many different people that it is a miracle if I ever get a letter at all

I seen in some of the Papers some Epistles from yours Truly   I had no Idea that they would come into print   Now dont dab this thing or any of the rest of them for I cant say that I am proud of them and I am obliged to pen them under very severe difficulties.

Well this is some three days later than I started this document and I am still prospering only I pulled up a bit lame after todays *Routine*. owing to the other Show Man being absent had an unusually steady whirl.

By the Way I received some Mail last Night   A Letter from Sister Sallie Written about July 1st to B.A. and one from Maud written about Aug 27 to Capetown. I certainly was pleased to get them for I had not heard from you for over three Months and more to hear that you were ▲ all ▲ well.

But here is what would drive you to the Beach   Every Night the Music strikes up over in *"his Largeness"* quarters. his daughter³ a damsel of some twenty winters (Which by the way must of been a bit hard) and ably assisted by whomever has the nerve to chime in will break forth on that "Gisard breaking" ballad entitled "After the ball." The Fatal wedding is After the ball   "Sweet Rosie Ogrady" is a close third and is gaining favor Nightly.⁴ "Sweet Marie" only comes on special occasions as it calls for special talent. Oh but one Maggie certainly does ▲ an ▲ injury to "The Girl I loved in Sunny Tenessee."

They have heard of the Lady that was bred in Kentucky and have written for particulars.

But when his Nibs Secretary (A *bloak* with a face like a pickle and a ~~sound~~ ▲ voice ▲ that well it dident need to be brought out it was out to far already) *piped* (All Coons looked alike to him.[)] (I was so enfatuated I lost my ~~seat~~ ▲ balance ▲ on the pailin⁵ fence and went down and out.[)] But never mind the tip is out that the first time there is no company we shall have access to the front yard and the Parlor Windows shall be *cast ajar* and we shall have a treat fit for the Gods.

All hands were chirping some kind of an Irish Pady Song (When I sniggered out in the Night Air) a *Mik* on the pailin next to me was going to *swat* me   he said you *yanks* dont appreciate good songs when you hear them

The Doxology is that loving little ditty christened "God save the King" when all *uncover* even to the Irish if they should have had the good fortune to be in the loft asleep. Complete words and music to any of the above can be had by examining the Music racks of any of the young ladies in these parts who are considered to be "up to ~~stuff~~ snuff" in the latest. above statement made under my hand and seal   this the longest day I ever seen   *"Amen"*

Well as the Tom Cat quartett has hushed it must be late   all hands join me in wishing you all a speedy Christmas and a Sunshiny *Fourth*.

dont be surprised if I beat this thing here⁶   you may still write to me at Capetown care of the American Consul as he is seeing after my Mail matter in my absence   From what I can hear all of those jender will be married pretty soon

Tell any of them that if they think they could subside as information that not to forget to deal me a hand but that is all I can offer.

9 P.M. some one day later than the above and I have had another fresh deal today as I have got to ride in the pastures all day up on a locoed horse and a gentlemens Saddle and I was glad to stop for it dident feel right in that garb

Oh I see by Mauds letter old Dick wont be back in Tahlequah   he told me for sure he was going to Texas from N.Y. and now he is heart mashing in Tahlequah   Well I hope all the boys will marry and settle down   Hurrah for

Spi   I knew he would pull through if he had a show. Tell Papa when he is in Oolagah to ask Lil Ellis to tell me where Jim Shepard ▲ is ▲   that is the boy that used to work for me. I think a lot of him and would write to him if I knew where he was   I last heard from him in California. By the way how is Kate[7]   I hope she has not married too   When you got to Novata[8] give my very best to all I know especially Jim Keys and the Phillips Girls   Tell Jim[9] he can rope on old Comanche next Fourth   Tell Jim Kell,[10] Booth and Hamp and all the old boys that I have as yet failed to see a place that has got a show with the old U.S. and to find a place there and stay there   Poor old Tom Lane   tell him to take that girl and quit making a living for that set of Bums (for I do know that he is the best boy I ever saw and I would rather hear of him doing well than any boy in that country but he is sorely handicaped[)][11]

I had a great time coming over on that cattle boat but I will not try to detain you with any of the facts as I will tell you that when I see you for I certainly had some curious times   I was Night Watchman   I could sleep all day and had to stay up all night   I will mail you a special edition of my Drama "25 days on a floating dung hill or where did he kick you." Oh them mules did play Ping Pong with them dagoes   they fed and worked all day and then mend up fresh kicks and bites and hooks at night.

Well I must stop   write me soon and a long letter   Give all my friends my best   tell them I will be there soon   Lots of love to all you

Your loving brother
Willie.

One of the boys here cut my hair off right short with a pair of horse clippers and when I get up on one of them long thoroughbreds with a little saddle and my stirrups up short I look like a monkey up a stick.

ALS, rc. OkClaW.

1. A reference to Will Rogers to the *Claremore Progress*, written 22 September 1902 and published 1 November 1902, above.
2. A reference to James Cleveland to Will Rogers, 25 June 1902, above.
3. Piccione had at least one daughter, mentioned here by Rogers and also in a British observer's account of Piccione's farm published in 1906. In the 1906 profile it was noted that Miss Piccione (whose first name was not given) had "her father's love of horses, and, as might be expected, is as much at home in the saddle as most people are on *terra firma*" (*Twentieth Century Impressions of Natal*, 540).
4. "After the Ball," words and music by songwriter-publisher Charles K. Harris, was published in 1892. A smash hit, the song was the first to sell in the millions of copies. It was a sentimental story ballad written to be sung with piano. The lyrics were tragic, describing a man who mistakenly rejects his sweetheart and years later dies alone with no home: "After the ball is over, / After the break of morn, / After the dancers' leaving, / After the stars are gone. / Many a heart is aching, / . . . Many the hopes that have

vanished, / After the ball" (*EV,* 4). Harris was a leading figure during the Tin Pan Alley period in the song-publishing business and an important songwriter for vaudeville. "After the Ball" had a resurgence of popularity when it was interpolated by Jerome Kern into his musical *Show Boat* in 1927. He was the author of a self-help book for rising composers called *How to Write a Popular Song* and of an autobiography, *After the Ball.* "The Fatal Wedding" was written by Gussie L. Davis. "Sweet Rosie O'Grady," an Irish waltz written by Maude Nugent, a singer at a night club called The Abbey in New York, was published by Edward B. Marke in 1896. It is a classic example of the romantic and sentimental spirit of Tin Pan Alley publications at the turn of the century. During the first decade of the twentieth century interest in popular sheet music reached a new high. Over one hundred songs written in the period sold over a million copies. Many of these have passed into the oral tradition (Bloom, *American Song,* 664; Ewen, *All the Years of American Popular Music,* 113, 116–117; *EV,* 4; Wenzel and Binkoswki, *I Hear American Singing,* 47, 50; Whitcomb, *After the Ball,* 3–5).

5. A paling fence (a fence made of wooden pales or pickets).

6. Some of Rogers's fellow contract workers apparently did as Rogers hinted he wanted to do himself. They "beat this thing here," either through such a mutual agreement with Piccione as Rogers reached or through desertion or deportation. A few weeks after Rogers wrote this letter, James Piccione filed notification with British colonial officials that one of Rogers's shipmates, "Pieter Smith whom he landed from the S.S. 'Kelvinside' has deserted his services" (minute paper from J. Piccione, Mooi River, 17 November 1902, NAD, IRD, vol. 13, ref. IRD 947/1902). Writing on Greenfield letterhead, Piccione wrote the inspector of immigration at Durban that Smith "got drunk and quarrelsome and refused to do any more work. He actually stole . . . Spirits out of the house and drunk it. He left Mooi River by 12 on train for Durban last night. This man is a thoroughly good worker when he is sober & has money." An immigration official noted at the bottom of the page to "Keep this at hand in case this man gives us trouble" (Jas. Piccione to the Inspector of Immigration, Durban, Natal, 17 November 1902, ibid.). In the following year Piccione had deported from South Africa two more laborers whom he had been brought from Argentina and landed in South Africa for service at his farm (minute paper from Consul for the Argentine Republic, Durban, 3 September 1903, NAD, IRD, vol. 20, ref. IRD 819/1903).

Drunkenness among workers was the cause for Piccione's complaint to the Colonial Office. Piccione asked for more police attention to the problem after one incident in 1897 when one of his laborers was served hard liquor at a local hotel on a Sunday, then collapsed drunk on the railroad track, narrowly escaping death when a railroad worker spotted his body and dragged him from the path of an oncoming train (James Piccione to the Colonial Secretary, 19 July 1897, minute paper from J. Piccione, NAD, C50, vol. 1523, ref. 1897/4942).

7. Kate Ellis.

8. Nowata was called Metz until the name of the post office there was officially changed in November 1899. "Nowata" is from the Delaware word *no-we-ata,* meaning "welcome." After statehood the town became the county seat of Nowata County, Okla. It was located on the Missouri Pacific Railroad line (Gideon, *Indian Territory,* 174; Shirk, *Oklahoma Place Names,* 152).

9. Probably a reference to James H. (Jim) Rider, who was taking care of Comanche.

10. James L. (Jim) Kell (b. 1875) attended the Willie Halsell College with Rogers. He was from Chelsea. He married another Willie Halsell student, Susan Cornelia Clark (b. 1876) from Adair in 1898 (*1894 Annual Catalogue of Willie Halsell School,* 7, 9; *OCF* 2:20).

11. Tom Lane, Rogers's boyhood friend, married Nora Matheson in June 1903 (*HRC*, 274; see also Biographical Appendix entry, LANE, Thomas Lipe).

From Clement Vann Rogers
21 October 1902
Claremore, I.T.

In this letter from his father, and in the following letter from his sister Sallie, Rogers was sent word of the procedures in the Cherokee Nation for the allotment of individual parcels of land. A few months before these letters were written, the Dawes Commission reported that it had received over fifty thousand applications "of Cherokees, Shawnees, Delawares, by blood and intermarriage, and freedmen for entry on the Cherokee rolls."[1] The dissolution of the Cherokee territorial government was slated for March 1906, but it continued in restricted form until June 1914, when Congress determined that the allotment of tribal properties had been completed.

Claremore, Ind. Ter., Oct. 21st *1902*

Dear Son

Cape Town
South Africa
care of the American Consul

Your letter come to me the other day & found me in good Health & Sallie Maude & May & children are all well. The Town is sorter quiet now. plenty of corn coming in. It is nice pretty weather out here. Cleveland & Yocum[2] is not on the Home place. I have 2 other men their. Your 2 Poneys are doing real well. Your Buggy Horse have grown quite a good deal. No one have used either of them.

Spi[3] is still at Okmulgee He havent been Home since he went their last Spring. Tahlequah have now got A Rail Road.

I still stay in my same rooms. Tom Lane[4] & Casper Lipe is going to School at Kansas City. Clem McSpadden is in Tennessee & Vandibuilt going to School.

Earnest Schrimsher is not trying to do any thing. Clem[5] went to St. Louis in Roping Contest but got nothing. Donnely[6] at Vinita got first money They are all at San an Tonia Texas to a big roping contest. not many from here went.

Big Show here at the opra Hall here tonight.[7] The Town Site questions & the Grade of the land is now going on. We only get 65 acres to each of us at the old Home place.[8] I will have to sell the balance to some one for we cant hold it. I will take the best of the field. Alf paid me in full for the Pasture & I paid up your insurance[9] I collected from Cleveland $24.00 & $7.50 from Yocum

The First National Bank building, Claremore, I.T. Clem V. Rogers was vice president of the bank. After his second wife, Mary Bibles Rogers, died in 1900, he lived in rooms on the second floor *(Scrapbook A2, OkClaW)*.

They claimed that were all they owed you. Earnest Schrimsher have not paid me yet.

I have all of my Houses Rented here in Town. Im going up Home in the morning. 60 acres of corn on the old Home place. I get one third. wheat did not amount to but very little. I will have your Poneys looked after this winter   Their is not a cow, Hog, chicken, or Turkey, on the old Home place. One Peafowell.

I give several Boys & Girls your address & they said they would write to you. I will write again soon, do write when you can.

your Father
C. V. Rogers

ALS, rc. OkClaW. On C. V. Rogers, Bank Building letterhead. Envelope addressed to W. P. Rogers, Cape Town South Africa, care of American Consul. Forwarded to Pietermaritzberg.[10] Return address printed C. V. Rogers, Room 9, Bank Bldg., Claremore, I.T.

1. Woodward, *Cherokees*, 322–23. On Will Rogers's participation in the enrollment and allotment process, see Will Rogers to Clement Vann Rogers, 21 May 1903, and Enclosures, Power of Attorney, 19 and 20 May 1903, below.

2. A reference to James Cleveland and to Pearl Yocum's family, who had been tenants at the old Rogers home ranch (see Pearl Yocum to Will Rogers, 25 June 1902, and James Cleveland to Will Rogers, 25 June 1902, above).

3. Spi Trent.

4. Will Rogers's friend Tom Lane occasionally made the news in Claremore in this period. The local paper confirmed that Lane was in business school in Kansas City and reported when he came home for the Christmas holidays in 1902. A week or so after Clem V. Rogers wrote this letter, Tom Lane was in town to see the Sparks' Circus, a traveling show that came to Claremore at the end of October 1902. He deliberately missed the train going back to Kansas City to see the performances on both weekend days (*CP* 1 November and 20 December 1902).

5. Clem Musgrove.

6. Possibly Thomas Austin Donnelly (b. 1878) or his brother James Henry Donnelly (1871–1958). Both attended Willie Halsell College (*OCF* 1:216; *Story of Craig County* 332–33).

7. The long-awaited opening of the new Windsor Opera House, part of Claremore's building boom, was scheduled for 18 October 1902, but the acting troupe that was supposed to appear canceled the performance. The opening went off instead on Tuesday of the next week. Will Rogers's sisters went to the performance, and Maud Lane wrote to her brother about it (see Maud Lane to Will Rogers, 31 October 1902, below).

8. According to the terms of the agreement ratified in the August 1902 Cherokee Nation elections, each officially enrolled citizen of the Nation was "entitled to a homestead equal in value to 40 acres of the average allotable land, inalienable and non-taxable for a period not exceeding twenty-one years, and such other land as would constitute an evaluation of a total of $325.60, inalienable for a period of five years. No individual allotment was to exceed more than 110 acres of average allotable land" (Wardell, *Political History of the Cherokee Nation,* 326). Town lots were separately evaluated by the Dawes Commission. Clem V. Rogers was allotted 69.93 acres of the old Rogers homestead and surplus land, and Will Rogers was allotted 78.84 acres (allotment records, Rogers ranch, box 7, OkClaW; see also Clement Vann Rogers to Will Rogers, 9 February 1903, below).

9. Alf Cunningham was a tenant on Rogers land. An Alfred Carroll Cunningham (b. 1860) is listed in *OCF* 2:99. Responding to urging from his father, Rogers had taken out a life insurance policy in 1898. According to Betty Blake Rogers, Rogers handed money "around to anyone who needed it and was creditor to half his acquaintances. However, he did take his father's wishes seriously enough to sign up for a twenty-year life-insurance policy which required him to meet a premium of $141.40 each year. But as far as responsibility was concerned, that was just what Willie didn't want" (Rogers, *Will Rogers,* 61). Clem V. Rogers was apparently attempting to collect on some of Will's debts in order to apply those funds to the premium payments on the life insurance policy (see Application to the Mutual Life Insurance Company of New York, 9 September 1898, above).

10. Pietermaritzburg, the capital, is located in southern Natal, some forty miles northwest of Durban. Founded in 1839, it is named for two leading Afrikaners, Pieter Retief, a Voortrekker leader, and Gert Martiz, president of the Voortrekkers' Council. The city was incorporated in 1853 and became the capital in 1856. It was linked by rail to Durban in 1880 and with Johannesburg in 1895. It is the seat of the provincial administration (*ESA,* 390–91; *WNGD,* 954).

"AFTER LIFE'S FITFUL DREAM"

Church Street, looking East, Pietermaritzburg

Postcard of Pietermaritzburg, South Africa, from Will Rogers's scrapbook of his trip (*Scrapbook 1902–4, CPpR*).

From Sallie McSpadden
30 October 1902
Chelsea, I.T.

Chelsea, I.T.
Oct. 30, 1902.

My Dear Brother

While every-body is asleep I am going to write you a little letter. Do you have any idea how much we all want to see you? Jim and Vance were out here the other night and were asking all about you. They were on their way to their farm across the river, to select allotments. Indeed that is the order of the day for every-body now. Maud and Cap made a flying trip to Nowata yesterday returning today. Visited Coz Gotts[1] family and also selected the childrens allottments. Clem thinks he is doing splendid in school. Says he has never been home-sick a single day. May, Herbert and Estelle are all getting along very nicely at the Academy. Irene, Estel, Gunter and Helen[2] are all together a gre ▲ a ▲t deal and get lots of comfort from each others society. That brings me to poor little Pauline[3] who two weeks ago had a severe illness which Dr. Bagby[4] called infantile paralysis and she can no more use her little feet than if she had none. We have great hopes of her getting over it, however. Dr. said it might be several months or a year, or two years, or she might never walk again, but I think she will recover after a while. Tom and Cap[5] you know never change. They are still the same henpecked husbands they have always been. . . .

I realize I am not writing you a newsy letter, but since the baby first took sick I have been right with her and hardly know what is going on — I just felt as if I wanted to write and tell you how much we all love you, how badly we want you to come home and that we talk about you, every day and wish we could see you. May God bless and keep you, dear brother, and bring you safely home to us Is the prayer of

Sister Sallie

ALS, rc. OkClaW. Envelope hand-addressed to Mr. W. P. Rogers, Cape Town, South Africa, c/o American Consul. Forwarded c/o Texas Jack's Wild West Show, East London, C.C.[6]

1. Alfred Mason Gott (b. 1844), a cousin of Will Rogers's father by marriage, married Sue Harris (b. 1849), a descendant through her grandmother in the Cordery family line, in 1869 (*OCF* 1:255; *WRFT,* 43).
2. References to Sallie McSpadden's children Clem, May, Herbert, Helen, and Maud Irene McSpadden and to Maud Lane's children Estelle and James Gunter Lane (see Biographical Appendix entries). May and Herb McSpadden and Estelle Lane were students at Chelsea Academy.
3. Sallie's one-year-old daughter, Pauline Elizabeth (later known as Paula), became severely ill in October 1902. She recovered from the illness and lived a long life in the Chelsea-Claremore area. She married Robert Love in 1937. Betty Blake asked her to become the curator of the Will Rogers Memorial when it was created in Claremore in 1938, and Paula Love and her husband served with the memorial for decades. She died in 1973 (see Biographical Appendix entry for LOVE, Pauline [Paula] Elizabeth McSpadden).
4. Dr. Oliver Bagby (1859–1937) was a leading citizen of Vinita and had treated members of the Rogers family for years. He was called to the bedside of Mary America Schrimsher Rogers during her final illness in May 1890. Bagby was born and raised in Missouri and, like Dr. Jesse Bushyhead, studied at the Missouri Medical College in St. Louis (later part of Washington University). Bagby graduated in 1881 and set up a practice in Vinita, I. T., in 1882. He married Mary Miller of Boles, Mo., in 1883, and the couple had two children. Oliver Bagby went into partnership with Dr. Morris Frazee, and the two answered calls on horseback or by horse and buggy over much of Indian Territory and sometimes into Texas. They were instrumental in vaccinating citizens of the Cherokee Nation against smallpox. Bagby entered into a new partnership with Dr. Benjamin Fortner in 1887 and practiced with Fortner until 1906. Dr. Bagby retired from active work as a physician in 1909 and became a businessman. He was one of the organizers of branches of the First National Bank in Vinita, Claremore, and Chelsea. He served on the board of directors of the bank and as president of the branch in Vinita for

over thirty years, and was active in bringing a hospital to Vinita. In the influenza epidemic of 1918 he returned to the practice of medicine in response to the acute local need. He delivered over a thousand babies in Indian Territory. His younger brother, Dr. Louis Bagby (1876–1943), also practiced medicine in Vinita, starting a practice there in 1900. Like his brother, Louis Bagby was involved in banking and in the establishment of the Vinita Hospital (Clinton, "Indian Territory Medical Association"; *CP,* 11 January 1902 and 10 January 1903; Keith, *Boy's Life of Will Rogers,* 43; *Story of Craig County,* 80, 242–43.

5. Will Rogers's brothers-in-law Tom McSpadden and Cap Lane.

6. East London is a South African seaport city in Cape Province, located at the mouth of the Buffalo River on the Indian Ocean. Originally called Port Rex when the British landed troops there in 1845, its name was changed to East London in 1847. In 1848 it was annexed, with its surrounding territory, to the Cape Colony. In 1858 a large contingent of German settlers immigrated to the area, and in 1874 a railway was begun. Major improvements were made to the harbor in the 1880s, and by the end of the century it was used by large ships. East London is approximately 150 miles from Port Elizabeth (*ESA,* 152–53; *WNGD,* 353).

From Maud Lane
31 October 1902
Chelsea, I.T.

Oct—31—1902.

My Own Dear Brother.

I have been thinking for some time I would write to you but we have had such a time all summer and it seems that we now are to have the coming event of the the year. some of Cap's folks have been here all summer and for the last month uncle Tom Lane[1] has been here and he is quite an invalid   we have to feed him most of the time and the care of his face is so bad one can hardly stand to look at it but I have to watch and help in the dressing of it many times a day   poor old man   I am so sorry for him he does hate to stay here so and he dislikes me so much but he has no money and no place to go so he is compelled to stay here. We were so glad to hear that you had landed safe and had found something you like to do but my how I do wish you was on your way home   I had hoped you would be home by XMas and we all talk of it but now that we have heard from you and you have not started home and did not say anything about comeing I fear we will be disspirited   The children talk of you all the time and want you to come home. We are all well but Sallies dear little baby she has been sick two weeks and they had Bagby come down from Vinita   he said both of her legs are parylized   we all had noticed she did not move them, the dr, said she might regain the use of them and walk after a while but if she did it would take a long while and then she might never walk but we all think she will get well   she has always been so strong and well and has just lived out with the other children. Papa is quite well   I went down there the other night to the opening of the new opera house and it is quite a nice one too   the play that night was the "Millionaire Tramp." I dont know what troop it was but the play was not as good as some I have seen here in Chelsea and they had made such a big blow about their opening.[2] you would hardly know Claremore they are getting so many new buildings and some nice stocks of goods   I love to go there every one is so nice to me. Papa writes you all the Claremore news I know. . . .

Jess has had a long and hard spell of fever this summer. he was treating Herb More who has just gotten up from the longest and worst spell of fever I ever knew of   While Jess was up there he took sick and there they were both in the same house   they sent to K.C. for a trained nurse for Herb and your little cousin Lizzie Triplet came up and nursed Jess[3]. . . .

Well Cap and I went up to K.C.[4] the first of this month. You know that was my first visit to that city and I must say I do not like it anything as well as I do St. Louis, but you may be sure we had a great time   any place you know is a show to me. Cap went up to buy his holiday goods so while he was busy I spent most of my time at Emery Byrd and Theyers John Taylors and some of the smaller places Then at night we took in a show the Salvation R Army and any old thing that came our way. Cap bought some very nice things for Christmas and we think the town is getting large enough now to handle some nice holiday goods. Well I came near forgetting to tell this, Cap and I went over to Nowata yesterday and back today, we went to see about the childrens allotments   we got the grade of our land over there and the most of it is graded at five dollars which will only give sixty five acres to the head, we will take all three alotments there for the children, Cap and I will take ours here and we get eighty one acres. . . .

May has given up the hotel at Talala and is now living in Oologah   I dont know what they are going to do I am sure papa has a new renter on the home place   he said when old uncle Jimmie left he took everything he could hall off and there was left only the old pecock and one rooster   they were there holding the place down all alone. Aunt Kate Daniels at Ft Gibson died some time ago   she had been up at Tahlequah for some time. Papa had intended takeing her alotment for her there at home but I dont know how it will be now   Vinita had a street fair. Cap and I went up and we sure had a fine time. . . .

We do so want to see you and I want you to write and tell us when to look for you for you surely do not intend spending your Christmas away from us. I must close now and I expect you are wondering why I have not stoped long ago. Pleas write to us soon and tell us all about your self and be sure you set a day for comeing home. Cap and the children join me in lots of love for your own dear self.

Lovingly

Maud Lane

ALS, rc. OkClaW. envelope hand-addressed to Mr. W. P. Rogers, Cape Town, South Africa, c/o American Consul. Forwarded c/o Texas Jacks Wild West Show, East London, C.C.

1. Tom Lane was Cap Lane's brother from Claremore. Maud Lane cared for him in his final illness (*CR*, 14 February 1902).

2. The new Windsor Opera House in Claremore got off to a bit of a rocky start with cancellations and rescheduling of its opening-night act. The opening was much anticipated, and the local paper had reported at the beginning of October that the scenery for the "new opera house arrived Saturday and has been put in place. There are five scenes as follows: parlor, kitchen, street, wood and prison" (*CP,* 4 October 1902). The show, *The Millionaire Tramp,* was scheduled to open 18 October 1902 with reserved seats at seventy-five, fifty, and thirty-five cents. The story of *The Millionaire Tramp,* set in nineteenth-century England and America, was published as a novel by Robert C. Givins in 1886 (Chicago: Laird and Lee). The opera troupe presenting the show canceled the engagement the week of 11 October 1902 and then rescheduled the opening for 21 October. The *Claremore Progress* reported that "Mrs. J. T. McSpadden, Mrs. C. Lane and Mrs. William Strange were among those down from Chelsea Tuesday night to take in the opening of the opera house" (*CP,* 25 October 1902). Most observers shared in Maud Lane's less-than-enthusiastic opinion about the performance; however, the second act that appeared at the house helped make up for the first. The Mahara Minstrels came to town next, and according to the *Progress,* their music, "bicycle riding and hoop juggling were the finest we ever witnessed. They will always be welcome in Claremore." The paper also promoted the next acting troupe by advising residents to "Miss your breakfast, miss your dinner, miss your supper, but don't miss 'A Chicago Tramp' at the Windsor Opera House next Tuesday night" (*CP,* 25 October 1902). Jim Baugh's National Stock Co. came to the Opera House in mid-November with the four-act drama *Colorado,* which had run in New York City, and *A Soldier's Sweetheart.* December brought the farce comedy *Two Married Men,* the drama *Convict's Daughter,* and promise of Clark's Lady Minstrels in January. By the end of 1902 the *Progress* proclaimed that "Claremore boasts of as fine an opera house as there is in the Cherokee and Creek nations" (*CP,* 20 December 1902, reprinted from the *So. McAlester Capital;* see also *CP,* 11 October, 18 October, 1 November, 8 November, 13 December, and 27 December 1902).

3. James Herbert Moore was a friend and business partner of Clem V. Rogers. He was the brother of Nell Moore Kates and the husband of Cora Musgrove, and he ran a hardware business in Claremore. He became very ill with typhoid fever in 1902, and Dr. Jesse Bushyhead also contracted the illness while caring for him. Lizzie Triplett was Jesse Bushyhead's sister, the daughter of Principal Chief Dennis Wolf Bushyhead and the sister of Will Rogers's mother, Elizabeth Alabama Schrimsher Adair Bushyhead. She married Thomas Triplett and lived at Westville, I.T., near the Arkansas border (*HRC,* 327; *WRFT,* 124).

4. A major railroad hub, stockyard, packinghouse and grain-storage center, Kansas City, Kans., is located at the joining of the Kansas and Missouri Rivers on the eastern

border of Kansas, across the state line from Kansas City, Mo. It was an important market for Indian Territory cattle, horses, and mules; corn, wheat, oats, and hay were also marketed there. The area was settled by Wyandot Indians in the 1840s, and by whites in 1857. The official city was created by combining several adjoining towns in 1886.

By the 1870s Kansas City was a thriving cattle market town; cattle ranchers were attracted to the city's stockyards and livestock exchange. At the end of the 1880s the city had eight meat-packing companies, including Armour and Swift. The city had strong links to Indian Territory. It was pivotal to the regional cattle industry, and its news-papers reported important Indian Territory news (see, for example, the article from the *Kansas City Journal* on the Matt Yocum murder, 18 July 1897, above). Kansas City was the nearest major urban center to the Verdigris country (it was approximately a two-hundred-mile train ride from Oologah), and members of the Rogers family frequently traveled there to shop, carry on business, or enjoy the city's amenities. After 1889 Clem V. Rogers often shipped his livestock to Kansas City on the Kansas and Arkansas Valley Railway (later the Missouri Pacific) and attended the cattle market there. Will Rogers made several trips to the city between 1899 and 1901, buying the latest fashions and popular sheet music and attending theater performances. In 1901 he also participated in a cowboy parade with the Zack Mulhall troupe down the city's main streets. Cap Lane went there to purchase wholesale goods to retail in his Chelsea pharmacy and general store. Emery, Bird, and Thayer (formerly Bullene, Moore, and Emery), one of the stores at which Maud Lane mentions shopping during the Lane trip in 1902, was located on Eleventh Street and Grand Avenue and was considered one of Kansas City's most lavish department stores. With a population of 163,752 in 1900 and many tall buildings, Kansas City must have offered the Rogers family a glaring contrast to the small towns to which they were accustomed in Indian Territory (Brown and Dorsett, *K.C.*, 50–53, 99, 102, 126–27; Collings, *Old Home Ranch*, 48; *WNGD*, 587). Will Rogers gave the following tongue-in-cheek account of the experience that he and another young cowboy, used to small town and ranch life in Indian Territory, had when they took some livestock up to Kansas City and encountered the unfamiliar technology of the big city:

> A cowpuncher and I went from my fathers ranch, where I was born and raised and live yet, which was then in what was called Cherokee Nation, now called Oklahoma, up to Kansas City with a train load of cattle to market. In the hotel that night where we went to get a room, they of course wanted us to sign the register but he was older and wiser than me, as I was only a yearling, and he winked at me and said Oh no we dont, thats a bill of sale to the cattle or some of your city tricks and I dont sign my name to one thing—and we dident—but the clerk gave us a bunk anyway.
>
> Well he established himself in my mind right there as about the wisest fellow I ever saw. Well they finally herded us into an elevator and that was some job too. I tell you they was 10 minutes getting us loaded into that old sister. When we got to the room and all ready to turn in, we couldent get the darn light out—it was electric light on a long cord. He was wise again and says—well by jacks I know enough not to blow it out cause I have heard tell of these rube fellows that have done that. I asked him if we couldent just turn it down a little bit, but nothing doing. He said—well we couldent sleep in the light. I told him to go see the fellow down stairs. He couldent never find downstairs and wondered if there was one of those things going down like that coming up or did people just jump down, and said he wouldent have people think we were a couple of country fellows by asking them anything (of course they naturally wouldent after what had already happened down there).

Well an idea finally hit me to put a boot over it and let it hang down in the boot as we had on boots of course. We tried that and it was great till he said—you darn fool that will set fire to the boot, so we took it down then he showed he was a genius—he untied all the loose cord above the globe and took the thing and gently placed it in the bureau drawer and shut the drawer and it was all to the merry.

We were walking across a crowded street—lots of traffic and dodging and ducking cars and all and he grabbed me and jerked me over on the side walk and said—get on this raised place here and we wont get run over by nothing bigger than a man anyway. We were standing way back next to the wall on a sidewalk and a street car passed and a wise motorman spied us and yelled—look, I am going to turn around, and we ducked ("The Hotel and Electric Light Episodes," transcriptions of autobiographical notes, OkClaW).

This electric light story is similar to the adventures that Rogers and another cowboy— both raised with kerosene lanterns—had with gas lights in a hotel room in San Francisco. That episode landed Rogers in the hospital (transcriptions of autobiographical notes, OkClaW; Rogers, *Will Rogers,* 58–59).

To Folks
17 November 1902
Durban, Natal, South Africa

Will Rogers writes home to let his family know he has left the employment of James Piccione and is back in the port city of Durban.

Durban, Natal, South Africa.
November 17, 1902.

My Dear Home Folks:

I will write you a short letter as you will get this about Christmas time, and will know that I am "proceeding magnificently." I am back at the port where I landed, I shoved off from that big "Stiff" I have been with. I have made a long trip up into the interior where the war was the hottest. I was in Ladysmith[1] and passed several English grave-yards that showed where there had been a battle and where probably one Boer horse was killed. It is a very pathetic sight to see the Boer families returning to their former homes and finding some all torn down and others occupied by the English. The Boers are as fine lot of people as one would wish to see; peaceful, law-abiding and friendly to all. They speak English as well as Dutch.

I am going up to Pretoria[2] in the Transvaal,[3] with a lot of stock for a man here and when I return I'll be ready to go home, as I will have seen a large part of the country. You get good pay here, but it costs more to live than at home, so you are none ahead. The weather is getting very hot here now and by Christmas will be at its hottest.

I am up against it good and hard now. Coming down the other day my "cargo of merchandise" was misplaced, consisting of clothes, saddle, and in fact my "whole works" except a small grip I had with me. They do not have a system of checking on the railways here; it is "catch as catch can," and I was caught for my roll. I have suspended operations till I hear from it, but it has been ten days and no tidings, so I have begun to prepare for the worst, which is to adopt the garb of my black neighbors. I have just investigated the contents of the small bag and find that it contains thirteen collars, one shirt—all soiled—one an unmarried sock and a clothes brush. The major part was occupied by a Spanish library of four volumes entitled, "How to Learn Spanish in a Day." by Antonio Pedro Gonzales; one little manual of 976 pages called "Spanish Made Easy."[4] By remembering these few hints and various others you will readily see I have not yet got next to their learning process. This grip also contained old letters and programs of every theatre from New York and London down to a magic lantern show in Zululand. I have gone to work brushing up the soiled linen, reading over the theatre bills and thinking what a discouraging scene I have just passed through.

Speaking of the song you wrote me about, here are some words I got up to the music of "Any Old Place I Can Hang My Hat is Home Sweet Home to Me:"

> I've traveled 'round this world a bit,
> I've been from coast to coast,
> Had every kind of food to eat
> From beans to quail on toast.
> There's not a land discovered yet
> But's good enough for me;
> So when I'm asked where I live
> I answer on the Q T—
>
> CHORUS
> I aint got no regular place
> That I can call my home;
> I can't go back to America
> She's far across the foam;
> Walking there's nothing doing
> Passages aint free,
> So any old place I can hand my Panama
> Is home, sweet home to me.
>
> There's not a song I haven't sung.
> From the I.T. to the Zulu

'Twas me that left my happy home
for you-oo-oo-oo-
But I aint a-going to weep no more
so good-bye Dolly Gray,
Just tell them that you saw me
And heard me sadly say—
I aint got no regular place
That I can call my home
Etc., Etc.

Owing to "the inclemency of the weather and the failure of crops" it will be folly for me to send you even a part of the priceless presents that I should, but am sure they would go down in mid-ocean. I will compromise, however by sending a "Good-Morning, Carrie,"[5] and wishing you a Happy Christmas and a cloudy Ground Hog Day.

As ever,
Will P. Rogers

PD. Printed in *CR*, 2 January 1903. Revised version printed in *CR*, 3 January 1903.

1. Ladysmith, a town on a tributary of the Tugela River in a farming region of northern Natal, was originally named Windsor when it was founded in 1861. It was renamed after the wife of Gov. Sir Harry Smith of the Cape. Located 115 miles northwest of Durban, it served as an important railhead for traffic to the Transvaal and the Orange Free State and as a center of trade for northern Natal. It was besieged by the Afrikaners during the first part of the South African War (October 1899–February 1900) and reoccupied by the British in 1900 (Pakenham, *Boer War; ESA*, 285; *WNGD*, 640).

2. Pretoria, the administrative capital of the Republic of South Africa and the capital of the Transvaal, is located on a tributary of the Limpopo River, some thirty-five miles north of Johannesburg. It was founded in 1855 by Marthinus W. Pretorius (1819–1901), the first president of the South African Republic (1857–60), and named after his father, the Voortrekker leader Andries Pretorius (1798–1853). It became the capital of the Boer confederation in 1860. The Afrikaner administration was forced to evacuate the capital in the second year of the South African War, and the British occupied the city under the command of Frederick Roberts (May 1900). The articles of peace that ended the war were signed in Pretoria at the end of May 1902. Pretoria became the seat of the Alfred Milner administration in 1905 and the administrative seat of the Union of South Africa in 1910. It was the home and burial place of S. J. Paulus (Paul) Kruger, president of the South African Republic from 1883 to 1902, and the location of the Voortrekker monument, a symbolic centerpiece of modern Afrikaner nationalism (*ESA*, 404; Harrison, *White Tribe of Africa*, 9–14; Pakenham, *Boer War*, 433, 551–53, 560–69; *WNGD*, 907).

3. The Transvaal, now the second-largest province in the Republic of South Africa, was formerly an independent state of the South African Republic (formed in 1856). Located in the northeast portion of South Africa, bordering on Portuguese East Africa (Mozambique) and Bechuanaland, the Transvaal was one of two Afrikaner (Boer) republics. Originally populated by Bantu peoples, there were few whites in the Transvaal region before 1835–36, when the Afrikaner Great Trek began. In 1867 the

discovery of diamonds near Pretoria made the area attractive to the British, who annexed the territory between 1877 and 1881.

After the Boer Rebellion of 1880–81 (also known as the First Anglo-Boer War or, by Afrikaners, the First War of Independence, or *Eerste Vryheidsoorlog*) the Transvaal was restored to independence under Afrikaner rule. The discovery of the Witwatersrand goldfields in 1886 brought great wealth to the republic, but also began a rush by *uitlanders* (foreigners) that threatened Afrikaners' dominance over the area. The Transvaal was the target of Jameson's Raid (1895–96), the precursor to the South African War. The Transvaal was the ally of the Orange Free State in that war against Britain. It was annexed as a British crown colony in 1900 and granted self-government in 1906. It became part of the Union (now Republic) of South Africa in 1910 (*ESA*, 534; Fisher, *Afrikaners;* Patterson, *Last Trek: A Study of the Boer People and the Afrikaner Nation; WNGD*, 1225).

4. Rogers brought home an edition of Laird and Lee's *Practical Spanish Instructor . . . A Common Sense System*, by F. M. Rivas (Chicago: Laird and Lee, 1898), a pocket guide. The inside of the book is enscribed "Santa Fe Land Company, San Christobal, Sante Fe Province, May 13, '02" (OkClaW).

5. "Good-Morning Carrie," written by Albert Von Tilzer and Cecil Mack (Robert McPherson, 1883–1944), was published in 1901. Mack, an occasional partner of Von Tilzer, was from Virginia. He wrote material for the vaudeville team of Bert Williams and George Walker (Kinkle, *Complete Encyclopedia of Popular Music and Jazz* 3:1358).

To Sallie McSpadden
17 November 1902
Durban, Natal, South Africa

Durban,
Natal
Nov 17. *1902*

View on the beach in Durban the place we landed from S. America when I was here before   This beach was full of wrecked ships & I think I told you that.[1]

APC, rc. OkClaW.

1. A severe storm stuck southern Africa in mid-August 1902 as Rogers was sailing to Durban aboard the *Kelvinside*. The *Buenos Aires Herald* reported that the storm had run ships aground in harbor at Cape Town and caused a British steamship to capsize. The vessels that were run aground included a British ship that had come from a port in Argentina (*BAH*, 19 August 1902).

From Maud Lane
24 November 1902
Chelsea, I.T.

Nov. 24—1902

Dear Willie

You dont know how blue your last letter made me feal   I had thought you if not then on your way home at least thinking of starting in time to reach home before Christmas and here came the letter that did not say when you would start for home   if you could just know how we all want to see you   Have you like some of the others signed contract to work for that man for five years, if not do please come home and if you have please see if he wont let you off. I think you know enough how to find work of some kind at home if you work at so many kinds of things there surely any one of them would make you a living here at home. We are all well and are all to eat this Thanksgiving dinner here with me   how we will miss you, I have Baked my fruit-cake and plum pudding salted pecans almons stuffed ten pounds of dates   how I do wish I could send you some of each. Willie some times I think that perhaps you havent money enough to bring you home   if that is the case please let me know and Cap and I will send you what you want. I saw Miss Kate C- last week in Claremore   she and her sister had gon down to attend a lecture given there by Ex govener Bob Taylor[1] of Tenn. Miss Kate looked so well in a white silk waist and the black silk collar you sent May, that was the first time I ever saw her.

Papa has not been up for some time. . . . I hear that Dick Parice is rushing Leila Morgan the young girl Cella Stapler is raising. I dont know who Dick Trent has. They say Spi is soon to take unto him self a companion she is a Oklmulgee girl[2]. . . .

Sallie and I are sending you a little Christmas greeting and do hope it will reach you safely. Do please come home   Just as soon as you can. We all send you just lots of love and am so very sorry we cant send you ▲ something ▲ more to advantage but we hope to see you very soon.

Lovingly
Maud

ALS, rc. OkClaW. Envelope hand-addressed to Mr. W. P. Rogers, Cape Town, South Africa, c/o American Consul. Forwarded to Pietermaritzburg, O.R.C. Stamped "unknown" and placed in Dead Letter Office under "R," letter no. 1524.

1. Robert Taylor (1850–1912), a popular governor of Tennessee, served three terms in office (1887–91, 1897–99). Taylor was the son of Methodist farmers who left Tennessee during the Civil War. Educated in Philadelphia, he moved to Washington, D.C., as a

young man when his father became the commissioner of Indian affairs in the Johnson administration. He returned to Tennessee to attend college, became a lawyer, and was elected as a Democrat to Congress in 1878. He was known for "his fiddling, joke-cracking and ludicrous antics" (Sobel and Raimo, eds., *Biographical Directory of the Governors of the U.S.* 4:1488–89). In 1886 his brother, Alfred A. Taylor, was nominated by the Republicans to run for governor. The Democrats replied by nominating Robert Taylor on their ticket, and the two brothers congenially conducted the gubernatorial campaign against one another. Robert Taylor was elected in 1887 and reelected for the following term. In 1907 he was elected to the U.S. Senate and returned to Washington, D.C. Taylor was popular on the lecture circuit. He spoke at the New Windsor Opera House in Claremore on 8 November 1902 to a sell-out crowd, giving a lecture entitled "The Fiddle and the Bow." The *Claremore Progress* reported that "Mrs. J. T. McSpadden and Mrs. C. L. Lane were down from Chelsea Saturday to attend the lecture" (*CP,* 15 November 1902; see also *CP,* 25 October, 1 November, and 8 November 1902).

2. Spi Trent married twice. He and his first wife had two daughters and a son. His second wife was Clarice L. Trent (Bill Hoge, "Oologah Oozings" column, *CP,* newsclipping, ca. 6 March 1960, OkClaW; see also Biographical Appendix entry, TRENT, Spi).

To Clement Vann Rogers
26 November 1902
Durban, Natal, South Africa

Durban. Natal.
South Africa.
Nov 26. 1902.

My Dear Father.

I will write you again and tell you how I am doing   I have only received one letter from you   that was when in Buenos Aires but I know that they have gone astray for you are so prompt about writing all the time

I have been at work all the time but quit and come in here to get a pass to go [to] another place (as you have to get a permit to go about in the country or on railway) and I lost all of my baggage   that is my saddle and outfit and in fact all but a little grip I had with it was lost or stolen off the train as they dont check things here and neither are they responsible for them   I have been hanging around here in hopes they would hear of them but I guess they were taken.

about the time you get this you should get a postal Money Order for 28 pounds in English Money   that is or should be in American $140.00 for my next insurance as I guess you had enough for the last out of what I was owed there I only send this now because I have it and I dont need any money now for I go to work for a man in a day or so. I think I will be there before it is time to pay that again but by sending it now we know that it will be provided for.

I have the job taking a bunch of mules to Ladysmith   that is 250 miles from here   I will have some of the Native Nigger boys to help me. they drive a world

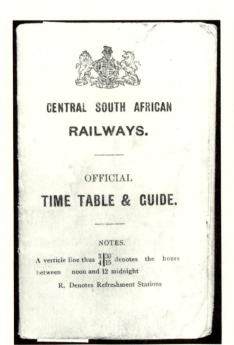

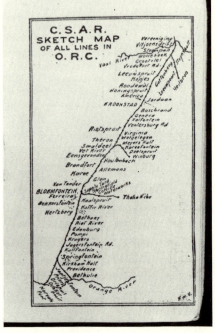

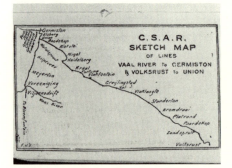

Among the possessions Rogers kept from his trip was a South Africa railway guide containing several maps of the country (*OkClaW*).

of stock from here as this is where it is landed from other places as they are trying to restock the country after the war. it costs to much to ship them and they only have to hire one white man and a lot of Niggers so it is much cheaper they often drive to Pretoria that is close to 1.000 miles cattle and horses both these little bit of South American Mules never sell under $125.00 to $200.00 apiece any kind of an old pony is worth that much too A good young all around horse will bring three or four hundred dollars and so do the big fine mules from home Oh cattle are up some there little cattle with a big hump on ther shoulder that all come from an Island a few hundred miles off the coast[1] they sell never less than $75.00 apiece and good cows as cows is what sells will bring $150.00 and $200.00 I have seen common old milk cows sell at auction for $350.00 apiece everything is high. Wages are fairly good you seldom do work for less than ~~2~~ 2 dollars a day that is for common but for a man that has a trade bricklayers carpenters and all them get 6 and 7 and never less than 5 a day but no one makes any money for you always board yourself out of that and ~~it are~~ ▲ they ▲ are falling for every ship brings from 5 hundred to a thousand and it is the job that is hard to get not the pay it is hard to get a job. oh it is a ruined country you should know what it was before the war. There is hundreds of men here without work.

Well I will close hoping to hear from you soon and if that [money order] dont turn up pretty soon write and I will see about it and have the receipt

from your loving son

Willie

address in care of consul at Capetown

Dont look for me for a couple or three months as I could do nothing by getting there in the Winter but expect to turn up about *April.*

Lots of love to all

Write me all the news and send me some of the papers as I got those you sent to B.A.

ALS, rc. OkClaW. Revised versions printed in *CR,* 9 January 1903, and *CP,* 10 January 1903.

1. A reference to Madagascar (the Malagasy Republic/Democratic Republic of Madagascar), an island in the Indian Ocean separated from southeastern Africa by the Mozambique Channel, populated by Malagasy peoples of Malayo-Indonesian and Afro-Arab ancestry. The Portuguese encountered the island in 1500, and French stations were established there in the seventeenth and eighteenth centuries, when the region became known for the activities of pirates. European control was effectively warded off until the 1860s. The Antenoro, Antesada, Betsileo, and Merina peoples were among the most important kingdoms before large concessions were granted to Europeans; by the end of the century the island was under French control. The Malagasy Republic (a member of the French Community) was established in 1958 and achieved independence

in 1960. The fourth-largest island in the world (excluding Australia), Madagascar is located some five hundred miles from the African coast. The island's most important products include coffee, rice, sugar, tobacco, and livestock (Brown, M., *Madagascar Rediscovered; WNGD*, 714).

To Clement Vann Rogers
15 December 1902
Potchefstroom, Transvaal, South Africa

After arriving in Ladysmith with the herd of mules he had helped drive from Durban, Will Rogers sought out the Wild West promoter Texas Jack at the showgrounds where his Wild West show was playing. Rogers demonstrated his skill with a rope, showing Texas Jack the Crinoline, a trick where a small loop is gradually enlarged as it circles until it makes a huge loop around the rope artist. After Texas Jack hired him, Rogers learned that he had a standing offer out to give a cash reward to anyone who could do the Crinoline. Rogers got a job roping, riding, and appearing as an actor in the Western sketches that made up part of Texas Jack's Wild West Show and Dramatic Company, which, like Buffalo Bill's Wild West show in the United States, combined the skills of the range and rodeo with circus, vaude-ville, and melodrama. After several years of experience performing before audiences in steer-roping contests, it was Rogers's first real introduction to show business. The company toured to several towns and cities in the South African provinces.[1]

Potchefstroom.[2] Dec. 15. [1902]

My Dear Father

I will write you and let you know how I am getting on and what I am doing.

Well since I last wrote you I left Durban with some horses that were shipped 6 hundred miles up this way and to the town where Texas Jacks Wild West Show was at and I went to him for work and as soon as I showed him what I could do with a rope he said he would take me so I am on the road with him now   he wants me to do roping in the ring but one of his riders that ride the pitching horses is laid off and I have rode a pitching horse every night since I have been with the show which is about 10 days   he also has a lot of Plays showing western life and I take the Indians part in some of them and some of them the Negro. I get $20 Twenty dollars a week and sleeping cars to sleep in but have to pay for my meals which are very dear at least 75 cents a meal   there is about 40 people with the show and about 30 horses.

We generally stay in a town two or three days and in the large ones longer   we have a crowded ~~house~~ ▲ Tent ▲ every night.

I like it fine and Jack himself is the finest old boy I ever saw and he seems to think a great deal of me[3]   he is a man about 40 years old and has traveled all

Rogers practices his roping in South Africa. In the two upper corners are cameos of
Rogers, which he hand labeled "Durban" *(Scrapbook 1902–4, CPpR).*

over the world showing   he is a much finer shot than Buffalo Bill and a fine
Rider and Roper   theres now about 7 or 8 Americans along

It isent a wild mob like them at home for he dont drink a drop or smoke or
gamble and likes for his men to be the same

I never did hear of all the things of mine   I lost my saddle and all and dont
suppose I ever will   I use his saddles and things. Did you ever get the Money I
sent to you   if you did not write me and I will have it looked up for I have the
receipt for it $140. in english Money for my next insurance.

Send this to the girls as I havent time to write them now   I hope you all had
a fine time Xmas   give my best to all the people and tell them I am doing
fine   write as usual to American Consul at Capetown

Lots of love to all

Your loving son
Willie.

ALS, rc. OkClaW. Revised versions printed in *CP,* 14 February 1903, and *CR,* 20 February 1903.

1. Some sources say Rogers joined Texas Jack's show in Ladysmith (see Ketchum,
Will Rogers, 81–84), others in Johannesburg (transcriptions of Rogers autobiographical

notes, OkClaW). Rogers recalled that his stage fright was so great the first night he appeared ("I was scared bleary eyed") that he fumbled badly in his attempts to do his rope tricks and "tangled myself up in the rope until they thought I was doing a Houdini. Why Jack took pity on me and come and drove me out. When he saw I was not going to be able to choke myself to death [with the rope] he came in and drove me out" (transcriptions of autobiographical notes, OkClaW). On Rogers's joining the show and the history of the show itself, see also Biographical Appendix entry, TEXAS JACK.

2. Potchefstroom, formed as a result of the Great Trek in 1838, was the first Afrikaner settlement in the Transvaal. Located in the southern Transvaal, some seventy-five miles southwest of Johannesburg, it became the capital of the Voortrekker community. Even after Pretoria became the new seat of government, Potchefstroom was referred to as the "Old Capital." It was located in the midst of a farming district and the largest cattle-raising region in the South Africa. The British besieged it in the Boer Rebellion (1880) and occupied it during the South African War (1900). Marthinus Pretorius, the first president of the South African Republic, died at Potchefstroom in May 1901. A British military camp was maintained there after the South African War. Since 1933 Potchefstroom has been a mining center (*ESA*, 401–2; *WNGD*, 976).

3. By all accounts Texas Jack was very fond of Will Rogers and treated him well. The respect was mutual, as Rogers felt that Texas Jack had a shrewd head for show business. Rogers had expected to ask for a job working with the show's horses and doing manual labor (helping to set up the tents, etc.) when the show traveled from town to town; instead, he ended up appearing in front of the audiences. He had his own roping act, rode bucking horses, and participated in a variety of roles in musical-variety and melodramatic numbers. He described Texas Jack as a "Regular Georgie Cohan" who "could do anything and always help anyone." He said Texas Jack got into a conversation with him when he approached him for a job and "found out I come from near where he did and he asked me if I couldent ride and rope so he got his old rope out and the fancy roping business was new to him and he fell for it and put me in that very night" (transcriptions of autobiographical notes, OkClaW). On the life of Texas Jack, see Biographical Appendix entry, TEXAS JACK.

To Sisters
28 December 1902
Standerton, Transvaal, South Africa

Will Rogers often credited Texas Jack with teaching him show business, including such performance tips as how to work an audience, when to end an act (always leave them wanting more), and how to develop his roping act for the stage. The impossibility of owning a ranch with little capital in Argentina, his difficulty finding employment as a wrangler or ranch hand, and his experience doing hard physical work with horses and stock in South Africa, all had altered Rogers's ideas of what he would try to do with his life. Rogers's new commitment to performance art is reflected in this letter home. Of Texas Jack and the show, he wrote, "I am going to learn things while I am with him that will enable me to make my living in the world without making it by day labor." Thus was born Will Rogers's new show-business identity as the "Cherokee Kid."[1]

FROM SOUTH AFRICA.

Standerton,[2] Transvaal,
December 28th, 1902.

My dear sisters and home folks: —

I will write and let you know how I am getting along. I am with Texas Jack's Wild West Shows yet. I have been with him almost a month and like it fine. We just got in here today and as this is Sunday we won't open up until tomorrow night and will be here about two weeks, as there are about five thousand troops here. We have showed at seven different towns since I have been with them. We stay two and three nights in a place. We have the best show in South Africa; about 23 horses and 35 people and only eight Americans with it. The play is partly a circus act and then they play blood curdling scenes of western life in America, showing encounters with Indians and robbers. I was an Indian but I screamed so loud that I like to scared all the people out of the tent. Then we have riders of bucking bronchos, roping and fancy shooting, and a little of every thing. I joined the show to do trick roping, but as our new tent without a center pole has not come yet, I have not commenced. I ride the bucking horses every night. I think I have a job as long as I want one. I never have got my saddle and clothes. I send you some of my little stamp pictures that I had taken a while back. I send papa $140 to pay September insurance, so I am all right for this year. I am getting $20 a week and sleeping quarters, but I have to buy my meals which are very dear. We had a real good time Christmas. They don't take on over Christmas and have trees and give presents here like they do at home. I went out to the Canadian soldiers camp and saw a base ball game. It is a sight out here, as America is the only country they play that game. I took supper and spent an enjoyable evening. I sung a lot of coon songs[3] and they thought the kid (as that is what Jack and the show men call me) was allright. I know you all had a fine time Christmas. It is certain that I will be with you next year, for Jack said he may sail for America from here. We will finish up this country about the last of July. We are supposed to finish up in Capetown where he started from, but he don't know for sure as he has India and Australia in mind.[4] I am going to learn things while I am with him that will enable me to make a living in the world without making it by day labor.

I have not got my mail from Capetown in three months. I will close with lots of love to all.

Your loving brother,
Will Rogers.

The " Cherokee Kid,"

FANCY LASSO ARTIST AND ROUGH RIDER,

Texas Jack's Wild West Show.

Will Rogers's The Cherokee Kid business card, from his scrapbook (3⅝ inches by 2⅜ inches) *(Scrapbook 1902–4, CPpR)*.

PD. Printed in *CP,* 21 February 1903. Revised version printed in *CR,* 27 February 1903.

1. As Rogers explained, "I thought to be a regular wild western[er] I had to have a name so I christened myself 'The Cherokee Kid' and had letterheads made" (transcriptions of autobiographical notes, OkClaW). He was billed as such on his business cards and on the playbills and programs for Texas Jack's show (see programs and business card, Texas Jack's Wild West Show, box 25, OkClaW). In choosing the name, Rogers combined the popular appeal of the two major players in Wild West performances — cowboys and Indians (much as Gordon William Lillie did in using "Pawnee Bill"). Wild West shows in the United States both exploited images of Native Americans and employed many actual Native Americans as part of their acts. Indian leaders such as Sitting Bull (who appeared with Buffalo Bill's Wild West in 1885) were reduced from their former grandeur to appearing as attractions in the shows that presented melodramatic and stereotyped visions of Indians and Indian life. Native Americans hired as extras (often playing warriors in battle scenes) were parodying the historical realities of their heritage (Deloria, "Indians"; Fiedler, "Legend"; Yellow Robe, "Menace of the Wild West Show").

2. Standerton is a town in the southeastern Transvaal some ninety miles from Johannesburg. Established on the Vaal River in the midst of a cattle-raising area in 1879, it was named after the owner of the first farm, Adriaan Stander. It was the scene of fighting during the Boer Rebellion (1880–81) and the South African War (1899–1902) and became a garrison town before World War I (*ESA,* 502; *WNGD,* 1151).

3. On coon songs as a genre of American popular music in this period, see Will Rogers to Sisters, 21 July 1902, nn. 5 and 6, above.

4. Texas Jack had toured through much of the British Empire and had been in Australia a few years before. He had family ties in Australia, including a daughter who lived there. Rogers later said, "I started in alphabetically and found Australia," regarding his move from South Africa later in 1903. The choice was not really so arbitrary. Texas Jack provided the young performer with contacts with the Wirth Brothers' Circus and other show-business people in Australia and New Zealand.

To Folks
28 January–6 March 1903
Harrismith, Orange Free State,
and Durban, Natal, South Africa

Harrismith[1]
Orange Free State[2]
South Africa
January. 28th. 1903

[Durban, South Africa
1 March — 6 March 1903]

My Dear Home Folks.

Well I will write you all again and let you know how I am getting on   I have not had any mail since the middle of October ▲ dated from home in August ▲ over three months ago but I guess I have a lot of mail at Capetown   I have written for it so hope to get it in the next town we stop in.

Well I am still with Texas Jacks Wild West and am getting on fine   I have been with them about two months now.

There is four of us that ride bucking horses and I do all the Roping now and it takes big   they all call me the *Kid* and that is what is ▲ I am ▲ on the Programe   The first time I come on to do my Roping act I was called back twice and they made a big to do over me   you see they dont use Ropes here to catch things and it is all a mystery to them to see it and I have learned to do quite a bit of fancy Roping that they think is wonderful   Then I play a nigger in a play that we put on some nights   do a cake walk[3] and sing a coon song.

I am going to Rope and tie down some steers in the next place in the ring.

Jack thinks I am all right   I dont have to do a thing all day only my work in the ring at night   I have had my wages raised to $25.*00* a week   I can save a little but it takes a good deal to buy food and clothes with in this country and you see I come to the show almost nacked after loosing all my things   I never did get a sign of a thing back   Saddle   bridle   clothes   blankets   tools   hat   and everything gone and after sending home that $140.00   When I went to the show I was broke to the world

I will only stick to this till I get money to go home which wont be long for I want to get there in the Spring.

Still this is as easy a job as you ever seen   go to the stables and order out one of the ponies and ride around   only have to be there when it is your time to go in the ring   you horse is saddled and at the entrance ready to go in   When you have finished go sit in the audience and watch the rest.

Left to right: Texas Jack, Mrs. Texas Jack, unidentified rider, and Will Rogers (*Scrapbook A1, OkClaW*).

We ▲ came ▲ here for two weeks and only have a couple of more nights then on to a big town where we will stop for probaly a month   you see we can put on so many different changes of programe that it makes a different show   but the Roping and Bucking horses are on every night

I will tell you how I missed making $250.00   Jack does a trick with a rope (the big whirl where he lets out all his rope around him) and he has been offering 50 pounds that is $250.00 for any one that could do it and he has been offering it for 5 years outside of America   Well I went down to the show one morning on getting into the town where it was and I seen him in the tent and asked him for a job   he asked me what I could do and I told him I could rope a bit so he sent for his rope and I got into the ring and the first thing I done was this trick which is common at home now.

Well I dident know anything of this 50 pounds he was offering so he give me a job and now he wont offer that and as I belong to the show I cant get it so it was my misfortune that I did not hear of it and then go to the show some night when he offered it and step down and do it   then I would of got the $250.00   oh but I was mad

Well I started this letter just one month ago as this is the 1st day of march   I kept putting off writing thinking of hearing from home   but I suppose the mail has been lost for I had it sent to me from Capetown to the last town and it never arrived   so I guess it is lost   the last letter I got from home was dated the latter part of August so you see that was about 7 months ago and I am getting in a hurry to hear   but no telling when I will.

When you dont hear from me dont worry for I am in good health and doing fine. Jack is talking of sending some one home for some fullbloods and a ~~cou~~ few more cowboys and to get a lot of Saddles and costumes and things and if he does he will send me   I dont know just when it will be   if it is at all   but at any rate it wont be long till I will see you all

We are showing in Durban ▲ now ▲ that is one of the biggest towns in South Africa   have been here one week and had packed houses every night   have just got a new and larger tent   we will be here two more weeks then we go to East London by boat   that is about 208 miles   then on down towards Capetown which we will reach in about 4 months from now

Children I am sitting out under the shade of the tent writing and all of the Monkeys and baboons are playing around me so I dont know what I am doing   they are all bigger than you Kids   some of them are five feet high when they stand on their hind legs   I have seen lots of wild ones out here   they are very common   these here ride horses and have races and pull each other off when one is passing another   I wish all you kids were here this evening for Matinee   we have the whole tent full of Kids on Saturday at Matinee for the children. On next Saturday afternoon We give a Medal to the little boy who can throw a rope the best so I am the Kids Ideal for they see me rope in the show and they follow me around to get me to show them so they can get the medal   You should be here Herb to show them. but you see these little boys never seen a lasso before   neither did their fathers   I like to rope at Matinee for it takes big with the Kids they applaud every throw till their hands are sore.

Oh I found my Saddle and bridle   Leggins and spurs[4] but could never hear if any of the other things   clothes and all that   it had been stolen and raffled off and I found it and love it now   oh but I was glad for it is so much better than any other one with the show

Well this is about a week later than the previous lines   it is now the 6th of March   We are still in Durban   will be here till the 16th   We have Tremendous crowds every night   I will send you some of the Programes   the one is Where I am on to ride the Bucking horses or Buck-jumping as it is called in this country is our opening programme in a town   then when they change I do the Roping instead of Jack as I do much more than him   you can see how I am billed up.

I havent time to write to all of you but send the letters and all to Papa and May for it is to all of you as I cant write to all as it would be the same   not a line of Mail and dont suppose I ever will get any   Well I will stop   lots of love to all I know   tell them all I am flourishing   living the life of a millionare but will see you before the 4th of July.

Papa dont let old Comanche be touched till I come home but do as you think best with the bay colt but dont let them take my buggy or harness   have him driven there in town but dont sell it him

There isent much use to write for I ▲ will ▲ never get it

Yours lovingly "The Kid"

Jack is crazy for Denney Lane and Booths brother[5] the one that rides and ropes   I have told him so much of their these people and would go crazy over them here   if I come home I will sho get them

ALS, rc. OkClaW. Envelope hand-addressed to Mrs. C. L. Lane, Chelsea, I.T., United States of America. Revised versions printed in *CR*, 17 April 1903, and *CP*, 18 April 1903.

1. Harrismith, a town in the northeastern Orange Free State, is located 153 miles northeast of Durban (Port Natal). It was founded in 1849 and named after Gov. Sir Harry Smith. Built at the base of Platberg Mountain at an altitude of some five thousand feet, the town became a strategic location during the South African War. It has developed into a trade center as well as a health resort (*ESA*, 220; *WNGD*, 489).

2. The Orange Free State, a province in the east-central Republic of South Africa, contains territory that was once the Orange River Republic. The Orange Free State is bounded on the southwest by Cape Province, on the southeast by Lesotho, on the east by Natal, and on the north by the Transvaal. A plateau, some four to five thousand feet above sea level, it is traversed by the Orange River and the Vaal River. There were few Europeans in the region before the Great Trek of 1836–38, when Afrikaner (Boer) settlers intruded upon the Zulus. The area was annexed by the British in 1848 and recognized as an independent Boer state in 1854. The Orange Free State was the ally of the Transvaal against the British in the South African War. It was reannexed by the British as the Orange River Colony at the end of May 1900, achieved self-government in 1907, and joined the Union of South Africa in 1910 (*ESA*, 374; *WNGD*, 896).

3. The cakewalk craze of the late 1800s was related to the popularity among whites of so-called coon songs and to the beginnings of white commercial exploitation of black ragtime music. The cakewalk as a popular dance craze began with Kerry Mills, who wrote "Rastus on Parade" in 1895 and "At a Georgia Camp Meeting" in 1897. Rogers and his young friends in Indian Territory had participated in the craze, holding cakewalk parties where favors were given to winning pairs of dancers. In the music-publishing industry as well as in the general public, the terms *ragtime* and *cakewalk* were interchanged in reference to sheet music written for the piano. The rhythm was like a march, in two-quarter time, with a top melody line played in syncopation. The stress falls between beats. Whereas pure, or "classical," ragtime began as the instrumental music of black composers and performers (notably, Scott Joplin), the term *ragtime* came

to be used in the early 1900s for an eclectic body of music that was produced or exploited by white composers and publishers and purchased by white consumers. Cakewalk music was often differentiated from other ragtime tunes by the satirical and discriminatory images of blacks conveyed in the lyrics and dance steps (Dennison, *Scandalize My Name*, 348, 350–54; Ewen, *All the Years of American Popular Music*, 119; Wenzel and Binkowski, *I Hear America Singing*, 51, 54, 57–58; for an illustration of African Americans performing a cakewalk, see Blassingame, *Black New Orleans, 1860–1880*, cover and 160–61; see also article in the *Claremore Progress*, 19 August 1899, above).

4. The railroad station in Durban finally located Rogers's prized saddle, but promptly auctioned it off as unclaimed baggage. Rogers was able to trace the man who brought it at auction. After hearing Rogers's story about the history of the saddle and its loss, the man kindly returned it to its rightful owner (Croy, *Our Will Rogers*, 80, 85).

5. Andrew Denny Lane was the youngest son of Dr. Andrew J. Lane and Lucinda Journeycake Lane. His oldest brother was Will Rogers's friend Tom Lane. Denny Lane married Odeyne Henry. Booth McSpadden had three brothers: Forrest (b. 1886), Theodore (b. 1887), and Oscar Lyle (b. 1892). Rogers is probably referring to either Forrest or Theodore. Forrest, like Lane, was a very good rider and roper. He was killed in 1904 in an accident when his horse fell on him while he was roping a steer. Theodore appeared with Rogers in Rogers's first stage trick-roping act in 1904 in St. Louis. Oscar became a rancher (*CR*, 7 October, 14 October, and 21 October 1904; *HRC*, 274–75, 299–300, 303–4; Ketchum, *Will Rogers*, 91, 93; *Statesman*, [Foyil, Okla.], 4 July 1908).

From Clement Vann Rogers
9 February 1903
Claremore, I.T.

In this letter Clem V. Rogers informs his son that he has participated in the Cherokee enrollment on his own and Will's behalf and will be taking land allotments in each of their names (he did so in August 1903). Portions of the old home ranch were to be subdivided between Clem V. Rogers and Will Rogers. A few hundred additional acres of the original ranch land were allotted to acquaintances with the understanding that Clem V. Rogers would then be able to buy or rent back the land.

Claremore, Ind. Ter., <u>Feb 9th</u>, *1903*

South Africa

Dear Willie

Your letter of Dec 15th come to me a few days ago & found us all well   All of our People are well & have been since you left. Chelsea People are doing all right. Stine & May are now living at Oolagah. They quit the Hotel at Ta.la.la. Stine is running a butcher Shop[1]   Yocum & Uncle Jim Cleveland quit my place & one is west of Ta la la & the other is on the Nat Skinner[2] Farm   John ~~Adair~~ Lipe[3] have got your Poneys at Ta la la taking care of them. He is sure taking care of them.

I have 2 Arkansaw Boys on my Home place. but I dont think they are much account. I keep old Minnie here at Claremore. she dont look well. she is getting to old to eat corn. Spi is still at oKmulgee & doing well   Dick Parris is at Tahlequah & wrote to me to send him a Dimon stud Pin that you had of his.[4] I did not send it, but put his letter with your things & you & him settle it on your return. Dick stays at Tahlequah. Clem Musgrove & Dick Steward are going to oKlahoma City to a big Roping contest in the morning   Jim Rider have been sick & stayed a long time at Hot Springs   Clem Mcspadden is now in Tennessee going to School. Little Charley McClellan died in Tennessee where he was going to School just before Christmas They brought him Home & Buried him here at Claremore Cemetary.[5]

Bunt Schrimsher is married to a man by the name of Robbinson   Earnest Schrimsher & Miss Phillips is married   Tom Cuningham & Miss Scott is married. Henry Starr is now at Home. old Uncle Tom Lane is very low here in Town. He wont live but a few days.

Tom Lane, Casper Lipe, & Frank Musgrove,[6] are all at Kansas City going to School. Gordon is running the Farm.

People commence to take their Allotments on the first of January. I havent taken mine yet. I got my & your no. They are about 3434 & 5   Willie if you dont come home this Fall you will have to send me a Power of Attorney to take your Allotment for you.[7] Every Person of age will have to take his own allotment, or give some one a Power of Attorney to take it for him. Me, you, & Spi will take the old Home place. I got the money you sent me   it were $135 82/100. I paid your insurance on your accident Policy you takin out at Talala before you went off. It were $13.00 for this year. your big Policy is not due until next September. Plenty more to pay it off here   I guess I have got every letter you wrote to me. & the Girls have got several. I publish yours in the Claremore Progress. Sallie & Maude wrote to you sometime ago & sent you some money. They banked it to Cape town care of American Consul. This only makes the 3th letter that I have wrote to you & only sent you Papers once. This winter havent been cold but has been awful wet, Rained all winter.

Sallie Maude & me will go to New Orleans in May to the big Confederate reunion.[8] The Ellis Girls says you must write to them. Every Body sends you Love for them & write to me when you can. your Pa

C.V. Rogers.

ALS, rc. OkClaW. On C. V. Rogers, Bank Building letterhead. Envelope typewritten to W. P. Rogers, American Consul, Cape Town, South Africa. Forwarded c/o Texas Jack's Wild West Show, East London, C.C.

1. Frank Stine had been running a butcher shop since at least December 1902, if not earlier. He and May Rogers Yocum Stine lived at Oologah, and he made frequent trips into Claremore on business (*CP*, 27 December 1902).

2. Nathaniel (Nat) Skinner (b. 1851), a Vinita-area rancher, was probably related to Jim Cleveland, one of the tenants at the Rogers ranch during the first year of Will Rogers's travels. Nat Skinner's mother's maiden name was Cleveland. He was born in Harrison County, Ky., and was educated in public schools in Kentucky and Missouri. He began his successful stock ranch in 1878 and became a major cattle broker in the Cherokee Nation. In 1879 he married Nannie Kell (1861–89) (perhaps some relation to Rogers's friend Jim Kell), who was half Cherokee and known as a "beautiful and accomplished woman" (O'Bierne, *Indian Territory*, 272). She was active as an officer in the Methodist Episcopal Church South Home Missionary Society. The Skinners had three sons: Louis, John, and Ray. Nannie Kell Skinner passed away on her twenty-eighth birthday in January 1889. The Skinner ranch grew into a huge enterprise, with seven hundred acres under cultivation and many thousands of head of cattle. Skinner also invested in the town of Vinita. He owned several pieces of real estate in the town and a large mercantile house called Skinner and Radcliffe. Nathaniel Skinner and Nannie Kell Skinner may have been related to Rogers's friend Heber Skinner, who, like Jim Kell, was a childhood friend and roping-contest buddy of Rogers's and became a Vinita-area rancher (O'Bierne, *Indian Territory*, 271–73, *OCF* 1:224; see also article from the *Indian Chieftain*, 2 August 1900, n. 4, above).

3. John Gunter (Johnny) Lipe (1864–1913) was the son of Clem V. Rogers's friend DeWitt Clinton Lipe and his first wife, Victoria Susan Hicks Lipe (d. 1867) (the niece of Principal Chief John Ross). John Gunter Lipe attended the Cherokee Male Seminary and the University of Arkansas at Fayetteville. He owned a large ranch at Talala and was married to Sarah (Lulu) Foreman (b. 1875) in 1899. He was the half brother of Nannie (b. 1872), Victoria (b. 1874), and Lola (b. 1877) Lipe, who, along with the Foreman girls, were part of Rogers's circle of friends (*HRC*, 281; Mihesuah, *Cultivating the Rosebuds*, 124, 127; *OCF* 1:158).

4. The whereabouts of the diamond stud pin had been the subject of earlier inquiry on Will Rogers's part when he wrote his father from Argentina; he and Dick Parris may have come to some agreement as to the disposition of the pin.

5. The death of Will Rogers's close childhood friend must have come as a shock to Rogers. Charles McClellan was twenty-three years old when he died of typhoid fever while at Cumberland College in Lebanon, Tenn. He was a junior at the college and president-elect of the local YMCA. His parents had been notified by telegram earlier in the month that their son was "dangerously ill," and they had left immediately for Tennessee. He died on 19 December 1902. He was buried with services in Claremore, and a notice of his death appeared in the *Claremore Progress* on 20 December, and an obituary on 27 December 1902. Will Rogers's friends Nannie Lipe and Ida Mae Collins wrote a tribute to McClellan on behalf of the Pocahontas Club. It was printed in the *Progress* on 1 January 1903 (see also *IC*, 25 December 1902, and Biographical Appendix entry, MCCLELLAN, Charles White).

6. Frank K. Musgrove (b. 1885) was the brother of Will Rogers's friends and cousins Clem Rogers (Clem) Musgrove and William (Will or Bill) Musgrove. He "died while still a young man" (*HRC*, 334). His father, Francis Marion Musgrove, was Clem V. Rogers's half brother (*OCF* 1:257; *WRFT,* 85). Frank Musgrove may have attended the same business college that Tom Lane went to in Kansas City.

7. Clem V. Rogers's roll number for enrollment and allotment was 11383; Will Rogers's number was 11384. Rogers sent his father a power of attorney from Port Elizabeth, Cape Colony, South Africa, in May 1903 (see Enclosure: Power of Attorney, 19 May 1903, enclosure to Will Rogers to Clement Vann Rogers, 21 May 1903, below). On 17 August 1903, Clem V. Rogers took out allotments in his and his son's names,

including sections of the old Rogers homestead. Martin (Spi) Trent, Jesse (Fred) Ross (a freedman), Rosa Wood Patterson, Jane S. Hicks, Perry Ross, Mariah Ross, and Gus Lowery also took out allotments of land that were originally part of the Rogers ranch. Clem V. Rogers bought back land from these individuals in the next few years (records of allotment, box 7, OkClaW; Collings, *Old Home Ranch*, 135; see also Testimony of Clement Vann Rogers on Behalf of William P. Rogers, 17 August 1903, and Certificates of Land Allotment, 17 August 1903, below).

8. Clem V. Rogers joined Tom and Sallie McSpadden and Cap and Maud Lane and several other Chelsea couples on an excursion to the Confederate veterans reunion in New Orleans in May 1903. They returned to the Cooweescoowee District at the end of the month (*CR*, 29 May 1903).

From Kate Ellis
15 February 1903
Oolagah, I. T.

Kate Ellis[1] and her sister Lillie (Lil) were close friends of Will Rogers. They lived in town in Oolagah, where their father, Jake Ellis, operated the Oolagah Hotel. Rogers was a regular visitor at their home. Although she was the go-between who formally introduced Rogers to the young Betty Blake at a party at the Ellis household in 1899, Kate Ellis and Will Rogers had been courting at the time, and in 1903 she was still widely assumed to be Will's "girl." Here she sends Will news of their mutual friends.

Sunday February fifteenth
1903. —
Oolagah
I. T.

My dear Will—

Just about this time one year ago since you left home and friends to see the world, and as you say, I guess the world doesn't look half as big to you as to some people—.

Your letter written Nov 28 and Jan 4— reached me only yesterday—Feb. 14—Valentines Day— quite a nice valentine wasn't it.

It found me still living in Oologah and signing myself Kate Ellis— spinster—tho' many times I've vowed I'd not live longer in single blessed-ness— but soon get over it—when I look at some married people—

We are not living at the hotel now— papa bought a right snug little nest here— I am teaching public school— Lillie is still Lillie[2] and helps me about 3 hrs a day.

There have been more changes than I can possibly mention, but will state ofen facts which will help you to while away the time, something to think of those long days—when you have nothing to do—

Will begin with Oologah— Bill Smith, first master married Annie Vineyard and they are now happy as can be— Mrs Clark, his sister married Jim Lowery—lives near Claremore and all kinds of other people here indulged in the matrimonial lottery— but dont know whether you know this or not— You must have had something in your eyes when you left home— if you really meant what you "observed" ~~aub~~ about my taking unto myself a husband in the form of The Right Honorable Casper[3]— You were only joking—of course—if you hadnt been you never would have written to me. . . .

Yes Spi is doing fine so your father says—he's assistant bookkeeper for some Mercantile Co. in Okmulgee. It was reported that he was to be married but guess Spi is like his cousin Willie in that respect and Dick— I know nothing of him the dear boy— only that he is still in his uncles drug store at Tahlequah— Tom[4] clerks in some store there too. Tahlequah is flourishing. Now has a R.R—and people say it is getting to be quite a little city— Perhaps I shall attend the Normal[5] there this summer. . . .

Sos McClellan[6] is not married either— there are some new girls in Claremore since you left the Misses Baker— I think Sol and Clem,[7] in fact all of Claremore's swells go down on their knees to them. Guess you would, too if you were here—if I'd let you—??? I know you're wishing I'd tell you about Ada[8]— or do you hear from her sometimes— she is teaching in Talala   I never see her—or havent for a long time but she was as beautiful and charming as ever when I did see her—

Old uncle Cleveland doesn't live on your place anymore— I think Johnny Lipe has your horses— Mr. Stine said they were looking as slick as a button the other day—

Mr. and Mrs Stine live right across the street from us—and they have the dearest little baby girl—just three days old— Jake says it looks like a baboon, but he loves it all the same. . . .[9]

Will— I havent said yet how glad I was to get your letter, nor can I—hard luck, good luck, *no beans*, beans, or anything couldn't make you anything but *Will*. Parts of your letter was so extremely ridiculous that I ~~nearly~~ alarmed the family with my spasmodic laughing— it reminded me of a letter you wrote me once from Hot Springs—at first I tho't probably you had turned Quaker— from your *thees* and *thines*— suppose you had just had an unusually good *feast* of some sort and were full of a spirit of devotion—

Tell Texas Jack *Hello* for me, and to make you be good—I hope he'll fire you before he goes much further—

Should you be so changed *I* wouldnt know you when you present yourself for your *handout*, in some manner let me know—*who thou art*—and you'll get two *hands out*.

It just seems like I'm writing to some one so far away— that it is impossible for you to ever get this— and more than likely you never will— that I'm going to quit and hope if you dont come home—it will reach you some how & some where— All send their love—and I say—"Oh Bill Bailey wont you come home."[10]

> Lovingly Your
>
> L. Kate

P.S. I forgot to mention the picture much as I have looked at it— are your *jams* really that fat— I'd just like to see— send me a *life size*— that one just fits my locket— suppose it will be preserved there for "future ref[erence]"

> by-by-
>
> Kate.

ALS, rc. OkClaW. Envelope hand-addressed to M. Willie P. Rogers, Capetown, South Africa, c/o American Consul. Forwarded to Texas Jack's Wild West Show, East London.

1. See Biographical Appendix entry, ELLIS, Kate.
2. The following summer Will Rogers's sister Maud wrote to him that "Lill Ellis has gotten into some trouble with Casper Lipe and that has most broken her mother's heart. Miss Kate has been teaching [at] the Oologah school and I think makes a fine teacher" (Maud Lane to Will Rogers, 12 July 1903, OkClaW).
3. Casper Lipe.
4. References to Spi Trent, Dick Parris, and Tom Lane.
5. As a result of reports on the inadequate preparation of Cherokee Nation teachers, the Nation's school board initiated summer normal school sessions for teachers. The Female Seminary was chosen as the site for the institute beginning in June 1899. The teachers had to take a required course called "Theory and Practice of Teaching." New teachers had to pass competency examinations. One hundred and fifty-four students were enrolled in the 1901 summer normal school (Mihesuah, *Cultivating the Rosebuds*, 65).
6. John Foreman (Sos) McClellan (b. 1872) was the older brother of Charles White McClellan. His Cherokee name was Wah-Shah-See, which was shortened to Shaw-See when he was a baby, and finally to Sos. He accumulated a great deal of land after allotment and raised horses and cattle. He ran the regional cattle-dipping vats for the Missouri Pacific Railroad and was officer of the Farmers Bank and Trust Co. He married Ethel Vivian Dennison, and they had two daughters and a son (*HRC*, 289–90).
7. Clem McSpadden or Clem Musgrove.
8. Ada Foreman.
9. Frank and May Rogers Yocum Stine had been living on a farm on the outskirts of Oolagah or in town off and on from the time of their marriage and their management of the Talala Hotel until they began their soda-fountain and butcher-shop businesses. Their new baby daughter Mattie Lane (Lanie) Stine (1903–78) was May Stine's sixth child. Jacob Edward (Jake) Stine, the baby's brother, was the Stine's three-year-old son (*WRFT*, 28; see also Biographical Appendix entries for MITCHELL, Mattie Lane Stine, and STINE, Jacob Edward).
10. "Bill Bailey Won't You Please Come Home" was written by Hughie Cannon and published as sheet music in 1902. The song became one of the most famous of the early ragtime compositions, which brought an increasing use of syncopation into popular

song. Bill Bailey was a black vaudevillian, and Cannon, himself a song-and-dance man, was a friend of his. The song was supposedly inspired one night when Bailey's wife locked Bailey out of their apartment because of his late-night partying with friends. The song was introduced on the minstrel circuit by John Queen in Newburgh, N.Y., and was eventually recorded by a number of star singers, including Ella Fitzgerald, Della Reese, and Jimmy Durante. Historian Sam Dennisen has pointed out that the original lyrics of "Bill Bailey" describe a woman who experiences domestic violence ("She married a B. and O. brakeman/Dat took and throw'd her down") and who passively accepts responsibility for her brutalization, only wishing her man would return home ("I know I'se to blame; well, ain't dat a shame?"). Dennisen categorizes "Bill Bailey" as a "bully song" that perpetuates white stereotypes of black men as violent and overly sexual and of black women as victims (Dennisen, *Scandalize My Name*, 372–73; Ewen, *All the Years of American Popular Music*, 169; Kinkle, *Complete Encyclopedia of Popular Music and Jazz* 1:11).

From Denny Lane
21 February 1903
Claremore, I. T.

Claremore, I. T.
Feb 21—1903.

Mr W. P. Rogers Esq.

My Dear Old boy—

If you ever get this letter you will be surprised to hear from me.

I read a long letter in the Progress from you to day. I saw Cousin Maud and Mrs McSpadden just a few day ago.

Willie every body is getting married   Old Scrim got married to Miss Philip's[1]   All these girls are getting put near grown. Mary Bullette and Alice Walkley and Byna Murphy. and the rest of them. You had better come home and pick out and step off. Every body would be glad to see you. I wish I was with you to ride some of those bronks and hoop right keen and tell them I was a wolf.

There was a roping contest at Oklahoma City about two weeks ago   Keys and Mus and Stewart went down and Clem[2] got third money. There has been several deaths since you have been gone   Little Charlie McClellen has died. Uncle Tom[3] has died. You wouldnt hardly know Claremore, it has grown so. You tell Jack that I am a wolf[4] and dont care who knows it. Willie I wish you would come home   I would give any thing to see you.

I will close with lots of love.

Your Friend
Denny Lane

Answer soon.

ALS, rc. OkClaW. Envelope hand-addressed to Mr. W. P. Rogers, Cape Town, South Africa, [c/o] American Consul. Forwarded c/o Texas Jack's Wild West Show, Port Elizabeth. Return address: "If not called for in 10 days return to Denny Lane, Claremore, I.T., U.S.A." Postmarked Claremore, 22 February 1903, and Capetown, 18 May 1903.

1. Ernest Schrimsher and Susan (Susie) Phillips Schrimsher.
2. Jim or E. B. Keys, Bill (Will) Musgrove, and Clem Musgrove.
3. Uncle Tom Lane's funeral was held in Claremore on 17 February 1903. Maud and Cap Lane and Sallie and J. T. McSpadden came down from Chelsea for the services (*CP,* 21 February 1903; *DC,* 19 February 1903).
4. A reference to Will Rogers talking with Texas Jack about Denny Lane's skills for the Wild West show. Rogers worried about being an impressive enough "wolf" himself when he first started with the show; he thought before "a fellow could go roping in the show [he] had to be a curley wolf and do all sorts of coureous [curious] things" that people have "all heard of but nobody has ever seen" (transcriptions of autobiographical notes, OkClaW).

From James H. Rider
26 February 1903
Talala, I.T.

Talala, I.T.
2—26—03

Mr Wm P Rogers
Capetown
South Africa
c/o American Consul
Friend Will: —

I received your letter about the 20th of Dec. but you told me not to write until you wrote again.

I sho would like to see you. I saw your father Some two weeks ago and he was showing me some pictures you had sent him   also a picture of your self. You must be getting lots to eat you are looking fine. It is raining here now and has been all winter   mud is ass deep to a camel in most places. We have had the worst spell of weather on cattle that we have had for about four years. Aud and Johnnie[1] have both got the blues. And old Dug is wintering his cattle principally on scenery and the scenery isnt the best in the country.

I tried to die all fall. I taken down with the rheumatism at Chelsea while I was on a round up. and they took me from there to Vinita. . . .

Your father wanted me to take Comanche and keep him for you until you come back. he said at that time he was looking for you home by April   I told him I didn't like to take the horse as he might get crippled or get an eye put out and I never would feel right over it. So I came on up to Talala   I hardly been home for over two months. I seen Clem and Bill Musgrove and they said them woolies were chasing hell out of your horse and they would turn him out on the range with McClellans old mares. Johnnie and the rest of them told me the same so I told your father I would take him not that I wanted to get any service out of him but taken him to keep them buttons off of him.

When I left for the Springs I left old Montie with Johnnie. So I told him when I came back he could keep either of the horses. Comanche or Montie as I knew he would care for him as good as I could or better as he has lots of oats and he decided to keep Comanche and he has sho got him fat. he looked awful bad and his hair was dead but he is looking good and feels fine.

They had a big time at Oaklahoma City the 10, 11, and 12 of this month. Of course they had a contest with the cat gut. Hop got 1st in 58 sharp   Jim 2d in one minut and some thing and Clem[2] got 3rd. . . . I guess you heard about Clem getting beat out of Robbin. They all went to St. Louis last fall to a contest and the boys all came home but the man that was to come back with the horses. When the horse came in old Robbin dident come back   Clem claims Mullhall kept him out on him but I think Mulhall must have bought the horse. As Clem wont talk much about him   There was seven rode him at Oaklahoma City. Clem says he is poor and has got his mane and tail chewed off. Clem rode him second and he come in bleeding at the nose. Some one asked Clem why he dident make Mulhall pay for the horse at Oaklahoma City. Clem said Mulhall offered him a draft for $250.00 But he wouldent take it.[3] That sounds funny. I saw Keys[4] here a while back. he is as big as mule. I think he is killing lots of booze from what I can hear. Miss Ada is as sweet as ever. Miss Vick is going to school at the Seminary. Miss Ada[5] is teaching school at Talala   I tried to get to go to school but they said I was much too large. Your girl Miss Ray[6] is attending school at Mexico Mo   she will be living out here on Caney[7] next summer so you had better come home and throw in with us. I havent saw your Ellis[8] girl but once and was at Talala the 4th of July.

Inclosed you will find a programme of what they are to have at El Paso, Tex. I havent got any cattle now. I dont know just what Ill do or where I will go yet. but when you write Mail my letter to Talala and if I am gone they will forward it to me   Well old pal I will close for this time   Hoping this will find you having a good time and enjoying good health as ever

Your friend
James H Rider
"Adios"

ALS, rc. OkClaW. Envelope hand-addressed to Mr. Wm. P. Rogers, Capetown, South Africa, c/o American Consul. Forwarded c/o Texas Jack's Wild West Show, Port Elizabeth. Return address, Box 54, Talala, Ind. Terr.

1. Probably references to Jim Rider's brothers, Austin Rider (b. 1871) and John Rider (b. 1874), although the other references to "Johnnie" that come later in the letter are to Will Rogers and Jim Rider's friend Johnny Lipe, who was watching Will Rogers's horses for him (Eastern Cherokee Application [Miller Roll #3756] of James H. Rider, 26 November 1906, OkTahN).

2. References to Jim Hopkins, Jim Keys or Jim Kell, and Clem Musgrove or Clem McSpadden. Rogers had gone to Oklahoma City to compete before he left on his travels (see article in the *Claremore Courier,* 15 June 1900, above).

3. This controversy over Rogers's horse Robin may have caused difficulty in Rogers's relationship with Zack Mulhall. Rider is probably referring to Clem Musgrove; however, he could also be referring to Will Rogers's nephew Clem McSpadden, who also sometimes participated in roping contests (see Biographical Appendix entry, MUL-HALL, Colonel Zack).

4. Jim or E. B. Keys.

5. Ada Foreman and her sister Victoria Lipe Foreman were both a few years younger than Will Rogers. Vic Foreman is listed among the graduates of the Cherokee Female Seminary in June 1903. Though Ada and Victoria's mother, Ada McClellan Foreman (Will Rogers's friend Charley McClellan's aunt), was widowed in 1891 with six surviving children, she was dedicated to seeing that they each received a good education. Both Ada and Vic Foreman attended Central College in Lexington, Mo. Will Rogers and Jim Rider's friend Johnny Lipe married Ada and Vic Foreman's older sister, Sarah (Lulu), in 1899 (*HRC*, 194–95, 281; Mihesuah, *Cultivating the Rosebuds*, 129; Starr, *History of the Cherokee Indians*, 237; see also Sallie Rogers McSpadden to Will Rogers, 25 April 1903, below).

6. Possibly a reference to Ada Gray, one of Will Rogers's girlfriends (see Ada Gray to Will Rogers, 8 July 1903, below).

7. A reference to the Caney River, which along with the Verdigris River, was one of the main tributaries in the Cooweescoowee District. The Caney River flowed near the western border of the district past Bartlesville, Sequoyah, and Ringo. Oolagah was located north of the fork of the Caney and the Verdigris, and Claremore was to the southeast. After meeting with the Verdigris, the Caney River continued to flow roughly parallel to the Kansas and Arkansas Valley Railway to the Arkansas River (Wardell, *Political History of the Cherokee Nation,* map of the Cherokee Nation, 274f.).

8. Kate Ellis.

To Sisters and Folks
17 March 1903
East London, Cape Colony, South Africa

LETTER FROM WILL ROGERS

Kings Hotel, East London, March 17, 1903.

My Dear Sisters and Home Folks: —

I wrote you only a few days ago, but will write you a short letter from here.

We were twenty-four hours coming from Durban by boat; then another twenty-four hours before we could land. With me it was the same old story — sick from start to finish. We open up here tonight. This is a very pretty place of

30 or 40 thousand inhabitants. We will be here about ten days then back inland. You see there are a great many towns in this country.

Jack is enlarging his show all the time and is making plenty of money. He carries a splendid band. I am getting on fine but expect to leave them when we reach Cape Town, which will be in three or four months. Then, I am off for home for I "sho want to see you all, good and plenty about now."

Sis, I don't like to impose on good nature, but I do want you to send me a lot of coon songs, and mix in a goodly number of sentimental songs with them for after making my debut as "The Champion Lasso Thrower of the World," I sing in a concert and as it is impossible to get the new songs over here you will all have to send them to me from there. New or old, they are all new over, here and all "take fine," so send a lot and send them at once.

Well, Good-Bye, hope you are all doing well. Give my love to all my friends and lots for yourself.

> Your Loving Brother,
> Will P. Rogers.

PD. Printed in *CR*, 24 April 1903. Revised version printed in *CP*, 25 April 1903.

To Clement Vann Rogers
22 March 1903
East London, Cape Colony, South Africa

Will Rogers sent his father a program for Texas Jack's Wild West Show in East London. The program advertised Will Rogers as the Cherokee Kid, "the marvelous lasso thrower" and "one of the leading characters in 'Texas Jack's Triumph,' a thrilling circus play."[1]

> East London
> March 22. 1903.

My Dear Papa

I will write you this short letter   I just wrote to you all a few days ago and will write you a longer letter in a day or so   this is to ask you to send me some Rope   I want about 100 feet of the best kind of hard twist rope   you can get it there   any of the boys will show you what I used to use   pretty small but hard twist   I cant get a thing here that we use some nights I rope with old tie ropes or any old things

Please send this at once   send it so it will come the quickest safest and surest way.

no matter the cost.[2]

I'm getting blooded aint I. Did you get the Money I sent home to you $140.00   I am getting along fine and will be home as soon as I make money enough which will be in a few months

Now papa please send this at once to me in care of the American Consul in Captetown   we will be there about the time that will get there for there is a big exibition on there then and I will have the rope to work with there   then I think I will go home and maby the show to.

Lots of love to all the folks and best regards to the friends.

your loving son Willie

[*P.S. at the top of first page:*] I havent had a letter from home yet. the last one was from Maud dated August 27. just seven months ago. but hope you are all as well as me.

[*P.S. at the top of last page:*] I wrote to Sallie for some Coon songs   if she dident get the letter tell her to send me a whole lot please

ALS, rc. OkClaW. Revised version printed in *CP,* 25 April 1903.

1. *CP,* 25 April 1903.
2. The *Indian Chieftan* reported that Lee Barrett mailed three lariat ropes to Rogers in South Africa in early May 1903. The paper erroneously reported that Will was "in the cattle business in the Transvaal" (*IC,* 7 May 1903). Mr. Barrett was the owner of a harness and saddle shop at Vinita, I.T. Clem V. Rogers paid $1.50 for the one hundred feet of rope and $6.15 for the postage, making it, as the *Claremore Messenger* put it, "rather an expensive piece of rope" (*CM,* 15 May 1903; see also *Story of Craig County,* 100, 603).

From Texas Jack
25 April 1903
Aliwal North, Cape Colony, South Africa

Will Rogers was already thinking of leaving Texas Jack's show in the first months of 1903; he signed on for part of a second tour for the next season before leaving South Africa for Australia and New Zealand in August. Here Texas Jack expresses his good opinion of Rogers. Rogers apparently used this letter of recommendation when he approached the Wirth Brothers' Circus for a job. Texas Jack knew the Wirth Brothers from previous tours of the Texas Jack Wild West Show and Dramatic Company in Australia.[1]

Aliwal North C.C.,[2]
25 Apl. 1903

I have very great pleasure in recommending Mr. W. P. Rogers. ("The Cherokee Kid") to circus proprietors. He has performed with me during my present South African Trip and I consider him to be the Champion Trick Roughrider and Lasso Thrower of the World. He is sober, industrious, hard-

TEXAS JACK'S WILD WEST SHOW
AND DRAMATIC COMPANY.

Aliwal North C.C.
25 Apl. 1903.

I have very great pleasure in recommending Mr W. P. Rogers ("The Cherokee Kid") to circus proprietors. He has performed with me during my present South African Tour and I consider him to be the Champion Trick Roughrider and Lasso thrower of the World. He is sober, industrious, hard-working at all times and is always to be relied on. I shall be very pleased to give him an engagement at any time should he wish to return.

(Signed)

Texas Jack

Letter of recommendation for Will Rogers written by Texas Jack (OkClaW).

working at all times and is always to be relied on. I shall be very pleased to give him an engagement at any time should he wish to return.

(Signed)
Texas Jack.

ALS, rc. OkClaW. On Texas Jack's Wild West Show and Dramatic Company letterhead, featuring a photograph of Texas Jack captioned "On Tour Round the World."

1. As Rogers put it, "Then I got Australia in my nut so Jack gave me a letter to the Worth [Wirth] Bros" (transcription of autobiographical notes, OkClaW).
2. Aliwal North was a Cape frontier town that became a transportation center and health resort in the midst of a farming district. Founded in the 1840s by the British, the town originated as a district headquarters that the British magistrate located at the site of Pieter Jacobus de Wet's farm, Buffelsvlei, near a strategic ford below the confluence of the Orange River and Kraai River that the Boers called Flotfontein. De Wet's farm had two large thermal mineral springs that people visited for treatment of rheumatism, arthritis, and similar painful ailments. Aliwal North became a municipality in 1882 and experienced a commercial boom in 1885, when it became the railhead of the railroad line from East London. As time passed, the town became a junction on the railway from Bloemfontein to East London and thus lost its trade advantage as a railhead, but it continued to develop as a resort known for its hotels, hot-spring spas, lawns, and gardens. The town was occupied by Afrikaner forces under Gen. J. H. Olivier during the South African War. Texas Jack's show no doubt was one of several touring entertainments that contributed to the town's tourist industry (Bulpin, *Discovering Southern Africa*, 374–75; Chantelle Wyley, History Subject Librarian, University of Natal, University Libraries, Durban, to WRPP, 28 August 1992; *SESA* 1:304–5).

From Sallie McSpadden
25 April 1903
Chelsea, I.T.

Chelsea Indian Ter. U.S.A.
April 25. 1903.

My Dear, Dear Brother:—

I'll begin my letter by telling you we are all well and I think we get every letter or card that you ever write. We are so sorry that no home mail ever reaches you. Papa has been sick occasionally this winter and Tom[1] was in bed for three weeks. but Papa is well again and so is Tom. I am getting along splendidly and so are Maud and May and their little folks. May and Frank have a little girl at their house about 3 mos. old named Mattie Lane Stine. They call her Lanie after Cap. We are always so anxious for your letters and every body is always asking about you. You can certainly have your pick of any of these girls when you come home. There will be sixteen girls to graduate at the Female Seminary the 2nd. of June. Among them are Vic Foreman, Scrap Lane, Janie

Hicks, Callie McNair and Maud and Lizzie McSpadden.[2] They are all making great preparations — "to dress" Kate Ellis seemed delighted over your letter. She is teaching in Oologah. Maud and I went over to see May about 5 or 6 weeks ago and seen the Ellis girls. May's husband runs a butcher shop in Oologah. Papa has your fine trotting horse in Claremore and is having old Commanche taken care of. Spi was up last Sunday from Okmulgee. He says he likes it down there Dick and George[3] have been down to visit him. Papa is going to take Maud and I to New Orleans to the Confederate Veteran Reunion, next month. Cap is going also. Only he pays his own way. Tom is going to keep house for me, with the assistance of a negro woman and sister May is coming over to keep house for Maud. We are anticipating a fine time. You know the world's Fair[4] was postponed and will not open till May 1904 but the Dedication Ceremonies take place next Thursday, Friday and Sat. Quite a lot of Cow-boys are going from here.[5] Mr. Poole goes with them. They have a roping contest. Maud and I sent you a little Christmas greeting in the form of a draft or exchange, for $10.00 each but it never reached you and was returned to us a month or so ago, but I have great hopes of this letter reaching you — Also the songs. So far I've not been able to get a single song that you left with any of the girls and as you are in such a hurry for them I send what I have, with some of Maud's Post Dispatch Songs. You will not be there any way but a very little while after getting these and they will probably tide you over till you come home again. I am mailing your song this morning and will send you some newer ones next week, as I'll order some from Kansas city to-morrow. So you may look out for them. All the boys want to join the show now, since you have — Every body is just wild to hear you talk of your travels. So hurry and come home, where we all love you so well and are anxiously awaiting you — Your loving Sister

Sallie C. McSpadden

ALS, rc. OkClaW. Envelope hand-addressed to Mr. W. P. Rogers with Texas Jack's Wild West Show, Cape Town, South Africa. Forwarded c/o American Consul, Bloemfontein, O.R.C.

1. Sallie's husband, Tom McSpadden.
2. Sallie's information was correct. Sixteen young women graduated from the Cherokee Nation Female Seminary on 9 June 1903. They included Victoria Lipe Foreman, Rosa Gazelle (Scrap) Lane, Janie Stapler Hicks, Caroline Quarles (Callie) McNair, Maude Hoyt McSpadden, and Elizabeth Peach (Lizzie or Peach) McSpadden. Caroline McNair (b. 1885) married James Walker McSpadden. Janie Hicks (b. 1886) married John Griffith Harnage (b. 1876), who attended Missouri State University in Columbia. Sisters Elizabeth Peach McSpadden (b. 1883) and Maude Hoyt McSpadden (b. 1885) were the siblings of Booth, Ella, Forrest, Theodore, and Oscar McSpadden, Will Rogers's friends; all were nieces or nephews of Sallie and John Thomas McSpadden. Lizzie McSpadden married Jessie Bartley Milam in April 1904. Maud McSpadden married Woodley Gail Phillips in 1905 and lived in Chelsea and later in Tulsa, Okla., and

San Diego, Calif. Gazelle (Scrap) Lane, the daughter of Dr. Andrew J. Lane and Lucinda Journeycake Lane and the sister of Will Rogers's friends Tom and Denny Lane, went on to college at Lexington, Mo., and Petersburg, Va. She became a teacher and city clerk in Claremore and was one of the leaders of the Pocahontas Club and the Claremore Presbyterian Church (*HRC*, 274, 300; Mihesuah, *Cultivating the Rosebuds*, 120, 129; *OCF* 1:41, 64, 184–85, 2:95; Starr, *History of the Cherokee Indians*, 237; Lane, interview, OkClaW; see also May McSpadden to Will Rogers, 31 August 1902, n. 5, above).

　　3. Siblings Spi, Dick, and Georgia (Georgie) Trent. Georgia Trent married Alfred Milton Pope, and their daughter, Madalyn K. Pope (1896–1977), married Sallie Rogers McSpadden's son Herbert Thomas (Herb) McSpadden in 1924 (*WRFT*, 16, 121).

　　4. Will Rogers would return home to the United States in order to participate in the Louisiana Purchase Exposition (St. Louis World's Fair) in 1904 (see Will Rogers to Sisters, 20 April 1904 below).

　　5. Zack Mulhall took his troupe to the dedication ceremonies in early May. Among the ropers were Jim Hopkins and Lucille Mulhall, who won third prize before a crowd of twenty thousand at the fair grounds. The Humane Society protested the killing of two steers in the contest (Koch, "Zach Mulhall, His Family, and the Mulhall Wild West Show," 36).

To Clement Vann Rogers
21 May 1903
Port Elizabeth, Cape Colony, South Africa

Here Will Rogers responds to his father's request for a power of attorney that will enable Clem V. Rogers to take out a land allotment on his son's behalf during Will's absence from the United States.

WILL ROGERS IN SOUTH AFRICA.

Port Elizabeth,[1] S. Africa, May 21.

C.V. Rogers, Claremore, I.T., U.S.A.

My Dear Father:

　　I will put this short letter in with the power of attorney that I am sending you in case I do not get back to the Cherokee Nation in time to take my allotment. I hope this will be all right, for a good lawyer over here said it would.

　　I sent you some money a few days ago, amounting to about $310 in American money. It was some I saved while with the show and don't need it here. I never got any letters, let alone money, from the girls. I don't think I ever got half my mail, so don't send any more money for it would get lost. Did they register it?

　　Well, I am getting along better all the time with Jack's show, and have promised to make another trip which will take four or five months, and then I will be ready to go home. I am getting homesick, but don't know what I would do there more than make a living. As it is, I am off here bothering and worrying no one, and getting along first rate.

Of course the show business is not the best business but so long as there is good money in it and it is honest, there to be no objection to it. I still keep sober and don't gamble, and Jack thinks a lot of me. I am taking his part in lots of things in the show, and he says as he is getting old I can take the show before long and do his work, He will furnish the capital and I think I would do well to try it a bit anyway.

Write when you can. Love to all. Your loving son,

Will Rogers.

Care American Consul, Capetown,
South Africa

PD. Printed in *CP,* 27 June 1903. Revised version printed in *CR,* 3 July 1903.

1. Port Elizabeth is a manufacturing and resort city in southeastern Cape Province. One of the major southern African seaports, it was named after Lady Elizabeth Donkin, the wife of a lieutenant-governor of Cape Colony. A fort was established at Port Elizabeth at the end of the eighteenth century, and British settlement began there in the 1820s. Development burgeoned after the completion of the Kimberley Railroad in 1873. By the end of the nineteenth century the area had become a center for exporting and manufacturing, especially of leather goods, boots and shoes. In the twentieth century a harbor was established and the city continued to be important in the overseas trade of manufactured goods, including automobiles and footwear (*ESA,* 399–400; *WNGD,* 971).

Enclosure:
Power of Attorney
19 May 1903
Port Elizabeth, Cape Colony, South Africa

POWER OF ATTORNEY

Know all men whom it may concern that I, William Penn Rogers, presently residing at Port Elizabeth in the Colony of the Cape of Good Hope, do hereby nominate, constitute and appoint my father, Clem Van Rogers, of Claremore, Indian Territory, U.S.A. with power of substitution to be my true and lawful attorney and agent, for me and in my name, place and stead, in due and customary form to receive for me and in my name a certain allotment of land in the Cherokee Nation, U.S.A., whereby the parties interested therein can receive a defined portion as his separate and exclusive property and on my behalf to sign, execute and make all documents and deeds necessary for that purpose.

And generally for effecting the purposes aforesaid, to do whatsoever may be requisite and necessary, as fully, amply and effectually, to all intents and purposes as I might or could do if personally present and acting therein;— hereby ratifying, allowing and confirming, and promising and agreeing to ratify, allow and confirm all and whatsoever my said attorney and agent shall lawfully do at cause to be done by virtue of these presents.

In Witness whereof, I have hereunto set my hand at Port Elizabeth in the Colony of the Cape of Good Hope on this 19th day of May, in the Year of Our Lord One Thousand Nine Hundred and Three (1903).

William Penn Rogers.

As Witnesses:

James Searle
BookKeeper
21 Main Street
Port Elizabeth

J. L. Watson
BookKeeper
21 Main Street
Port Elizabeth

ADS, rc. OkClaW.

Enclosure:
Supplemental Documents to Power of Attorney
20 May 1903
Port Elizabeth, Cape Colony, South Africa

To all whom these presents shall come.

I, Wilfred Lawson Brown of Port Elizabeth, Cape Colony, Notary Public, by lawful authority, duly admitted and sworn, do hereby certify and attest that I was present on the 19th day of May 1903 and did see William Penn Rogers, the person named in the Power of Attorney hereunto annexed, duly sign, seal and execute the said Power of Attorney and that the name, William Penn Rogers thereto subscribed is of the proper handwriting of the said William Penn Rogers and that the names James Searle and J. L. Watson thereto subscribed as the attesting Witnesses thereto are of the respective proper handwriting of James Searle and James Lawrence Watson.

In faith and testimony whereof I, the said Notary, have hereunto sub-scribed my name and set and affixed my seal of office at Port Elizabeth foresaid, this 20th day of May in the year of our Lord One Thousand Nine Hundred & Three (1903).

[*word illegible*] Attestor
W. Lawson Brown
Notary Public

[seal affixed]

To all whom it may concern I John Anthony Chabaud, Consular Agent of the United States of America at Port Elizabeth in the Colony of the Cape of Good Hope do hereby certify that Wilfred Lawson Brown, is a Notary Public, duly sworn and admitted under lawful authority and that to all acts, instruments, documents and writings subscribed by him in that capacity full faith and confidence are given in this Colony, in Court and thereout.

Given under my hand and seal of Office at Port Elizabeth afore-said this 20th day of May in the Year of Our Lord One Thousand Nine Hundred & Three: —

John A. Chabaud
Consular Agent at Port Elizabeth
of the United States of America

ADS, rc. OkClaW.

From Annie Greenslade
6 June 1903
Graaff Reinet, Cape Colony, South Africa

River Street
Graaf Reinet[1]

June 6th 1903

My Dearest-loveing boy
only these few words to let you know that I do love you so much   I realy dont know what to do when you are going to leave me   my heart will break all over   you my Dear this is what I must tell you   please dont follow me to-night because the child father is coming to fetch me to night after the play   I will come and see you tomorrow afternoon and take you out for a walk for the last   you must kindly give me your address this is mine

Annie Greenslade

ALS, rc. OkClaW. On personal stationery with bouquet of flowers in upper right corner.

1. Graaff Reinet is a historic frontier town in Cape Province on the Sundays River. First settled in 1786 on the site of the farm of Dirk Coetzee, it was named for Cape Colony Gov. Cornelis Jacob van de Graaf and his wife, Cornelia Reynet. It became the principal town of the magisterial district and division of Graaff-Reinet and a stop on the railway line between Port Elizabeth and De Aar. The district "gave birth to a hardy, independent and rugged assembly of human beings," and the town in its early days was "peopled by a picturesque crowd of wanderers, hunters, explorers and pioneers" (Bulpin, *Discovering Southern Africa*, 327). Three well-known Afrikaner leaders lived in Graaf Reinet before the Great Trek began: Gert Maritz, Sarel Cilliers, and Andries Pretorius. The town is known for its late-eighteenth- and early-nineteenth-century Cape Dutch–style buildings, and the area remains a center for cattle, dairy, horse, and sheep farming (Bulpin, *Discovering Southern Africa*, 327–28; *SESA* 5:292–94; Chantelle Wyley, History Subject Librarian, University of Natal, University Libraries, Durban, to WRPP, 29 August 1992).

To Sisters and Folks
20–27 June 1903
Bloemfontein, Orange Free State, South Africa

Bloemfontein.[1] S.A.
Orange Free State
June 20.[–27] 1903

My Dear Sisters and home folks

I have just received the songs and also your letter and of course it is useless to say how glad I was to get the music   also to hear from you for it had been about 5 months since I had a letter   so glad to hear you all were well

Well I am as usual doing all right   am still with the show   We are on a second tour of the country now but these places are all new to me as they showed there before I joined them   We are going into Portugese East Africa[2] on this trip as all the country we have been in is British Territory that formerly belonged to the Boers   This town we are in was the capitol of the Free State that the English took from the Boers   then we go to Pretoria[3]   that is the Transvaals Capitol   they are large towns   we will be here 10 days. The country is getting settled down now and it is as great a place as you could find   only you see lots of Soldiers are still in the country. The frequency of English Graveyards remind one that there has been something doing around these parts

There is a great boom on in these towns to give you an Idea of things   in a town no larger than Vinita with only on[e] Rail Road one lot with 150 foot but no improvements sold for £200.000 pounds that is equivalent to one million dollars at home   Well we consider that a dollar at home is worth as much as a pound here even though it is 5 of our dollars   carpenters Brick layers and all kinds of skilled labor get a pound and a half and two pounds a day   that is $7.50 to 10.00 but then when you go to buy anything away it goes   you have no Idea how little regard money that one would think a lot at home is thought of here and most all of it is carried on your person   that is by the working class   it is in belts worn around your waist or small ones on your arms above the elbow or below the knee   you will often see an old fellow pull out his old belt and count out a hundred pounds that is 5 hundred dollars and ofttimes as much as two thousand and still no one is robbed at all. but still you see just as many poor men for while it is easy made it is just as easy spent

Well here it is the 27 and I havent posted this letter yet.

Oh it is cold here now   of course not like it is there but it seems cold   for it is disagreeable   there is sometimes a sheet of ice over the water.

Well I will send you some pictures that a friend of mine took   they are not very good but will answer   send two to papa and also one to May

Will also send you a couple of clippings telling you of the fire and also of our opening night in this place

Well I will close   write soon and a long letter for I am always so anxious to hear from home

My best to all my friends and will see you all in a very few months.

Your loving brother
Willie

c/o American Consul Capetown

Tell Papa I got the Rope and I also got 3 bundles of songs   only one letter   that was from Sallie

ALS, rc. OkClaW. Envelope hand-addressed to Mrs. C. L. Lane, Chelsea, Indian Territory, United States of America.

1. Bloemfontein, the capital of the Orange Free State, was founded as a village in 1846. A British fort was built there in 1848. Though still a small settlement, it became the capital of the Orange Free State and seat of the Orange River Volksraad in 1854. It is located almost three hundred miles west of Durban on a tributary of the Modder River. It is now the seat of the Appellate Division of the South African Supreme Court (*ESA*, 60; *WNGD*, 153).

2. Portuguese East Africa, or Mozambique, came under European influence when it was sighted by Vasco da Gama in 1498. Six years later the Portuguese established a fort there, a precursor to Portuguese settlement and political control. At the end of the nineteenth century Portuguese East Africa was connected to South Africa with a railway line that ran between its capital, Lourenço Marques, and Pretoria (*ESA*, 347–49; *WNGD*, 797–98).

3. Texas Jack's Wild West Show played in Pretoria (which was, as Rogers points out, the capital of Transvaal) at the end of July 1903 (see *PN*, 24 July, 27 July, and 31 July 1903).

From Ada Gray
8 July 1903
Fairview, [I.T.]

Fair View[1]—
July 8th 1903

My boy:

Do you with-hold your self from me longer, and will you refuse to write to me after I have made you this confession. Forgive me Will this one time for the last. for as I forgive you now—you shouldn't deny me this plea of my heart forgiveness.

Are you ever coming home? write me in your letter when you are coming. I hope it will be before another letter can get to you. though it will be a pleasure for me to write you; but a far greater pleasure to see you. Will if you can understand in these few words all that is ment you will never have a right to believe again as you wrote John.

Will when you come home I shall be the happiest person the world holds— if I am forgiven. and if not then I shall be very unhappy.

I will not give you your choice of these statements, but if it is the latter, then you will never know how miserable I am. and if I never receive an answer to this I'll know you have accepted the latter . . .[2] Though I am still your most affectionate

Ada Gray . . .[3]

ALS, rc. OkClaW. Envelope addressed to American Consul, Cape Town, South Africa, forwarded to Sydney, Australia, and then care of Wirths' Circus.

1. There were three Fairviews in Indian Territory/Oklahoma around the turn of the century: one in Beaver County, one in southwest Logan County near Seward, and one that is the county seat of Major County. All had post offices established at the end of the 1800s; the first two Fairviews are no longer in existence (Shirk, *Oklahoma Place Names*, 76).
2. Ellipses in original document.
3. Ellipses in original document.

From Maud Lane
12 July 1903
Chelsea, I.T.

Will Rogers's father became a Downing Party candidate for the Cherokee Nation Senate as a representative of the Cooweescoowee District in the campaign of the summer of 1903. Clem V. Rogers was elected to the position at the beginning of August 1903 and thus became a member of the last Cherokee National Council before statehood.

July 12—1903.

Our Own Dear Brother,

what an age it has been since ~~wh~~ we have had a letter from you, but I fear it has been eaven longer since you have heard from us. We keep hopeing you will soon be home, but as long as you are well and doing well I guess we hadent aught to expect you soon.

We go on day in and day out just the same as when you were here   have had very few changes. Sallie papa Cap and I went to New Orleans the 17 of May   stayed a week and just had the finest kind of a time, went down to the gulf and about five miles out on a little tug boat   that little trip gave me a great longing for a sea voige and if you stay over there very much longer I fear I will attempt a trip across the deep to see you. . . .

Papa was up here the other day, he is so full of business since he was anominated for the senit he and Joe LeHay[1] with Bill Rogers,[2] for Chief papa had not been felling at all well this spring but now he never has an ache or pain and to let him tell it Bill is the very best man on earth. . . .

I do hope you have long before this received at least some of the music we have sent you, and papa sent you some rope in May guess you have it now. Papa said you had written to John Lipe and were mad at Sallie and I because we have parts of all your letters published. Yes we have been, because if you could know how all your friends love to hear from you and how they all look for a letter from you, still if you dont like it we will not put any more in the papers, just anything so you write to us often.

I have no cook this summer and you should see me mooving around these hot days   I tell you everything has to come up all O.K. or they hear from me. Papa has your young horse down at Claremore. I tell you he is just fine, what would you take for him? Papa bought a place there in Oologah for May to live in   it is the place the Elliss bought and then found they did not want to live there always. papa did not give the place to May because the first chance she had she would sell it and spend the money. . . .

How I do hope you will get some of our letters but the most of them have been returned   the letter Sallie and I sent you a Christmas greeting in was returned with the draft in it all O.K. Write when you can. All joins me in a world of love to our own dear boy.

Loveingly Maud.

ALS, rc. OkClaW. Envelope hand-addressed to W. P. Rogers, Cape Town, South Africa, c/o American Consul. Forwarded to Sydney, Australia, and on c/o Wirths' Circus, Murchison, Victoria. Printed return address: C. L. Lane, Prescription Druggist, Chelsea, Ind. Ter.

Joseph Martin (Joe) LaHay *(center)*, shown with committee members who lobbied for separate statehood for the Indian Territory. An influential politician and Rogers family friend, LaHay served as treasurer of the Cherokee Nation and as the first mayor of Claremore *(Ferguson Collection, OkU)*.

1. Clem V. Rogers and his friend Joe (Joseph Martin) LaHay were chosen as candidates for the Cherokee Nation Senate at the Downing district convention held in Claremore at the end of June 1903. After William Little declined the honor of a nomination, Clem V. Rogers's name was put forward. Rogers rose and "stated while he was not a candidate in any sense of the word, but if the delegates thought he would add any strength to the ticket, he would accept." His announcement was greeted with applause and "amid much enthusiasm, he and Mr. LaHay were unanimously named as the candidates for the senate" (*CP,* 4 July 1903).

William Charles (W. C.) Rogers of Skiatook (who was no relation to Will Rogers's family) was the Downing Party candidate for principal chief of the Cherokee Nation (*DC,* 5 August 1903). The *Claremore Messenger,* a Republican organ, took some criticism from its political allies for an editorial that stated that, in making the "selection of C. V. Rogers and J. M. LaHay [two Democrats] as candidates for Senators for Cooweescoo-wee district, the Downing party have selected two men who have led in offical and public life for many years, and against whom not one word or even insinuations, as to their integrity has been said, or even intimated" (*CM,* 10 July 1903; see also *CM,* 31 July 1903). The opposition (pro-Democratic) *Claremore Progress* also heartily endorsed the two men during the campaign (*CP,* 4 July and 25 July 1903). Clem V. Rogers campaigned for W. C. Rogers as principal chief, and both the Rogerses were elected. Clem V. Rogers later became one of the delegates from Indian Territory to serve at the 1906 constitutional convention for the new state of Oklahoma (Collings, *Old Home Ranch,* 94 n. 1; Keith, "Clem Rogers and His Influence on Oklahoma History," 35, 36, 60, 68–69, 81, 82).

2. William Charles Rogers (1849–1917) became the last acting principal chief of the Cherokee Nation before statehood. He defeated the National Party candidate E. L. Cookson for the position and succeeded Chief Thomas M. Buffington. W. C. Rogers represented the Cooweescoowee District in the Cherokee National Council in 1881 and 1883 and became a senator from the district in 1882 and 1895. He married Nannie Haynie in the early 1890s. His career was very similar to that of Clem V. Rogers. Like Clem V. Rogers, he began as a farmer-rancher with a general store–trading post in the Verdigris valley, served in Stand Watie's regiment of the Confederate Army, became a successful stockraiser, entered Cherokee politics and held a variety of offices, and later owned a hardware store and was a bank officer. His hardware store was in Skiatook, I.T., and he was the president of the First National Bank of Skiatook. He remained principal chief of the Cherokees until his death (Dewitz, *Notable Men of Indian Territory,* 72; Meserve, "Chief Thomas Mitchell Buffington and Chief William Charles Rogers"; *OCF* 1:215; Starr, *History of the Cherokee Indians,* 251, 263).

Performance Reviews from the *Pretoria News*
27 and 31 July 1903
Pretoria, Transvaal, South Africa

Texas Jack's Wild West Show played in Pretoria in July and August 1903. The Pretoria News *reported on 22 July 1903 that "To-morrow night 'Texas Jack, the Cowboy King,' so dear to the heart of the youth of Pretoria, will open his show at the old spot in Vermuelen street" with new personnel added since the show's last tour. An advertisement on the following day promised that "TEXAS JACK is Coming: Entire New Company, including AJAX The Flexible Marvel, Miss Williams and her Trained Pony. Clarence Welby Cook in his famous Jockey Act. Constant,*

Daring Trapeze; and a Splendid Mounted Cowboy Band . . . Exhibition on Bucking Bronchos Nightly." The show opened on the evening of 23 July and received a very positive review that cited Texas Jack's skill with a lasso and a gun and the *"intensely exciting"* dramas that left the audience *"spellbound."[1]* Will Rogers received special notice in a 25 July 1903 Pretoria News *review, which stated that "the lassooing of the Cherokee Kid and the Bucking Bronchos . . . were especially good."* The show continued in evening and matinee performances through 5 August. The following two documents are examples of performance reviews of the Pretoria show.

TEXAS JACK
Matinee Performance
(By a Contributor.)

A matinee performance was given on Saturday afternoon when there was a crowded audience of enthusiastic children and many grown up, to witness the show, amongst whom were noticeable the daughters of the Lieut. Governor. Wonderfully successful matinees attend Texas Jack always, owing no doubt to the fact that the performance presented falls nothing short of the evening's entertainment. The turns have already been noticed in these columns, but mention must again be made of Ajax, whose marvellous contortions drew great applause. His gracefulness is not the least pleasing part of his performance. Texas Jack gave an exhibition of his skill as marksman, and the Cherokee Kid proved himself a champion with the lasso.

Saturday Night

On Saturday night the above circus was more crowded than ever, and the artists seemed to even surpass any of their former performances. The show opened with an exhibition of vaulting from a spring board, the clowns causing roars of laughter in their funny imitations of the other acrobats. The vaulting was first started off the spring board on to a padded cushion, then one by one eight horses were added, over which all went successfully. Then Mr. Turner gave an exhibition of turning a double somersault in mid-air and falling on his feet. Mr. Constance then came and did some wonderful balancing feats on the trapeze, his balancing of the chair on its two hind legs and swinging from side to side being especially good. The introduction of monkeys riding on horses and the zebra caused much amusement, but the zebra was a little refractory, and after the first jump refused to take the rail again. Apollo performed some wonderful feats of strength. He opened his performance by throwing about a 56lb. weight with as much ease as a child would an indiarubber ball. A 100lb. weight seemed almost as nothing in this strong man's hands. He then bent a

TEXAS JACK'S

..GREAT..

American Circus

AND

WILD WEST SHOW.

Monday, August 3rd,

AND FOLLOWING NIGHTS.

PROGRAMME.

1. GARLAND MANOEUVRE by Ladies and Cowboys on Horseback
2. AVARRO and RICARDO on the Double Trapeze ...
3. CLOWN ADOLPH and his Pony " BILLY "
4. TABLE VAULTING ACT by DANNIE and BOGIE YELDING
5. JEU DE ... ROSE played on Horseback ...
6. ALVAREZ and TONY will cause some Amusement ...
7. Champion High-Leaping Pony " Tenny " Trained and Introduced by Miss WILLANS
8. AJAX, the Flexible Marvel ...
9. MADAME YELDING and her Celebrated High School Horse " Cosmo "
10. LYSTER, Xylophone Expert ...
11. Mr. ERIC WARD, Dashing Rough Rider ...
12. CONTEST in imitation of Mr. Eric Ward's Act for a Prize of a Mexican Saddle ...
13. LASSOING EXTRAORDINARY by the CHEROKEE KID ...
14. The BUCKING HORSES will attempt to get rid of their Riders ...

INTERVAL OF TEN MINUTES.

15. BAR ACT by 1st ... NNIE YELDING ...
16. MISS VIOLET WELBY COOKE, Queen of the Wire ...
17. WESTERN SKETCH—" The Massacre by Indians " ...
18. APOLLO will show his tremendous strength ...
19. Mr. J. KOCH'S Zebras and Riding Monkeys ...
        GOD SAVE THE KING.

This Programme is subject to Alteration.

Will Rogers was listed as act 13 in Texas Jack's Wild West Show program from 3 August 1903, Pretoria, South Africa (*Scrapbook 1902–4, CPpR*).

solid pile of steel over his arm, and he challenged any man to do the same for £20. He also gave a further challenge of £20 that no four men could straighten the same piece when bent, which he did himself, seemingly with perfect ease. His next act was the breaking of a horse-shoe. After these acts he tore in half a pack of playing cards, and to further show his strength he did a feat that only one other man in the world is credited to have done, and that was the tearing of three whole packs of cards at the same time (Sandow[2] is the only other credited with this). He then lifted a man of 11 stone 6lbs. with one arm, after which he tackled and was successful in lifting to the full extent of his arm a weight of 200lbs (one arm only).

The next item was the introduction of the high leaping pony "Penny," which with no rider cleared a gate of 6ft 1 in. This pony is solely trained by Miss Williams.

Ajax, the Flexible, is simply a marvel, and his acts are quite beyond description. To see him once you want to see him again. This man has a wonderful expansion of chest measurement, his normal size being 40in., and he can expand to 46 3/4 in., his neck is also rather large, being 17½ in., and his weight 11 stone 2lbs.

The Cherokee Kid performed some wonderful feats with the lasso, his double act of catching first the horse and then the man with two lassos being very clever.

His last performance was that of enveloping himself and horse in a crinoline letting the hoop touch the ground and then bringing it back over the horse and himself and allowing the loop to return to its former size.

For the riding of bucking horses three aspirants came forth, but none were successful in winning the £5.

Then Montana Brown gave an exhibition on a bucking horse, which did all in its power to unseat its rider, but was not successful. Texas Jack gave a fine exhibition in marksmanship, and after the interval the programme was brought to a close by a scene in prairie life, which was much appreciated by all present.

To-night a complete change of programme is to be presented, when new artists, who have just arrived from Australia, will appear. These include Miss Violet Welby Cooke,[3] who has just finished a contract with Harry Rickards[4] and received the most favourable of Press notices.

TEXAS JACK
A BOXING BOUT.

A large number of people attended Texas Jack's show last night. The double trapeze act by Avarro and Ricardo was both daring and amusing. The Risley act by Azide, a lad of 14 years, was very good, and the lad gives promise of becoming an acrobat of no mean repute. The bucking horse was again mastered last night by one of our well-known footballers, to wit, Thomas of the Thistle. The second horse that was brought in was of a very vicious disposition, and after getting rid of one of his riders, tried very hard to get rid of the Cherokee kid, but without success. The attraction of the evening no doubt was the three-round spar between Cook,[5] the light-weight champion of South Africa, and Jim Walker, the champion middleweight of Rhodesia. The time-keeper, in introducing the contestants to the audience, gave out a challenge on behalf of Cook to knock out in six rounds all comers up to the weight of 11st 4lbs. This challenge was accepted by J. Sharpe.[6] This man is well known in South African fistic circles. He is the man who fought and beat Cooper at Krugersdorp[7] for the ten-stone championship of South Africa. Cook and Sharpe have met before in Johannesburg in a six-round fight, which Cook won.

This fight is to take place at the circus to-night, both men being in fairly good trim.[8]

Miss Violet Welby Cook is giving a very clever exhibition of wire walking.

PD. Printed in *PN*, 27 July and 31 July 1903.

1. *PN*, 24 July 1903.
2. Eugene Sandow (1867–1925) was a well-known German-born strongman who performed in burlesque and vaudeville. In 1889 Sandow first gained fame in London, where he beat Samson, known then as the most powerful strongman. As a young showman, Florenz Ziegfeld, Jr., discovered Sandow and had him appear in his variety show at the 1893 Chicago World's Fair. Ziegfeld used his promotional skills to make the strongman a popular sensation. Dressed in skimpy silk shorts, Sandow performed such acts as holding a man in one hand, lifting a dumbbell with a person hidden in each ball, and wrestling a lion. Sandow retired in England in 1907 and invested in several consumer products that carried his name, including a health oil and corset (Chapman, *Sandow the Magnificent*; Gragert, *Will Rogers' Weekly Articles*, 5:78–80; Higham, *Ziegfeld*, 12–18, 168; *EV*, 452–53; Toll, *On with the Show*, 297–99).
3. The Cookes were an old and famous family in the English circus world. Beginning with Thomas Cooke, they had operated one of the earliest traveling circuses, or tent companies, in eighteenth-century Scotland. Thomas Cooke's son, Thomas Taplin Cooke, brought the Cooke family circus to New York in 1836. It featured forty members of the Cooke family among its 130 artists, including Cooke's 12 children. At the time of Thomas Taplin Cooke's death in 1866 almost all of his (then) 19 children were performing in the circus, many of them specializing in rope or wire walking or in equestrian acts. By the end of the century generations of Cookes had intermarried with members of other prominent circus families. Brothers John and Clarence Welby Cooke joined the Wirth Brothers' Circus in its tour of South America in 1896, and both came to Australia with the circus in 1900. Marizles Wirth recalled that in Rio de Janeiro the "Cookes' mother and two sisters were with the show."

Violet Welby Cooke, a wire walker, may possibly have been one of the two sisters to whom Wirth referred, or she may have been married to one of the Welby Cooke brothers. Violet Welby Cooke toured with Wirth Brothers' Circus in Australia for a time, worked on the Rickards' theater circuit, and then went to South Africa, where she joined Texas Jack's show. Meanwhile, John Welby Cooke married the Wirth brothers' niece, Edith, and they toured India with Harmston's Circus in the early 1900s. They returned to Australia, and John Welby Cooke became the Wirth Brothers' Circus ringmaster and remained with them for many years before his death in 1924. Like Violet Welby Cooke, Clarence Welby Cooke (an expert equestrian like his brother) appeared with Texas Jack's show on its South Africa tour. The English-speaking show-business world was linked in that era with an international vaudeville circuit that included networks in Australia, New Zealand, South Africa, India, the United States, and England. The Cookes, the Wirths, and Texas Jack were all involved in that circuit (Mark St Leon, Gelbe, Australia, to WRPP, 28 April 1993; on members of the Cooke family, see Croft-Cooke and Cotes, *Circus: A World History,* 96–99; Greaves, *Circus Comes to Town,* 82; St Leon, "Bareback Queen").

4. Harry Rickards (1843–1911), whose real name was Benjamin Leete, was a well-known comic singer, theater proprietor, and impresario. Born in England, Rickards first performed in British music halls and became noted for his interpretations of Cockney songs. He formed his own companies, which toured South Africa (1876) and Australia (1885–86). In 1892 Rickards permanently moved to Sydney, where he bought several theaters and other showplaces in Australian cities. Known as the most important popular vaudeville manager and theater owner in Australia, he brought many famous variety performers to the country. In 1908 he purchased a large English estate near Margate, Kent, and he died from apoplexy in England on 12 October 1911 (*ADB* 11:387–88; Leavitt, *Fifty Years in Theatrical Management,* 217).

5. In a series of shows a man described as Jewey Cook, reportedly the lightweight champion of England, sparred with "unknowns" from the audience who challenged him in an effort to win a ten-pound note. The act drew large audiences of men (*PN,* 25 July, 30 July, 31 July, and 1 August 1903).

6. Possibly a reference to Johnny Sharpe, who fought in England in 1910 and later managed world flyweight champion Terry Allen (Carpenter, *Masters of Boxing,* 164).

7. Krugersdorp is a town on the West Rand in the southern Transvaal, South Africa, about twenty miles from Johannesburg. It was founded in 1887 by Abner Cohen and developed into a gold- and manganese-mining and industrial center. The Paar-dekraal monument, an important site in Afrikaner society, was erected there (*ESA,* 281; *WNGD,* 630).

8. On the history of prizefighting as a sport in the English-speaking world (bare-knuckle pugilism and boxing) see, for example, Brailsford, *Bareknuckles: A Social History of Prize-Fighting* (on eighteenth- and nineteenth-century England and on the international dimensions of prizefighting as a world sport), and Gorn, *Manly Art* (on the United States). Brailsford points out that the development of international connections in the boxing world (i.e., between Britain and areas under British colonial influence such as the United States, Australia, and South Africa) was just one example, like horse racing, "of organised sport crossing national frontiers" (139). Unlike horseracing or cricket, which became more exclusive, appealing to an elite, pugilism (especially in the bare-knuckle era) appealed primarily to working-class "Anglo-Saxon communities overseas" that "were more receptive" to the more "rugged" kinds of sports entertainment (141). The kind of three-round spectator spar that Texas Jack set up for his show's appearances in Pretoria became popular at the end of the nineteenth century, when

> sparring exhibitions were a more legitimate means of entertaining the public than prize-fights. . . . At the humblest levels, in the travelling fairground booth, there was more than mere sparring on offer for the local worthies who sought to stand up to the resident

pugilist for three rounds to earn a sovereign or two and much local glory. Fighters who had made their reptuations usually toured in groups of four or five to make a full programme of entertainment possible. Public halls, hotels, swimming baths and even theatres were among their varied venues as they trekked through the provinces. . . . At the top end of the entertainment scale, as star circus performers giving sparring and fitness displays in that other ring, the best-known pugilists would command the salaries of top-billed theatrical performers—they were the precursors of the general move of spectator sport into its eventual ambit of show business.

These pugilists had their own press agents and took on the "air of popular entertainers" (Brailsford, *Bareknuckles*, 153–54).

From Mamie S.
ca. July 1903
Pretoria?, Transvaal, South Africa

Wednesday

Dear Kidd:

I am very sorry you dissipointed me this afternoon   had you come round where I asked Brown to tell you, you would have been quite safe as it is the back entrance to the Hotel & nobody would have seen us, oh my darling I am dying to see you   sure I know you will laugh at me saying that but it is true all the same. I suppose the boys told you what had happened up there so of course I will not go there again   Now darling will you do me this favor & come here tonight about an hour after show or say half past twelve then I will come out to see you.

instead of coming up the street that the train runs   turn off the other street   you will see a lane   wait there fore me   I will not dissipoint you   now will you my darling? I know you will my darling old Kid

yours loving
as always
Mamie

turn over

p s

I just almost forgot to ask you this, you seem to have cut me since last night & I heard you remark this morning about looking for a boat   well darling if you wish to cut loose frome me come tonight & tell me so even if it is a great blow to me anything would be better than for to look at me as you did this morning   it does hurt me because I love you more than I can ever tell anyone perhaps it is not my place to tell you how I love you but I cant help it   I must let my mind out to some one & I trust you more than anyone else   now sweet heart write me a note & let me know if you will come Bill will give it to me

M. S.

Dear Kiddie

I have come to the conclusion now I want to make a proposition to you   oh my darling I can not let you leave me   dont you think that this would be a good idea if you have not given Jack notice yet then dont do it just stay with the show to work & I will go back to Syd & let both of us try & save as much money as we can. & if you you think it advisable send to your people and get some money & then we will also have saved a bit then we could go away   sweetheart I could live much better if you were in the show   we need not be intamate we could just make out as if ~~anything~~ everything is over between us   now dont you think it is a good plan. send me an answer by Harry & then I will know what to do   oh my darling dont say no to this then I will realy begin to believe you dont love me   now darling I love you so much that it seems to me I should die if you leave me so tata my darling   think it over well & let me know   oh I wish we had last night over

yours lovingly
Mamie

ALS, rc. OkClaW.

To Clement Vann Rogers
2 August 1903
Pretoria, Transvaal, South Africa

Pretoria. South Africa
Aug. 2. 1903.

My Dear Father.

After so long a time I will again write to you but there is nothing of importance to write of   I am still at work and doing very well and enjoying the best of health.

I have not had any mail from home for some time   I got the rope alright that you sent and was glad to get it

This place Pretoria is the capitol of the Transvaal and the home of Paul Kruger[1]   it was before the war the principal Dutch town and a very pretty little city too   We have just left Johannesburg[2]   that is the great gold fields[3] and the largest of all the African towns. We next go into Portugese Territory[4]   that is over in the east part on the coast   Jack himself is leaving the show for a trip to America to bring out some new people   he wants me to stay till he gets back as I take his parts in the show while he is away   he says he may get down that way and if so he will come around and see you.

I will come as soon as he gets back for I am getting in a hurry to get home. Did you get the Money I sent you about three months ago[?] it was 65. Pounds.

I will drop you in a newspaper notice or two that I have got out of the last paper or so and you can see how I am getting on

Give all the Sisters and folks my best love and regards to all my old friends. and most of all to my Dear Father who has ▲ always ▲ done all in his power for me and for which I am certainly thankful.

I will close   *write when you can* to your *contented* son

Willie

Capetown S.A.
c/o American Consul.

Dont any one write until you hear from me again as I wont be here that long.

ALS, rc. OkClaW. Revised version printed in *CP,* 12 September 1903.

1. Pretoria was the home and burial place of Afrikaner hero Stephanus Johannes Paulus (Paul) Kruger, president of the Transvaal Republic from 1883 to 1902. Kruger (1825–1904) was of German heritage, born in the Cape Colony. His parents were Voortrekkers, and he joined them on the Great Trek from the Cape Colony to the interior. He participated in Afrikaner raids against the Ndebeles and the Zulus in the mid and late 1830s and led attacks against Sechele, Moshweshwe, and other African chiefs in the following decades. He became a farmer near Rustenburg, Transvaal, and a lay preacher in the Dopper sect while holding various offices in the developing Afrikaner administration. He was a leader in the resistance movement against British annexation of the Transvaal in the late 1870s and was central to negotiations that led to Afrikaner independence in 1881. In 1883 he began the first of four terms as president of the Transvaal Republic. Campaigns against Tswana chiefs resulted in British annexation of Bechuanaland in 1885, and in the following year the politics of the region were transformed by the discovery of gold on the Rand. The development of the goldfields brought the migration of *uitlanders* (white, mostly English-speaking foreigners or outsiders) and the financial impact of foreign capital. Kruger sought to maintain Afrikaner political and economic control and cultural dominance. He limited the political rights of newcomers and was faced with increased tensions with the British that foreshadowed the South African (Anglo-Boer) War. He anticipated that war, built up Afrikaner forces with profits from the gold mines, and directed the Afrikaner war effort in 1899–1900 until he was forced into exile from Pretoria in May 1900. Kruger worked futilely to win support for the Afrikaner cause in Europe and died in Switzerland in July 1904, two years after the Afrikaner alliance was defeated by Britain (Fisher, *Paul Kruger;* Hillegas, *Oom Paul's People;* Kruger, *Memoirs of Paul Kruger;* Mavais, *Fall of Kruger's Republic;* Wilson and Thompson, eds., *Oxford History of South Africa* 2:307–14).

2. Johannesburg, the largest city of southern Africa and one of the largest in all of Africa, is located south of Pretoria in the Orange Free State. An industrial and mining center, it was founded by Europeans as a camp in 1886 after the discovery of gold in the region. The tent city that was established in 1886 was named after Johannes Petrus Meyer. The city was located at the center of the Witwatersrand goldfield. Johannesburg and the surrounding goldfields, which were mined by several companies, were located on a plateau in the southern African high veld, some six thousand feet above sea level. The goldfields were developed initially along an outcrop line of gold deposits that were roughly equidistant east and west of Johannesburg. By 1895 Johannesburg had a population of over 100,000 people. In May 1900 it was occupied by the British, and it continued under British rule until 1901. Lord Alfred Milner maintained his headquarters there. The area was subject to extensive development, and by 1911 its population was more than double the 1895 figures ("Johannesburg under the Boers" and "The Fall of Johannesburg," chaps. 3 and 5 in Cammack, *Rand at War,* 61–82; Richardson and Van-Helten, "Gold Mining Industry in the Transvaal"; *ESA,* 255–56; *WNGD,* 574).

3. The mineral resources had been used by African peoples, who worked deposits on a small scale for centuries before European discovery. People of European descent discovered coal in Natal in the 1840s and diamonds in the Orange and Vaal River areas in the 1860s. Gold was discovered on the Witwatersrand in 1884, causing a rapid expansion of mining and related industrialization. The mining boom brought an influx (and dominance) of foreign, especially British, capital, more pointed political and economic imperialism on the part of the British toward African peoples and the Afrikaners, and massive changes in the South African labor structure (including the importation of Chinese labor and the use of African labor in gold mines). A new bureaucratic and technological infrastructure had to be created to mine and market the new wealth and to accommodate the surge of new migrants that the discovery of gold attracted. These developments resulted in a virtual revolution in the political economy of South Africa during the decades around the turn of the century. Even in areas politically dominated by Afrikaners, diamond and gold fields and the railways (essential for transport of the mineral wealth) were under British ownership and control. The goldfields were opened to public digging in 1886, and by the end of the century gold-mining companies were utilizing deep-mining production. In 1899 there were 156 mines on the Rand, most on the Main Reef of the Witwatersrand fields. By 1910 gold comprised 80 percent of South Africa's exports and its major source of foreign exchange (Houghton, "Mining Revolution"; Johnstone, *Class, Race, and Gold;* Magubane, *Political Economy of Race and Class in South Africa,* 102–18; Richardson and Van-Helten, "Gold Mining Industry in the Transvaal").

4. A reference to Portuguese East Africa (Mozambique).

Testimony of Clement Vann Rogers on Behalf of William P. Rogers, to the Department of Interior, Commission to the Five Civilized Tribes 17 August 1903 Tahlequah, I.T.

Here Clem V. Rogers testifies on behalf of Will Rogers before Dawes Commission officials, claiming part of the family homestead in his son's name. The lands allotted to Will Rogers are documented in the following certificates of allotment. Clem

Rogers was allotted a total of 69.93 acres of the home-ranch land, a 19.93-acre homestead, and 50 acres in surplus land. Will Rogers was allotted 78.84 acres, a 30.04-acre homestead, and 48.80 in surplus land. His homestead allotment included the core part of the old home ranch, including the house in which he was born.[1] Allotment brought an end to the large cattle ranches and open grasslands that had dominated the area, and gave rise to a new norm of fencing and small tenant farming. The ranch that Will Rogers had managed before leaving for South America shrank from a 60,000-acre spread to a farm of a few hundred acres, and the cattle range on which he had grown up was divided into hundreds of separate allotments.[2]

Cherokee Allotment

No. 11384.

DEPARTMENT OF THE INTERIOR,
COMMISSION TO THE FIVE CIVILIZED TRIBES,
CHEROKEE LAND OFFICE.

Tahlequah, I.T., August 17, 1903.
Testimony of Clement V. Rogers in the matter of the request of William P. Rogers to the Commission to the Five Civilized Tribes to make a discretionary allotment and designation of homestead to himself as shown herein and on attached application form.

Clement V. Rogers, being first duly sworn by Samuel Foreman,[3] a Notary Public in and for the Northern District of Indian Territory, testified as follows:

Q What is your name?   A Clement V. Rogers.

Q What is your age?   A 64 last January.

Q What is your post office address?   A Claremore.

Q Are you a citizen of the Cherokee Nation?   A By blood, yes, sir.

Q About whose allotment and designation of homestead do you desire to give testimony?

A For my son, William P. Rogers.

Q Why does your son, William P. Rogers, not appear in person and make this application?

A He is in South Africa with a show.

Q Is he familiar with this land that you are applying to the Commission to have allotted to your son?   A Yes, sir, he was raised on it.

Q Did he request you to make this application for him?   A Yes, sir.

Q You advise the Commission to designate and select the following described land: the SE 9.20 acres of Lot 5, and the W 20 acres of Lot 5, and the SE 10 acres of Lot 3 of Section 19; and the S 9.60 acres of Lot 9, of Section 18, Township 23 N., Range 16 E., containing 48.80 acres and valued at $205.20, and designate as a homestead: the NE 20 acres of Lot 3, and the W 20.04 acres of Lot 3, of Section 19, Township 23 N., Range 16 E., containing 30.04 acres and valued at $120.16, for your son, William P. Rogers, is this correct?   A Yes, sir.

Q Are there any improvements on this land?   A Yes, sir, all of the improvements are on the homestead, outside of the fences.

Q What do the improvements consist of?   A A dwelling house, barn, granaries and out buildings.

PD. DNA, RG 75.

1. See the following certificates for the exact size and location of Will Rogers's allotments. The allotments for Clem V. Rogers, Enrollment No. 11383, were as follows. The first entry represents homestead land, the last three surplus land.

W 19.93 acres of Lot 4	Sec. 19	Twp. 23N	Range 16E	Acres 19.93
SE 10 acres of Lot 10	Sec. 18	Twp. 23N	Range 16E	Acres 10.00
E 20 acres of Lot 4	Sec. 19	Twp. 23N	Range 16E	Acres 20.00
N2 of NE4 of SW4	Sec. 19	Twp. 23N	Range 16E	Acres 20.00

Total acres: 69.93

A total of 352.34 acres were allotted from the old Rogers ranch to Will Rogers, Clem V. Rogers, and seven other individuals. Over time Clem V. Rogers bought this acreage back so that it was under Rogers family ownership (allotment records and certificates of allotment, box 7, OkClaW; Collings, *Old Home Ranch*, 135).

2. The maximum amount of land allotted varied among the Five Tribes, according to separate allotment agreements drawn up with the Dawes Commission. Choctaw and Chickasaw citizens received 320 acres; Cherokees, 110 acres (or less acreage equal to a maximum valuation of $325.60); Creeks, 160 acres; and so forth. Cherokee, Creek, and Seminole freedslaves and their descendants shared with Indian citizens in the various sizes of allotment, but former slaves in the Choctaw and Chickasaw Nations were restricted to 40 acres. The final rolls, completed in July 1907, included the names of 41,798 people, including 31,400 Cherokees, 197 Delawares, 286 whites who had married Cherokees, 4,991 Cherokee minors, and 4,305 minor descendants of former slaves (Collings, *Old Home Ranch*, 101; Commission, *Final Rolls of Citizens and Freedmen of the Five Civilized Tribes in Indian Territory;* Gibson, *History of Oklahoma*, 118; Hewes, *Occupying the Cherokee Country of Oklahoma*, 57).

3. Samuel Sunset Foreman (b. 1873) married Minnie Ola Smith (b. 1875) in 1894 (*OCF* 1:173).

Certificates of Land Allotment
17 August 1903
Tahlequah, I. T.

DEPARTMENT OF THE INTERIOR
COMMISSION TO THE FIVE CIVILIZED TRIBES

Roll Number	Certificate of Homestead Allotment	Certificate
Cherokee Roll I Freedman Roll.		No. 23839
11384		

CHEROKEE LAND OFFICE

Tahlequah, *I. T.* Aug 17 *1903*

This certifies that <u>William P. Rogers</u> has this day selected the following described land as a HOMESTEAD, viz:

Sub-Division of	Section	Town	Range
NE 10.00 acres of Lot 3 of	19	23	16
W 20.04 acres of Lot 3 of	19	23	16

containing <u>30.04</u> acres more or less, as the case may be according to the United States survey thereof. Total appraised value of land described in this certificate $ <u>120.16</u>

This certificate is not transferable.[1] Commission to the Five Civilized Tribes.

[initials illegible]
Chairman

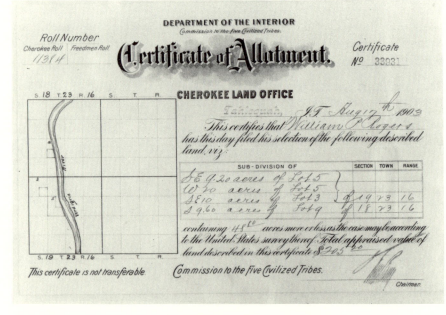

Certificates of land allotment for William P. Rogers (*OkClaW*).

DEPARTMENT OF THE INTERIOR
COMMISSION TO THE FIVE CIVILIZED TRIBES

Roll Number   Certificate of Allotment.   Certificate
Cherokee Roll | Freedman Roll.   No. 33931
11384

CHEROKEE LAND OFFICE

Tahlequah, *I. T.* Aug 17th *1903*

This certifies that William P Rogers has this day filed his selection of the following described land, viz:

Sub-Division of	Section	Town	Range
SE 9.20 acres of Lot 5			
W 20 acres of Lot 5			
SE 10 acres of Lot 3 of	19	23	16
S 9.60 acres of Lot 9 of	18	23	16

containing 48.80 acres more or less, as the case may be according to the United States survey thereof. Total appraised value of land described in this certificate $ 205.20

This certificate is not transferable.[2] Commission to the Five Civilized Tribes.

[*initials illegible*]
Chairman

PD, with autograph insertions. OkClaW.

1. The homestead certificate included a map detailing the acres of lot 3 in section 19, town 23, range 16, claimed by Clem V. Rogers on Will Rogers's behalf.
2. The certificate of general allotment included a map detailing the acreage claimed: lots 3, 5, and 9 in sections 18 and 19, town 23, range 16, along the Verdigris River.

From Maud Lane
17 August 1903
Chelsea, I. T.

Aug 17—1903.

Our Dear Old Boy.

I keep thinking of you more and more, the nearer fall comes the worse I want to see you. Well things are mooveing on here very much as they always do   just as fast as any of our girls and boys grow up a bit they have to get married and the most of them could not buy a pound of soap. Papa was elected to the senate   he and Joe Le Hay from Cooweescoowee[1] with Will Rogers a Chief and Mr Dave Faulkner assistant   they say this was the hottest election we have had for a long time.[2] All the [U.S.C.?] people were natinols and wanted Cookston,[3] they called the Dowan party[4] Democrats and the Nat. Republicans so everyone took a hand in it. Mr. W. E. Halsell worked so hard for Cookston and they say he spent about $10000.00   but ▲ in ▲ it it has done him no good he and papa have fallen out over it. . . .

Some time a go papa saw a man in Claremore who just came from S. Africa and he had been to Texas Jack's show and he remembered the Cher. Kid   some how I wanted to send for him and have him come up but I know he could tell us nothing about you for he only saw you while you were preforming. but I would give anything in the world to see some one who could tell me all about you. . . .

Dear Brother please do write to us just as often as you can. I heard you did not like it because we have been publishing your letters   well we did not mean to offend you but if you could know how all your friends love to hear from you and how they all watch for your letters and one paper coppies it from another till it has gone all around so you see you are a great boy at home, but if you dont want us to print any more we want only to please   write to us often

Loveingly
Maud.

ALS, rc. OkClaW. Envelope hand-addressed to W. P. Rogers, Capetown, South Africa, c/o American Consul. Forwarded to Sydney, Australia, and on c/o Wirths' Circus, Murchison, Victoria. Printed return address, C. L. Lane, Prescription Druggist, Chelsea, Ind. Ter.

1. Clem V. Rogers and Joe M. LaHay received hearty support among the Democrat-Downing Party supporters in the Claremore area. The local *Claremore Progress* declared that "a vote for C. V. Rogers and J. M. LaHay is a vote for a speedy settlement of the Cherokee estate. Rogers never in his political life wronged his people out of a dollar, and you can rest assured he never will" (*CP,* 25 July 1903). The pair were less popular in Vinita. The *Daily Chieftain* criticized LaHay for his "lofty ambition" to become a candidate for principal chief at the Downing convention and reminded its readers that LaHay "has held the office of treasurer of the Cherokee nation for nearly four years after the functions of the office, all except the salary, had been abolished," accusing him of drawing a salary for "services never rendered" (27 July 1903). The same paper reminded voters that in the spring of 1903 Clem V. Rogers had been asked to support keeping the land office in Vinita and instead had urged the Department of the Interior to move it elsewhere—"a fact that should be recalled in the polling booth" (*DC,* 1 August 1903). The paper also reasoned that "those who vote for Cookson for chief and Clem Rogers and Joe LaHay for senate, are in a measure nullifying their own votes. John Franklin and George Mayes should be elected, men who will sustain Cookson's administration" (*DC,* 20 July 1903). Despite these criticisms, both Clem V. Rogers and LaHay were elected to the Senate with strong support in Cooweescoowee District at the beginning of August 1903—Rogers with 1,207 votes to Franklin's 683, and LaHay with 1,292 votes to Mayes's 849. W. C. Rogers and David Faulkner also prevailed in district tallies. As the

tallies. As the *Daily Chieftain* put it, in "Cooweescoowee district the Downings elected a straight ticket from head to tail" (*DC,* 5 August 1903; see also 4 August 1903; *IC,* 6 August 1903). The *Progress* commented wryly on how Rogers's candidacy had been viewed in regard to the statehood issue. A few days after the election it announced that "C. V. Rogers was elected and still we are not a part of Oklahoma yet!" (*CP,* 8 August 1903).

2. In the Cooweescoowee District, in the election tallies for principal chief and assistant principal chief, W. C. Rogers received 1,302 votes to E. L. Cookson's 783, and David Faulkner became assistant chief with 1,363 votes to Wolfe Coon's 708 (*DC,* 5 August 1903). The *Claremore Progress* exulted that "Claremore does things right. She gave W. C. Rogers, C. V. Rogers and J. M. LaHay, each, one hundred and five majority" (8 August 1903).

David McNair Faulkner (1841–1914) had been approached to run for principal chief in the past, as had Clem V. Rogers. His mother, Aursakie Potts Faulkner, was a full-blood Cherokee. He was a veteran of the Second Cherokee Mounted Volunteers and had served as a councilor from the Sequoyah District in 1869 and 1877. He was elected to the Cherokee Senate in 1879, 1881, 1889, 1895, and 1901 and was a Cherokee Nation delegate to Washington, D.C., in 1897. He owned a ranch near Claremore, and his family moved to Claremore in 1912 during his tenure as assistant principal chief. His first wife, Rachel Louvenia Adair Faulkner (1844–99), was the mother of a daughter and three sons (including David Jesse Faulkner [b. 1874], a long-time resident of Claremore who in 1900 married Jennie McClellan Foreman [b. 1878]); his second wife, Emma Winfred Faulkner (whom he married in 1900), was the mother of three daughters and one son and was a member of the Pocahontas Club. David McNair Faulkner remained assistant principal chief until shortly before his death in August 1914 (*CM,* 15 August 1903 and 18 August 1905; *CP,* 27 June 1993; *CV,* 12 May 1899; Faulkner, "Story of Bertha Lillian Faulkner-Starr," *As I Recollect,* 117–18; *HRC,* 33; *OCF* 1:211, 2:93; Starr, *History of the Cherokee Indians,* 559).

3. Edley Levi Cookson (b. 1854), a Progressive backed by the Republican Party in the Cherokee Nation elections of August 1903, was a senator from the Illinois District in 1891, 1895, 1899, and 1901. He had previously served as a judge in the Illinois District in 1893. His candidacy for principal chief was strongly supported in the Vinita area in 1903, and he lost to W. C. Rogers in the Vinita precinct by only one vote (114 to Rogers's 115) while losing overwhelmingly in the Cooweescoowee District as a whole (*DC,* 4 August and 5 August 1903; *OCF* 2:4).

4. Clem V. Rogers had long been active in the Downing Party, the dominant political party among the Cherokees. The party had been formed as a reform party in 1866–67 as a result of the Reconstruction process, realignments in the factionalization between Northern Cherokees and Southern Cherokees around the issue of Cherokee sovereignty, and the political crisis that occurred upon the death of John Ross. Southern Cherokee leaders of the Southern Rights, or Watie, Party (former Treaty, or Ridge, Party supporters) joined with some elements of the Ross Party to support the successful candidacy of Keetoowah Society member Lewis Downing, an army officer during the Civil War and assistant principal chief under John Ross. Downing was opposed by John Ross's nephew, W. P. Ross, who represented the National Party. Several other Cherokee parties also existed in the 1870s, including the Independent-Conservatives, the Union National Independents, the Boys, and the People's Party. Downing died only two months into his second term as principal chief (1872), and the Downing Party fell into temporary disarray during the administration of National Party chief Dennis Wolf Bushyhead, who was principal chief from 1879 to 1887.

In the early 1880s the Downing Party was effectively submerged for a time by the rise of the Union Party. Both the National and the Union (sometimes called the Keetoowah) Party were "alike in having a Keetoowah organization among the fullbloods and in their political prejudice against the Negro," though the National Party was considered more "progressive" and the Union Party more "conservative," that is, supportive of traditional ways and opposed to white intrusion (Wardell, *Political History of the Cherokee Nation*, 342). In the mid-1880s the Downing Party was reorganized. After a bitter campaign in 1887, Downings dominated the head Cherokee offices until the transition to statehood. Even though both houses of the National Council sometimes had a National Party majority, each principal chief was a Downing, including Joel B. Mayes (replaced upon his death by C. J. Harris), S. H. Mayes, T. M. Buffington, and W. C. Rogers, who served as principal chief from 1903 to 1917, during the period of dissolution of Indian Territory and the first years of statehood (Caywood, "The Administration of William C. Rogers"; Littlefield, *Cherokee Freedmen*, 111, 232–35, 254; Litton, "Principal Chiefs of the Cherokee Nation"; Mankiller and Wallis, *Mankiller*, 170; McLoughlin, *Champions of the Cherokees*, 441–43, 468, 476–77, 478; Starr, *History of the Cherokee Indians*, 120, 251, 262–63, 273; Wardell, *Political History of the Cherokee Nation*, 209, 343–48; Wright, *Guide to the Indian Tribes of Oklahoma*, 72).

6. AUSTRALIA AND NEW ZEALAND
September 1903–April 1904

Dressed in a red velvet suit made by Margaret Wirth, wife of circus promoter George Wirth, to highlight his performance as the Mexican Rope Artist, Rogers displays his roping skills to children in either Australia or New Zealand *(Scrapbook 1902–4, CPpR).*

CARRYING A LETTER OF RECOMMENDATION FROM TEXAS JACK, ROGERS SET sail across the Indian Ocean for Australia in early August 1903. After approximately a year in South Africa he wrote his sister Sallie that he had "enough" of the country.[1] Texas Jack asked him to remain with his show, but he declined the opportunity. Rogers felt the need to return home and also to explore more of the world—to see, as he wrote, if "this old Globe . . . really is round."[2] He planned to stay a couple of months in Australia and return home before December 1. Instead, he spent nearly seven months in New Zealand and Australia, eventually obtaining a job as a performer with the Wirth Brothers' Circus, a prominent Australian company.

Rogers's decision to travel to Australia and New Zealand was consistent with his interest in exploring frontier life in other nations. Much like South Africa and Argentina, Australia offered Rogers an opportunity to see firsthand a country with large cattle and horse holdings. After sailing for twenty-five days in rough waters and experiencing acute sea sickness, he stopped in New Zealand, where he commented on the large sheep-raising stations and dairy farms. From Australia, Rogers penned several letters describing the huge properties of owners engaged in the sheep and cattle industries. He spent considerable time in the cities of Sydney and Melbourne and in the interior. Although Rogers did not travel far into the outback, he did stay at a large cattle station in northern Victoria near Benalla and Murchison. Here he came into direct contact with the rugged stockmen, drovers, and shearers who played a major role in Australian frontier history.[3]

In his letters home Rogers compared the life on the Australian frontier to his experiences in the Indian Territory and Argentina. He noticed that the Australian cowboy used a smaller padded saddle without a horn and controlled his stock with a cattle whip instead of a rope. He was impressed by the quickness of Australian horses and their jumping ability. Rogers, however, was disappointed with Australian ranch life and felt that the quality of the livestock was better in Argentina. "I don't like this country very much except for farming," he wrote home.[4]

Rogers was especially interested in the Maoris and the Aborigines, the indigenous peoples of New Zealand and Australia, respectively. He sent home

On the Wanganui River   Photo by Denton

Postcard of New Zealand from one of Will Rogers's scrapbooks (*Scrapbook 1902–4, CPpR*).

a pictorial card featuring a Maori woman in a native costume and another featuring a Native Australian man with a boomerang and a mallet. In his observations on these groups Rogers evokes the social Darwinist racial stereotypes of his time.[5]

A note of homesickness and appreciation for the United States appears in Rogers's letters. After being away for nearly two years, he writes Spi Trent that he is "longing to see the old home country again, for there is no country like home."[6] In Australia he found himself in situations defending American manners and customs. He wrote his father, "I was always proud in America to own that I was a Cherokee and I find on leaving them that I am equally as proud to own that I am an American for if there is any nation earning a *rep* abroad it is America."[7]

Around Christmas time Rogers found employment as a lariat artist and trick rider with the Wirth Brothers' Circus. The Wirth Brothers was a well-known international circus based in Australia that had made several world tours to South Africa (1893–94, 1899), South America (1895), England (1897–98), and Asia (1900).[8] Owned by George and Philip Wirth, the circus was extremely popular in Australia and New Zealand. Its program offered audiences a variety of entertainment from weight lifters and trapeze artists to wild-animal acts and plays.[9]

Rogers joined the Wirth Brothers during a time when circuses were attracting large crowds all over the world. The years from 1870 to 1914 marked the golden age of the circus. The traveling circus, which appealed to both rural and urban audiences, offered inexpensive, razzle-dazzle entertainment emphasizing daring and physical action. The multi-ringed circus reached its peak in the United States with the Barnum and Bailey and Ringling Brothers circuses. The big top was especially popular in New Zealand and Australia, where over sixty circuses flourished over the years. In Australia the circus was largely a family tradition, with shows owned by the Wirths, the FitzGeralds, the Ashtons, the Soles, the Perrys, and the Bullens.[10] Historically, the circus had evolved from equestrian exhibitions by English riding masters in the eighteenth century. Since that time horsemanship acts had been a regular feature of circus performances. In the United States and other countries Wild West acts were a popular feature on circus bills, and some companies often presented equestrian exhibitions in their programs.[11]

Rogers probably began performing with the Wirth Brothers' Circus during its Christmas-season engagement in Melbourne in 1903. Afterwards he toured with the company in other Australian towns and in New Zealand during January and February of 1904. Rogers must have been delighted that he

Left to right, Betty and Will Rogers with Margaret and George Wirth. Will Rogers grew close to the Wirths while performing with their circus in 1904. Here they visit the Rogerses in September 1929 *(OkClaW).*

obtained a job with such a prominent circus; certainly, it gave him more confidence in pursuing a career in show business. Texas Jack undoubtedly knew of the Wirth Brothers troupe, and his letter of recommendation probably helped Rogers get a job with the circus. As in South Africa, Rogers was billed not only as the Cherokee Kid but also as a Mexican rope artist doing "fancy rough riding and unique lassoing."[12] Australian and New Zealand newspapers gave Rogers favorable reviews for his lasso artistry.

By March Rogers had decided to leave the circus and return home in time for the upcoming Louisiana Purchase Exposition (St. Louis World's Fair), scheduled to open on April 30. He booked third-class passage on the steamship *Ventura*, which left Auckland on 18 March 1904 and after a rough voyage arrived in San Francisco in early April.[13] From there he took a train home, arriving in Oologah on April 11. He had been away for over two years and had traveled over fifty thousand miles. His trip abroad made Rogers more mature and worldly, and his performances with Texas Jack and the Wirth Brothers gave him substantial introductions to the limelight of show business. When he returned to Indian Territory in 1904, the foundations for his remarkable career were in place.

1. Will Rogers to Sallie McSpadden and All, 5 September 1930, below.
2. Will Rogers to Clement Vann Rogers, 4 September 1903, below.
3. For a comparison of frontier history in Australia and New Zealand see Allen, *Bush and Backwoods*.
4. Will Rogers to Sisters and All, 27 November 1903, below.
5. Will Rogers to Clement Vann Rogers and Folks, 28 September 1903; see also Will Rogers to Spi Trent, 4 December 1903, below.
6. Will Rogers to Spi Trent, 4 December 1903, below.
7. Will Rogers to Clement Vann Rogers and Folks, 28 September 1903, below.
8. *ADB* 12:544–55; *AE* 6:344; Wirth, P., *Life of Philip Wirth;* Wirth, G., *Round the World with a Circus*. For information on the Wirth brothers, see also Biographical Appendix entry, WIRTH, George and Philip Peter Jacob.
9. The With Brothers' Circus staged plays called *Cinderella and the Glass Slipper* and *Dick Turpin's Ride to York*. Their animal acts included a wrestling bear, named Jack; a bucking white elephant, called Ghunisah; and high-jumping greyhounds. (See Will Rogers Scrapbook, 1902–4, CPpR.)
10. Greaves, *Circus Comes to Town*, 15.
11. In 1890 the Wirth Brothers' Circus had featured a Wild West show starring American cowboys (Wirth, P., *Life of Philip Wirth*, 49–52). On circus history, see Croft-Cooke and Cotes, *Circus: A World History;* Nye, *Unembarrassed Muse*, 188–91; Toll, *On with the Show*, 49–79; Wilmeth, *Variety Entertainment and Outdoor Amusements*, 48–65.
12. Wirth Brothers' Circus clipping, Will Rogers Scrapbook, 1902–4, CPpR.
13. "Ventura Battled with Storm Seas," unidentified clipping, Will Rogers Scrapbook, 1902–4, CPpR.

———

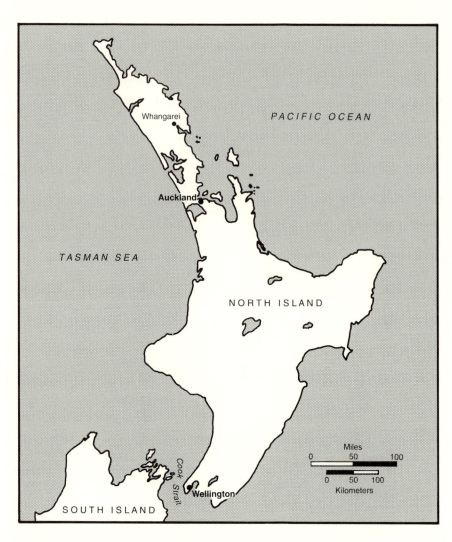

New Zealand, North Island (*map art by Gigi Bayliss*).

To Clement Vann Rogers
4 September 1903
Wellington, New Zealand

The ship Rogers took from Capetown, South Africa, across the Indian Ocean to Australia stopped in New Zealand. From Wellington he penned his father a letter on a pictorial letter card in which he makes many observations about the country and its inhabitants.

Wellington[1]
New Zealand
Sept 4th 1903.

My Dear Papa.

Dont get excited when you look on the map and see where I am now. left Africa ▲ and the show ▲ for I had seen it all and I was afraid you all would think I had permanently located there as I was there for a year but I must see a bit more and get back home consequently must be on the move. I went east from Africa to here across the Indian Ocean went to the south of Australia   we touched the Island of Tasmania[2] then on here   landed yesterday Sep. 3rd after 25 days rough weather and a distance of over 7 thousand miles   Tomorrow I leave for Auckland[3] about 400 miles north of here   will be over here a week or so then drop over to Australia. will be there a couple of months then as you see I am heading around this old Globe to see if it really is round. I will land in America on the west coast then on home which will not be later than Dec 1st. In regard to this country it is as prosperous and good a little country as I ever seen   sheep raising and farming are the principal industry[4] This place is the capitol   a nice little city of 60 thousand. of course all New Zealand belongs and is governed by the english and English is spoken.[5] it is supposed to be the best of the English Colonies according to its size   The natives are more like the mexican tribes of Indians than any I know of and are called Maori[6] [*word illegible*] Indians   I will close   lots of love to all   your loving son

Willie.

Write at once and address me in care of the American Consul   Sydney   Australia

P.S. [*at the top left margin of first page*] Please tell me if you got the money I sent you about 4 months ago. about $300

APCS, rc. OkClaW. Revised versions printed in *CP,* 10 October 1903, and *CR,* 13 October 1903. On New Zealand Pictorial Letter Card featuring a photograph captioned "A representative type of a modern Maori Woman in Native Costume."[7] Hand-addressed to C. V. Rogers, Claremore, Indian Territory, United States of America *Via Frisco.*

"Queen of the Plains"

S. M & Co. Series

Maori Canoeist   Photo by Denton

Postcard of a Maori woman, from Rogers's scrapbook *(Scrapbook 1902–4, CPpR)*.

1. Located at the southern tip of North Island at the country's geographical center, Wellington is New Zealand's capital and a principal economic, transportation, communications, and cultural center. Because of a fine harbor, the city was founded there in 1839 by the New Zealand Company, a British colonization land company, and its agent, Col. William Wakefield. To underscore its connection to the British empire, Wellington

was named in honor of the first duke of Wellington, who supported the colonization of the city. It quickly grew in population and importance and succeeded Auckland as the capital of New Zealand in 1865 (*ENZ*, 610–14; *WNGD*, 1327).

2. Tasmania is located in the South Pacific Ocean about 150 miles south of the state of Victoria, Australia. Discovered in 1642 by the Dutch navigator Abel Tasman, who named it Van Diemen's Land, the island was taken over by Great Britain as a colony in 1803. Renamed Tasmania in 1856, it became a state in the Federal Commonwealth of Australia in 1901. The population of Tasmania was 170,000 in 1901 (Townsley, "Tasmania"; *WNGD*, 1190).

3. Located on North Island, Auckland is New Zealand's chief port and industrial center and the country's largest city. The attraction of a harbor and the surrounding agricultural resources prompted its founding on 18 September 1840 by Gov. William Hobson. The city was named for George Eden, earl of Auckland (*ENZ*, 120–35; *WNGD*, 91).

4. New Zealand's prosperity has largely depended on its farm-based economy. Wool production and the export of lamb, mutton, and dairy products are important to its economy. The wool industry began in 1834 when the Australian John Bell Wright shipped 105 Merino sheep to the country. Sheep farms comprise nearly half of New Zealand's agricultural lands, and sheep stations are primarily located on the drier eastern sections of the two islands. New Zealand is the world's second-leading exporter of wool after Australia. The country is known especially for its Corriedale breed of sheep (*ENZ*, 682–85; Holmes, "New Zealand Economy").

5. New Zealand was originally occupied by native Maoris from Polynesia. European interest in the island first began in 1642 when Able Tasman discovered it for the Dutch East India Company. The island was mapped by Capt. James Cook in 1769. The British and Australians conducted extensive trade with the Maoris, who then numbered about 100,000 to 250,000. By 1839 about 2,000 Europeans were living in New Zealand. In the Treaty of Waitangi in 1840, Maori native leaders ceded the island to the British and it became a crown colony under British sovereignty. New Zealand became a dominion in 1907 and achieved independence as a state in the British Commonwealth in 1931 (Sorenson, "Historical Outline"; *WNGD*, 842).

6. An ancient Eastern Polynesian race, the Maoris migrated to New Zealand, where their culture flourished before colonization by the British. Archaeological evidence suggests that they inhabited New Zealand about 900, but accounts suggest they arrived sometime between 1200 and 1400. They are known for their elaborate ceremonies, rituals, mythology, folklore, music, and crafts, which include carving in wood, stone, or bone; cave paintings; geometrical textile designs; and tattooing. Having been victims of discrimination and fearing confiscation of their lands, the Maoris resisted colonization and fought the British in a series of wars from 1843 to 1848 and from 1860 to 1872. When Rogers was in New Zealand, there were about 50,000 Maoris in the country; their population had been reduced by two-thirds as a result of intertribal wars and conflicts with the Europeans. Today they represent about 9 percent of the population (ca. 350,000) and are mostly engaged in unskilled labor, trades, and farming. The present Maori rights movement is especially directed toward land rights and political equality (Berndt, "Maori"; *EA* 18:252, 20:249; *ENZ*, 408–77; McCreary, "Maori"; *WNGD*, 842).

7. The letter included four pictorial cards as well as a cover pictorial, and writing space. Photographs featured a composite of portraits of Maori leaders and official and ceremonial sites; prospectors panning for gold; a portrait of Sophia, a Ngapuhi tribe member who was a famous guide in the Hot Lakes district; mountaineers near the Great

Tasman Glacier; a laundress working at a naturally hot lake; and composite photographs of Maori peoples of different classes, with a social Darwinist caption claiming that "the difference between the chiefs and the lower-class Maori" could be distinguished from their facial features. Rogers finished writing the letter in the margins of the photograph of Sophia.

To Sallie McSpadden and All
5 September 1903
Wellington, New Zealand

Wellington
New Zealand
Sep. 5

My Dear Sister and all

(Notice)

Please Procure one of the childrens Geographics and acquaint yourself with the where abouts of this particular place.

I just yesterday completed another jump in my Roving trip by crossing the Indian Ocean from Capetown   off to the east and south of Australia calling in at The island of Tasmania   then to this prosperous little city of 60 thousand souls   the capitol of New Zealand. after 25 days of pitching and tossing intermingled with Sea Sickness as usual and also Toothache ~~united~~ ▲ all togeather ▲ formed a hard combination

The Show in Africa wanted me for another tour over the same country ▲ but I wouldent go ▲ and as I had had enough Africa I thought I had better be going if I was ever going to get any where for I will be with you before long.

This may seem at first to be a long way from home and every where else but the fact is it is really closer and much more easily reached to and from America than Africa was as there is a direct line of steamers from here and Australia to frisco which go the six thousand miles to frisco in 17 days from New Zealand or 20 from Australia   so you see I am really nearer   so write to me at once and I will get the letters before I leave for I missed all of my mail from Africa   that music was the last thing I got or will get out of that mail for it could not reach us here   I would be gone. I am in the best of health and feel fine but getting quite homesick

Write to me at once and tell me all the news

Your loving Brother Willie

c/o American Consul. Sydney. Australia.

APCS, rc. OkClaW. New Zealand Pictorial Letter Card hand-addressed to Mrs. J. T. McSpadden, Chelsea, Indian Territory, United States of America, via Frisco.

From Sallie McSpadden
14 September 1903
Chelsea, I.T.

Chelsea, Indian Ty.
September 14, 1903.

Dear Dear Brother:

We were all so glad to get news of you through the letter papa received last Tuesday. All your friends are so anxious to hear from you, as well as our-selves. Oh, we want to see you so badly. We all enjoyed the pictures you sent home Of course we show them to every body. You say in your letter that "Jack" is coming to America.[1] Well that means that you won't be home for several months then. But if he does come here we will certainly "feed him on the fat of the land," for being so nice to "our boy" over there. I cant understand why you don't get more mail from home, for we write often, and send papers also. And I don't think we have ever missed a single thing, either letter or paper, pictures or money that you have sent to us. . . .

Did you get the last two songs I sent you? They were "In the Good Old Summer Time" and "Under the Bamboo Tree"[2] I hope you found several that you could use among the number I sent you, and I am going to order some more in about ten days and will send them right on to you.

Well, I am not going to write such long letters but will write oftener than before and you will stand a better show of getting more in quantity at least, if not quality. We are all very, very well and want you to be home in time to go to the St. Louis World's Fair with us which opens next May.[3] Every one sends you bushels of love and hopes to have you with us soon again.

Lovingly Yr. Sister
Sallie C. McSpadden,

ALS, rc. OkClaW. Envelope hand-addressed to Mr. W. P. Rogers, c/o American Consul, Cape Town, South Africa. Forwarded to Sydney, Australia, and on c/o Wirths' Circus, Murchison,[4] Victoria.

1. Although Texas Jack had appeared in the United States as a performer with a traveling circus in the late nineteenth century before he formed his own traveling Wild West show, no evidence has been found that Texas Jack's Wild West Show and Dramatic Co. performed in the United States in 1904–5 before Texas Jack's death in South Africa in October 1905.
2. "In the Good Old Summer Time" (lyrics by Ron Shields and music by George Evans) was one of the most popular songs of 1902 and was introduced by Blanche Ring in the musical *The Defender.* "Under the Bamboo Tree," words and music by Robert Cole and J. Rosamond Johnson, was also a top hit of 1902 and was introduced in the musical *Sally in Our Alley.* Johnson, an African American composer, wrote many songs with his

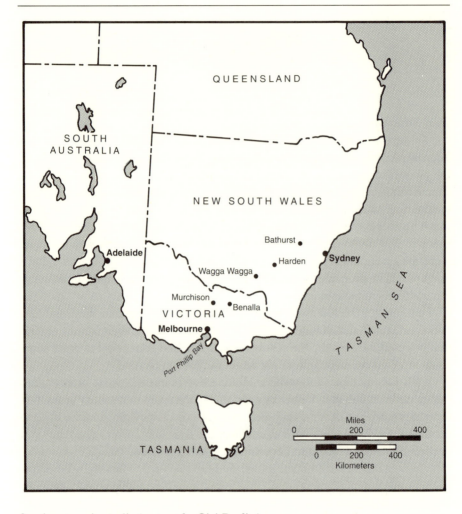

Southeastern Australia *(map art by Gigi Bayliss)*.

brother, James Weldon Johnson (1871–1938), an influential author, statesman, and civil-rights leader (Lax and Smith, *Great Song Thesaurus*, 28, 282, 403).

3. Rogers later performed as a trick roper with Wild West shows at the Louisiana Purchase Exposition (St. Louis World's Fair) in 1904 (Rogers, *Will Rogers*, 82).

4. Located in north-central Victoria, Murchison is a railroad junction eighty-five miles north of Melbourne. It is situated in an agricultural region that produces oats, barley, and livestock (*CLG*, 1266).

To Clement Vann Rogers and Folks
28 September 1903
Sydney, New South Wales, Australia

Sydney.[1] Australia.
Sept 28. 1903.

My Dear Father and home folks.

I suppose you received my cards from New Zealand so you will not be surprised to hear of me out here   I went from Wellington to Auckland by boat   was there a short time then over to Sydney which is $1500[2] miles from New Zealand   was four and a half days on that boat. New Zealand is the most prosperous little country I have ever seen since I left. very good stock and farming and nice cities and towns. Australia though much larger is not so good   they have had a drouth here for the last 5 or 6 years and most all the stock are dead. It was the greatest sheep country in the world and lots of cattle but in the last year it has just began to rain and it will take years for it to be what it was.[3] The tracts of land here held by ▲ the ▲ ranches I think are the largest in the world for it takes so much to keep a sheep or cow on and the ranches here hold hundreds of miles[4]   it is a great timbered country   most all the land is covered by thick timber[5]   it is an enormously big country and very few people only in the cities and away back in the interior is nothing but Negroes[6] and they are still a bit skittish.

The Natives of New Zealand is a kind of Indian called the Mouira but the Natives of Australia are Niggers and the way they can *toss* that Boomerang[7] aint slow. it will shave your hat of agoing and your head of a coming ~~come~~ back. Kangaroos are as common as Rabbits at home. They dont handle stock here like at home   they ride just little flat padded saddles and dont know what a Rope is   they use long stock whips to drive them with. They are not near so good stock men as ▲ even ▲ the *Gouchos* of the Argentine are ~~even~~ but the most conceited set of people on the face of the globe in regard to what they can do and what they know.[8]

Sydney and Melbourne[9] are the principal cities of about $500.000 five hundred thousand ▲ each. ▲ and are greatly like American cities more up to date than any I have been in ▲ since I left home ▲ much more so than England

It is very amusing in ▲ all ▲ these countries any thing new or what they havent had before will be called American. you hear electric street cars called American Tram cars. All the refreshment places are advertised in box car letters "American cold Drinks   American Soda fountain["]   the bars will have up drinks mixed on the American plan. the barber will advertise "American barber chair." you see if it is one of their kind it will be just a strait old stool chair where you sit up as straight as if you were in church and they will shave you and that shave is something chronic. I was always proud in America to own that I was a Cherokee and I find on leaving them that I am equally as proud to own that I am an American for if there is any nation earning a *rep* abroad it is America

I have had arguments with every nationality of man under the sun in regard to the merits of our people and country   from prize fights to the greatest internation questions of which I *knew all* about for you are not an American if you dont know. no matter what it concerns you must know whether you know right or not   for all these big fish stories are traced to the Americans   so you have got to uphold the *rep*

I was out to the races the other day   this is the greatest racing country under the sun everybody man woman and child bets on the races   the very poorest must have their small bet on the races. oh but the ▲ race ▲ courses are pretty ones   all their tracks where the horses run are left with pretty grass are not cleaned out like ours and there is no dust.

I seen the great Australian Derby ▲ worth 40 thousand $ ▲ run and there were 44 starters a mile and a half and at the finish the last horse was not 15 feet behind the first   they were all locked togeather around the track   think of 44 horses running like that   Ive seen two and three race around a track togeather but not 44   the horse that finished 10th head was at the winners hips   it was the greatest sight I ever saw   The tracks are much wider here than at home   In the hurdle or steeplechase races the horses had to run up and down a steep hill and the jumps were 5 ft solid rock   8 horses fell over different jumps   1 horse and one rider killed

Well it is just Spring time here and things look very pretty. I am going out into the country in a few days   then down to Melbourne. If you have already written in reply to my last from N.Z. you had better not write again I dont think I will be here over two months yet   My last letter from home was dated the middle of April. I am in the best of health   feel fine and hope you all are same   I hope I will be able to see you all before many more months   I am as ever your loving son

Willie.

My best to all   (Tell Kates[10] I dont know any news to write him but he can publish this one if he likes[)][11]

ALS, rc. OkClaW. Revised version printed in *CP,* 31 October 1903.

1. Founded in 1788 by the British as a penal colony at Botany Bay on the continent's southeast coast, Sydney is the capital of the state of New South Wales and the largest city in Australia. In 1901 Sydney had a population of about 480,000 people. It was named after the Lord Sydney who was British home secretary from 1784 to 1789 and was instrumental in founding the original convict settlement. Possessing a natural harbor, Sydney is Australia's most important port (Bolton, ed., *History of Australia*, 4:36; *CAE*, 618–20; Clark, M., "Historical Outline"; *WNGD*, 1175).

2. Rogers included a dollar sign in the original letter.

3. Australia is the world's leading producer of wool and exporter of meat, beef, veal, mutton, and lamb. Both sheep and cattle were brought to Australia by European settlers. The most common breed of sheep is the Merino. Primarily because of a severe drought between 1891 and 1902, as well as the proliferation of rabbits and a worldwide depression, sheep declined in Australia from 106.4 million to 53.7 million. It took about thirty years for the wool industry to recover fully (Bolton, ed., *History of Australia*, 4:25–27; *CAE*, 64–66, 573–81; *EA* 2:724).

4. Australian agriculture has been traditionally dominated by large grazing properties. The sheep and cattle stations owned by landlords often totaled hundreds of thousands of acres. Under the Australian land system, wealthy settlers and land syndicates had received from the crown huge grants of leasehold lands, some of which they were eventually able to purchase. Beginning in 1831, the crown lands could be sold at public auction, but in order to prevent widespread settlement, land was sold at a high price. Such factors as the high cost of shipping to distant markets and the risk of floods, bushfires, and droughts underscored the need for ranchers to have considerable wealth and discouraged small property owners. Even in the frontier or bush country, squatters engaged in sheep raising occupied large areas of land in the midnineteenth century. Despite land-reform legislation encouraging ownership of small tracts, Australian agricultural landholding remained in the possession of a few thousand wealthy families (Bolton, ed., *History of Australia*, 4:53–55; Bowen, "Western Australia"; *CAE*, 368–69; Herbert, "Queensland"; Shaw, A., *Story of Australia*, 75; Spate, *Australia*, 46).

5. Australia's main forests are primarily in the highlands and the coastal regions of the country, where there are large tropical rain forests. An indigenous tree common in Australia is the eucalyptus, which was exported to California. Australia has a flourishing timber industry (*CAE*, 638–39; *EA* 2:725–26).

6. Archaeological evidence suggests that the Aborigines have been in Australia for over forty thousand years, having migrated to the continent from Southeast Asia. A nomadic hunting, fishing, and food-gathering people, the Aborigines developed a rich, ceremonial culture with a strong religious orientation toward animism, ancestor worship, magic, totemism, and fertility cults. Tribes lived in separate territories, and all tribal members were linked through kinship. Known for their craftmanship, painting, cave decoration, and carving, including rock engravings, sculptural posts, and figures, the Aborigines were the first people to adopt ground-edge tools. Cooperation and sharing were highly regarded among the Aborigines, and they expressed in their attitude toward the environment a reverence for nature. Their population was around 251,000 when the first white settlers (primarily convicts) arrived from England in 1788. European settlement led to the occupation of much of their land, depopulation, and destruction of their culture. Although the Aborigines were officially British subjects, white settlers committed considerable atrocities against them on the Australian frontier. In 1901, two years before Rogers was in Australia, there were about 66,950 Aborigines in the country; currently there are about 125,000, of whom some 50,000 are full-bloods. Today Aborigines suffer from segregation, poverty, unemployment, and disease. Legal-

ly Australian citizens, they are able to vote and receive government benefits, and Aborigines currently have a strong protest movement calling for land rights, housing and health legislation, equal political representation, and bilingual education (Berndt, "Aborigines, Australia"; Berndt and Berndt, *World of the First Australians; CAE*, 1–5; *EA* 2:709–11; Elkin, "Aborigines").

7. A curved throwing stick indigenous to the Australian Aborigines, the boomerang originated as a weapon for hunting and war and is now mainly used for sport. The art of throwing a boomerang depends on the thrower's ability to have it return to the starting point (*EA* 4:256).

8. Equivalent to the American cowboy and the Argentinean gaucho was the Australian drover, who lived a rugged life moving his herds of sheep and cattle across the Australian outback as he attempted to survive in a desolate landscape and harsh climate. Rogers keenly noted the drover as a different type of stockman. Author Keith Willey wrote: "Instead of fancy cowboy suits and silver-mounted spurs he [the drover] wore an ordinary work-shirt, moleskin trousers, serviceable riding boots and a hat designed to keep off the sun rather than attract attention. And as an antidote to hardship and disappointment, ever-present in his environment and way of life, he cultivated an attitude of social pessimism about the nature of things" (*Drovers*, 3).

9. Melbourne is the capital of the state of Victoria and a principal financial, industrial, transportation, and cultural center. In 1837 the city was named after William Lamb, Lord Melbourne, who was then British prime minister. Melbourne's port, Port Phillip Bay, was discovered in 1802, but it was not until the 1830s that the area was first settled by the British. Melbourne had a population of 494,129 in 1901 (Bolton, ed., *Oxford History of Australia* 4:36; *CAE*, 414–15; *WNGD*, 748).

10. A reference to A. L. Kates, publisher of the *Claremore Progress* (see Biographical Appendix entry, KATES, Albert L.).

11. The version of this letter printed without a postscript in the *Claremore Progress* (31 October 1903) reads: " . . . if he desires. Hoping to hear from you soon, with kindest regards to all my friends, believe me, as ever your loving son, William."

From Sallie McSpadden
3 October 1903
Chelsea, I.T.

Chelsea Indian Territory <u>Oct. 3 1903</u>

My Dear Willie:

We just received your card[1] a few minutes ago and we are all so glad you are coming home. I have just written the fact to papa who is not very well. but I think when he really knows you are on your way home he will be like a boy again. . . . You would be surprised at the inquiries made for you, not only by relatives and intimate friends, but by people you would think hardly knew you. We want you home by Thanksgiving, if possible. We all spend that time with me and if you are only with us it will be a real and true Thanksgiving. Christmas we all go over to Mauds and we are sure you will be home by then. I am just writing to tell you how anxious we are to see you, and will tell you the news when you come. All send bushels of love and echo the cry—"Hurry Hurry Home."

Lovingly Yr. Sister
Sallie C. McSpadden
Chelsea,
Ind. Ty.

ALS, rc. OkClaW. On Bank of Chelsea[2] letterhead, J. T. McSpadden, president, W. G. Milam,[3] vice president, John D. Scott, cashier, and Charles H. Windham, assistant cashier. Envelope hand-addressed to Mr. W. P. Rogers, Sydney, Australia, c/o American Consul. Forwarded to Wirths' Circus, Murchison, Victoria. Return address, J. T. McSpadden, Chelsea, U.S.A., I.T.

1. Will Rogers to Sallie McSpadden and All, 5 September 1903, above.
2. Prominent citizens of Chelsea met on 18 January 1896 in the Odd Fellows Hall for the purpose of organizing a private bank. The Bank of Chelsea was granted a perpetual charter by the federal government under Arkansas law and was the first state bank in the Cherokee Nation. It officially opened on 23 March 1896 with a cash balance of $1,808.41. John Thomas McSpadden, the husband of Sallie McSpadden and the brother-in-law of Will Rogers, was a founder of the bank and its first president (DuPriest et al., *Cherokee Recollections*, 152–53; *HRC*, 301; see also Biographical Appendix entry, MCSPADDEN, John Thomas).
3. William Guinn (Willie) Milam (1860–1934) was a founder of the Bank of Chelsea as well as a businessman, cattleman, and public official. He served as councilman and mayor of Chelsea and as Rogers County commissioner from 1907 to 1913, helping to develop school districts, townships, and the county government immediately after statehood. In 1908 Milam and his son acquired control of the bank, and members of the Milam family have been involved in its operations for several generations (*HRC*, 316–17; Starr, *History of the Cherokee Indians*, 575).

From May Stine
4 October 1903
Oolagah, I.T.

Oolagah, I.T.
Oct 4 '03.

My dear Brother,

Well we Recieved your dear letter yestaday, and was so glad to here from you again, but we hope and pray we will see you soon. Well it has been so long sence you left and I have written and I have so much to tell you I hardly no where to begin. We quit the Hotel and moved to Oolagah   Frank runs a butcher shop in the winter and a Ice Cream parlor in Summer. Johnnie[1] goes to School to Miss Kate Ellis. Jack runs over town and our daughter Laney[2] is the sweetest thing   everybody says she looks like you   she is seven months old. . . . You just much be at home by Christmas are it wont seem like Christmas.

May Rogers Yocum Stine and family members in 1909, the year of her death. *Back row (left to right):* May; her second husband, Frank Stine (who is holding their baby, Owen, born in 1909); and their eldest son, Jake Stine, born in 1900. Their daughter Lanie, named in honor of Cap Lane, is in the front row on the far right. She was born in 1903 (*OkClaW*).

Johnny Yocum (1893–1952), Will Rogers's nephew, was the only surviving child of Rogers's sister May's first marriage to Matthew Yocum (*OkClaW*).

Papa hasent be up in quite awhile   he was real sick the last time he was up. he had Irean and Ethel[3] with him. I havent been to Chelsea sence May. I tell you Oolagah is building and they is folks wanting houses here every day and cant get them. they is lots at the coal banks[4]   they are sure at work. When ever we here from you why Frank just takes it up to the shop for every body wants to no what you had to say and when you are comeing home. Well I will close for I don't no nothing to write of Intrest for I never do leave Oolagah. All I hope is the next news you give us will be in person. May God bless and pretect, and return you save to the ones that love you so. They all join me in love,

May.

ALS, rc. OkClaW. Envelope hand-addressed to William P. Rogers, Sydney, Australia, c/o American Consulate. Forwarded c/o Wirths' Circus, Murchison, Victoria. Return address printed, Crescent Meat Market, Oolagah, I.T.

1. John Vann Yocum (1893–1952) was the son of May Rogers Yocum Stine and her first husband, Matthew Yocum (see Biographical Appendix entry, STINE, May Rogers Yocum).
2. Mattie Lane (Lanie) Stine (see Biographical Appendix entry, MITCHELL, Mattie Lane Stine).
3. Clem V. Rogers's granddaughters Maud Irene McSpadden (1896–1973), daughter of J. T. McSpadden and Sallie Rogers, and Ethel Lindsey Lane (1894–1975), daughter of C. L. Lane and Maud Rogers (see Biographical Appendix entry, MILAM, Maud Irene McSpadden).
4. Oologah grew in population in the early 1900s largely because of coal-mining industry. Coal was discovered as early as 1890, and by the next decade there were many strip-pit coal mines producing eight to ten carloads of coal daily. Coal mined in the area was shipped on the Kansas and Arkansas Valley Railway (later the Missouri Pacific). Edward Sunday and his son, W. E. Sunday, operated a productive coal mine in the area, loading eight to ten carloads a day until 1933 (*History of Oologah*, 10–11; see also Biographical Appendix entry, SUNDAY, William Esther).

To Clement Vann Rogers and Folks
22 November 1903
Benalla, Victoria, Australia

Banella.[1] Victoria. Australia
Nov. 22. 03.

My Dear Father and old [all] the folks

I will drop you this card and tell you how I am getting on and tell you how sorry I am to not be able to be at home Xmas but it will be impossible and cant be helped   I know you people dont want to see me any worse than I want to see you   I leave here about the 1st of Feb   I am getting on O.K. in this country am away back in the Interior. am going down to Melbourne soon. I am out on

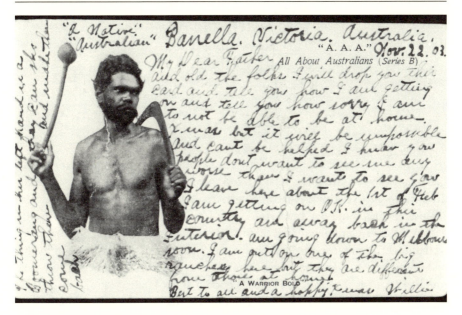

Postcard of an Aborigine man, sent by Rogers to his father *(OkClaW)*.

one of the big ranches here but they are different from those at home. Best to all and a happy Xmas

Willie

[*Note beside photograph of*] "A Native Australian"   The thing in his left hand is a Boomerang and they can sho throw these and make them come back

APCS, rc. OkClaW. On an "All About Australians (Series B)" pictorial postcard featuring a photograph of a Native Australian man with a boomerang and mallet, described as "A Warrior Bold."

1. Located in the northern part of the state of Victoria, the town of Benalla is 104 miles northeast of Melbourne, situated on the Broken River. The town had 2,509 people in 1891. It is centered in a farming region noted for sheep, cattle, and pig raising and for the production of wheat, barley, flax, and potatoes. The Aborigines, resenting white intrusions on their territory, attacked and killed sheepherding squatters near the town in 1838. The name of the town comes from an Aborigine word meaning "big waterholes" (*AEP,* 406, 410; *CAE,* 69; *WNGD,* 135).

To Sisters and All
27 November 1903
Murchison, Victoria, Australia

WILL ROGERS HEARD FROM AGAIN

Murchison, Victoria, Australia
November 27, 1903.

My Dear Sister and all the Troop: —

At last I have received a few of the letters you have written me, four of them that has followed me from Africa, and one each from you and sister May, directed to me to Sydney, Australia, written on October 4. Some of these were six months old, but it had been eight since I had last heard. Oh, no! It was only a rumor that I wasn't glad to get them, and more than glad to know you were all well and getting on nicely. Well, as for me, I am as usual in the best of health and doing very well out here in Kangaroo land. I don't like this country very much except for farming. It is not as good a stock country as the Argentine Republic. Nothing but trees, no open country. All just like a grove, with very little underbrush. All big trees. There is about as rotten a government here as one would wish to see.[1] I am now out here with a friend of mine on one of the big ranches or stations as they call them. I am going down to Melbourne soon, will be there about Christmas.

I think I will depart from here about the last of January or the first of February.

There is a native camp of black fellows here, and I was trying to throw the boomerang. About the best way I could get it to come back was to send one of the little black fellows after it. Have been out chasing kangaroos on some of the fastest horses I ever rode. Out here all of the horses are jumpers. The fences are all rail fences, and you are no horseman at all if you go to the gate; you just top the fences, which are five feet high, and which is considered no jump at all. The horses are part thoroughbred, as all the ranches have their horses bred up like that, but they ride only one or two horses each. The saddles are little plain padded ones, only it has big pads in front of your knees, like wings, so you can grip it good. They have no horn or back. They don't use a rope at all; but, say, they use a cattle whip, not like our old big ones, but they are small and long, about twenty or twenty-five feet. Oh, but they did paralyze me when I saw them use them. I did not know what a whip was made for until I saw these fellows use them. I tried one, but only succeeded in tying knots around my own neck. But that wasn't so bad as the Bolos[2] that I tried in South America. I knocked knots on my head so that I could not get my hat on for a week.

I still have my saddle and outfit with me; these fellows call it a rocking chair.

Well, I have seen the horsemanship of all these countries, and it is all on somewhat different principles, but they all accomplish the same thing, and in the end get their cattle work done, and that is all that is required. I think the cowboys are the kings of the lot.

I see by your letter that papa still has my young horse, but you don't mention old Comanche. You don't mean to say there is no Comanche, or that he is dead. If so, I will never come home, for it would not be home if he was not there.[3]

You were both saying in your letters that I was mad at you for publishing my letters or parts of them. You are mistaken. I don't care, if you like to have them published, or the parts of them that might interest any of my friends. I was only ashamed of them, is why I didn't like them published.

I got a nice letter from May,[4] which told me all the news. You all only write about two pages, then stop. You used to write long letters. I have received only two from papa since I left home.

I know you people are planning to attend the World's Fair. Don't be alarmed but what I will be there. I will be by your side. I did not get the last songs you mentioned. I only got two packages at the same time. As for papers, I never received any since those first ones I got in South America.

I can't tell you where to write, for I may not be here to receive it, so wait until you hear from me again.

Your loving brother.

Will.

PD. Printed in *CP,* 23 January 1904.

1. The six separate colonies of Australia united into the first Australian Common-wealth in 1901. There was considerable political turmoil after the Commonwealth's formation with three political parties contesting for popular support: the Conservative free-traders, the Liberal protectionists, and the Labor Party. At the time Rogers wrote, the nation was preparing for its second federal election on December 16, in which the Labor prime minister, Alfred Deakin, was reelected. Women voted in the election for the first time (*AEP,* 118; *AZSP,* 13–14).

2. Bolas were weapons used by the gauchos of Argentina to hunt and entangle wild cattle, horses, and ostriches. They consisted of rawhide thongs tied together at one end with heavy stone or iron balls at the other end (Slatta, *Cowboys of the Americas,* 133).

3. Comanche, Rogers's favorite roping pony, was well taken care of by several friends while Rogers was away. Rogers rode the horse in roping events through 1905, including the Madison Square Garden horse show of that year. After the event Zack Mulhall had a dispute with Rogers and in retaliation sent Comanche to a farm in the South without Rogers's permission. Comanche died around 1914 (Collings, *Old Home*

Ranch, 61, 85; McSpadden, "Horses and Horse Collars," and Marquis, "Will Rogers and His Horses" in Horses file, OkClaW; see also Biographical Appendix entry, MULHALL, Colonel Zack).

4. May Stine to Will Rogers, 4 October 1903, above.

To Clement Vann Rogers
November 1903
Harden, New South Wales, Australia

STILL IN AUSTRALIA.

C. V. ROGERS HAS RECEIVED THE FOLLOWING LETTER
FROM HIS SON WILLIE:

Harden,[1] New South Wales, Australia, Nov. 1903.

My Dear Father.

I will write you again and tell you where I am and that I am doing all right. I wrote you a few weeks ago from Sydney. I suppose you got it. I am away back in the interior of the country where all the stock ranches are located. This was a great stock country before the drouth which lasted for years. It is a timbered country, trees all over but not thick like a grove. This is a good year here, and the country looks very pretty. It is getting summer here now. It is the greatest sheep country in the world. I will be out here a short time longer, and then go to Melbourne and will leave this country just after Christmas, as I can't get home for Christmas. I am awfully sorry I will not be there, but when I do come it will be to stay, for have I certainly seen a bit and learned some things since I left, but have had a very good time.

I am looking for some mail from you all to come out here in a few days in answer to the one I wrote you from New Zealand. Hope it comes, for my last news from home was dated in April seven months ago.

I will write to the girls. A mail leaves here every three weeks. If you don't get them before Christmas, I do so hope you will all have a pleasant time and remember that I am as usual enjoying myself, even though I am thousands of miles away. Lots of love to all. Your loving son,

Willie.

PD. Printed in *CP,* 12 December 1903. Also printed in *CR,* 18 December 1903.

1. Located in the state of New South Wales on Murrimboola Creek, Harden is about 238 miles southwest of Sydney. A railway-junction town surrounded by a farming community, Harden is noted for dairy and wheat farming, lamb raising, and wool production. The town was named after a railway surveyor (*AE,* 310).

To Spi Trent
4 December 1903
Murchison, Victoria, Australia

STILL IN AUSTRALIA.

SPY TRENT HAS RECEIVED THE FOLLOWING LETTER FROM WILL ROGERS.

Manachusin [Murchison], Australia,
Dec. 4

Mr. S. E. Trent:

My Dear Old Friend: —

It has been quite awhile since I heard from or about you. I answered your letter which I received a year or so ago, but did not get a reply. Well, I should think that by this time you are one of the firm, if you are still at your same job.[1] I know it is useless to ask you if you are doing well, for I always predicted that you would. As for me, I am the same old Will, doing very well and seeing the biggest part of the world. I am away back in the interior on one of the big ranches with a friend of mine, having quite a time.

It is all English-speaking white people in Australia, but a few blacks who are still a bit cranky. There is a camp of them close here. They are not kinky headed like negroes but have straight hair, more like an Indian. Say, but they can throw a boomerang. It sails all about the place, then back and they catch it in their hands. There are lots of stock in this country. I have seen a lot of it since I landed, and will see a lot more before I leave, which will be about the first of February, 1904. So I will have traveled 34,000 miles since I left home, and seen quite a bit of the world. Still I look forward, longing to see the old home country again, for there is no country like home.

Well, I hope this will find you married and settled down.[2] How is old Paris and R.O.?[3] I hope they are not starving some good girl to death. When you write home tell them I will try and write to them before long. Also to Paris. I guess he is still taking in roping contests. They don't know what a rope is in this country. Well, I will stop. Hoping to see you soon, I am, as ever your old friend and cousin.

Will.

P.S. Give my very best love to cousins Mollie, Georgia, Tom, R.O. and all the rest.[4] Tell them old Will is enjoying himself as usual.

Will.

PD. Printed in *CP,* 30 January 1904.

1. Spi Trent worked as a bookkeeper at the Parkinson-Trent Mercantile Co. in Okmulgee, I.T., until 1904, when he took a job in Oklahoma City (Trent, *My Cousin Will Rogers*, 145–49; see Biographical Appendix entry, TRENT, Spi).

2. Trent married twice. This first wife was Allie Belle Williams; his second wife's name was Clarice (*WRFT*, 121).

3. References to Dick Parris and possibly to Spi Trent's father, Dr. Robert Owen (R.O.) Trent.

4. References to Mollie Minx Brown Trent (b. 1854), Spi Trent's mother; Georgia Trent, Spi Trent's sister; Thomas Trent (b. 1887), Spi Trent's brother; and Robert Owen Trent, Spi Trent's father. Will Rogers and Spi Trent were distant cousins. Mollie Trent was the daughter of John Lowery Brown and Ann E. Schrimsher, who was the half sister of Mary America Schrimsher Rogers, Will Rogers's mother (*OCF* 2:156; *WRFT*, 120–21).

Performance Review from the *Melbourne Age*
28 December 1903
Melbourne, Victoria, Australia

The first notice of Rogers's employment with the Wirth Brothers' Circus was printed during the show's annual Christmas engagement in Melbourne. Owned and operated by George and Philip Wirth, this popular Australian entertainment was considered Australia's largest and most outstanding circus. Rogers performed a rope and horse-vaulting act and continued to be billed as the Cherokee Kid.[1]

WIRTH'S CIRCUS

A brief season was entered upon by Messrs. Wirth Bros.' circus on Saturday, and during the ensuing fortnight two performances will be given each day. So far as several of the artists are concerned the season will take the nature of a farewell, as their engagements have expired and they propose to leave Australia at an early date. The Howard Bros., whose mystifying performance still baffles all who witness it, Herr Pagel and others are bound for fresh fields.[2] They went through their turns on Saturday in a manner which gave great delight to the large audiences which filled the big tent both afternoon and evening. Some novel features were introduced by Mons. Ragoul, with the wild beasts which play such a prominent part in the show. A tiger essaying the act of Blondin, two others indulging in see saw, and drawing a third in a chariot at full gallop, were all given with that neatness and promptness which denoted the completeness of their training. It was equally astonishing to see such a miscellaneous collection of animals, as a lion, pony, dog and goat, going through a variety of acts by word of command or gesture. The Cherokee Kid made his first appearance, and gave an interesting display of rough riding and lassooing. A picturesque turn was that presented by Miss Phyliss Wirth. After going through the serpentine dance on horseback, she reappeared as a human butterfly, circling round the ring by the aid of a simple contrivance, finally alighting on the ground amid most cordial marks of recognition of the merit of her act. The flying Eugenes gave an excellent display of single and double somersaults, and Mr. P. Wirth gave further evidence of the success of his training of the beautiful white mustang Moncrief. Herr Pagel again displayed his mighty strength, carrying a horse estimated to weigh nearly half a ton up a ladder. The show is full of excellent features.

PD. Printed in *Melbourne Age*, 28 December 1903.

1. The Wirth Brothers' Circus played in Melbourne beginning on 26 December 1903 and staged performances through 8 January 1904 (letter from Mark St Leon to WRPP, 9 February 1993; advertisements and reviews, *Melbourne Argus*, 26 December 1903–8 January 1904). Rogers was in the city over Christmas as his letter to his father indicates (3 January 1904). An undated program in Rogers's 1902–4 scrapbook lists Rogers as number 16 on the bill: "Fancy Rough Riding and Unique Lassoing (first appearance in Australia), the American Cowboy. The CHEROKEE KID." An unidentified clipping (ca. 26 December 1903) mentioned that the show opened on Boxing Night and that a "fresh feature was the rough riding of the 'Cherokee Kid'." Other scrapbook clippings also mentioning Rogers's name reveal that he played with the circus in Wagga Wagga and Bathurst, Australian towns in New South Wales. On the circus, see clippings, box 25, OkClaW; clippings, Will Rogers Scrapbook 1902–4, CPpR; *ADB* 12: 544–55; *AE* 6: 344; Brennan, "Australia's Biggest Circus," 49; Rogers, *Will Rogers*, 79–80; Wirth, P., *Life of Philip Wirth;* Wirth, G., *Round the World with a Circus*. See also Biographical Appendix entry, WIRTH, George and Philip Peter Jacob).

2. Andrew and James Howard did an act in which one brother sat blindfolded in the ring and identified articles his brother found in the audience (clipping, box 25, OkClaW). A weight lifter, Herr Pagel was advertised as "the German Hercules" who could wrestle five-hundred-pound lions and carry a full-grown horse up a twenty-foot ladder (clippings, box 25, OkClaW, and Will Rogers Scrapbook 1902–4, CPpR). Born in February 1878 in the Pomeranian town of Plathe near the Baltic coast, Frederick Wilhelm August (William) Pagel is considered the most famous circus name in South Africa, where he became a naturalized citizen about 1918. Before forming his own circus, Pagel was a star attraction as a strongman in circuses around the world. After performing with the popular FitzGerald Brothers' Circus in Australia, Pagel signed a contract with the Wirth Brothers' Circus in 1903–4. It was at this time that he and Rogers performed on the same bill. Shortly thereafter, Pagel returned to South Africa, where he created his own circus. He traveled with his own troupe throughout South Africa and other African nations. Africans called the show "istrongimani" after his strongman act and the name "istrongimani" eventually became synonymous with all circuses in the region. Pagel acted as ringmaster in his own show and was a noted animal trainer. He became known especially for wrestling his favorite lion, Hopetoun. William Pagel died on 13 October 1948 from complications of a cerebral hemorrhage at Knysna, Cape Province, South Africa (Birkby, *Pagel Story*).

To Clement Vann Rogers and Folks
3 January 1904
Melbourne, Victoria, Australia

STILL IN AUSTRALIA

Melbourne, Australia
Jan. 3 1904.

My Dear Father and all the Home Folks: —

Christmas has come and gone, and I hear you all had a good old time up to Chelsea. I would have given anything to have been there but I could not; still I had a right good time away off down here. I was in Melbourne the largest city of Australia, and a very pretty place to put in Christmas. Out in these countries are as nothing compared with at home. No Christmas trees, scarcely any presents given, only cards sent to your friends, and to cap the climax it is as hot as the 4th of July. This is the last old Christmas away from home for me. I received some letters from May and Sallie dated Oct. 3, a few weeks ago; have been looking for more; but they haven't come yet. I have been writing to you all regular, and I hope you gotten all the letters. I am in the best of health and feeling fine; have got a good job[1] here but will leave soon. I can't tell you just when I will land up there, but I can tell you that I will be there in plenty of time for the opening — not closing — of that "St. Louis Street Fair."[2] I will drop in on you all some of these days when you are not looking for me or thinking anything about me. Well, I will close. Give my best love to all my folks and friends.

Ever your affectionate son,
Will.

P.S. — You need not write for I would not get it. W.

PD. Printed in *CP,* 30 January and 13 February 1904.

1. A reference to Rogers's employment with the Wirth Brothers' Circus.
2. Will Rogers was in St. Louis when the Louisiana Purchase Exposition (St. Louis World's Fair) officially opened on 30 April 1904 (Ketchum, *Will Rogers,* 90).

Review from the *Auckland Star*
20 January 1904
Auckland, New Zealand

Rogers performed with the circus during its tour of New Zealand in January and February and received a favorable review in the Auckland paper.

AMUSEMENTS.
Wirths' Circus.
A Successful Opening.

The love of the circus seems to be inherent in man, if only openly enthusiastic in early youth, and veiled hypocritically in later years. It would be interesting no doubt to trace the causes of the deep hold the circus has upon the average human being, but this article is intended to be a notice of the new show put on by the Wirth Bros. The firm's name is a household word in Auckland, for their lengthy residence here last winter is well remembered. The initial performance of this tour of New Zealand was given before a huge crowd which filled every corner of the great tent, and the frequent applause the spectators gave was hearty and genuine. It has been said cynically that all circuses are the same circus, but Messrs. Wirth certainly belong to the better order of circus proprietors, and their show on this occasion is far from wearisome. One is inclined to think the programme unnecessarily overloaded, there being no less than 27 acts, but the performance ended before eleven o'clock, and the sequence was so quick that one had scarcely time to get tired. The great grievance the critic usually has to prefer against average circuses—the unvarying sameness of the different acts—is in large measure absent and one can confidently recommend the two newest acts—Herr Pagel's and the Cherokee Kid's—as well as the performance of the Howard Brothers. These are distinctly good, and would mark the advent of the circus as a thing of moment anywhere.

Herr Pagel's strength appears on the face of it almost superhuman, and certainly Samsonian. He claims to be a naturally strong man—not developed by any particular system, unless it be hard work. Without question Herr Pagel is a splendid specimen of the muscular human, and his feats excite wonder and admiration in everyone who sees them. There is a convincing indentation and shaking of the earth when his mighty dumbbells fall, and one cannot deny the strength of a man who, as Herr Pagel did, holds a matter of seventeen men on his chest for the space of a minute. Herr Pagel lifted weights up to 280 lbs. with one hand to the limit of his reach; he heaved up a heavy solid bell with a man on it similarly; and he carried a 1050 lb. horse up a ladder. He also effected a truly exciting feat: he entered the cage of a raging lion, forced open its mouth by sheer strength and drove the startled animal back to its kennel. Prolonged applause followed this act, and the equally effective one of supporting the seventeen men. The other new act is, like most of our new things, American—a lassooing business. The Cherokee Kid is a gentleman with a large American accent and a splendid skill with lassoos. He demonstrated what could be done with the whirling loop by bringing up a horse and its rider from impossible position, once throwing together two lassos encircling man and horse separately. He also showed the spectators how to throw half-hitches on to objects at a distance, and did other clever work with the ropes. It was a very interesting performance.[1] One need not be concerned to know how the clever Howard Brothers effect their mysterious communication with one another—some will favor the memory system, and others the more esoteric theory of thought-transference; but the essential fact remains that these clever men have never been found out in a mistake. They pass from one person to another with lightning rapidity, the one inquiring and the other, sitting blindfolded in the ring, answering questions with particularity concerning articles selected from amongst the spectators. If it be a system, it reflects the greater credit on the workers of it, as well as the creators. This act never palls on the spectators.

The newest idea put forward by the management amongst the animals is "something unique in animal training," to wit, the performance in the same cage of a lion, a dog, a pony, and a goat, the whole ultimately lying down together quite peacefully—under the eye and whip of their brilliantly successful trainer, M. Jean Rogalle [Ragoul]. He startled the spectators into a mighty thrill when he seized the lion by its feet and walked across the ring with it coiled about his neck. The performance of the tigers in the chariot and the rest of their tricks we have seen before, but custom does not dull the interest in them. The other acts are much the same as before, save that they are all distinctly better done. On the whole the performance was honestly good, and the new turns and the animals alone make the circus worth a couple of visits; and no one should miss seeing Herr Pagel. The circus is located at Freeman's Bay, and trams run to and from it every night before and after the performance.

PD. Printed in *Auckland Star,* 20 January 1904.

1. In one program Rogers was advertised as the "Cherokee Kid, America's Champion Mexican Cowboy, Expert Lasso Thrower and Rough Rider." To accent Rogers's appearance as a "Mexican Cowboy," Mrs. George Wirth made Rogers a colorful red velvet suit with a gold braid. He later wore it to impress Betty Blake when she saw him perform at the 1904 St. Louis World's Fair. Rogers also supposedly performed tricks on horseback, locking his feet around the saddle's horn, leaning down, and grabbing a handkerchief on the ground as his horse raced at full speed (Croy, *Will Rogers,* 86; Rogers, *Will Rogers,* 83).

To Sisters and Folks
4 February 1904
Whangarei, New Zealand

GONE INTO THE SHOW BUSINESS AGAIN.

Whangarhei,[1] New Zealand,
February 4, 1904.

My Dear Sister and all the Home Folks: —

I will write you all and let you hear how I am doing and to tell you that I am coming home very soon now, sure. I will be there certain before the opening of the St. Louis Fair, honest.

Well, since I last wrote I am back over in New Zealand, where I was when I first came from Africa. Have been here about two weeks. You see that is on my way home, as it is five days nearer Frisco than Australia.

I didn't have quite enough money after touring Australia to come home, so I was offered an engagement with Wirth Bros. big circus at a very good salary and I told them I would go over to New Zealand with them for a few weeks only. They want me for twelve months, but I have seen enough for me and want to come home.

We played the first place over here at Auckland. I am doing a roping and a trick riding act and have been a big success, for it was never done here before. I will send you a sheet with some of the newspaper clippings, also lithograph photos of myself with some fancy roping and a program of the show, which will show you and all my friends what I am doing.

This little New Zealand is the prettiest place I ever saw. Oh, such beautiful scenery! We are away up a river tonight; just came in by a little steamboat about an hour ago.[2] We are not showing till tomorrow. There are high mountains all around us. This is just a small town. I am up in my hotel all alone writing this. I want it to catch the Frisco boat that leaves Auckland, which is fifty miles from here, on the 5th of February. I have not had mail but once since I left Africa; that was a letter from Mae, dated Oct. 3d. I won't get any now, I don't suppose. I hope you are all as well as I am. I will see you all for sure this time not later than May 1st.

Well, I will close but will write again soon. You needn't write, for you won't have time. Lots of love to all of you and my friends.[3]

Brother Willie.

PD. Printed in *CP,* 5 March 1904.

1. Located on the coast of North Island and surrounded by hills, Whangarei is situated on the banks of the Hatea River, about 180 miles by road north of Auckland. The capital of the Northland region and a transportational center, Whangarei is a farming community involved in sheep and cattle farming, fruit growing, and dairy farming as well as various small industries. The town's name is derived from *whanga* meaning "laying in wait" and *rei* meaning "charge," suggesting northern peoples anticipating invasion from the south (*ENZ* 3:644; *WNGD*, 1337).

2. The Northland Main Trunk railway, connecting Whangarei to Auckland, was not built until 1923 (*ENZ* 3:644).

3. The article went on to include a review of the Wirth Brothers' Circus from the *Auckland Herald*, which repeated information similar to the review in the *Auckland Star* on 20 January 1904.

Notice from the *Vinita Leader*
14 April 1904
Vinita, I.T.

On 25 March 1904 the Claremore Messenger *reported that Will Rogers had written to his father from New Zealand that he would "arrive home early in May." Will apparently made better time in his travels than he had hoped, traveling steerage on the steamship* Ventura *from New Zealand to San Francisco. The boat left Auckland on 18 March 1904 and encountered stormy seas in the Pacific.[1] Rogers arrived home on 11 April 1904 from his experiences in the Southern Hemisphere. To welcome his son home, Clem V. Rogers hosted a family reunion dinner.[2]*

HOME FROM THE ANTIPODES.

Will Rogers, son of C.V. Rogers of Claremore, has returned from the other side of the world. For some time he has been engaged with a wild west show in Australia, South Africa and New Zealand. He also worked on ranches. His work with a lariat was a revelation to the people over there.

PD. Printed in *VL*, 14 April 1904.

1. An article in Will Rogers's scrapbook described how "monster combers continually climbed over the steamship's brow and sides and swept along the decks. All the cabins forward were flooded and for twenty-one hours the steamer only maintained enough speed to keep her head-on to the seas." An officer on the bridge nearly fell overboard. On its way to San Francisco the ship stopped in Pago Pago, Fanning Island, and Honolulu. The *Ventura* listed only eight cabin passengers and one steerage (Rogers) to Honolulu. It carried eighty-six cabin, sixty-three second-cabin, and forty steerage passengers from Honolulu to San Francisco, many of whom were bound for the St. Louis World's Fair ("Ventura Battled with Storm Seas," unidentified clipping, Will Rogers Scrapbook, 1902–4, CPpR).

2. On 16 April 1904 the *Claremore Progress* reported: "Col. C.V. Rogers was here Monday [11 April 1904] and unexpectedly his son, Will, came in the same evening and he went home and called in all of his children to attend a dinner at Claremore the next day." On 15 April 1904 the *Claremore Messenger* also reported that Rogers had returned and

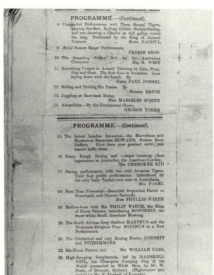

Rogers was listed as act 16 in the Wirth Brothers' Circus program *(Scrapbook 1902–4, CPpR)*.

"has many interesting things to say of his trip, the customs of the people, their mode of living, etc." The *Claremore Progress* likewise noted that the "Progress has in the past year contained many letters of interest from his pen of his travels and hope as soon as he is rested up and has a respite from the importunities of his friends for a recital of his adventures to receive further descriptive accounts of his travels" (16 April 1904).

To Sisters
20 April 1904
Claremore, I. T.

Shortly after his arrival home Rogers wrote his sisters that he was joining Zack Mulhall's Congress of Rough Riders and Ropers at the St. Louis Louisiana Purchase Exhibition. In doing so, he began another major turning point in his career, appearing as a lasso artist in Wild West shows and vaudeville in the United States.

Claremore, I.T. Tuesday Night 1904

My Dear Sisters

Will write you to let you hear where I am   have been up to Talala Mays Halls Ranch the Farm Lanes Lipes and all and will leave for Tahlequah in the a.m. will only be there a bout two or three nights. then back and by Chelsea for a day or so   then onto the Fair[1] I heard from Mulhall and he wants me   they will send old Comanche in a day or so with a shipment that he is bringing from Sapulpa[2] but I wont go for a few days   Papa says it is all right with him and he seems well pleased. I will close

Love to all

Willie

ALS, rc. OkClaW. On Lindel Hotel, E. H. Gibbs, Proprietor, letterhead.

1. On 29 April 1904 the *Claremore Messenger* reported that "Will Rogers left Monday night [25 April 1904] to join a wild west show which will hold forth at the exposition at St. Louis this summer."

2. Sapulpa, thirteen miles southwest of Tulsa, is the county seat of Creek County, Okla. Its post office was established on 1 July 1889, and the town was named for James Sapulpa, a Creek Indian. *Sapulpa* in Creek means "sweet potato." Incorporated in 1897, Sapulpa in its early years attracted many outlaws (including the Dalton and James gangs), and its Stockade Hotel was the scene of considerable revelry. The town grew as a result of its location on the St. Louis and San Francisco Railroad, which transported cattle to St. Louis and Kansas City (Gideon, *History of Indian Territory*, 156; Shirk, *Oklahoma Place Names*, 187; *WNGD*, 1079).

Biographical Appendix

Rogers Genealogy

WILL ROGERS'S EARLY FAMILY LIFE, THE EXPERIENCES OF HIS PARENTS, AND the marriages of his sisters and their establishment of their own families, form an important part of this volume. The following four family trees chart the relationships of Will Rogers's family members. The first chart begins with Rogers's maternal and paternal grandparents, the Schrimshers and the Rogerses, and ends with Will Rogers and Betty Blake Rogers's four children. The second shows the nuclear family of Rogers's eldest sister, Sallie Rogers McSpadden, followed by the family trees of his other two sisters, Maud Rogers Lane and May Rogers Yocum Stine. Profiles of many of these family members appear in the Biographical Appendix.

Will Rogers Family Tree

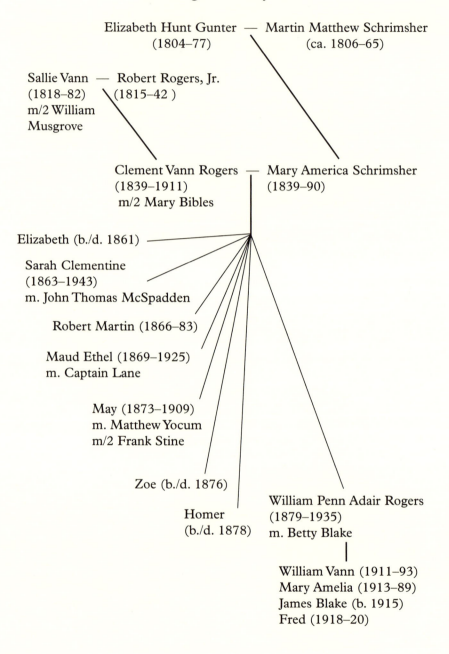

Elizabeth Hunt Gunter — Martin Matthew Schrimsher
(1804–77)   (ca. 1806–65)

Sallie Vann — Robert Rogers, Jr.
(1818–82)   (1815–42)
m/2 William
Musgrove

Clement Vann Rogers — Mary America Schrimsher
(1839–1911)   (1839–90)
m/2 Mary Bibles

Elizabeth (b./d. 1861)

Sarah Clementine
(1863–1943)
m. John Thomas McSpadden

Robert Martin (1866–83)

Maud Ethel (1869–1925)
m. Captain Lane

May (1873–1909)
m. Matthew Yocum
m/2 Frank Stine

Zoe (b./d. 1876)

Homer
(b./d. 1878)

William Penn Adair Rogers
(1879–1935)
m. Betty Blake

William Vann (1911–93)
Mary Amelia (1913–89)
James Blake (b. 1915)
Fred (1918–20)

McSpadden Family Tree

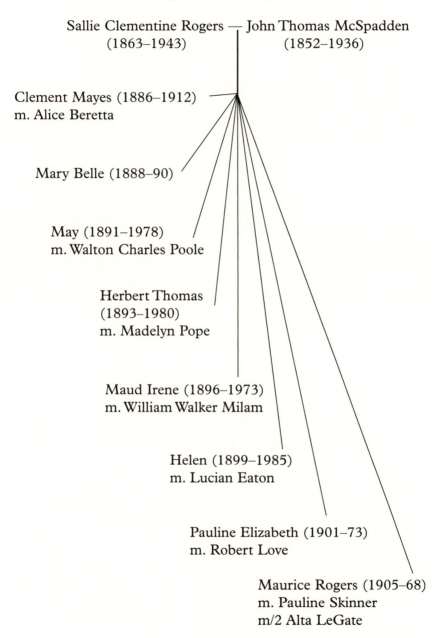

Sallie Clementine Rogers — John Thomas McSpadden
(1863–1943)   (1852–1936)

Clement Mayes (1886–1912)
m. Alice Beretta

Mary Belle (1888–90)

May (1891–1978)
m. Walton Charles Poole

Herbert Thomas
(1893–1980)
m. Madelyn Pope

Maud Irene (1896–1973)
m. William Walker Milam

Helen (1899–1985)
m. Lucian Eaton

Pauline Elizabeth (1901–73)
m. Robert Love

Maurice Rogers (1905–68)
m. Pauline Skinner
m/2 Alta LeGate

Lane Family Tree

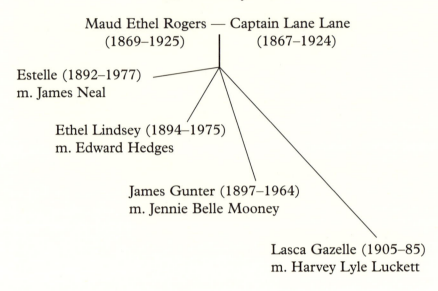

Maud Ethel Rogers — Captain Lane Lane
(1869–1925)   (1867–1924)

Estelle (1892–1977)
m. James Neal

Ethel Lindsey (1894–1975)
m. Edward Hedges

James Gunter (1897–1964)
m. Jennie Belle Mooney

Lasca Gazelle (1905–85)
m. Harvey Lyle Luckett

Stine Family Tree

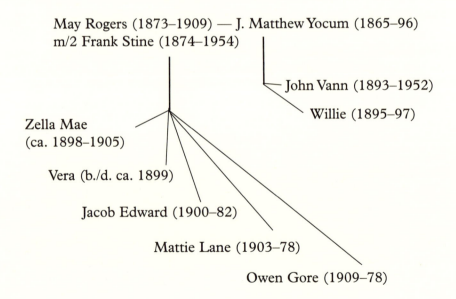

May Rogers (1873–1909) — J. Matthew Yocum (1865–96)
m/2 Frank Stine (1874–1954)

John Vann (1893–1952)

Willie (1895–97)

Zella Mae
(ca. 1898–1905)

Vera (b./d. ca. 1899)

Jacob Edward (1900–82)

Mattie Lane (1903–78)

Owen Gore (1909–78)

Name Index

THE FOLLOWING INDIVIDUALS ARE PROFILED IN THE BIOGRAPHICAL APPENDIX.

Adair, Elizabeth Alabama Schrimsher. See BUSHYHEAD, Jesse, and ROGERS, Clement Vann.

Adair, Susannah McIntosh Drew (1844–1939)

Adair, William Penn (1830–80)

Barrett, Victoria Lipe. See LIPE, DeWitt Clinton.

Bibles (Bible), Mary. See ROGERS, Mary Bibles.

Blake, Betty (Bettie). See ROGERS, Betty Blake.

Buffalo Bill. See CODY, William F.

Bushyhead, Dennis Wolf. See BUSHYHEAD, Jesse Crary.

Bushyhead, Jesse Crary, M.D. (1870–1942)

Cody, William F. (Buffalo Bill) (1846–1917)

Eaton, Helen McSpadden (1899–1985)

Ellis, Kate (b. ca. 1879)

Ewing, Frank (1879–1965)

Halsell, Ewing (1877–1965)

Halsell, William Electious (W. E.) (1850–1934)

Hedges, Ethel Lane (1894–1975)

Hopkins (O'Donnell), James Dennis (Jim) (1875–1966)

Johnson, William A. (Bill) (b. 1880)

Kates, Albert L. (A. L. or Pop) (1861–1938)

Knight, Lythe A. (Light) (ca. 1861–1924)

Lane, Andrew Jackson, M.D. (ca. 1851–96)

Lane, Captain Lane (Cap or C. L.) (1867–1924)

Lane, Estelle. See NEAL, Estelle Lane.

Lane, Ethel. See HEDGES, Ethel Lane.

Lane, James Gunter (1897–1964)

Lane, Lasca Gazelle. See LUCKETT, Lasca Gazelle Lane.

Lane, Lucinda Elliott Journeycake. See LANE, Andrew Jackson, and LANE, Thomas Lipe.

Lane, Maud Ethel Rogers (1869–1925)

Lane, Thomas Lipe (Tom) (ca. 1879–1924)

Lillie, Gordon William (Pawnee Bill) (1860–1942)

Lipe, DeWitt Clinton (D. W. or Major) (1840–1916), and the Lipe family

Lipe, Lola Vann. See LIPE, DeWitt Clinton.

Lipe, Nancy Eva (Nannie). See LIPE, DeWitt Clinton.

Lipe, Oliver Wack. See LIPE, DeWitt Clinton.

Lipe, Victoria Susan. See LIPE, DeWitt Clinton.

Love, Pauline Elizabeth (Paula) McSpadden (1901–73)

Luckett, Lasca Gazelle Lane (1905–85)

McClellan, Charles White (Charley) (1879–1902)

McGonigle, Henry Clay (1879–1921)

McSpadden, Clement Mayes (Clem) (1886–1912)

McSpadden, Helen. See EATON, Helen McSpadden.

McSpadden, Herbert Thomas (Herb) (1893–1980)

McSpadden, Irene. See MILAM, Maud Irene McSpadden.

McSpadden, John Thomas (Tom or J. T.) (1852–1936)

McSpadden, Maurice. See MCSPADDEN, Sallie Clementine Rogers.

McSpadden, May. See POOLE, May McSpadden.

McSpadden, Pauline. See LOVE, Pauline Elizabeth (Paula) McSpadden.

McSpadden, Sallie Clementine Rogers (1863–1943)

Milam, Maud Irene McSpadden (1896–1973)

Mitchell, Mattie Lane Stine (1903–78)

Mulhall, Lucille (1885–1940)

Mulhall, Colonel Zack (1847–1931)

Nay, Margaret. See VEERKAMP, Margaret (Maggie) Nay Price.

Neal, Estelle Lane (1892–1977).

O'Donnell, James. See HOPKINS, James Dennis.

Oropeza, Vincente (1858–1923)

Parris, Richard (Dick) (1877–1922)

Pawnee Bill. See LILLIE, Gordon William

Piccione, James (J. J.) (ca. 1856–post 1918)

Poole, May McSpadden (1891–1978)

Price, Margaret Nay. See VEERKAMP, Margaret (Maggie) Nay Price.

Rider, James Hall (Jim) (b. 1877)

Robinson, Juliette (Bunt) Schrimsher (1878–1963)

Rogers, Betty Blake (1879–1944)

Rogers, Charles (Rabb) (b. 1837) and Houston (b. 1840)

Rogers, Clem. See ROGERS, Charles and Houston.

Rogers, Clement Vann (C. V., Clem, or Clem V.) (1839–1911)

Rogers, Houston. See ROGERS, Charles and Houston.

Rogers, Mary America Schrimsher (1839–90)

Rogers, Mary Bibles (1866–1900)

Rogers, Maud Ethel. See LANE, Maud Ethel Rogers.

Rogers, May. See STINE, May Rogers Yocum.

Rogers, Robert Martin (Bob) (1866–83)

Rogers, Rhoda (Rody). See ROGERS, Charles and Houston, and WALKER, Agnes (Babe) Rogers.

Rogers, Sallie. See McSPADDEN, Sallie Clementine Rogers.

Rogers, Susannah McIntosh Drew Adair. See ADAIR, Susannah McIntosh Drew.

Schrimsher, Ernest Vivian (1875–1942)

Schrimsher, John Gunter (1835–1905)

Schrimsher, Juliette Melvina (Bunt). See ROBINSON, Juliette (Bunt) Schrimsher.

Stine, Frank (1874–1954)

Stine, Jacob Edward (1900–1982)

Stine, Mattie Lane (Lanie). See MITCHELL, Mattie Lane Stine.

Stine, May Rogers Yocum (1873–1909)

Stine, Owen Gore. See STINE, May Rogers Yocum

Sunday, Edward (Ed). See SUNDAY, William Esther

Sunday, William Esther (1877–1959)

Texas Jack (1865–1905)

Timberlake, Margaret (Peggy) Rogers. See ROGERS, Clement Vann, and LIPE, Dewitt Clinton.

Trainor, Leonard Edward (1879–1940)

Trent, Richard Owen, M.D. (ca. 1853–88)

Trent, Spi (Martin) (1884–1959).

Veerkamp, Margaret (Maggie) Nay Price (ca. 1882–1979)

Walker, Agnes (Babe) Rogers (b. 1862)

Walker, Dan (b. ca. 1852)

Wirth, George (1867–1941) and Philip Peter Jacob (1864–1937) (Wirth Brothers)

Yocum, John (Johnny). See STINE, May Rogers Yocum.

Yocum, J. Matthew (Matt) (1865–96)

Biographical Entries

The following alphabetical entries feature profiles of individuals named in this volume who were members of Will Rogers's family, close friends, or of special significance to the Rogers family or Will Rogers's career.

ADAIR, Elizabeth Alabama Schrimsher. See BUSHYHEAD, Jesse, and ROGERS, Clement Vann.

ADAIR, Susannah McIntosh Drew (1844–1939). Susannah McIntosh Drew Adair was a close friend of Clem V. Rogers and Mary America Schrimsher Rogers. Present at the birth of Will Rogers at the Rogers ranch in November 1879, she suggested the new baby boy be named after her husband, Cherokee politician and Confederate Army veteran William Penn Adair, a colleague of Clem V. Rogers (see ADAIR, William Penn). Involved in Cherokee politics through her marriage, Susannah Adair also served in regional Indian Territory political positions in her own right.

Susannah McIntosh Drew was of Creek-Cherokee descent and a member of a wealthy slaveholding family. Her father was a druggist. She grew up in the Creek Nation and was educated in Texas, Alabama, and Mississippi. Like the Schrimsher family, the Drews became refugees in Texas during the Civil War, when the Cherokee Nation was wracked by violence among Cherokee factions and by the invasion of federal forces. Susannah McIntosh Drew married William Penn Adair in 1868, and lived in Washington, D.C., where she participated with him in social affairs connected to his position as a Cherokee Nation diplomat. She was in Indian Territory on 4 November 1879, when Will Rogers was born at the Rogers ranch, and "Aunt Sue," as she was known by friends and family, assisted Mary America Schrimsher Rogers at the birth. Clem V. Rogers was in Washington, D.C., at the time with William Penn Adair. The baby boy was named William Penn Adair Rogers in honor of Aunt Sue's husband and Clem V. Rogers's longtime friend. Aunt Sue remained at the Rogers ranch for two weeks after the birth to help care for the infant. The Cherokee Nation rolls taken when Will Rogers was a seven-month-old baby in 1880 list him as "Col. W. P. Rogers," using William Penn Adair's military title from the war.

After William Penn Adair's death in 1880, Susannah Adair was remarried to

William H. Rogers, a wealthy Muskogee man (no relative to the Clem V. Rogers family). When William H. Rogers passed away in 1889, he left her most of his fortune, but the will was contested and broken. She became the clerk of the Creek Nation Supreme Court (1894–97) and served as a commissioner in the three-person Creek Nation commission that determined individual rights of citizenship for the purpose of issuing land allotments.

Like Will Rogers, Aunt Sue was taken by aeronautics. She was deeply shaken by the news of Rogers's death, but stated that knowing Rogers, "he probably made some joke just before the plane crashed." She happily accepted two airplane rides at the local airfield at Muskogee as gifts for her ninety-first birthday a few months later (15 October 1935), telling reporters that Rogers's death had been a terrible loss, but "we can't hold it against aviation and progress" (unidentified newspaper clippings, Muskogee, August and October 1935, OkClaW; Foreman, C., "Creek Pioneer").

ADAIR, William Penn (1830–80). William Penn Adair was a prominent Cherokee Nation lawyer and politician in the mid–nineteenth century. He and his wife, Susannah McIntosh Drew Adair (see above), also a figure in Cherokee Nation politics, were friends of Clem V. Rogers and Mary America Schrimsher Rogers. Will Rogers, Clem V. Rogers's youngest son (b. 1879), was named for him.

William Penn Adair was the son of George Washington Adair and Martha Martin Adair. George Washington Adair's maternal grandmother was Gehoga Foster, a Cherokee, and the rest of his heritage was Scotch-English. William Penn Adair was born in Georgia on 15 April 1830, the year President Andrew Jackson signed into law legislation for the removal of the Cherokees and other Indian peoples from the southeastern states to the Indian Territory west of the Mississippi River. The politics of removal thus framed the young William Penn Adair's life. His father signed the Treaty of New Echota in December 1835. Many saw the treaty as fraudulent and as a betrayal of Cherokee interests, but a small number of others accepted it as a pragmatic recognition of the realities of federal political power, agreeing to the terms for the sale of Cherokee lands in preparation for removal under the provisions of the 1830 Indian Removal Act. Homelands were ceded in exchange for a promise of lands in the region already occupied by the western Cherokees, or Old Settlers. Adair's maternal grandfather as well as his father supported the New Echota treaty. Backed by a minority of mostly upper-class, largely acculturated slaveholders who had large farms and operated fisheries, mills, ferries, and other Cherokee Nation East businesses, the treaty was opposed by Chief John Ross and the majority of Cherokee people. Over fifteen thousand people later signed a memorial opposing the treaty. The treaty thus marked the beginning of a longstanding split in Cherokee politics between the National (or Ross) Party, which had fought the legislation through the courts and resisted removal, and the Treaty (or Ridge) Party, of which the Adairs, as well as John Ridge, Elias Boudinot, and Stand Watie were supporters. Ross, also known as Cooweescoowee (which became the name of the district of the Indian Territory where the Rogers family lived) had fought with the Cherokee regiment under General Andrew Jackson in the Creek war and was the author of much of the Cherokee constitution of 1827. The Treaty of New Echota was ratified in Washington in May 1836, setting a deadline of May 1838 for completion of the removal process; backers of the Treaty Party, including the Adair family, left their eastern homes circa 1836–38. The more elite, many of whom were slave-holders, emigrated themselves; others went in groups under government auspices. The Ross Party resisters stayed until forced to depart by government troops, arriving over the Trail of Tears in the Cherokee Nation West in 1838–39, suffering severely from illness, the lack of provisions, and the harsh winter.

William Penn Adair was seven years old when his family voluntarily made the trip from Georgia in 1837. The Adairs settled near Salina, and William Penn Adair was educated in Cherokee Nation schools and outside the Indian Territory. He earned a degree in law and became a member of the Cherokee Supreme Court. He was active in the Masons, first as a member of Flint Lodge No. 74 in the 1850s and later of the Indian Territory Grand Lodge. He was elected to his first term in the Cherokee Senate in 1855 and was reelected in 1857 and 1859. Like many other Treaty Party supporters, he was sympathetic to state's-rights arguments and the southern cause. He was a member of the group of leaders who supported the antiabolitionist sentiments of the Knights of the Golden Circle, a secret society advocated by his close friend Stand Watie. He was among those politicians who called for the expulsion of antislavery missionaries working under the auspices of Northern missionary boards within the Nation in 1859. With the onset of the Civil War, he, along with his brothers Brice and Benjamin Franklin Adair, and his father, George Washington Adair, served with the Confederate Cherokees. William Penn Adair was assistant quartermaster and later colonel of Stand Watie's Cherokee Mounted Regiment of the Confederate army (the same regiment in which Will Rogers's father, Clem V. Rogers, was first lieutenant and later promoted to captain). Adair led guerilla raids across federal lines in April and May 1864, earning the name "Gray Ghost" because his men were spotted in different sections of Arkansas and Missouri disrupting Union activities and supply lines. In the following year Adair was taken into custody by the Keetoowah Cherokees (or

"Pins"), full-bloods loyal to the Union, and held at federal army headquarters at Tahlequah for the last several weeks of the war.

Adair was a member of the delegation of Confederate Cherokees selected to negotiate with Northern, or Federal, Cherokees (supporters of the Union) in Washington, D.C., after the war. John Ross died at the end of the negotiations in August 1866, and after the delegations returned to Indian Territory, Lewis Downing, who had served in the Union army, was elected the new principal chief of the Cherokee Nation. Adair was among those in the Watie (or Southern Rights) Party who, like Clem V. Rogers, joined in the Downing-Party coalition with former Ross-Party and Treaty-Party members, unified in their opposition to territorial status. He became the "foremost lobbyist for the Nation in opposing all territorial bills" (McLoughlin, *Champions of the Cherokees*, 441). He became friends with John B. Jones, a Baptist missionary and adopted Cherokee citizen who became the federal agent to Indian Territory in the years after the war, and worked closely with Jones in support of Cherokee sovereignty and appropriations (despite calling for Jones's expulsion from the Nation before the war).

Adair married twice; his first marriage, in 1861, was to Sarah Ann Adair (a second cousin). She died in the last years of the Civil War. His second marriage was to Susannah McIntosh Drew in 1868. William Penn Adair was frequently a delegate from the Cherokee Nation to Washington, D.C., between 1866 and 1879, and after their marriage the Adairs split their time between living near Adair, I.T., and in Washington. They attended the inaugural ball of President Ulysses S. Grant and were frequent guests at the White House during his administration. William Penn Adair was elected assistant principal chief of the Cherokee Nation in 1879.

Adair's time in that Cherokee Nation office was short. He died unexpectedly in Washington, D.C., in October 1880 after contracting pneumonia while suffering from a bout of typhoid fever. There is no evidence that he ever saw his namesake. Clem V. Rogers was a member of the Cherokee Senate committee that officially commended Adair after his death for his long service to the Nation. The committee announced that Adair would be buried in Tahlequah and that the Cherokee National Council and the Capitol building would observe a month-long official mourning in his honor (see proclamations issued on the death of William Penn Adair, Cherokee National Records, OkHi, microfilm CHN 12, vols. 273, 274, 275A; Croy, *Our Will Rogers*, 7; Dale and Litton, eds., *Cherokee Cavaliers*, 252; Fischer and Gill, "Confederate Indian Forces Outside Indian Territory," 275–78, 279; Foreman, C., "Creek Pioneer"; Franks, *Stand Watie and the Agony of the Cherokee Nation*, 117, 127, 151,

158, 167, 174, 182, 184–85; *HRC,* 88; Keith, "Clem Rogers and His Influence on Oklahoma History," 15 n. 1, 40–41; McLoughlin, *Champions of the Cherokees,* 365–66, 367, 441–42, 464, 482; Moore, "William Penn Adair"; Perdue, *Slavery and the Evolution of Cherokee Society,* 50–69, 111, 141–45; Starr, *History of the Cherokee Indians,* 143, 183, 296; Woodward, *Cherokees,* 157–81, 182–91, 192–218).

BARRETT, Victoria Lipe. See LIPE, DeWitt Clinton.

BIBLES (BIBLE), MARY. SEE ROGERS, Mary Bibles.

BLAKE, Betty (Bettie). See ROGERS, Betty Blake.

BUFFALO BILL. See CODY, William F.

BUSHYHEAD, Dennis Wolf. See BUSHYHEAD, Jesse Crary.

BUSHYHEAD, Jesse Crary, M.D., (1870–1942). Jesse Bushyhead was Will Roger's first cousin and a member of one of the leading families in Cherokee Nation politics. Born on 29 June 1870, he was the grandson of Rev. Jesse Bushyhead (d. 1844) (a Baptist preacher and colleague of the influential missionary Evan Jones, a translator and printer in the Cherokee language, a leader of a contingent from the East on the Trail of Tears, and a Ross Party politician) and the son of Principal Chief Dennis Wolf Bushyhead (1826–98) and Elizabeth Alabama Schrimsher Adair Bushyhead (1835–82) (Mary America Schrimsher Rogers's sister). His father, a member of the National Party (successor to the Ross Party and opposition party to the Downings) was elected principal chief for two terms in 1879 and 1883. Dennis Wolf Bushyhead (whose middle name was alternately spelled "Wolf" or "Wolfe" within the family and by others) and Elizabeth Alabama Schrimsher Bushyhead's four children were Mary Elizabeth (b. 1873) (she married Thomas William Triplett [b. 1869]), Sarah Catherine (Kate) (b. 1876), and Dennis Wolf (b. 1880), all of whom lived at Westville, I.T., and Jesse Crary, who became a Claremore physician.

Dr. Bushyhead had a medical practice in Claremore for over fifty years (beginning in 1891), with offices on the second floor of the bank building and over Hill's Drug Store. He married Fay Ione Reynolds (b. 1870) of Cane Hill/Boonsville, Ark., in 1898. Born in Shelby County, Tenn., Fay Reynolds was a graduate of the University of Arkansas and had been assistant principal at the Claremore public school for two years. She was the only non-Indian woman to be invited to become a member of the Pocahontas Club. She was a friend of Mary Bibles Rogers, and the Bushyheads and the Rogers often socialized, celebrating holidays and birthdays together. The Bushyheads continued to be close to Clem V. Rogers and his children after Mary Bibles Rogers's death in 1900. They had five children of their own: Oowala Eliza (b. 1900), Edward Reynolds (1902–1923 or 1924), Jesse Crary (b. 1903), Dennis Wolf (b. 1905), and George Davis (b. 1908). Like fellow Claremore leader and Cherokee politician Joe LaHay, Jesse Bushyhead in his bachelor days had been friends with May Rogers Yocum Stine's first husband, Matthew Yocum, who died in 1896. Jesse and Fay Bushyhead purchased a house from Clem V. Rogers in April 1906.

Dr. Bushyhead graduated from the Cherokee Male Seminary in 1887 and received his medical degree from Washington University–Missouri Medical College in St. Louis, Mo. He stayed abreast of new developments in medicine and continued to take postgraduate courses at Missouri Medical College, Tulane University in New Orleans, and hospitals in New York. He was also active in Cherokee Nation politics. He served as the last treasurer of the Cherokee Nation before statehood. He was elected in 1903, succeeding friend Joe LaHay in the office. Whereas Clem V. Rogers and most Downing Party advocates became strong supporters of the Democratic Party, Bushyhead was a Republican leader and sometimes one of Clem V. Rogers's political rivals. They were the nominees of their respective parties in the 1906 elections that chose district delegates to attend the upcoming state constitutional convention. Like most of the Democratic candidates, Rogers won the election (he received 815 votes to Bushyhead's 615), but the tally was very close in Claremore, where both men were highly respected.

Jesse Bushyhead was one of the original members of the Will Rogers Memorial Commission. He has been remembered as "a man of gentle and compassionate heart and skilled beyond his time in medical practice and techniques" (*As I Recollect,* 138; see also 138–42). He remained a close friend of Betty Blake Rogers after Will Rogers's death (Will Rogers to May McSpadden, ca. 21 December 1934, and Sallie McSpadden to Betty Blake Rogers, 6 February 1939, SRM-OkClaW; Bell, *Genealogy of Old and New Cherokee Indian Families,* 92–94; *CC,* 28 June 1899; *ChC,* 18 January 1901; Collings, *Old Home Ranch,* 87; *CP,* 1 July 1893, 21 September 1895, 17 September, 24 September, 3 October, and 26 November 1898, 19 October 1901, 18 January and 10 May 1902, 12 October and 4 November 1906; *CR,* 17 January 1901; *CWM,* 20 April and 27 April 1906; *DC,* 3 October 1898 and 5 November 1903; DuPriest et al., *Cherokee Recollections,* 179–80; *HRC,* 461; McLoughlin, *Champions of the Cherokees;* Meserve, "Chief Dennis Wolfe Bushyhead"; *OCF* 1:40, 56, 2:149, 178; Starr, *History of the Cherokee Indians,* 120, 256–58, 262–63, 292; *WRFT,* 124).

CODY, William F. (Buffalo Bill) (1846–1917). One of the United States's most prominent show-business entrepreneurs, William F. Cody commercialized the myth of the West through his famous Buffalo Bill's Wild West show. The show shaped international images of the cowboy as the so-called American character, and the Plains Indian as the quintessential Native American—conceptions that were perpetuated in popular culture, song, and film well into the twentieth century.

Born near Le Claire, Iowa, Cody moved to Kansas in 1854 and, when still a young boy, ran away to work with freight outfits in the West. He was a Pony Express rider in 1860–61 and served in the cavalry and as a scout to General Sherman in Kansas during the Civil War. During the war he became a stage driver and scout for the U.S. Army. Cody was given the name Buffalo Bill as he gained a reputation for leading buffalo hunts with army officers out of Fort Hays and with employees of the Union Pacific Railroad Co., which used buffalo meat to feed construction crews.

Cody began building his status as a western icon in the popular mind when he met the eastern writer Ned Buntline (Edward Judson) and became the subject of a series of best-selling dime novels (*Buffalo Bill, the King of the Border Men*, 1869, was the first of 550 novels featuring Buffalo Bill as the hero). In 1872 he appeared with his friend and fellow scout Texas Jack Omohundro in a melodrama, *The Scouts of the Prairie*, written by Buntline, that opened in Chicago. After a shaky start, the play toured the East with a new writer. The cast (which, for a time, included Wild Bill Hickock), the scripts, and scenarios went through several incarnations, focusing on conflict between white plainsmen (the heroes) and stereotypical war-whooping American Indians (the villains). Unemployed white New York actors often were employed in parts as Native Americans. In addition to this entrée into show business, Cody continued to scout and had his own large ranch in Nebraska.

The idea of developing a Wild West show emerged around a Fourth of July celebration Cody helped plan in North Platte, Neb., in 1882. He organized cowboys from his own and surrounding ranches to do bronco and bison riding, trick roping, mock shoot-outs and an imitation Pony Express ride. He received financial backing and founded his own show in 1883. In 1884 it went on tour, featuring "real" plainsmen and cowboys, marksmen, expert ropers, and Indians. Annie Oakley was the show's sharpshooter, and Sitting Bull toured with the cast of Indians in 1885. The show sold out many thousands of seats in its performances, including those in Madison Square Garden in 1886–87. It made popular tours to Europe from the late 1880s through 1906, and in towns across the United States, including Claremore in 1900. It reached its apex at the

Chicago World's Columbian Exposition in 1893, where Will Rogers attended the show, either with his father or a group of young friends. They had box seats in a huge ampitheater seating twenty-two thousand people. The young Rogers was impressed with the spectacular acts, especially that of Vincente Oropeza, who starred in a roping act featuring Mexican vaqueros (see OROPEZA, Vincente). He remained a fan and knew many individuals who at one time appeared with the Buffalo Bill show. When he was in Europe in June 1906 he probably saw the Buffalo Bill Wild West show in Vienna (he kept a schedule of the show's 1906 European tour among his effects from the trip), and he may possibly have done his roping act as a special appearance on that occasion (see Mort Shea, interview, HCP-MoU). Almost two decades after he enjoyed the show at the Chicago Exposition Rogers appeared with Buffalo Bill (in one of many of the promoter's supposed farewell seasons) in the combined Buffalo Bill's Wild West and Pawnee Bill's Far East show at Madison Square Garden, New York, in April 1910. He performed a version of the act he was then doing in vaudeville.

Despite Cody's claim that his show offered the "real picture, with real characters" (Cody, *Adventures of Buffalo Bill*, 152), Buffalo Bill's Wild West show combined aspects of the rodeo and circus with melodrama to create a stylized and mythic image of manliness and the American West. While creating and furthering sterotypes of both the American cowboy-pioneer and the American Indian, Buffalo Bill's show also consciously sought to depict its own brand of bravery and heroism in Native American culture and to laud the golden age of the unsettled West. After a long career, Cody finally retired from show business. He founded the town of Cody, Wyo., now the home of the Buffalo Bill Historical Center, an important repository for historical documents and material culture of the American West (Buffalo Bill's Wild West schedule for Official Route 4, Season 1906, OkClaW; Blackstone, *Buckskins, Bullets, and Business* and *Business of Being Buffalo Bill; Buffalo Bill and the Wild West;* Cody, *Adventures of Buffalo Bill; EFB,* 1:293–94; *IC,* 21 September 1899; Keith, *Boy's Life of Will Rogers,* 67–72; Leonard and Goodman, *Buffalo Bill; NYT,* 26 April 1910; Russell, *Lives and Legends of Buffalo Bill* and *Wild West;* Sell and Weybright, *Buffalo Bill and the Wild West; Variety,* [30 April 1910], 17, and as clipping, Vaudeville Scrapbook, CPpR).

EATON, Helen McSpadden (1899–1985). The sixth child of John Thomas (Tom) McSpadden and Sallie Rogers McSpadden, Helen McSpadden was born on 11 October 1899. She graduated from Chelsea High School in 1917, attended the Central College for Women in Lexington, Mo., and graduated from Tulsa

University. She married Lucian A. Eaton (1893–1930) of St. Joseph, Mo., on 12 October 1921, and they made their home in St. Louis, Mo. After her husband's death she moved back to Maplewood, where her daughter, Lucia, was born prematurely. The house burned down in the fall of 1932 and Sallie and Helen spent some time living with Will and Betty Rogers while a new home was being prepared. Helen was still living with her mother when Sallie Rogers McSpadden became gravely ill in 1942. Sallie willed the McSpadden home to her (Will Rogers to Sallie McSpadden, ca. October–November 1932, SRM-OkClaW; Bell, *Genealogy of Old and New Cherokee Indian Families,* 357; Eaton, interview, OkClaW; *HRC,* 301; *WRFT,* 14).

ELLIS, Kate (b. ca. 1879). Kate Ellis was a close friend of Will Rogers's and was for a time romantically linked with him when they were in their late teens and early twenties. She lived in Oolagah with her parents and her younger sister, Lil, and the young Will Rogers was often a guest in the Ellis home. Her parents ran the Oolagah Hotel. In 1903 Will Rogers's sister May Rogers Yocum Stine and her family moved into a house across the street from the Ellises. Kate Ellis was responsible for Will Rogers's having the opportunity to get to know Betty Blake in the fall of 1899. After a first bashful meeting with Blake in the Oolagah train station, Rogers was invited to a taffy-pulling party at the Ellises' at which Blake was the guest of honor. (He had stopped at the station to pick up a banjo that had arrived for him by rail, and Blake waited on him at the desk. She was in town visiting her sister Cora Blake Marshall and brother-in-law Will Marshall, the Oolagah station manager.) Kate Ellis was of a cheerful disposition and was a good friend to Rogers, writing to him when he traveled abroad in 1902–04, and becoming friends with the Stine family when they became her neighbors. During his absence she became a schoolteacher in Oolagah and was very well respected. Kate Ellis was locally perceived as Will Rogers's "girl." As Rogers biographer Homer Croy has put it, Rogers saw a number of Indian Territory young women, but "Kate Ellis was *the* one. There was talk that the two were going to get married, but her father [Jake Ellis] was opposed to it. Will was too wild, he said; even his own father couldn't control him" (Croy, *Our Will Rogers,* 55; see also 71). A man who had been a student in Ellis's class described her as "Will's first sweetheart. He was quite gone on her. She was the prettiest girl in Oologah." He went on to explain that Rogers and Ellis had been dating when Betty Blake came to town, and that Blake was initially reluctant to respond to Rogers's interest in her not only because of his wild reputation but also because of her loyalty to Ellis, who had become her close friend. Jake Ellis apparently had words with Rogers when he brought Kate

Ellis home very late from a date one evening, and during the altercation forbade Rogers and his daughter from seeing one another again (interview with Cal Tinney by Homer Croy, ca. 1930–31, quoted in Croy, *Our Will Rogers*, 342; see also Bill Hoge to Homer Croy, n.d., HCP-MoU). When she was in her midtwenties Ellis married another man (after Rogers had returned to the States and was pursuing his vaudeville career). She moved away from Oklahoma, made her home in Kansas with her husband, Robert W. Lewis, and lost touch with Rogers. She later declined to speak about her years of friendship with him (Croy, *Our Will Rogers*, 109, 218, 219, 342, 343; Ketchum, *Will Rogers*, 69; see also Kate Ellis to Will Rogers, 15 February 1903, and Maud Lane to Will Rogers, 12 July 1903, OkClaW).

EWING, Frank (1879–1965). Ewing first met Will Rogers in 1898 when Rogers worked on Frank Ewing's father's (W. P. Ewing's) Little Robe Ranch near Higgins, Tex. Rogers had just left the Kemper School after learning about the ranch from schoolmate William Johnson, who was a friend of Frank Ewing (see JOHNSON, William A.). The Ewing ranch was located twelve miles southeast of Higgins in present-day Ellis County, Okla. Rogers and Frank Ewing were inseparable companions while Rogers worked as a cowpuncher on the ranch. They would rope, bust steers, work cattle together, and play games of tug-of-war on ponies. Ewing remembered that Rogers had such a fun time that he refused a paycheck for his work (Croy, *Our Will Rogers*, 46–47). Their most exciting adventure was accompanying four hundred head of cattle to Medicine Lodge, Kans. Rogers spent several months on the Ewing ranch in 1898 and visited his friend on additional occasions before he left for Argentina in 1902. Ewing wrote: "Will came to see me at various times and would stay two or three weeks at a time, or a month or two at a time for about five years. We worked together and camped together for several years" (Frank Ewing to Homer Croy, 15 August 1952, HCP-MoU). Ewing's father later bought another ranch north of Higgins on Camp Creek, where he was a successful rancher. Frank Ewing also became a prominent rancher in the Panhandle area. On 1 June 1902 he married Laura Garnet Word (b. 1882) of Higgins, and they were the parents of two sons, Franklin and Thomas. Learning of Rogers's speaking engagement at Amarillo in February 1926, Ewing wired him: "If you could ride an old give-out horse from Higgins to Amarillo in '98, I certainly ought to make it in a Ford, so if you have somebody in your audience you will know it's me" (*TDW*, 7 March 1926). The reunion also included their mutual friend, William Johnson. In 1958 Ewing made a nostalgic visit to the Will Rogers Memorial at Claremore (Frank Ewing, interview, 79:498–99, IPH-OkHi;

Croy, *Our Will Rogers*, 45–47; *History of Lipscomb County,* 411; Keith, *Boy's Life of Will Rogers,* 117–37; "Notes and Documents [Little Robe Township, Ellis County]," 344; Rogers, *Will Rogers*, 50–53; "Texan's Visit to Memorial Recalls His Days with Will," clipping, Frank Ewing file, OkClaW).

HALSELL, Ewing (1877–1965). A successful rancher and businessman in Oklahoma and Texas, Halsell was a lifelong friend of Will Rogers. Halsell was born in Jacksboro, Tex., on 12 February 1877. When his father, William E. Halsell, moved to Vinita, I.T., he sent his son to Willie Halsell College, a primary and secondary school (see HALSELL, William Electious). As schoolmates, Rogers and Halsell spent considerable time together and shared a mutual passion for roping and riding horses. The two practiced roping at the Halsell house in Vinita, where they would have fun trying to lasso Ewing's three sisters as they ran around the house. After attending Willie Halsell College, Halsell studied at a business school in Poughkeepsie, N.Y. In 1898 his father appointed him manager of his Bird Creek Ranch near Tulsa, and the following year he became sole operator of the ranch. He also managed his father's Mashed-O Ranch in Amherst, Tex., and, with his sisters, became co-owner of the property, which was deeded to them in 1903. In 1899 Halsell married Lucile Fortner (d. 1963), a Willie Halsell schoolmate and the daughter of Dr. Benjamin F. Fortner, a prominent Vinita physician. The Ewing Halsell family made their home in both Texas and Vinita. A prosperous cattle trader and breeder, Halsell at one time owned and operated four huge ranches, including the Big Creek Ranch in Craig and Nowata Counties in Oklahoma, and gas and oil properties. In 1944 Halsell purchased the Farias Ranch at Eagle Pass, Tex., comprising ninety-seven thousand acres near the Mexican border, and subsequently he moved to San Antonio. Halsell donated the family home in Vinita to the town's public school system. He enjoyed visiting Rogers at his Pacific Palisades ranch, where the two would rope together as in their youth. Rogers also visited Halsell at his Texas Mashed-O Ranch in the summer of 1934. According to Richard Ketchum, Halsell witnessed Will Rogers's final will while visiting the Rogers ranch in 1935 just before Rogers left for Alaska on his fatal trip (*Will Rogers*, 368–69). After Rogers's death, the Halsells were very supportive friends to Betty Blake Rogers. Ewing Halsell was a member of the committee for the establishment of the Will Rogers Memorial and played a major role in the completion of the building in Claremore. He was an original member of the Memorial Commission and helped fund the construction of Rogers's tomb. Halsell died of a heart attack in Texas on 16 December 1965; his estate formed the Ewing Halsell Foundation, headquartered in San Antonio

(Betty Blake Rogers to Sallie Rogers McSpadden, 31 August and 20 September 1937, and Will Rogers, Jr., to Sallie Rogers McSpadden, 29 September 1939, SRM-OkClaW; Holden, *Ranching Saga;* Rogers, *Will Rogers,* 57, 268; *Story of Craig County,* 378).

HALSELL, William Electious (W. E.) (1850–1934). W. E. Halsell was a prominent and prosperous cattleman, rancher, and banker in the Indian Territory and Texas. The son of Electious Halsell (1816–67) and Elizabeth Jane Mays (1818–70), William Halsell was born in a log house in Decatur, Ala., on 7 June 1850. In 1855 the family moved to Wise County, Tex., where William Halsell grew up. After attending school until the age of eighteen, Halsell entered the livestock business and became a Texas trail driver on the Chisholm Trail, accompanying cattle to northern markets. With his brother John Glenn Halsell (1845–86), he operated a large ranch in Texas and stocked it with an extensive herd of cattle. Halsell married Mary Alice Crutchfield (1854–94) on 24 January 1872 and moved to the Cooweescoowee District of the Cherokee Nation in 1882. His marriage to Crutchfield, who was part Cherokee, enabled him to claim a homestead that eventually became the largest ranch in the Tulsa area in the 1880s and 1890s. Called the Bird Creek Ranch, or the Mashed-O because of its brand in the shape of a flattened O, its headquarters were located about eight miles north of Tulsa, where Halsell employed fifty-five cowhands to oversee thirty thousand cattle on his range. Each spring Halsell would ship thousands of longhorns from Texas to his ranch, where they grazed on bluestem grass in preparation for shipment to market. The Halsell family resided in a large Vinita mansion containing twenty rooms. The property also featured four outbuildings and a large barn. After the death of his wife in 1894, Halsell married Josephine (Josie) Crutchfield (1875–1946), a niece of his wife and a graduate of Willie Halsell College. An imposing figure, Halsell was over six feet tall with sharp black eyes and snow-white hair. He played a large role in the town's public affairs as a board member of the Vinita Fair Association and the Worcester Academy, and as a benefactor of Willie Halsell College, named after his daughter, Willie Edna Halsell, who died in 1884. He also helped build a theater and opera house in the town. Halsell befriended Clem V. Rogers when they first met in Tahlequah around 1882. Soon thereafter he visited the Rogers ranch and remembered seeing three-year-old Will Rogers "with a mop of unruly hair, a big mouth which turned up slightly at the corners, an infectious smile, good-humored, well-mannered. . . . He was constantly riding a stick horse which he would make gallop, trot, pace, back-up, rear-up, and pitch, all with amazing pantomime" (Holden, *Ranching Saga,* 127). In 1894 Halsell and

Clem V. Rogers organized the First National Bank in Claremore and both served on its original board of directors. The two, however, sometimes disagreed over political matters. In the election of 1903 for principal chief of the Cherokee Nation, Halsell supported and funded the defeated National Party candidate, Edley Levi Cookson, whereas Clem V. Rogers backed William Charles Rogers (no relation), who was the Downing Party candidate (see Maud Lane to Will Rogers, 17 August 1903, above). A leading entrepreneur of the Indian Territory, Halsell was one of the founders of the First National Bank of Vinita (1892) and the First National Bank of Tulsa (1898), serving as the latter's president for five years. In addition, Halsell financed a grocery wholesale firm (1898), organized the Indian Telephone Co. (1899) to construct long-distance lines, and headed the Metropolitan Lumber Co. (1901). He also made considerable money in real estate holdings as the population increased in the Indian Territory due to railroad expansion and the burgeoning oil and coal industries. He purchased numerous blocks of lots in Chelsea, Claremore, Fort Gibson, Muskogee, Vinita, and other towns, selling them for enormous profits. In 1910 Halsell moved to Kansas City, where he owned considerable city property and stock in the National Bank of Commerce.

On 23 December 1901 Halsell became one of the largest landowners in Texas when he bought 184,155.3 acres of the famous XIT Ranch from the Capitol Freehold Land and Investment Co., Ltd., of England for $368,310. Established in 1885, the XIT Ranch consisted of 3,050,000 acres of land traded by the state of Texas to the Capitol Syndicate in return for the construction of a new capitol building in Austin, completed in 1888. Considered one of the largest fenced ranches in the world with 160,000 head of cattle, the XIT was located in the western Texas Panhandle and covered nine counties. In 1901 the Capitol Syndicate began to sell its holdings in order to meet its financial obligations. The newly acquired Halsell property was located in Lamb and Castro Counties and belonged to the Spring Lake and Yellow House divisions of the XIT Ranch. During the next few years Halsell bought another 100,000 acres from the XIT holdings. These new acquisitions also became known as the Mashed-O Ranch. A real estate speculator, Halsell established the towns of Amherst and Earth in Texas and also owned banks, hotels, and cotton gins. He started selling his Mashed-O landholdings in Texas in the 1930s; the last acres were sold by the family in 1972. Will Rogers visited the Halsell family several times at their large Texas ranch, where he liked to help with the roundup; and his son, Jim Rogers, also spent considerable time there. W. E. Halsell also visited Will Rogers in California. Halsell died in Santa Monica, Calif., on 25 November 1934 (HFP-TxLT files; Atherton, *Cattle Kings*, 214–15; *OCF* 1:243;

CWM, 28 January 1910; Dale, *Range Cattle Industry*, 113–15; Debo, *Tulsa*, 67–68; Haley, *XIT Ranch of Texas*, 218; Holden, *Ranching Saga; IC*, 14 August 1890; "Mashed O Ranch Extends to Buffalo Days," *West Texas Livestock Weekly*, copy, HFP-TxLT; O'Beirne, *Indian Territory*, 193–94; Rogers, *Will Rogers*, 57, 306; *Story of Craig County*, 378; *TDW*, 14 August 1927, 29 July 1934; Webb, ed., *Handbook of Texas* 1:293, 2:940–44).

HEDGES, Ethel Lane (1894–1975). Ethel Lane was the second child of Maud Ethel Rogers Lane and Cap Lane of Chelsea. She attended Northeast Teachers College, Tahlequah, and earned her degree at Oklahoma University. She worked at the Claremore Telephone Co. and taught school in Sequoyah and Tiawah until her marriage to Edward E. Hedges in 1917. She died in Wichita, Kans., on 30 October 1975 (*CR*, 8 November 1975; *CWM*, 17 July 1908, 27 January 1911, 12 October 1917; *HRC*, 275; Love, "The Rogers Family"; *WRFT*, 26).

HOPKINS (O'Donnell), James Dennis (Jim) (1875–1966). World-record steer roper and equestrian, Jim Hopkins was born on 2 January 1875 in Bastrop County, Tex. His father and mother operated a general merchandise store. Hopkins lived in several small Texas towns as a boy, including Colorado City and Midland. About the age of fourteen or fifteen he went to work as a horse wrangler for the Deep Creek Outfit, a large cattle operation. As a young man he moved to the Claremore/Oologah area in Indian Territory, where he was employed as a cowhand on several ranches, including those of Charles McClure McClellan and Clem V. Rogers. The first time he saw Will Rogers was around 1890–91 when Hopkins was unloading a trainload of steers which were driven to Clem V. Rogers's ranch. Hopkins and Will Rogers competed in many roping contests, including the Rough Riders reunion in Oklahoma City in July 1901. They were also together in the Zack Mulhall show at the 1904 St. Louis World's Fair. An expert roper and winner of many steer-roping contests, Hopkins was considered to be among the best ropers of his time. He broke the steer-roping record at the Confederate Veterans reunion in Memphis in May 1901, tying a steer in 18.2 seconds on Rogers's horse, Comanche. Hopkins toured with many Wild West and rodeo shows as a trick roper and bronco rider, including the Mulhall show, Buffalo Bill's Wild West, and the 101 Ranch show. For unknown reasons, he changed his name to O'Donnell, which he derived from a town in Texas where he once lived. Hopkins worked for Will Rogers for many years, taking care of his polo ponies when Rogers lived on Long Island in 1918–19. Around 1921 Hopkins moved to California, where he continued to care for Rogers's horses and helped teach Will and Betty Blake Rogers's children how to ride. Hopkins wrote several poems about Rogers after he died. Upon retiring, Hopkins lived in Lawndale and Escondido, Calif., and then spent his remaining years living with a nephew, James G. Hopkins, and his wife in Garwood, Tex. He wrote the following poem, "To Will Rogers," in 1959:

> For we have been partners all these many long years,
> A'riding the ranges and rounding up steers.
> So when I check in and lay down my rope;
> When I slip through the darkness, along trails that are strange,
> I'll find Will and our old ponies, waiting there on the range.

(see Hopkins, "To Will Rogers"; Hopkins, "My Friend Will"; Hopkins, interview, OkClaW; Jim Hopkins [O'Donnell] file, OkClaW; Jim Rogers, conversation with Arthur Wertheim, Los Angeles, 7 June 1993; Will Rogers, Jr., to Mrs. James G. Hopkins, 29 April 1966, OkClaW; Collings, *Old Home Ranch*, 39, 91–92; Rogers, *Will Rogers*, 257; *TDW,* 16 December 1934.)

JOHNSON, William A. (Bill) (b. 1880). A banker and cattle rancher, Johnson was born in Bell Buckle, Tenn., on 15 August 1880. He moved with his parents in 1885 to the Panhandle town of Higgins, where they became pioneer settlers. His father, J. F. Johnson (1858–1927), operated the Johnson Hotel (where Rogers stayed in 1898) and a grocery store in Higgins. In 1897 the family moved to nearby Canadian, Tex. Bill Johnson was sent to the Kemper School in Boonville, Mo., where he befriended Will Rogers. There Johnson told Rogers about opportunities to work in the Texas Panhandle, including the Perry Ewing ranch near Higgins. Johnson returned to the Panhandle area, where he entered the cattle business. In 1904 he organized the Johnson McQuiddy Cattle Co. with his brother-in-law A. V. McQuiddy. In 1903 Johnson married Maude Baker, the daughter of the First District judge and superintendent of schools in the Canadian District. Johnson succeeded his father as president of the Southwest National Bank of Canadian in 1927. He was also vice-president of the Canadian Oil Co. and director of the All-American Insurance Co. of Amarillo. In February 1926, Rogers performed in Amarillo and visited with Johnson and Frank Ewing (Frank Ewing, interview, 79:498–99, IPH—OkHi; *Amarillo Daily News-Globe,* 20 February 1926; *History of Lipscomb County;* Keith, *Boy's Life of Will Rogers*, 115–16; Rogers, *Will Rogers*, 52–53; Stanley, *Higgins Texas Story,* 5, 8; *TDW,* 7 March 1926).

KATES, Albert L. (A. L. or Pop) (1861–1938). As the publisher of the *Claremore Progress,* Kates was instrumental in publishing Will Rogers's letters from South America, South Africa, Australia, and New Zealand between 1902 and 1904. Born in New Jersey and educated in rural public schools, Kates became a printer's apprentice for the Woodstown, N.J. *Register* in 1882, and later found employment as a journeyman printer and journalist in the East. Suffering from tuberculosis and desiring to own his own newspaper, he bought the *Claremore Progress* in June 1893 by telegraph without visiting the town and inspecting the business. The newspaper had been founded in March 1893 by the cowboy Joe Kline (who later became a Theodore Roosevelt Rough Rider and a Buffalo Bill performer), but after a few issues he sold it to J. G. Cash. "Pop" Kates, as he became known, arrived in Claremore on 29 June 1893 with his wife, the former Nellie C. Moore, and two young sons. "On alighting from the train my heart sank within me as I viewed the scene," Kates recalled. "A town of about 125 population, hogs wallowing in the main street, board sidewalks . . . all buildings were cheap, false fronted shacks. I was not very enthusiastic over my prospects" (*CP,* centennial edition, 27 June 1993). Two days later on 1 July 1893 he published his first edition of the *Progress,* using an old army sheet-fed press. Under Kates's management the *Claremore Progress* soon became one of the best newspapers in the Indian Territory and Oklahoma. It was first a weekly, independent in politics, and had a circulation of six hundred in 1907. Kates featured both local and national news in the paper, relying at first on his son to gather news on horseback from other pony express riders. Kates purchased the *Claremore Courier,* the paper's competitor, in 1900. With his friend Clem V. Rogers, he supported statehood and was chair of his district for the drafting of the state constitution. He was an avid supporter of renaming the Cooweescoowee District, Rogers County, after Will Rogers's father. Kates remembered visiting with Will Rogers from the time he was seventeen. "I always had a love for travel," Kates said, "and admired Will for wanting to see the world. The greatest education a newspaper man can get is to travel as much as possible" (*CP,* centennial edition, 27 June 1993). Kates also regularly published Rogers's weekly and daily articles in the Claremore paper. A community and civic leader and a member of the Commercial Club, Kates was on the Legislative Committee as well as chair of the Indian Territory Press Association, and later he was an influential member of the Oklahoma Press Association. He also served as Claremore postmaster for eight years during the Woodrow Wilson administration. Kates published the *Claremore Progress* until his death in 1938, when it was taken over by his two sons, Bill and Harry. The paper is now a daily. It belongs to the Donrey Media Group, and Dave Story is the publisher (Carter, E., *Story of Oklahoma Newspapers,* 31; *CP,* centennial edition, 27 June 1993; Dewitz, *Notable Men of Indian Territory,* 127; Foreman, C., *Oklahoma Imprints, 1835–1907,* 63–64; *HRC,* 9; Thoburn, "Albert L. Kates," 131).

KNIGHT, Lythe A. (Light) (ca. 1861–1924). A prosperous Texas Panhandle cattleman, Knight employed the young Will Rogers in 1898 as a cowhand accompanying cattle on a trail drive to Kansas. At the time Knight was in partnership with Henry Slaton. According to one story, Rogers approached Knight, who said, "Here kid. You look hungry. Take this [five dollars] and get you something to eat. Then come back and we'll talk job" (*Amarillo Sunday News Globe,* 14 August 1938). A long-time resident of Hale County, Tex., Knight became a foreman on the Spade Ranch owned by Dudley Sudyer in 1886. He was sheriff of Hale County from 1890 to 1895. Knight owned eighteen thousand acres in the Plainview area, where he grazed a large herd of cattle and employed numerous cowhands. A prosperous farmer, he also grew abundant crops of wheat and cotton and established the first cotton gin in the area. Knight was also a successful banker in Plainview, where he organized the First National Bank in 1900 and was president of the Third National Bank. In 1891 he married Betty Lester of Hale Center. Knight's wife remembers the two of them seeing Rogers perform in the *Ziegfeld Follies* and going backstage to visit Will. "Always after that he never came through Plainview without coming to the house or calling us," Mrs. Knight remembered (Luron Brown file, PHM). Knight died in Plainview in 1924 (*Amarillo News Globe,* 14 August 1938; Croy, *Our Will Rogers,* 47; Keith, *Boy's Life of Will Rogers,* 138–40).

LANE, Andrew Jackson, M.D. (ca. 1851–96). Dr. Lane, graduate of Tulane University, was a pioneer physician in the Oowala and Claremore areas of the Indian Territory. Born in Tennessee and raised in Texas, he was practicing medicine in Fort Gibson, I.T., when C. W. Lipe urged him to move to Oowala in 1876. According to a letter from Paula Love to Rogers biographer Homer Croy, Dr. Lane was the uncle of Cap Lane, who married Will Roger's sister Maud (see also *HRC,* 331–32). Croy writes in *Our Will Rogers* that Dr. Lane was the doctor present at Will Rogers's birth. His evidence comes from Dr. Lane's daughter, Gazelle (Scrap) Lane, but her version of the events has not been confirmed. Other evidence points to Dr. Richard Owen Trent as the physician in attendance at the birth. Dr. Lane was a friend of the Rogers family and served as their family physician. He married Lucinda Elliott Journeycake, a Delaware Indian, on 25 December 1877. Their children, Thomas Lipe, Nancy Shasta, Gazelle (Scrap), Fortner Gordon, and Andrew Denny, were friends of Will Rogers during his youth (Gazelle Lane to Lewis J. Moorman, M.D., 19 February 1954, Moorman Collection, OkU; *As I Recollect,* 19–24; *CR,* 7 November 1896; Croy, *Our Will Rogers,* 18; DuPriest et al., *Cherokee Recollections,* 230–31; *HRC,* 274–75; Keith, *Boy's Life of Will Rogers,* 42–43; Lane, interview, OkClaW; see also Biographical Appendix entry for LANE, Thomas Lipe, and Record of the Birth of Will Rogers, 4 November 1879, n. 10, above).

LANE, Captain Lane (Cap or C. L.) (1867–1924). A Chelsea pharmacist and church and civic leader, Cap Lane married Will Rogers's sister, Maud Ethel Rogers, in 1891. Cap Lane was born in Clarksville, Tex., and was the son of Robert Gordon Lane, M.D. He graduated in 1885 from Kemper Military School, Boonville, Mo. (where the young Will Rogers also attended school in 1897–98). He earned a pharmacology degree in 1887, apprenticed briefly at an Indian Territory drugstore, and then owned and operated Lane's Corner Drug Store at Sixth and Olive Streets in Chelsea. In addition to pharmaceuticals, the store offered schoolbooks, stationary, and other retail goods for sale. He was also on the board of directors of the Bank of Chelsea with his brother-in-law John Thomas McSpadden and served as its president for a time.

An observer described Cap Lane as a "bright, intelligent and well educated man, of courteous manner and kindly disposition" who owned livestock and did "a good business." The same source reported his wife, Maud Rogers Lane, as "a cultured lady" who had been well educated (O'Bierne, *Indian Territory,* 107). In 1905 Cap Lane built two new brick buildings and moved his drugstore, complete with soda fountain, into a new two-story establishment at the corner of Sixth and Pine Streets. The local paper took the occasion to praise him for being generous and fair in his business dealings and for offering quality products, thus earning the large and loyal patronage that he enjoyed. Later, he owned the OK Rexall store in Chelsea.

Cap Lane's popularity was demonstrated in 1911 when he was tried by a local jury for selling Jamaica ginger, which had a high alcohol content. Cap honestly acknowledged on the witness stand that he had sold the item in question. The judge then deemed the sale a violation of the law. The jury nevertheless returned an immediate verdict of "not guilty." The case may have represented something of a local mandate in regard to Chelsea citizens' view on government regulation of alcohol, as well as a testament to the high regard enjoyed by Mr. Lane.

In the last decade of his life Cap Lane retired from his drugstore and spent his time farming and operating a small dairy business delivering milk on a rural route to neighbors and friends. He died of a cerebral hemorrhage on 19 July 1924 (on the 1911 court case, see *RCL,* 15 September 1911; on Mr. Lane and his business, see *CC,* 18 August 1905; *CR,* 6 February, 3 April, and 8 May 1903, 7 April 1905, 16 November 1906; Hitch, *Will Rogers, Cadet,* 23; *HRC,* 275, 332–33; on Cap Lane's family life, see LANE, Maud Ethel Rogers).

LANE, Estelle. See NEAL, Estelle Lane.

LANE, Ethel. See HEDGES, Ethel Lane.

LANE, James Gunter (1897–1964). Gunter Lane was the only son of Will Rogers's sister, Maud Rogers Lane, and Cap Lane. Born on 12 May 1897 in Chelsea, Gunter attended the Chelsea public schools and graduated from the Agricultural and Mechanical College at Stillwater. He married Jennie Belle Mooney (1897–1982) in 1917, and they had five children. Their son was named Robert Rogers Lane after Clem V. Rogers's father and one of his sons, and one of their four daughters was named Maud in honor of Gunter's mother. They resided in Bartlesville, Okla. (*HRC*, 275; Love, "The Rogers Family"; *WRFT*, 26).

LANE, Lasca Gazelle. See LUCKETT, Lasca Gazelle Lane.

LANE, Lucinda Elliott Journeycake. See LANE, Andrew Jackson, and LANE, Thomas Lipe.

LANE, Maud Ethel Rogers (1869–1925). Maud (sometimes spelled Maude) was the fourth child of Mary America Schrimsher Rogers and Clem V. Rogers. She was born 28 November 1869 in Fort Gibson, I.T., where her parents had temporarily relocated to regain economic security following the Civil War. She was still a baby when the family moved to their new home on the Rogers ranch on the Verdigris River. Maud boarded with her sister Sallie and brother Robert at their uncle John Gunter Schrimsher's house on Dog Creek in order to attend West Point School, a tiny rural school taught by John Vann. At the age of fourteen she began attending Worcester Academy in Vinita; later she went to the Cherokee Female Seminary, where she roomed with her cousin Elizabeth Musgrove (daughter of Clem V. Rogers's half brother, Frank Musgrove). Both girls were in residence at the school when it burned down on Easter Sunday in 1887. Maud transferred to Howard Payne College in Fayette, Mo., and studied there from 1888 to 1890.

When her mother died in May 1890, Maud was bedridden at the Rogers ranch with the typhoid fever that had struck many in the valley. Upon recovery she stayed home for a time to comfort her mourning father and to help raise young Willie, who was ten years her junior. On 14 October 1891 she married Captain Lane (known as Cap or C. L.) Lane (1867–1924), a Chelsea pharmacist (see LANE, Captain Lane). The Lanes were married at the Rogers ranch in an intimate ceremony with only immediate relatives invited. Clem V. Rogers gave his daughter and new son-in-law a team of horses, and other family members and close acquaintances gave them household items, including a quilt and a wardrobe. Mary Bibles, the housekeeper who would in a few years become Maud's stepmother, gave the wedding couple five dollars.

The Lanes established a home in Chelsea and became prosperous civic leaders known for their hospitality and charity toward others. They had four children: Estelle (1892–1977), Ethel Lindsey (1894–1975), James Gunter (1897–1964), and Lasca Gazelle (1905–1985) (see HEDGES, Ethel Lane; LANE, James Gunter; LUCKETT, Lasca Lane; and NEAL, Estelle Lane). In May 1901 the Lanes' newly remodeled and painted home was destroyed by a fire that began when workmen were burning a pile of debris left from the recently completed renovations; the family escaped unharmed but lost all their possessions. They built a new, larger home on the outskirts of town, which they called Sunset Farm. The third-floor attic of the house was left empty so that children could use it for roller skating, and the first floor had a double parlor, hall, and music room with sliding doors designed so that people could dance through all the rooms. The house often had visitors, and much of Maud Lane's life was devoted to providing for them. She also took in ill family members and cared for them, and visited shut-ins as a church worker. Her niece, Paula McSpadden Love, observed that "she spent much of her time looking after the poor, afflicted and discouraged much better than the paid welfare worker of today" ("The Rogers Family"). She taught women's Sunday-school classes, whereas Cap taught high-school and men's classes, at the Episcopal Methodist Church South. She had the reputation of being "an excellent business woman" and was the treasurer of the Women's Home Missionary Society of the Episcopal Methodist Church South, an organization her sister Sallie Rogers McSpadden headed (ibid.). She attended the missionary society conferences as a delegate, including those at Pryor Creek in May 1901 and at Chickasha in June 1904.

Like her sister Sallie, she wrote lovingly to her brother Will during his time abroad in 1902 and 1903, telling him how eagerly the family and neighbors received news of his travels and experiences. She also expressed to Will some wistfulness about her own life, her inability to see the world as he was free to do, and the burden she sometimes felt from the demands of her household work and of the many people who expected her care ("I am quite tired and there has not been three days at one time I have not had company in the house and now to cap it all Cap and each of the children is sick. . . . you cant know how very tired I am of company and . . . I am so behind with my sewing and all my summers work. . . . How I do wish I was with you and seeing all the wonderful things you are seeing" (Maud Lane to Will Rogers, 27 August 1902, above).

During World War I, Maud Lane opened a Red Cross sewing room in the Episcopal Parish House (her sister Sallie was director of the Chelsea Red Cross at the time). Cap Lane retired from the drugstore and devoted himself to a small farm, plowing and planting his field, raising a Jersey and Guernsey herd, starting a dairy, and delivering milk by buggy as he drove Maud into town to work at the sewing room. When the family purchased a car, Maud and her daughter Lasca learned to drive, but Cap refused to do so, continuing his business with the buggy. Maud suffered a stroke soon after her husband's death from a cerebral hemorrhage in 1924 and was paralyzed as a result. She lived the last months of her life as an invalid. She died on 15 May 1925 at the age of fifty-five.

According to Will Rogers's son, Jim Rogers, Will Rogers was especially fond of his sister Maud and took every opportunity to spend time with her when he was in Chelsea. He had come to visit her for several days in December 1924. When he received news of her death, he traveled to Chelsea from New York, where he was appearing in the *Ziegfeld Follies*, in order to attend his sister's funeral service. He eulogized her in a May 1925 McNaught Syndicate column, noting the mass of people who had come to the funeral and stating that "all the honors that I could ever in my wildest dreams hope to reach would never equal the honor paid on a little western prairie hilltop, among her people to Maud Lane. If they will love me like that at the finish, my life will not have been in vain" (*TDW,* 24 May 1925). This sentiment was an accurate forecast of Rogers's own belovedness at his death ten years later; it was, however, in contrast to the feeling that Maud expressed in 1917, when she confided to an old friend that she was worried over "losing her eyesight and felt no one cared for her" (Jim Rogers, conversation with Arthur Wertheim, Los Angeles, WRPP; 7 June 1993; memoirs of Mary Newcomb, OkClaW; see also scrapbook of Sallie Rogers McSpadden, SRM-OkClaW; Collings, *Old Home Ranch,* 23–24; *CP,* 4 May 1901; *CR,* 30 May and 12 October 1901, 10 June 1904; *IC,* 14 June 1888, 22 October 1891; *HRC,* 275; Ketchum, *Will Rogers,* 38, 39; Love, "The Rogers Family at Worcester Academy" and "The Rogers Family"; Starr, *History of the Cherokee Indians,* 642; *WRFT,* 26–27).

LANE, Thomas Lipe (Tom) (ca. 1879–1924). The son of Dr. Andrew J. Lane and Lucinda Elliott Journeycake Lane, Tom Lane was one of Will Rogers's closest friends during his youth. He was educated at the community school at Oowala, attended Willie Halsell College with Will Rogers in 1891 and 1894, and was also a student at the Cherokee National Male Seminary in 1892 and 1893. He roomed with Will Rogers at Willie Halsell College. After the death of his father in 1896, he attended school in Claremore, and in 1902 he went to business school in Kansas City. Like Will Rogers, he was an honorary member of the Pocahontas Club and served as club president in 1903 and 1904. A talented musician, he often sang at club functions. Lane married Nora Matheson on 1 June 1903 and the couple were the parents of four children. For several years he was employed as cashier at the Bank of Foyil in Oklahoma (*As I Recollect*, 20–24; *CP,* 1 November and 20 December 1902; DuPriest et al., *Cherokee Recollections*, 63; *HRC*, 274–75; Keith, *Boy's Life of Will Rogers*, 57–59).

LILLIE, Gordon William (Pawnee Bill) (1860–1942). The Wild West show entrepreneur and early frontiersman Bill Lillie was born in Bloomington, Ill. His family moved to Kansas, and at the age of sixteen he became a trapper on the Great Plains. He worked as a cowboy on cattle drives and roundups, and in the early 1880s became a teacher at a Pawnee Agency industrial-training school in Indian Territory. He later joined a party of "land boomers" in Oklahoma. He was a member of a syndicate that attempted to buy the Cherokee Outlet from the Cherokee Nation in 1888 (Congress refused the offer). He worked as a Pawnee interpreter for Buffalo Bill's Wild West in the mid-1880s, and in 1886 married sharpshooter May Manning, a graduate of Smith College. In 1888 he organized his own traveling show. The Pawnee Bill Wild West Show was one of the best known, and Lillie toured with it for over twenty years. It traveled to Claremore in October 1905 and included an airship as one of its attractions. Between 1908 and 1913 Lillie was in a partnership with William Cody, establishing the Buffalo Bill's Wild West and Pawnee Bill's Far East show, which toured Illinois, Iowa, Nebraska, Colorado, and Wyoming. Rogers appeared with the combined show at Madison Square Garden in April 1910. The partnership between Lillie and Cody was dissolved in July 1913, and Lillie retired to a two-thousand-acre ranch in Pawnee, Okla. He set up a well-known trading post there, invested in oil, and became a vice-president of the Fern Oil Co. Concerned with the preservation of the wild life of the West, he was a backer of the Wichita Wildlife Refuge and worked for the protection of the buffalo. He became a friend of Clem V. Rogers and of Sallie Rogers McSpadden as well as of Will Rogers. Will Rogers visited him on his ranch at Pawnee, Okla., as well as at get-togethers at the Miller Brothers' 101 Ranch in the 1920s (scrapbook of Sallie Rogers McSpadden, SRM-OkClaW; *CP,* 18 October 1905; *EFB;* "Father of Will Rogers Came to County in 1857," unidentified newsclipping, Claremore, 4 November 1937; *HRC*, 29; Keith, "Clem Rogers and His Influence on Oklahoma History," 93; Keith, *Boy's Life of Will Rogers*, 217–18; Leonard and Goodman, *Buffalo Bill*, 278–80; Lillie, *Life Story of Pawnee Bill;*

Metcalf, "Historic Sites in the Cherokee Strip," 393, 394; Russell, *Wild West,* 50–51; Shirley, *Pawnee Bill: A Biography; TDW,* 7 November and 19 June 1928; *Variety,* [30 April 1910], 17).

LIPE, DeWitt Clinton (D. W. or Major) (1840–1916) (and the Lipe family). As a rancher, merchant, and Cherokee Nation politician, D. W. Lipe was, like his friend and business partner Clem V. Rogers, a veteran of the Confederate army and one of the pioneers of the Verdigris country. He and his family lived near the Foreman, McClellan, and Rogers families along the Verdigris River, and their children grew up socializing together.

D. W. Lipe was Catherine Gunter Lipe and Oliver Wack Lipe's first son, the eldest of seven children. He was born in Eureka, near Tahlequah, I.T., on 17 February 1840. He attended Cherokee Nation schools and studied in Cane Hill, Ark., before going to the Cherokee Male Seminary at Tahlequah. He came to the Verdigris country in 1858 and had a ranch on the Caney River until the Civil War. He served in the Confederate army along with Clem V. Rogers, and after the war he lived in the Choctaw Nation until 1867. He married twice. His first wife was Victoria Susan Hicks (1839–67) of Tahlequah, the niece of Principal Chief John Ross. She graduated in 1856 in the same Cherokee National Female Seminary class as Mary America Schrimsher Rogers's sister, Elizabeth Alabama Schrimsher, and Clem V. Rogers's sister Margaret (Peggy) Rogers. The Lipes were married in September 1861. Victoria Hicks Lipe died of cholera in August 1867, shortly after she and her husband had moved from the Choctaw Nation to a place on Dog Creek near Claremore. She and D. W. Lipe had one child, John Gunter Lipe (b. 1864). After her death D. W. Lipe moved back to Fort Gibson and went into business with his father, while his mother cared for his young son.

The Gunters (Mary America Schrimsher Rogers's mother's family) and the Lipes were long related by marriage: Will Rogers's grandmother's sister, Catherine Gunter (1811–76), who came to Indian Territory in 1838, married Oliver Wack Lipe (D. W. Lipe's father) in 1839. Oliver Wack Lipe, born in New York in 1814 of Dutch descent, was a captain in the New York State Guards in 1833, and came to Indian Territory in 1837. He and Catherine Gunter Lipe lived first in Eureka, not far from Tahlequah, and then on a farm two miles northwest of Tahlequah. In 1854 they moved into town and Oliver Wack Lipe began operation of the O.W. Lipe and Son mercantile stores in Tahlequah and Fort Gibson. He became one of the Indian Territory's leading entrepreneurs. He was a commissar in Stand Watie's regiment during the Civil War. After the war he employed his son's friend Clem V. Rogers, who was a fellow veteran and married to Lipe's niece, Mary America Schrimsher Rogers, to haul merchandise for his businesses. Clem V. Rogers worked in partnership with D. W. Lipe moving freighted goods to the Choctaw Nation and trading them for cattle, which he drove back to Fort Gibson. Rogers had extensive knowledge of the Verdigris country, and Lipe had capital; together they formed a partnership to graze the Choctaw cattle in the Cooweescoowee District. The venture encouraged Rogers to return to the area, and he began to reestablish a ranch there beginning in 1868, and he moved his family from Fort Gibson to the renovated place in 1870. D. W. Lipe soon did the same, and in 1872 they dissolved their partnership.

D. W. Lipe's second wife was Mary Elizabeth Archer, one of five daughters of Mary Vann Archer and Edwin Archer, all of whom were schoolteachers. Soon after their marriage in March 1871, D. W. Lipe left his father's mercantile business and moved with his new wife to the Verdigris valley, where they built a home near what became known as Oowala, on Sweetwater Creek, and established a ranch and cattle business. Their ranch was just across the Verdigris River from the Rogers ranch.

The Lipes had three daughters, Nancy Eva (Nannie) Lipe (1872–1956), Victoria Susan Lipe (1874–1923), and Lola Vann Lipe (1877–1923). All relatively close to Will Rogers in age, the "Lipe girls," as both Sallie McSpadden and Maud Lane referred to them in their letters to Will Rogers in 1902 and 1903, were friends of the Rogers family. All three attended Cherokee Nation schools. Nannie and Victoria attended the Cherokee Female Seminary and the Presbyterian Oswego School for Girls in Oswego, Kans. Nannie graduated in 1895 or 1896; Victoria was forced to leave school because of ill health; and Lola transferred from Cottey College, Nevada, Mo., to Oswego and graduated in 1896 or 1898. Both Nannie and Lola became teachers and taught school in Claremore and Watova. Nannie Lipe was an active member of the Pocahontas Club and was elected president of the club in 1900. She became the assistant county superintendent of schools of Rogers County, Okla. Victoria was the only "Lipe girl" to marry. She married John Barrett (b. 1872) in 1898.

D. W. Lipe owned the small store and post office that was a stage stop in Oowala. He donated a one-room log building (a former granary) for use as a local rural school for Oowala children beginning in 1881, and the C. M. McClellans brought out a schoolteacher from Arkansas to teach in it. Like his friend Clem V. Rogers, Lipe was a rancher who was also active in Cherokee Nation politics. He was the district clerk for the Cooweescoowee District from 1874 to 1877 and treasurer of the Cherokee Nation for two four-year terms (1879–83 and 1895–99). He was elected to the Cherokee Nation Senate in 1877 and 1885 and was a commissioner on several Cherokee Nation commissions. Like Clem V. Rogers, he was a delegate to the 1906 constitutional convention. After statehood he became the county clerk of Rogers County (1907–10). And, in another parallel to Clem V. Rogers's life, he left his ranch (in 1908) and moved into the town of Claremore and became active in business and civic affairs there (Aldrich, "General Stores, Retail Merchants, and Assimilation"; *CP,* 19 May 1900; Collings, *Old Home Ranch,* 16, 18, 19, 30 nn. 13 and 14, 41; DuPriest et al., *Cherokee Recollections;* Gideon, *Indian Territory,* 606–7; *HRC,* 60, 194, 280–81; Lipe, "History of the Lipe Family," in *As I Recollect;* Walker, interview, IPH-OkHi; McSpadden, "Clement Vann Rogers," 393; Mihesuah, *Cultivating the Rosebuds,* 124, 125; O'Bierne, *Indian Territory,* 241–42; *OCF* 1:57, 82, 177, 224, 2:114; Starr, *History of the Cherokee Indians,* 233, 292, 299, 498; *WRFT,* 78, 114, 126, 127).

LIPE, Lola Vann. See LIPE, DeWitt Clinton.

LIPE, Nancy Eva (Nannie). See LIPE, DeWitt Clinton.

LIPE, Oliver Wack. See LIPE, DeWitt Clinton.

LIPE, Victoria Susan. See LIPE, DeWitt Clinton.

LOVE, Pauline Elizabeth (Paula) McSpadden (1901–73). The niece of Will Rogers and the seventh child of John Thomas (Tom) McSpadden and Sallie Rogers McSpadden, Pauline Elizabeth McSpadden was born near Chelsea on 13 September 1901. She was a toddler when her uncle Will Rogers went to live abroad in Argentina, South Africa, Australia, and New Zealand. During his absence she suffered an incident of infantile paralysis that deeply alarmed the family. At age seven she was sent to a sanitarium in St. Louis for a year, and eventually she recovered from the illness. She grew up at Maplewood, the McSpadden home in Chelsea, was a member of the Pocahontas Club, and graduated from Chelsea High School in 1922. She graduated from the Oklahoma College for Women at Chickasha in 1926 and received her master's degree in English from the University of Missouri in 1930 (her tuition and expenses at the latter were paid by Will Rogers). She taught English, speech, and music at the Chelsea and Vinita high schools and English at Northeastern State College in Tahlequah. Between 1927 and 1929 she lived with the Rogers family in Beverly Hills, where she was a companion to their daughter, Mary. In Chelsea on 24 November 1937 she married Robert Love, the third child of Samuel and Flora Love of Vinita. Like his father, he became an architect and building contractor. Paula McSpadden met him when she was teaching in the Vinita school system. In the year after their marriage the Loves were asked to direct the newly built Will Rogers Memorial in Claremore, which opened to the public on 4 November 1938. They operated the Memorial for the next thirty-five years, hosting researchers and a series of distinguished guests. Paula Love was responsible for developing the archive housing Rogers's papers, and she collected other valuable reference material. She wrote many profiles of Will Rogers, his family, and Oklahoma/Indian Territory history, including *The Will Rogers Book* (1961) of sayings. She dedicated herself to the preservation of public knowledge of her famous uncle's character and career. Paula Love passed away after a brief illness in Tulsa on 28 April 1973, and Robert Love resigned from the Memorial two years later (Maud Lane to Will Rogers, 31 October 1902, OkClaW; Paula and Robert Love to Betty Blake Rogers, various correspondence, 1930s, SRM-OkClaW; Betty Blake Rogers to Sallie McSpadden, 7 December 1937, SRM-OkClaW; Bell, *Genealogy of Old and New Cherokee Indian Families,* 357; Collins, "Paula McSpadden Love"; *HRC,* 283–84; Love, interview, OkClaW; *WRFT,* 14).

Luckett, Lasca Gazelle Lane (1905–85). Gazelle Lane, a niece of Will Rogers, was the youngest daughter of Maud Ethel Rogers Lane and Cap Lane. She was born in Chelsea on 19 June 1905, attended the Chelsea schools, and graduated from the Cherokee Female Seminary in 1903. She became a schoolteacher and taught school in Indian Territory/Oklahoma. She married Harvey Lyle Luckett (1900–1961), and they had two sons, one of whom died as a small child. They made their home in Boulder, Colo. (*CP,* 13 June 1903; *CR,* 12 February 1904; *CWM,* 5 February 1904; *HRC,* 275; Love, "The Rogers Family"; *WRFT,* 26).

McClellan, Charles White (Charley) (1879–1902). Charles McClellan was Will Rogers's closest friend during his early years and the recipient of letters Rogers wrote while attending the Willie Halsell College. He was the son of Charles McLure McClellan (1845–1927), a prosperous cattleman, and Jennie Lind Foreman McClellan (1850–1911), the youngest daughter of the influential Cherokee Presbyterian missionary Rev. Stephen Foreman (1807–81), and his wife, Sarah W. Riley (d. 1861). Clem V. Rogers told Charles McLure McClellan about the marvelous opportunities for ranching in the Cooweescoowee District while the two were serving in the Confederate army, and as a result the elder McClellan moved to the area around 1875. Charles White McClellan was born six days after Will Rogers. He grew up on his parents' ranch in the Oowala community, located across the Verdigris River several miles from the Rogers ranch. He attended school at the Cherokee National Male Seminary in Tahlequah and with Will Rogers at the Willie Halsell College in Vinita. Like

Rogers, McClellan enjoyed riding and roping, and he participated in steer-roping contests with Rogers, including the Confederate reunion at Memphis in May 1901. He and Rogers were among the first male honorary members of the Pocahontas Club. A one-quarter Cherokee who identified closely with his Indian heritage, McClellan often dressed in Native American clothing and wore his hair in a traditional manner, shaved on the sides or in long braids, using a white buckskin thong for a clip. Friends remember him building a tipi and bonfire near his home for neighborhood stomp dances participated in by Rogers and their friends and attended by many residents of Claremore. McClellan spent several weeks each year visiting the Shawnees northeast of Chelsea and other Indian peoples, learning their traditional dances. He would then teach those dances to his friends, including Will Rogers; Gordon, Tom, Denny, Shasta and Gazelle Lane; Bill McClellan; and the Lipes. The stomp dances would then be held on a knoll outside the Lane home, drawing audiences from nearby communities who came to see the young people dance in native dress. McClellan also participated with Rogers in local roping contests. While attending Cumberland College at Lebanon, Tenn., McClellan grew ill and died from typhoid fever. He was buried with services in Claremore. His sister, Mary Ermina Comer (1875–1934), donated Rogers's letters to Charles McClellan to the Will Rogers Memorial (Lane, interview, OkClaW; Wear, interview, OkClaW; *As I Recollect,* 25–30, 33–34, 68–77; Collings, *Old Home Ranch,* 27, 60, 83, 91; *CP,* 20 December, 25 December, and 27 December 1902; 1 January and 3 January 1903; *HRC,* 289; Keith, *Boy's Life of Will Rogers,* 73–88; Starr, *History of the Cherokee Indians,* 637).

McGONIGLE, Henry Clay (1879–1921). (Newspaper accounts alternately spell Clay McGonigle's last name McGonagill, McGonigall, and McConagil.) A champion steer roper, McGonigle was born at Old Sweet Home, Lavaca County, Tex. He grew up on his father's horse ranch in Odessa, Tex., where his father bred quarter horses. A top cowhand, bronco rider, and roper, McGonigle set many records in steer and calf roping, and performed in roping contests in both North and South America, winning hundreds of contests. In 1901 he roped a steer that had a one-hundred-foot start in twenty-three seconds. In a well-publicized competition in San Antonio for the steer-roping championship in January 1905, McGonigle lost to J. Ellison Carroll, another great roper. In another famous match in Muskogee in 1907, McGonigle beat world champion Bob Gentry by tying eleven steers in less time than it took Gentry to tie ten animals. After steer roping was outlawed in most states, McGonigle turned to calf roping. In 1900 McGonigle and other cowboys went to Argentina to perform. Rogers competed against McGonigle in steer-roping contests at the 1901 San Antonio International Fair and Exhibition. After retiring from the rodeo circuit, McGonigle became a rancher in Texas, New Mexico, and Arizona. In 1921 McGonigle was killed when he accidently came in contact with an electric power line at Sacaton, Ariz. During a visit to Texas in 1926, Rogers lamented McGonigle's death and wrote that he missed seeing his roping buddy. "Clay was acknowledged by everyone to be the funniest Cowboy that ever lived," he wrote in his weekly article (*TDW,* 7 March 1926). McGonigle was inducted into the Rodeo Hall of Fame, in the National Cowboy Hall of Fame in Oklahoma City, in 1975 (McGonigle file, NCHF; Porter, W.H., *Who's Who in Rodeo,* 84–85; "Rivals Are Friends," clipping, 16 January 1905, scrapbook A1, OkClaW; Westermeier, *Man, Beast, Dust,* 45–46).

MCSPADDEN, Clement Mayes (Clem) (1886–1912). The eldest son of John Thomas (Tom) McSpadden and Sallie Rogers McSpadden, Clem McSpadden carried high expectations for achievement placed upon him by his family. He attended Kemper School, Boonville, Mo., and graduated with highest honors in June 1902. His younger sister May reported to her uncle Will Rogers when Rogers was living in Argentina that Clem would start at Vanderbilt University, Nashville, in the fall 1902 term (May McSpadden to Will Rogers, 31 August 1902, above). Clem wrote himself on the same day, informing his uncle that there had been a big celebration in Tahlequah to welcome the new railroad and that the young people at the dance at the opera house had missed Will being there (Clem McSpadden to Will Rogers, 31 August 1902, above). McSpadden became a civil engineer. He studied at Vanderbilt for the 1902–3 school year and at the State School of Mines in Rolla, Mo., in 1903. He worked on the Oklahoma and Cherokee Central Railroad in 1904 and traveled to Mexico in 1906. He married Alice May Beretta of San Antonio, Tex., in Los Angeles on 3 July 1912, and died of typhoid fever in California not long after the wedding, on 20 August 1912. He was working for the Santa Fe Railroad Co. as a surveyor near Chaves, N.M., when he became ill and the company brought him to Los Angeles for treatment. He was buried in Chelsea (death record and marriage record, McSpadden family Bible, SRM-OkClaW; *CC,* 30 September and 14 October 1904, 28 December 1906; *CP,* 31 May 1902; *CR,* 7 September, 12 October, and 24 December 1901; 3 January, 6 June, and 12 September 1902; 19 June, 18 September, and 25 December 1903; 29 July and 19 August 1904; 29 September 1912; *CWM,* 23 September 1912; *DC,* 28 May and 30 May 1902; *HRC,* 301; *IC,* 14 January 1904; *RCL,* 23 August 1912; *Vinita Republican,* 11 June 1902; *WRFT,* 14).

McSPADDEN, Helen. See EATON, Helen McSpadden.

McSPADDEN, Herbert Thomas (Herb) (1893–1980). Will Rogers's nephew and the fourth son of John Thomas (Tom) McSpadden and Sallie Rogers McSpadden, Herb McSpadden was raised on a ranch and, like his mother and father, loved horses and the cattle business. He was in the last graduating class of the Cherokee Male Seminary at Tahlequah in 1910 and served in World War I. He married Madelyn Pope of Orange, Calif., (1898–1977) in Oklahoma City on 20 August 1924. His father turned over his ranching interests to him in 1914. He participated regularly as a stockman with rodeos in the Southwest in the 1920s.

After Clem V. Rogers moved to Claremore in 1898, the Rogers ranch was occupied by a series of tenants in addition to being managed for a brief time by the young Will Rogers before he went abroad. In the 1920s Will Rogers wanted to rebuild the old ranch to something of its former splendor, and he asked Herb McSpadden to become foreman of the ranch in the fall of 1927. McSpadden moved his family to the ranch and directed restorations according to Rogers's wishes. Fences and buildings needed repair, weeds were rampant, and the roads had deteriorated so that they were difficult to use. The wonderful herds of cattle and horses that Clem V. Rogers had kept on the property were long gone, and the ranch boasted less than one hundred cows. Rogers went about buying land and reassembling old sections of grassland along the Verdigris River to meet his dream of reestablishing some semblance of the bluestem grasses and cattle range of his youth. Other acreage was leased, so that Rogers had regained over seventeen hundred acres of his father's old ranch land before his death in 1935. Herb McSpadden oversaw the restocking of the ranch and the reconstruction of its outbuildings, fences, and equipment while Madelyn Pope McSpadden redecorated the old home, restoring it to resemble the way Mary America Schrimsher Rogers once had it furnished. After Will Rogers's death ownership of the ranch went to Betty Rogers, who retained Herb McSpadden as manager. He bred quarter horses, including a string of palominos, under Clem V. Rogers's old J4 brand, and built up a herd of Hereford cattle, branded with Will Rogers's Dog Iron Brand. McSpadden also participated in civic affairs and served on the Oologah school board.

In 1958 sixteen hundred acres of the ranch land were condemned and deeded for government use in connection with the construction of the Oologah dam and reservoir. In 1959 the Rogers family donated the old ranch house and a tract of land to the state of Oklahoma. Herb McSpadden left the ranch in the fall of 1960. The state of Oklahoma moved the ranch house to land several miles from the old site and reassembled it for public use as a state park where today the birthplace, known as the Dog Iron Ranch, is visited by many tourists and schoolchildren each year (marriage record, McSpadden family Bible, SRM-OkClaW; Sallie McSpadden to Will Rogers, 27 July 1902, OkClaW; scrapbook of Sallie McSpadden, SRM-OkClaW; Bell, *Genealogy of Old and New Cherokee Indian Families*, 357; Collings, *Old Home Ranch*, 63, 110–12, 114–15, 122, 123, 137; *HRC*, 301; McSpadden, H., "The Importance of Faith and Belief," "Horses and Horse Collars," and talk, OkClaW; *WRFT*, 14).

McSPADDEN, Irene. See MILAM, MAUD IRENE McSPADDEN.

McSPADDEN, John Thomas (Tom or J. T.) (1852–1936). A Chelsea cattle rancher, banker, and civic leader, Tom McSpadden was a member of a prominent non-Cherokee Indian Territory family. He collaborated with Clem V. Rogers in cattle and horse drives in the 1870s, bringing up livestock from Texas to the Verdigris valley. He married Will Rogers's sister Sallie Clementine Rogers in 1885. He was one of seven sons of Elizabeth Jane Green McSpadden (1821–89), who was born in Tennessee, and Rev. Thomas Kingsbury McSpadden (1825–77). His father was a circuit rider in Alabama who came to Indian Territory in 1869 as a Southern Methodist missionary. Reverend McSpadden established churches in the Cherokee Nation affiliated with the Methodist Episcopal Church South, the faith of Will Rogers's mother, Mary America Schrimsher Rogers. Tom McSpadden was born on 15 March 1852 in Alabama and educated at public schools and the Phoenix Academy, near Fort Payne, Ala. After coming to Indian Territory, he worked first as a schoolteacher and then as a blacksmith, before entering the cattle business. During the time he was a blacksmith, he served for one term as the mayor of Vinita. He and his brothers, Joe, Sam, and Fair, eventually settled in the Chelsea area, while his other brothers, Jim, Frank, and Magnus, lived in Tahlequah. Sam McSpadden became the Chelsea postmaster while Tom McSpadden became one of the largest landowners and cattle raisers in the area. Tom McSpadden maintained several farms with some thousand head of cattle and hundreds of acres under cultivation. He helped found the Bank of Chelsea in March 1896, served on the board of directors, and was president of the bank in 1903. He was an owner of the Chelsea Mercantile Co., a grocery and general-goods store, and he was director of the Chelsea Fair from 1901 to 1915. A local biographer described him as "a representative citizen, progressive, liberal and wide-awake" (O'Bierne, *Indian Territory*, 148). A real-estate developer, McSpadden had the largest number of rental units of any individual in Chelsea at the turn of the century. He and his wife were very active in the Methodist Episcopal Church South and in Chelsea educational campaigns. In combining stockraising and banking, property ownership, and political interests, Tom McSpadden's career was similar to that of Sallie Rogers McSpadden's father, Clem V. Rogers (scrapbook of Sallie McSpadden and McSpadden family correspondence, SRM-OkClaW; Helen McSpadden to Betty Blake Rogers, 5 November 1936, SRM-OkClaW; Collings, *Old Home Ranch*, 60; *CC*, 15 February 1901, 20 January 1905, 10 March 1906; *CR*, 17 January 1901, 15 August, 17 October 1902; 6 February, 7 August, 2 October, 23 October, and 30 October 1903; 28 April, 16 June, 13 October, and 27 October 1905; *HRC*, 301–2; Starr, *History of the Cherokee Indians*, 571; on McSpadden family and civic life, see also MCSPADDEN, Sallie Clementine Rogers).

MCSPADDEN, Maurice. See MCSPADDEN, Sallie Clementine Rogers.

MCSPADDEN, May. See POOLE, May McSpadden.

MCSPADDEN, Pauline. See LOVE, Pauline Elizabeth (Paula) McSpadden.

MCSPADDEN, Sallie Clementine Rogers (1863–1943). Sallie Rogers was the oldest daughter of Mary America Schrimsher Rogers and Clem V. Rogers to live to adulthood. Her sister, Elizabeth, the Rogers's first-born, had died in infancy two years before Sallie's birth. Sallie was born during the Civil War on 16 December 1863, when her father was fighting with the Confederate army and her mother was a refugee from Indian Territory, living with her parents and other family members in a farmhouse near the refugee camp in Bonham, Tex. Her early childhood was spent in Texas and at Doaksville and Fort Gibson in Indian Territory, where her parents lived at the war's end. She was seven years old when the family moved back to the Verdigris valley onto the new ranch Clem V. Rogers had established a few miles from the site of his old trading post and home.

Of all the children, Sallie responded the most strongly to her mother's tutoring in music, and she became an accomplished pianist, often playing with her mother for the family or entertaining at social gatherings. She was also comfortable on the back of a horse, spending many of her childhood days riding on the open ranch land, going to fetch the mail from the post office in Oowala, or heading out to visit people at nearby ranches. As she recalled later in life, "I almost lived in a saddle in those days—a side-saddle, of course. No nice young lady would have thought of riding astride." Before her baby brother Will could walk, she often galloped with him in her lap (Ferguson, "Let Me Rest in Oklahoma"). Like most daughters of wealthy Cherokee ranchers, she was home mostly in the summer months and boarded elsewhere during the school year to be in closer proximity to the best Indian Territory schools.

Sallie and two other older Rogers children, Robert and Maud, lived with their uncle John Schrimsher in order to attend West Point School near Dog Creek. She later lived with her aunt Martha Gulager near Tahlequah so that she could go to Eureka School. At the age of twelve she started at the Cherokee Female Seminary at Park Hill, near Tahlequah, and graduated in 2 July 1880. She began teaching school at the Cooweescoowee District school at Oowala in the fall of 1880, when her little brother Will was a baby. From 1881 to 1885 she taught high school at the Cherokee Orphan Asylum at Salina.

Sallie was close to her father as well as to her mother, and she often accompanied Clem V. Rogers on his trips to Coffeyville, Kans., where he went to buy supplies for the ranch. She also contributed to the refined spirit of beauty and hospitality that her mother created at the ranch. She had read extensively and studied music at the seminary, and she was "like her mother . . . gay, charming, and accomplished," adding "graciousness to the social life of the Rogers home" (Collings, *Old Home Ranch,* 24). Music was an avid interest that Sallie shared with not only her mother but also her brother, Will. In later years, when Will Rogers traveled to Argentina and Africa, Sallie was his conduit for sheet music of the latest songs. She wrote to him about which songs were currently popular and he asked her to send him certain titles.

Sallie married John Thomas (Tom) McSpadden (1852–1936), at the Rogers ranch just before Christmas on 16 December 1885, her twenty-second birthday (see McSpadden, John Thomas). Mary America Schrimsher Rogers organized the wedding. For the ceremony she created an altar beautifully adorned with mistletoe, bittersweet, and geraniums that she had grown in pots inside the house. Will Rogers, who had just turned six years old, assisted his sisters Maud and May in serving a turkey dinner to the guests after the ceremony was completed. The local Vinita *Journal* reported that with the wedding the "county lost its most popular belle" (16 December 1885). The couple honeymooned in New Orleans and returned to live at the McSpadden ranch, across the Verdigris River from the Rogers ranch. Will Rogers came to live with them so that he could attend the Drumgoole School, a one-room rural school for Cherokee children located a few miles from the McSpadden place. This was an impressive event in the young boy's life because his oldest sister became a kind of second mother to him; the relationship would remain important, particularly after the death of Mary America Schrimsher Rogers in 1890.

In 1892 the McSpaddens moved to Chelsea, where they built a home that they called Maplewood. They became deeply involved in church, cultural, and civic affairs in Chelsea. They were both active in the local Methodist Episcopal Church South, where Tom was the first superintendent of the Sunday school (from 1889 to 1894) and Sallie played the organ and directed the primary school for fifty years. She also organized and taught the "Madonna" class, a course designed for mothers with small children. She was president of the Chelsea branch of the Women's Home Missionary Society (from ca. 1889 to 1940).

Sallie was a charter member of the Chelsea Delphian Review Club, a study and service club for women, and she was well known for her ability as an extemporaneous speaker and book reviewer, drawing large crowds when she spoke in cities in Oklahoma. An undated newsclipping in her scrapbook reports that she "filled the pulpit at the Ketchum Methodist church Sunday in the absence of the pastor and gave a very inspirational sermon." One friend who eulogized her stated that "her talks sparkled with the same wit and humor that made her brother, the late Will Rogers, famous" (Fullerton, "Sallie Rogers McSpadden," 127). The *New York Times* called her a "humorist in petticoats" (26 August 1943). She wrote and directed a pageant on women in the Bible that was performed in Tulsa and other cities. McSpadden was sought as an expert on local and state history; in 1910 the *Oklahoma City Times* published an article she wrote on the history of the Cherokee Male and Female Seminaries. Like her mother, she was an inspired gardener and talented in crafts. She began a movement in the Cherokee Nation to revive traditional arts, especially basket making. She also was an excellent storyteller. She directed the local Red Cross for sixteen years, was a charter member of the American Legion Auxiliary, and during World War I was in charge of the Red Cross production rooms in town.

McSpadden was active with the women's-club movement and was a leader in the Oklahoma Federation of Women's Clubs. In 1935 she worked for the election of Roberta Campbell Lawson (of Tulsa) to the presidency of the National Federation of Women's Clubs, and she became the National Secretary of Bible Literature for the federation during Lawson's tenure. She hosted a conference of the Business and Professional Women's Clubs of the Oklahoma Federation in 1937, soon after the local Chelsea club had completed their drive on behalf of "The Business Woman as Citizen," which promoted the "advancement of women in many economic and political fields" and encouraged acceptance of women "assuming the full stature of citizenship" (Chelsea newsclipping, 1 April 1937, scrapbook of Sallie McSpadden, SRM-OkClaW). Her friend Eula Fullerton remembered, "Politically she was a Democrat, but when candidates came to her soliciting her aid, she never avoided the issue but told them exactly where she stood on any questions at stake. Her utter fearlessness in such matters was startling" (Fullerton, "Sallie Rogers McSpadden," 128).

Sallie and her husband, Tom McSpadden, as well as Sallie's sister Maud Lane, were in a group of Chelsea residents who brought the Redpath Horner Chautauqua Circuit to Chelsea, and both the McSpaddens and the Lanes hosted visitors who came to town for the chautauqua meetings. The McSpadden property included some small ponds, and the town children would come to their house for ice-skating in winter. Like Clem V. Rogers, who donated land in Claremore for a children's park, the McSpaddens gave a tract of land immediately adjoining Maplewood to the town for a city park.

Sallie maintained her interest in education issues, based on her experience teaching in the Cherokee Nation schools. She and Tom McSpadden were committed to public education and were very involved in the city schools, where they sent their younger children. They also contributed money for the building of the Cumberland Presbyterian church and academy, which became a nonsectarian school, and saw that their own children had the opportunity to attend college. As one journalist put it, "In some families the mother trains her daughters to be domestic. In other families she trains them to be intellectual. Mrs. McSpadden trained her daughters to be both" (Davis, K. M., "Will Rogers and His Sister"). Sallie was an honorary member of Beta Sigma Phi, a sorority centered around local study groups founded for young businesswomen supporting families and for homemakers who had not had the opportunity to go to college. Members pursued a four-year course of study including literature, music, public speaking, and the arts. In 1950 one of the women's dormitories at the University of Oklahoma campus was named for Sallie McSpadden.

The McSpaddens had eight children. Their eldest son, Clement Mayes McSpadden (1886–1912), was close to his uncle Will Rogers and wrote to him about his school and dating life when Rogers lived abroad in 1902–3 (see McSpadden, Clement Mayes). Their first daughter, Mary Belle (1888–90), died in the same typhoid-fever epidemic that killed Sallie McSpadden's mother. Their third child, May, was born in 1891 (see Poole, May McSpadden). Their fourth child, Herbert Thomas (Herb) (1893–1980), became the manager of the Rogers ranch at Oologah in 1927 and lived there for over thirty years (see McSpadden, Herbert Thomas). Their next three children were Maud Irene (1896–1973), Helen (1899–1985), and Pauline Elizabeth (Paula) (1901–73) (see Eaton, Helen McSpadden; Love, Pauline Elizabeth (Paula) McSpadden; Milam, Maud Irene McSpadden). Paula McSpadden Love and her husband later became the first directors of the Will Rogers Memorial. The last child born to Tom and Sallie McSpadden was Maurice Rogers McSpadden (1905–68). Born after Will Rogers had returned to the United States from his adventures abroad, Maurice graduated from the Agricultural and Mechanical College in Stillwater, Okla. (now Oklahoma State University) and earned a master's degree at Iowa State University of Science and Technology, Ames, Iowa. He became a lieutenant in the U.S. Army Medical Corps.

Tom McSpadden died a year after he and Sallie McSpadden celebrated their fiftieth wedding anniversary at Maplewood in December 1935. Sallie McSpadden died on 25 August 1943 from heart disease. The local newspaper described her as "Chelsea's most eminent resident." The oldest Rogers child to have survived to adulthood, she outlived all her siblings, including her beloved little brother, Will. She was the only one of his seven siblings still alive when he was killed in the plane crash in August 1935, and she represented the family at some events held in his honor. Sallie McSpadden and Betty Blake Rogers became good friends and grew especially close after Will Rogers's death. They exchanged warm and frequent correspondence about their feelings, well-being, and families. Betty Blake also contributed generously to Sallie McSpadden's material well-being in McSpadden's old age (Sallie Rogers McSpadden, interview, 76:158–59, IPH-OkHi; scrapbook and correspondence of Sallie McSpadden, SRM-OkClaW; Sallie McSpadden to Will Rogers, 1 September 1902 and 14 September 1903, above; Will Rogers to Folks, 17 November 1902 and 17 March 1903, above; *Christian Science Monitor,* 20 October 1961; Collings, *Old Home Ranch,* 23–24, 29, 31 n. 62; *CR,* 13 March 1903; Davis, K. M., "Will Rogers and His Sister"; Ferguson, "Let Me Rest in Oklahoma"; DuPriest et al., *Cherokee Recollections,* 238–39; Fullerton, "Sallie Rogers McSpadden," 126–28; *HRC,* 301–2, 303; Kaho, *Will Rogers Country,* 24–26; Love, "Rogers Family"; *NYT,* 26 August 1943; *RCL,* 19 January 1912; Starr, *History of the Cherokee Indians,* 571–72; *TDW,* 15 December 1935; Thoburn and Wright, *Oklahoma* 3:244; *VJ,* 16 December 1885; *WRFT,* 14, 20).

MILAM, Maud Irene McSpadden (1896–1973). Will Rogers's niece, Irene McSpadden, was the fifth child of John Thomas (Tom) McSpadden and Sallie Rogers McSpadden. Born on 5 April 1896 near Oolagah, Maud graduated from Chelsea High School in 1916 and attended the Agricultural and Mechanical College at Stillwater. She married Walker William Milam (1896–1967) of Chelsea on 19 May 1917. W. W. Milam, who had been educated in Chelsea, in the Kemper Military School in Boonville, Mo., and at Oklahoma University, became president of the Milam Oil Co. The Milams had two sons. Irene McSpadden Milam wrote her memoirs of her uncle, published as an article and in pamphlet form in 1935, in which she recalled how her grandfather, Clem V. Rogers, would take her mother, Sallie Rogers McSpadden, and her aunt Maud

Rogers Lane to New York and Boston to see Will Rogers perform. She happily remembered going to see his acts herself when the nieces and nephews would travel to a midwestern city, stay in a hotel, and go to see Will Rogers perform when he was on the Keith and Orpheum circuits ("to me in my early teenage it was as if Aladdin had rubbed his lamp"). She recalled also Rogers's kindness and financial generosity toward his sisters' children, helping make possible the things they aspired to and desired, and visiting them whenever possible. Later, during his film career, he invited their families to visit him on the set and arranged for them to stay at his ranch in Pacific Palisdades. Irene McSpadden Milam was living in Oklahoma City at the time of Will Rogers's death and in Claremore when her mother became gravely ill in 1942 (scrapbook of Sallie McSpadden, SRM-OkClaW; Bell, *Genealogy of Old and New Cherokee Families*, 357; *CWM*, 25 May 1917; *HRC*, 301; Milam, "Will Rogers as I Knew Him"; Starr, *History of the Cherokee Indians*, 575–76).

MITCHELL, Mattie Lane (Lanie) Stine (1903–78). Lanie Stine was May Rogers Yocum Stine's sixth child. Born when the Stines lived in Oolagah across the street from the Ellis family, she was named in honor of Maud Lane's husband, Cap Lane. Will Rogers funded the education of Lanie Stine after her mother's death in 1909. She attended Ursuline College in Cleveland, became a teacher in Florida, and worked in education for fifty years. She married Eldon E. Mitchell, and they had one daughter, named Sallie Mitchell (perhaps after Sallie McSpadden), who also became a teacher. Lanie Stine Mitchell died in Miami in 1978 (*WRFT,* 28).

MULHALL, Lucille (1885–1940). Lucille Mulhall, the daughter of Wild West showman Zack Mulhall (see MULHALL, Colonel Zack), and Mary Agnes Locke Mulhall (1859–1931), is recognized as America's first major professional cowgirl. Born in St. Louis, Mulhall grew up on her parents' large ranch in Oklahoma Territory and was sent to a boarding school at St. Joseph's Convent in Guthrie. When she was seven, her father told her she could have all the steers she could rope, and immediately she collected a herd with the LM-Bar brand. Publicity stories state that by age ten she was helping out on the ranch, branding calves, roping steers, breaking in colts, and capturing coyotes and wolves with her rope. She started her professional career in 1899 and was an immediate teenage sensation with her father's Wild West show, acclaimed for her roping and riding skills on her sorrel horse, Governor. Although other women performed in Wild West shows before 1900, she became the country's first well-known equestrian, and her feats popularized the word *cowgirl*. Theodore Roosevelt, who was then running for vice-president on the Republican ticket, admired her riding skills at the Rough Riders reunion in Oklahoma City in 1900. She and her sisters, Agnes (Bossie) and Georgia, were honored at a dinner Roosevelt gave after the event. Legend has it that after the reunion Roosevelt went to the Mulhall ranch, where Lucille lassoed a wild wolf. The hide was presented to Roosevelt and became one of his prize collections. Lucille Mulhall gained national fame in many of the shows her father produced between 1900 and 1910. She entered regional and national competitions, winning the thousand-dollar gold medal at the 1902 cattlemen's convention in Fort Worth by roping and tying three steers in three minutes, thirty-six seconds. At the Frontier Day celebration at Pendleton, Ore., in 1905 she won a large silver belt buckle as the women's world roping champion by tying a steer in twenty-two seconds. Rogers frequently visited the Mulhall ranch as a young man. He and Lucille Mulhall were reported to be very fond of each other, and he taught her some fancy roping tricks. They performed together in the Mulhall show between 1899 and 1902, at the St. Louis Louisiana Purchase Exposition in 1904, and at New York's Madison Square Garden in 1905. At the latter event Lucille Mulhall lead a parade up Fifth Avenue in a ranch costume and thrilled the large crowds at the Garden with her skills on horseback. In June 1905 the Mulhall Wild West show troupe acted in several Thomas A. Edison Kinetograph short films shot at Bliss in Oklahoma Territory. Among them was *Lucille Mulhall Roping and Tying Steer, Great Buffalo Chase,* and *Western Bad Man Shooting Up Saloon.* In 1906 she became the star attraction in Lucille Mulhall and Her Ranch Boys, a vaudeville touring act in which she did fancy roping tricks on horseback and on foot. On the vaudeville circuit she was noted for wearing a white outfit while mounted on her white horse, Eddie C. She appeared at the Calgary Stampede in September 1912 in one of the first trick-roping contests between women. In 1913 she organized a vaudeville act called Lucille Mulhall and Co., which was booked in vaudeville houses around the country until 1915. Known as the first woman producer of rodeos, she created an outdoor show called Lucille Mulhall's Round-up, which played at fairs, conventions, and livestock shows in 1916 and 1917. Mulhall was often featured in rodeos at fairs and conventions and starred in other Wild West shows, including the Buffalo Bill and the 101 Ranch Wild West Combined in 1916. A champion steer roper and winner of many gold medals, she twice broke the world record in competitions against men ropers and often roped and tied a steer in under thirty seconds. Stories and photographs referred to her as "America's Greatest Horsewoman." Her marriages, to Martin Van Bergen, a singer (m. 1907–14) and Tom Burnett, a wealthy Texas rancher (m. 1919–22) both ended in divorce. She had at least two children, William Logan Van

Bergen (b. 1909) and Margaret Mulhall (1906–1928), who was raised by Mary
Agnes Locke Mulhall as if she were her own. After her divorce from Burnett in
1922, Lucille Mulhall returned to the Mulhall ranch. Semiretired from the
rodeo circuit, she appeared only sporadically as a specialty act in the late 1920s
and made few public appearances in the 1930s. She cared for her aged parents
until their deaths in 1931 and made her final appearance in a parade in Guthrie
in 1935. She was killed in a car-truck collision near the Mulhall ranch on 22
December 1940 and was buried in the family mausoleum on the ranch. Today
Lucille Mulhall is recognized as one of the nation's foremost horsewomen and
ropers and as an important figure in rodeo history for opening up the sport to
women. In December 1975 she was inducted into the Rodeo Hall of Fame, part
of the National Cowboy Hall of Fame in Oklahoma City, and she was named a
honoree of the National Cowgirl Hall of Fame in Hereford, Tex. (Fisch, oral
history, WRPP; MFC; Mulhall file, OkClaW; Cheney, "Lucile Mulhall,
Fabulous Cowgirl"; Jordan, *Cowgirls*, 193; Koch, "Zack Mulhall, His Family,
and the Mulhall Wild West Show"; Musser, *Before the Nickelodeon*, 323; Olds,
"The Story of Lucille"; Porter, *Who's Who in Rodeo*, 90–91; Roach, *Cowgirls*,
84–89; Russell, D., *Wild West*, 79–80; Stansbury, *Lucille Mulhall;* see also
MULHALL, Colonel Zack).

MULHALL, Colonel Zack (ca. 1847–1931). A pioneer showman and producer of
Wild West shows, Mulhall played a pivotal role in Rogers's early show-business
career. Rogers's first public appearances were as a steer roper in cowboy
competitions organized by Mulhall between 1899 and 1902.

Accounts differ on Mulhall's birth. One writer states that he was born
Zachary Taylor Vandevere in New Orleans in 1848. Another suggests he was
born Zachariah P. Vandeveer on 22 September 1847 in either Texas or Cooper
County, Mo. His mother and father died when Mulhall was a youth; conse-
quently, he was reared by an aunt and uncle, Mr. and Mrs. Joseph Mulhall, in
St. Louis, and he adopted their name.

Zack Mulhall was educated in local parochial schools and attended at
Christian Brothers' College in St. Louis, and by many accounts also studied at
Notre Dame in Indiana, but was not interested in schooling and preferred the
life of a cowboy. In 1875 he married Mary Agnes Locke, who also had been
reared by the Mulhalls. Zack and Mary Agnes Locke Mulhall were the parents
of five children, including twin girls, Madeline and Mildred, who died in
infancy, and a son, Logan (1881–95), who died of diphtheria while a boy. Only
two daughters lived to adulthood, Agnes (1877–1916), nicknamed Bossie, and
Lucille (1885–1940) (see MULHALL, Lucille). The Mulhalls also cared for a

young girl, Georgia Smith (1872–1955) for a short time. She became Zack's mistress, and they had two children, Charley (1888–1958) and Mildred (1895–1957), who were raised by Mary Agnes Locke Mulhall as her own son and daughter.

Mulhall worked as a general livestock-purchasing agent, first for the Atchison, Topeka, and Santa Fe Railroad and then in 1896 for the St. Louis and San Francisco Railroad. During the famous 1889 Land Run in the Unassigned Lands, he claimed a homestead of 160 acres in Alfred, Oklahoma Territory, about eleven miles north of Guthrie. On 6 June 1890 the town was named Mulhall in his honor. Over the years Mulhall bought more property near the town and eventually accumulated thousands of acres in what is now Logan County. On his ranch, which included a race track and a large stable, he and his wife conducted a lucrative cattle business and bred racehorses. Rogers, who spent considerable time at the Mulhall ranch between 1899 and 1902, was considered a member of the family. He was particularly fond of Mary Agnes Locke Mulhall and performed chores for her at the ranch. He had lost his mother as a boy, she had lost a son, and they formed a special and warm relationship. He was known to have played the piano with one finger while singing a tune for Mary Agnes Locke Mulhall.

Mulhall started organizing cowboy competitions in 1899, calling his troupe the Congress of Rough Riders and Ropers, a group of working cowhands from the Indian Territory and neighborhood states. His first large cowboy tournament was in October 1899 at the St. Louis annual fair in which Will Rogers appeared as a steer roper. Later Rogers claimed that this was the start of his show-business career. The Mulhall group performed at expositions, conventions, county fairs, carnivals, and other events in the Indian and Oklahoma Territories and states in the Midwest and Southwest. Rogers performed with the Mulhall company at the Rough Riders reunion in Oklahoma City in 1900, the Confederate Veterans reunion at Memphis in May 1901, the Elks convention at Springfield, Mo., in September 1901, the Des Moines Seni-Om-Sed Carnival, and the San Antonio International Fair and Exhibition in October 1901.

Mulhall also had a popular cowboy band, who, dressed in bright outfits, performed at the events. Mulhall placed some of his top ropers in the band, including Rogers, and would bet anyone in the audience to compete against his band members in steer roping. Theodore Roosevelt became a fan of the Mulhall show after seeing Lucille Mulhall perform at the Rough Riders reunion. He invited Mulhall and his cowboy band to march in the 1901 inaugural parade celebrating his election as vice president with President McKinley. In the fall of 1901 Roosevelt, who had become president as a result of the assassination of McKinley, endorsed Mulhall as governor of Oklahoma Territory, but withdrew his selection because of mounting opposition to Mulhall's Democratic Party affiliation. Roosevelt visited the Mulhall ranch several times (once for a wolf hunt) and Mulhall's daughter, Agnes, a talented musician, sang at his inaugural ball in 1905. Mulhall wrote Theodore Roosevelt several times in early 1912, urging him to again seek the presidency and citing Roosevelt's popularity in the South.

After returning from Australia and New Zealand, Rogers performed with the Mulhall troupe at the Louisiana Purchase Exposition (the 1904 St. Louis World's Fair). In St. Louis the Mulhall performers joined the Col. Frederic T. Cummins's Indian Congress show at the fair. Mulhall became involved in a shooting incident arising from a quarrel with an employee of the Cummins show over a question of authority and the treatment of his horses. He shot three men, including seriously wounding an innocent bystander. The show was consequently forced to move outside the fairgrounds at Delmar Gardens. Mulhall stood trial for the shooting and was sentenced to three years in prison, but successfully appealed the case, arguing self-defense, and in 1907 was finally acquitted. In April 1905 Rogers appeared with the Mulhall Wild West show at New York's Madison Square Garden. This show brought Rogers considerable publicity when newspapers reported that Rogers had roped a wild steer that had run into the stands. After this engagement Rogers entered vaudeville and never again performed with the Mulhall troupe on a regular basis. Rogers's decision to leave the show angered Mulhall, and he shipped Comanche, Will's horse, with the rest of his stock from New York. Rogers's favorite roping pony eventually ended up on a farm in the South. The incident precipitated a misunderstanding between Mulhall and Rogers that endured for several years.

In June 1905 the Mulhall troupe performed at the large roundup rodeo at the Miller Brothers' 101 Ranch in Oklahoma Territory, a performance held for the meeting of the National Editorial Association. For the next several years Mulhall promoted a vaudeville act called "Lucille Mulhall and Her Ranch Boys." This indoor stage act played in vaudeville houses around the country. The outdoor Mulhall Wild West show was revived in 1910 and went on national tour, appearing in St. Louis and Des Moines, and at the Appalachian Exposition in Knoxville. It featured Mulhall's daughter Lucille, his son Charley, and other family members in rough riding, lariat trick roping, and steer roping. The bill also included a Mexican bullfight, a trapeze act, skits portraying the Pony Express and the Deadwood stagecoach robbery, and an act called the Mountain Meadow Massacre with Sioux and Cheyenne Indians in full battle dress. Among the other star cowboys appearing with the Mulhalls in 1910 were Tom Mix (also a performer with the 101 Ranch Real Wild West Show), who had recently completed *The Range Rider* (1909), a silent western film for the Selig Co.; Sam "Sunny Jim" Garrett, a trick roper; and J. Ellison Carroll, a champion steer roper.

When the show disbanded in 1915, Mulhall joined his wife in managing their large ranch, although he did appear sporadically with other shows. In the 1920s he was the advance man and parade leader for the Miller Brothers' 101 Ranch Real Wild West Show. In 1923 he was appointed chief bodyguard to Oklahoma governor Jack Walton and occasionally worked as a state health-department inspector. Rogers saw Mulhall in April 1930 during the unveiling of *The Pioneer Woman* memorial in Ponca City; then again on 5 February 1931 at Stillwater, Okla., where Rogers was appearing on a benefit tour for the Red Cross. The old friends embraced one another with tears in their eyes, and Rogers gave Mulhall money to help him with his financial difficulties. Mulhall's wife had died from cancer in January 1931, and his ranch had been reduced to about 480 acres. In April 1931 Mulhall made his final appearance when he and Lucille rode at the head of the parade for the '89er Celebration in Guthrie, Okla. He died on 18 September 1931 at his ranch, and his funeral was reportedly attended by four thousand mourners, including many Oklahoma pioneers and notables. Rogers wrote eulogies for both Mary Agnes and Zack Mulhall. When he learned of Mulhall's passing, Rogers wrote in his weekly article: "We lost a might fine old Western Character a few weeks ago. . . . He always kept in touch with me, and was very interested in my little carryings on. He was a natural showman, loved the spectacular, but never had any fakes. Every boy was a real one. His Shows were of the very best" (*TDW*, 11 October 1931; see also Zack Mulhall to Theodore Roosevelt, 6 January and 12 February 1912, in *Theodore Roosevelt Papers*, reels 122s.1, 128s.1; Fisch, oral history, WRPP; MFC; Mulhall file, OkClaW; *TDW*, 4 May 1930; Cheney, "Lucile Mulhall, Fabulous Cowgirl"; Collings and England, *101 Ranch*, 142–44; Day, *Will Rogers*, 266–67; Keith, *Boy's Life of Will Rogers*, 186–97; Koch, "Zack Mulhall, His Family, and the Mulhall Wild West Show"; Mix, *Life and Legend of Tom Mix*, 68; Mix and Health, *Fabulous Tom Mix*, 68–80; Olds, "The Story of Lucille"; Rogers, *Will Rogers*, 84–88; Russell, *Wild West*, 79–80; Stansbury, *Lucille Mulhall*; Thoburn and Wright, *Oklahoma* 3:764; see also MULHALL, Lucille).

NAY, Margaret. See VEERKAMP, Margaret (Maggie) Nay Price.

NEAL, Estelle Lane (1892–1977). The eldest child of Maud Rogers Lane and Cap Lane, Estelle Lane was born in Chelsea on 20 September 1894. She married James T. Neal (1886–1948), and they had a son and a daughter. She resided in Tulsa in 1975 (Love, "The Rogers Family"; *HRC*, 275; *WRFT,* 26).

O'DONNELL, James. See HOPKINS, James Dennis.

OROPEZA, Vincente (1858–1923). Born on a large ranch in the state of Puebla, Mexico, Oropeza was considered one of the great charros and trick ropers of all time. His father supposedly taught him the art of roping, and as a boy he roped horses and cattle and broke in mustangs on his father's ranch. He and his brother, Augustin, were also talented picadors in the bullfight ring. Oropeza was also a skilled matador and toured Mexico as the head of a group of bullfighters. The Mexican cowboy and roping tradition strongly influenced cowboy culture in the Southwest, and Oropeza especially personifies the Hispanic impact on North American rodeo cowboys. Indeed, the Mexican *charriada,* popular in the eighteenth and nineteenth centuries and a tradition still celebrated today, featured daring performances of horsemanship and roping that were introduced by charros from northern Mexico traveling in the Southwest and influenced the rodeo's development in the United States ("Ride 'Em Charro," *LAT,* 17 April 1994). Oropeza and his team of charros toured with Buffalo Bill's Wild West for many years (see CODY, William F.). Using a Mexican riata made of fibre from the maguey plant, he was known to throw the lasso forty feet and to catch objects fifty feet away with ease. As described in a newspaper clipping in Rogers's early scrapbook, Oropeza was especially noted for three very intricate tricks: " 'The Salute' . . . consists in throwing the rope out with a big loop at the end, retaining control of it like a hoop, so as to permit a running horse to pass through it, and then catching a second horse in the loop. In a second trick, called 'The Umbrella,' Señor Vi[n]cente whirls the rope around his head, letting the loop go in such a manner that it falls from above round his body, and whirls about him while he dances inside it. A third trick, called 'Oropeza's Dreams,' is to toss the loop of the lasso far out, and retain such control of it that it goes rolling around the thrower in mid-air like a rapidly revolving wheel" (clipping from the *Illustrated Mail,* n.d., Scrapbook 1902–4, CPpR). Rogers later used these roping stunts in his performances in Wild West shows and on the vaudeville stage.

Rogers first saw Oropeza perform with this show at the 1893 World Columbian Exposition in Chicago, and his roping skills influenced the young boy. He was particularly impressed with the graceful manner in which Oropeza spun his rope and danced in and out of a twirling loop. Rogers watched intently as Oropeza, dressed in a dashing, embroidered jacket, a red sash, and a hat with gold braid, wrote his name in the air with his rope, one letter at a time.

After seeing Oropeza, Rogers was determined to practice his roping skills. Six years later Rogers and Oropeza competed together in a steer-roping contest at the 1899 St. Louis annual fair. While appearing with the Wirth Brothers' Circus in New Zealand, Rogers was sometimes billed as "The Mexican Rope Artist" and dressed in a bright velvet costume. Oropeza was the winner of the oldest trick-roping contest on record in New York City in 1900 and was crowned champion of the world in this event. Journalists and advertising flyers often misspelled his name as "Orapeza," "Oro Peso," and "Orespo." The type of trick and fancy roping that Oropeza practiced became a standard feature at rodeos and Wild West shows. He spent about sixteen years with Buffalo Bill's Wild West. In 1923 Oropeza retired in Puebla, Mexico, and died in December 1923. Today he is considered an influential pioneer of the *charriada*. In 1975 he was inducted into the Rodeo Hall of Fame, a branch of the Cowboy Hall of Fame in Oklahoma City. "He was the first roper that any of the present day fancy ropers ever saw, and up to this day I have never seen a man exhibit the same accuracy and style that he did," Will Rogers wrote in 1913 (Rogers, "Various Styles of Roping," 71; see also Byers, *Roping*, 105; Dean, "Magueys, Myths, and Men"; Keith, *Boy's Life of Will Rogers*, 62–72; Ketchum, *Will Rogers*, 43, 92; Porter, W. H., *Who's Who in Rodeo*, 94, 95; Russell, *Lives and Legends of Buffalo Bill*, 376–77, 442, and *Wild West*, 105).

PARRIS, Richard (Dick) (1877–1922) (last name sometimes spelled Paris). A close friend of Will Rogers from Tahlequah I.T., Dick Parris accompanied Rogers on his trip to Argentina in 1902. Like Rogers, Parris was part Cherokee. His Indian name was Ook-squl-luke. He was born and raised in Tahlequah, the eldest of five children. His parents, Noah Parris (b. 1848) and Polina Virginia Williams Parris (b. 1850), were both born in the Cherokee Nation of Old Settler families; his mother died in April 1899, and his father was still living in 1906. Dick Parris attended the Cherokee Male Seminary in Tahlequah. He worked as a cowboy on several area ranches and was one of the ranch hands who worked for Will Rogers on the Rogers family ranch near Oolagah in the early 1900s. He joined Rogers and other Cherokee Nation young men in regional bronco-busting and cattle-roping contests. He was a popular figure around Oolagah, known for his sardonic smile, quick wit, and humor. Rogers invited Parris to go with him to Argentina and paid his friend's way with funds he had earned by selling cattle from the old Rogers home ranch, which he had been managing before he decided to go abroad. The two set out for New Orleans in March 1902, mistakenly believing they could find passage to South America from that southern port. They learned that there was no direct ship to Argentina from New Orleans, and after a brief stay in Louisiana they took passage to New York. Over the next month they traveled from New York to England, spent time in London, and then shipped to Buenos Aires via various European ports, the Cape Verde Islands, and Brazil, arriving in Argentina in early May 1902. Though Parris did not suffer from seasickness as Rogers did, he was homesick and depressed on the trip and soon let Rogers know he wanted to return home. After less than a month in South America, Rogers paid for Parris's trip home and sent various gifts for the Rogers family along with him. Parris left Buenos Aires on 24–25 May 1902 (as Rogers put it in his autobiographical notes, "I was plum busted—in the mean time the other old hand [Dick] had lit a schuck for Old Glory," OkClaW). When Parris arrived in the United States and found he did not have the money to pay customs fees on the gifts Will had asked him to deliver to the folks at home, he cabled Clem V. Rogers for help, and Rogers's father sent him the funds he needed. Parris wrote to Will Rogers on Independence Day 1902 from Tahlequah to let him know he had arrived at home safely and had visited the Rogers family. He reported that none of the girls they knew had married yet and that he hoped to "tie up with some of them and that very quick" (Richard Parris to Will Rogers, 4 July 1902, above). Parris returned to the social and work routine to which he was accustomed in Indian Territory, and Rogers's sisters sometimes sent word of him to Rogers as Rogers continued his adventures abroad. In August 1903 the *Claremore Progress* reported that Parris's left hand (his dominant hand) had been seriously mutilated in an accident that occurred while he was roping a cow when he was working near Roseberry, Idaho. If the report was accurate, he evidently recovered well from the accident, because Will Rogers recalled roping with Parris in a Wild West show organized by the Miller Brothers' 101 Ranch and held in Kansas City about a year later. Dick Parris appeared on the Authenticated Roll of Cherokee Citizens of 1880. He was not married at the time of the Dawes Commission enrollments and was not named in the federal census of Indian Territory in 1900. He moved to Bartlesville, I.T. (a town of some three hundred people in the northern part of the Cherokee Nation, near the Kansas border) in 1904 and worked in ranching. He and his wife, Alta Parris, had at least one son, Dick Parris, Jr. According to Rogers's friend and fellow roper, Jim Minnick, "it was Dick's adopted boy that got killed, and they say it was the death of this boy that drove Dick crazy" (Jim Minnick, interview, HCP-MoU). After statehood Dick Parris became a deputy sheriff of Washington County under Sheriff Griff Graham in Bartlesville. He became seriously ill in 1919 and was hospitalized for the last three years of his life. He died of complications of syphilis in December 1922 at the Elks Nursing

Home in Vinita and was buried in Bartlesville (Will Rogers to Folks, 23 May 1902, above; Maud Lane to Will Rogers, 24 July 1902, above; Eastern Cherokees application of Richard J. Parris [for appropriations by Act of Congress], 6 October 1906, OkTahN; record of funeral of Richard Parris, 7 December 1922, BPL; Victoria Sheffler, University Archivist, Northeastern State University, Tahlequah, to WRPP, 10 December 1992; *Bartlesville Morning Examiner*, 7 December and 8 December 1922; *CP*, 23 June 1900, 18 May 1901, 21 June 1902, 1 August 1903; *DC*, 5 September, 6 September, and 5 October 1901; *CR*, 7 May 1902; *IC*, 12 September 1901; Croy, *Our Will Rogers*, 73, 76–78; Day, ed., *Autobiography*, 16–19, 28–29; Day, *Will Rogers*, 41–42; Hewes, *Occupying the Cherokee Country of Oklahoma*, 53; OCF 2:133; Rogers, *Will Rogers*, 63–65).

PAWNEE BILL. See LILLIE, Gordon William.

PICCIONE, James (J. J.) (ca. 1856–post 1918). One of Will Rogers's employers in South Africa, James Piccione was a wealthy farmer, livestock breeder and dealer, and thoroughbred-horse owner and trainer. He operated a large prosperous farm in Natal, where he hired Will Rogers as a cattle handler for a shipment of livestock he was transporting from Argentina to South Africa in August 1902. He then kept the young Rogers on as a horseman and ranch hand for the first few months that Rogers spent in South Africa.

Piccione was born in Belfast, Ireland, and immigrated to South Africa in December 1879. After several years of traveling in different regions of the country and working at various jobs, including contract labor in Pietermaritzburg, Piccione purchased property in Natal in 1894. Over the next several years he developed it into a large modern estate and stock farm. The farm was called Greenfields (or sometimes Greenfield or Greenlands). It was located a few miles away from the British garrison of Mooi River Station on the Mooi River. Piccione amassed a fortune trading in sheep, cattle, and mules in the late 1890s. He supplied the government and local farmers with imported mules and donkeys, and also bred horses (James Piccione, Greenfield, Mooi River, to the Surveyor General, 1898, NAD, SGO, vol. III/1/132, ref. SG 5760/1898; Jas. Piccione to the Colonial Secretary of Natal, 23 July and 28 July 1897, minute paper re J. Piccione, NAD, C50, vol. 1524, ref. 1847/5039; see also minute paper re Jas. Piccione, Mooi River, 26 September 1909, NAD, SNA, vol. I/1/448, ref. 3607/1909). The *Buenos Aires Herald* credited him (in racist fashion) with establishing the "live stock trade between this country and South Africa, having come over several years ago with a cargo of Zulus, who were the object of great curiosity in the Boca" (24 July 1902). He made several trips to Argentina, replacing Irish-bred horses on his stock farm with South American ones, which he felt were better suited for military purposes and the South African climate. He maintained lucrative contracts to supply remounts to British colonial forces in South Africa and to the Portugueses in Portuguese East Africa (Mozambique), becoming in the process what one British source called "one of the large landed proprietors of the Colonies" (*Twentieth Century Impressions of Natal*, 538).

During the South African (Anglo-Boer) War (1899–1904), many farmers' livestock were scattered or decimated as horses were seized for use in the war or destroyed by the British in order to prevent their use by Afrikaners. Piccione supplied British mounts and also renewed the stock of the more-wealthy farmers with beef and dairy cattle, sheep, and horses purchased from South America. He began thoroughbred racing around the turn of the century and owned some renowned racehorses, including Bonnie Dundee, a horse that was shipped from Argentina to Natal on the same boat that carried Will Rogers to Africa. His state-of-the-art stables impressed observers, including Rogers, as palatial in scale and quality, grand almost to a ludicrous degree.

Piccione employed Zulu farm workers and also hired English-speaking immigrant laborers from Argentina and India on a contract or indentured basis, regularly employing about fifty laborers at Greenfields and more at his other additional farms. He dealt fairly regularly with colonial officials and local police in maintaining social control over his workers, sometimes in an adversarial relationship to local constables. In 1908, for example, he protested that police who came to make arrests on his Grobelaar's Kloof farm at Colenso had entered the farm improperly instead of using the gate ("I consider it a disgrace that the police should show such a bad example to the natives by entering farms by climbing through fences"), and he informed officials, "I have instructed my people to shoot at any persons found entering the farm by climbing in through the fences . . . be they police or civilians, Black or White." The local magistrate replied to Piccione that "in the future the Police will make use of the gate." In 1897 he chastised police for failing to uphold ordinances that should have been effective in regulating the drinking habits of Greenfields employees who traveled into the local town on their day off (Jas. Piccione to the Resident Magistrate, Ladysmith, 20 June 1908, in minute paper re J. Piccione, Mooi River, 20 June 1908, NAD, 1/LDS, vol. 3/3/19, ref. L851/1908; James Piccione to the Colonial Secretary, 19 July 1897, in minute paper re J. Piccione, NAD, C50, vol. 1523, ref 1897/4942).

Piccione was well known in elite agricultural and ranching circles in Buenos Aires while Will Rogers was living in Argentina, seeking work on the ranches, and making friends with sailors and other immigrant workers in the city, whose social life often centered around the docks. Rogers was hired at the shipyards to travel to South Africa as a caretaker for one of Piccione's shipments of livestock. He left Buenos Aires aboard the *Kelvinside* on 5 August 1902 and had a difficult time with seasickness during the rough voyage. Upon Rogers's arrival in South Africa, Piccione arranged for his work permit, allowing his legal entry into the country in exchange for further labor. Rogers was contracted to help transfer the shipped animals—some two thousand head—from the port in Durban to Piccione's farm near Ladysmith. Rogers worked at Greenfields for several weeks in a variety of capacities, including grooming and walking or riding horses for inspection by prospective buyers, breaking green horses, exercising racehorses in morning workouts on Piccione's private training course, doing maintenance work in the stables, and serving as an assistant to the farm blacksmith and veterinarian. Piccione called Rogers "Yank."

In many ways working at Greenfields would have seemed somewhat familiar to Rogers, despite the foreign surroundings. Like Will's father, Clem V. Rogers, James Piccione had started a ranch with black labor, became properous dealing in livestock and farming, and was a breeder and buyer of fine horses. (Clem V. Rogers's mother's family, the Vanns, had owned and raced horses in the East before the Cherokee removal, and Clem V. Rogers avidly supported racing in the country-fair circuit, bred and dealt in horses, and after retiring from his ranch, had a modern livery stable built in Claremore that housed some of his best horses.) Will Rogers was thus accustomed to the livestock business and to the social and racial hierarchies that existed within Indian Territory. Piccione's farm in Natal exposed him to various economic and racial strata of South Africa, including the elite of British descent and large property owners; fellow English-speaking immigrant laborers; professionals like the farm veterinarian, manager, trainers, and jockeys; British soldiers at the nearby station; Zulu residents and workers; and indentured workers from India. Rogers's social life and his observations of Piccione's stock business and of the surrounding region also acquainted him with the realities of the recent South African War, leading him to sympathize and identify with the lives and recent history of the Afrikaners (Rogers to Folks, 5 October 1902, above; see also unidentified newsclipping sent to Will Rogers by E. B. Camp, Buenos Aires, August 1902, Will Rogers Scrapbook, 1902–4, CPpR; primary documents regarding the conduct of Piccione's estate and his role as an employer of foreign laborers, NAD, Pietermaritzburg, 1897–1918, vol. nos. 1/1/448, 1/112, 2/167, 3/1/132, 3/3/195, 11, 13, 20, 26, 48, 92, 102, 126, 127, 136,

152, 159, 166, 247, 328, 1523, and 1524; Chantelle Wyley, History Subject Librarian, University Libraries, University of Natal, Durban, to WRPP, 28 August 1992; Chief, Natal Archives Depot, Pietermaritzburg, to WRPP, 8 October and 30 November 1992; Croy, *Our Will Rogers,* 79–80; Day, *Will Rogers,* 44; "J. Piccione," in *Twentieth-Century Impressions of Natal,* 537–42; Ketchum, *Will Rogers,* 79; Rogers, *Will Rogers,* 69–75; on Clem V. Rogers as a breeder of horses, see Collings, *Old Home Ranch,* 60).

POOLE, May McSpadden (1891–1978). One of Will Rogers's favorite nieces, May McSpadden (who in her youth was often called Mazie) was the third child of John Thomas (Tom) McSpadden and Sallie Rogers McSpadden. As a child, she wrote to her uncle Will as he traveled in South America and Africa, telling him about local news in Chelsea, her education, family affairs, and the status of the animals he had left behind. In one letter she informed him that her brother "Herb and I started to Chelsea Academy August, 18, 1902. I am in the sixth grade this term, and Herb is in the fourth" (May McSpadden to Will Rogers, 31 August 1902, above; see also Sallie McSpadden to Will Rogers, 30 October 1902, above). After going through the Chelsea Academy, May graduated from the Cherokee Female Seminary in Tahlequah on 29 May 1907 and earned a degree at Northeastern State Normal School in Tahlequah. Family photographs depict May as a young woman in traditional Indian dress, her hair plaited in two long braids with headband. She followed in her mother's footsteps and became a teacher in Indian schools. She was head of the primary department of the Foyil, Okla., public school from 1908 to 1910 and taught at the Bloomfield Academy in Ardmore, Okla., in the former Chickasaw Nation in 1917–18. Bloomfield Academy had the "reputation of being one of the best schools in the Indian Service"; many of the "children in this school had no money, or very little money, and . . . a good portion of the children were full-bloods" (report of H. M. Gillman, Jr., Field Representative, to the Commissioner of Indian Affairs, Indian Field Service, 28 April 1930, Bloomfield School Records, DNA, RG 75, box 150-1929). She sought government clerical work in 1918 after completing the school year at Bloomfield. May McSpadden married Walton Charles Poole (1889–1945) of Chelsea on 22 May 1919. Her friend Fay Reynolds Bushyhead, wife of Dr. Jesse Bushyhead, gave her an engagement party before the wedding. Walton Charles Poole was the eldest son of Emma Musick Poole (1864–1944), a former teacher who after her husband's death operated an insurance agency, and Charles Walton Poole (1859–1910), a graduate of the Cherokee Male Seminary in Tahlequah who was a cattle rancher and storekeeper in Vinita and one of the organizers of the First

National Bank of Chelsea. The Poole and McSpadden families were both active in the Methodist Episcopal Church South, and Emma Poole and Sallie McSpadden were members of many of the same organizations. Like Sallie and May McSpadden, Emma Poole was a schoolteacher before her marriage. May McSpadden Poole and Walton Charles Poole had two children, Lula Elizabeth (Bettee or Betty) and Charles Walton Poole. May McSpadden Poole lived in Chicago (scrapbook and correspondence of Sallie McSpadden, SRM-OkClaW; Department of Interior Records on Indian Schools, Indian Field Service, Shawnee, Okla., DNA, RG 75, boxes 70691-07-162 to 48869-13-165; Bell, *Genealogy of Old and New Cherokee Indian Families*, 357; *CM*, 25 February 1910, 3 January and 23 May 1919; *Foyil City Breeze*, 24 May 1912; *HRC*, 353–54; Mihesuah, *Cultivating the Rosebuds*, 130; *RCL*, 1 April, 24 June, 12 August, and 2 September 1910, 12 May and 18 September 1911; *Statesman* [Foyil, Okla.], 31 October 1908; *WRFT*, 14–15).

PRICE, Margaret Nay. See VEERKAMP, Margaret (Maggie) Nay Price.

RIDER, James Hall (Jim) (b. 1877). A rancher and steer roper, Rider was a good friend of Will Rogers during his youth. Part Cherokee, Rider was born in the Cherokee Nation on 6 January 1877, the son of Elizabeth Gunter (d. 1879) and Alexander McCoy Rider (d. 1883). His father was a judge in the Cooweescoowee District in 1879. Rider attended Willie Halsell College in Vinita while Rogers was enrolled in the school. His brothers, Austin (b. 1871) and John (b. 1874), were also friends of Rogers. A resident of Talala, Rider participated with Rogers in many steer-roping contests, including the Confederate Veterans reunion at Memphis. During this time Rider worked as a cowpuncher on the Jim Hall ranch. He was known for his expert use of the "Johnny Blocker" head throw, in which the loop was thrown turned over instead of flat, which was especially effective in roping hornless or short-horned cattle. The throw was named for John Rufus Blocker, a Texas cattleman who originated the throw. Rogers saw Rider throw the "Blocker" in a contest and afterwards got his friend to teach it to him. Always on the lookout for a good horse and saddle, Rogers once bought one of Rider's horses, and before leaving for Argentina, he purchased Rider's California oak-tanned leather saddle, considered one of the finest in the Indian Territory. Rider corresponded with Rogers while he was in South Africa. Later, Rider moved to Watova, Okla., and took up ranching. He was the father of seven children, including five girls. When his last child was born he telegraphed Rogers: "Hog dog! I got another boy. What should I name him?" Rogers replied: "Put boots and spurs on him and name him Will Rogers" (undated clipping, James Rider file, box 42, OkS). Rogers saw Rider occasionally during his visits to the state. He met Rider at the dedication of *The Pioneer Woman* memorial on 22 April 1930 in Ponca City. Rogers wrote in his weekly column, "Jimmy Rider, an old hand that ranched right side of me in those days, and forgot more about roping than I will ever know, well Jimmy brought his 'Remuda' over, had a Ford full of the finest Kids you ever saw, one wild one named Bill Rogers" (*TDW,* 4 May 1930). When Rogers died, Rider wrote Homer Croy: "I was truly living in hopes, that Will and I would eventually live nearer each other as we enjoyed one another. His likes were my likes, ponies, roping, and handling cattle" (J. H. Rider to Homer Croy, 27 October 1935, HCP-MoU; see also James Rider to Will Rogers, 2 September 1902 and 26 February 1903, above; *1894 Annual Catalogue of Willie Halsell College,* 10; Eastern Cherokee Application (Miller Roll no. 3756) of James H. Rider, 26 November 1906, OkTahN; James Rider, enrollment no. 4103, Census of 1890, Cooweescoowee District, OkHi, 185; Collings, *Old Home Ranch,* 85, 91; Croy, *Our Will Rogers,* 55, 77; Keith, *Boy's Life of Will Rogers,* 148–67; *OCF* 1:61; Starr, *History of the Cherokee Indians,* 286).

ROBINSON, Juliette (Bunt) Schrimsher (1878–1963). Will Rogers's cousin Bunt Schrimsher was the daughter of Mary America Schrimsher Rogers's older brother (and Clem V. Rogers's good friend), John Gunter Schrimsher (1835–1905), and his wife, Juliette Melvina Candy Schrimsher (1841–1930) (see SCHRIMSHER, John Gunter). The Schrimshers had a ranch-farm near the Rogers ranch in the Cooweescoowee District, and the Schrimsher children grew up with the Rogers children. Bunt Schrimsher, like Will Rogers, was the baby of her family, but was one year older than him. Bunt was educated at the West Point School near her parents' home on Dog Creek in the Verdigris country and at the Cherokee Female Seminary at Park Hill. She graduated in 1898 and taught school until her marriage. She married Abraham Van Dyke Robinson (known as Dyke) on 10 May 1902. The Schrimsher and Rogers families were initially somewhat ill at ease with the match—perhaps because of Robinson's origins outside of Indian Territory and the Cherokee Nation. Dyke Robinson (1878–1941) was from Lexington, Mo., and was educated at Wentworth College there. He worked in his family's flour-mill business before coming to Indian Territory, where he took a job in Claremore at a hardware store owned by Clem V. Rogers. There he met Bunt Schrimsher, a favorite in the Schrimsher-Rogers families. Their marriage was evidently a successful one, and they lived in Claremore for the rest of their lives and were among the town's leading citizens. Dyke Robinson became active in the Democratic Party and local politics after statehood. He was court clerk of Rogers County (in 1918 and from 1920 to 1941) and postmaster of Claremore. Bunt Schrimsher Robinson also was active in civic affairs. She was the registrar of voters in her ward, a leader in the Methodist Episcopal Church South, and a member and president of the Pocahontas Club and other organizations. She and Dyke Robinson had four children, all of whom were raised and educated in Rogers County. Their two sons became bankers, and one daughter was a teacher in Claremore and Muskogee and married another Claremore educator. Bunt Schrimsher Robinson has been described as "a proud and lovely lady" with "long black hair" who "showed her Indian blood quite plainly" and identified strongly with her Cherokee heritage (DuPriest, et al., *Cherokee Recollections*, 75; see also Bell, *Genealogy of Old and New Cherokee Indian Families*, 370–71; *HRC*, 371–72, 385; *WRFT*, 122, 123).

ROGERS, Betty Blake (1879–1944). The wife of Will Rogers, Betty Rogers was the daughter of James Wyeth Blake (1845–82) and Amelia J. Crowder (1845–1922). The Blake family came from eastern Tennessee, while the Crowder family originated in North Carolina. Born in Missouri, James Blake operated a saw and grist mill during the 1870s at Silver Springs valley in Benton County, Ark. Betty Rogers was born there on 9 September 1879, two months before Will Rogers's birthday. After the death of James Blake in 1882, the family moved to Rogers, several miles from Silver Springs. A fledgling town at the time, Rogers had been founded on 10 May 1881 as a depot station on the St. Louis and San Francisco (Frisco) railway line and was named after Captain C. W. Rogers, vice-president and general manager of the railroad. To provide for her large family, Amelia Blake became a dressmaker. Betty Rogers was the seventh child in a family of seven girls and two boys. Her six sisters included Cora (b. 1869), who married Will Marshall, a railroad telegraph operator; Anna (b. 1871), a telegraph operator, who married Lee H. Adamson, a railroad bridge foreman; Waite (b. 1873), who married Arthur Ireland, a railroad mail clerk; Theda, nicknamed Dick (1875–1966), a teacher; Virginia (1881–1975), who married Bruce W. Quisenberry, a druggist; and a half sister, Zuleki (1885–1969), whose father was J. O. Boyd and who married Everett Stroud. Her two brothers were John (1867–1889), a brakeman who was killed in a railroad accident at Purdy, Mo.; and James (Sandy) K. Blake (b. 1877), a railway agent who later helped manage the Rogers family's affairs. The Blake family was considered one of the most socially prominent families in Rogers, Ark. Betty's mother owned a large house at 307 East Walnut Street. All the daughters were active in the town's social affairs. Betty Blake was educated at the Rogers Academy, a Congregational school. Afterwards, she worked as a typesetter on the *Rogers Democrat,* the local newspaper; as a clerk at Parks' Dry Goods store and at the H. L. Stroud Mercantile Co. in Rogers; and as a billing clerk at the Frisco station in Jenny Lind, Ark. Attractive and charming, she was a popular young lady in Rogers, known as Bettie by family and friends during her youth. The local newspaper reported her winning the cakewalk contest at the Miller Opera House in May 1898. She was also very proficient on the guitar and piano and performed with the Bentonville Young Ladies Orchestra. Betty had several beaux, including Tom Harvey, son of the free-silver advocate William Hope (Coin) Harvey who built the lavish resort, Monte Ne, in Silver Springs in 1901.

Recovering from a bout of typhoid fever, Betty traveled to Oologah in the fall of 1899 to visit her sister Cora and Will Marshall, who was the stationmaster at the railway depot. One day Rogers entered the station to pick up a package and was entranced by the new arrival. Soon they developed a friendship, playing the latest popular tunes together; and he escorted her to local parties. Late in December she left Oologah, and Rogers wrote her two letters that suggest his affection for her. Although she liked him, they came from different backgrounds, and her friends teased her about her "Wild West Indian Cowboy." He saw her twice before he left for Argentina in 1902, once in Springfield, Mo., where Rogers was competing in a steer-roping contest, and at a street fair in Fort Smith, Ark. While he was abroad, their relationship cooled, and it was not until he saw her again at the Louisiana Purchase Exposition (St. Louis World's Fair) in 1904 that they resumed their courtship. For the next several years Rogers traveled around the country performing a rope act on the vaudeville circuit, and he would write her regularly from different cities. These letters reveal their growing fondness, but they also suggest tensions in their relationship, primarily jealousy over other men and women each was dating. After a long courtship, Rogers married Betty Blake on 25 November 1908; the ceremony occurred at Rogers in the home of Amelia Blake, the bride's mother. Will and Betty Rogers were the parents of four children: William Vann (Will, Jr.) (1911–93), Mary Amelia (1913–90), James Blake (b. 1915), and Fred (1918–20).

Often described as modest and self-effacing, Betty Rogers stayed away from publicity and tried to remain in the background of her husband's career. Nonetheless she played a major role behind the scenes and assumed multiple responsibilities as mother, homemaker, and manager of the family's financial affairs. She sometimes accompanied her husband on trips across the nation and abroad. An important silent partner in his career, Betty Rogers offered her husband advice about his stage material, his writing, and his choices of movie scripts. She urged her husband to joke about the day's headlines when he joined the *Ziegfeld Follies* in 1916, which led to Rogers's becoming a renowned topical humorist. Betty Rogers was active in charity work with the Women's Club of Beverly Hills and helped establish the first church in Beverly Hills. After her husband's death in 1935 she assumed a more public role by speaking at statue unveilings, memorial dedications, and ship christenings. She was also instrumental in the establishment of the Will Rogers Memorial in Claremore. During World War II she opened a section of her Pacific Palisades, Calif., ranch home to tourists for the benefit of the Red Cross. Polo games on the grounds were also conducted for charity. She wrote a memoir of her husband, entitled *Will Rogers: His Wife's Story,* (1941), which was serialized in the *Saturday Evening Post* in 1940 and published in a new edition by the University of Oklahoma Press in 1979.

Following an extended illness from an influenza attack, she died on the evening of 21 June 1944 at the Rogers ranch in Pacific Palisades. Faced with mounting taxes on the ranch property, she had approved a conveyance agreement on 8 June 1944 donating a large portion of the Rogers ranch to the state of California to be used as a historical monument and public park. This gift creating the Will Rogers State Park was announced the day after her death. The remainder of her estate was left to her three children. Her funeral was held at Forest Lawn Memorial Park and was attended by close relatives and friends, including the western film star William S. Hart and the actress Billie Burke. The services were conducted by Hazel Houseman, a Christian Science reader. On her death the Oklahoma State Society of Washington, D. C., issued a resolution that read in part, "A loyal and inspiring companion to Will Rogers, distinguished Oklahoman, she played an important part in his successes as a showman, humorist, philosopher, philanthropist and world traveller and she shared with him a profound love for Oklahoma, its people and its traditions" (Snelling, "One of the Blake Girls," 72–73; see also clippings and miscellaneous material, BBC-RHM; Chestnut, "That Tomboy Who Married Will Rogers"; Croy, *Our Will Rogers,* 60–69; *LAT,* 22 June 1944, 23 June 1944, 27 June 1944; *NYHT,* 22 June 1944; *NYT,* 22 June 1944; Poole, Eaton, and Milam interviews, OkClaW; Rogers, *Will Rogers;* Snelling, "One of the Blake Girls"; *WRFT,* 135–38).

ROGERS, Charles (Rabb) (b. 1837) and Houston (b. 1840). Brothers Rabb and Houston Rogers were the slaves of Clem V. Rogers's father, Robert Rogers. Houston Rogers was born in Tahlequah, and his brother may have been born there as well. The two spent their youths working on the Rogers and Musgrove farms in the Going Snake District of Indian Territory. After Robert Rogers's death in 1842, ownership of Rabb and Houston Rogers passed to Clem V.

Rogers's mother, Sally Vann Rogers, who soon thereafter (1844) married William Musgrove, one of the leading slaveholders of the Cherokee Nation West. Rabb and Houston Rogers were in turn deeded to the young Clem V. Rogers in 1855 or 1856, and their labor was instrumental in the establishment of his farm and trading post in the Cooweescoowee District in the years just before the Civil War.

While Clem V. Rogers managed the ranching and commercial aspects of his claim near the Caney River, Rabb and Houston Rogers planted, maintained, and harvested the crops (used to feed the livestock) and the garden. At the outbreak of the war, Rabb Rogers accompanied Mary America Schrimsher Rogers out of harm's way when she fled the first Rogers ranch on horseback with her infant daughter. Rabb and Houston Rogers reportedly supported opposite sides during the Civil War. Evidence implies that Rabb Rogers remained through all or much of the war on the land that he had occupied with his brother and Clem V. Rogers before the conflict began, while Houston Rogers and his family spent some of the war years in Fort Gibson. After the war ended both brothers were employed by Clem V. Rogers at the second Rogers ranch near the Verdigris River. (Homer Croy reports that Clem V. Rogers sent "word to Rabb and Huse to come to see him and said about as follows, 'Well, Rabb's side won. My side lost. I would like for you to work for me. I will pay you wages' " [Croy, *Our Will Rogers,* 15]). The brothers each worked their own small farms (located not far from the Rogers ranch and the town of Talala) as well as doing hired jobs for Clem V. Rogers.

Agnes Rogers Walker has related that Clem V. Rogers "gave my Uncle Rabb Rogers the spot where the old homestead and trading post had been because he liked him and knew him to be dependable" (Walker, interview, IPH-OkHi). The land where the first Rogers ranch was located was held by the Cherokee Nation in common and thus technically could not be owned or given; however, when Clem V. Rogers returned to the Cooweescoowee District after the war he traded the improvements—most of which had been made by Rabb Rogers— for some of Rabb Rogers's cattle, and chose another site some miles away to establish his new ranch. (See Collings, *Old Home Ranch,* 22–23.) The tributary of the Caney River that ran through the property where the first Rogers ranch had been established, and where Rabb and Rhody Rogers's family was raised, became known as Rabb's Creek. Rabb Rogers built a two-story frame house with seven rooms in a locust tree grove near the creek.

Houston Rogers married Sidney Ross. A former slave of Oliver Ross, she was the daughter of a full-blood Cherokee mother and an African American father who had a home on Spring Creek, twenty miles northwest of Tahlequah.

Houston Rogers and Sidney Ross-Rogers's daughter Agnes Rogers Walker (b. 1862) recalled that their "home in Rogers County [then the Cooweescoowee District] was a one room log cabin with a log summer kitchen. The cabin faced the east and was built of hewed logs and the kitchen of round logs. We obtained our water supply from a spring near the house. Our furniture was all home-made with the exception of one bed, and we cooked on a fireplace. My parents were farmers and we raised most of our living. The chief crops in our vicinity were corn, potatoes, and vegetables. Our principal foods were corn bread, milk, butter, sorghum, hog meat and beef" (Walker, interview, IPH-OkHi). Agnes Rogers Walker remembered that Houston Rogers made his own farming implements (plough and harrow) and that he owned a horse and a yoke of steers. Agnes was one of several children, including Samuel (b. 1873), Charles (b. 1875), Eli (b. 1877), Robert (b. 1880), and Anderson (b. 1882). The latter raised Comanche, who was branded with an A.R. on the left shoulder, before Clem V. Rogers bought the horse from Houston Rogers.

Rabb Rogers married Rhoda (Rody) Rogers (b. 1846). The couple has six sons—Nick (b. 1868), Jack (b. 1870), Houston (b. 1872), Clem V. (Clem) (b. 1874), Jasper (b. 1876), and Isaac (Ike) (b. 1883)—and five daughters: Clara, Rosa (Rose) (b. 1880), Lucy (b. 1882), Grace (Gracie) (b. 1888) and Margaret (b. 1889). Agnes Rogers Walker recalled that "these children and my daughter and two sons were Will Rogers's playmates. This was not unusual for there were few white people in the unsettled country at that time" (Walker, interview, IPH-OkHi; Will Rogers later said that he was not only raised among African Americans in Indian Territory, "I was raised *by* them. And Lord, I was five years out on the ranch before I ever knew there was a white child" [Rogers to Mr. Tobias, n.d., OkClaW, cited in Yagoda, *Will Rogers,* 309]). Will Rogers remained close to the Rabb and Houston Rogers families and visited them when he made trips to Oklahoma in the years after he had gained fame.

In 1897 Rabb and Rody Rogers's sons Clem (who was named for Will Rogers's father, Clem V. Rogers), Houston (named for Rabb's brother), and Jasper became embroiled in the controversy surrounding the murder of Will Rogers's sister May's husband, Matthew Yocum. The three Rogers brothers were arrested for the crime (along with Albert Tucker and Ben Greenleaf, who were also African Americans), but were later released for lack of evidence. Those participating in local gossip wondered whether Clem V. Rogers might have ordered the killing out of disgust with his son-in-law's business habits, or surmised that Yocum may have been killed because of bad business debts, suspected embezzlement, or money he owed from gambling (see *Kansas City Journal,* 18 July 1897, above).

Homer Croy interviewed Clem Rogers in 1952 and described him as a dignified man "with a white mustache and a pleasant way of talking." Clem Rogers was at the time of the interview "on relief but added to his income by doing light hauling and small jobs." He recalled that when he was young Clem V. Rogers sent for him, pleased that he was his namesake, and gave him "two cows and two calves, a horse, saddle and bridle, a suit of clothes," and a twenty-five dollar gold piece. He also remembered a wild wagon ride as a little boy when he hurriedly traveled with his aunt Sidney Ross-Rogers and cousin Agnes Rogers from Rabb's Creek to the Rogers ranch on 4 November 1879, when Will Rogers was brought into the world (notes of 1952 interview with Clem Rogers [b. 1874] by Homer Croy, HCP-MoU; 1890 Census of the Cherokee Nation, OkHi; Walker, interview, IPH-OkHi; Collings, *Old Home Ranch*, 11, 22–23, 61; Croy, *Our Will Rogers*, 12, 15, 353; see also Introduction, pt. 1, "Cherokee Heritage," above; and ROGERS, Clement Vann, and WALKER, Agnes Rogers).

ROGERS, Clem. See ROGERS, Charles and Houston.

ROGERS, Clement Vann (C. V., Clem, or Clem V.) (1839–1911). The father of Will Rogers, Clem V. Rogers was a successful rancher-farmer and Verdigris-country pioneer, Confederate army veteran, Cherokee Nation politician, and Claremore investor and civic leader.

Clem V. Rogers's parents, Robert Rogers (1815–42) and Sallie Vann Rogers (1818–82), migrated from the Cherokee Nation East to Arkansas in 1832 and on to Indian Territory in 1835, thus preceding the forced removal of the Cherokees from the East in 1838–39. Robert Rogers was, through the matrilineal kinship system of the Cherokees, a member of the Blind Savannah Clan. His father, Robert Rogers, Sr. (ca. 1785–before 1828), was Scotch-Irish-English and was from Georgia; his mother, Lucy Cordery Rogers (b. ca. 1784), was half Cherokee and was born in the Cherokee Nation East (probably Georgia). Robert Rogers, Sr., was selected as a delegate from the Hickory Log District to the Cherokee Nation Constitutional Convention at New Echota in 1826 (the convention took place in July 1827). Sallie Vann Rogers, a member of the Wolf Clan, was the daughter of Avery Vann (b. ca. 1770s) and Margaret McSwain Vann (b. ca. 1775), a Cherokee full-blood. Robert and Sallie Vann Rogers lived in the Going Snake District of Indian Territory, near the Arkansas border, in a large log home near the Baptist Mission Church and School on the outskirts of what became the town of Westville (Adair County). Clem V. Rogers was born there on 11 January 1839. He was the Rogers's second child; his sister, Margaret, was born in 1836 (known as Peggy, she married Allison Timberlake in 1856 and lived in Vinita). Their father, a "big, loud, dark-skinned, mustached man from whom Clem got much of his temper and bluntness," was killed in 1842 in an altercation with a supporter of Chief John Ross over a Cherokee political issue stemming from Rogers's support of the Treaty of New Echota (Keith, "Clem Rogers and His Influence on Oklahoma History," 2; see also ADAIR, William Penn). Two years later Sallie Vann Rogers remarried. She wed William Musgrove (ca. 1815–80), a wagonmaker and farmer, and they had two children, Francis Marion (Frank) Musgrove and William Due (Will or Bill) Musgrove. The Musgroves had a small mercantile business, manufactured plug tobacco, kept beehives, and ran wagon-, furniture-, and cabinet-making shops. Clem and Margaret attended the Baptist Mission School about a mile from their home, where they were taught by Rev. William Upham and Rev. Evan Jones; and when they were older, they went to the Cherokee Male and Female Seminaries at Tahlequah and Park Hill. Much as his son Will would feel and do decades later, Clem had little love for his step-parent; he reacted bitterly to his mother's remarriage. Also like his son, he heartily disliked school, was frequently truant, and "soon gave it up and went to work as a cowboy for Joel Mayes Bryan (1809–99), a large cattle dealer" of Choteau, I. T. (Love, "The Rogers Family at Worcester Academy"; see also Meredith, "Will Rogers' Roots"; *OCF* 2:77–78). He was sixteen years old when he drove cattle for Bryan on a drive from Choteau to Kansas City and on to St. Louis in 1855.

When Clem V. Rogers returned home, his mother gave him property to help him begin his own cattle business, including several head of cattle and some horses. She also deeded him two African American men whom his father had owned as slaves. These men, Charles (Rabb) Rogers and Houston Rogers, were brothers and had been given the last name of the Rogers family (see ROGERS, Charles and Houston). Clem V. Rogers began his own enterprise in the Cooweescoowee District in 1856. He chose a site up the Caney River, a branch of the Verdigris, near a tributary that came to be known as Rabb's Creek (after Rabb Rogers), not far from what became the town of Talala. A friend of his from the Cherokee Male Seminary, John Gunter Schrimsher, was the nearest neighbor. He had a place about ten miles south on Dog Creek (see SCHRIMSHER, John Gunter). Rabb and Houston Rogers managed the farming on the Rogers place, growing abundant crops of corn for wintering the livestock, while Clem V. Rogers oversaw the herd of longhorn cattle on the range and managed trade in a small trading post he established in a log house his stepfather, William Musgrove, had helped him build. He freighted merchandise for the trading post from Coffeyville, Kans., and carried on trade with the Osages and a growing number of Cherokee settlers. Business went well, and Clem V. Rogers courted Mary America Schrimsher, John Gunter Schrimsher's sister, when she came to visit her brother at his nearby ranch. They were married in 1858 at her grandmother's home in Fort Gibson, and they lived at the place near Rabb's Creek for three years. The first child, Elizabeth, was born there in September 1861, in the midst of regional hostilities at the beginning of the Civil War that included Union raids on the Rogers and Schrimsher ranches. Mary America Schrimsher Rogers and baby Elizabeth left the ranch and, escorted by Rabb Rogers, went to Clem V. Rogers's mother near Westville on horseback. The baby died there in December 1861. Mary Rogers spent the remainder of the war with her parents as a refugee in Texas (see ROGERS, Mary America Schrimsher).

The Confederacy recognized the strategic importance of Indian Territory as a base for the invasion of Kansas and as protection for Arkansas and Texas. Members of the Cherokee Nation split in their allegiance to the Confederate or the Union cause, while others argued, at least at the beginning of the conflict, for neutrality. Two Cherokee governments operated during the war, one loyal to the exiled Principal Chief John Ross, who represented in abstentia full-blood Indians and Union Cherokees, and the other in support of the Confederate Stand Watie. Clem V. Rogers, as a mixed-blood slaveholder from a well-to-do, long-time slaveholding family, with ties of birth and culture to the South and political loyalty to the Treaty (or Ridge) Party, supported the Confederacy. He and his brother-in-law John Gunter Schrimsher were two of three delegates from the Cooweescoowee District who attended a special convention held by Confederate Cherokees after Chief John Ross was removed from the Indian Territory in the summer of 1862. The convention chose Stand Watie as principal chief of the Confederate Cherokees. Rogers enlisted in Watie's Regiment of Cherokee Mounted Rifles in July 1861 and served with it throughout the war as part of the Confederate army. He saw action in battle near his own ranch that December. He was a superb equestrian. He became a first lieutenant under Captain James Butler and three years later was promoted to captain of the cavalry division under General Stand Watie. Watie's forces participated in skirmishes against Union Cherokees in Indian Territory, burning the capitol and other governmental buildings at Tahlequah and the home of John Ross. They made several raids north of the Arkansas River in Missouri and Arkansas and along the Kansas border, and disrupted the supply lines of federal troops. During the war the Indian nations were twice invaded by federal forces, but the Confederate Cherokees fought largely independent of military or financial aid from the Southern states. Rogers began a long political association and friendship with Cherokee statesman William Penn

Adair while both were serving in the war; they were both members of the Confederate Cherokee Council from 1862 to 1865 (see ADAIR, William Penn). Rogers was honorably discharged in 1865 after Watie surrendered to federal authorities in June 1865.

Rogers was twenty-six years old at the war's end. He went to Texas to rejoin his wife. The Cherokee Nation had been devastated by the internal and external conflicts of the war, and conditions in the Verdigris country had changed radically from those that had existed before the war. The Rogers ranch and trading post at Rabb's Creek had been destroyed; the livestock driven away or confiscated. Rabb and Houston Rogers had been made free men. Clem and Mary Rogers moved near her family in Fort Gibson, and Clem V. Rogers went to work for Oliver Wack Lipe (a prosperous businessman who was an uncle by marriage to Mary Rogers). He hauled freight on a mule wagon train from Kansas City to Sedalia, Mo., and on to Fort Gibson. He saved his money and invested it in partnership with Oliver Wack Lipe's son, DeWitt Clinton (D. W.) Lipe, in cattle in the Choctaw Nation. Both Rogers and Lipe moved their families back to new ranches in the Verdigris valley circa 1869–70 (see LIPE, DeWitt Clinton).

The second Rogers ranch was located on the Verdigris River about seven miles from the site of Rogers's old trading post, near what became the towns of Oologah and Talala. Several families of Rogers's acquaintance came to the valley to establish stock-raising ranches and farms near the new Rogers ranch, including the McClellans, Foremans, Lanes, Lipes, and Clem's half-brother, Frank Musgrove. Clem and Mary Rogers had three children before they moved back to the Verdigris country (Sallie, Robert, and young Maud); their remaining children (May, Zoe, Homer, and Will) were born at the Rogers ranch between 1873 and 1879 (see LANE, Maud Ethel Rogers; MCSPADDEN, Sallie Clementine Rogers; ROGERS, Robert Martin; STINE, May Rogers Yocum).

These were boom years at the ranch as the family grew, a large new ranch house was completed, and Rogers engaged in the range-cattle business on a grand scale. He ran several thousand head of Texas cattle until the coming of the Kansas and Arkansas Valley Railway (later the Missouri Pacific) in 1889, when the railroad split his range in two and the town of Oologah came into being as a railroad stop not far from the ranch; and he continued to make large profits in the cattle business into the 1890s. The 2 May 1877 *Cherokee Advocate* described the extreme beauty of the ranch with its timbered hills and rolling grasslands and meadows of flowers, its 180 acres of rich level land in cultivation, and the house, "a happy combination of ancient and modern conveniences," from which "Mr. Rogers and his worthy family dispense a large benevolence." Men who worked at the Rogers ranch included Dan Walker, an African American cowboy from Fort Gibson who was an expert roper and taught the young Will Rogers how to rope; Ed Sunday, a Cherokee cowboy, who was an excellent rider and in charge of the spring roundups that Will Rogers helped with as a boy; and Alf Cunningham, the ranch foreman (see SUNDAY, William Esther, and WALKER, Dan). Will Rogers's friends and relatives Jim Hopkins, Clem Musgrove, Doc Payne, Spi Trent, Matt Yocum, and others also loved the ranch or worked there (see HOPKINS, James Dennis; TRENT, Spi; and YOCUM, J. Matthew). Clem V. Rogers is credited with being the first farmer to raise wheat in the Verdigris valley and the first to build barbed-wire fencing; he also was among the innovators who employed modern farm machinery and regularly rotated their crops. He held the contract to supply meat for the Cherokee Orphan Asylum. He was a promoter and member of the board of directors of the Vinita Fair, and president of the Livestock Association of the Cherokee Nation in 1891. He retired from the ranch in 1898. Tenants (and, for a short time, his son, Will) took over the ranch and its crops, and Rogers invested the wealth he had accrued from cattle in businesses and real estate in the town of Claremore.

Clem V. Rogers was an important political figure in the Cherokee Nation. After the war and the death of Principal Chief John Ross he supported the Downing Party. His postwar political career began in 1877 when he was elected district judge for the Cooweescoowee District. He served one two-year term in the one-room log courthouse at Kephart Springs on Dog Creek. He was a senator in the Cherokee Senate from his district for five terms beginning in 1879, 1881, 1883, 1899, and 1903. His brother-in-law John Gunter Schrimsher was his fellow senator from the Cooweescoowee District in 1879 and 1883. With the help of political organizing by Rabb and Houston Rogers, he also developed something of a political machine among African American residents of his district. In one of his more important legislative acts, he wrote and introduced a bill leasing land in the Cherokee Strip to the Cherokee Strip Live Stock Association (May 1883), bringing the huge tract of land under the control of organized cattle interests and formalizing the collection of tax monies for its use. Throughout the 1880s he resisted the transitions taking place within the Nation as non-Indian intruders settled in Indian Territory and utilized its resources. When it came to regarding his African American constituents as intruders, however, he opposed efforts by his colleagues to deprive ex-slaves and minority Indians (Shawnees and Delawares) of their rights as citizens to receive federal payments distributed to members of the

Nation. Although his recommendations on this issue, made as part of a council committee report in 1883, were ignored by the National Council, the citizenship rights of former slaves and Shawnees and Delawares were later upheld by federal law (1888). Rogers was a candidate for the office of treasurer of the Cherokee Nation in 1887, but lost the election to his National Party opponent, Robert Bruce Ross, by one vote of the National Council. He split from the Downing Party temporarily in the 1891 elections, when he supported Dennis Wolf Bushyhead (National Party principal chief from 1879 to 1887) as a third-party Liberal candidate against Downing Party candidate Joel B. Mayes, who had come into conflict with the Cherokee Strip Live Stock Association over rates for leasing the Cherokee Strip. In July 1893 Principal Chief C. J. Harris appointed Rogers to serve with Joshua Hutchins of Georgia and P. H. Pernot of Indiana to appraise improvements made by intruders on Indian land (the latter two were appointed by President Grover Cleveland). In 1898 Rogers was appointed by Principal Chief Samuel H. Mayes to a Cherokee Nation commission to confer with the federal Dawes Commission regarding land allotment in preparation for the dissolution of the Cherokee Nation. He campaigned for William C. Rogers, the Downing Party candidate for principal chief in 1903, the last elected chief before statehood, and was himself elected to the final Cherokee Senate. He was one of the fifty-five delegates from Indian Territory who met with colleagues from Oklahoma Territory in the 1906 constitutional convention at Guthrie to develop the legislative basis for Oklahoma statehood. During the convention proceedings Cooweescoowee District was renamed Rogers County in his honor (January 1907). When it came to federal politics, one turn-of-the-century source described him as "a Democrat and an admirer of William J[ennings] Bryan" (Gideon, *Indian Territory,* 298; see also Keith, "Clem Rogers and His Influence on Oklahoma History," 82). As a Democrat, he belonged to the dominant party in the new state of Oklahoma. Democrats represented a large majority of those elected as delegates to the 1906–7 convention, and as a group they supported a Jim Crow platform of separate schools and facilities for African American citizens, antimiscegenation mandates, restrictions of black voting rights, and opposition to blacks in public office. Rogers was also "bitterly opposed to woman suffrage and the people who came to Guthrie from Washington to lobby for it" during the constitutional convention (Keith interview with Judge O. H. P. Brewer, 10 March 1938, cited in "Clem Rogers and His Influence on Oklahoma History," 84; see also Littlefield, *Cherokee Freedmen,* 216, 254).

Clem V. Rogers's first wife, Mary America Rogers, died in May 1890. In January 1893 he was remarried to his young housekeeper and neighbor, Mary

Bibles. He gave up the active management of the farm to renters and he and Mary moved to Claremore in August 1898. They lived in a home at Sixth Street and Muskogee Avenue until Mary Bibles Rogers's death in 1900 (see ROGERS, Mary Bibles).

Rogers was described as kindly but stern, always immaculately dressed in vest, wing collar, and four-in-hand tie, and demonstrating an innate ability to command. Other less-admiring observers found him to be "rich and haughty—awful haughty," a man who during his ranching days "thought he was monarch of all he surveyed, and he pretty nearly was" (Roach, "Will Rogers' Youthful Relationship with His Father," 327). In his biography of Clem V. Rogers, Keith describes him as a "strong tempestuous man" (Keith, "Clem Rogers and His Influence on Oklahoma History," 1). Roach and other writers have suggested that Will Rogers's relationship with his father was strained, and certainly there were sometimes strong disagreements between father and son. Clem V. Rogers initially did not approve of his son's show-business career, but gradually he became quite proud of Will's success in vaudeville. Clem V. Rogers's private letters also reveal an emotional and caring side that he may not have shown in public.

Clem V. Rogers owned considerable real estate in Claremore, including rental houses, a livery stable, and shares in a hardware store and a hotel; and he donated property for a public playground for children. He was a member of the board of trustees of Willie Halsell College (1894–95) and of Worcester Academy (1882) in Vinita; in 1899 he became president of the Claremore School Board. He was a vice president and member of the board of directors of the First National Bank of Claremore from 1894 to 1911. After the death of his second wife he lived in furnished rooms in the First National Bank Building. He was a member of the city council and of the Claremore Board of Equalization. He remained active in political and civic affairs and was close to his family, spending each weekend with his daughters. He died at his daughter Maud Lane's home in Chelsea on 28 October 1911 (certificate of eligibility for Cross of Honor application, United Daughters of the Confederacy, by Sallie Rogers McSpadden, descendant of Clement Vann Rogers, Second Lieutenant, Co. G, 1st Regiment, Cherokee Mounted Volunteers, C.S.A., 1 December 1935, SRM-OkClaW; documents, Clem Vann Rogers miscellaneous file 7, OkClaW; Bell, *Genealogy of Old and New Cherokee Indian Families,* 354–55; *CA,* 2 May 1877; Clark, B., "Delegates to the Constitutional Convention"; Collings, *Old Home Ranch,* 6–10, 16–19, 35–36, 38–39; *CP,* 12 September 1896, 20 February and 31 July 1897, 26 February and 10 December 1898, 8 July 1899, 12 April and 19 April 1902, 4 April 1903; Croy, *Our Will Rogers,* 9–16, 19–20;

CV, 28 October 1898, 5 May and 12 May 1899; *CWM,* 18 April 1902, 8 June, 23 November, and 14 December 1906; "Father of Will Rogers Came to County in 1857," unidentified newsclipping, Claremore, 4 November 1937, OkClaW; Fischer and Gill, "Confederate Indian Forces Outside of Indian Territory"; Gaines, *Confederate Cherokees,* 8–9, 13, 15, 33, 77, 120; Gideon, "Clem Vann Rogers," in *Indian Territory,* 296–97; *IC,* 26 June, 11 September, and 2 October 1890; 26 February, 30 April, and 2 July 1891; 18 August 1892; 14 June, 26 July, and 18 October 1894; 27 August and 1 October 1896; 17 August 1899; 2 August 1903; Kaho, *Will Rogers Country,* 19–22, 27–28; Kaho, "Uncle Clem," and "Willie's Dad," unidentified newsclippings, November 1942 and 1945, OkClaW; A. L. Kates, "Early Campaigning in Oklahoma," unidentified newsclipping, 7 February 1930, OkClaW; Keith, "Clem Rogers and His Influence on Oklahoma History"; Keith interviews with Charles Galbreath, 11 March 1938, Ed Hicks, 11 March 1938, and George Mayes, 9 March 1938, Ed Sunday, 10 March 1938, cited in Keith, "Clem Rogers and His Influence on Oklahoma History," 28, 34, 70, 73; Keith, *Boy's Life of Will Rogers,* 1–9, 16–19, 24; Love, "The Rogers Family at Worcester Academy" and "The Rogers Family," in *As I Recollect;* McSpadden, P., "Clement Vann Rogers"; Meredith, "Will Rogers' Roots"; Moore, "William Penn Adair," 37; Perdue, *Slavery and the Evolution of Cherokee Society,* 119–40; Poole, interview, OkClaW; Roach, "Will Rogers' Youthful Relationship with His Father"; Starr, *History of the Cherokee Indians,* 52, 151, 272; *Stillwell Democrat-Journal,* 28 June 1973; Thoburn and Wright, *Oklahoma* 3:244–45; *Tulsa Democrat,* 30 October 1911; Walker, interview, IPH-OkHi; *WRFT,* vi, 8, 59, 85).

ROGERS, Houston. See ROGERS, Charles and Houston.

ROGERS, Mary America Schrimsher (1839–90). Will Rogers's mother, Mary America Schrimsher Rogers, was the daughter of the Eastern Cherokee Elizabeth Hunt Gunter Schrimsher (1804–77) and Martin Matthew Schrimsher (1806–65) of Fort Gibson, I.T. Her parents were wealthy slaveholders, and she was raised on one of the larger plantations in the region. Her father was either a Welsh immigrant or was of Welsh descent born in Tennessee. He and Mary's mother came to Indian Territory from Alabama. Her mother, Elizabeth Hunt Gunter Schrimsher, was half Cherokee, the daughter of a full-blood Cherokee of the Paint Clan (Catherine Gunter, d. 1835, who was the daughter of Ghi-go-ne-li, a Cherokee chief) and a white Welsh immigrant father (John Gunter), who was a trader and gunpowder maker in Creek Path (Guntersville), Ala. Elizabeth and Martin Schrimsher were married in Creek Path in September 1831 and had moved to Fort Gibson by 1835.

Mary America Schrimsher was born at her parents' plantation at Eureka, near Tahlequah, on 9 October 1839. She was educated at the academy at Cane Hill, Ark., a school many privileged Cherokee children attended, and perhaps she also attended the Cherokee Female Seminary in Park Hill. With a fine contralto voice, she excelled in music, studying piano. She also was known in town as a good dancer, and her vivaciousness, wit, and good humor made her popular at local gatherings. She was very religious and a member of the Methodist Episcopal Church South. She sang in the church choir and was active in charity and social work. She met Clem V. Rogers, a school friend of her brother John, at the Cherokee Male Seminary in Tahlequah. John Gunter Schrimsher soon established a ranch not far from the site in the Verdigris valley where Clem V. Rogers began a small trading post. Clem also built a two-room saddlebag-style log house that was separated from the trading post by a corral. When Mary America Schrimsher came to visit her brother at his place on Dog Creek, Clem rode over from his trading post on Rabb's Creek to court her. She and Clem V. Rogers were married in 1858 at her grandmother Schrimsher's house in Fort Gibson.

Mary's presence at the remote trading post in the Cooweescoowee District transformed the Rogers's small house into something of a social center in the region. After three years of married life at the ranch, the Rogers's first child, Elizabeth (named in honor of Mary's mother) was born on 11 September 1861. The baby came as the sectional hostilities of the Civil War heightened in the region as Cherokee loyalties split between the Union and the Confederacy and Union forces massed in nearby Kansas. The Rogers place at Rabb's Creek was raided by Union soldiers stationed in Kansas, who drove away the horses and cattle. The log home was later burned to the ground. Clem V. Rogers had joined a Cherokee unit of the Confederate army in July, and in December 1861 he was involved in a battle not far from John Gunter Schrimsher's ranch. The women and children in the Schrimsher and Rogers families were sent away to the eastern part of Indian Territory. Mary traveled by horse with the baby in midwinter, under the protection of Rabb Rogers. Baby Elizabeth was ill during the journey and died shortly after Mary reached Clem's mother's home in December 1861. Mary then joined her own parents and siblings in Fort Gibson, and they soon moved to their plantation near Tahlequah. They hoped to spend the war there, but increasing violence by Union soldiers and raids mounted by rival members of the Cherokee Nation resulted in the destruction of the family home and crops. The Schrimshers fled to Texas, becoming residents at the refugee camp at Bonham in 1862. Clem V. Rogers visited them there when on furlough during the four years of the war, and Mary gave birth to their second child, Sallie Clementine, in Bonham in December 1863.

At the war's end Clem V. Rogers came to Texas to reclaim his family. He and Mary and young Sallie traveled to the Choctaw Nation, where Clem's mother, Sallie Vann Rogers Musgrove, had spent the war living near Doaksville. They stopped there to put in a crop, and their third child, Robert, was born at her place in April 1866. Mary's father, Martin Schrimsher, died on the trip back to Indian Territory from Texas in 1865. In the fall of 1866 the Rogerses moved to a farm they rented from Mary's sister, Elizabeth Alabama Schrimsher Adair (later Bushyhead), east of Fort Gibson. They worked the farm for a year, then moved to the Schrimsher home in Fort Gibson, where their fourth child, Maud Ethel, was born in November 1869. During this time Clem V. Rogers had entered into partnership with his friend DeWitt Clinton Lipe to develop herds of cattle in the Verdigris country. He hired local men living near his old trading post to help develop a second ranch in the Cooweescoowee District, up the Verdigris River and some seven miles east of his first property on Rabb's Creek. In the fall of 1870 Mary, Clem, and the children moved to the remodeled log house on the new ranch. May, the Rogers's fifth child, was born there in May 1873.

Mary maintained a household in the log home until 1875, when the grand two-story main ranch house was completed with its log walls plastered inside and weatherboarded outside, its parlor, porches, and four fireplaces. The Rogers ranch prospered in this period, and Mary decorated the new house with fine furnishings including lace curtains, carpets, and a grand piano in the parlor. The piano had been freighted from St. Louis, down the Mississippi River and up the Arkansas River, and then moved overland from Fort Gibson. The yard was landscaped with rows of cedars, a grass lawn, and elaborate flower beds gardened by Mary. She crystallized wild grasses and was famed in the neighborhood for her beautiful winter bouquets of dried and preserved flowers, leaves, and grasses. Two more children were born in the house, but died in infancy: Zoe (January–July 1876) and Homer (July–September 1878). In November 1879 Mary gave birth to her eighth and last child, a boy, William Penn Adair Rogers. (Rogers later noted that he was born on election day, and since his mother was prohibited from voting, she felt she should make a statement of some kind and so gave birth to him). She was assisted in the birth by Susannah McIntosh Drew Adair, and the baby was named for "Aunt Sue's" husband, William Penn Adair, a prominent Cherokee Nation politician who was a close friend of the family (see ADAIR, Susannah McIntosh Drew, and

ADAIR, William Penn). When young Will was four years old, his brother, Robert, died suddenly after having seemed to recover from typhoid fever (see ROGERS, Robert Martin).

Mary had become closely acquainted with other Cherokee families who had moved into the area, including the Foremans, Lanes, Lipes, McClellans, and Musgroves. Ada Foreman, a neighbor who was out gathering wild grapes with Jennie McClellan across the river from the ranch home on the day of Rogers's birth, was one of the first to see the new baby. Jennie McClellan was expecting at the time, and six days later gave birth to her son Charley, who became Will Rogers's best friend. Mary Rogers was known for bringing a different family home from church each Sunday to enjoy dinner with the Rogerses, and for opening her home for parties and community socials, including joyful square dances on the ranch lawn. She kept a tight household with the help of cooks, her daughters, and local hired girls, preparing huge meals for the ranch hands and visitors and maintaining high sanitary standards in the kitchen. The linens and dish towels were boiled after every meal, and the kitchen was scrubbed from floor to ceiling each day. She also regularly provided food, clothing, supplies, and nursing assistance to neighbors in need. Agnes Rogers (Aunt Babe) Walker, a respected cook who worked in the Rogers household, recalled that Mary America Schrimsher Rogers "would go horseback or in a buggy to the rescue of folks night and day whether they was colored, Indian, or white, or whether their trouble was birth, sickness, or death" (Keith interview with Agnes [Babe] Walker, 27 June 1936, quoted in Keith, "Clem Rogers and His Influence on Oklahoma History," 29; see also WALKER, Agnes Rogers). When some elderly low-income neighbors lost their home to a fire, the community rebuilt the house and the Rogerses provided them with new furnishings and provisions. A fine but practical dresser who preferred tailored simplicity over ruffles and frills, Mary Rogers was also known among the people of the Verdigris country as an excellent baker and cook, renowned for her gifts of delicious canned goods and pies. She taught her children to sing and play the piano, and made music and Bible study—as well as dancing, good eating, and horsemanship—important parts of family life. An accomplished musician, she played by ear, and it is from her that Will Rogers developed his love of singing.

Her son Will shared many aspects of her personality. As a man who had been a playmate of Will's in the 1880s remembered, "Willie favored his mother more'n he did his father; she was more on the entertain' and joke side; his father was all business; wasn't a man to laugh much" (Croy interview with Clem Rogers, son of Rabb Rogers, quoted in *Our Will Rogers*, 6). Or, as biographer Homer Croy has put it, their marriage was a case of the attraction of opposites: "Clem was gruff, domineering and demanding. Mary Schrimsher was lighthearted, with an extraordinary sense of humor," a deeply religious outlook, and "great human sympathy" (Croy, *Our Will Rogers*, 13, see also 24; and Keith, "Clem Rogers and His Influence on Oklahoma History," 8–9). Will Rogers also had his father's stubbornness and rebelliousness, especially in his youth, and developed both his mother's charitable nature and, eventually, his father's business sense, if not some of his demeanor.

In the spring of 1890 simultaneous typhoid fever and measle epidemics hit the Verdigris valley. Both Maud Rogers and Sallie Rogers McSpadden (who had married in 1885) became very ill. The daughters were brought to the Rogers ranch to be nursed by their mother. Will Rogers, eleven years old at the time, had been suffering from the measles, and he was sent away to the home of Gracey Greenleaf, who was working as a cook at the Rogers ranch. Sallie's three-and-a-half-year-old son, Clem McSpadden, also was ill with the measles. Her two-and-a-half-year-old daughter, Mary Belle McSpadden, died of typhoid fever on 22 May, she and Maud lay bedridden. Mary America Schrimsher Rogers was tireless in her care for the others and soon, exhausted, was stricken herself with the fever and what Dr. Oliver Bagby diagnosed as amoebic dysentery. She died one week after her granddaughter, on 28 May 1890. She was fifty years old.

Her death profoundly affected the family and ranch life. Agnes Walker said her death was a "great blow" to Will Rogers, "as well as to the entire community, for Mary Rogers was loved by all who knew her," and that when "Mary died this country just went down" (Walker, interview, IPH-OkH; and Keith interview with Agnes [Babe] Walker, 27 June 1936, cited in Keith, "Clem Rogers and His Influence on Oklahoma History," 64). As one family historian has put it, "All that her children knew of joy and beauty was embodied in her" (Tacker, "Rogers Family," pt. 1; see also Roach, "Will Rogers' Youthful Relationship with His Father"). Will, the youngest, had been devoted to his mother and was hit hard by her passing. He had lost his only brother, then his mother; and a dozen years later his best friend, Charley McClellan, would also die as they had, from typhoid fever (see McCLELLAN, Charles White). May, previously a carefree young woman with her mother's good humor, was the only daughter spared from the illness and had a grim responsibility as the only child able to attend Mary Rogers's funeral (see STINE, May Rogers Yocum). Clem V. Rogers, often depicted as a stern man toward others, deeply mourned his wife. He lived at the ranch for another two and a half years, then began a new phase of his life, remarrying and moving to

Claremore (see ROGERS, Clement Vann, and ROGERS, Mary Bibles). The Rogers ranch house was stripped of Mary America Schrimsher Rogers's furnishings and rented out. The house and yard declined into barrenness and neglect, ceasing to be the center of celebration and hospitality it had been during her life (Lane, interview, OkClaW; memoirs of Mary Newcomb, OkClaW; Poole, interview, OkClaW; Rogers family birth register, Bible of Sallie McSpadden, SRM-OkClaW and above, 4 November 1879; Walker, interview, OkClaW; Collings, *Old Home Ranch,* 9, 10–12, 16–22, 79; Croy, *Our Will Rogers,* 4–5, 8–9, 17, 21, 24, 25–26; Day, ed., *Autobiography,* 2–3; *HRC,* 374–75; Keith, *Boy's Life of Will Rogers,* 5–6, 12, 43–44; Keith, "Clem Rogers and His Influence on Oklahoma History," 7–8, 21, 24, 27, 29, 62–63; Ketchum, *Will Rogers,* 25, 39; Love, "Rogers Family at Worcester Academy," and "Mary America Schrimsher"; Roach, "Will Rogers' Youthful Relationship with His Father," 325–26, 328; Tacker, "Rogers Family," pts. 1 and 2; *WRFT,* 110–14, 120).

ROGERS, Mary Bibles (1866–1900). The second wife of Clem V. Rogers, Mary Bibles was a neighbor of the Rogerses' and the youngest daughter of George Bibles (1837–1917; sometimes spelled "Bible"), who was part Cherokee. Mary's parents came to the Cooweescoowee District from Texas and settled on a farm near Talala; her father's brother, William Henry Bible (1852–1933), who was born in the Cherokee Nation, and his wife Mary E. Locker Bible (1853–1917), who was from Texas, also settled in the area in 1883. Mary Bibles's mother, Annie Bibles, was a teacher at the Sunnyside School near Talala. The same age as Clem V. Rogers and Mary America Schrimsher Rogers's son Robert, Mary Bibles was born shortly after the Civil War near Alluwee in the Cherokee Nation. She had an older sister, Margaret or Eliza (1857–90), who married Salul or Rory McCoy Nicholson (1848–91), and they had six children; among them, Richard Edward (1878–1969), who once worked on Clem V. Rogers's ranch. She is listed along with her father and brother John in the 1883 Pay Roll by Right of Cherokee Blood for the Cooweescoowee District (DNA, RG 21, FARC). The Bible family is also listed in the *Final Rolls of Citizens and Freedmen of the Five Civilized Tribes* (1907), 303.

The Bibles families were well acquainted with the Rogers family, and Mary Bibles became a housekeeper at the Rogers ranch, probably after Mary America Schrimsher Rogers's death in 1890. She was present at the small gathering of close friends and relatives who were invited to the wedding of Maud Rogers to Cap Lane held at the Rogers ranch in 1891. Mary Bibles and Clem V. Rogers were married on 15 January 1893. He was fifty-four years old, and she was twenty-seven, only thirteen years older than Clem's youngest son,

Will, who was away at school at the time of the wedding. The wedding apparently took place with little advance warning to Rogers's daughters, and young Will Rogers was reportedly not told that it had occurred until he returned home from school for summer vacation several months later. Historian Fred Roach, Jr., writes that Will Rogers disliked Mary Bibles Rogers and, when given the news that she had become his stepmother, he "registered deep shock, hurt, and alienation," doing little to cooperate with the new arrangement while he was at the ranch and continuing to be deeply rebellious at school (Roach, "Will Rogers Youthful Relationship with His Father," 331; see also Croy, *Our Will Rogers*, 30, 92). Mary Bibles Rogers received little if any mention in the Rogers children's accounts of their family's history.

Clem V. and Mary Bibles Rogers moved from the ranch land into the town of Claremore, taking up residence in a two-story house that Clem had purchased from Ed Williams at Sixth Street and Muskogee Avenue. They gained some local fame by being the first couple to have gaslight installed in their home in 1899. Mary Bibles Rogers was active in the Methodist Episcopal Church South and apparently was very well regarded in the community. In 1899 she suffered from a severe case of meningitis and underwent surgery for treatment of side effects of the disease. She fell down a flight of stairs in the Rogers home during her recuperation and never recovered her health. Clem V. Rogers brought her to several health resorts, including Hot Springs, Ark., and Colorado Springs, Colo., in hopes of a recovery. She died on 17 January 1900. An obituary in a local paper reported that her suffering had been great and that at her funeral service "the church would scarcely seat the large number of sympathizing friends who came to pay their final respects to the deceased lady." The notice also stated that Mary Bibles Rogers's mother and two sisters were deceased and that she was survived by her father *(CP,* 20 January 1900). She was also survived by her brother, for Clem V. Rogers wrote to him after her death to assure him of his love and affection and continued support. Rogers promised to give Mary's brother the legal papers establishing Bibles's ownership of the farm where Bibles and his family were living, which apparently had been owned either by Mary Bibles or by Clem V. Rogers himself. "Dont you think for a moment that I will ever rob your wife and little children out of this farm. The Love I had for your Dear Sister, who is now gone, I . . . also have the same for you all." He went on to say that he would help the Bibles family in any way. He wrote that he had moved from the house he shared with Mary Bibles Rogers to rooms above the town bank and was "getting very tired of it, but my lovely companion [is] now gone." He then wrote of his assurance that Mary Bibles Rogers had "gone to the Home of Love" and ended his letter with the sentiment "Hoping you are prepared to see your sisters in Heaven is the wish of a true friend, C. V. Rogers" (C. V. Rogers to [John] Bibles, Claremore, 31 May 1900, OkClaW).

Clem V. Rogers never remarried. He remained living in furnished rooms over the First National Bank Building and made frequent visits to his daughters' homes until his own death in 1911. As administrator of his second wife's estate, he reported that sales of the property she held at the time of her death had yielded the following: one field near Oologah, $120; a second adjacent field on the south, $140; one box house in Oolagah, $60; and seven head of cattle, $120; for a total of $440. He also detailed medical and funeral expenses totaling $355.40, charged against the above, and stated that Mary Bibles Rogers had no debts other than the expenses related to her final illness (death notice and probate estate record of Mary Rogers, Clem V. Rogers, administrator, U.S. Court, Indian Territory, 3 February 1900 and 5 January 1903, OkClaW; *CC*, 1 September and 13 September 1899, 20 April 1900; *CP*, 28 January, 25 February, 11 March, 8 April, 1 July, 12 August, 2 September, 23 September, 7 October, 14 October, 21 October, and 2 December 1899; 13 January, 20 January, and 27 January 1900, 29 October 1911; *CV*, 27 January, 10 March, and 7 April 1899; Gideon, *Indian Territory*, 297; *HRC*, 110, 111, 119–20, 294, 336–37, 375; *IC*, 19 January 1893 and 19 October 1899; *Inola Register*, 25 January 1907; Keith interview with Ed Sunday, 11 March 1938, cited in "Clem Rogers and His Influence on Oklahoma History," 76; Keith, "Clem Rogers and His Influence on Oklahoma History," 79; *OCF* 1:158; McSpadden, P., "Clement Vann Rogers," 397; Starr, *History of the Cherokee Indians*, 646; *WRFT*, 11).

ROGERS, Maud Ethel. See LANE, Maud Ethel Rogers.

ROGERS, May. See STINE, May Rogers Yocum.

ROGERS, Rhoda (Rody). See ROGERS, Charles and Houston, and WALKER, Agnes Rogers.

ROGERS, Robert Martin (Bob) (1866–83). The oldest son of Clem V. Rogers and Mary America Schrimsher Rogers, Robert Martin Rogers was born in the Choctaw Nation at Boggy Depot, near Clem V. Rogers's mother's place at Doaksville, on 15 April 1866. Mary America Rogers and Clem V. Rogers, with toddler Sallie, had joined Sallie Vann Rogers Musgrove and Will Musgrove after returning to Indian Territory from Texas, where Mary had spent most of the Civil War years. Robert was named in honor of his paternal grandfather and great-grandfather, both named Robert Rogers, and his maternal grandfather, Martin Schrimsher.

Robert spent the first few years of life in the Fort Gibson area and moved with his family to the Rogers ranch in the Verdigris valley in 1870. He attended West Point School near Dog Creek, east of Claremore, the first school established in the area after the war. Robert, his friend Dick Mayes, his older sister Sallie, and his cousins Kate and Robert Timberlake and John Adair, were the only students at the school. All of the students boarded with John Schrimsher, Mary America Schrimsher Rogers's brother and an old friend of Clem V. Rogers. Unlike his sandy-haired and blue-eyed little brother Will, Robert physically resembled his mother, with her black hair and dark eyes. He has been described as both a lonely and serious child and tough, hardy, and fearless. He loved ranch life, got along well with the cowboys who worked the Rogers herds, and was an excellent roper, participating wholeheartedly in the work on the range. He seemed destined to inherit his father's cattle business and farm, and as an excellent horseman and roper he was a role model for his little brother, who watched him before he was old enough to ride himself.

Robert began attending Worcester Academy in Vinita at the age of sixteen, boarding with his Aunt Peggy Timberlake. His name, as well as those of his cousins Jennie and Robert Timberlake and his sisters May and Maud, was listed in the 1882–83 school catalogue. He was at Vinita at the time of his death on 13 April 1883 just before his seventeenth birthday. Weakened by a recent bout of typhoid fever, he became feverish while branding calves on a roundup at the Hall ranch on Rock Creek, not far from town, and he died that evening. After his son's sudden death, Clem V. Rogers arranged for Robert's teenage school friends to come to the Rogers ranch for the funeral service, and Robert was buried in the family cemetery near the house. His body was later moved to the family plot at the Chelsea cemetery (Lane, interview, OkClaW; Poole, interview, OkClaW; Collings, *Old Home Ranch*, 16, 23, 24–25, 31n.47; Keith, interview with Sallie Rogers McSpadden, 11 March 1938, cited in "Clem Rogers and His Influence on Oklahoma History," 58; Love, "Rogers Family" and "Rogers Family at Worcester Academy"; *Worcester Academy Catalogue, 1882–1883*, 8–9; *WRFT,* 10).

ROGERS, Sallie. See MCSPADDEN, Sallie Clementine Rogers.

ROGERS, Susannah McIntosh Drew Adair. See ADAIR, Susannah McIntosh Drew.

SCHRIMSHER, Ernest Vivian (1875–1942). A cousin of Will Rogers on his mother's side, Schrimsher was born on 24 July 1875 near Claremore. He was the son of Juliette Melvina (Candy) Schrimsher (1841–1930) and John Gunter Schrimsher (1835-1905) (see SCHRIMSHER, John Gunter). Ernest Schrimsher was educated in the Cherokee Nation public schools, Willie Halsell College, and the Cherokee National Male Seminary. In 1902 he married Susan Phillips (1878–1959), and they had six children. Schrimsher participated with Rogers in many steer-roping contests between 1899 and 1901. A successful rancher, Schrimsher served as postmaster of Collinsville during the presidency of Woodrow Wilson (*As I Recollect*, 41–44; Bell, *Genealogy of Old and New Cherokee Indian Families*, 369–72; Starr, *History of the Cherokee Indians*, 509, 526–27, 651; *WRFT,* 120–23).

SCHRIMSHER, John Gunter (1835–1905). Will Rogers's maternal uncle, John Gunter Schrimsher was the son of Martin Matthew Schrimsher (1806–65) and Elizabeth Hunt Gunter Schrimsher (1804–77). He was born in Blount County, Tenn., and came to Indian Territory with his family as an infant. Schrimsher was educated in Tahlequah schools and at the Cherokee Male Seminary. As a teenager he left school to accompany his father to California during the gold rush in 1849. He returned to Indian Territory and worked briefly as a schoolteacher before meeting Juliette Melvina Candy, whom he married in Spavinaw in 1859. They moved to his fledgling ranch on Dog Creek in the Cooweescoowee District. Juliette Melvina Candy's mother (Elizabeth Bell Candy) had died when she was young, and she had been raised in part by Sarah Bell Watie, wife of Stand Watie. With the coming of the war, John Gunter Schrimsher (like his friend and neighbor Clem V. Rogers) enlisted in Watie's Cherokee Mounted Regiment and served as a member of the Cherokee Confederate Council from 1862 to 1865. Like Mary America Schrimsher Rogers, Juliette Candy Schrimsher spent much of the war as a refugee in Texas, and like the Rogerses, the Schrimsherses reestablished their ranches in the Verdigris country after the war. John Gunter Schrimsher was elected sheriff of Cooweescoowee District in 1867 and 1877, and he served (in conjunction with Clem V. Rogers) as senator from the district to the Cherokee National Council in 1879 and 1883 (and again in 1897). He also was a delegate on Cherokee commissions to Washington, D.C. (1883, 1885), and became a district judge in 1893. He was active in the Masons. John and Juliette Schrimsher had three daughters and one son: Sarah Catherine (Kitty) (1866–92), Elizabeth Belle (Bessie) (1873–1957), Ernest Vivian (1875–1942), and Juliette Melvina (Bunt) (1878–1963) (see SCHRIMSHER, Ernest Vivian, and SCHRIMSHER, Juliette Melvina). Will Rogers was especially close to Ernest and Bunt, who were closest to him in age and shared many mutual friends. John Gunter Schrimsher was killed when struck by lightning while riding horseback at his son Ernest's ranch in July 1905. Juliette Melvina Candy Schrimsher died at her daughter Bunt's home in Claremore in December 1930 (discharge certificate of John Gunter Schrimsher, 12 July 1864, signed by C. V. Rogers, company commander, Confederate army, Clem Vann Rogers miscellaneous file 7, OkClaW; *CP,* 8 July 1905; Schrimsher-Robinson, "Brief History and Narratives of the Schrimsher and Candy Families"; Starr, *History of the Cherokee Indians,* 296, 509, 527; *WRFT,* 120, 122, 123; see also ROGERS, Mary America Schrimsher; ROGERS, Clement Vann).

SCHRIMSHER, Juliette Melvina (Bunt). See ROBINSON, Juliette Schrimsher.

STINE, Frank (1874–1954). The second husband of Will Rogers's sister May Rogers Yocum Stine, Frank Stine was born in Washington County, Ky. He was the cousin of May Rogers Yocum's first husband, Matt Yocum (see YOCUM, J. Matthew). He lived in Fort Worth, Tex., and May married him there in 1898. Frank and May managed hotels near where she had grown up, and also helped to manage the Rogers ranch. They lived in Oologah, where Frank opened a small soda fountain and butcher business. They had five children.

After May Rogers Yocum Stine's death, Frank Stine worked in Oklahoma oil fields until he was injured in 1914. He returned to the Fort Worth area to open a small garage and rented a thirty-acre farm, which he worked with his second wife, Leoma Allen (d. 1975), whom he met in Texas. Leoma Allen Stine's sister, Mary Allen, married Frank and May Rogers Stine's son Jake Stine in 1919 or 1920 (see STINE, Jacob Edward). Frank and Leoma Allen Stine made their home in Fort Worth and had three daughters, Mary, Lillian, and Joann. Leoma Allen Stine corresponded with Betty Blake Rogers and her brother J. K. (Sandy) Blake, Will Rogers's office manager, reporting on the family's status. Rogers had helped the family financially in the years before Frank Stine's remarriage, and during the depression the Stines, hard-hit like many working families, often sent the Rogerses appeals for assistance with bills they were unable to pay (Frank Stine to Will Rogers, Ochelata, Okla., 19 March and 26 October 1914, and other letters, Stine family correspondence file, OkClaW; Mary Allen Stine to Reba Collins, 25 March and 12 May 1982, OkClaW; *CDM,* 26 September 1901; *CP,* 4 April and 10 October 1903; *OCF* 1:158; see also STINE, May Rogers Yocum).

STINE, Jacob Edward (Jake) (1900–1982). The first son of Frank Stine and Will Rogers's youngest sister, May Rogers Yocum Stine, Jake Stine was born at the Rogers ranch at Oologah on 3 July 1900. The Stines often oversaw matters at the ranch when Will Rogers was away at roping contests. When Jake was a young child, they moved to Talala, where they renovated and managed the Talala Hotel, and then to a house in Oolagah, where Frank Stine began a business. After his mother's death when he was nine years old, Jake Stine was taken in by Maud and Cap Lane. Then he went to live with Frank Stine's family in Fort Worth, Tex. He met Mary Allen at church in Fort Worth when they were both thirteen years old, and they married seven years later. They moved to Goleta, Calif., where—following in Jake Stine's parents's footsteps—they worked in the restaurant and hotel business for over fifty years. They had one daughter, Betty Pauline Stine (1922–44), who was born in Texas and graduated from Santa Barbara High School in 1939. She was named for Jake Stine's aunt, Betty Blake Rogers, and his first cousin Pauline McSpadden Love (see Love, Pauline Elizabeth McSpadden, and Rogers, Betty Blake). Betty Pauline Stine was a student at the University of Arizona when World War II began. Fascinated with flying, she entered the second class of the new Women's Air Service Pilot (WASP) program and was the first WASP to be granted a uniform. She was on her final solo cross-country flight before receiving her wings when her plane caught fire over Quartzsite, Ariz. She parachuted out, but was dragged through mountainous terrain and died later the same day in a hospital. She was awarded her wings posthumously. Jake Stine suffered a stroke in 1979 and was cared for by his wife until his death in Goleta in March 1982 (Mary Allen Stine to Reba Collins, 2 March, 25 March 1982, OkClaW; *WRFT,* 28; see also Stine, May Rogers Yocum).

Stine, Mattie Lane (Lanie). See Mitchell, Mattie Lane Stine.

Stine, May Rogers Yocum (1873–1909). Named Mary after her mother, but known all her life as May for the month in which she was born, May Rogers was the youngest daughter of Mary America Schrimsher Rogers and Clem V. Rogers to live past infancy. She was born on 31 May 1873 on the Rogers ranch near Oologah and lived in the region all her life. Like her brother Robert, she resembled her mother, with black hair and dark eyes. Very popular as a child, she was described as a very "care-free and light-hearted" person until the death of her mother in May 1890 (Love, "The Rogers Family"). She attended kindergarten at Worcester Academy in Vinita in 1882–83, and by 1886 she was studying at the Cherokee Female Seminary at Park Hill with her older sister Maud. In January 1888 she began a teacher's training program at the Harrell International Institute at Muskogee, where she was a classmate of Ella Foreman and Mamie and Victoria Lipe, girls from other families close to the Rogerses in the Verdigris country. Her young brother Will joined her at the

Harrell International Institute in September 1888. May was at the Rogers ranch with her ill sisters and mother when Mary America Schrimsher Rogers passed away in May 1890. Subsequent events of her life somewhat estranged her from her family. Neither her father nor her sisters cared much for either of her husbands, whom they regarded as exploitative. They were not as well-to-do as the McSpaddens or Lanes and relied frequently on the generosity of Clem V. Rogers. May's personal life was marked by a series of tragedies, beginning with the sudden death of her mother when May was just seventeen.

May married a local farmer, J. Matthew (Matt) Yocum (1865–96), on 9 October 1892 at the Rogers ranch (see YOCUM, J. Matthew). She was nineteen years old, and her husband was twenty-seven. The wedding was performed by Judge Watt Starr. Matt Yocum was described at the time of the wedding as a "royal good fellow" who "has a host of friends who will congratulate him on his good fortune in securing such an estimable partner for life's journey" (*IC*, 13 October 1892). The Rogers family saw him as a bit of a ne'er-do-well who benefited from his father-in-law's financial standing and business connections; he worked at a series of jobs that Clem V. Rogers secured for him or that were connected to Clem's investments. He and May managed the DeVann Hotel in Claremore in addition to having the small farm near Oolagah. They had two children, John Vann Yocum (1893–1952) and Willie Yocum, who was born in 1895.

In January 1896 the DeVann Hotel was destroyed in a great fire that burned down six adjoining buildings. Clem V. Rogers lost thousands of dollars in his investment in the renovated hotel. At the same time Matt Yocum's financial dealings had been called into question, and he was charged with embezzlement. At the end of the year, in December 1896, he was murdered at the Yocum farm by shots fired through his and May's bedroom window. He was struck by one bullet as he was preparing for bed, and cried out to his wife before dying. May and their son Willie narrowly escaped harm from a second shot that penetrated the headboard of the bed in which they had been sleeping.

In the following months, May, a young widow with children to support, returned to the hotel-management business she had previously shared with her husband, purchasing the Oologah Hotel from J. Epsy Bell in February 1897. In the following June, William Cheatham, who had been courting May after her husband's death, was returning on foot, either from an evening visit to May's home or from escorting her home after a social affair in town, when he was shot and killed. His body was found near the railroad tracks on the outskirts of Oologah on 11 June 1897 (the *Indian Chieftain*, 22 July 1897, places Cheatham's death in April, not June, of 1897). The case caused a stir in Indian Territory when the *Kansas City Journal,* building a story on rumor and innuendo, printed an article implicating Clem V. Rogers in Cheatham's murder and accusing Will Rogers of being an accomplice. It further accused May of having earlier been an accessory to her husband's murder, by allegedly pinning up the curtain of the bedroom window on the night of his death, and went on to claim that, when she was informed of Cheatham's death, she exclaimed with bitterness and brief that her "father's money had killed her husband and now had killed the only man she loved" (*KCJ,* 18 July 1897). Walter Desky (a.k.a. W. E. Milstead), a stranger who had spent just a few months in town, was arrested for Cheatham's murder. The *Kansas City Journal* reported that, under questioning, he claimed that Clem V. Rogers had hired him to commit the act. Yocum's murder, meanwhile, had gone unsolved, with five local African American men falsely accused and arrested for the crime—including Clem Rogers, a childhood friend of Will Rogers and the son of Charles (Rabb) Rogers (see ROGERS, Charles and Houston). The men were in custody when the second murder occurred, and they were released by the court shortly after, with the court citing lack of evidence linking them with Yocum's death. The *Kansas City Journal* article was proved to be a fabrication, and Clem V. Rogers successfully sued the paper, and others that had picked up the falsified story, for libel. Less than two months after the demise of her friend Cheatham and the family scandal that followed his death, May's youngest son, Willie, passed away from illness (30 August 1897).

A year later (August 1898), May remarried in Texas. Her second marriage was to a cousin of Matt Yocum's, Frank Stine (1874–1975) of Fort Worth (see STINE, Frank). The Stines lived in May's home in Oologah and at the Rogers ranch. Frank Stine was employed for a time in nearby oil fields. Frank became a father to young Johnny Yocum, and together he and May Stine had five children. Two, Zella Mae and Vera, died in infancy or early childhood. The other children were Jacob Edward (Jake) (1900–1982), Mattie Lane (Lanie) (1903–78), and Owen Gore Stine (1909–78) (see MITCHELL, Mattie Lane Stine, and STINE, Jacob Edward). The Stines took over the management of the Talala Hotel, renovating it to attract a better class of clientele. Frank Stine opened a soda fountain in Oolagah in 1903. In June of that year the family moved into the McDaniel Hotel, and Frank moved his soda-fountain business into the new Lipe family store; he also added a butcher shop to the facilities. Tragedy returned to the family when young Zella Mae Stine died in December 1905, and in the summer of 1909 May became severely ill. Frank took her to Sallie McSpadden's home in Chelsea to be cared for, and she passed away there on 25 July 1909 at the age of thirty-six. Will Rogers later listed "confinement" as her cause of death on an insurance application form, and the *Claremore Progress* reported her death as a result of a "lingering illness" (Statements fo Medical Examiner, Will Rogers application for insurance, Mutual Life Insurance Co. of New York, 23 September 1918, in Mutual Life Insurance Co. of New York, "Gift to the Nation"; *CP,* 30 July 1909). The illness may possibly have been related to complications from childbirth.

J. T. McSpadden became the legal guardian of Johnny Yocum, while Frank Stine retained guardianship of the other children, who were taken in by relatives. Jake Stine was sent to Texas to be raised by Frank Stine's family, Lanie stayed with the McSpaddens, and Owen, the baby, was taken in by the Lanes. Clem V. Rogers remembered each of May's children in his will, and Will Rogers took on the financial responsibility for their education. Lanie Stine attended the Ursuline Academy in Paola, Kans., where Rogers paid for music and art lessons in addition to her room and board. In 1912–13 Rogers purchased May's children's shares in property in Claremore and Oologah left to them by Clem V. Rogers. He doled out the purchase money in the form of periodic support payments for the children, made care of Frank Stine.

Frank Stine remarried and lived in Texas. Johnny Yocum lived in Dallas in the 1910s, when his half-brother Jake Stine lived in Fort Worth. Around 1920 Yocum moved to an Indian reservation in Arizona, where he died in 1935. His sister-in-law Mary Allen Stine has described him as "good looking, black hair and eyes and proud of his Indian blood" (Mary Allen Stine to Reba Collins, 12 May 1982, OkClaW). Owen Stine married in Fort Worth and lived there until his death in 1978.

Owen Stine had difficulty in the management of money. An attractive man with a winning personality, he also had a problem with drinking and in the early 1930s was jailed on forgery charges. Betty Blake Rogers's brother, J. K. (Sandy) Blake, was fond of Owen Stine and repeatedly helped him, including posting his bond on appeal of the criminal charge and working in conjunction with local lawyers in Hempstead, Tex., to keep Stine from serving a two-year penitentiary sentence. He also helped secure a job for Stine as a rural delivery person for Amon Carter's Fort Worth *Star-Telegram.* He continued to deal with the consequences of many of Stine's numerous financial and personal indiscretions in the 1930s, working with Stine's supervisor at the *Star-Telegram,* who, like many others, cared for Stine and looked out for his welfare. Blake protected Will Rogers from knowledge about Owen Stine's problems. During negotiations regarding Stine's criminal case, Blake wrote: "I do not want to ask Mr. Rogers for a letter unless absolutely necessary. He does not know anything about Owen's trouble and I don't want to tell him" (J. K. Blake to William F.

Jackson, attorney, Hempstead, Tex., 8 November 1931, Stine family correspondence file, OkClaW; see also guardians deeds, John T. McSpadden, guardian of Johnny Yocum, and Frank Stine, guardian of Jake Stine, Mattie Lane Stine, and Owen Stine, 24 October 1912, Claremore, Okla.; list of deeds belonging to W. P. Rogers and orders confirming sale of interest of minor in real estates, Walter W. Shaw, judge, Rogers County Court, 7 April 1913, Will Rogers and Johnny Yocum, Jake Stine, Mattie Lane Stine, and Owen Stine, parties, Stine family correspondence file, OkClaW; miscellaneous notes on family history by Paula Love, OkClaW; Mary Allen Stine [wife of Jake Stine] to Reba Collins, 2 March, 25 March, and 12 May 1982, OkClaW; Sallie McSpadden to Betty Blake Rogers, July 1909, SRM-OklaW; *CM*, 30 July 1909; *CP*, 27 October and 17 November 1894; 18 January, 15 February, and 2 May 1896; 6 February, 13 February, 10 April, and 17 July 1897; 6 August 1898; 18 October 1902; 4 April, 20 June, and 10 October 1903; 30 July 1909; *HRC*, 376; *IC*, 23 December 1886; 14 June 1888; 13 October 1892; 13 February and 17 December 1896; 7 January, 22 July, and 12 August 1897; 3 February 1898; Love, "Rogers Family"; *OCF* 1:158; *OS*, 25 November 1904, 20 January 1905; *Talala Topic*, 21 July 1905; *VL*, 10 December 1896, 22 July 1897; *WRFT*, 28).

STINE, Owen Gore. See STINE, May Rogers Yocum.

SUNDAY, Edward (Ed). See SUNDAY, William Esther.

SUNDAY, William Esther (1877–1959). William Sunday was the son of Nancy Wilkerson (d. 1886) and Edward Sunday (1853–1943). His father, Uncle Ed Sunday, as he was commonly called, was a founder of Oologah and its first mayor, and operated a livery stable and general merchandise store in the town. Ed Sunday discovered coal on his property in the 1890s and operated a coal mine until 1933. He was also a Cherokee public official, a member of the Nationalist Party, and was elected to the Cherokee National Council in 1887. He was a friend of Clem V. Rogers and worked as a line rider for him in the early 1870s, an experience he described in his memoir, *A Line Rider in the Cherokee Nation* (1942). Ed Sunday had a large farm (located two miles northwest of the present site of the Will Rogers Memorial), which was where his son, William Sunday, was born. William Sunday was educated at the Cherokee National Male Seminary and the Kansas City Business College. The young Sunday and Will Rogers became boyhood friends. Sunday was serving as mayor of Oologah in the winter of 1900 when he fined Rogers for violating a smallpox quarantine. He helped his father operate the general merchandise store in Oologah, called Sunday and Son. Later he helped found the Claremore

Federal Building and Loan Association, was appointed to the Cherokee National Council in 1946, and established a claims commission to represent Cherokees before the federal government. With Maude DuPriest he wrote *Gah Dah Gwa Stee* (1953), a book about his family and other pioneers from the Oologah/Claremore area. In 1911 he married Elizabeth Lee Allen; they were the parents of two daughters. As the owner of a real-estate and loan business, he helped Will Rogers buy the property in Claremore that became the site of the Will Rogers Memorial. Sunday was one of the original members of the Will Rogers Memorial Commission (*CP,* 3 February 1900; Sunday et al., *Gah Dah Gwa Stee; A History of Oologah,* 9, 11, 201; *HRC,* 413–14; Starr, *History of the Cherokee Indians,* 654; Sunday, *Line Rider in the Cherokee Nation; TDW,* 23 August 1931 and 28 August 1932).

TEXAS JACK (1865–1905). Wild West promoter Texas Jack took his name from his benefactor, Texas Jack Omohundro (1846–80), a scout who worked out of Fort McPherson and other U.S. Army installations with William Cody in the 1860s and 1870s. Omohundro was born in Virginia and lived in Texas. Over six feet tall, dark-haired, and handsome, he accompanied Cody to Chicago in 1872 to appear on stage in *The Scouts of the Plains.* He married the heroine of that drama, Guiseppina Morlacchi, a beautiful Italian actress who was hired to play the part of an Indian maiden. According to biographer Hershel Logan's account of the legend of young Texas Jack's origins, while a scout on the Plains, Omohundro came across a Kansas homestead where a husband and wife had been killed in an Indian attack that left their young son alive. He rescued the orphan and brought him to Fort Worth, Tex., where he was raised by a foster family. The child, who did not know his real family name, took the name Texas Jack.

The younger Texas Jack became a performer with a traveling circus and gained a reputation for his sharpshooting and rough-riding act. Billed as "a noted American Scout," Texas Jack was said to have performed his act in "nearly every city of the world, including San Francisco, Honolulu (Sandwich Islands), Auckland (N.Z.), Sydney (Australia), Java, India, Egypt, Paris, London, and New York" ("Texas Jack," in *Prominent People,* n.d., n.p., viii, box 25, OkClaW). He began his own show and toured with it to South Africa and England. Texas Jack had performed in Australia in 1890 and returned with his Wild West Show and Dramatic Co. in 1898–99 (and during that time he made circus-world connections that Will Rogers used a few years later to get a job with the Wirth Brothers' Circus during its 1903–4 tour of Australia and New Zealand; as Rogers put it, "Jack gave me a letter to the Wirth Brothers," which Rogers took with him when he went from South Africa to Australia) (autobiographical notes of Will Rogers, WR Notes Autobiography file, OkClaW). During the 1899 tour of England, Texas Jack's show was billed as "Savage South Africa." He returned to South Africa in the following year and ran a show that pitted mock Pony Express riders on horses against cyclists, in races of various lengths. He began a new version of Texas Jack's Wild West Show and Dramatic Co. in 1902, shortly before Will Rogers came to South Africa. He leased land and sheds "for the purpose of giving Exhibitions of Horse Training etc. therein" in Cape Town in June 1902 (Texas Jack to Frank Kobb, Esq., Secretary, Table Bay Harbour Board, Cape Town, South Africa, 6 June 1902, CAD, CHB, vol. 294, ref. 337, pt. 1). The company included performers from the United States, Australia, Argentina, and South Africa. In 1902–3 various versions of the traveling show featured horseback tricks (including an act by Mrs. Texas Jack), a trapeze act, horse races, clown acts, a contortionist, magicians, singers and musicians, jugglers and acrobats, a rough-riding display, sharpshooting by Texas Jack, bronco riding, a "realistic Western Sketch," and Will Rogers, "The Cherokee Kid, Lasso Expert" (playbills and programs, ca. 1902–3, box 25, OkClaW). In addition to his rope-trick act, Will Rogers was also sometimes billed with Montana Brown or Buckskin Bill (W. F. Hampton) as a bucking-bronco rider. In some engagements the featured western sketch was "Texas Jack's Triumph," starring Texas Jack as himself with Will Rogers sometimes playing an African American character named Sam or another called by the stereotypical nickname Coaley (a name used for black characters in Texas Jack productions). Rogers reported that he was regularly cast as either a black person or an American Indian in the show's historical sketches. Texas Jack was by all accounts fond of Rogers. Rogers credited Texas Jack with teaching him a great deal about show business and how to move and win a crowd, as well as with having given him the idea of appearing on stage with his pony.

Texas Jack died at a Kroonstad, South Africa, district hospital on 25 October 1905, two years after Will Rogers left his Wild West show. E. Collins, an "intimate friend" of the deceased, supplied the information given on Texas Jack's death notice. Collins reported that Texas Jack was a widower; that he believed that the marriage of Texas Jack and his wife, Lily Dunbar, had taken place in Australia; and that there was one daughter, Hazel Jack, "aged about fourteen years." Collins listed Texas Jack's occupation as "Circus Proprietor and Farmer" (Death Notice of Texas Jack, death book no. 292, fol. 10, 26 October 1905, Kroonstad, South Africa, TAD, ref. no. MHG 7681). Texas Jack's will, deposited in Pretoria on 11 August 1903, made his daughter, Hazel Jack, "at present residing in Prahran near Melbourne, Australia, to be the sole and universal heir of all my Estate," and Wilfred Percy Fawcett and Thomas Joseph Fitzsimmons his executors (Last Will and Testament of Texas Jack, 5 August 1903, Pretoria, South Africa, TAD, ref. no. MHG 7681; see also FSAD, estate file of Texas Jack, ref. no. MHG J1067). Fawcett and Fitzsimmons were witnesses to a legal document involving a breach-of-contract suit against Texas Jack in Johannesburg in March 1904 (Special Power of Attorney in the Supreme Court, 15 March 1904, Johannesburg; and Summons Issued for Texas Jack by Bert Willison, 24 February 1904, Pretoria; *Bert Willison v. Texas Jack,* TAD, ref. no. ZTPD 5/562, no. 170/1904).

Like Buffalo Bill Cody, Texas Jack helped create and preserve an international mythology of the American cowboy. As he wrote in a poem that he sometimes used in his western sketches: "I was raised among the cowboys, my saddle is my home, / And I'd always be a cowboy no matter where I roam; / And like my noble namesake, my help I'll volunteer, / And try to be of service to the Western Pioneer / I am a roving cowboy, I've worked upon the trail, / I've shot the shaggy buffalo, and heard the coyote wail, / I've slept upon my saddle, and covered with the moon, / And I expect to keep it up until I meet my doom" ("Texas Jack," in *Prominent People*, n.d., n.p., viii, box 25, OkClaW; see also Will Rogers to Clement V. Rogers, 15 December 1902, and Will Rogers to Folks, 28 January–6 March 1903, above; clippings, Will Rogers Scrapbook, 1902–4, CPpR; playbills and programs for Texas Jack's Wild West Show and Circus, Texas Jack's Wild West Show and Dramatic Co., etc., box 25, OkClaW; *Texas Jack's Romance: A Sketch from Real Life,* Pretoria, n.d., script, box 25, OkClaW; C. Van Niekerk to Will Rogers, Jr., 31 May 1940, box 25, OkClaW; Herschel C. Logan to Paula McSpadden Love, Curator, Will Rogers Memorial, 10 September 1952, box 25, OkClaW; Chief, FSAD, to WRPP, 30 October 1992; Chief, CAD, to WRPP, 5 November 1992; Chief, TAD, to WRPP, 11 November 1992; Mark St Leon, Glebe, Australia, to WRPP, 9 February and 26 February 1993; "Buffalo Bill Behind the Footlights," chap. 7 in Sell and Weybright, *Buffalo Bill and the Wild West;* Croy, "Texas Jack"; Day, ed., *Autobiography,* 21–23; Logan, *Buckskin and Satin: The Life of Texas Jack,* 22–26; *PN,* 22, 23, 24, 25, 27, 29, 30 and 31 July 1903, and 1, 4, and 5 August 1903; *Punch* [Melbourne], 22 December 1898; reminiscences of Marizles Wirth in St Leon, *Australian Circus Reminiscences,* 21–23).

TIMBERLAKE, Margaret (Peggy) Rogers. See ROGERS, Clement Vann, and LIPE, DeWitt Clinton.

TRAINOR, Leonard Edward (1879–1940). Trainor was born in the Cherokee Strip and attended the Cherokee National Male Seminary at Tahlequah. He worked as a cowpuncher and participated regularly with Will Rogers and other Indian Territory young men in roping contests and Wild West shows at the turn of the century. Trainor eventually joined Pawnee Bill's Wild West and Far East show in 1902. Gordon Lillie (Pawnee Bill) called him "the wildest cowboy that ever 'topped a bronc' in my show" ("Will Rogers' Double Dies," *LAT,* 29 July 1940).

Trainor made his home in Chelsea, Okla., where he was town marshal and later U.S. deputy marshal. He married Laura May Rider (b. 1881) in 1898. In 1914 he moved to Hollywood, where he became a cowboy actor and extra in the movies. Rogers hired his old friend as his stand-in in his films and he gained fame as Rogers's double. Trainor appeared in Westerns and other films in the 1920s and 1930s, including *You Never Know* (1922), *Galloping Jinx* (1925), *Fast Lightnin'* (1925), *The Border Sheriff* (1926), *Hi-Jack Rustlers* (1926), *Headin' for Danger* (1928), and *Terror Trail* (1933). After Rogers's death Trainor was employed by Fred Stone, and he portrayed Rogers in the Santa Monica Will Rogers pageant. He died on 28 July 1940 from heart disease (*CP,* 16 June 1900; *DC,* 23 July 1901; *IC,* 12 September 1900; *LAT,* 29 July 1940; *OCF,* 1:39, 167; Ragan, *Who's Who in Hollywood* 2:1694; Truitt, *Who Was Who on the Screen,* 458; unidentified clipping, Leonard Trainor file, Harvard University Theatre Collection).

TRENT, Richard Owen, M.D. (ca. 1853–88). Born in Richmond, Va., Trent was sent by the federal government to a post as a physician at Fort Gibson, I.T. In 1876 or 1877 Trent married Mary Katherine (Mollie) Brown (1859–1952), whose mother, Ann E. Schrimsher, was a half sister of Will Rogers's mother. The Trents had four children: Dick, Georgia, Tom, and Spi (see TRENT, Spi). For a time Dr. Trent served as a secretary to Principal Chief Dennis Wolf Bushyhead at council meetings in Tahlequah. According to some accounts, Dr. Trent, a personal friend of the Rogers family, was possibly the attending physician at Will Rogers's birth (see Record of Birth of Will Rogers, 4 November 1879, n. 10, above). Trent was noted for his excellent baritone voice and was a popular singer at social occasions. He died on 12 January 1888 as a result of gangrene contracted from a gunshot wound (Madelyn Pope McSpadden to Lewis Moorman, M.D., 2 February 1954 and 23 March 1954, Lewis J. Moorman Papers, OkU; Collins, *Roping Will Rogers,* 120–121; Trent, *My Cousin Will Rogers,* 14.

TRENT, Spi (Martin) (1884–1959) (also known as Martin Trent, Isparschecher Trent, Spi E. Trent, Spi M. Trent). A distant cousin of Will Rogers through the Schrimsher line, Spi Trent was born at Fort Gibson, I.T., on 21 December

1884, the son of Richard Owen Trent, M.D. (ca. 1853–88) and Mary Katherine (Mollie) Brown (1859–1952). Some documents indicate that his given name was Martin (see, for example, Commission, *Final Rolls . . . Indian Territory,* 269; *OCF* 2:156; records of allotment, Rogers ranch, 1903, box 7, OkClaW). Spi Trent and his brothers Richard Owing (Dick) (b. 1880) and Thomas Brown (Tom) (b. 1887) were boyhood pals of Will Rogers. When Rogers returned to his father's ranch in 1898, his father put him in charge of the property. Rogers did not like living in the main house with a tenant farmer's family, and so he and Spi built a log cabin on the Rogers ranch, probably during the summer of 1900. Here the two lived together, enjoying cooking their own food, sorghum molasses and flapjacks for breakfast and navy beans with pork for dinner. Trent and Rogers participated in many social activities in Claremore and Oologah, attending dances and other events. They also joined in various steer-roping contests in 1900 and 1901, including the Rough Riders reunion at Oklahoma City in July 1900 and at Springfield, Mo., in September 1900. They also traveled together to the Pan-American Exposition in Buffalo in 1901. With the financial help of Clem V. Rogers, Spi Trent attended Spaulding Business College in Kansas City. Rogers asked Trent to go to Argentina with him, but instead Trent went to work as a bookkeeper at the Parkinson-Trent Mercantile Co. in Okmulgee, I.T., a general hardware store operated by Josiah Charles Trent (1868–1920) and James Parkinson. Spi (Martin) Trent received an allotment of acreage from the Rogers ranch in 1903, but Clem V. Rogers later bought the property back from him.

Later Trent's relationship with Will Rogers and his wife was not always cordial. Apparently, Trent used his relationship as a distant cousin to advance his career. Often unemployed during the Great Depression, Trent borrowed money from Rogers. One time Rogers received a letter from a disgruntled landlord in Los Angeles stating that Trent and a friend had left their apartment without paying their rent and other bills (Olive Williams to Will Rogers, 1 March 1933, Spi Trent correspondence file, OkClaW). After Rogers's death Trent continued to borrow money from Betty Rogers. She received letters from people inquiring about Trent's whereabouts and asking for her assistance in the collection of Trent's unpaid bills.

In 1938, Trent wrote a reminiscence of Rogers called *My Cousin Will Rogers,* published by G. P. Putnam's Sons. Written in western slang, the book contains many comic anecdotes about Rogers, many of them impossible to prove. Before its publication and hoping to gain her support, Trent sent Betty Rogers the manuscript. When Betty Rogers read it, she immediately objected to the book and sought unsuccessfully to stop its publication. She particularly disliked the book's title, the author's claim that he was a boyhood and lifelong friend of Will Rogers, the book's dedication to her, and Trent's use of copyrighted material (letters and sayings). She called on Will H. Hays, Jesse Jones, and Patrick J. Hurley, three of her husband's associates, and her attorney, Oscar Lawler, to help her. Through their efforts, she was able to have the dedication and Rogers's sayings deleted (Will H. Hays to Betty Rogers, 16 December 1938; 5 January, 27 January, and 7 May 1939; Betty Rogers to Jesse Jones, 9 December 1938; Patrick J. Hurley to Betty Rogers, 15 December 1938; Betty Rogers to Patrick J. Hurley, 9 December 1938, Spi Trent correspondence file, OkClaW). She wrote Madeline McSpadden that Trent "had so many times embarrassed Will by using his name out here that I naturally hated to have him armed with a book which is based entirely on a life-long friendship and close association with Will—something we know did not exist" (30 January 1939, SRM-OkClaW).

Trent was a founder and publisher of *Highway 66 Magazine and Guide*, a travel journal that dealt with the Will Rogers Memorial Highway (Route 66) from Santa Monica to Chicago. From his first marriage to Allie Belle Williams Trent, Trent had three children; his second marriage was to Clarice L. Trent. In 1938 Trent was living in Brooklyn, and around 1940, he returned to California, where he died in Yucaipa on 12 January 1960 (Hoge, "Oologah Oozings" column, *CP,* ca. 6 March 1960, clipping, OkClaW; Spi Trent to Will Rogers, 11 September 1902, and Will Rogers to Spi Trent, 4 December 1903, above; Thoburn and Wright, *Oklahoma* 3:630; Trent, *My Cousin Will Rogers; WRFT,* 121).

VEERKAMP, Margaret (Maggie) Nay Price (ca. 1882–1979). Maggie Nay was a friend of Will Rogers when he was a student at Scarritt Collegiate Institute in Neosho, Mo. When she was fourteen and Will Rogers was seventeen they often socialized as a pair within a larger group of young people (as she later explained, "We were of the gang stage and would meet and all go in a crowd"; Margaret Nay Price to Homer Croy, 16 July 1952, HCP-MoU). Her mother objected to her dating Will Rogers, who had gained a reputation for his somewhat wild ways. When Rogers asked her out to a party, she was thrilled but her mother forbade her going. When told of Mrs. Nay's disapproval, Rogers was deeply offended and wrote to Maggie about his feelings of rejection (see Will Rogers to Margaret Nay, 27 November 1896, above). A negative assessment of his Indian heritage, as well as an unsupported assumption about his indulging in bootlegged alcohol, were factors in Maggie Nay's mother's censure of the budding relationship.

Maggie Nay later married Garland Price, and they lived in Neosho, where he was employed in drug stores. During the 1930s and early 1940s they moved to Fayetteville, Ark., where she worked as a caseworker. She wrote a diary of her experiences caring for poor farm families, called "Leaves from a Rural Case Worker's Diary." The manuscript reveals a sensitive, kind person who was deeply concerned about the people she tried to help. On May 29 she wrote:

> These old people get me. I can't stand it. Old age is more or less a tragedy at very best, but poverty stricken and sightless old age—why do such things have to be? Yesterday an old man came to the office to make application for aid. He told me he was seventy five years old and had never asked for help in his life. He had thought maybe he could get by until old age pensions were granted, but he had been eating only one meal a day and finally there was no food left at all. I tried to cheer him up with my inane chatter, but, as he signed the necessary blanks, the tears kept dropping on the paper.

And on July 15 she wrote:

> The thing that simply breaks your heart in this relief work is that nothing really constructive can be done for the people. We cannot even give them enough to keep them from being hungry and certainly can do very little toward setting them on their feet again. One longs, most of all, to do things for the children. In cities where there are free clinics and institutions of various kinds a little something can be done, but out here in the hinterland it seems impossible. We finally succeeded in holding a clinic for crippled children and worked for weeks notifying the families and drove miles and miles bringing the children in. We got a few of the children into various hospitals and institutions for treatment, but most of the parents refused to send their small children so far from home, and of course they do not have the money to go and stay with them—and so it all seems rather hopeless.

The Prices later returned to Neosho, where Margaret worked in a bank and as a librarian. She also was a book reviewer and a charter member of Neosho's Fortnightly Study Club. After Garland Price died (when Margaret was around the age of eighty-one), she married her second husband, Franz Veerkamp. She was over ninety when she died in 1979 (Carol Hamilton [Margaret Nay Price's grandniece] to WRRP, 14 November 1993, with enclosure, "Leaves from a Rural Case Worker's Diary"; Bonnie Martin to WRRP, 28 March 1993; Louise D. Prettyman to Homer Croy, 11 July 1952, HCP-MoU; Croy, *Our Will Rogers*, 31–32, 336; Ketchum, *Will Rogers*, 42).

WALKER, Agnes (Babe) Rogers (b. 1862). Agnes Rogers was the daughter of Houston Rogers, a former slave who was owned by Clem V. Rogers at the time of her birth during the Civil War (see ROGERS, Charles and Houston). Her mother was Sidney Ross-Rogers, the daughter of a full-blood Cherokee mother and an African American father, who was at the time of Agnes Rogers's birth the slave of Oliver Ross.

Agnes Rogers was born 8 December 1862 and lived for the first two years of her life in Fort Gibson, I. T. She was raised from the age of two in a log cabin on land near Talala, across Talala Creek from the Dalton family of outlaw fame. Her parents' place included picnic grounds that were used for an annual community get-together. Agnes was educated at a one-room Cherokee school on Rabb's Creek, run by Sally Bingham, a Cherokee teacher with some twenty Indian and African American students. After Clem V. and Mary America Schrimsher Rogers returned to the Cooweescoowee District a few years after the Civil War, Agnes Rogers worked as a cook at their ranch. When interviewed about her experiences late in her life, she expressed very high admiration for Mary Rogers and discussed the positive influence she felt Mrs. Rogers had on the Oologah area (see ROGERS, Mary America Schrimsher). According to her nephew, Clem Rogers, Agnes Rogers Walker (along with either her mother, Sidney Ross-Rogers, or her aunt Rhoda Rogers, or both women) was called to the side of Mary Rogers during the birth of Will Rogers in 1879.

In addition to working at the Rogers ranch, Agnes Rogers Walker helped her husband with their farm and, during the busy cattle-shipping season, worked at the Talala Hotel as a cook. She married Dan Walker, an African American cowboy from Fort Gibson, who came to the Verdigris country to work at the Rogers ranch and became one of its principal ranch hands (see Walker, Dan). Their children (Charlotte, Charlie, and Mack), as well as the younger children of her uncle and aunt Rabb and Rhoda Rogers, were playmates of the young Will Rogers. The children hunted and fished together, and Dan Walker taught them to rope and ride. Dan and Agnes Walker (whom Will Rogers called Uncle Dan and Aunt Babe) helped care for Will after the death of his mother in 1890. In the Cherokee Rolls for Cooweescoowee District, 1890, Daniel Walker is listed as a farmer, and Agnes (called Aggie), twenty-seven years of age, is listed as his wife. Neither could read or write. They had five children at the time the rolls were prepared.

In 1933 Will Rogers responded to a distressed request from Agnes Walker to help her son, Eli Walker, win a retrial after a shooting incident that occurred in Bartlesville, Okla. Rogers gave funds to help in the case and recommended a lawyer, William F. Hurt, who succeeded in having the conviction overturned on grounds of insufficient evidence, freeing Eli Walker from jail (1890 Census of the Cherokee Nation, Cooweescoowee District, OkHi; notes of 1952 interview with Clem Rogers [b. 1874] by Homer Croy, and Oklahoma Historical Society to Homer Croy, 8 August 1952, HCP-MoU; Walker, interview, IPH-

OkHi; Croy, *Our Will Rogers,* 4–5, 19, 250–53; see also Birth Record of Will Rogers, 4 November 1879, n. 10, above).

WALKER, Dan (b.ca. 1852) One of the key ranch hands at the Rogers ranch for seven years, Dan Walker was instrumental in teaching the young Will Rogers how to ride and care for horses and how to use a rope. He came to the Cooweescoowee District from Fort Gibson, I.T., after the Civil War. He had a small farm of his own and worked at the ranch of Charles M. McClellan as well as at the Rogers ranch. He married Agnes Rogers. In addition to his ranch work, he became a U.S. deputy marshal (Collings, *Old Home Ranch;* Croy, *Our Will Rogers,* 19–20, 24–25; Walker, interview, IPH-OkHi; see also ROGERS, Charles and Houston, ROGERS, Clement Vann, and WALKER, Agnes Rogers).

WIRTH, George (1867–1941) and Philip Peter Jacob (1864–1937) (Wirth Brothers). The sons of John Wirth (1834–80) and Sarah Phillips, the Wirth brothers were well-known Australian circus proprietors. A musician from Bavaria, John Wirth immigrated to Victoria in 1855 and later settled in Dalby, Queensland, where he formed a band that played in circuses and processions and at balls and other events. Philip and George Wirth joined their father's band, called the Wirths Tourist Band, and traveled around the country giving concerts. Philip played the trombone, and George the tenor horn. In 1878 John Wirth and his four sons, John, Harry, Philip, and George, formed a small circus called Star Troupe of Varieties, which toured New South Wales and Queensland. In 1880 the circus played in Sidney, where it staged many forty-five-minute shows throughout the day. Its popularity grew and the show was renamed the Wirth Brothers' Circus. By 1888 it was considered among the largest circuses in Australia, with sixty horses and fourteen wagons. In 1890 the Wirth Brothers staged a successful combined circus and Wild West show with cowboys and Indians imported from the United States.

The Wirth Brothers' Circus was truly a family affair. Philip Wirth, a noted horse and animal trainer, and his wife, Sarah Jane Hodgson (d. 1929), performed acts on horseback. George Wirth was also an excellent equestrian, but after injuring his knee, became business manager in 1899. Philip Wirth's daughter, Phyllis, did a dance on horseback, and his sister Mary Elizabeth (Marizles) Wirth (1868–1948) performed a famous acrobatic act jumping through fifty paper hoops from a bareback horse. May Emmeline Wirth (1894–1978), the adopted daughter of Marizles Wirth, became a famous bareback rider and somersault equestrian with the Ringling Brothers' Circus. A star for many years, May Wirth was elected to the Circus Hall of Fame in 1964.

The Wirth Brothers' Circus included a large menagerie and many animal acts. The circus appeared in several places between 1893 and 1900, including South Africa (1893–94, 1899), South America (1895), England (1897–98), India (1899), and Java (1899). With the death of their brothers, John Jr. (1894) and Harry (1895), ownership of the circus went to George and Philip and their sister Mary Wirth. The Wirths' nearest competitor in Australia was the FitzGerald Circus, owned by two brothers, but this circus lost its importance in 1906 when its proprietors died, and it was eventually bought by the Wirths. After 1900 the Wirth Brothers' Circus primarily performed in Australia and New Zealand.

Will Rogers appeared with the circus in Australia in December 1903 and in January and February 1904 during its engagement in New Zealand. Texas Jack's letter of recommendation (25 April 1903) probably helped Rogers obtain the job. Since the Wirth Brothers' Circus had toured South Africa, the brothers undoubtedly knew of Texas Jack. Also, Texas Jack had appeared in a Wild West show in Australia in 1898–99 (Mark St Leon, Glebe, Australia, to WRPP, 9 February 1993). Billed as "The Cherokee Kid" and "The Mexican Rope Artist," Rogers performed a roping and trick-riding act, often wearing a red velvet embroidered suit that Mrs. George Wirth (Margaret Bain) had made. Rogers's engagement with the circus must have given him confidence to continue his show-business career, knowing that his talents might be recognized by other companies.

In 1907 the Wirth Brothers' Circus performed in Melbourne in the large Olympia amusement complex, where the Victorian Arts Center now stands. The circus had a popular engagement each November in conjunction with the Melbourne Cup. In 1916 the circus opened at the elegant Hippodrome in Sydney. The Wirth Brothers' Circus continued to flourish in the 1920s and 1930s as it imported the best circus acts from all over the world. By 1933 the Wirth Brothers' Limited Circus, as it had been renamed, was so large that it traveled using a special train with eight coaches and twenty trucks, carrying ten elephants, forty horses and ponies, fourteen cages of wild animals, and eight tents. The company numbered 150 people, including 40 performers who staged twenty-five acts. Both brothers acted as ringmasters; in addition, Philip Wirth was a noted trainer of horses and somersault equestrians. The Wirth brothers participated in Australian horse-racing organizations and traditionally presented a gold whip to the winning jockey in the prestigious Melbourne Cup. After the death of the two brothers the circus was operated by the family of Philip Wirth. During World War II it was the only circus permitted to travel within Australia. The Wirths' circus continued after the war, but the advent of television caused its demise in 1963 (clippings, box 25,

OkClaW; clippings, Will Rogers Scrapbook, 1902–4, CPpR; *ADB* 12:544–55; *AE* 6:344; Brennan, "Australia's Biggest Circus," 49; Brisbane, ed., *Entertaining Australia*, 133, 153, 191; Greaves, *Circus Comes to Town;* Ketchum, *Will Rogers*, 85, 92; Rogers, *Will Rogers*, 79–80, 83; Wirth, G., *Round the World with a Circus;* Wirth, P., *Life of Philip Wirth*).

YOCUM, John (Johnny). See STINE, May Rogers Yocum.

YOCUM, J. Matthew (Matt) (1865–96). Matt Yocum was the first husband of Will Rogers's youngest sister, May Rogers Yocum Stine. Yocum married May Rogers in October 1892, and they had two children. He was a small farmer and hotel manager who developed financial problems. He was killed one night at their Oolagah farm when shots came through their bedroom window as May was sleeping with their youngest son in the bed beside her and Yocum was preparing to retire. The murder caused considerable local speculation but went unsolved. May later remarried, marrying Yocum's first cousin, Frank Stine (*CP,* 29 December 1894, 5 January, 26 January, 2 February, 16 February, 13 April, 21 September 1895, and 18 January 1896; *IC,* 6 October and 13 October 1892; *VL,* 10 December 1896; see also STINE, Frank, and STINE, May Rogers Yocum).

Bibliography

THE SOURCES USED IN THIS VOLUME ARE LISTED HERE IN THE FOLLOWING THREE categories: books, articles and chapters in anthologies, and unpublished and miscellaneous sources. Readers may find the titles in quotation marks in the document endnotes and in the Bibliographical Appendix entries cited below in either the Articles and Chapters section or among the Unpublished and Miscellaneous Sources. See also the list of Manuscript Collection and Repository Symbols and the Guide to Abbreviated Citations for Published Sources in the front matter of the volume.

BOOKS

Abel, Annie H. *Slaveholding Indians*. 3 vols. Cleveland: Arthur H. Clark, 1915–25.

———. *The American Indian as Slaveholder and Secessionist*. Cleveland: Arthur H. Clark, 1915.

———. *The American Indian as Participant in the Civil War*. Cleveland: Arthur H. Clark, 1919.

———. *The American Indian under Reconstruction*. Cleveland: Arthur H. Clark, 1925.

Allen, H. C. *Bush and Backwoods: A Comparison of the Frontier in Australia and the United States*. East Lansing: Michigan State University Press, 1959.

Allwood, John. *The Great Exhibitions*. London: Studio Vista, 1977.

Alworth, E. Paul. *Will Rogers*. New York: Twayne Publishers, 1974.

Anderson, Bonnie S., and Judith P. Zinsser. *A History of Their Own: Women in Europe*. Vol. 2. New York: Harper and Row, 1988.

Anderson, William L., ed. *Cherokee Removal Before and After*. Athens and London: University of Georgia Press, 1991.

Armitage, Susan, and Elizabeth Jameson, eds. *The Women's West*. Norman: University of Oklahoma Press, 1987.

Arnesen, Eric. *Waterfront Workers of New Orleans: Race, Class, and Politics, 1863–1923*. New York: Oxford University Press, 1991.

As I Recollect. Claremore, Okla.: Pocahontas Club, 1949.

Atherton, Lewis. *The Cattle Kings*. Bloomington: Indiana University Press, 1961.

Babcock, Sidney Henry, and John Y. Bryce. *History of Methodism in Oklahoma: Story of the Indian Mission Annual Conference of the Methodist Episcopal Church, South*. Vol. 1. N.p.: Privately printed, 1935.

Bailey, Minnie Thomas. *Reconstruction in Indian Territory*. Port Washington, N.Y.: Kennikat Press, 1972.

Baird, W. David, and Danney Goble. *The Story of Oklahoma*. Norman: University of Oklahoma Press, 1994.

Barreto, Margarita. *El mate: Su historia y cultura*. Buenos Aires: Ediciones del Sol y Ediciones de Aquí a la Vuelta, 1989.

Bass, Althea. *Cherokee Messenger*. Norman: University of Oklahoma Press, 1968.

Becco, Horacio Jorge, and Carlos Dellepiane Calcena. *El gaucho: Documentacion-iconografia*. Buenos Aires: Editorial Plus Ultra, 1978.

Bell, George Morrison, Sr. *Genealogy of Old and New Cherokee Indian Families*. Bartlesville, Okla.: Privately printed, 1972.

Benedict, John D. *Muskogee and Northeastern Oklahoma*. 2 vols. Chicago: S. J. Clarke, Publishing Co., 1922.

Berndt, R. M., and C. H. Berndt. *The World of the First Australians*. 4th ed. Adelaide, Australia: Rigby Publications, 1985.

Betjeman, John. *Victorian and Edwardian London from Old Photographs*. New York: Viking Press, 1969.

Bhana, Surendra. *Settling Down Roots: Indian Migrants in South Africa, 1860–1911*. Johannesburg, South Africa: Whitwatersrand University Press, 1990.

———. ed. *Essays on Indentured Servants in Natal*. Leeds, England: Peipal Tree Press, 1990.

Bhana, Surendra, and Bridglal Pachai, eds. *A Documentary History of Indian South Africans*. Capetown, South Africa: D. Philip; and Stanford, Calif.: Hoover Institution Press, 1984.

Birkby, Carel. *The Pagel Story*. London and Cape Town, South Africa: Hodler and Stoughton, 1948.

Blackstone, Sarah J. *Buckskins, Bullets, and Business: A History of Buffalo Bill's Wild West*. New York and Westport, Conn.: Greenwood Press, 1986.

———. *The Business of Being Buffalo Bill: Selected Letters of William F. Cody, 1879–1917*. New York: Praeger, 1988.

Blassingame, John W. *Black New Orleans, 1860–1880*. Chicago: University of Chicago Press, 1973.

Bloom, Ken. *American Song: The Complete Musical Theatre Companion*. 2 vols. New York: Facts on File, 1985.

Bloomfield, Julia K. *The Oneidas*. 2d ed. New York: Alden Brothers, 1907.

Bolton, Geoffrey, ed. *The Oxford History of Australia*. Vol. 4, *1901–1942: The Succeeding Age*, by Stuart Macintyre. 1986. Reprint, Melbourne, Australia: Oxford University Press, 1990.

Brailsford, Dennis. *Bareknuckles: A Social History of Prize-Fighting*. Cambridge: Lutterworth Press, 1988.

Branda, Stephen Eldon. *The History of Texas: A Supplement*. Vol. 3. Austin: Texas State Historical Association, 1976.

Brisbane, Katherine, ed. *Entertaining Australia*. Sydney, Australia: Currency Press, 1991.

Brookes, Edgar H., and Colin de B. Webb. *A History of Natal*. Pietermaritzburg, South Africa: Natal University Press, 1965.

Brown, A. Theodore, and Lyle W. Dorsett. *K.C.: A History of Kansas City, Missouri*. Boulder, Colo.: Pruett Publishing Co., 1978.

Brown, Mervyn. *Madagascar Rediscovered: A History from Early Times to Independence*. Hamden, Conn.: Anchor Books, 1979.

Buffalo Bill and the Wild West. Brooklyn: Brooklyn Museum, in conjunction with the Museum of Art, Carnegie Institute, and the Buffalo Bill Historical Center, 1981.

Bulpin, T. V. *Discovering Southern Africa*. 4th ed. Muizenberg, South Africa: Treasury of Travel, 1986.

Burns, Louis F. *A History of the Osage People*. Fallbrook, Calif.: Ciga Press, 1989.

Byers, Chester. *Roping: Trick and Fancy Rope Spinning*. New York and London: G. P. Putnam's Sons, 1928.

Cammack, Diana. *The Rand at War, 1899–1902: The Witwatersrand and the Anglo-Boer War*. Berkeley and Los Angeles: University of California Press; Pietermaritzburg, South Africa: University of Natal Press, 1990.

Campbell, O. B. *Vinita, I.T.: The Story of a Frontier Town of the Cherokee Nation*. Oklahoma City: Colorgraphics, 1969.

Campisi, Jack, and Laurence M. Hauptman, eds., *The Oneida Indian Experience*. Syracuse, N.Y.: Syracuse University Press, 1988.

Carlson, Leonard. *Indians, Bureaucrats, and Land: The Dawes Act and the Decline of Indian Farming*. Westport, Conn.: Greenwood Press, 1981.

Carpenter, Harry. *Masters of Boxing*. London: Heinemann, 1964.

Carter, Edward L. *The Story of Oklahoma Newspapers, 1844 to 1984*. Muskogee, Okla.: Western Heritage Association, 1984.

Carter, Hodding, William Ransom Hogan, John W. Lawrence, and Betty Werlain Carter, eds. *The Past as Prelude: New Orleans, 1718–1968*. New Orleans: Tulane University Press, 1968.

Carter, Joseph H. *Never Met a Man I Didn't Like: The Life and Writings of Will Rogers*. New York: Avon Books, 1991.

Cass, James, and Max Birnbaum. *Comparative Guide to Junior and Two-Year Community Colleges*. New York: Harper and Row, 1972.

Castagnino, Raúl H. *Centurias del circa criollo*. Buenos Aires: Colección Nuevo Mundo, 1959.

Chapman, David L. *Sandow the Magnificent: Eugene Sandow and the Beginnings of Bodybuilding*. Champaign: University of Illinois Press, 1994.

Cherokee National Male Seminar Catalogue, 1883-1884. St. Louis: Robert D. Patterson and Co., 1883. (Copy, OkU.)

Clegg, Leland, and William B. Oden. *Oklahoma Methodism in the Twentieth Century*. Nashville, Tenn.: Parthenon Press, 1968.

Cody, William F. *The Adventures of Buffalo Bill*. New York and London: Harper and Brothers, 1905.

Collings, Ellsworth. *The Old Home Ranch: Birthplace of Will Rogers*. 2d ed. Claremore, Okla.: Will Rogers Heritage Press, 1986.

———, and Alma Miller England. *The 101 Ranch*. Norman: University of Oklahoma Press, 1937, 1989.

Collins, Reba. *Roping Will Rogers Family Tree*. Claremore, Okla.: Will Rogers Memorial, 1982.

———. *Will Rogers: Courtship and Correspondence, 1900–1915*. Oklahoma City: Neighbors and Quaid, Inc., 1992.

Commission and Commissioner to the Five Civilized Tribes and the Secretary of the Interior. *Final Rolls of Citizens and Freedmen of the Five Civilized Tribes in Indian Territory*. Washington, D.C.: Government Printing Office, 1907.

Cope, Trevor. *Izibongo: Zulu Praise-Poems*. Oxford: Clarendon Press, 1968.

Cotterill, R. S *The Southern Indians: The Story of the Civilized Tribes before Removal*. Norman: University of Oklahoma Press, 1954.

Cowles, Virginia. *Gay Monarch: The Life and Pleasures of Edward VII.* New York: Harper, 1956.

Croft-Cooke, Rupert, and Peter Cotes. *Circus: A World History.* London: Paul Elk Ltd., 1976.

Cronon, William, George Miles, and Jay Gitlin, eds. *Under an Open Sky: Rethinking America's Western Past.* New York: W. W. Norton, 1992.

Crowl, Philip A. *Guide to Historic Britain.* New York: Congden and Weed, 1983.

Croy, Homer. *Our Will Rogers.* New York: Duell, Sloan and Pearce; Boston: Little, Brown and Co., 1953.

Cunningham, Frank. *General Stand Watie's Confederate Indians.* San Antonio, Tex.: Naylor Co., 1959.

Dale, Edward Everett. *The Range Cattle Industry: Ranching on the Great Plains from 1865 to 1925.* Norman: University of Oklahoma Press, 1930, 1960.

Dale, Edward Everett, and Gaston Litton, eds. *Cherokee Cavaliers: Forty Years of Cherokee History as Told in the Correspondence of the Ridge-Watie-Boudinot Family.* Norman: University of Oklahoma Press, 1939, 1969.

Dale, Edward Everett, and Morris L. Wardell. *History of Oklahoma.* New York: Prentice-Hall, Inc., 1948.

Darwin, Bernard. *The Lure of London: Being a Treatise on the Historic and Social Features of "The Mighty City of the Thames."* London: Hotel Cecil, 1925.

Davidson, Basil. *No Fist Is Big Enough to Hide the Sky: The Liberation of Guinea and Cape Verde.* London: Zed, 1981.

Day, Donald. *Will Rogers: A Biography.* New York: David McKay Co., 1962.

————, ed. *The Autobiography of Will Rogers.* Boston: Houghton Mifflin Co., 1949.

Debo, Angie. *And Still the Waters Run: The Betrayal of the Five Civilized Tribes.* Princeton: Princeton University Press, 1940, 1972.

————. *Tulsa: From Creek Town to Oil Capital.* Norman: University of Oklahoma Press, 1943.

————. *A History of the Indians of the United States.* Norman: University of Oklahoma Press, 1970, 1989.

Dennison, Sam. *Scandalize My Name: Black Imagery in American Popular Music.* New York and London: Garland, 1982.

Deutsch, Sarah. *No Separate Refuge: Class, Culture, and Gender on an Anglo-Hispanic Frontier.* New York: Oxford University Press, 1987.

Dewitz, Paul W. *Notable Men of Indian Territory at the Beginning of the Twentieth Century, 1904-1905.* Muskogee, I.T.: Southwestern Historical Co., n.d. [1905?]. Micro-published in "Western Americana: Frontier History of the Trans-Mississippi West, 1550–1900." New Haven, Conn.: Research Publications, Inc., 1975.

Directory of Oklahoma State Almanac, 1989–1990. Oklahoma City: Oklahoma Department of Libraries, 1989.

Donaldson, Thomas, comp. *The Six Nations in New York.* Supplement for the Eleventh Census of 1890. Washington, D.C.: Interior Department, 1892.

Duke, Cordia Sloan, and Joe B. Frantz. *6,000 Miles of Fence: Life on the XIT Ranch of Texas.* Austin: University of Texas Press, 1961.

DuPriest, Maude Ward, Jennie May Bard, and Anna Foreman Graham. *Cherokee Recollections: The Story of the Indian Women's Pocahontas Club and Its Members in the*

Cherokee Nation and Oklahoma Beginning in 1899. Stillwater, Okla.: Thales Micro-university Press, 1976.

Ehle, John. *Trail of Tears: The Rise and Fall of the Cherokee Nation*. New York: Anchor-Doubleday, 1988.

1894 Annual Catalogue of Willie Halsell College, A School for Boys and Girls. Vinita, I.T.: The Indian Chieftain Printers, 1894. (Copy, OkClaW.)

Estrada, Marcos de. *Apuntes sobre el gaucho Argentina*. Buenos Aires: Ministerio de Cultura y Educacion, 1981.

Evants, Jeremiah. *Cherokee Removal: The "William Penn" Essays and Other Writings*. Edited by Francis Paul Prucha. Knoxville: University of Tennessee Press, 1981.

Everett, Dianna. *The Texas Cherokees*. Norman: University of Oklahoma Press, 1990.

Ewen, David. *All the Years of American Popular Music*. Engelwood Cliffs, N.J.: Prentice-Hall, 1977.

Faulkner, Harold U. *Politics, Reform, and Expansion*. New York: Harper and Row, 1959; Harper Torchbooks, 1963.

Federal Writers' Project of the Works Progress Administration for the City of New Orleans. *New Orleans City Guide*. 1938. Rev. ed. Boston: Houghton Mifflin, 1952.

Ferns, Henry Stanley. *Britain and Argentina in the Nineteenth Century*. Oxford: Oxford University Press, 1960.

Fields, Ronald. *W. C. Fields by Himself*. Engelwood Cliffs, N.J.: Prentice-Hall, 1973.

Filler, Louis, and Allen Guttmann, eds. *The Removal of the Cherokee Nation*. Boston: D. C. Heath and Co., 1962.

Fisher, John. *The Afrikaners*. London: Cassell, 1969.

_____. *Paul Kruger*. London: Secker and Warburg. 1974.

Foreman, Carolyn Thomas. *Oklahoma Imprints, 1835–1907: A History of Printing in Oklahoma before Statehood*. Norman: University of Oklahoma Press, 1936.

Foreman, Grant. *Indian Removal: The Emigration of the Five Civilized Tribes of Indians*. Norman: University of Oklahoma Press, 1932, 1956.

_____. *Advancing the Frontier: 1830–1860*. Norman: University of Oklahoma Press, 1933.

_____. *The Five Civilized Tribes*. Norman: University of Oklahoma Press, 1934, 1986.

_____. *Indians and Pioneers: The Story of the American Southwest before 1830*. Norman: University of Oklahoma Press, 1936.

_____. *Muskogee: The Biography of an Oklahoma Town*. Norman: University of Oklahoma Press, 1943.

Franklin, Jimmie Lewis. *The Blacks in Oklahoma*. Norman: University of Oklahoma Press, 1980.

_____. *Journey Toward Hope: A History of Blacks in Oklahoma*. Norman: University of Oklahoma Press, 1982.

Franks, Kenny A. *Stand Watie and the Agony of the Cherokee Nation*. Memphis, Tenn.: Memphis State University Press, 1979.

Frantz, Joe B., and Julian Ernest Choate, Jr. *The American Cowboy*. Norman: University of Oklahoma Press, 1955.

Frederiksson, Kristine. *American Rodeo: From Buffalo Bill to Big Business*. College Station, Tex.: Texas A & M University Press, 1985.

Fritz, Henry Eugene. *The Movement for Indian Assimilation, 1860–1890*. Philadelphia:

University of Pennsylvania Press, 1963.

Fulford, Roger. *Queen Victoria*. London: Collins, 1951.

Gaines, W. Craig. *The Confederate Cherokees: John Drew's Regiment of Mounted Rifles*. Baton Rouge and London: Louisiana State University Press, 1989.

Gibson, Arrell Morgan. *A Guide to the Regional Manuscript Collections in the Division of Manuscripts, University of Oklahoma Library*. Norman: University of Oklahoma Press, 1960.

_____. *Oklahoma: A History of Five Centuries*. Norman: Harlow Publishing Corp., 1965.

_____. *The History of Oklahoma*. Norman: University of Oklahoma Press, 1984.

Gideon, D. C. *Indian Territory: Descriptive, Biographical, and Geneological, Including the Landed Estates, County Seats, etc., with a General History of the Territory, etc.* New York and Chicago: Lewis Publishing Co., 1901.

Gilbert, Douglas. *American Vaudeville: Its Life and Times*. New York and London: Whittlesy House, McGraw-Hill Book Co., 1940; New York: Dover, 1963.

Gipson, Fred. *Fabulous Empire: Colonel Zack Miller's Story*. Boston: Houghton Mifflin Co., 1946.

Goodwin, Gary C. *Cherokee in Transition*. Chicago: University of Chicago Department of Geography, 1977.

Gorn, Elliott. *The Manly Art: Bareknuckle Prize Fighting in America*. Ithaca: Cornell University Press, 1986.

Gragert, Steven K., ed. *Will Rogers' Weekly Articles: The Hoover Years, 1931–1933*. Ser. 4, vol. 5, of *The Writings of Will Rogers*. Stillwater: Oklahoma State University Press, 1982.

_____, ed. *Will Rogers' Weekly Articles: The Roosevelt Years, 1933–1935*. Ser. 4, vol. 6, of *The Writings of Will Rogers*. Stillwater: Oklahoma State University Press, 1982.

Greaves, Geoff. *The Circus Comes to Town: Nostalgia of Australian Big Tops*. Sydney, Australia: Reed Books, 1980.

Green, Benny. *The Streets of London*. London: Pavilion Books, 1983.

Guy, Jeff. *The Destruction of the Zulu Kingdom: The Civil War in Zululand, 1878–1884*. London: Longman, 1979.

Haley, J. Evetts. *The XIT Ranch of Texas and the Early Days of the Llano Estacado*. Western Frontier Library, no. 34. Norman: University of Oklahoma Press, 1953.

Halliburton, R., Jr. *Red over Black: Black Slavery among the Cherokee Indians*. Westport, Conn.: Greenwood Press, 1977.

Hardie, Frank. *The Political Influence of Queen Victoria, 1861–1901*. 1938. 2d ed. London: Frank Cass, 1963.

Harris, John, Geoffrey de Bellaigue, and Oliver Millar, *Buckingham Palace and Its Treasures*. New York: Viking, 1968.

Harrison, David. *The White Tribe of Africa: South Africa in Perspective*. Berkeley and Los Angeles: University of California Press, 1981.

Haw, Joseph L., III. *The McSpad(d)en Family Ancestry*. Lincoln, Nebr.: Augustums Printing Service, Joseph L. Haw III, 1982.

Hewes, Leslie. *Occupying the Cherokee Country of Oklahoma*. University of Nebraska Studies, n.s., no. 57. Lincoln: University of Nebraska Press, 1978.

Higham, Charles. *Ziegfeld*. Chicago: Henry Regnery Co., 1972.

Hillegas, Howard C. *Oom Paul's People . . . A History of the Boers.* 1899. Reprint, New York: Negro Universities Press, 1969.

Historic San Antonio, 1700–1900. San Antonio, Tex.: American Institute of Architects, 1963.

A History of Lipscomb County, Texas, 1876–1976. Lipscomb, Tex.: Lipscomb County Historical Society Committee, 1976.

A History of Oologah: Our First One Hundred Years, 1890–1990. Oologah, Okla.: Privately printed, 1990.

The History of Rogers County, Oklahoma. Claremore, Okla.: Claremore College Foundation, 1979.

Hitch, Lt. Col. A. M. *Will Rogers, Cadet: A Record of His Two Years as a Cadet at the Kemper Military School, Boonville, Missouri.* Boonville, Mo.: Kemper Military School, 1935.

Hobsbawm, Eric. *Workers: Worlds of Labor.* New York: Pantheon Books, 1984.

Holden, William Curry. *A Ranching Saga: The Lives of William Electious Halsell and Ewing Halsell.* San Antonio, Tex.: Trinity University Press, 1976.

Jackson, Joy. *New Orleans in the Gilded Age: Politics and Urban Progress, 1880–1896.* Baton Rouge: Louisiana State University Press, 1969.

James, Edward T., Janet Wilson James, and Paul S. Boyer, eds. *Notable American Women, 1607–1950.* 2 vols. Cambridge, Mass.: Harvard University Press, Belknap Press, 1971.

Jeffries, Graham M. *A Century of Buckingham Palace, 1837–1937.* London: Hutchinson, 1937.

Johnstone, Frederick A. *Class, Race, and Gold: A Study of Class and Racial Discriminations in South Africa.* London: Routledge and Kegan Paul, 1976.

Jones, Virgil Carrington. *Roosevelt's Rough Riders.* Garden City, N.Y.: Doubleday and Co., 1971.

Jordan, Teresa. *Cowgirls: Women of the American West.* Garden City, N.Y.: Anchor Press, 1982.

Kaho, Noel. *The Will Rogers Country.* 2d ed. Claremore, Okla.: Privately printed, 1950.

Katz, William Loren. *Black Indians: A Hidden Heritage.* New York: Atheneum, 1986.

Keith, Harold. *Boy's Life of Will Rogers.* New York: Thomas Y. Crowell Co., 1937.

Kennedy, Carolee. *The Art and Material Culture of the Zulu-Speaking Peoples.* UCLA Museum of Cultural History Pamphlet Series, vol. 1, no. 3. Los Angeles: University of California, 1978.

Ketchum, Richard M. *Will Rogers: The Man and His Times.* New York: American Heritage Publishing Co., 1973; Touchstone/Simon and Schuster Paperback, 1973.

King, Duane H. *The Cherokee Indian Nation: A Troubled History.* Knoxville: University of Tennessee Press, 1979.

Kinkle, Roger D. *The Complete Encyclopedia of Popular Music and Jazz, 1900–1950.* 4 vols. New Rochelle, N.Y.: Arlington House, 1974.

Koebel, W. H. *Argentina, Past and Present.* London: Adam and Charles Black, 1914.

Kruger, S. J. Paulus. *The Memoirs of Paul Kruger.* 2 vols. London: T. Fischer Unwin, 1902.

Kuper, Hilda. *Indian People in Natal.* Pietermaritzburg, South Africa: Natal University Press, 1960.

Lamar, Howard, ed. *The Reader's Encyclopedia of the American West.* New York: Thomas Y. Crowell Co., 1977.

Lamar, Howard, and Leonard Thompson, eds. *The Frontier in History: North America and Southern Africa Compared.* New Haven and London: Yale University Press, 1981.

Larden, Walter. *Estancia Life: Agricultural, Economic, and Cultural Aspects of Argentine Farming.* London: T. Fisher Unwin, 1911.

Larra, Raul. *Jorge Newbery: El conquistador del espacio.* Buenos Aires: Editorial Futuro S.R.L., 1960.

Lawrence, Elizabeth Atwood. *Rodeo: An Anthropologist Looks at the Wild and the Tame.* Chicago and London: University of Chicago Press, 1984.

Lax, Roger, and Frederick Smith. *The Great Song Thesaurus.* 2d ed. New York: Oxford University Press, 1989.

Leavitt, M. B. *Fifty Years in Theatrical Management.* New York: Broadway Publishing Co., 1912.

Lee, Sidney. *King Edward VII: A Biography.* 2 vols. London: Macmillan, 1925–27.

Lefebvre, Irene Sturm. *Cherokee Strip in Transition: Circumstances, Conflicts, and Challenges.* Enid, Okla.: Cherokee Strip Centennial Foundation, 1991.

Leonard, Elizabeth Jane, and Julia Cody Goodman. *Buffalo Bill, King of the Old Wild West.* New York: Library Publishers, 1955.

Levine, Robert M. *Historical Dictionary of Brazil.* Metuchen, N.J.: Scarecrow Press, 1979.

Lillie, Gordon William. *Life Story of Pawnee Bill.* Topeka, Kans.: Arthur Capper, 1916.

Limerick, Patricia Nelson. *The Legacy of Conquest: The Unbroken Past of the American West.* New York: W. W. Norton, 1987.

Limerick, Patricia Nelson, Clyde A. Milner II, and Charles E. Rankin, eds. *Trails: Toward a New Western History.* Lawrence: University Press of Kansas, 1991.

Lipschutz, Mark R., and R. Kent Rasmussen, eds. *Dictionary of African Historical Biography.* 2d ed. Berkeley and Los Angeles: University of California Press, 1986.

Littlefield, Daniel F., Jr. *The Cherokee Freedmen: From Emancipation to American Citizenship.* Westport, Conn.: Greenwood Press, 1978.

Littlefield, Daniel F. and James W. Parins. *American Indian and Alaska Native Newspapers and Periodicals, 1826–1924.* Westport, Conn.: Greenwood Press, 1984.

Lobban, Richard. *Historical Dictionary of Guinea-Bissau and Cape Verde.* Metuchen, N.J.: Scarecrow Press, 1979.

Loftie, William J. *Westminster Abbey.* London: Seeley, 1890.

Logan, Herschel C. *Buckskin and Satin: The Life of Texas Jack.* Harrisburg, Pa.: Stackpole Co., 1954.

Magubane, Bernard Makhosezwe. *The Political Economy of Race and Class in South Africa.* New York and London: Monthly Review Press, 1979.

Malone, Henry Thompson. *Cherokees of the Old South: A People in Transition.* Athens: University of Georgia Press, 1956.

Mankiller, Wilma, and Michael Wallis. *Mankiller: A Chief and Her People.* New York: St. Martin's Press, 1993.

Mardock, Robert W. *The Reformers and the American Indian.* Columbia: University of Missouri Press, 1971.

Marlowe, Julia. *Julia Marlowe's Story.* As told to E. H. Sothern. New York: Rinehart and Co., 1954.

Masterson, V.V. *The Katy Railroad and the Last Frontier.* Norman: University of Oklahoma Press, 1952.

Mavais, Johannes S. *The Fall of Kruger's Republic.* Oxford: Clarendon, 1961.

McAfee, George F. *Missions Among the North American Indians.* New York: Woman's Board of Home Missions of the Presbyterian Church, 1890.

McArthur, Benjamin. *Actors and American Culture, 1880–1920.* Philadelphia: Temple University Press, 1984.

McLoughlin, William G. *Cherokees and Missionaries.* New Haven: Yale University Press, 1984.

———. *The Cherokee Ghost Dance: Essays on the Southeastern Indians, 1879–1861.* Macon, Ga.: Mercer, 1984.

———. *Cherokee Renascence in the New Republic.* Princeton: Princeton University Press, 1986.

———. *Champions of the Cherokees: Evan and John B. Jones.* Princeton: Princeton University Press, 1990.

———. *After the Trail of Tears: The Cherokees' Struggle for Sovereignty, 1839–1880.* Chapel Hill and London: University of North Carolina Press, 1993.

McReynolds, Edwin C. *Oklahoma: A History of the Sooner State.* Norman: University of Oklahoma Press, 1954.

Mihesuah, Devon A. *Cultivating the Rosebuds: The Education of Women at the Cherokee Female Seminary, 1851–1909.* Urbana and Chicago: University of Illinois Press, 1993.

Millan, Sarah Gertrude. *The People of South Africa.* New York: Alfred A. Knopf, 1954.

Miner, Craig H. *The St. Louis–San Francisco Transcontinental Railroad: The Thirty-fifth Parallel Project, 1853–1890.* Lawrence: University Press of Kansas, 1972.

Mix, Olive Stokes, and Eric Heath: *The Fabulous Tom Mix.* Englewood Cliffs, N.J.: Prentice-Hall, Inc., 1957.

Mix, Paul E. *The Life and Legend of Tom Mix.* South Brunswick, N.J., and New York: A. S. Barnes and Co., 1972.

Moncrieff, A. R. Hope. *London.* London: A. and C. Black, 1910.

Mooney, James. *Historical Sketch of the Cherokee.* Washington, D.C., and Chicago: Smithsonian Institution Press, Aldine Publishing Co., 1975. (A selected portion of *Myths of the Cherokees.* N.p.: U.S. Bureau of American Ethnology, 1900).

Morris, John W., Edwin C. McReynolds, and Charles R. Goins. *Historical Atlas of Oklahoma,* 3d ed. Norman: University of Oklahoma Press, 1986.

Moulton, Gary E. *John Ross: Cherokee Chief.* Athens: University of Georgia Press, 1978.

———, ed. *The Papers of Chief John Ross.* 2 vols. Norman: University of Oklahoma Press, 1985.

Mullen, Richard, and James Munson. *Victoria: Portrait of a Queen.* London: BBC Books, 1987.

Munck, Ronaldo, with Ricardo Falcon and Bernardo Galitelli. *Argentina, from Anarchism to Peronism: Workers, Unions, and Politics, 1855–1985.* London: Zed Books, 1987.

Musser, Charles. *Before the Nickelodeon: Edwin S. Porter and the Edison Manufacturing Company.* Berkeley and Los Angeles: University of California Press, 1991.

Neosho, City of Springs. Rev. ed. Neosho, Mo.: Newton County Historical Society, 1984.

Nichols, David A. *Lincoln and the Indians.* Columbia: University of Missouri Press, 1978.

Nichols, Madaline Wallis. *The Gaucho.* Durham, N.C.: Duke University Press, 1942.

Nye, Russel. *The Umembarrassed Muse: The Popular Arts in America.* New York: Dial Press, 1970, 1971.

Oakley, Ann. *Woman's Work: The Housewife Past and Present.* 1974. 1st American ed. New York: Pantheon/Vintage, 1975.

O'Beirne, H. F. *The Indian Territory: Its Chiefs, Legislators, and Leading Men.* St. Louis: Privately printed, 1892.

O'Neill, Perez, Lance, Larcade. *San Antonio Historic Survey, 1972.* San Antonio, Tex.: City Planning Department, 1972.

Osvaldo Cutolo, Vicente. *Nuevo diccionario biografico argentino (1750–1930).* 6 vols. Buenos Aires: Editorial Elche, 1978.

Otis, D. S. *The Dawes Act and the Allotment of Indian Lands.* 1934. Edited by Francis Paul Prucha. Norman: University of Oklahoma Press, 1973.

Our 75th Year of Community Service (1892–1967). Vinita, Okla.: First National Bank and Trust Company, 1967.

Pakenham, Thomas. *The Boer War.* London: Weidenfeld and Nicolson, 1979.

Parins, James W. *John Rollin Ridge: His Life and Works.* Lincoln: University of Nebraska Press, 1991.

Patterson, Sheila. *The Last Trek: A Study of the Boer People and the Afrikaner Nation.* London: Routledge and Kegan Paul, 1957.

Paullada, Stephen. *Rawhide and Song: A Comparative Study of the Cattle Cultures of the Argentinian Pampa and North American Great Plains.* New York: Vantage Press, 1963.

Perdue, Theda. *Slavery and the Evolution of Cherokee Society, 1540–1866.* Knoxville: University of Tennessee Press, 1979.

———. *The Cherokee.* New York and Philadelphia: Chelsea House, 1989.

Piccirilli, Ricardo, Francisco Romay, and Leoncio Gianello. *Diccionario historico argentino.* 6 vols. Buenos Aires: Ediciones Históricas Argentinas, 1953–54.

Pillay, Bala. *British Indians in the Transvaal: Trade, Politics, and Imperial Relations, 1885–1906.* London: Longman, 1976.

Porter, Kenneth Wiggins. *The Negro on the American Frontier.* New York: Arno Press, 1971.

Porter, Willard H. *Who's Who in Rodeo.* Oklahoma City: Powder River Book Co., n.d. [ca. 1982–83].

Ragan, David. *Who's Who in Hollywood: The Largest Cast of International Film Personalities Ever Assembled.* 2 vols. New York: Facts on File/Oxford University Press, 1992.

Rainey, George. *The Cherokee Strip.* Guthrie, Okla.: Co-operative Publishing Co., 1933.

Rasmussen, Steen Eiler. *London: The Unique City.* Rev. ed. London and Cambridge, Mass.: MIT Press, 1982.

Roach, Joyce Gibson. *The Cowgirls.* Denton: University of North Texas Press, 1990.

Robertson, Donald B. *Encyclopedia of Western Railroad History.* Vol. 2, *The Mountain*

States: Colorado, Idaho, Montana, and Wyoming. Dallas: Taylor Publishing Co., 1991.

Robertson, M.S. *Rodeo: Standard Guide to the Cowboy Sport.* Berkeley, Calif.: Howell-North, 1961.

Robertson, Pauline Durrett, and R. L. Robertson. *Panhandle Pilgrimage: Illustrated Tales Tracing History in the Texas Panhandle.* 2d ed. Amarillo, Tex.: Paramount Publishing Co., 1978.

Rodriguez Molas, Ricardo E. *Historia social del gaucho.* Buenos Aires: Ediciones Marv, 1968; Buenos Aires: Centro Editor de América Latina Capítulo, 1982.

Rogers, Betty. *Will Rogers: His Wife's Story.* 1941. Norman: University of Oklahoma Press, 1979.

Rolinski, Charles J. *Historical Dictionary of Paraguay.* Metuchen, N.J.: Scarecrow Press, 1973.

Rollins, Peter C. *Will Rogers: A Bio-Bibliography.* Westport, Conn.: Greenwood Press, 1984.

Roosevelt, Theodore. *The Rough Riders.* 1899. Reprint, Williamstown, Mass.: Corner House Publishers, 1979.

Rosenberg, Daniel. *New Orleans Dockworkers: Race, Labor, and Unionism, 1892–1923.* Albany: State University of New York Press, 1988.

Royce, Charles C. *The Cherokee Nation of Indians.* 1887. Reprint, Chicago: Aldine, 1975.

Russell, Charles Edward. *Julia Marlowe: Her Life and Art.* New York: D. Appleton and Co., 1926.

Russell, Don. *Lives and Legends of Buffalo Bill.* Norman: University of Oklahoma Press, 1960.

———. *The Wild West: A History of the Wild West Shows.* Fort Worth, Tex.: Amon Carter Museum of Western Art, 1970.

Rydell, Robert W. *All the World's a Fair: Visions of Empire at American International Expositions, 1876–1916.* Chicago and London: University of Chicago Press, 1984, 1987.

Sargent, Charles. *The Spatial Evolution of Greater Buenos Aires, Argentina, 1870–1930.* Tempe: Arizona State University Center for Latin American Studies, 1974.

Satz, Ronald N. *American Indian Policy in the Jacksonian Era.* Lincoln: University of Nebraska Press, 1975.

Savage, William W., Jr. *The Cherokee Strip Live Stock Association: Federal Regulation and the Cattleman's Last Frontier.* Columbia: University of Missouri Press, 1973.

———. *Singing Cowboys and All That Jazz: A Short History of Popular Music in Oklahoma.* Norman: University of Oklahoma Press, 1983.

Scobie, James R. *Argentina: A City and a Nation.* New York: Oxford University Press, 1964.

———. *Revolution on the Pampas: A Social History of Argentine Wheat, 1860–1910.* Austin: Institute of Latin American Studies by the University of Texas Press, 1964.

———. *Buenos Aires: Plaza to Suburb, 1870–1910.* New York: Oxford University Press, 1974.

Sell, Henry Blackman, and Victor Weybright. *Buffalo Bill and the Wild West.* New York: Oxford University Press, 1955.

Shaw, A. G. L. *The Story of Australia*. 3d ed. London: Faber and Faber, Ltd., 1967.

Shaw, Caroline. *Cape Verde*. World Bibliographical Series, no. 123. Oxford, Denver, and Santa Barbara: Clio Press, 1991.

Shirk, George H. *Oklahoma Place Names*. Norman: University of Oklahoma Press, 1965.

Shirley, Glenn. *Pawnee Bill: A Biography of Major Gordon W. Lillie*. Lincoln: University of Nebraska Press, 1958.

Slatta, Richard W. *Gauchos and the Vanishing Frontier*. Lincoln and London: University of Nebraska Press, 1983.

———. *Cowboys of the Americas*. New Haven: Yale University Press, 1990.

Slide, Anthony. *The Encyclopedia of Vaudeville*. Westport, Conn.: Greenwood Press, 1994.

Smith, Harvey. *The Charm of Old San Antonio: A Spanish Settlement of the Southwest*. New York: R. F. Whitehead, 1931.

Smith, Peter. *Politics and Beef in Argentina*. New York: Columbia University Press, 1969.

Sobel, Robert, and John Raimo, eds. *Biographical Directory of the Governors of the United States, 1789–1978*. Six vols. Westport, Conn.: Meckler Books, 1978.

Sober, Nancy Hope. *The Intruders: The Illegal Residents of the Cherokee Nation, 1866–1907*. Ponca City, Okla.: Cherokee Books, 1991.

Spalding, Hobart. *La clase trabajadora Argentina (documentos para su historia: 1890–1912)*. Buenos Aires: Editorial Galerna, 1970.

Spate, O. H. K. *Australia*. London: Ernest Benn Ltd., 1968.

Stanley, F. *The Higgins Texas Story*. Nazareth, Tex.: Privately printed, 1975.

Stansbury, Kathryn B. *Lucille Mulhall: Her Family, Her Life, Her Times*. 2d ed. Mulhall, Okla.: Heirloom Pub. Co., 1992.

Starr, Emmett. *History of the Cherokee Indians and Their Legends and Folk Lore*. 1921. Reprint, New York: Kraus Reprint Co., 1969.

St Leon, Mark Valentine. *Australian Circus Reminiscences*. Sydney, Australia: Privately printed, 1984.

The Story of Craig County: Its People and Places. Vinita, Okla.: Craig County Heritage Association, 1984.

Stuart, Paul. *The Indian Office: Growth and Development of an American Institution, 1865–1900*. Ann Arbor, Mich.: UMI Research Press, 1978.

Stultz, Newell M. *South Africa*. Ann Arbor: Pierian Press, 1988.

Sunday, Edward. *A Line Rider in the Cherokee Nation*. Tulsa: Standard Printing Co., 1942.

Sunday, William E., Marcel M. DuPriest, Marilee Brenhardt, and Quannah Archer Chu-lee-wah. *Gah Dah Gwa Stee*. Pryor, Okla.: Byron Smith Printing Co., 1953.

Sweet, William Warren. *Methodism in American History*. New York: Methodist Book Concern, 1933.

Tawa, Nicholas E. *The Way to Tin Pan Alley: American Popular Song, 1866–1910*. London: Collier Macmillan; New York: Schirmer, 1990.

Taylor, Carl C. *Rural Life in Argentina*. Baton Rouge: Louisiana State University Press, 1948.

Teall, Kaye M. *Black History in Oklahoma*. Oklahoma City: Oklahoma City Public Schools, 1971.

Thoburn, Joseph B., and Muriel H. Wright. *Oklahoma: A History of the State and Its*

People. 4 vols. New York: Lewis Historical Publishing Co., 1929.

Thompson, Leonard. *The Unification of South Africa, 1902–1910.* Oxford: Clarendon Press, 1960.

———, ed. *African Societies in Southern Africa.* New York: Praeger, 1969.

Thornton, Russell. *The Cherokees: A Population History.* Lincoln: University of Nebraska Press, 1990.

Tinker, Edward Larocque. *Life and Literature of the Pampas.* Latin American Monographs Series, no. 13. Gainesville: University of Florida Press, 1961.

Toll, Robert C. *Blacking Up: The Minstrel Show in Nineteenth-Century America.* New York: Oxford University Press, 1974.

———. *On with the Show: The First Century of Show Business in America.* New York: Oxford University Press, 1976.

Tolson, Arthur L. *The Black Oklahomans: A History, 1541–1972.* New Orleans: Edwards Printing Co., 1974.

Trennert, Robert. *Alternative to Extinction: Federal Indian Policy and the Beginnings of the Reservation System.* Philadelphia: Temple University Press, 1975.

Trent, Spi M. *My Cousin Will Rogers.* New York: G. P. Putnam's Sons, 1938.

Truitt, Evelyn Mack. *Who Was Who on the Screen.* New York and London: R. R. Bowker Co., 1974.

Twentieth-Century Impressions of Natal: Its People, Commerce, Industries, and Resources. Natal, South Africa: Lloyd's Greater Britain Publishing Co., 1906.

Utley, Robert. *The Indian Frontier of the American West.* Albuquerque: University of New Mexico Press, 1984.

Vilakazi, Absolom. *Zulu Transformations: A Study of the Dynamics of Social Change.* Pietermaritzburg, South Africa: University of Natal Press, 1965.

Wardell, Morris L. *A Political History of the Cherokee Nation, 1838–1907.* Norman: University of Oklahoma Press, 1938.

Warwick, Peter, ed. *The South African War: The Anglo-Boer War, 1899–1902.* London: Longman, 1980.

Webb, Walter Prescott, ed. *The Handbook of Texas.* 2 vols. Austin: Texas State Historical Association, 1952.

Weil, Thomas E., Jan Knippens Black, Howard I. Bluestein, Hans J. Hoyer, Kathryn T. Johnston, David S. McMorris, eds. *Area Handbook for Argentina.* Foreign Area Studies of American University, DA pam. 550-73. Washington, D.C.: Government Printing Office, 1974.

Wenzel, Lynn, and Carol J. Binkowski. *I Hear America Singing: A Nostalgic Tour of Popular Sheet Music.* New York: Crown Publishers, 1989.

Wertheim, Arthur Frank, ed. *Will Rogers at the Ziegfeld Follies.* Norman and London: University of Oklahoma Press, 1992.

West, C. W. "Dub". *Muskogee: From Statehood to Pearl Harbour.* Muskogee, Okla.: Muskogee Publishing Co., 1976.

Westermeier, Clifford P. *Man, Beast, Dust: The Story of Rodeo.* N.p.: World Press, 1947.

Whitcomb, Ian. *After the Ball.* London: Penguin Press, 1972.

White, G. Edward. *The Eastern Establishment and the Western Experience: The West of Frederic Remington, Theodore Roosevelt, and Owen Wister.* New Haven and London: Yale University Press, 1968.

White, Richard. *"It's Your Misfortune and None of My Own": A New History of the American West.* Norman and London: University of Oklahoma Press, 1991.

————. *The Middle Ground: Indians, Empires, and Republics in the Great Lakes Region, 1650–1815.* London: Cambridge University Press, 1991.

White, William W. *The Confederate Veteran.* Tuscaloosa, Ala.: Confederate Publishing Co., 1962.

Wilkins, Thurman. *Cherokee Tragedy.* 1970. Rev. ed. Norman: University of Oklahoma Press, 1985.

Willey, Keith. *The Drovers.* Melbourne, Australia: Macmillan Co. of Australia, 1982.

Willis, Jean L. *Historical Dictionary of Uruguay.* Metuchen, N.J.: Scarecrow Press, 1974.

Wilmeth, Don B. *Variety Entertainment and Outdoor Amusements: A Reference Guide.* Westport, Conn.: Greenwood Press, 1982.

Wilson, Derek. *The Tower, 1078–1978.* London: H. Hamilton, 1978.

Wilson, Garff B. *A History of American Acting.* Bloomington: Indiana University Press, 1966.

Wilson, Monica, and Leonard Thompson, eds. *The Oxford History of South Africa.* Vol. 2, *1870–1966.* New York and Oxford: Oxford University Press, 1971.

Wirth, George. *Round the World with a Circus.* Melbourne, Australia: Troedel and Cooper Printers, 1925.

Wirth, Philip. *The Life of Philip Wirth.* Melbourne, Australia: Troedel and Cooper Printers, n.d. [ca. 1933].

Wit and Philosophy from the Radio Talks of America's Humorist, Will Rogers. New York: E. R. Squibb and Sons, 1930.

Woodward, Grace Steele. *The Cherokees.* Norman: University of Oklahoma Press, 1963.

Worcester Academy Catalogue of Pupils and Teachers with Courses of Study. Vinita, Indian Territory, 1882–1883. St. Louis: Slawson and Co., 1988. (Copy, OkU.)

Workers of the Writers' Program of the Works Projects Administration in the State of Arkansas, comp. *Arkansas: A Guide to the State.* New York: Hastings House Publishers, 1941.

Workers of the Writers' Program of the Works Projects Administration in the State of Oklahoma, comp. *Oklahoma: A Guide to the Sooner State.* Norman: University of Oklahoma Press, 1941.

Worster, Donald. *Under Western Skies: Nature and History in the American West.* New York and London: Oxford University Press, 1992.

Wright, Muriel H. *A Guide to the Indian Tribes of Oklahoma.* Norman and London: University of Oklahoma Press, 1951, 1986.

Yagoda, Ben. *Will Rogers: A Biography.* New York: Alfred A. Knopf, 1993.

ARTICLES AND CHAPTERS IN ANTHOLOGIES

Agnew, Brad. "A Legacy of Education: The History of the Cherokee Seminaries." *Chronicles of Oklahoma* 63 (Summer 1985): 128–47.

Aldrich, Duncan M. "General Stores, Retail Merchants, and Assimilation: Retail Trade in the Cherokee Nation, 1838–1890." *Chronicles of Oklahoma* 57 (Summer 1979): 119–36.

Bailes, Howard. "Military Aspects of the War." In *The South African War: The Anglo-Boer War, 1899–1902,* edited by Peter Warwick, 65–102. London: Longman, 1980.

Ballenger, T. L. "The Cultural Relations between Two Pioneer Communities." *Chronicles of Oklahoma* 34 (Autumn 1956): 286–95.

Berndt, Ronald M. "Aborigines, Australian," and "Maori." In Academic American Encyclopedia [database online]. Danbury, Conn.: Grolier Electronic Edition, 1993. Available from GE Information Services (GEnie), Rockville, Md.

Billington, Monroe. "Black Slavery in Indian Territory: The Ex-Slave Narratives." *Chronicles of Oklahoma* 60 (Spring 1982): 56–65.

Blanch, M. D. "British Society and the War." In *The South African War: The Anglo-Boer War, 1899–1902,* edited by Peter Warwick, 210–38. London: Longman, 1980.

Bloom, Leonard. "The Acculturation of the Eastern Cherokee: Historical Aspects." *North Carolina Historical Review* 19 (October 1942): 328–58.

Bowen, Ian. "Western Australia." In *Australia, New Zealand, and the South Pacific: A Handbook,* edited by Charles Osborne, 78. London: Anthony Blond, 1970.

Brennan, Martin C. "Australia's Biggest Circus." *Billboard,* 7 November 1925.

Brewer, T. H. "Necrology: Rev. Theodore Frelinghuysen Brewer." *Chronicles of Oklahoma* 9 (September 1931): 349–51.

Brown, Loren N. "The Dawes Commission." *Chronicles of Oklahoma* 9 (March 1931): 71–105.

———. "The Establishment of the Dawes Commission for Indian Territory." *Chronicles of Oklahoma* 18 (June 1940): 171–81.

Campbell, Harry. "Reminiscences." *Chronicles of Oklahoma* 28 (Autumn 1950): 379–81.

Caywood, Elzie R. "The Administration of William C. Rogers." *Chronicles of Oklahoma* 30 (Spring 1952): 29–37.

Chapman, B. B. "Cherokee Allotments in the Outlet." *Chronicles of Oklahoma* 59 (Winter 1981–82): 401–21.

Cheney, Louise. "Lucil[l]e Mulhall, Fabulous Cowgirl." *Real West* 12 (March 1969): 13–15, 58–59, 73.

Chinoy, Helen Krich. "Art versus Business: The Role of Women in American Theatre." In *Women in American Theatre: Careers, Images, Movements,* edited by Helen Krich Chinoy and Linda Walsh Jenkins, 1–9. New York: Crown, 1981.

Clark, Blue. "Delegates to the Constitutional Convention." *Chronicles of Oklahoma* 48 (Winter 1970–71): 400–14.

Clark, Manning. "An Historical Outline." In *Australia, New Zealand, and the South Pacific: A Handbook,* edited by Charles Osborne, 5–17. London: Anthony Blond, 1970.

Clinton, Fred S. "The Indian Territory Medical Association." *Chronicles of Oklahoma* 26 (1948): 23–55.

Collins, Reba. "Paula McSpadden Love." *Chronicles of Oklahoma* 51 (Fall 1973): 362–64.

Conser, Walter H., Jr. "John Ross and the Cherokee Resistance Campaign, 1833–1838." *Journal of Southern History* 44 (May 1978): 191–212.

Croy, Homer. "Texas Jack." *Westerner's Brand Book* (New York) 2 (1955): 29.

Dale, Edward Everett. "The Cherokees in the Confederacy." *Journal of Southern History* 13 (1947): 159–85.

Davis, J. B. "Slavery in the Cherokee Nation." *Chronicles of Oklahoma* 11 (1933): 1056–72.

Davis, Kenneth Penn. "Chaos in the Indian Country: The Cherokee Nation, 1828–

1835." In *The Cherokee Indian Nation: A Troubled History*, edited by Duane H. King, 129–47. Knoxville: University of Tennessee Press, 1979.

Davison, Oscar William. "Oklahoma's Educational Heritage." *Chronicles of Oklahoma* 27 (Winter 1949–50): 354–72.

Dean, Frank. "Magueys, Myths, and Men." *Western Horseman* 31 (March 1966): 58–59, 96, 98.

Debo, Angie. "Southern Refugees of the Cherokee Nation." *Southwestern Historical Quarterly* 35 (1932): 255–66.

Deloria, Vine, Jr. "The Indians." In *Buffalo Bill and the Wild West*, 45–56. Brooklyn: Brooklyn Museum in conjunction with Museum of Art, Carnegie Institute, and Buffalo Bill Historical Center, 1981.

Derrick, Patty S. "Julia Marlowe: An Actress Caught between Traditions." *Theatre Survey* 32 (May 1991): 85.

Deutsch, Sarah. "Landscape of Enclaves: Race Relations in the West, 1865–1990." In *Under an Open Sky: Rethinking America's Western Past*, edited by William Cronon, George Miles, and Jay Gitlin, 110–31. New York: W. W. Norton, 1992.

Doran, Michael. "Population Statistics of Nineteenth-Century Indian Territory." *Chronicles of Oklahoma* 53 (Winter 1975–76): 492–515.

Duncan, James. "The Keetoowah Society." *Chronicles of Oklahoma* 4 (1926): 251–55.

Eaton, Rachel Caroline. "The Legend of the Battle of Claremore Mound." *Chronicles of Oklahoma* 8 (December 1930): 369–70.

Elkin, A. P. "The Aborigines." In *Australia, New Zealand, and the South Pacific: A Handbook*, edited by Charles Osborne, 279–84. London: Anthony Blond, 1970.

Fabian, Ann. "History for the Masses: Commercializing the Western Past." In *Under an Open Sky: Rethinking America's Western Past*, edited by William Cronen, George Miles, and Jay Gitlin, 223–56. New York: W. W. Norton, 1992.

Fiedler, Leslie. "The Legend." In *Buffalo Bill and the Wild West*, 84–95. Brooklyn: Brooklyn Museum in conjunction with Museum of Art, Carnegie Institute, and Buffalo Bill Historical Center, 1981.

Fischer, LeRoy H. "The Civil War Era in Indian Territory." *Journal of the West* 12 (1973): 345–55.

———. "Oklahoma Territory, 1890–1907." *Chronicles of Oklahoma* 53 (Spring 1975): 3–8.

Fischer, LeRoy H., and Jerry Gill. "Confederate Indian Forces Outside of Indian Territory." *Chronicles of Oklahoma* 46 (Autumn 1968): 249–84.

Fogelson, Raymond D. "On the Varieties of Indian History." *Journal of Ethnic Studies* 2 (1974): 105–12.

Foreman, Carolyn Thomas. "Mrs. Laura E. Harsha." *Chronicles of Oklahoma* 18 (June 1940): 182–84.

———. "A Creek Pioneer: Notes Concerning 'Aunt Sue' Rogers and Her Family." *Chronicles of Oklahoma* 21 (September 1943): 271–79.

———. "Dr. and Mrs. Richard Moore Crain." *Chronicles of Oklahoma* 35 (Spring 1957): 72–79.

Foreman, Grant. "Clifton R. Breckinridge (1846–1932)." *Chronicles of Oklahoma* 12 (March 1934): 118–19.

Fowler, Gene. "Will Rogers: The Texas Connection." *Texas Highways,* January 1994, 32–37.

Fullerton, Eula. "Sallie Rogers McSpadden." *Chronicles of Oklahoma* 22 (Spring 1944): 126–28.

Garrett, Kathleen. "Worcester, Pride of the West." *Chronicles of Oklahoma* 30 (Winter 1952–53): 386–96.

Gibson, Arrell Morgan. "Ranching on the Southern Great Plains." *Journal of the West* 6 (January 1967): 135–53.

———. "The Cowboy in Indian Territory." In *The Cowboy: Six-shooters, Songs, and Sex,* edited by Charles W. Harris and Buck Rainey, 139–53. Norman: University of Oklahoma Press, 1976.

———. "America's Exiles." *Chronicles of Oklahoma* 54 (Spring 1976): 3–15.

———. "The Centennial Legacy of the General Allotment Act." *Chronicles of Oklahoma* 65 (Fall 1987): 228–51.

Graebner, Norman Arthur. "History of Cattle Ranching in Eastern Oklahoma." *Chronicles of Oklahoma* 21 (September 1943): 300–11.

———. "The Public Land Policy of the Five Civilized Tribes." *Chronicles of Oklahoma* 23 (July 1945): 107–18.

Halliburton, Rudi, Jr. "Origins of Black Slavery among the Cherokees." *Chronicles of Oklahoma* 52 (1974–75): 483–96.

———. "Black Slave Control in the Cherokee Nation." *Journal of Ethnic Studies* 3 (1975): 23–36.

Herbert, H. W. "Queensland." In *Australia, New Zealand, and the South Pacific: A Handbook,* edited by Charles Osborne, 68–74. London: Anthony Blond, 1970.

Hexham, Irving. "Afrikaner Nationalism 1902–1914." In *The South African War: The Anglo-Boer War, 1899–1902,* edited by Peter Warwick, 386–403. London: Longman, 1980.

Holm, Tom. "Cherokee Colonization in Oklahoma." *Chronicles of Oklahoma* 54 (Spring 1976): 60–76.

Holmes, F. W. "The New Zealand Economy." In *Australia, New Zealand, and the South Pacific: A Handbook,* edited by Charles Osborne, 373–84. London: Anthony Blond, 1970.

Hopkins, Jim. "To Will Rogers." *The Ranchman* (July 1959): 71.

Houghton, D. Hobart. "The Mining Revolution." In *The Oxford History of South Africa,* edited by Monica Wilson and Leonard Thompson, 2:10–21. New York and Oxford: Oxford University Press, 1971.

Jackson, Joe C. "Church School Education in the Creek Nation, 1898 to 1907." *Chronicles of Oklahoma* 46 (1968): 312–19.

Johnson, N. B. "The Cherokee Orphan Asylum." *Chronicles of Oklahoma* 44 (Autumn 1966): 275–80.

Lipe, Nannie. "History of the Lipe Family." In *As I Recollect,* 3–11. Claremore, Okla.: Pocahontas Club, 1940.

Litton, Gaston L. "The Principal Chiefs of the Cherokee Nation." *Chronicles of Oklahoma* 15 (September 1987): 253–70.

Lott, Eric. "Love and Theft: The Racial Unconscious of Blackface Minstrelsy." *Representations* 39 (Summer 1992): 23–50.

Love, Paula McSpadden. "The Rogers Family." In *As I Recollect*, 110–16. Claremore, Okla.: Pocahontas Club, 1940. (See also draft manuscript of same title, manuscript section).

Mahnken, Norbert R. "Old Baptist Mission of Evan Jones." *Chronicles of Oklahoma* 67 (Summer 1989): 174–92.

Marquis, Arnold. "Will Rogers and His Horses." Pt. 1. *The Western Horseman* 28 (February 1963): 28–30, 71–73.

Martin, George. "The Wit of Will Rogers: The Story of a Cowboy Who Has Become a Famous Comedian." *American Magazine*, November 1919, 4–35, 106–10.

"Mashed O Ranch History Extends to Buffalo Days." *West Texas Livestock Weekly*, 10 July 1975.

Maxwell, Amos. "The Sequoyah Convention (Part II)." *Chronicles of Oklahoma* 28 (Autumn 1950): 299–340.

McCreary, J. R. "The Maori." In *Australia, New Zealand, and the South Pacific: A Handbook*, edited by Charles Osborne, 446–52. London: Anthony Blond, 1970.

McFadden, Marguerite. "Intruders or Injustice?" *Chronicles of Oklahoma* 48 (Winter 1970–71): 431–49.

McLoughlin, William G. "Red Indians, Black Slavery, and White Racism: America's Slaveholding Indians." *American Quarterly* 26 (1974): 367–85.

———. "Thomas Jefferson and the Beginning of Cherokee Nationalism." *William and Mary Quarterly* 3 (October 1975): 562–80.

———. "Experiment in Cherokee Citizenship." *American Quarterly* 33 (1981): 3–25.

McLoughlin, William G., and Walter H. Conser, Jr. "The Cherokees in Transition." *Journal of American History* 64 (1977): 678–703.

McSpadden [Love], Paula. "Clement Vann Rogers." *Chronicles of Oklahoma* 48 (Winter 1970–71): 389–99.

Meredith, Howard L. "Will Rogers' Roots." *Chronicles of Oklahoma* 57 (Fall 1979): 259–65.

Meserve, John Bartlett. "Chief Dennis Wolfe Bushyhead." *Chronicles of Oklahoma* 14 (September 1936): 349–59.

———. "The Mayes." *Chronicles of Oklahoma* 15 (March 1937): 54–56.

———. "Chief Colonel Johnson Harris." *Chronicles of Oklahoma* 17 (March 1939): 17–21.

———. "Chief Thomas Mitchell Buffington and Chief William Charles Rogers." *Chronicles of Oklahoma* 17 (June 1939): 135–47.

Metcalf, C. E. "Historic Sites in the Cherokee Strip." *Chronicles of Oklahoma* 59 (Winter 1981–82): 392–400.

Miles, George, "To Hear an Old Voice: Rediscovering Native Americans in American History." In *Under an Open Sky: Rethinking America's Western Past*, edited by William Cronon, George Miles, and Jay Gitlin, 52–70. New York: W. W. Norton, 1992.

Miner, Craig. "East-West Railway in Indian Territory." *Chronicles of Oklahoma* 47 (Spring 1969): 560–81.

Moore, Cherrie Adair. "William Penn Adair." *Chronicles of Oklahoma* 29 (Spring 1951): 32–41.

Nasson, William. "Tommy Atkins in South Africa." In *The South African War: The Anglo-Boer War, 1899–1902*, edited by Peter Warwick, 123–38. London: Longman, 1980.

"Notes and Documents (Little Robe Township, Ellis County)." *Chronicles of Oklahoma* 30 (Autumn 1952): 343–45.

Olds, Fred. "The Story of Lucille." *The War Chief of the Indian Territory Posse of Oklahoma Westerners* 8 (December 1974): 3–12.

Perdue, Theda. "Cherokee Planters: The Development of Plantation Slavery before Removal." In *The Cherokee Indian Nation*, edited by Duane H. King, 110–28. Knoxville: University of Tennessee Press, 1979.

———. "Cherokee Planters, Black Slaves, and African Colonization." *Chronicles of Oklahoma* 60 (Fall 1982): 322–31.

———. "The Conflict Within: Cherokees and Removal." In *Cherokee Removal Before and After*, edited by William L. Anderson, 55–74. Athens, Ga., and London: University of Georgia Press, 1991.

Porter, Bernard. "The Pro-Boers in Britain." In *The South African War: The Anglo-Boer War, 1899–1902*, edited by Peter Warwick, 239–57. London: Longman, 1980.

Pretorius, Fransjohan. "Life on Commando." In *The South African War: The Anglo-Boer War, 1899–1902*, edited by Peter Warwick, 103–22. London: Longman, 1980.

Richardson, Peter, and Jean Jacques Van-Helten. "The Gold Mining Industry in the Transvaal, 1886–99." In *The South African War: The Anglo-Boer War, 1899–1902*, edited by Peter Warwick, 18–36. London: Longman, 1980.

Roach, Fred, Jr. "Will Rogers' Youthful Relationship with his Father, Clem Rogers: A Story of Love and Tension." *Chronicles of Oklahoma* 57 (Fall 1980): 325–42.

Robinson, Ella. "Burning of Spaulding Institute, Muskogee, September 25, 1899." *Chronicles of Oklahoma* 46 (Autumn 1968): 336–37.

Roediger, David R. "Black Skins, White Masks: Minstrelsy and White Working Class Formation before the Civil War." In *The Wages of Whiteness: Race and the Making of the American Working Class*, 115–32. London and New York: Verso, 1991.

Scheurer, Timothy E. "Thou Witty: The Evolution and Triumph of Style in Lyric Writing, 1890–1950." In *American Popular Music: Readings from the Popular Press*, vol. 1, *The Nineteenth Century and Tin Pan Alley*, edited by Timothy E. Scheurer, 104–19. Bowling Green, Ohio: Bowling Green State University Popular Press, 1989.

Schrimsher-Robinson, Juliette. "Brief History and Narratives of the Schrimsher and Candy Families." In *As I Recollect*, 41–44. Claremore, Okla.: Pocahontas Club, 1949.

Scobie, James R. "Buenos Aires as a Commercial-Bureaucratic City, 1880–1910." *American Historical Review* 77 (October 1972): 1035–73.

Self, Nancy Hope. "Building of the Railroads." *Chronicles of Oklahoma* 49 (Summer 1971): 180–205.

Slatta, Richard. "Cowboys and Gauchos." *Américas* 33 (March 1981): 3–8.

Smith, Brian Lee. "Theodore Roosevelt Visits Oklahoma." *Chronicles of Oklahoma* 51 (Fall 1973): 263–79.

Sorenson, M. P. K. "An Historical Outline." In *Australia, New Zealand, and the South Pacific: A Handbook*, edited by Charles Osborne, 339–48. London: Anthony Blond, 1970.

Spies, S. B. "Women and the War." In *The South African War: The Anglo-Boer War, 1899–1902*, edited by Peter Warwick, 161–85. London: Longman, 1980.

Stewart, Martha. "The Indian Mission Conference of Oklahoma." *Chronicles of Oklahoma* 40 (Winter 1962–63): 330–36.

Suthern, Orrin Clayton, II. "Minstrelsy and Popular Culture." In *American Popular Music: Readings from the Popular Press,* vol. 1, *The Nineteenth Century and Tin Pan Alley,* edited by Timothy E. Scheurer, 75–85. Bowling Green, Ohio: Bowling Green State University Popular Press, 1989. (Reprinted from *Journal of Popular Culture* 4 [Winter 1971]: 658–73.)

Tacker, Ann. "The Rogers Family—Our Heritage." *Rogers County Observer,* 21 November, 5 December, and 26 December 1968.

"Theodore F. Brewer." *Chronicles of Oklahoma* 6 (June 1928): 232–33.

Thoburn, Joseph B. "Albert L. Kates 1861–1938 (Necrology)." *Chronicles of Oklahoma* 16 (March 1938): 131.

Thornton, Russell. "The Demography of the Trail of Tears Period: A New Estimate of Cherokee Population Losses." In *Cherokee Removal Before and After,* edited by William L. Anderson, 75–95. Athens, Ga., and London: University of Georgia Press, 1991.

Tinnin, Ida Wetzel. "Influences of the Cherokee National Seminaries." *Chronicles of Oklahoma* 37 (Spring 1959): 59–67.

Townsley, W. A. "Tasmania." In *Australia, New Zealand, and the South Pacific: A Handbook,* edited by Charles Osborne, 85–91. London: Anthony Blond, 1970.

Vernon, Walter N. "Methodist Beginnings among Southwest Oklahoma Indians." *Chronicles of Oklahoma* 58 (Winter 1980–81): 391–411.

Warwick, Peter. "Black People and the War." In *The South African War: The Anglo-Boer War, 1899–1902,* edited by Peter Warwick, 186–209. London: Longman, 1980.

Willan, Brian. "The Siege of Mafeking." In *The South African War: The Anglo-Boer War, 1899–1902,* edited by Peter Warwick, 139–61. London: Longman, 1980.

Williams, Ronnie. "Pictorial Essay on the Dawes Commission." *Chronicles of Oklahoma* 53 (Summer 1975): 225–38.

Wilms, Douglas C. "Cherokee Land Use in Georgia before Removal." In *Cherokee Removal Before and After,* edited by William L. Anderson, 1–28. Athens, Ga., and London: University of Georgia Press, 1991.

Wilson, L. W. "A History of Wagoner, Oklahoma." *Chronicles of Oklahoma* 50 (Winter 1972–73): 486–96.

Witcher, Esther. "Territorial Magazines." *Chronicles of Oklahoma* 29 (Winter 1951–52), 484–97.

Yellow Robe, Chauncy. "The Menace of the Wild West Show." *Quarterly Journal of the Society of American Indians* 2 (July–September 1914): 224–28.

UNPUBLISHED AND MISCELLANEOUS SOURCES

Abbott, Devon Irene. "History of the Cherokee Female Seminary: 1851–1910." Ph.D. diss., Texas Christian University, 1989.

"As Schoolboy, Rogers Hated Routine but Always Was Brilliant at History." Press Release 3, Morning Newspapers, 12 December [1935]. PD. OkClaW.

Baker, Jack D. "Major Cherokee Genealogical Records," n.d. TMS. OkClaW.

Ballenger, T. L. "Early History of Northeastern State College," n.d. TMS. OkTahN.

Campisi, Jack. "Ethnic Identity and Boundary Maintenance in Three Oneida Communities." Ph.D. diss., State University of New York at Albany, 1974.

Carseloway, James R. "Some Interesting Facts about Will Rogers." n.d. TMS. IPH-OkHi.

Chestnut, Edgar. "That Tomboy Who Married Will Rogers," n.d. Clipping. Free Library of Philadelphia, Will Rogers personality file.

Collins, Reba. "Will Rogers, Writer and Journalist." Ed.D. diss., Oklahoma State University, 1967.

Davis, Katherine Murdoch. "Will Rogers and His Sister." *Christian Herald* clipping, May 1935. OkClaW.

Eaton, Helen McSpadden. Interview by Paula Love. Chelsea, Okla., 5 April 1966. OkClaW.

Ferguson, Mrs. Walter. "Let Me Rest in Oklahoma." Interview with Sallie Rogers McSpadden. Unidentified newspaper clipping, n.d. Scrapbook of Sallie McSpadden, SRM-OkClaW.

Fisch, Martha. Oral history interviews by Barbara Bair. Guthrie, Okla., January 1994. WRPP.

Geier, Philip Otto. "A Peculiar Status: A History of Oneida Indian Treaties and Claims . . . 1775–1920." Ph.D. diss., Syracuse University, 1980.

Hogue, Bill. "Oologah Oozings" column. *Claremore Progress,* ca. 6 March 1960. Clipping, OkClaW.

Holland, Cullen Joe. "The Cherokee Indian Newspapers, 1828–1906." Ph.D. diss., University of Minnesota, 1956.

Hopkins, Jim. Interview by Will Rogers, Jr. Los Angeles, Calif., 10 August 1955. OkClaW.

Keith, Harold. "Clem Rogers and His Influence on Oklahoma History." Master's thesis, University of Oklahoma, 1938. (Copy, OkClaW.)

Koch, Iris. "Zack Mulhall, His Family, and the Mulhall Wild West Show." Master's thesis, Oklahoma Agricultural and Mechanical College, 1940.

Lane, Gazelle (Scrap). Interview by Paula Love. Chelsea, Okla., 30 December 1964. OkClaW.

Love, Paula McSpadden. "Mary America Schrimsher," n.d. TMS. OkClaW.

_____. "The Rogers Family." n.d. Included in scrapbook of Sallie McSpadden, SRM-OkClaW. (Draft ms. for published essay in *As I Recollect;* see article section.)

_____. "The Rogers Family at Worcester Academy," n.d. TMS. OkClaW.

_____. "The Pocahontas Club," 1968. TMS. OkClaW.

_____. Interview. n.d. OkClaW.

McSpadden, Herb. "The Importance of Faith and Belief." *Ranchman,* n.d., 8, 10, Clipping. In scrapbook of Sallie McSpadden, SRM-OkClaW.

_____. "Horses and Horse Collars." *Ranchman,* n.d. Clipping. Horses file, OkClaW.

McSpadden, Sallie Rogers. *Oklahoma City Times* article, ca. April 1910. Clipping. Misc. file 7, OkClaW.

"Memoirs of Mary Newcomb." n.d. TMS. OkClaW.

Milam, Irene McSpadden. "Will Rogers as I Knew Him." *Chelsea Star,* 1935. Clipping. Misc. file 7, OkClaW.

Mulhall scrapbook. Clippings, ca. 1904–10. MFC.

Mutual Life Insurance Company of New York. "Gift to the Nation: Celebrating 150

Years, 1843–1993: Famous Policyholders' Files: William Penn Rogers, 'Will Rogers,' (1879–1935)." New York: Mutual Life Insurance Co. of New York, 1993. Microfilm, OkClaW.

Odell, Marcia Larson. "Divide and Conquer: Allotment among the Cherokees." Ph.D. diss., Cornell University, 1975.

O'Donnell (Hopkins), Jim. "My Friend Will." n.d. TMS. OkClaW.

Oskison, John M. "A Tale of the Old I.T." n.d. TMS. JMO-OkU.

Poole, May McSpadden. Interview with Paula Love. Chelsea, Okla., 5 April 1966. OkClaW.

Poole, May McSpadden, Helen McSpadden Eaton, and Irene McSpadden Milam. Interviews. Chelsea, Okla., 12 June 1970. OkClaW.

Reed, Gerard Alexander. "The Ross-Watie Conflict: Factionalism in the Cherokee Nation, 1838–1865." Ph.D. diss., University of Oklahoma, 1967.

Roach, Samuel Frederick, Jr. "Lariat in the Sun: The Story of Will Rogers." Ph.D. diss., University of Oklahoma, 1972.

Roethler, Michael. "Negro Slavery among the Cherokee Indians." Ph.D. diss., Fordham University, 1964.

Rogers, Will. "How I Got into Show Business." Unpublished autobiographical manuscript, ca. 1912. Typed transcription by Ben Yadoga. WRPP.

Rogers, Will. "Various Styles of Roping." In *The Stampede: Canada's 2d Annual World's Greatest Frontier Days' Celebration*, 71, 73. Winnipeg, Canada: Official Program, 9–16 August 1913. URL-CLU.

Snelling, Lois. "One of the Blake Girls: The Story of Betty Blake (Mrs. Will Rogers) and Her Benton County Family." Ca. 1977. TMS. OkClaW.

St Leon, Mark Valentine. "The Bareback Queen." Biography of May Wirth. TMS. Author's copy, Glebe, Austalia.

Theodore Roosevelt Papers. Presidential Papers Microfilm. Washington, D.C.: Library of Congress, 1967.

Tompkins, Charles H. "My Association with Will Rogers." *Old Trail Drivers Convention Program*, October 1953, 7–12.

Tyner, Howard Q. "The Keetoowah Society in Cherokee History." Master's thesis, University of Tulsa, 1949.

Walker, Agnes. Interview by Alene D. McDowell. 13 January 1938. Works Progress Administration Biography. 75:32–41. IPH-OkHi.

Wear, Susan McClellan. Interview. Pocahontas Club audiotape 16. OkClaW.

Weisiger, Marsha. "National Register Lists Oklahoma Properties." *Mistletoe Leaves* (newsletter of the OkHi), February 1993.

"Will Rogers Chronology," n.d. TMS. OkClaW.

Will Rogers Scrapbook, 1902–04. Original, CPpR. Microfilm copy, no. 559-1-5785, URL-CLU.

Wilms, Douglas C. "Cherokee Indian Land Use in Georgia, 1800–1838." Ph.D. diss., University of Georgia, 1973.

Wyche, Sue Martin. "History of Chelsea: Research Report." Northeastern State College, Okla., 1974. CPL.

Index

References to illustrations are printed in **boldface** type.

References to notes or appendix entries that provide primary biographical information about an individual are preceded by an asterisk (*).

For page numbers of correspondence between given individuals and Will Rogers, see list of Documents in the preliminary matter of the volume (pages ix–xiv).

ma City, 10, 153, 193–94&n.1, **195,
196**, 198nn.7,9, 203, 494; reunion, in
Las Vegas, N.Mex. Terr., 194n.1
Rowsey, Eva Patton, 108, 106n.1, 120
Rowsey, William Eugene, 105, *106n.1,
107, 108, 114
Rucker, Frank Marshall, 214, 215n.6,
216&n.1
Rucker, John Garther (M.D.), 215n.6
Rucker, May Dora Taylor, 215n.6
Russel, Maggie, 125
S., Mamie (friend of Will Rogers in
South Africa), 423–24
Saddler, P. E., 211
San Antonio, Tex., 172n.2, 173n.3; an-
nual fairs in, 11, 172, 227, 229n.1,
229–30, 232n.2, 262, 265n.7
Sanders, George, **150**
Sanders, William Edward, 84, *89n.19
Sandow, Eugene, 420, *421n.2
Sapulpa, I.T., 470n.2
Saunders, George W., 229n.2
Scarritt, Rev. Nathan, *127, 129n.1
Scarritt Collegiate Institute, Neosho,
Mo. (Neosho Seminary/Neosho Colle-
giate Institute), 8, **70**, 75, 77, 127,
129n.1; football team, 129n.1, **132**
Schrimsher, Ann E., 54n.10
Schrimsher, Bess. *See* Lewis, Elizabeth
Belle Schrimsher
Schrimsher, Elizabeth Alabama. *See*
Adair, Elizabeth Alabama Schrimsher
Schrimsher, Elizabeth Hunt Gunter, 32,
32, 38, 44n.11, 170n.2, 180n.9
Schrimsher, Ernest Vivian, 119, 194,
197n.5, 204n.1, 214, 224, 282, 284,
290n.15, 367, 368, 399, *551–52
Schrimsher, John Gunter, **32**, 35, **66**, 73,
82, *552–53
Schrimsher, Juliette Melvina (Bunt).
See Robinson, Juliette Melvina
Schrimsher
Schrimsher, Martin, 32, 37, 170n.2,
180n.9
Schrimsher, Sarah Catherine (Kitty), 84,
86n.6
Schrimsher, Susan Philips (Susie),
*290n.15, 399, 400n.1
Scott, Gen. Winfield, 44n.11
Scudder, Ida, 316

Seni-Om-Sed Carnival, Des Moines,
Iowa, 11, 12, 223n.2, 224, 225&n.1
Sequoyah (George Guess), 71
Sequoyah Convention (1905), 213n.3
Sequoyah Hotel, Claremore, I.T.,
221n.4, 283, 284, 286–87n.4, 291n.16
Sharpe, Jim, 214, 216
Shelton, J. C., 77
Shenandoah, Chapman, 306, *311n.8
Skinner, Heber, 202 & *n.4, 203,
203n.11, 216, 349, 350n.7
Skinner, John Kell, 222, *223n.3
Skinner, Louis, 120
Skinner, Martha (Mattie) Riley, 202n.4,
349, 350n.7
Skinner, Nannie Kell, 223n.3
Skinner, Nathaniel (Nat), 223n.3, 393,
*395n.2
Slavery. *See* Cherokee Nation West: and
slaveholding
Slaves, freed, citizenship rights of, 38,
46–47n.16, 50–51n.27, 57–58n.3, 121,
123–24n.5, 206n.1, 208n.1, 428n.2
Smith, John, 90
Smith, Riley, 228
Smith, Thomas A., 191n.7
So This Is London (1930 film), 31, 39n.2
South Africa, **332**, 351; African labor in,
326, 355, 357, 381, 383, 426n.3; British colonialism in, 324, 355; and frontier, 323, 329n.4; and gold/diamonds/
mineral resources, 324, 330n.9, 378–
79n.3, 425n.1, 426nn.2,3; history of
Cape Colony, 406n.2, 409n.1, 412n.1;
history of Orange Free State, 351,
392nn.1,2, 413n.1; history of Natal,
325, 351, 369n.10, 378n.1; history of
Transvaal, 351, 378–79n.3, 386n.2,
388n.2, 424; Indian immigration/labor
in, 326, 330n.10, 354, 357, 360–61n.9,
363; political economy of, 381, 383,
412–13; population of, 324, 354, 359–
60n.8; railroads in, **382**; Union of, 32,
379n.3. *See also* Afrikaners; First War
of Independence; South African War;
Zululand/Zulu peoples
South African (Anglo-Boer) War, 10,
238, 256n.4, 323, 325, 329; civilian
concentration camps/refugees in, 325,
330n.8, 357–58n.1; devastation of,